Frisians to America, 1880-1914

# Frisians

Annemieke Galema

# to America

# 1880-1914

## With the baggage of the fatherland

REGIO-PRojekt Uitgevers, Groningen 1996
The Netherlands

*Colophon*

Research for this publication was made possible by
financial support of the Netherlands Organization for
Scientific Research in The Hague.

*This book was realised thanks to financial contributions from:*

Boelstra-Olivier Stichting
Commissie van Beheer P.W. Janssen's Friesche Stichting
Cultuurfonds provincie Friesland
Gravin van Bylandt Stichting
Ottema-Kingma Stichting
Provincie Friesland

| | |
|---|---|
| *Design* | H. Dorgelo, Kielwindeweer |
| *Pre-press* | Von Hebel bv, Groningen |
| *Printing* | De Bruin, Noordbroek |
| *Publication* | REGIO-PRojekt Uitgevers, Groningen |
| *Front cover photo* | Dutch family waiting at Ellis Island around 1900 (postcard). |

ISBN 90-5028-076-5

© REGIO-PRojekt Uitgevers, Groningen,
the Netherlands, 1996

Distributed in the United States and Canada by
Wayne State University Press, Detroit, Michigan

*Cover: Dutch family waiting at Ellis Island around 1900*

# Contents

# List of tables, figures, and maps

# Acknowledgments

The origins of this study go back to a celebration. In 1982, it had been 200 years ago that two nations, the Netherlands and the United States, entered into diplomatic relations and concluded a Treaty of Amity and Commerce. To commemorate this bilateral bicentennial a conference with prominent American and Dutch scholars was organized in Amsterdam. Robert P. Swierenga gave a lecture about Dutch immigration and settlement in the United States, and it was from this that I drew inspiration for the research project, which has resulted in this book.

*With the Baggage of the Fatherland* deals with Frisians who are part of the bilateral history of the Netherlands and the United States, and who are comers and goers at the same time. It is about Frisians as just one small ingredient in a trans-Atlantic migration process, of which we can get an adequate picture only by paying attention to both the sending and receiving communities. Therefore, I owe a debt of gratitude to many people on both sides of the ocean.

Friends and colleagues in the history department of the University of Groningen have provided a valuable and stimulating environment. Especially, professor Marten G. Buist and professor Pim Kooij were in the frontline during the beginning stages of this study, and an inducement along the road. Also, committee members of Wereldcontact were interested in this research and they have continued to be so over the years.

During the long process of research and writing, many people got involved. Staff members at the municipal archives in the Frisian clay area, friends and colleagues at Kent State University where I started this research project under supervision of professor Robert P. Swierenga, and employees in the Calvin College Archives, at the National Archives in Washington DC, and at many other archives and libraries, have all been very helpful. Numerous people in the Dutch-American communities have shown great hospitality and been good company during my research in the United States.

It is not possible for me to mention everyone individually for their interest and help. To a special few, however, I owe a particular debt. Professor Hille de Vries from the University of Leiden and Professor Robert Swierenga who supervised the research process gave generously of their time, advise, criticism, continuous encouragement and friendship, for which I am truly grateful. Professor Herbert Brinks of Calvin College was very inventive in showing me the real stories of individual migrants with roots in different worlds. I highly appreciate his comments and hospitality, and his good fellowship during the immigrant-letter campaign.

I also owe a great debt to George Welling, who from the beginning spent countless hours patiently and skillfully helping me in handling the data with the computer. The same was true for Hans Galema.

During the last phase of completion, Kate Delaney spontaneously offered her editorial qualities. Her comments saved me from countless errors in English. It should be made clear at this point that the translation of immigrant letters used in this volume is my own.

Lastly, I would like to thank my parents who gave me all the possible opportunities in their own natural way. Hans and Hannah did the greatest job by making life a joyful and interesting happening in a seemingly endless research journey.

# Preface

## Introduction

Population movements have become one of the most pressing issues of our time, forcing their way on to political agendas throughout the world. Renewed scholarly interest in the history of international migrations followed naturally. The movement of large numbers of people from Europe to the United States in the nineteenth century stimulated much research, while fostering curiosity about the meaning of ethnic identity, the process of ethnic group formation, and the effects of migration on the native country as well as on the country of settlement.

Enthusiasm for explorations into the history of emigration to the Americas has been nourished by the transformation of Europe into an immigration continent in recent decades. In the Netherlands immigration has become of topical interest now that it has become clear that immigrants who came after World War II would stay permanently.[1] We are debating matters of immigration policy, assimilation or integration, and effects of cultural diversity like bilingualism and denominational affiliation. In this contemporary discussion, a plea is made for an historical approach toward the study of international migrations.[2]

There are several reasons to adopt such an approach. The pitfalls of ad hoc research can be avoided because long-term developments can be analyzed. Also, contemporary developments become part of a broader, historical context. Furthermore, the voices of nativism and racism can be combatted by creating a more positive image of newcomers that, simultaneously, can help them achieve equal status in the new land. Immigrant communities abroad can become potential markets for tourism and goods, making the long-term study of immigration important for the economy.[3]

In the 1960s, when emigration from the Netherlands to traditional destinations like the United States, Canada, Australia, and New Zealand, became marginal, historians showed increasing interest in the subject. The quantitative-oriented research of Robert P. Swierenga, an American historian of Dutch origin, gave momentum to this interest.[4] Attention focused not only on emigration; social scientists and historians examined the phenomenon of immigration to the Netherlands and its history, including the pioneering comparative studies by Jan Lucassen and Rinus Penninx.[5]

Over the last century scholars have examined immigrant groups in the
United States from different perspectives. Around 1880 nationalism
dominated and immigrants were portrayed as undesirable foreigners whose
maladjusted behaviour threatened the Anglo-Saxon lifestyle. In the
beginning of the twentieth century, immigrants started to combat this vision,
and different ethnic groups pointed to the contributions of their cultures to
American society. Scholars emphasized the desire of newcomers to
assimilate. In the interbellum era, progressive historians like Frederick
Jackson Turner promoted a harmonious society in which nationality groups
would melt into a new mixed race.
Some scholars felt that the "real immigrant truth" was displayed by
sociologists. In 1951 in his book *The Uprooted* the historian Oscar Handlin
used sociological theories to explain the assimilation process. He introduced
the interdisciplinary approach to migration research. Handlin considered
immigrants as products of uprooting and dislocation. He painted a picture
of extreme disorientation and discontinuity of European laborers and
farmers. Handlin's immigrants seemed like isolated molecules in American
society, with their direction determined by coincidences. Then, in the 1960s,
the historian Frank Thistlethwaite presented a new concept by which
immigration was considered a *process* that should be studied in its entirety.

Within Europe many different regions lost inhabitants who left for the
Americas. The migratory process showed similarities as much as differences,
and in most cases it was not entirely related to a national context.[6]
Emigration regions raise the question of the most appropriate unit of
analysis. The national or provincial context does not meet research demands
because these units contained areas of both high and low emigration.
Municipalities and particularly villages may have been the real emigration
units and deserve further scholarly attention.[7]

This research deals with the migration of Frisians to the United States
between 1880 and 1914. The specific area of concentration is the northern
coastal farming region of sea clay soils, known as *De Bouwhoek*. The Frisians
form a distinct ethnic group, that faced trilingualism in the United States.
Furthermore, in the pre-migration period, these Frisians were a strongly
agrarian-oriented rural population, which suggested profitable research
opportunities concerning social and occupational mobility. Therefore, this
study will follow the migration process from the time of leaving the
homecountry into the settlement phase.
The traditional sea clay areas were the cockpit of Dutch migration to the
United States in the last quarter of the nineteenth century. Most emigrants
came from this type of soil in the provinces of Groningen, Zeeland, and
Friesland. Over half (55 percent) of all emigrants in the period 1835-1880
originated from the countryside of these provinces.[8] The choice of a rural
clay area is also dictated by socio-economic factors. In his pioneering
quantitative research dealing with Dutch overseas migration, R.P. Swierenga
concludes that despite some religiously driven emigration, ultimately

economic conditions in the countryside were decisive.[9] Unemployment rates are usually higher in regional centers. The clay areas can be considered as very peripheral with high unemployment rates and hence likely to produce a high percentage of overseas migrants.

To put Dutch overseas migration in regional perspective, I chose to study the northern Frisian area because the agrarian depression particularly affected this part of the province. The stagnation in the business cycle took a more serious turn in Friesland than in Zeeland or Groningen, and it lasted longer.[10] Since individual and local factors in migration are usually influenced by major socio-economic forces, the agrarian depression seems to be an important circumstance to take into account.

R.P. Swierenga found that in the 65 years before 1880, the occupation most frequently listed by Dutch emigrant males of 20 years and older was laborer (*werkman, dagloner*).[11] Another factor in the choice of the Frisian clay area was that in the last two decades of the nineteenth century Friesland faced many labor disputes, which suggests a causal relation between labor unrest and migration to the United States. The Frisian labor movement contributed greatly to the Dutch labor movement as a whole.[12] One must investigate whether it really was laborers who left the province, and whether Frisians brought their labor activism to the United States.

Furthermore, Frisians have long been known for their devotion to the soil. They are enamored of tradition and attachment to the fertile cultivated lands. The Frisian national anthem contains the phrase: "Flean op! Wij sjonge it bêste lân fen 'e ierde, It Fryske lân fol eare en rom" [Arise and sing, the best country on earth, the Frisian land filled with honor and glory]. If this is an apt characterization, one wonders why so many exchanged their native soil for the unknown spacious American lands. What was promised to them? "Nobody emigrates without a promise!"[13] This also raises the question to what extent was Frisian ethnic identity preserved. These were questions and data that fascinated me and guided this research.

In the following chapters the term *migration* designates the permanent free movement of people over international borders. The focus will be on the migration of a group of Dutch Frisians to the United States. I will speak of *emigrants* when dealing with this group or individuals of this group in Friesland, and of *immigrants* when dealing with them in their place of settlement overseas. The *nuclear family*, i.e. husband, wife, and children, appeared to be an important unit in the migration process, as was the *family* at large, i.e those sharing blood kinship.

Considarable attention will be given to socio-economic and demographic factors in the Frisian case-study area (chapters 1 and 2), following which theoretical concepts concerning motivating circumstances and personal characteristics of the migrants are discussed (3). Unraveling the image of America provides the theme for the essay dealing with fantasy and realism in the migration process (4). In examining the actual move to the other side of the Atlantic the focus is on occupational and geographical mobility of the migrants (5), and the effects of chain migration are made clear through community studies (6 and 7). The ethnic baggage is weighed at the last station of the trans-Atlantic trip (8).

*Baggage from emigrants on Rotterdam's quay*

### Sources of migration data

This study of northern Frisian migration to the United States relies heavily on two data sets. The first covers the emigrant population of the sending area from 1880 to 1915. The so-called *Bevolkingsregisters* or Population Registers provide a rich source of information concerning the departing emigrant. They list family name and first name, sex, relation to the head of the household, date of birth, place of birth, civil status, religious affinity, occupation, date of emigration, place of last residence, and intended destination. People who planned to leave had to obtain a Migration Certificate from the local authorities, although there was no penalty for not doing so. After this they were removed from the Population Registers with a firm deletion by the local official and marked as "left for America" or -when known- "left for Grand Rapids, Michigan". If a prospective emigrant had neglected to get such a Certificate, he was removed from the Population Registers with the remark "removed officially" [*ambtshalve geroyeerd*] when the local official became aware of the departure.

Thus, it was possible to glean from the Population Registers all the marked names of persons who intended to leave for the United States. The archival journey included the city hall of Franeker for the records of the municipality of Barradeel, the townhalls of Ferwerd and St. Annaparochie for the municipalities of Ferwerderadeel and Het Bildt, the regional archives [*Streekarchief*] in Dokkum for the municipalities of Oostdongeradeel and Westdongeradeel, and the townhall of Witmarsum for the municipality of Wonseradeel. In this way, one by one, I was able to collect data on emigrants for the years 1880-1914. The resulting data set – named "Frisians in America, 1880-1914" – contains almost 10,000 northern Frisians who left for the United States of America. This quantitative information meets the demands of social research by allowing individual level time-series analyses of demographic and social differentials. Total in- and out-migration can also be compared to the total population.[14] For this study all of the variables in the Population Registers will be analysed.

The reliability and individual variables in the *Bevolkingsregisters* will be discussed later. However, some comments on the use of the Population Registers should be made. The whole administrative procedure of the emigrant registration was complicated and led to considerable unregistered or "clandestine" emigration. R.P. Swierenga, after comparing international data sets of Dutch migrants, concluded that most likely one out of three emigrants left unregistered.[15] But this does not necessarily indicate *inaccurate* registration, but rather the *incompleteness* of the data. M.L. Samson in his study of Wisch in the Dutch Achterhoek around the turn of the century, comments that his source-critical analysis of the population data revealed clearly that the migration data were highly reliable, especially as compared with that of many other countries.[16] Y. Schreuder noted that the Dutch *Landverhuizerslijsten* [and therefore the Population Registers from which they are derived] are valuable because they are the only source that recorded place of last residence methodically, which makes it possible to link the place of origin in the Netherlands and the initial settlement in the United States.

The second data set is titled "Frisians in the USA, 1900/1910" and contains detailed demographic, social and economic information on Frisian immigrants in the United States. This data was collected from the manuscripts of the decennial U.S. Census for the years 1900 and 1910. The 1890 federal manuscripts were destroyed by fire. The U.S. Census contains information about places of residence and tenure, names, personal data including children born and living, length of marriage, the relationship between the members of the household, place of birth, parents' origin and citizenship, education, and occupation and ownership of the house or farm. With this information the immigration historian can seek to answer questions concerning geographical and regional aspects, the material living sphere, the family and household structure, demographic information and the occupational structure of the Frisian ethnic group.

It is not an easy job to distill the northern Frisians from the census manuscripts. First of all, the places of settlement are not known precisely and secondly the Frisians are only a small ingredient of the total U.S.

population of about 76 million souls in 1900. The details and usefulness of the Census as a source also will be discussed later, but some general remarks are appropriate here.[17] As happened with the Population Registers, most data entry of the Censuses involved straightforward transcriptions, but several value judgments had to be made. For example, Frisian names written by an American census taker were not always accurate and the date of birth of the immigrant was recorded by month and year in the 1900 Census and by age only in the 1910 Census. These inadequacies led to linkage problems and required personal judgments.[18] However, the combination of the Dutch and American databases provides a linked file that is called "Linked Files: Frisians to America and Frisians in the U.S.A. Computer Compilation." This data file makes possible the reconstruction and analysis of the trans-Atlantic experience of the northern Frisian immigrant group. In the linkage file each emigrating Frisian family or single person is identified in his place of origin and also in his place of settlement in the United States. The Dutch Population Registers and the U.S. Census Manuscripts, as well as their combined linked file provide the structural basis for more impressionistic or narrative information of qualitative sources.

There is a third *possible* quantitative source for the study of Frisian overseas migration. This is the American passenger arrival lists which contain information of historical and demographic interest. These U.S. ship passenger lists, held by the Balch Institute in Philadelphia, were sworn documents that captains of ships were required by law to deliver to Customs upon arrival in the United States from any foreign port.[19] For the period 1820-1955 they provide information concerning names, relationship with other family members, sex, age, nationality, town of origin, occupation, literacy, type of immigration, class of travel, port of embarkation, port of debarkation, and date of arrival.[20] Unlike the Dutch Emigrant Records or *Landverhuizerslijsten*, the U.S. passenger lists give information (like year of birth, occupation, nationality) concerning *all* family members, including women and children. However, the U.S. passenger lists did not add enough new information pertinent to this study to require their inclusion here. The passengers lists do *not* usually include the very valuable information of the (intended) destination in the United States of the Frisians. And personal information on *all* the northern Frisian family members of emigrating households could be obtained from the data of the Dutch Population Registers. Passenger lists from the Dutch port of embarkation – Rotterdam – are not available before 1900 and would not have been complete because the Frisian immigrants occasionally left via other ports.[21] Consequently, the quantitative basis of this study is an analysis of the data from the Dutch Population Registers in combination with the U.S. Census Manuscripts.

Besides the quantitative orientation, this research also deals with the social, informational, and opinion-making aspects of Frisian overseas migration. Some important trends can be reconstructed only by integrating quantitative sources with the more qualitative ones like the local press dealing with emigration, immigrant letters, personal documents, diaries, autobiographies, immigrant newspapers, church records, county histories, and oral traditions. In my search for these archival documents I relied heavily on the specialized local archives on the Dutch in the United States like the Calvin College Archives in Grand Rapids, Michigan. In the Netherlands many primary sources were collected by organizing a national immigrant letter campaign, which provided letters written to the native country and many other personal documents.

The massive trans-Atlantic migration to the United States around the turn of the century has been the subject of research for a long time. In the study of Frisian migration I have used these secondary sources often, especially because they show different historiographical approaches. In some cases the literary approach to the subject gave a refreshing perspective. These primary and secondary sources have yielded a great deal of valuable information about Frisian migration to the United States around the turn of the century.

*Painting of C. van der Zwalm, 1914.*
*View of the river Maas with the steamer 55.* Statendam II, *Collectie Maritiem*
*Museum 'Prins Hendrik', Rotterdam*

# Chapter 1 Not gone yet:
# the different municipalities and their local distinctions, 1880-1914

## 1.1 Introduction

> Looking to last years' harvest, we may conclude that it was almost a total disaster. Potatoes are of very bad quality and minor yield. Corn is very cheap and at the moment also flax only makes 1.00 to 1.20 guilders per bundle. Cattle still are pretty expensive. You can understand that for farmers and *gardeniers* [former land laborers who cultivated their own piece of land to make a living] the outlook is none too bright and this also affects the working class in a highly negative sense. Consequently, there are many families who make up their minds to leave Friesland to seek their fortune in the new fatherland: America.[1]

This personal letter was written in 1891 by R.J. Algra from the village of Ee in the province of Friesland to J.D. Douma in the village of Pella, Iowa, on the other side of the Atlantic Ocean. The letter does not reflect a very flourishing perspective. Should we consider Algra's judgment exceptional for his time? What can we say about the social and economic conditions in the northern Frisian clay area in the late nineteenth and early twentieth centuries? Friesland, seventh province of the Netherlands, is bordered on the north by the North Sea, on the north east by the Lauwers Sea, on the east by the provinces of Groningen and Drenthe, on the south by the province of Overijssel and the Zuiderzee, and on the west by the Zuiderzee. J.H. Veenendaal writes in his description of the Netherlands in 1880: "The greatest length from West to East is a thirteen hours' walk, the longest latitude from North to South takes fourteen hours."[2]

The province of Friesland can be divided into three geographical districts: clay, sand, and peat-soil topped with clay. The clay area stretches alongside the North Sea and is divided into an agricultural region [*De Bouwhoek*] and a grassland region [*De Greidhoek*]. The sand area lies on the east side of the province and is called *De Wouden*. In between these areas lies the peat-bog soil, or *Het Lage Midden* with the famous frisian lake district. On the west side of this center the peat is topped with a layer of clay, which becomes thinner going east. In *De Greidhoek* one finds grasslands, because the clay, and peat soils are not suited for agriculture.[3]

To gain an insight into Frisian economic activity in the second half of the nineteenth century, it is useful to examiné foreign trade for the year 1870. From the list of foreign trade (*Staat van Buitenlandse Handel*) of 1870, it is possible to distill the Frisian share in the Dutch trade balance.

Map I. *The province of Friesland with the different municipalities*

Table 1.1    **Import and export of the Frisian economy in 1870:**

| products | export | import | export surplus |
|---|---|---|---|
| agricultural | ƒ.  9,040,000 | ƒ.  1,290,000 | ƒ.  7,750,000 |
| dairy and cattle | ƒ. 26,075,000 | ƒ.     80,000 | ƒ. 25,995,000 |
| hunting and fishing | ƒ.     228,000 | ƒ.      1,000 | ƒ.     227,000 |
| Total | ƒ. 35,343,000 | ƒ.  1,371,000 | ƒ. 33,972,000 |

**Source:** *Staat van buitenlandse handel, 1870*

Table 1.1 reveals that the province of Friesland profited from agricultural trade. Hunting and fishing were of secondary importance. In every other branch the imports totally outran the exports, except for some businesses of minor importance like (roofing) tiles and Dutch gin (*jenever*). Friesland clearly was an agricultural province.

Frisian agriculture underwent modernization in the late 19th century. Even before 1870 there had been shifts in cultivation patterns. Peas and oats replaced cole seed, and in the 1890s sugar beets became the best solution for the drop in profits from madder (*meekrap*). Farmers increasingly turned to potatoes. It became possible to vary the cultivation scheme, and the use of fertilizer made cropping choices more flexible.

There were numerous regional differences in Frisian agriculture.[4] Some regions suffered from a decline of arable land. Between 1880 and 1910 there was an absolute decrease of 7,000 hectares (from 50,000 to 43,000 hectares) in arable land in the province. The grassland however, increased in these years from 199,000 hectares to 215,000. This is in contrast to the province of Groningen, where in the same period the proportion of arable land increased from 119,000 to 131,000 hectares. In a third province with heavy overseas migration, Zeeland, the arable land was enlarged from 107,000 to 111,000 hectares.[5]
The total production of grains in Friesland occupied 25,650 hectares in 1851/1860. In 1914 it had decreased to 13,155 hectares. Generally in the period 1880-1914, the grassland expanded at the expense of agricultural land, and so did the cattle-farms at the expense of the growing of grain. The use of arable land changed; cultivation of wheat, oats, barley, buckwheat, cabbage seed, and flax decreased, while the growing of potatoes, sugar beets, canary-seed, mangold and clover increased.[6]

Between 1849 and 1914 the Dutch government organized occupational censuses in the years 1849, 1859, 1889, 1899, and 1909. This counting was connected with the population census, except for the years 1869 and 1879 in which no occupational census was taken.
The following table is based on data from occupational censuses of 1899 and 1909.

Table 1.2  **Percentage of persons in the labor force in three economic categories in three different provinces in the northern Netherlands:**

| Province | Industry | | Agriculture | | Trade | |
|---|---|---|---|---|---|---|
| | 1899 | 1909 | 1899 | 1909 | 1899 | 1909 |
| | % | % | % | % | % | % |
| Friesland | 24 | 24 | 41 | 41 | 10 | 10 |
| Groningen | 30 | 29 | 36 | 33 | 10 | 10 |
| Overijssel | 41 | 44 | 35 | 33 | 6 | 5 |

**Source:** *Uitkomsten der beroepstelling in het Koninkrijk der Nederlanden op den 31sten December 1899 en 1909*

In 1889, 31.8 percent of the Dutch labor force worked in agriculture and 33.6 percent in industry.[7] Industrialization in the province of Friesland was not very significant, even less than in the provinces of Groningen and Overijssel. In 1889 only 3.5 percent of the labor force worked in small-scale industry.[8] Handicraft and industry never held influential positions in the Frisian countryside. Although carpenters were necessary, a village could consider itself privileged if a shoemaker or a weaver were present. Usually these craftsmen settled in the cities or the major municipal centers, where the farmers and rural folk gathered at the weekly market to do business with the local traders and shopkeepers.[9]

Leeuwarden is the only major city in Friesland that had a certain standing and a varied occupational structure. In 1890 its population was about 30,000. The main factory was a straw-board factory, with a work force of 144 persons. This provincial capital also had a gas company (46 laborers) and a cigar factory (42 persons). All the other businesses in 1890 had fewer than 40 laborers.[10] Each of the cities of Harlingen, Franeker, Sneek, and Bolsward had a population of more than 4,500 souls. For the remaining eleven cities of the province the population figure was lower.[11]

In the whole province at the turn of the century, the clay industry or *tichel-werken* (brick yards, roofing tiles companies, and finer pottery), the cigar factories, and the oil mills were the businesses with the highest number of laborers.[12] Frisian cities were trade and provision centers for their agricultural hinterland.

In 1909, 41 percent of the Frisian labor force still worked in agriculture, a figure which does not include workers in the dairy industry. In the provinces of Groningen and Overijssel industry was relatively more developed than in Friesland.

The industrial breakthrough began in the dairy business. In 1879 the first private dairy factory opened in the village of Veenwouden and within a few years there were other private initiatives. In 1886 Warga was the first to get a cooperative dairy factory. By 1900 there were 126 different dairy factories and the industrial revolution had come to the countryside.[13] After 1880 a total shift from home production to factory production had taken place and from the turn of the century the dairy business became the most important industry in the province of Friesland.[14]

Some attention should be paid to Frisian cattle industry. The specific marine climate and the nineteenth century business cycle favored the expansion of stock breeding. According to the cattle census of 1910, Friesland had the highest total in the Netherlands, 118 cows per 100 hectares of cultivated soil, compared to the national average of 94.[15] Most of the cattle served the dairy industry and were used for breeding. In the nineteenth century exporting fat cattle for food became a less important export product than pedigree ("herd-book") cattle, and the Frisian black-patched cows became world famous.[16]

The agrarian crisis of the late nineteenth century had a great impact on Dutch agriculture. The drop in prices during this depression affected the diverse agricultural products differently, but it finally resulted in the adaptation of new cultivation schemes. In 1899 in a letter to his family in Paterson, New Jersey, Broer J. Soolsma from Franeker mentioned some changes:

> Nowadays in this environment a lot of sugar beets have been raised and this has been real profitable for farmers and laborers because it is easy raising for the farmers and many laborers are needed for this crop. This time of year hardly enough hands are available for lifting, decapitating and transport, thus the workman makes good money nowadays... Green peas now are raised a lot too, this is important for the poor people too, while there are households that earn 7 to 8 Guilders a week with that, with selecting the peas. This is done by the wife and children, the husband has another job too, so the situation here is not burdensome at the moment.[17]

Between 1878 and 1895 the Frisian clay areas were heavily affected by the depression, and it was not until 1905 that the region regained its strength. In the *Bouwhoek*, where the farmers became very wealthy during the boom period of the 1870s, the drop of prices had a huge impact. The situation of the land laborers became untenable and because of the agricultural nature of the province, these workers did not easily find employment outside of agriculture.

Since there was a very high percentage of land laborers among the migrants to the United States, their position in the Frisian clay area deserves special attention. The best study of the Frisian laboring class is T. van der Wal's *Op zoek naar een nieuwe vrijheid* [Search for a new freedom]. Van der Wal concludes that between 1870 and 1895 wages and working hours were too low and too long. In the eighties and nineties complaints were drowned by the all-important desire for employment. Many farm laborers did not have steady contracts.[18] Housing in the clay area was not very comfortable with poor heating and lighting and families were usually big. Nutrition was insufficient and unbalanced. The food of laborers, for example, consisted of

*Clay country around Ooster-Nijkerk*

rye bread with grease or syrup in the morning and potatoes with mustard sauce for dinner. Vegetables or meat were rarely tasted. The drinking water supply was very poor. The waterworks of the *Leeuwarder Waterleiding Maatschappij* [The Leeuwarder Waterworks Company] came into use in 1888 and at that time a new chapter in public health began. Generally speaking, health insurance was not very common among the laboring class. In most factories workers had to rely on the uncertain "charity" of their employer when illness struck.

Van der Wal concludes that one can not speak of a rising prosperity for Frisian laborers between 1870 and 1895.

He finds some improvement in the personal well-being of the laborers, but at the same time he plays down this aspect by stating: "People's well-being just has to be paid from people's prosperity, which was lacking in Friesland after 1878."[19] As we turn to the occupational structure of Frisian overseas migrants, we will discuss specific laborers and their working conditions more directly.

The conclusion must be drawn that in the nineteenth century the Frisian economy became increasingly one-sided, and this poor economic structure caused a relative decline. The pillars of the 18th century Frisian economy: the carrying-trade, the peat-digging, agriculture, and the industry for a local market, had lost their strengths as well-integrated segments of a healthy economy. At the turn of the century only agriculture retained its role. Except for the dairy industry, hardly any new industries became established in Friesland. The position of Friesland in the national and international trade became very unfavourable because the *Zuiderzee* lost its importance to the *Noordhollandsch* and the *Noordzee* channel.

Friesland lost its independent economic – as well as political – position and according to J.L. van Zanden this can be attributed to the processes of economic and political integration in which the province got involved in the nineteenth century.[20]

The region of greatest emigration was the *Bouwhoek* in the northern part of Friesland. Nine municipalities [*gemeenten*] belonged to this area: Kollumerland, Oostdongeradeel, Westdongeradeel, Ferwerderadeel, Het Bildt, Menaldumadeel, Franekeradeel, Franeker, and Barradeel. In a few municipalities of the *Greidhoek* some lands were also used for agriculture. For example, in Wonseradeel in the north in the *Lytse Bouhoeke* [the small *Bouwhoek*], the small towns of Pingjum, Arum, Witmarsum, and Kimswerd, all bordering *De Bouwhoek*, had clay lands. The heavy clay soil is hard to farm and in times of heavy rainfall fieldwork is very difficult. But the heavy clay also has advantages: it does not demand such intensive manuring and summer weeds do not come up so easily as in sandy soil areas.[21]

The area of research is defined by clay and sea. The selected municipalities all have a rural character. For the purpose of a comparative analysis the urban regions such as the cities of Harlingen, Dokkum, and Franeker have been left out. The municipalities of Oostdongeradeel, Westdongeradeel, Ferwerderadeel, Het Bildt, Barradeel, and Wonseradeel form a bloc in the northwest of the province. What follows is a brief geographical, socio-economic and religious description of each of these municipalities. Together they offer a general picture of the Frisian clay area. I will not answer a standardized questionaire for each municipality. The idea is to focus on a specific typology. Migration data will be discussed in the following chapters dealing with demographic factors and with the migratory movement of each municipality.

## 1.2 Oostdongeradeel: religion

Around the turn of the century the village of Anjum was the largest of the 13 villages in the municipality of Oostdongeradeel. In 1879 Anjum had 1,643 inhabitants but then declined to 1550 by 1913. Transport services in the region were poor. The only possibility over land was the stage coach from the city of Dokkum to the village of Oostmahorn and the local railway from Dokkum to Metslawier. Steamships brought people, cattle, and trading goods from the village of Ee to the cities of Leeuwarden and Dokkum. Those who did not have their own carriage walked many miles.
The villages were quite isolated. The majority of the labor force worked in agriculture which meant that in summertime a lot of work had to be done and in wintertime people often were unemployed. Among the agricultural professions, the farm laborers represented the highest percentage.[22]
Housing was poor and it was 1912 before the first public housing was built. The supply of houses between 1880 and 1900 generally equalled the number of households, but the quality was poor.[23]
According to Van der Wal's study of the Frisian labor movement, the

*The* Gereformeerde *church in Metslawier.*

situation of the laborers was depressed. In 1892 one of the editors of the journal *Het Vaandel* reported that the situation in Friesland was worse than in Ireland. He pointed to Oostdongeradeel where 1,434 people received poor relief out of a population of 8,000, and more than half (770) of those on poor relief were 12 to 60 years of age and able to have a full time job.[24] Remarkable in this perspective is a citation from the annual report of the municipality [*gemeenteverslag*] of 1910:

> The higher demands of life which can be more easily met in America with its higher wages than here on our soil are more responsible for the increasing emigration to that continent than the desire to escape poverty. Still, concerning aging and illness etc., the laborers' certainty of subsistence leaves much to be desired and therefore people become subject to public charity. However a specific needy class does not exist in this municipality. Compared to earlier days, the situation of the laborer in this municipality has really improved.[25]

The report also refers to the reasons for this progress: agriculture is flourishing again, better economic conditions, cooperation between public and religious poor relief, and the the provision of work for the unemployed.[26]

Around 1900 more people were still members of the Dutch Reformed [*Hervormde*] church than of the more orthodox, *Gereformeerde* church. By 1909, according to the census, the more Calvinistic adherents outnumbered the Reformed (table 1.3). In 1880 this ratio was totally different: at the start

of that year the Reformed made up 90 percent of the total population of Oostdongeradeel.[27]
Between 1880 and 1914 the proportion of *Hervormden* decreased in contrast to the *Gereformeerden*.[28]

Table 1.3  **Proportional percentage for every municipality of the total number of persons belonging to the most important religious denominations:**

|  | N.H. | R.K. | C.G. | None | Other |
|---|---|---|---|---|---|
| Barradeel | 54 | 2 | 26 | 14 | 4 |
| Ferwerderadeel | 44 | 0 | 48 | 3 | 5 |
| Het Bildt | 30 | 0 | 24 | 35 | 11 |
| Oostdongeradeel | 44 | 0 | 50 | 2 | 3 |
| Westdongeradeel | 55 | 0 | 31 | 7 | 6 |
| Wonseradeel | 54 | 9 | 24 | 10 | 4 |
| Average | 47 | 2 | 34 | 12 | 6 |

**Source:** *Census of 1909. Uitkomsten der negende tienjaarlijkse volkstelling*

In the same years when a large part of the Frisian proletariat left the *Hervormde Kerk* to join Domela Nieuwenhuis, another part joined Abraham Kuyper and his sympathizers and left the same church through a different gate. Some orthodox clerics sought for an alternative and the mass of their followers flocked from the *Hervormde Kerk*. The *Doleantie* was a fact. Soon it became clear that the *Doleantie* and the *Afscheiding* of 1834[29] had a lot in common and this resulted in the merger of both persuasions in 1892 with the name: *Gereformeerde Kerken in Nederland*. From the beginning of this massive fusion, resistance appeared among certain clergyman who did not want the *Christelijk Gereformeerde Kerk* to lose their identity. This resistance finally made sure that this denomination was preserved as an independent church.[30] Table 1.4 shows the main religious groups in the province during the time of mass migration to overseas destinations.

Table 1.4  **Religious denominations in the province of Friesland (December 31, 1879):**

| | |
|---|---|
| Hervormd/Reformed | 256,184 |
| Christelijk Gereformeerd/Christian Reformed | 22,471 |
| Doopsgezind/Mennonite | 17,553 |
| Evangelisch Luthers/Evangelical Lutheran | 1,193 |
| Rooms Katholiek/Roman Catholic | 26,161 |
| Nederduitse Israëliet/Jewish | 2,199 |
| Other/None/Unknown | 4,116 |
| Total Population | 329,877 |

**Source:** *Census of 1879. Uitkomsten der zesde tienjarige volkstelling*

### 1.3 Westdongeradeel: fishing

The municipality of Westdongeradeel was situated west of Oostdongeradeel.[31] In the 1880s it had many small towns and hamlets, but no major city. The villages of Holwerd, Nes and Ternaard were the most important and the latter was the municipality center. Most inhabitants made a living in agriculture, although fishing was quite important too. In Paesens-Moddergat and Wierum along the *Waddenzee* coast, the families mostly gained their income through fishing in the North Sea.[32] Around 1880 Paesens-Moddergat had a fleet of 22 ships and Wierum had 17. The women also worked in the

*House behind the dikes between the villages of Holwerd and Ternaard*

fishing business, searching for the sea worms that the men used for bait and selling the catch door-to-door. A contemporary writer reported that most fishermen quit fishing in the summer months because they worked on the farms, mainly digging potatoes. In wintertime the fishermen had no employment to fall back on, unlike the farm laborers who spun flax. If fishing was poor, there was often no alternative to the public dole.[33]

In 1883 the Paesens-Moddergat fleet experienced a major disaster. In the first week of March, because of very bad weather, 17 of the 22 ships were wrecked and 83 of the 109 fishermen perished at sea. The Frisian chronicler G.A. Wumkes described 200 families in mourning.[34] Although a fund was created to support the afflicted area, the fishing business never regained its strength, and suffered also from competition from steamships.

Later in 1893 the village of Wierum also met disaster. And as in Paesens-Moddergat it was the final blow for a profitable fishing business.[35] In 1915 a governmental report concerning coastal fishing did not even mention the villages of Paesens-Moddergat and Wierum.[36]

According to the estimates of 1891 the municipalities of Oostdongeradeel and Westdongeradeel had the highest expenditure for poor relief in the province. This was in fact a strange situation because these regions were totally rural, while normally the cities housed the masses of the poor. Nevertheless, in 1891 the city of Leeuwarden budgeted ƒ 1.77 per inhabitant for poor relief, while Oostdongeradeel reserved ƒ 4.12 and Westdongeradeel ƒ 3.36. Compared to the rural municipalities with their heavier burdens, the cities therefore had a rather favorable position.[37]

In 1892 A. Rauwerda concluded that 30 percent of the Frisian population received poor relief.[38] In the *Bouwhoek* this was related to seasonal work. In 1850 J.H. Beucker Andreae noted that in Westdongeradeel the average workforce per farm was 4 men, 6 found temporary jobs, while 5 laborers did not find any employment. In winter most of the casual laborers were on poor relief and in summer they worked on the land. In the municipality of Ferwerderadeel, the proportion was 12-14 laborers with permanent jobs per 100 laborers with casual jobs.[39] In other parts of the province, as in *De Greidhoek*, the proportion of permanent to casual laborer was 1 to 4. This more favorable situation was due to the fact that not so many seasonal laborers were needed and that the labor force was smaller than in the clay area. J.J. Spahr van der Hoek characterizes Beucker Andreae's description as typical for *De Bouwhoek* in the nineteenth century. Because of the surplus of laborers, wages remained low and the gap between employer and employee widened.[40]

The people of Westdongeradeel mostly belonged to the *Hervormde Kerk*. According to the census of 1879 88 percent of the inhabitants were Reformed [*Hervormd*]. In 1909 this figure had dropped sharply to 55 percent because of a membership shift, and at that time 31 percent belonged to the *Gereformeerde Kerk* (see table 1.3). As in other Frisian villages almost every village in Westdongeradeel had its own church, the pride of the community. Most often, it was the only public building in the neighborhood and people gathered in the church for many important community matters. Although the first purpose of the church was worship, the building was also used for elections and town meetings.[41] Furthermore, most villages had some shopkeepers and trade people. Usually, there was a smithy, a house painter's workshop, one or more taverns, and a carpenter shop. These businesses were very much involved in the weal and woe of agriculture.[42]

According to Van der Wal, socialism did not attract much support in Oost- and Westdongeradeel. Maybe this had something to do with the high percentage of *Gereformeerden* in these municipalities. Some authors emphasize that *De Dongeradelen* have a long conservative tradition. In 1891 the village of Holwerd served as the center of action for the labor movement because at that time it was the only community in northeast Friesland where socialists had a considerable following.[43]

### 1.4 Ferwerderadeel: education

The municipality of Ferwerderadeel was bounded on the east by West-dongeradeel, on the west by Het Bildt, on the north by the Waddenzee and on the south by the municipalities of Dantumadeel, Tietjerksteradeel, and Leeuwarderadeel. The landscape is characterized by dikes and mounds [*terpen*]. As in other regions in the clay area, as the years passed by the sea deposited large quantities of soil on the shore and enlarged Ferwerderadeel with polders. In 1872 the municipality covered a little more than 8,259 hectares. The accretion of land at that time was estimated at 700 to 800 hectares. About 3,800 hectares were used for grass and hay lands, while 3,350 hectares functioned as arable land with 19 percent given over to flax.[44] There were no major cities. Around the turn of the century the most important villages were Ferwerd, Marrum, Hallum, and Blija.[45]

*Birthplace in Ferwerd, Friesland (Zeedijk 23) of Sybren Lubberts Westra, who emigrated in 1899 to Michigan. Members of the* Sterk-*family are photographed around 1911. Photo donated by J. Hoekstra in Ferwerd*

Like other places in Friesland, Ferwerderadeel had its share in the development of the dairy industry. In 1891 a decision was made to erect a cooperative dairy factory in Wester-Nijkerk in the neighboring municipality Westdongeradeel. This had to be enlarged in 1893 because of the many farmers who subscribed. In the same year a new steam dairy factory was built in the hamlet of Bartlehiem close to the village of Hallum. Most of the traditional butter and cheese production at the farms lost their meaning because they were transferred to the factories. The department of agriculture reported in 1904, that the farm production of butter was 1.9 million kilograms against 11.7 kilograms in the dairy factories of Friesland.[46] This rapid change also indicates that butter and cheese farmers did not need as many laborers.

As in the Dongeradelen, there was much seasonal labor in Ferwerderadeel and many workmen were unemployed in winter. The cultivation of flax helped to fill the off-season days. Some entrepreneurs bought large quantities of flax to treat during wintertime. Only during certain months in spring and summer was the entire labor force able to find work, a situation that had already lasted at least a decade, writes a well-educated farmer in 1892.[47] Indicative of the endemic unemployment problem is the creation in 1892 of a commission for the unemployment relief by the *Friesche Maatschappij van Landbouw* [Frisian Society for Agriculture] in Ferwerderadeel. This commission was subsidized by the municipality and by absentee landlords.[48]

The educational system in the *fin de siècle* period was based on public and private schools. The public schools had a long tradition and almost every village had its own elementary school. The first denominational school was established in Ferwerd in 1865 and Wanswerd followed in 1866. In 1914 Ferwerderadeel counted eight public and eight denominational schools.[49] The quality of education continued to improve in the last quarter of the century.

But did the whole Frisian population profit from the educational system? If we read the comments of Jan Stap, one of the leaders of the Frisian labor movement, we learn that the field workers in the northern clay area struggled with the choice between school and fieldwork for their children. "Indeed, women's and children's labor in the fields is the main cause of the desultory school attendance in the countryside", wrote Stap in 1890.[50] And two years later A. Rauwerda stated that because of the fieldwork, absenteeism at school sometimes rose to 40 percent. He gives an example based on his own experience in the municipality of Het Bildt; in wintertime he had to deal with 80 children in his classes, while he had to be glad when 50 to 60 of them appeared in summertime. With fine irony Rauwerda added that this "gladness" was relative, because when he was confronted with the extra 20 to 30 'land guys' ["*landgasten*"] in wintertime, he had his hands full with youths "almost as big as himself."[51] Rauwerda was convinced that, although a municipal regulation forbade fieldwork for children under twelve, most farm laborers ignored this regulation because of financial need. A 1906 report concerning the economic situation of the farm laborers described the 1901 school-age act [*leerplichtwet*] as a "blessing" for the children of the laboring class.[52]

## 1.5 Het Bildt: laborers and strikes

If the observant traveller looks to the landscape of Het Bildt, he does not find the tortuous roads, the curved ditches or the fancifly-created pieces of arable or grasslands of the "Old" land. Het Bildt is polderland shaped by architects with rulers. Its roads run in straight lines from village to village and the dikes are fairly straight too. Compared to the other municipalities, the soil of Het Bildt is still young: the inpoldering began only in the early sixteenth century. The inspiration and funds for this huge project came from farmers and authorities in Holland[53], which led to outside functionaries becoming residents of this region. The inhabitants of Het Bildt therefore speak a different language than the Frisian used by other people in the northern clay area.[54]

The municipality of Het Bildt bordered Ferwerderadeel and Leeuwarderadeel in the east, Menaldumadeel and Barradeel in the south, and the Waddenzee in the northwest. The most important villages, St.Jacobiparochie, St.Annaparochie, and Lieve Vrouwenparochie lay from west to east along one road [*Middelweg*]. The grasslands were mostly situated in the *Zuidhoek*, south of the *Blikvaart*. The proportion of arable land to grassland was about three to one; agriculture was the most important source of income. Het Bildt did not have much industrial activity. Four corn mills, two dairy factories, a fruit canning factory, a few oil mills, a printing office, a brick yard, and some chicory drying-houses were the principal industries that served agriculture.[55] Fishing was also a source of income. In 1904 a fleet of 33 boats and 500 fish traps was available. Generally herring were the target, while salmon and seals were prized. But the risks assumed by the fishermen were quite high; storms readily destroyed their equipment.[56] The catch also varied immensely, and income was unstable. S.H. Buwalda, who studied the history of fishing in Het Bildt, noted that the income of one fisherman, Kees Jaaps Tjepkema, between 1846 and 1890, fluctuated between ƒ 68 to ƒ 700 per year.[57]

In characterizing Het Bildt, the position of laborers and the religious affinity of the population uniquely mark this municipality. "How can we describe the position of the laboring population in 1910," asks H.S. Buwalda. He concludes that agriculture flourished again after the languishing period of Jan Stap, but the laborers continued on the "old footing"[58]. What does Buwalda mean by "the old footing"? In fact, he points to generally miserable conditions of life among agricultural laborers in the eighties and nineties. Van der Wal concludes that one can hardly speak of a rising prosperity of the labor population in these years.[59] The laborers of Het Bildt were active in promoting better circumstances for laborers. The ideas of Ferdinand Domela Nieuwenhuis (universal suffrage and an eight hour working day) already were widespread in the area in 1885, especially because this "prophet of the laborer" had visited Het Bildt several times that year. P.J. Troelstra, poet and later chairman of the Frisian Social Democratic Labor Party [*S.D.A.P*], also spoke in Het Bildt as a spirited advocate of universal suffrage. In the winter of 1888-1889 the population of Het Bildt shared radical newspapers and speeches.[60]

The severe winters of 1888 and 1890 brought the pinch of poverty. Houses of laborers in the clay area became vacant as inhabitants moved to America. In the years from 1881 to 1883, for example, respectively 224, 162, and 132 registered persons left for the United States, a total of 518 emigrants in three years, which was 6 percent of the average total population of Het Bildt. From 1889 to 1893, respectively 176, 100, 97, 128, and 112 registered people moved overseas in a five-year time period. This totaled almost 7 percent of the average total population in those years.[61]

*Pieter Jelles Troelstra*

In the spring of 1888 in the peat areas of Friesland and Drenthe, peat diggers went on strike for better terms of employment. The laborers finally realized that they had to organize themselves to get ahead. In Het Bildt this conviction resulted in the creation of *Broedertrouw* [Brother Loyalty], a labor union that tried to prevent the *koppelarbeid* or labor broker system and field labor by married women and young children. G. van Tuinen was chairman and the laborer Jan A. Stap vice chairman.[62] In the spring of 1890, after unsuccessful talks with the farmers concerning better wages for the field workers, *Broedertrouw* organized the first strike. They demanded a wage of 12 cents per hour for men and 6 cents for unmarried women. The farmers reluctantly agreed and the laborers went back to work. The successful strike activated not only all the laborers in Het Bildt, but also those in other parts of the northern clay area. Money was collected everywhere; financial aid reportedly even came from America.[63]

But these developments widened the gap between employer and employee. The farmers began to avoid places where laborers gathered, such as the local barber shop. In the language of Het Bildt S.H. Buwalda describes the atmosphere like this:

> It is understandable that many farmers from Het Bildt are cautious concerning this
> movement [the labor movement, A.G.]. Many farmers who rented their farms considered

the demands of the laborers as an attack on their already sober existence of those years, while the owners of the land were afraid that higher wages would lower the rents. Until then, these matters had usually been discussed in the barber shop and on the bench in the barn where the farmlaborers sat warm and cosy on Sundays during winter (not attending church services anymore). That some farmers refused to let the laborers in the barn – when there was pleading for the rights of laborers, while formerly they only had duties – was understandable. Also the employers avoided the barber shop on Saturday night when the employees came in to have their beards removed. But now the meetings of *Broedertrouw* replaced these gatherings, usually on Sunday. Attendance grew, also by the women. Only the orthodox *Hervormden* and the *Gereformeerden* stayed away.[64]

The farmers also started to organize themselves and the high unemployment rate among the laborers was their weapon. Although at first some farmers sympathized with the miserable position of the laborers, in the end they had to show solidarity with other farmers. More strikes took place, but the success of *Broedertrouw* did not last. In 1892 a decision was made to make *Broedertrouw* a regular division of the *Sociaal Democratische Bond* [Social Democratic Union]. Most of the laboring population continued to live precariously and unemployment rates remained high.[65]

Socialism was fed by this depressing situation. H. Sannes concludes that the early labor movement not only was anti-religious, but also anti-monarchical. For example, when the young queen and her mother visited Friesland in 1892, a demonstration took place with slogans like: "Open the ballot box, people are ready!" and: "Wealth at your house, hunger at ours!". The result was that the ladies of Orange returned to Leeuwarden and cancelled their trip to Het Bildt.[66]

In the late nineties, Domela Nieuwenhuis increasingly turned towards anarchism, but Troelstra and others became leaders of a socialist movement that tried to reach goals by parliamentary action. In 1894 Troelstra also was the co-architect of the Social Democratic Labor Party [*Sociaal Democratische Arbeiders Partij*]. But in Het Bildt, especially on the west side, people sympathized with Domela. The situation in Het Bildt cannot be separated from other happenings in Friesland or the Netherlands. Unrest among laborers appeared in many places and proceedings against socialists, who threatened law and order, increased alarmingly.[67] G.A. Wumkes reports that at a conference of socialists in December 1893, Domela Nieuwenhuis and Troelstra fought about whether or not to participate in the general elections.[68] This difference of opinion among the leaders of the labor movement did not facilitate the uniting of the laborers themselves.

The labor movement in Het Bildt was also anti-religious. This was closely connected with the fact that in this municipality non-church affiliation was more widespread than in the other municipalities of the clay area. In 1879 0.4 percent of the population of Het Bildt did not report any religious conviction: they joined the category "none".[69] Most of the inhabitants of Het Bildt at that time belonged to the *Hervormde Kerk*.[70] Thirty years later the category "none" contained 35 percent of the population [table 1.3].[71] In 1909 one out of three persons in this municipality did not belong to any church. In his research concerning non-church affiliation in Friesland, M. Staverman draws the conclusion that both the Reformed revival or *Doleantie* (1886)[72] and the turning away from church demonstrated the disintegration of society. The secularization was caused by sociological factors like the drifting apart of the elite leaders of the *Hervormde Kerk* and the rural masses. The *Hervormde Kerk* showed little affection for the social movement of the laborers. Staverman is also convinced that the disintegration of church life originated in religious contradictions. Religious as well as social differences led to the decline of the *Hervormde Kerk*.[73]

Like irreligiousness, the *Doleantie* was a symptom of the deadly crisis in the *Hervormde Kerk* at the end of the nineteenth century. Staverman emphasizes that the mentality of leading socialists like Domela Nieuwenhuis, Pieter Jelles Troelstra, Vitus Bruinsma, Waling Dijkstra and Oebele Stellingwerf was far from ecclesiastical. Their ideas originated in the liberal milieu that was awakened by Multatuli's spirit of *De Dageraad*. For them the church was an institution without any values to offer to the individual or society.[74]

### 1.6 Barradeel: farmers and soil

The municipality of Barradeel bordered the *Waddenzee* in the northwest; Het Bildt in the northeast; Menaldumadeel, Franekeradeel, Franeker, and Wonseradeel in the south and southeast; and in the west Harlingen and the *Zuiderzee*. The width of the municipality was 17.5 kilometers. Originally Harlingen with its harbor was part of Barradeel, but because of its successful economic development Harlingen became an independent city. Barradeel counted nine villages, of which Sexbierum and Tzummarum competed for the designation: largest municipal village. In 1908 the former had 1,516 inhabitants, while the latter had 1,442. From 1867 on, "púndyken" or gravel roads connected the villages and in the eighties public transport brought the people to the Friday market in Leeuwarden. The waterways also carried passengers by boat. From different villages weekly boat services were available to the cities of Leeuwarden, Harlingen and Franeker.[75]

An observer walking along one of the two main roads in the municipality the gravel road between the villages or the "Oudedijk" that paralleled that road-would discover two different landscapes divided by the row of villages. The land north of this interface mainly was used as arable land, especially for potatoes, while the area south of this line was grassland. On both sides of the road, large farms stood like fortresses in the field. In smaller farmhouses scattered around "gardeniers" or cottagers tried to make a living.

In painting the portrait of the northern Frisian clay area, the farmer himself should not be forgotten. What was the world like for him in the second half of the nineteenth century? Spahr van der Hoek cites E. Allershof, who in 1880 thought that the farmer of Friesland was conservative. Many of them wanted other people to do the technical and scientific experiments, and were prejudiced against everything new. Allershof was convinced, however, that most farmers hoped for progress, but they did not want to take economic risks.[76] Although Allershof was describing the *woudboeren*, Spahr van der Hoek shows that this also characterized the *kleiboeren* who were influenced by the high unemployment rates of the last two decades of the nineteenth century. The introduction of new technologies and labor saving machinery surely must have been slowed down by the large labor surplus. In the *Bouwhoek* three different types of farmers can be distinguished: the *eigenboeren* who owned their farms and cultivated them themselves; the *huurboeren* who were tenants and usually rented house and land from a landlord, and the *gardeniers*, laborers who managed to rent or buy a small piece of land and cultivate it intensively. Around 1890 flax and early potatoes were commonly grown. The *gardeniers* ranked between the laborer and the "real" farmers. They often rented their land from year to year not directly from the landlord, but from the *huurboer*, or tenant farmer who profited greatly.[77] In the clay area the normal period of rent usually was seven years. But five years – like in *De Wouden* – was no exception and the seven years did not apply to *gardeniers*.[78]

In 1890, according to Spahr van der Hoek, the percentage of *eigenboeren* with one hectare or more in Friesland was the lowest in the whole country [table 1.5].

Table 1.5  **Users of one hectare or more by province:**

|  | total users | *eigenboer* % |
| --- | --- | --- |
| Friesland | 13,136 | 38,7% |
| Groningen | 9,460 | 77,7% |
| Drente | 9,253 | 60,8% |
| Overijssel | 19,185 | 67,6% |
| Gelderland | 29,961 | 56,9% |
| Utrecht | 5,557 | 48,3% |
| N-Holland | 13,784 | 53,5% |
| Z-Holland | 12,549 | 46,5% |
| Zeeland | 6,466 | 39,4% |
| N-Brabant | 29,024 | 67,7% |
| Limburg | 17,930 | 57,7% [79] |

**Source:** Spahr van der Hoek, *Geschiedenis van de Friese landbouw*, 1: 684

If we compare Friesland with its neighboring province Groningen, the percentage of farmers who owned their farms was barely half. Within Friesland the percentage of *eigenboeren* also varied. In 1890-1891 in the grasslands [*Greidhoek*] the percentage was 29, in the clay area [*Bouwhoek*] 27 and in the sandy east region [*Wouden*] 53 percent or nearly twice as high.[80] A high percentage of tenant farmers does not in itself always have to be disadvantageous. It very much depends on the regulations and circumstances under which the tenancy takes place. In Friesland many landlords did not live near their farms. This meant that the absentee landlord had no personal view or knowledge of his possessions, and the relationship between owner and tenant was not face to face. The following municipalities had absentee landlords who owned more than 30 percent of the land [table 1.6]:

Table 1.6 **Absentee landlords in 1897 who owned 30 percent or more of the land in the following municipalities:**

| Municipality | Total hectares | Absentee owned |
|---|---|---|
| Oostdongeradeel | 8,100 | 33% |
| Westdongeradeel | 6,600 | 45% |
| Ferwerderadeel | 8,600 | 57% |
| Het Bildt | 7,700 | 62% |
| Barradeel | 6,100 | 82% |

**Source:** V. Bruinsma, "De Friesche gemeenten en het wetsontwerp betreffende gemeente-financiën," *Vragen des Tijds* 2 (1897): 21. No figures are extant for the municipality of Wonseradeel

Barradeel had by far the most landowners living outside the municipality. Spahr van der Hoek also mentions that in 1893-1894 in the whole of Friesland 57 percent of the landed proprietors lived outside the province.[81] These owners considered their estates a long-term investment from which they hoped to get the highest possible profit for the lowest possible costs. Within Friesland the owning of land was also seen as a good investment, especially among retired farmers. Every new renting period, the landowners tried to raise the rent. In the 1870s the available statistics show an increase in rents even when land prices were falling. If the farmer was not able to pay, he was ordered to leave. In 1879-1880, farm rents declined, but not in proportion to the sharp drop in crop prices caused by the depression.[82] The phenonemon of the absentee landlord put an administrator or solicitor between landowner and tenant.

At public auctions these *strikjildskriuwers* or brokers earned a percentage of every higher bid for the rent, which sometimes inflated the prices enormously. The lease often contained many restrictions, like conditions for cultivating the farmyard, the maintenance of land and buildings, or a ban on fertilizers. Often the farmer was unsure about the continuation of the lease which could result in the neglect of the farmhouse and lands.[83]

In this context the social position of the different types of farmers in the clay area deserves attention. Spahr van der Hoek describes a landowner who forbade his tenant to wear a white collar on Sunday. The motto was "der moat ûnderskied wêze" [there has to be distinction].[84] However, the argument that the *eigenboer* had a higher social status than the *huurboer* [tenant] in the second half of the nineteenth century cannot be sustained. Th. van Welderen Rengers and J.H. Faber argued against this as early as 1913.[85] The arable farmer as well as the grassland farmer was classified according to the size of his farmhouse and land. This also determined his position in the local society and, as Spahr van der Hoek subtly recounts, the attention from potential suitors for his daughters. In the clay area the bigger farmers, both tenant or owner, set the fashion, even without taking part in the local life. Historically the *bouwboer* had a higher social status than the *greidboer*.

In the third quarter of the nineteenth century the social distance between farmer and laborer in the clay area (in Het Bildt particularly) became greater. This was caused by the fact that the farmers more often acted as managers.[86] It is also said that the farmers in the hey-day before 1877 prospered and were spoiled. H. Twerda voiced this as follows:

> Our farmers became rich. If one visited the farms in those days, it was all pomp and circumstance. A lot of money, beautiful clothes, nice things, and very often away from home, which became for many of them the most important thing to do. And in the evenings often to the bars. Why should one work hard and do one's best? Everything turned out right anyway, didn't it?[87]

Indeed, many farmers became more materialistic in those prosperous years, but the laborers did not get their share. Spahr van der Hoek blamed the widening gap between the farmer and laborer on the increasing prosperity of the farmer, but also on the fact that farmers had to pay for poor relief. In 1870 the Poor Relief Act [*Armenwet*] was changed, and the municipalities were given the responsibility for taking care of their own poor. The municipalities introduced new regulations and imposed a tax [*Hoofdelijke Omslag*] on the inhabitants to make poor relief possible.[88] The *Hoofdelijke Omslag* differed per municipality. Especially in the clay area where unemployment rates in wintertime were high, this was a heavy burden. Churches and private foundations also gave benefits to the poor and some poor people received money from civil as well as private foundations. Absentee landlords were not charged the municipal tax if they lived outside the municipality. The taxes for poor relief resulted in the flight of landowners to the cities where they sometimes could live on the same amount of money they had to pay on their estates for poor relief.[89]

The phenomenon of the absentee landlord imposed a heavier tax load on the remaining municipal population. Van der Wal refutes the idea that the cities had the heaviest burden because of the supposed crowding of the poor. He calculated the municipal expenditures for poor relief in 1891 in proportion to the total municipal expenditures and the population, and then compared the different municipalities. The comparison leads to the conclusion that the city of Leeuwarden had a much more advantageous position than the rural municipalities. Leeuwarden, for example, paid 7 percent of total municipal expenditures for poor relief, while Oostdongeradeel paid 43 percent, Westdongeradeel 35 percent, and Ferwerderadeel and Het Bildt 31 and 28 percent respectively. Van der Wal also notes that only a few wealthy people lived in the Frisian rural municipalities and that in the 1890s more than half of the Frisian soil was owned by persons living outside the municipalities.[90] Needless to say, the call for taxes on the absentee landlords became stronger and stronger.

"That Friesland's poverty and unemployment rates have risen sharply is not what I want to prove," wrote the socially-motivated Vitus Bruinsma in an article in 1894 entitled '*Hoe is Friesland te helpen?*' [How can Friesland be given a hand?]. Bruinsma documented the increasing poverty by noting that the Dutch government gave the amount of ƒ 15,770 to the needy municipalities in 1891, ƒ 166,390 in 1892 and ƒ 245,225 in 1893. In 1893 five of the six Frisian municipalities were classified as "needy" – except Wonseradeel – and the state subsidies to Friesland added up to about $^5/_6$ of the total state subsidies to needy municipalities in the whole country.[91] Van der Wal notices that between 1875 and 1890 the expenditures of the charitable institutions remained at almost the same level, while the total number of paupers increased. A contemporary calculated that in 1890 about 30 percent of the Frisian population received poor relief.[92]

How inadequate the system of poor relief still was before the turn of the century is also shown by writers in the municipality of Barradeel:

> Two quarters, a guilder when it was a large family, sometimes with rye bread but mostly without, this was how a family had to get by the whole week. They had potatoes in the cellar, sometimes peat in the loft, credit at the baker and the storekeeper and that was how they were making both ends meet. As soon as the earnings came in early summer, they paid the debts. That was how they suffered, year by year, without ever saving a penny. And as long as they were young and strong, this was possible. But when they aged, when they became aware that they could not supply their own wants anymore, what then? For them the old days held a terrifying prospect. Live with the kids and eat the bread of charity over there? Or pass the last days of life in the poor house, however good it could be? Then rather, much rather to the cemetery.[93]

One writer mentions, that 11 percent of the population of Barradeel was on poor relief in 1881.[94] There were limited possibilities to find work in trade and industry. In 1880 the most important factories in the municipality were five chicory drying-houses, a chicory distillery, a hulling mill [*stoomgrutterij*], a saw mill, and three corn mills. In 1911 the report for trade and industry [*Verslag van den Toestand van Handel en Nijverheid*] mentioned two cement factories, one chicory factory, five straw pressers, three saw mills, three corn mills, seven brick-yards (including tiles), an oil-mill, a lime-kiln, a tannery, a fishing-trade, and two dairy factories.[95] Although industry became more important around the turn of the century, agriculture and related businesses remained the most important source of jobs.

At the end of December 1879, 85 percent of the population in Barradeel belonged to the *Hervormde Kerk*. A few people were *Christelijk Gereformeerd,* and some Catholic. The latter is explained by the fact that Barradeel contained monasteries dating from the Middle Ages. Table 1.3 shows that in the first decade of this century, the municipality still had 54 percent *Nederlands Hervormden* and the *Gereformeerden* comprised 26 percent. Along with Het Bildt, Barradeel had the greatest percentage of non-church population in 1909: 14 percent. This had been a negligible category in 1879.

### 1.7 Wonseradeel: clay and grass

The southernmost region of the study area is the municipality of Wonseradeel. Laying south of the port of Harlingen and almost encircling the city of Bolsward, its territory is mainly sea clay. In the north around the villages of Kimswerd, Arum, Pingjum and Witmarsum one finds arable land, where mainly potatoes, corn, and flax were planted in the eighties. The cultivation scheme around 1910-1920 had changed more towards sugar beets, beans, and peas at the cost of corn.[96] The remainder of the municipality is covered with grasslands above which rise the towers of the different village churches. Around the turn of the century, average farm size was 25-35 hectares. A lot of energy was spent in draining the soil and using fertilizer. In the first decade of this century, both efforts led to higher profits, qualitatively as well as quantitatively. Cattle stock improved and increased. Farmers in the grassland area had turned to cattle-breeding in the second half of the nineteenth century and from 1879 on, the Frisian Herd-Book [*Fries Rundvee Stamboek*] stimulated their search for quality. However, the production of milk remained the main source of income.

In this context it is useful to say something about butter production in the late nineteenth century.[97] While sailing in Friesland in 1891, the Englishman Reginald Brougham met a man in the village of Grouw:

> I fancy he was what is called a butter agent, who buys butter here and sends it over to England, where whoever receives it mixes it with about eighty per cent. of filth, and sells it as "excellent Brittany butter," or under some other name, and pockets the difference. Anyway, the butter here is far the best I have ever tasted, and one doesn't, and moreover can't get it in England, so some one must play the fool with it, and certainly not my old man. This is a great butter centre; there are over sixty farms which "grow" nothing but butter and cheese, and it all goes to England, and I want to find the happy man who ultimately eats it in its native purity, for it's divine.[98]

The longtime-famous Frisian butter industry became threatened by Danish competition. The Danes succeeded in obtaining a higher price, mainly due to Frisian bungling in the production process as well as in the commission business. In addition, butter of poor quality from other provinces was brought to market labeled with Frisian certificates.

In the meantime the invention of margarine became a real competitive factor. For a long time the division between "natural" and "artificial" butter was not clear to the consumer.[99] Complaints became louder and louder in the late seventies and the idea spread that something had to be changed to save the trade. No agricultural area in the Netherlands was as dependent on the butter trade as the Frisian dairy area. Almost all the butter was exported. Van Zanden mentions that in 1912 Friesland produced on 12 percent of the Dutch cultivated land, about 24 percent of the national butter production.[100] He is convinced that the factory production of dairy products arose out of technical innovation rather than as a response to poor quality or low reputation. The first butter factory started in Veenwouden in 1879. Other initiatives soon followed. The biggest farmers set the trend which led to huge steam dairy factories with large capitalizations.[101]

At the same time the idea of co-operation took form among the farmers. In every realm where farmer and farm business came into contact with the market, co-operative societies were started to buy fertilizer, seeds, machines, and fodder, and also to sell and process agricultural products, and provide credit. Smaller farmers could profit from centralized buying of supplies. Co-operatives also worked to prevent monopolistic gains by buyers and suppliers. The result was that the co-operative dairy factories predominated even before the turn of the century, although, as Spahr van der Hoek states, the idealistic co-operative movement had to wait until the end of the agricultural crisis [i.e. more prosperity] to gain a permanent hold among the farmers.[102] The rise of the dairy factories and the co-operative movement were processes that strengthened each other. As a result butter production flourished again and Friesland was not oriented entirely to England as its export area. Germany also became an important market for Frisian dairy products, and from 1895 till 1912 Friesland reached its historical peak in butter production, while cheese production doubled between 1893 and 1913.[103] More and more laborers were able to find employment in the dairy factories, which was a welcome relief from the burden of unemployment.

The village of Makkum was an exception in Wonseradeel and even in Friesland as a whole. Although the municipality mainly was agriculturally-oriented, Makkum had a long tradition in specific handicrafts and industry.

| Datum | Namen | Volw. | Kind | Stoomschip | Klasse | Sp.Vracht | Bestemming | Comm. Spoorvracht |
|---|---|---|---|---|---|---|---|---|
| 1912. | Overgebracht | 49 | 16 | | | | | |
| 16 Feb. | Gebr. Wen J. Ybema | 2. | | | 2de p.p | | Racine Wisc. | |
| 9 Maart | Tjerk Kuipers | 2. | | | 2de | | Passaic N.J. | |
| 9 „ | W. Beenders | 3. | | Potsdam | 2de | | Hartford Con. | |
| 2 „ | R. Sevensma | 2. | | Rotterdam | 2de | 19.63 | Rochester N.Y. | |
| 24 Feb | Rein de Boer | 1. | | Rijndam | 2de | 69.25 | Treton Iowa. | |
| 24 „ | Rouke de Boer | 1. | | Rijndam | 2de | 69.25 | Treton Iowa | |
| 24 „ | Pier Abe Smit | 1. | | Rijndam | 2de | 69.25 | Treton Iowa | |
| 9 Mrt. | Wed. Tj. Dijkstra | 3. | | Potsdam | 2de | 128.25 | Grand Rapids Mich | |
| 9 „ | A. Hoos | 2. | | Potsdam | 2de. | 85.50 | Grand Rapids Mich | |
| 2 „ | A. Minks | 1. | | Rotterdam | 2de | 19.63 | Rochester N.Y. | |
| 27 April | Pieter vd. Plaats | 1. | | Noordam | 2de | 43.13 | Hudsonville Mich | |
| 27 „ | Riens Wiarda | 1. | | Noordam | 2de | 69.88 | Rock Valley Iowa | |
| 27 „ | Sijtse Hilt | 1. | | Noordam | 2de. | 69.88 | Rock Valley Iowa | |
| 27 „ | Haltje Wiarda | 2. | | Noordam | 2de p.p | | Rock Valley Iowa | |
| 18 Mei | Gosse Reinsma | 1 | | Potsdam | 2de | | Goshen Indiana | |
| 24 Aug. | Harmen Bloemsma | 1 | | Rijndam | 2de | 170.38 | Imperial Cal. | |
| 24 „ | Laas Bloemsma | 1 | | Rijndam | 2de | 170.38 | Imperial Cal. | |
| 24 „ | Watze Oostenveld | 1. | | Rijndam | 2de | 170.38 | Imperial Cal. | |
| 14 Dec | Jacob de Vries | 1 | | Rotterdam | 2de | | | |
| 1913. 1 Maart | Melle de Boer | 1 | | Rotterdam | 2de. | | | |
| 1 „ | R. Joustra | 1 | | Rotterdam | 2de | | | |
| 1 „ | Over te brengen. | 79 | 16 | | | | | |

*Page from a notebook of Douwe Reitsma, agent of the Holland America Line in Makkum*

It had ship-yards, brick-yards (four roof-tile factories in 1892), lime-kilns, a paper- and oil-mill, saw-mills, a corn-mill, a ropeyard, and a sailing-loft. The *tichelwerken* [finer pottery], which had a 300-year tradition, had become famous.[104] Certainly many laborers found jobs in these businesses, but not all the industries operated all year long. For example, in the lime-kilns the laborers worked about ten months a year, while the brick-yards, depending on the weather, operated only eight months a year.[105] Van der Wal in his analysis of wages concluded that farm laborers in the western clay area (northern part of Wonseradeel) had the highest pay level. This may be due to the competition from the industries and crafts in Harlingen and in Makkum.[106] The wages in these sectors were higher than in agriculture and therefore pushed all wages higher.

In most of the 28 villages of the municipality little industrial activity took place, and the church was the biggest building in town. Wonseradeel followed the general pattern of religious affiliation of northern Friesland. In 1879 83 percent of the inhabitants belonged to the *Hervormde Kerk* while 10 percent were Catholics. This picture changed by 1911 in favor of the *Gereformeerden*, who by then made up 24 percent, against the *Hervormden* with 54 percent.[107] The *Doleantie* also left its traces in this area. Many orthodox communities of the Reformed Church changed to follow the leaders of the *Doleantie*. As a result some Reformed communities became so small that for years they could not afford to call a minister.[108] It is obvious that the divisions within many religious communities had major consequences for the social life in the village. The corporate life was arranged according to religious affiliation. That meant that the village as a social unit often suffered severely. The struggle for spiritual independence was fought inside as well as outside the church.

In conclusion, the province of Friesland can be divided into three geographical districts: clay, sand, and peat-soil topped with clay. The case-study clay area is divided into an agricutural and a grassland region. Around the turn of the century almost half of the Frisian labor force worked in agriculture. Industrialization had had little effect. The agricultural nature of the province meant that the Frisian clay area was heavily affected by the agrarian depression in the two decades before 1900, which provided push factors for emigration.

The six municipalities with heavy emigration between 1880-1914 can be categorized by religious affiliation, circumstances of labor, economic nature, educational institutes, farmers and soil. Besides agriculture, the region was economically dependent on fishing. There were limited possibilities to find work in trade and industry, and the agrarian depression fed widespread labor unrest. Absentee landlords were a common phenomenon, which emphasized the physical and psychological distance between farmers and laborers. The majority of the people in the clay area affiliated with the *Hervormde Kerk*, and the good educational system was based on public and private schools, although not everybody profited. In this *fin de siècle* climate emigration appeared to be not only exceptional but a normal behavior.

## *Chapter 2* The demographic factor and the structure of migration

### 2.1 Introduction

After 1750 population levels in Europe and elsewhere increased rapidly. Historians have not fully explained this increase, although many agree that the demographic transition was caused by a drop in death rates, which resulted in a birth surplus. There were exceptions. For example Ireland's population decreased by 1 percent between 1800 and 1900 because of the potato famine and the system of primogeniture that determined the number of children who could hope to inherit land. While waiting for their inheritance, these children often delayed marriages, thus effectively reducing the period of female fertility. Some remained celibate or emigrated, because their hopes of receiving land had been in vain.[1]

For the Netherlands, a different picture developed. B.H. Slicher van Bath, J.A. Faber, and A.M. van der Woude have shown that between 1500 and 1650 the Netherlands experienced a relatively rapid population expansion, followed by a stagnation that lasted until 1815. The demographic transition took place around the period of French rule. Between 1815 and 1875 the natural annual population increase was about 10 per 1000 of the total population. In those years, "normal" rates were sometimes displaced by exceptional rates due to epidemics or potato disease such as in 1847.[2] After 1875 the natural increase in population grew slowly to 15.6 per 1000 in 1901-1905. Then it started to decrease gradually to 12.3 in 1916-1920.[3] Between 1879 and 1920 the Dutch population expanded from 4.0 to 6.9 million, an increase of 58 percent in forty years. E.W. Hofstee compared the population figures of the Netherlands with those of Belgium and concluded that after 1875 the increase in the Netherlands was extremely high. In the century after 1875, the Dutch population advanced by almost 10 million while the Belgians expanded only by 4.5 million. The Netherlands thus held an exceptional position within the Western European world and the search for causes of this development has been much debated among demographers. Birth and marriage, death, settlement and departure generally determine the size of the population and its increase or decrease.

While the causes of European population growth are complex, it is important to note that local variations can lead to different outcomes. "The rise of the population had distinct implications for peasant families and farms throughout Europe," argues John Bodnar, who points out that these farms usually relied on family labor. He adds that some birth control was practiced even by preindustrial peasant families, mainly by remaining unmarried for a certain time.[4] This Malthusian pattern of birth control originated in the preindustrial agrarian system (or as Hofstee calls it: *het agrarisch ambachtelijk patroon*), which resolved itself into a system of adjustment to the means of subsistence through low marriage frequency and high age of marriage. This was more or less a long-term policy linked with morals and manners.[5] After 1850 a new pattern appeared, the neo-Malthusian birth control, which was rooted in the change of mentality caused by modern dynamic cultural ideas. This resulted in more marriages as well as more marriages at a younger age, which according to Hofstee, was linked with the proletarianization of the labor class and with the growing resistance against a patriarchal society. However, the idea that one was allowed to marry only when able to support a family remained widespread. And it was not until 1880 that a real decrease of birth rates took place in the Netherlands (as well as in Germany and England). This decrease varied by region and by philosophy of life.[6]

## 2.2 The phantom of depopulation

If population figures at the national level are compared, specific regional patterns show up. In Friesland (as well as in Groningen, Noord- and Zuid-Holland and Zeeland) we find high percentages of young married persons and low percentages of never married people, while these percentages are respectively low and high in the eastern provinces of the country and very low and very high in Noord-Brabant and Limburg. Generally, comparing the Dutch provinces, we can speak of three characteristics for Friesland as well as Groningen in the nineteenth century: a relatively low age of marriage, a relatively high marriage frequency, and relatively low fertility rates.[7]

"The power of a country exists for the most part in the population total, because what good are large quantities of fertile land if no hands are available to harvest the fruits," stated a demographer in a geographic journal in 1885.[8] Studying the demographic literature concerning Friesland (and the Netherlands) in the late nineteenth century, many scholars saw a problem in the depopulation of the countryside. Articles with titles like *the exodus of people from rural areas*, and *flourish and decline of the Frisian municipalities based on population figures*, were no exception.[9] According to the census of 1879, Friesland together with Gelderland, Noord-Brabant, Overijssel, and Drenthe, belonged to the least densely populated provinces of the Netherlands. On every 1000 hectares an average of 993 persons were present in Friesland, while in Zuid-Holland this figure was 2,659 and Groningen 1,102.[10] However, in the period 1860-1880, the Frisian population increased at almost the same percentage as the average in the Netherlands as a whole.[11] This means that before the eighties we can not speak of an "alarming" situation in Friesland. For the same period J. Kuyper concluded that urbanization was noticeable in big cities like Amsterdam, Rotterdam, The Hague, Utrecht, Arnhem, and Groningen with an average increase of 36 percent. Kuyper did not record an alarming depopulation in the countryside in 1885 and therefore he thought that urbanization in the Netherlands was not as harmful to the rural areas as it was in other European countries at that time.[12]

If we take a closer look at the actual population figures of the different Dutch provinces based on the censuses, the Frisian case can be viewed in national perspective.

Table 2.1    **Population of the Netherlands and its provinces, 1869-1920 (in thousands):**

| Year | 1869 | 1879 | 1889 | 1899 | 1909 | 1920 |
|------|------|------|------|------|------|------|
| Groningen | 225 | 253 | 273 | 300 | 328 | 366 |
| Friesland | 292 | 330 | 336 | 340 | 360 | 383 |
| Drenthe | 106 | 119 | 131 | 149 | 173 | 210 |
| Overijssel | 254 | 274 | 295 | 333 | 383 | 439 |
| Gelderland | 433 | 467 | 512 | 567 | 640 | 730 |
| Utrecht | 174 | 192 | 221 | 251 | 289 | 342 |
| N-Holland | 577 | 680 | 829 | 968 | 1,108 | 1,298 |
| Z-Holland | 688 | 804 | 950 | 1,144 | 1,391 | 1,679 |
| Zeeland | 178 | 189 | 199 | 216 | 233 | 245 |
| N-Brabant | 429 | 466 | 510 | 554 | 623 | 734 |
| Limburg | 224 | 239 | 256 | 282 | 332 | 440 |
| Netherlands | 3,580 | 4,013 | 4,511 | 5,104 | 5,858 | 6,865 |

**Source:** Hofstee, *Korte demografische geschiedenis van Nederland,* 124-25

Table 2.2    **Increase in percentage of population of the Netherlands and per province:**

|  | 1869-1920 | 1879-1909 |
|------|------|------|
| Groningen | 62% | 30% |
| Friesland | 31% | 9% |
| Netherlands | 92% | 46% |

**Source:** Hofstee, *Korte demografische geschiedenis van Nederland,* 124-25

Tables 2.1 and 2.2 make clear that Friesland's population increased more slowly than the national rate or the other provinces. The contrast with the other Dutch provinces become particularly marked in the decades around the turn of the century: between 1879 and 1909 Friesland grew by 9 percent, while the national population grew by almost 46 percent. Even in Groningen, a neighboring province with similar socio-economic patterns, the population increased at a rate more than triple the Frisian figure. Some years even showed a population decrease for Friesland: 1881, 1882, 1883, 1889, 1890, and 1892. The same pattern was not found in any other province of the Netherlands, which justifies the conclusion that the Frisian population advanced at a slow pace and in some years even diminished.

Looking more closely at the regional differences within the province, it appears that the municipalities north of the railway from Harlingen to Groningen mostly lost population between 1880-1914. Friesland's depopulation occurred mainly in the very fertile clay area.[13] To explain the causes of Frisian population changes, a closer look at birth, marriage, and death rates is essential.

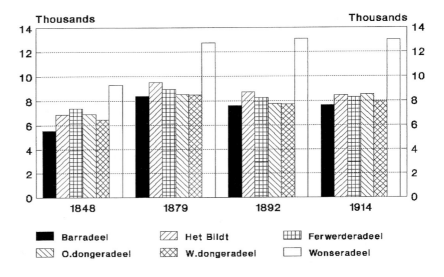

*Figure 2.1*

**Source:** *table constructed from V. Bruinsma,* "De vermindering der bevolking in Friesland," *Vragen des Tijds 2 (1894), table E, 124, and from A. Vondeling,* "Eat oer it tal biwenners," *table 1, 8-9*

### 2.3 Demographic variables and the Frisian clay area in Dutch perspective

Table 2.3 and figure 2.1 compare the population changes in the six Frisian municipalities.

Table 2.3  **Population of six Frisian municipalities 1848-1914:**

| Year | 1848 | 1879 | 1892 | 1914 |
|---|---|---|---|---|
| Barradeel | 5,550 | 8,354 | 7,611 | 7,658 |
| Het Bildt | 6,873 | 9,503 | 8,725 | 8,451 |
| Ferwerderadeel | 7,394 | 8,938 | 8,267 | 8,277 |
| O-Dongeradeel | 6,898 | 8,515 | 7,755 | 8,512 |
| W-Dongeradeel | 6,468 | 8,490 | 7,709 | 7,915 |
| Wonseradeel | 9,270 | 12,736 | 13,079 | 12,999 |
| Province | 245,784 | 327,720 | 336,296 | 368,088 |
| Netherlands | 3049,685 | 4037,010 | 4669,576 | 6212,697 |

**Source:** see figure 2.1

Table 2.3 shows that all the municipalities had a population increase in the period 1848-1879, which is analogous to the national population development. However, all the municipalities, except Wonseradeel, had in 1914 because of migration not even regained their population level as of 1879 (see figure 2.1).[14] This was in contrast to the rising provincial and national totals for that period.

Another picture appears when looking at birth and death rates in national and provincial perspective. E.W. Hofstee compiled the numbers of birth, death, and birth surplus. From this source table 2.4 is constructed:

Table 2.4  **Birth rates (A), death rates (B), and birth surplus (C) in the Netherlands and in the sea clay provinces per five year periods:**

| Period | Friesland | | | Groningen | | | Zeeland | | | Netherlands | | |
|---|---|---|---|---|---|---|---|---|---|---|---|---|
| | A | B | C | A | B | C | A | B | C | A | B | C |
| 1871/75 | 34.4 | 20.9 | 13.4 | 34.6 | 23.0 | 11.6 | 41.3 | 26.4 | 14.9 | 35.9 | 25.5 | 10.4 |
| 1876/80 | 34.3 | 19.3 | 15.0 | 35.9 | 20.4 | 15.5 | 38.2 | 22.4 | 15.8 | 36.3 | 23.0 | 13.3 |
| 1881/85 | 30.7 | 17.7 | 13.0 | 32.6 | 17.9 | 14.7 | 35.2 | 19.3 | 15.9 | 35.0 | 21.6 | 13.4 |
| 1886/90 | 29.5 | 17.7 | 11.8 | 31.0 | 17.4 | 13.6 | 34.0 | 18.8 | 15.2 | 33.7 | 20.6 | 13.2 |
| 1891/95 | 28.9 | 16.7 | 12.2 | 31.2 | 17.2 | 14.0 | 34.4 | 18.7 | 15.8 | 33.2 | 19.7 | 13.5 |
| 1896/00 | 27.9 | 14.8 | 13.1 | 30.7 | 15.0 | 15.7 | 33.2 | 16.8 | 16.4 | 32.3 | 17.3 | 15.0 |
| 1901/05 | 27.9 | 14.4 | 13.5 | 30.5 | 14.8 | 15.7 | 31.5 | 15.2 | 16.4 | 31.8 | 16.2 | 15.6 |
| 1906/10 | 25.8 | 13.1 | 12.8 | 28.8 | 13.0 | 15.8 | 28.7 | 13.8 | 14.9 | 29.7 | 14.4 | 15.3 |
| 1911/15 | 24.5 | 11.9 | 12.6 | 26.8 | 12.3 | 14.6 | 26.0 | 12.7 | 13.3 | 28.0 | 12.9 | 15.0 |
| 1916/20 | 23.9 | 13.0 | 10.9 | 25.3 | 13.5 | 11.7 | 24.3 | 12.9 | 11.4 | 25.9 | 13.6 | 12.3 |

**Source:** Hofstee, *Korte demografische geschiedenis van Nederland*, table 1, 122-23

This table shows that in the decade before 1881 birth rates in Friesland are only slightly lower than in the Netherlands as a whole. Zeeland shows remarkably high birth rates. In the beginning of the eighties birth rates drop

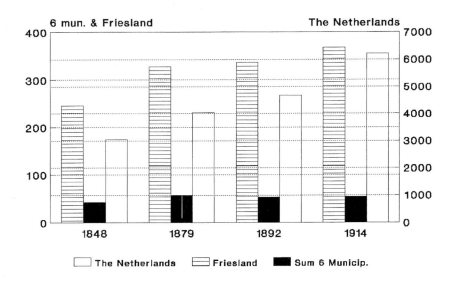

*Figure 2.2*

*Increase in population in national, provincial and regional perspective, in thousands, 1848-1914.*
**Source:** *table constructed from V. Bruinsma,* "De vermindering der bevolking in Friesland,"
Vragen des Tijds 2 *(1894), table E, 124, and from A. Vondeling,* "Eat oer it tal biwenners,"
*table 1, 8-9*

in Friesland and it is not before 1920 that Frisian birth rates would again
approach the national level. Indeed in the years 1881-1915 the table makes
clear that compared to the national rates, there was in Friesland an average
of 4.07 fewer births per 1000 people. But this can not be the whole story.
The average annual population increase in Friesland between 1879 and 1909
was (based on table 2.3) 0.28 percent and the national increase was 1.34
percent or, for Friesland 2.8 and for the Netherlands 13.4 per 1000. A
difference of about 10.6 still has to be accounted for, and that is a reason
why an average of 4.07 births per 1000 cannot fully explain the stagnation
of the Frisian population around the turn of the century.
The death rates can also be a reason for Friesland's drop below the national
population level. However, table 2.4 shows that from 1871 until 1920 death
rates in Friesland and Groningen were *always* lower than the national rates.
Against 17.5 deaths per year per 1000 people in the Netherlands between
1881 and 1915, Friesland had 15.2, which gives the province an advantage of
2.2. It should be remarked that the table also makes clear that this positive
difference was getting smaller in the first decades of the twentieth century.[15]

Can the same picture be painted for the municipalities in the clay area?
Table 2.5 shows the situation for the clay area.[16]

Table 2.5    **Birth rates (A), death rates (B), and birth surplus (C) in 6 municipalities:**

| Period | Oostdongerad. | | | Westdongerad. | | | Het Bildt | | |
|--------|------|------|------|------|------|------|------|------|------|
|        | A | B | C | A | B | C | A | B | C |
| 1881/85 | 26.7 | 14.9 | 11.7 | 27.2 | 15.5 | 11.7 | 31.3 | 18.5 | 12.8 |
| 1886/90 | 25.9 | 16.5 | 9.3 | 26.5 | 16.3 | 10.3 | 30.2 | 18.6 | 11.6 |
| 1891/95 | 27.7 | 16.7 | 11.0 | 25.5 | 16.4 | 9.2 | 28.5 | 14.0 | 14.5 |
| 1896/00 | 28.4 | 14.2 | 14.2 | 24.3 | 14.5 | 9.8 | 25.2 | 13.5 | 11.8 |
| 1901/05 | 27.9 | 17.3 | 10.7 | 26.3 | 15.2 | 11.1 | 23.1 | 13.9 | 9.1 |
| 1906/10 | 26.5 | 13.9 | 12.6 | 24.8 | 14.9 | 9.9 | 20.5 | 12.8 | 7.6 |
| 1911/15 | 23.9 | 12.3 | 11.6 | 23.9 | 12.1 | 11.8 | 20.3 | 11.1 | 9.2 |
| | Ferwerderadeel | | | Barradeel | | | Wonseradeel | | |
| 1881/85 | 30.4 | 19.1 | 11.3 | 34.2 | 17.6 | 16.6 | 31.3 | 17.1 | 14.2 |
| 1886/90 | 29.0 | 17.9 | 11.1 | 34.4 | 19.8 | 14.6 | 30.1 | 16.3 | 13.8 |
| 1891/95 | 27.1 | 16.9 | 10.2 | 29.7 | 15.9 | 13.7 | 28.2 | 14.7 | 13.5 |
| 1896/00 | 26.6 | 15.6 | 10.9 | 25.4 | 12.7 | 12.6 | 25.7 | 13.3 | 12.5 |
| 1901/05 | 27.7 | 15.7 | 12.0 | 24.8 | 12.6 | 12.2 | 26.4 | 13.1 | 13.2 |
| 1906/10 | 24.5 | 14.0 | 10.4 | 23.1 | 11.6 | 11.5 | 24.1 | 10.7 | 13.4 |
| 1911/15 | 24.0 | 12.4 | 11.5 | 21.2 | 10.9 | 10.2 | 24.1 | 10.9 | 13.2 |

**Source:** *Statistiek van den loop der bevolking in Nederland, 1881-1915.* Wageningen, Landbouwuniversiteit

Compared to the figures of Friesland as a whole, it is clear that between 1881 and 1915 the average birthrate in the different municipalities of the northern clay area always was lower. In the same period the clay area had an average birthrate of 1.3 per 1000 lower than the province.[17] Death rates were lower too for the clay municipalities: Ferwerderadeel was an exception in its higher average death rate compared to the province (15.9 compared to 15.2). The clay area as a whole annually counted 14.8 deaths per 1000 average between 1881 and 1915, or 0.4 less than in the province.

In summary, the average birth surplus in the clay area between 1881 and 1915 was 11.8 per 1000. For Friesland this number was 12.7 per 1000. It is clear that the clay area had a slightly lower birth surplus, but this does not account for the stagnation in the population on the provincial as well as the municipal level.

The conclusion for the province is obvious too; the smaller number of births in Friesland compared to the nation in the years 1881-1915 is almost totally compensated for by the smaller number of deaths. This means that the minimal increase, and sometimes even regional decrease of the Frisian population has to be ascribed to other factors like migration.

A direct cause that remains to be examined is the comparison of in- and out-migration. The following numbers are relevant:

Table 2.6   **In- and out-migration of Friesland in 5-year periods 1881-1915:**

| Period | In- | 0/00 | Out- | 0/00 | Surplus | 0/00 |
|---|---|---|---|---|---|---|
| 1881/85 | 85608 | 51.9 | 104976 | 63.6 | -19368 | -11.7 |
| 1886/90 | 83214 | 49.5 | 98982 | 58.8 | -15768 | - 9.4 |
| 1891/95 | 86494 | 51.4 | 104073 | 61.8 | -17579 | -10.4 |
| 1896/00 | 91088 | 53.5 | 108096 | 63.5 | -17008 | 10.0 |
| 1901/05 | 100478 | 57.5 | 110222 | 63.1 | - 9744 | - 5.6 |
| 1906/10 | 105959 | 58.8 | 118520 | 65.8 | -12561 | - 7.0 |
| 1911/15 | 112125 | 60.9 | 121117 | 65.8 | - 8992 | - 4.9 |

**Source:** *Statistiek van den loop der bevolking in Nederland*

Table 2.7   **In- and out-migration of the different municipalities 1881-1915:**

| Period | In- | 0/00 | Out- | 0/00 | Surplus | 0/00 |
|---|---|---|---|---|---|---|
| Oostdongeradeel | | | | | | |
| 1881/85 | 1717 | 42.5 | 2628 | 65.0 | - 911 | - 2.5 |
| 1886/90 | 1526 | 38.3 | 2091 | 52.5 | - 565 | -14.2 |
| 1891/95 | 1459 | 37.5 | 1845 | 47.5 | - 386 | - 9.9 |
| 1896/00 | 1586 | 40.2 | 2019 | 51.2 | - 433 | -11.0 |
| 1901/05 | 1905 | 47.2 | 2063 | 51.1 | - 158 | - 3.9 |
| 1906/10 | 1895 | 45.6 | 2227 | 53.6 | - 332 | - 8.0 |
| 1911/15 | 1956 | 46.1 | 2343 | 55.2 | - 387 | - 9.1 |
| | | | | | | |
| Westdongeradeel | | | | | | |
| 1881/85 | 1301 | 32.1 | 2226 | 54.8 | - 925 | -22.8 |
| 1886/90 | 1202 | 29.9 | 1791 | 44.6 | - 589 | -14.7 |
| 1891/95 | 1179 | 30.5 | 1732 | 44.8 | - 553 | -14.3 |
| 1896/00 | 1254 | 33.0 | 1802 | 47.4 | - 548 | -14.4 |
| 1901/05 | 1520 | 39.9 | 1698 | 44.5 | - 178 | - 4.7 |
| 1906/10 | 1545 | 39.5 | 1849 | 47.2 | - 304 | - 7.8 |
| 1911/15 | 1876 | 47.6 | 2251 | 57.1 | - 375 | - 9.5 |
| | | | | | | |
| Het Bildt | | | | | | |
| 1881/85 | 1540 | 34.7 | 2594 | 58.4 | - 1054 | -23.7 |
| 1886/90 | 1283 | 28.8 | 1950 | 43.7 | - 667 | -15.0 |
| 1891/95 | 1350 | 31.0 | 2079 | 47.7 | - 729 | -16.7 |
| 1896/00 | 1605 | 37.2 | 2182 | 50.6 | - 577 | -13.4 |
| 1901/05 | 1870 | 43.6 | 2118 | 49.4 | - 248 | - 5.8 |
| 1906/10 | 2107 | 48.9 | 2377 | 55.1 | - 270 | - 6.3 |
| 1911/15 | 2139 | 50.4 | 2417 | 56.9 | - 278 | - 6.5 |

| Ferwerderadeel | | | | | | |
|---|---|---|---|---|---|---|
| 1881/85 | 1498 | 36.3 | 2402 | 58.2 | - 904 | -21.9 |
| 1886/90 | 1273 | 30.5 | 1547 | 37.1 | 247 | - 6.6 |
| 1891/95 | 1436 | 34.6 | 1698 | 40.9 | - 262 | - 6.3 |
| 1896/00 | 1798 | 42.9 | 2024 | 48.3 | - 226 | - 5.4 |
| 1901/05 | 2071 | 49.8 | 2515 | 60.5 | - 444 | -10.7 |
| 1906/10 | 1958 | 47.2 | 2577 | 62.1 | - 619 | -14.9 |
| 1911/15 | 2040 | 49.5 | 2420 | 58.7 | - 380 | - 9.2 |
| | | | | | | |
| Barradeel | | | | | | |
| 1881/85 | 1921 | 8.9 | 2672 | 68.1 | - 751 | -19.1 |
| 1886/90 | 1799 | 46.0 | 2559 | 65.4 | - 760 | -19.4 |
| 1891/95 | 1834 | 48.2 | 2449 | 64.4 | - 615 | -16.2 |
| 1896/00 | 1855 | 48.6 | 2310 | 60.6 | - 455 | -11.9 |
| 1901/05 | 1963 | 51.6 | 2241 | 58.9 | - 278 | - 7.3 |
| 1906/10 | 1986 | 52.0 | 2473 | 64.8 | - 487 | -12.8 |
| 1911/15 | 2241 | 58.6 | 2412 | 63.0 | - 171 | - 4.5 |
| | | | | | | |
| Wonseradeel | | | | | | |
| 1881/85 | 2920 | 45.3 | 3819 | 59.3 | - 899 | -13.9 |
| 1886/90 | 2847 | 43.9 | 3571 | 55.1 | - 724 | -11.2 |
| 1891/95 | 2773 | 42.6 | 3519 | 54.0 | - 746 | -11.5 |
| 1896/00 | 2726 | 42.1 | 3574 | 55.2 | - 848 | -13.1 |
| 1901/05 | 3083 | 47.5 | 3773 | 58.2 | - 690 | -10.6 |
| 1906/10 | 3182 | 48.7 | 4084 | 62.6 | - 902 | -13.8 |
| 1911/15 | 3187 | 49.2 | 3950 | 60.9 | - 763 | -11.8 |

**Source:** *Statistiek van den loop der bevolking in Nederland*

What catches the eye is that during every five year period between 1881 and 1915 Friesland had an out-migration deficit. For the entire period this deficit averaged -8.4 per 1000 inhabitants. For the various municipalities this deficit was even higher: Barradeel had 13 more persons per 1000 inhabitants per year who left the municipality than who settled in the municipality. For Ferwerderadeel this number was -10.7.[18] This means that the clay area relatively lost more people to other regions than did the province as a whole. Compared to the departure from the province as a whole, more Oostdongera-deel inhabitants left this thinly populated municipality, and the same was true for the other clay municipalities. Every year many people left the clay area. If we study the actual numbers, we see that in each 5-year period, average about 150 to 1,015 more people left this area than moved into it. In the municipality of Het Bildt between 1881 and 1915 the difference between in- and out-migration even was 3,823 in favor of the emigrants. That means that in a little more than thirty years almost 45 percent of the municipal population departed![19]

In conclusion, it is clear that the population of Friesland since 1879 increased extremely slowly compared to other provinces in the Netherlands. Secondly, this slow increase or sometimes even decrease was especially evident in the municipalities with very fertile soil in northern Friesland. Thirdly, while the relatively low birth rate in the clay area contributed to this result, the death rate is also lower in this area, which means that death rates functioned as a compensating factor. Fourthly, the main point is that the clay area lost its inhabitants because they left the area for other places in the country but also for the land overseas.

A comparison of the total out-migration and the emigration in the clay area leads to the conclusion that in the time period 1880 to 1914 the proportion of emigrants to the United States diminished.

Table 2.8  **Total out-migration in Friesland and the clay area compared to the total emigration from the clay area (percentage of emigrants compared to total out-migration in clay area):**

| Period | Out-Frl | Out-clay | Em.U.S. | % |
|--------|---------|----------|---------|---|
| 1881/1885 | 104976 | 16341 | 2050 | 12.5 |
| 1886/1890 | 98982 | 13509 | 1740 | 12.9 |
| 1891/1895 | 104073 | 13322 | 1804 | 13.5 |
| 1896/1900 | 08096 | 15930 | 932 | 5.9 |
| 1901/1905 | 110222 | 14408 | 822 | 5.7 |
| 1905/1910 | 118520 | 15587 | 1047 | 6.7 |
| 1911/1915 | 121117 | 15793 | 933 | 5.9 |

\* note: the emigration figures for the period 1911/1915 are not complete because a total of the year 1915 is not available in the data file of Frisian emigrants from the clay area

**Source:** *Statistiek van den loop der bevolking in Nederland;* J.B.E. Galema, "Frisians to America, 1880-1914. Computer Compilation," (Groningen, 1992)

Table 2.9  **Total out-migration in the different municipalities of the clay area, compared to the emigration to the United States in 5-year periods:**

| | 1881/85 | | 1886/90 | | 1891/95 | | 1896/00 | | 1901/05 | | 1906/10 | |
|---|---|---|---|---|---|---|---|---|---|---|---|---|
| | Out | Em | Out | Em | Out | Em | Out | Em | Out | Em | Out | Em |
| Oostdo. | 2628 | 321 | 2091 | 157 | 1845 | 282 | 2019 | 84 | 2063 | 111 | 2227 | 180 |
| Westdo. | 2226 | 182 | 1792 | 151 | 1732 | 228 | 1802 | 76 | 1698 | 77 | 1849 | 85 |
| Bildt | 2594 | 619 | 1950 | 405 | 2079 | 399 | 2182 | 236 | 2118 | 180 | 2377 | 261 |
| Ferwer. | 2402 | 586 | 1547 | 381 | 1698 | 227 | 2024 | 113 | 2512 | 170 | 2577 | 147 |
| Barrad. | 2672 | 107 | 2559 | 472 | 2449 | 391 | 2310 | 330 | 2241 | 129 | 2473 | 124 |
| Wonser. | 3819 | 235 | 3571 | 174 | 3519 | 277 | 3574 | 93 | 3773 | 155 | 4084 | 250 |

Percentages: emigration with regard to total municipal out-migration:

| | | | | | | |
|---|---|---|---|---|---|---|
| Oostdo. | 12.2 | 7.6 | 15.3 | 4.2 | 5.4 | 8.1 |
| Westdo. | 8.2 | 8.4 | 13.2 | 4.2 | 4.5 | 4.6 |
| Bildt | 23.9 | 20.8 | 19.2 | 10.8 | 8.5 | 11.0 |
| Ferwer. | 24.4 | 24.6 | 13.4 | 5.6 | 6.8 | 5.7 |
| Barrad. | 4.0 | 18.4 | 16.0 | 14.3 | 5.8 | 5.0 |
| Wonser. | 6.2 | 4.9 | 7.9 | 2.6 | 4.1 | 6.1 |

**Source:** *Statistiek van den loop der bevolking in Nederland*

Did the proportion of emigrants to the United States differ from the total out-migration per municipality? Studying table 2.9 it appears that the municipality of Het Bildt had a relatively high proportion of overseas emigrants compared to the total out-migration. From all the people who left the municipality, in the 1880s about one quarter to one fifth left for the United States. The same tendency appears for the municipality of Ferwerderadeel. If one out of four people who left the municipality went to the United States, a rather special trend was set. The other municipalities showed a lower share in overseas migration compared to their total out-migration.

### 2.4 Six municipalities and the America-trek, 1880-1914

In order to define the variables which determined the socio-economic characteristics of the northern Frisian migration to the United States around the turn of the century, it is essential to present the statistics of the departure from this area. The data of the original Population Registers (*Bevolkingsregisters*) proved to be the only good source for collecting the quantitative information about emigration from Friesland to the United States.

The often-used Emigration Records (*Landverhuizerslijsten*) are not available for the province of Friesland.[20] These documents are apparently lost, but the determined researcher can recover the data. The official Emigration Records were derived annually from the Population Registers and are convenient because they list all overseas emigrants. Using the Population Registers requires examining thousands of records to distill the actual people who were listed as "vertrokken naar Amerika".

In the nineteenth century Population Registers, the members of each family were recorded, including servants and boarders.[21] By official decree all municipal departures and settlements had to be noted. By striking out or incorporating the name and personal information on all movers, the government official compiled with the decree.[22]

The information in the Population Registers may be judged sufficiently representative for the purpose of this study, because these registers were kept rather precisely in the northern clay area. There are hardly any missing data. Other scholars who have used Population Registers were also content with their reliability.[23]

Of course some reservations about the use of the Population Register for the study of migration have to be made. Not every emigrant was recorded properly. From 1861 on, every person who intended to leave had to obtain an official Migration Certificate, but control and enforcement were far from perfect. R.P. Swierenga found, after putting the Dutch Emigration Records of 1835-1880 together, that one out of three emigrants did not register. In particular, single adult males could be found among the unregistered or clandestine migrants. Swierenga assumes that this had partly to do with avoiding military service.[24] In Friesland this happened as well. Thomas Burmania who was *Afgescheiden*, for example, left the village of Ferwerd in March 1892 because he did not want to serve the army.[25] For other than religious reasons, Gerrit Roorda also wanted to go to America to avoid military service:

> I looked for a solution and found it: I would, like Tsjerk, go to America, to make some money. And after I had earned some cash, I would return, to be able to study architecture. Furthermore there was the case of military service. In 1908 I drew by lot. My friend Freerk Loopstra had gone free, but I had not.[26]

Military service was one possible reason for leaving clandistinely. It is also likely that single persons often left unnoticed more than did whole families because no specific passport or border crossing registration was required. For the purpose of administration, the Dutch registration system was based on voluntary co-operation of the migrant, and hence was not totally reliable. However, in the northern Frisian clay area small scale social networks would have prevented many from leaving without being noticed. Their travel accounts often report the presence of friends and family at the moment of departure. Johannes van Dijk from the municipality of Ferwerderadeel tells us something about a departure in 1881:

> Thursday morning at six o'clock, accompanied by M.Fokkema, I left the village of Ferwerd. A great many people were about, to see many of us for the last time and to say goodbye. And no wonder! This morning fifty persons were about to leave the village.... The crowd in Leeuwarden with many emigrants, put our meditation to an end. What a people who were traveling with us!...Old and young, men, women and children, youngsters and girls, all ages were ready to reach their goal...Many were very sad, the circumstances forced them to leave family and friends, village and the home they loved.[27]

Certainly, the transatlantic migrants did get local attention; but we cannot be sure that the local official indeed scratched them from the Population Registers as "vertrokken naar Amerika."

Swierenga states in his analysis of Dutch migration to the United States, that "the secret weapon of contemporary scholarship in social and economic history is exploitation of the computer's capacity to process large bodies of information on individual persons."[28] Indeed, without automation, it would be impossible to generalize about a group of emigrants of the size described in this study. Apart from this generalization and also the primary gains of

*A farewell from P.J. Buwalda and wife, October 10, 1886, to Hartwerd, Friesland before going to North Yakima, Washington State*

speed, accuracy, and ease in handling large quantities of data, the use of computers also enables one to ask new research questions.

But since men and events are complex and in many cases not very predictable, quantitative methods have limitations. These methods by no means preclude the use of value judgments or speculations. Therefore, the historian has to rely on qualitative sources as well and as J. Marczewski concludes: the quantitative methods by no means can be opposite or competative to qualitative research.[29] The two approaches have to be complementary and should go hand in hand. First I will discuss the quantitative data files. Later the integration with the qualitative sources will be pursued.

In the case of the Frisian case-study group, there are two final data files with biographical information on overseas migrants that will be linked to compare information before departure from Friesland and after settlement in the United States. As mentioned above, the first data file is compiled from the official Population Registers in the Netherlands. The second data file is derived from the Population Schedules of the U.S. Federal Census for the years 1900 and 1910, which will be discussed later.

The Population Registers from 1880 till 1914 give considerable personal information on the migrant: Family Name, First Name, Sex, Relation to Head of Household, Date of Birth, Place of Birth, Civil Status, Religion, Occupation, Date of Emigration, Place of Last Residence and Intended Destination. Rather than sample a certain percentage of the overseas migrants, I accumulated all recorded persons who left for the United States between 1880 and 1914. Their biographical information has been stored in a data file which combines first and last name with 17 variables containing the specific characteristics of the emigrant. In order to systematize the huge quantity of data, a codebook was constructed [see Appendix I].[30]

Based on the resulting datafile, a total of 9,467 emigrants left the northern clay area [see table 2.10].
More men than women left for America: 5,347 against 4,093, or a ratio of 131:100 (see figure 2.3). The total number of officially recorded overseas migrants made up 2.5 percent of the Frisian population of December 31, 1914 (372,625 inhabitants) and 17.5 percent of the population in the six municipalities of the clay area (54,030 inhabitants).
The number of emigrants from the clay area was about 8 percent of the total number of Dutch emigrants who left for the United States in that same time period.[31]

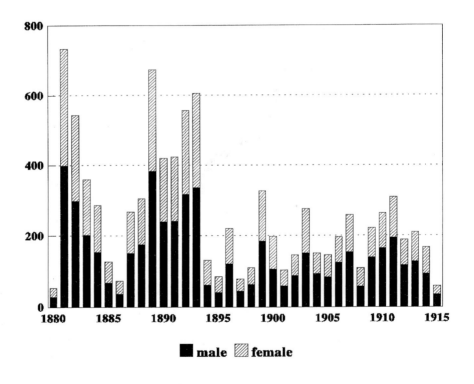

*Figure 2.3 Male-female ratio of emigrants, all municipalities 1880-1914.*
**Source:** *J.B.E. Galema, "Frisians to America. Computer Compilation." (Groningen, 1992)*

Studying the table of the emigrants of all municipalities, it appears that in some years many more people left for the United States than other years: 1881, 1882, 1889, 1892, and 1893 were the peak years. Over the whole period the great number of emigrants between 1881 and 1893 catches the eye. In those 13 years, almost 60 percent of the total overseas emigration over 35 years from the clay area occurred. This time period corresponds with the period of severe agricultural crisis in Friesland and also with the peaks in internal mobility.[32] Compared with internal mobility, the emigration to North America showed a very different pattern; the essence of this difference is that with emigration there is no exchange; people from Friesland did settle in the United States, but the in-migration of Americans to Friesland is nil.

Taking a second look at the table, it becomes clear that within the 13 years of heavy emigration, there are two years of relatively low departure. In 1885 and 1886 about 200 people altogether were removed from the Population Registers, which was less than half that between 1881 and 1894. This fits the national pattern of overseas migration. For the Frisian clay area this decline possibly can be explained by the relatively positive agricultural output in those years. The annual report of the municipality [*gemeenteverslag*] of Oostdongeradeel in 1885 and 1886 mentioned that the state of agriculture was "very good" and "generally speaking satisfactory, a bit more unfavourable than in 1885."[33] Years with good harvests can be expected to have created more employment as well as better prospects for the future, which in turn could discourage the willingness to migrate.

In 1890-1891 a severe winter hit the farmers and laborers heavily.[34] An escalating labor conflict in Het Bildt was one of the results. This winter could well be one of the causes for the increase in emigration in 1892 and 1893. In spite of the agricultural crisis, which still had its impact, the overseas migration dropped sharply in 1894, although a considerable number of people continued to depart. The decline may have been caused by new possibilities for seasonal work in Germany which came on the horizon. In the second half of the nineties Frisian land laborers or farm workers went to Germany to find work as milkers at dairy farms, as laborers on canal works, or as unskilled workers in mines and factories.[35] The decline may also have been caused by two other factors: in 1893 America plunged into an economic depression and in the same year Friesland learned about the unsuccessful attempt of a group of 200 families to settle in San Luis Valley, Colorado. These settlers were cheated by directors of The Holland American Colonization Company, [*De Hollandsch-Amerikaansche Landverhuizing-Maatschappij*], who used the deposits for their swindling schemes:

> When they [these two hundred families] arrived in that far away land and expected to come into possession of their alleged property, it appeared very sadly that they could consider their money as thrown away. They did not get any land and the *maatschappij* [The Holland American Colonization Company] had no penny to repay.[36]

In the first decade of the twentieth century, emigration from the clay area to the United States was rather stable. A moderate number of 190 per year left and this pattern continued in the economically prosperous and progressive years before World War I. Even in times of prosperity there were still Frisians who decided to venture overseas. This probably had everything to do with the tradition of migration in the late nineteenth century, which will be discussed in Chapter 3.

Table 2.10 shows the annual overseas emigration per 100,000 population of the Frisian clay area and of the Netherlands.

Table 2.10 **Annual overseas emigration per 100,000 population of the Frisian clay area and of the Netherlands:**

| Year | Absolute clay area population Dec 31 | Absolute clay area migration to US | Rate per 100,000 clay Frisians | Rate per 100,000 Netherlanders |
|------|------|------|------|------|
| 1880 | 55809 | 54 | 97 | 73 |
| 1881 | 54318 | 734 | 1351 | 179 |
| 1882 | 53936 | 544 | 1009 | 138 |
| 1883 | 53546 | 359 | 670 | 79 |
| 1884 | 53697 | 286 | 533 | 58 |
| 1885 | 53915 | 127 | 236 | 40 |
| 1886 | 54291 | 73 | 134 | 39 |
| 1887 | 54535 | 267 | 490 | 92 |
| 1888 | 54500 | 305 | 560 | 95 |
| 1889 | 53230 | 675 | 1268 | 160 |
| 1890 | 53345 | 420 | 787 | 62 |
| 1891 | 53217 | 424 | 797 | 79 |
| 1892 | 53166 | 557 | 1048 | 124 |
| 1893 | 52872 | 606 | 1146 | 116 |
| 1894 | 53183 | 132 | 248 | 23 |
| 1895 | 53320 | 85 | 159 | 21 |
| 1896 | 53167 | 220 | 414 | 29 |
| 1897 | 53259 | 78 | 146 | 13 |
| 1898 | 53265 | 110 | 207 | 15 |
| 1899 | 52676 | 326 | 619 | 22 |
| 1900 | 52724 | 198 | 378 | 28 |
| 1901 | 52880 | 104 | 197 | 36 |
| 1902 | 53030 | 146 | 275 | 38 |
| 1903 | 53237 | 275 | 517 | 58 |
| 1904 | 53418 | 151 | 283 | 49 |
| 1905 | 53794 | 146 | 271 | 49 |
| 1906 | 53840 | 196 | 364 | 61 |
| 1907 | 53796 | 258 | 480 | 101 |
| 1908 | 54020 | 109 | 202 | 49 |
| 1909 | 53548 | 221 | 413 | 73 |

| | | | |
|---|---|---|---|
| 1910 | 53406 | 263 | 492 | 90 |
| 1911 | 53428 | 309 | 578 | 87 |
| 1912 | 53577 | 188 | 351 | 68 |
| 1913 | 53812 | 210 | 390 | 70 |
| 1914 | 54030 | 167 | 309 | 49 |
| other | | 144 | | |
| **Totals:** | | | | |
| 1880-14 | | 9467 | 498 | 68 |

**Source:** 1. Population figures for the municipalities from the Agricultural University in Wageningen.

2. Frisian emigration data derived from Galema, "Frisians to America, 1880-1914. Computer Compilation."

3. Annual rate per 100,000 Dutch overseas migration derived from Swierenga ed., *The Dutch in America*, 28-30 combined with the annual number of Dutch emigrants to the U.S. found in Swierenga, "The Delayed Transition," tables 3 and 5

Over the entire period the Netherlands shows a moderate rate of 68 emigrants per 100,000 population who went to the United States. The rate for the Frisian clay area per 100,000 population was 498 between 1880 and 1914, again showing the need of research into the regional pattern of Dutch overseas migration and the need to analyze these patterns in depth

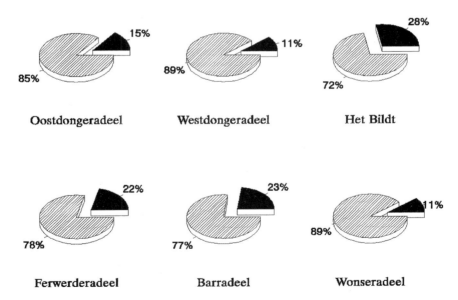

*Figure 2.4 Emigrants from clay area, 1880-1914, compared to the population in 1914.*
**Source:** *Galema, "Frisians to America, 1880-1914. Computer Compilation." Vondeling, "Eat oer it tal biwenners," 8-9*

and to refine our understanding of Dutch emigration. The emigration to the United States was especially important for the agrarian provinces with alluvial soil and at the periphery of the country, where the possibilities for expansion of agriculture were minimal and where there was little industrial development.

Appendix II shows the municipalities in the clay area with their proportion of people who left for the United States between 1880-1914 [see Appendix II].

Het Bildt delivered the largest proportion of emigrants from the clay area. The population of the municipalities – except Wonseradeel – fluctuated around 8,000 inhabitants in 1914 [figure 2.4].[37] Sometimes – as in Het Bildt – even more than one out of four inhabitants left for the United States. In Wonseradeel the proportion of grassland was much larger than in the other municipalities. It is striking that Wonseradeel had the lowest relative proportion of emigrants; only 1 out of 10 inhabitants left.

A closer look at the regional pattern of Frisian emigration shows that the rate of departure from some villages was much higher than from others [Appendix III]. In Blija in Ferwerderadeel, for example, a quarter of the population – based on the Census of 1909 – emigrated to the United States between 1880-1914. In the village of Jislum half of the population decided to leave for America. But in the same municipality only 7 percent left from Genum. Other municipalities also show an unbalanced distribution of emigrants. The causes for these patterns can mainly be found in the tradition of migration, in the propriety ratio and – related to that – in the occupational structure.

If a village had a large proportion of home- or landowners, the rate of emigration was lower than in a village where landless land laborers and craftsmen made up the largest part of the population. Property possibly was an extra barrier to the decision to move, especially in times with poor economic prospects. This could also be the explanation for the fact that in Wonseradeel – the only municipality that was clearly divided into an agricultural and a grassland region – the villages that were part of the *Bouwhoek* (agriculture) had a far larger proportion of emigrants than the villages in the *Greidhoek*. From agriculturally-oriented Arum more than 23 percent of the population in 1909 left between 1880-1914, from Witmarsum a little more than 20 percent and from Pingjum 10 percent, while from the grasslands of Burgwerd 7 percent left, from Tjerkwerd 4 percent and from Greonterp only 1 of the 161 villagers. This supports the general idea that the agricultural depression had a larger impact in the agricultural areas than in the grassland areas. It also makes clear that in some villages within one generation sometimes more than one of five people left for spacious America. To relate the propriety ratio to the rate of emigration, the example of Greonterp shows that in a rural area with a high proportion of farm ownership, people were less willing to migrate overseas. It was hard to sell property at a profit in times of economic distress. One would expect emigration to be decreasing or nil in economically profitable times. But if the village of Arum is studied in time, it appears that even after the agrarian depression the departure for overseas continued. In 1907 even 34 people left, almost as many (36) as in the 1893, a year of heavy emigration from Friesland as well as the Netherlands. As mentioned before, part of the explanation might be the tradition of migration. But it could very well be that farmers who were owners and landlords did not want to divide their property further among sons and daughters (impartible inheritance).[38] Ideas of large scale economic and agricultural units already affected the spirit of the Frisian farm owners and landlords in the nineteenth century. Although industrialization came rather late in the Netherlands, modernization already had its impact on agricultural progress around the turn of the century and in many ways the last quarter of the nineteenth century cannot be described as a period of *general* stagnation.[39]

To see which group made up the largest part of the emigrant stream, it is interesting to study the age-specific migration rates. One would expect that younger people left and that the older people stayed in Friesland. However, the age-specific migration rates indicate that even people older than 65 decided to look for fortune overseas [table 2.11].

Table 2.11   **Absolute age-specific migration: Frisian clay area 1880-1914 and percentage of total group of emigrants:**

| Age | Males | Females | Total | % Total |
|-----|-------|---------|-------|---------|
| 0-14 | 1675 | 1586 | 3261 | 35% |
| 15-24 | 1591 | 796 | 2387 | 26% |
| 25-34 | 937 | 704 | 1641 | 18% |
| 35-44 | 475 | 434 | 909 | 10% |
| 45-54 | 348 | 279 | 627 | 7% |
| 55-64 | 189 | 172 | 361 | 4% |
| 65> | 69 | 49 | 118 | 1% |
| Total | 5284 | 4020 | 9304 | 100%[40] |

**Source:** Galema, "Frisians to America, 1880-1914. Computer Compilation"

Children constituted the largest group of emigrants. Over one third of both males and females belonged to this group. Men and women between the ages of 15 and 24 formed the second largest share. The difference between the sexes is striking: almost twice as many males as females in the same age group left. This indicates that young men were more eager to leave indepently. Men were more often looking for labor possibilities outside the home and also outside Frisian borders.
If emigration had something to do with the economic possibilities especially for young men during the agricultural crisis, it should be expected that after 1900 – as the agrarian crisis began to fade – the difference between the sexes would be minimized. This is not the case. Division in two time periods of the age-specific migration rates for the age-group between 15 and 25, indicates

that women were less eager to migrate even after the agrarian crisis [table 2.12].

Table 2.12   **Absolute age-specific migration by sex, age-group 15-25, clay area, 1880-1900 and 1901-1914:**

| 1880-1900 | | | 1901-1914 | | |
|---|---|---|---|---|---|
| Male | Female | Total | Male | Female | Total |
| 952 | 560 | 1512 | 639 | 236 | 875 |
| 63.0% | 37.0% | 100% | 73.0% | 27.0% | 100% |

**Source:** Galema, "Frisians to America, 1880-1914. Computer Compilation"

The explanation for this difference between the sexes in this age-group of young people cannot be found only in economic trends like the hard hitting agrarian crisis. It is more likely that social and cultural traditions were determinants of this development. If it was not extremely necessary for

*Clara De Young (Klaasje de Jong) from St. Annaparochie and her fiancé George (Gerrit Gerrits) Brolsma in 1913, before they left to the U.S.A., where they married and finally settled in Minnesota. Photo donated by J. Brolsma, Leiden*

financial means, women in the clay area stayed home to care for the children and to provide the infrastructure for home- and family life. Between 1849 and 1909 the number of women working as day laborers sharply declined.[41] Studying the occupational structure of the agrarian professions, it appears that Friesland compared to other provinces in 1909 did not have a high proportion of women in the labor force.[42] Only when poverty was standing in the doorway, did women work with men as field laborers, servants, peddlers, factories, or in fishing, as is described in the case of the municipality of Westdongeradeel.[43] Contemporary reports indicate that it generally was seen as a pernicious situation when married women worked for wages outside the home. "May there come a time, that the husband earns enough money to let the wife run the house and let the child stay with the mother, school and play. How would we have a different world!", was one of the statements of a report concerning women's and children's labor around 1890.[44] The late nineteenth century civic ideals that women should devote themselves to family life, began to dawn on the rural society as well. The immigrant D. Dijkstra wrote in a letter of 1900 from Chicago that he knew for sure, that "I would not want to go to a place where Rieka [his wife] also had to work to earn a living. In former days at farms I have seen how the women had to work. And this is not necessary here. And therefore I don't think that we will come back to Holland soon."[45]

The religious affinity of the emigrants from the clay area is also a datum that can be derived from the Population Registers. Within the group of emigrants it appears that the greatest number are affiliated with the *Nederlands Hervormde* Church [table 2.13].

Table 2.13    **Religious affilliation among Frisian clay emigrants 1880-1914: numbers and percentage:**

| Religion | number | percentage |
|---|---|---|
| Nederlands Hervormd | 5959 | 62.9 |
| Gereformeerd | 1355 | 14.3 |
| Christelijk Gereformeerd | 1207 | 12.7 |
| Doopsgezind (Mennonite) | 218 | 2.3 |
| Catholic | 13 | 0.1 |
| None | 692 | 7.3 |
| Other/Missing | 23 | 0.2 |
| Total | 9467 | 100.0 |

**Source:** Galema, "Frisians to America, 1880-1914. Computer Compilation"

In 1881 about 78 percent of the Frisian provincial population was affiliated with the *Nederlands Hervormde* Church, while 7 percent was *Christelijk Gereformeerd*, 5 percent was Mennonite and 8 percent was Catholic.[46] Taking the census of 1909 as a source, it appears that there are hardly any Catholics in the clay area. The *Nederlands Hervormde* people made up an average of 47 percent of the municipal clay population in 1909. This means that the religious distribution among emigrants did not exactly reflect the pattern in the clay area, because *Nederlands Hervormde* emigrants were overrepresented and *Gereformeerde* emigrants were underrepresented.

Knowledge about the geographical mobility of the group of emigrants and also of the individual emigrant, can give insight into the mobility structure of the clay population in general. It appears that over the whole period 1880-1914 more than half of all the emigrants (almost 59 percent) emigrated directly from their place of birth. Some 16 percent left from the neighborhood of their birthplace, while about 6 percent left from a village in the same municipality. A few (13 percent) emigrated from a neighboring municipality. Only the extremely low percentage of about 5 percent departed to the United States from a municipality not neighboring their place of birth. If the figures are combined, the following simplified table 2.14 shows the extra-ordinary low local mobility among the group of emigrants before departure.

Table 2.14 **Emigration geographic rate of all the emigrants from the Frisian clay area 1880-1914:**

| Same municipality | Neighboring municipality | Non-neighboring municipality | Unknown |
|---|---|---|---|
| 81.2 % | 13.2 % | 5.4 % | 0.2 % |

**Source:** Galema, "Frisians to America, 1880-1914. Computer Compilation"

It is striking that more than four-fifths of the emigrants left from the same municipality where they were born. One is inclined to think that these people left a static society, where any mobility outside the municipal borders was rare. But this does not fit the general mobility pattern of the Frisian clay area at all. From 1870 on Friesland was a demographic expulsion area. Between 1880 and 1914 all the clay municipalities had an out-migration surplus. It also does not fit one of the general characteristics of the rural migration. According to H. de Vries, the study of a certain regional units, like the municipality, shows that native people [autochtonen] usually were less eager to migrate than non-natives.[47] Concerning emigration from the Dutch province of Brabant, Schreuder stated that emigrant families were a potentially mobile segment of society and that migrants transferred residence prior to emigration.[48] For the group of Frisian emigrants from the clay area these characteristics do not hold.

In this context the static element has to be restricted to the group of overseas emigrants. It could very well be that we are dealing with people who in a way had no choice except emigration, to escape their economic, social or psychological burdens. This group in general does not show mobile characteristics before departure to America.[49] Many of them never saw the provincial borders and some of them never stepped over the municipal border. This can be illustrated by the travel accounts, many of which had a sound of surprise and astonishment once the home town was left. Catharinus

Hoekema who emigrated from Wommels in 1915 wrote on the steamship to America: "On that little trip [through the Netherlands] I have seen quite a bit of the Netherlands, and I never thought that such wide uninhabited lands were present in this densely populated Netherlands." And about walking in the city of Rotterdam, he mentioned: "From two to four in the afternoon, we saw a lot that we had never seen before."[50]

We can question to what extent this emigration can be judged a totally free decision, if the conditions of life were so bad that people psychologically and morally were forced to leave their home country.

It is also plausible that the people who left for America followed the accustomed paths of their neighbors, their family and their friends, who had left before them. The ties of the family or the community network could have been so strong that the decision to emigrate was made more easily. The fact that people were aware that emigrants seldom returned made potential emigrants more eager to cross the ocean, to be reunited with those with whom they had the strongest social ties. It probably made no sense to change places within the Frisian borders to achieve family reunification because the possibility of gathering with family and friends was assured anyway.

In addition to the strikingly high percentage of emigrants who emigrated from the municipality of their birth it is also noted that the number of people who left a municipality not neighboring their place of birth, was extremely low. Only slightly more than 500 persons out of the more than 9,000 emigrants had moved to a different part of Friesland before their departure for the United States. Comparing the municipalities the pattern does not show much variety: the percentage of people who emigrated from a place not closely connected with their birthplace fluctuated between 4.3 percent in Het Bildt and 6.2 percent in Oostdongeradeel. It is clear that they did not rush from place to place before the decision to go overseas was taken. Only 1 percent of the whole group of emigrants had not been born in the province of Friesland. In conclusion, people were extremely attached to their native soil before making the longest journey of their lives.

## *Chapter 3* Signal for departure: motivating factors and personal characteristics

### 3.1 Migration tradition

"Send these to me!," the image of Miss Liberty seemed to shout to Europe's "tired, poor and huddled masses yearning to breath free."[1] The same spirit which would inspire Emma Lazarus in 1883 had already infected Frisian emigrants like Dirk Jans Miedema. In the spring of 1881 he put an advertisement in the journal *Het Noorden* to gather people interested in joining him on his journey to America. It was at a time when French and American artists and politicians were still arguing about the physical and emotional appearance of the huge Statue of Liberty that would be created on Bedloe's Island at the entrance of New York's harbor.

Dirk Jans Miedema was already well acquainted with the New World. In 1852 he left his northern Frisian homeland and emigrated with wife and child to the United States. Tradition has it that he was fleeing poverty. He settled in Holland, Michigan, among other Dutch immigrants, and it was almost thirty years before he returned to his native country.

Miedema surely was not the first Frisian emigrant who left for America.[2] At the end of the 1840s migration began to attract the Dutch, inspired by the moves of clergymen like A.C. van Raalte and H.P. Scholte, who went with groups of religiously like-minded people to Holland, Michigan, and Pella, Iowa, respectively. In Friesland prominent individuals like Sipke Osinga from the village of St. Annaparochie, the Reverend Marten Annes Ypma from Hallum and Worp van Peyma from Ternaard together with family and friends had already left before Miedema. Indeed, at the time when Miedema returned to Friesland his emigration had been far from unique. In 1881 he was in fact part of a Frisian migration tradition of four decades. Between 1835 and 1880 almost 4,000 people from the province of Friesland migrated to the United States.

To put late nineteenth-century Frisian migration into historical perspective, it is useful to reflect upon these earlier migratory moves. The experiences of people who left the Frisian clay area before 1880 must have been an important ingredient in the motivation of later ocean crossers. Although some Frisians left before the 1840s, it will be adequate to start with the mass emigration in the time period of Scholte and Van Raalte to establish the context of the tradition of migration.

America on October 15, 1846, among them nine Frisians from the cities of Franeker and Sneek.[3] In the spring of 1847 the emigrant Sjoerd Aukes Sipma left the village of Bornwerd in the municipality of Westdongeradeel to join the group of one of the Seceder's [*Afgescheiden*] leaders, Rev. H.P. Scholte, bound for the prairies of Iowa. Scholte and the members of his Association sailed in chartered vessels from Rotterdam early in April. One of the two leaders on board of the *Pieter Floris* was the Frisian Hierke Ypes Viersen, Sipma's brother in law. Viersen, a tradesman from the village of Driesum, was an active supporter of Scholte's Association and helped Frisians emigrate by advancing money for their passage and for the purchase of land in the settlement.[4] Sipma has left a picture of the journey and of the life the Dutch immigrants had to adopt. In his *Belangrijke Berigten uit Pella...* [Important Messages from Pella...] Sipma reported about the trip overseas, about the area of settlement, the relation to Scholte's Association, the typical Frisian neighborhood in Pella, the possibilities of finding jobs and housing, churchlife, and American women.[5] From Sipma we also know that most of the Frisian passengers were emigrants from the municipalities of West- and Oostdongeradeel and Dantumadeel. "In spite of formidable initial difficulties, some of the Friesians who came with Sipma succeeded admirably, or at least so it must have seemed to them in their penury," writes H.S. Lucas.[6] Sipma accounted himself and his wife as successful immigrants. They were contented and wished their relatives and friends from Friesland were living with them in Iowa.[7]

More Frisian emigrants came to Pella. In 1849 Anne, the brother of the well-known poet Tjibbe Geerts van der Meulen, landed in Pella with a group of people from the village of Bergum and surroundings.[8] Six years later the teacher and publisher of Sipma's letters in Friesland, Jelle Pelmulder from Bornwerd, arrived. Together with Sipma he helped to consolidate and carry forward the oft-discussed plans of establishing a new colony. He became the first one to draft definite plans for the formation of the new Dutch colony of Orange City in northwest Iowa. Letters from Pelmulder about his journey and first impressions were also published in 1859 in northern Friesland.[9] Pelmulder remarked on the motivation of the emigrants: people did not leave the Frisian soil because of their religious principles, but only to improve their material circumstances.[10] In the introduction of Pelmulder's letters it is said that he himself as a teacher did not earn enough money to support his large family and that he did not see any future for his children.[11] Very detailed travel accounts have been left by a number of emigrants from the municipalities of Het Bildt and Barradeel. Among them, according to the introduction, were "in their circles very respectable members of society."[12] Sipke Osinga was one of those who left from the village of St. Annaparochie on March 26, 1847 accompanied to the port of Harlingen by some friends. Osinga wrote letters in which he reported about the poor accommodation on board the sailing ships. Deeply moved, he described the foul air and the bad drinking water for the steerage passengers, which lead to deaths of many children, including his daughter Houkje. After the trip Osinga's letters came from Albany, New York, where he met other Frisian immigrants and where he found a job in a bookshop. As early as October 1847 Osinga was signing his letters with the words: "your American Friend S. Osinga."[13] Some of these emigrants from Barradeel went to Vriesland in Michigan, others from Het Bildt later arrived in Lafayette, Indiana, where they met with immigrants formerly from the province of Groningen.

Other travel accounts of bad experiences come from a number of Frisians who traveled to North America via Liverpool with the *William and Mary* in order "to free themselves from that general recession that is so clearly in evidence in our fatherland."[14] Oepke Bonnema, a grain dealer from Kimswerd in Wonseradeel, left with 92 persons, and recounts the bad situation on board: the captain and his crew continually held back on the provisions that were agreed upon.[15] This led to fights on the vessel and later on when the ship ran aground near the Bahama Islands because of "dead-drunk" mates, the captain was the first to flee the ship. The chaos that resulted is not hard to imagine. Some people drowned and after a few days of great anguish the shipwrecked were picked up by an English schooner. The 66 Frisian emigrants and others who survived were put ashore on the Bahamas without any luggage, but with the help of natives they were transported to New Orleans where they started the inland trip to the state of Wisconsin.

The settlement of Bonnema's group near La Crosse in Wisconsin was called Frysia. The travel account as well as the first information and experiences in Frysia, including hints for future emigrants were written down by B.B.

*Travel journal of Oepke Bonnema,*
*written by B.B. Haagsma, 1853*

Haagsma, Bonnema's bookkeeper and a former schoolteacher from Arum (Wonseradeel). The two booklets were respectively published in 1853 and 1855 in Friesland.[16] However, according to Van Hinte who claimed to have first-hand information from Bonnema's cousins, the farming colony of Frysia did not prosper. Although Lucas first mentions it as a successful settlement, he later says that its best years were over by 1880.[17] The Rev. John H. Karsten had yet another opinion in 1897. He mentioned that "the colony at present numbers between 400 and 500." He admitted though that when the lumbering business ceased, the settlers in Frysia (later called New Amsterdam) fell back upon farming but the sandy soil was far from ideal for this purpose. Karsten added: "But there are other reasons perhaps for the partial failure of New Amsterdam – reasons which relate to the moral condition of the settlers. But of these we need not speak here." Later Karsten referred to the lack of regular church services in this community.[18] The analysis of Bonnema's failure or success is not the most important question here. It is interesting to mention that other emigrants from Minnertsga and St. Annaparochie joined Bonnema's settlement.

Another emigration that was much in the public eye around the middle of the nineteenth century was the departure of Rev. Marten Annes Ypma from Minnertsga and his followers, who wanted to join the colony of Van Raalte in Michigan. Ypma had been a minister of the Seceders in Hallum when he was called to lead a group of emigrants. His congregation of 49 adults and a number of children left for the United States on April 7, 1847, sailing with the English ship *Vesta*.[19] Twelve miles east of Van Raalte's village of Holland they found a fertile clay region where they set up the village of Vriesland. It was situated deep in the forest and in the pioneering days, it was so isolated that provisions could be obtained only with difficulty. Other Frisians arrived in Vriesland, but also people from the province of Gelderland which resulted in the creation of *'de Geldersche buurt'* or neighborhood. At the same time emigrants who had been living in the east decided to join Ypma's colony. Klaas de Vree and Jeltje Ypma (sister of Marten Annes), originally from the village of Sexbierum, and Tede Ulberg, with his family from Minnertsga, came to Vriesland, and they left written accounts of their pioneering days in America.[20] Their stories show the difficult conditions some immigrants experienced in the beginning: at night Ypma's house was locked with a blanket and a box in front of it, because they were afraid of wolves or even sometimes of bears. There was little furniture and interiors were most primitive. Reverend Ypma in later years served other Dutch immigrant communities, among them Graafschap in Michigan, and Roseland, a south Chicago suburb. Ypma ended his religious career and his immigrant life in Alto, Wisconsin, where he died in 1863. During his years in America he had served old and new immigrants both Frisians and people from other parts of the Netherlands. His migration was typical in that it included religiously like-minded people of sparse financial means.

There were other migrations to America. According to a Frisian historian the departure of the well-situated farmer Worp van Peyma in 1849 with his people received much attention in Friesland.[21] Van Peyma belonged to a prominent farmer's family from Ternaard. He had had a good education and at a young age held political positions in the area.[22] His interests in technical, economic, and mathematical sciences leaned more to theoretical approaches than to practical applications. He became famous for his ideas concerning hydraulics and dikes. There was another aspect too: according to J. Swart who studied Van Peyma's life and ideas, this farmer had a romantic side to him that led him to read Dutch poetry and works of well-known thinkers like Pascal and Rousseau. In fact, Van Peyma belonged to the scientific and intellectual elite in Friesland and had many friends in those circles. However, his spiritual and materialistic position did not prevent him from emigrating to the New World. In the spring of 1849 he left with family, friends, other farmers including some from the neighboring province of Groningen, via the city of Groningen to Bremerhaven in Germany, where they took a steamer to New York. Van Peyma was driven by his dissatisfaction with the political and social climate in the Netherlands and by his imagination of America as a free country. He settled in the town of

Lancaster, close to the city of Buffalo. His communication with his old friends in the fatherland remained intensive and therefore his emigration became a well-known phenomenon in northern Friesland.[23] The "Farewell" poem by his friend and brother-in-law Rinse Posthumus had the following phrases:

How hard it is, thus to take leave of one another,
Consoled that you went to the land of Washington,
And Franklin, through whose counsel and deeds
Freedom won out over servitude...

We people can only thrive in freedom;
That's how God wants it, he makes us free:
That's what America tells us in the gladdening
Of those who come to freedom's school and shelter.
There we are human beings and citizens; before the law
No one has an advantage, except by their virtue.
No citizens are crushed by a new burden:
There a new world is growing in happy youth.

Oh Frisians! Netherlands! across the sea, to the west,
lies the land where there is room for you to work.
To forget the land, where Mother cradled me and fed me
With mother's milk, where my parents' remains lie.
No one can: Nay! The human heart must bleed
When it, for the last time, bids that land farewell!

That the old and new world help each other,
And that America may awake us from our doze
And give new life to our aged [obsolescent?] mind.[24]

These are words of consolation, a hymn to freedom on the other side of the ocean, a song of lamentation for the old fatherland, and finally words of expectation. All the ingredients of a well-considered departure are there and these must have been representative for many overseas emigrants at the time.

There is at least one more northern Frisian emigration in the decades before the 1880s that attracted attention. In 1854 Tjisse Tillema from Hiaure in Westdongeradeel travelled with his parents to the United States and settled for one year close to the Van Peymas in Lancaster. In 1855 his family went west to Milwaukee, Wisconsin, and a few years later Tjisse moved with his bride Sarah van der Velde, originally from Blija in Ferwerderadeel, to an area southwest of Alto in Columbia County. There they developed the village of Friesland and zealously urged other Frisians to come to their settlement. Many from the *Dongeradelen* responded and because of the lack of new land, a new village was founded nearby and called Randolph. Agriculture and

*Hessel O. Yntema*                    *Klaaske van der Kooi (married Yntema)*

cattle raising were the most important sources of income and Van Hinte is convinced that Tillema became a prosperous man.[25] Different writers emphasize the "Frisian character" of these villages in Wisconsin. Even in the beginning of the nineteenth century Van Hinte and others mention the use of the Frisian language in Randolph and Friesland.[26] I will turn to these more culturally-tinged characteristics of the immigrant communities in a later chapter.

It is certainly not true that before the 1880s only emigrants from the northern Frisian clay area left for the United States. In other parts of Friesland the tradition of overseas migration can be found as well. On April 21, 1847, Hessel O. Yntema and his wife Klaaske van der Kooi, both born in the municipality of Wonseradeel, emigrated with seven children from the village of Koudum. They were Mennonites, leaving to flee the military service and taxes, and they established themselves near Drenthe, about eight miles east of Holland, Michigan, and very close to Ypma's Vriesland.[27] In the same year of Oepke Bonnema's departure, another group of 17 Mennonites from the south-western part of the province left and finally settled in New Paris close to Goshen, Indiana. According to contemporaries, these people from the village of Balk in 1853 mainly emigrated for religious reasons and freedom from bearing arms.[28] One year later about 80 persons from the region of Gaasterland joined this settlement in Indiana.[29] Some children of the immigrants in this colony later settled in the state of California close to the Sacramento River. We know about their economic achievements and spiritual well-being from Jan de Jong, who spent a few years in America. Around 1882 this visitor reported extensively to a Frisian newspaper called *Hepkema's Courant* about the Mennonite farmers' colonies in Indiana and California and about other Frisian settlements.[30]

According to R.P. Swierenga's findings, the overseas emigration between 1830 and 1878 from other parts of Friesland was relatively low. The tradition of migration was mainly located in the municipalities of Barradeel, Het Bildt, and Ferwerderadeel and also in the southwestern region of Gaasterland. From 1830 to 1878 about 34 to 92 emigrants per 1000 average population left for America from these areas, while the rest of Friesland had a number lower than 34. There was a concentration of areas of departure in the Netherlands. Before the 1880s the primary emigration fields were in the Achterhoek in the province of Gelderland, in the sea clay farming regions of Groningen and Friesland, in the Zeeland islands, and in the Peel in the province of Noord-Brabant.[31]

As mentioned above, concentrated fields of settlement in the United States existed too. In the third quarter of the nineteenth century, northern Frisian immigrants could be found in areas close to cities like Chicago and Paterson, New Jersey. Preserved immigrant letters give notice of these settlements and their early histories are mentioned by Van Hinte and Lucas. All these Frisians made a contribution to the conquest of the frontier and to the development of the American continent. Whether we can speak of a substantial contribution, as some writers do, is not yet proven.[32]

There was a tradition of overseas migration in the Frisian clay area before departure of the emigrants who are the subject of this research. Whatever the motivation of these earlier settlers may have been, whether they were rich, poor, young, old, or crippled, it is clear that they often maintained contact with their fatherland and that they often shared their intentions and experiences with those who had remained behind. It is also clear that the departure of emigrants in groups was not unnoticed by their fellow villagers and other people in the region. At the time of Oepke Bonnema's emigration, his bookkeeper said that there were enough rumors and discussions "to fill about twenty booklets" and the group was given a farewell by "hundreds of family members and friends."[33] Worp van Peyma's leaving was reported in the provincial newspaper the *Leeuwarder Courant,* and even the *Provinciale Groninger Courant,* the newspaper of the province of Groningen, mentioned it in some articles.[34] The life story of Hendrik Kroes who left at the age of 26 in 1891 from the village of Ferwerd contains the following phrases concerning his youth:

In 1865 our *Christelijke Gereformeerde Gemeente* had a vacancy. Reverend L.J. Hulst had gone to Stadskanaal. He later on went to America. Before him reverend D.J. v.d. Werp served in Ferwerd – he also left for America. Earlier reverend S. Baron was in Ferwerd – who also left for America. Later on reverend K. Kuiper served in Ferwerd. I went to his confirmation classes. He later on went to America too...Is it then such a great miracle that later on I left for America too?[35]

The stories of the America-trekker have been told and retold and they encouraged the creation of the tradition of migration in the area.

## 3.2 Migration theory

The phenomenon of migration is a complex matter. For more than a century scholars in many different disciplines have tried to find causes and effects of migration. Different disciplines have used different approaches.[36] As early as 1885 and 1889, E.G. Ravenstein presented his celebrated papers on the "laws of migration before the Royal Statistical Society."[37] Since then, his ideas have stood the test of time and are still considered as the starting point for the study of migration theory.

Prior to Ravenstein European scholars recognized the beginning of large scale migrations, but they mainly concentrated on the move to the cities and the phenomenon of depopulation of the countryside.[38] These investigations did not specifically focus on international migration and often dealt with regional matters. Their general impact on the theory of permanent crossing of national borders has therefore been small.

E.G. Ravenstein came to his generalizations by analyzing the data of the English censuses of 1871 and 1881. His Laws contain the following elements: migratory moves depend on distance, travel by stages, migration produces a counterstream, it originates more in the countryside than in urban regions, and economic motives are primary. Although Ravenstein used the national perspective, his ideas already for more than a century give body to research into migration in all kinds of areas and places. P. Kooij in his study of mobility in the city of Groningen, comments:

> From Dahomey to Dokkum population movements are studied within the framework of the distribution of age, the differences in sex, distance, migration by stages, economic necessity, etcetera. Of course this also provided results that did not correspond with Ravenstein's conclusions. But except for the distribution of age, these studies never referred to the time period that was described by Ravenstein.[39]

Kooij concludes that Ravenstein formulated his Laws in the same period as the one he studied (*fin de siècle*), which is also true for this research. Some of the Laws are still usable, especially those focusing on causes and consequences in migrations.

In 1969 E.S. Lee stated that this century has brought no excursion into migration theory comparable to that of Ravenstein. As derived from Ravenstein, Lee created "a general scheme into which a variety of spatial movements can be placed and, from a small number of what would seem to be self-evident propositions, to deduce a number of conclusions with regard to the volume of migrations, the development of streams and counterstreams, and the characteristics of migrants".[40]

Lee admitted that before the launching of his theory some other scholars had made some usable generalizations. Dorothy Thomas and her associates in the 1930s concluded that migrants tend to be young adults or persons in their teens.[41] In 1940 S.A. Stouffer was convinced that migratory moves between A and B become smaller as more intervening opportunities are present between A and B. Also, the longer the distance, the greater the number of such opportunities.[42]

Motivation and characteristics, conditions and consequences of international migration have been studied in the Netherlands too.[43] There was considerable research into the motivation of Dutch migrants during the time of the overseas exodus after World War II. N. Frijda, G. Beijer, B.P. Hofstede, and R. Wentholt all tried to unravel the determinants of overseas migration, but their studies led J.E. Ellemers to conclude that migrants were not special types, but "fairly normal" people.[44]

E.W. Hofstee found that, more than personal characteristics, it was the circumstances in which people live which determine the advancement or impediment of migration.[45] Ellemers is convinced that structural tension within a bigger group of migrants is very influential, once a structural process of loosening from the environment already exists. For example, urbanization and industrialization can cause social tension that fosters migration.[46]

The synthetic migration theory of H. ter Heide stresses push- and pull factors which determine the circumstances of migration. According to P. Kooij, Thomas was probably the first to distinguish the circumstances that caused migration from a certain area [push] and the situation that caused seductiveness and attraction from the area of settlement [pull].[47] Ter Heide bases his statement on the idea that potential emigrants are aware of the situation in the area of departure as well as the area of settlement.[48] Their intention is to find a better life. This improvement is not only economic; social and psychological motives also will influence the decision. But Ter Heide totally overlooked the fact that immigrants often make up or justify their decision to migrate *after* they moved. In that respect, I am more willing to rely on the *standaardmotief* or the standardized motive of H.M. in 't Veld-Langeveld. She takes the line of an individual motive for migrating persons, which is formed by individual as well as group aspirations. Others are being informed of this individual motive, through which the motive starts to function as an independent influence on the willingness to migrate. In this way, the individual motive lies ready to operate as an answer to expressions of general frustrations or dissatisfaction. In that manner, according to In 't Veld-Langeveld, the *standaardmotief* will coincide with the cherished desires of many people.[49]

Much has been written about the consequences of migration, especially concerning ethnicity and assimilation in the host country. In the Netherlands the work of J.J.M. van Amersfoort about immigration and ethnicity after World War II is a substantial contribution to this side of the story.[50] In the United States there have been numerous studies concerning immigrant groups. For decades after World War II, these rarely made

*Bjetje Postma with her son Charles F. van der Meij (picture 1964). Bjetje left with her husband Fedde Scheltes van der Meij in 1912 for a honeymoon to America. Her husband died 35 years old, and Bjetje went back to Friesland. She returned to the U.S.A. with Sijtze (Sam) Wassenaar, her second husband. Both died in Rock Valley, Iowa. Photo donated by K. Postma, Damwoude*

theoretical connections with motivation, circumstances and consequences in the area of departure. Lately all new studies try to do so.[51]

In many of the recently published mobility studies there is a complaint about the lack of substantial theoretical generalizations for the phenomenon of migration. Or as S. de Schaepdrijver notes in her study of foreign migration to mid-nineteenth century Brussels: "many statements, no theory".[52] H. van Stekelenburg, after discussing some economic and sociological theoretical approaches, even concludes that real laws are not useful in migration studies: one can only speak of tendencies. Van Stekelenburg states that the theoretical approach has shifted from mono-causal explanations like Malthus' absolute over-population, to recognition of the complicated and dynamic forces in society that structure the decision to migrate.[53]

This corresponds with my strategy of integrating research into individual and collective factors for migration. It is still valuable to follow in the track of other scholars who classified the factors in migration, especially Lee's approach based on Ravenstein's Laws.[54] For the comparative study of two sides of the ocean I will also rely on the analysis by Joed Elich of Dutch emigration to Australia and a theoretical concept of Charles Tilly concerning networks and categories in migration.

E. Lee classifies the following factors which determine the decision to migrate and the process of migration as follows: factors associated with the area of origin; factors associated with the area of destination; intervening obstacles; and personal factors.

Lee is convinced that "in every area there are countless factors which act to hold people within the area or attract people to it, and there are others which tend to repel them".[55] This means that pull and push factors, as well as neutral factors determine the decision to migrate. Although migration may result from a combination of factors at origin and destination, Lee warns that the decision is not merely a matter of combining pluses and minuses. He mentions the natural inertia that always exists before the move, but also the intervening obstacles between every two points of departure and destination. Obstacles that are trivial to some people, such as poor food on the road, may be prohibitive to others. Lee makes the very important remark that there are many personal factors that influence the individual decision and therefore we must recognize that "it is not so much the actual factors at origin and destination as the perception of these factors which result in migration."[56] Personal aspirations, preferences, sensations, or appreciations contribute to the evaluation of the situation at origin as well as destination and this makes one thing clear: the personal factors that hold and attract people are not perfectly understood either by the scientist or the person directly involved in the process of migration.

The integration of Lee's factors in the act of migration produces a dynamic theory of migration. Based on these factors, Lee himself formulated a series of hypotheses about the volume of migration, the development of stream and counterstream, and the characteristics of migrants. Not all these hypotheses are interesting for this study, but it makes sense to assay the following for the Frisian migrants:

1   The volume of migration is related to the difficulty of surmounting the intervening obstacles.
2   The volume of migration varies with fluctuations in the economy.
3   The volume and rate of migration vary with the state of progress in a country or area.
4   Migration tends to take place largely within well-defined streams.
5   Migration is selective.
6   Migrants responding primarily to plus factors at destination tend to be positively selected.
7   Migrants responding primarily to minus factors at origin tend to be negatively selected.
8   The degree of positive selection increases with the difficulty of the intervening obstacles.
9   The heightened propensity to migrate at certain stages of the life-cycle is important in the selection of migrants.

Lee's hypotheses are mainly a matter of causes. I will try to relate these hypotheses to the sources of Frisian migration later. The consequences of migration have been studied as well, but as J. Elich properly observed, the perspective usually is one sided: either causes *or* consequences, either the accent on the sending *or* the receiving community.[57] In fact the perspective is even broader: the social psychological aspects of migration are an important acknowledged component.[58] Culture and social structure are closely related and in a constant state of dynamic interaction, or as M. Gordon states, "it is the norms and values of the society which, for the most part, determine the nature of the social groupings and social relationships which its members will create; and, conversely, frequently it is through the action of men in social groups that cultures undergo change and modification."[59]

Elich defines in the context of migration the concepts of social structure and culture in a division of social reality on the one side and cultural reality on the other. In his view, social reality represents "the whole of groups, organizations, social positions, and social relations that is developed and preserved by human beings". Cultural reality stands for "the whole of institutions developed and preserved by human beings, based on rules, values, manners and customs, loyalties, esthetical and ethical considerations, in short: based on motivated, meaningful acting and thinking."[60] With this definition of social reality, it is possible for the researcher to focus on social stratification of individual migrants, on the way migrants organize their move, and on the factor of power which is a determinant in migratory moves. With the concept of cultural reality it is possible to research elements of the process of identification by language, religion, norms, and values, but also elements of cognizance like the images of America before departure and the image of the old fatherland after settlement.[61] Elich's division seems useful to me because both concepts help to order the empirical research. In fact, of course, social and cultural reality are one totality and the lines between the two cannot be strictly drawn. But for the purpose of analysis Elich's division seems beneficial.

In the reality of American immigration, immigration produced an acute perplexity, the problem of Americanization. Immigration also created the problem of inequality among racial and ethnic groups. Many scholars believe that significant aspects of American inequality resulted from the social organization of immigration. But the old conceptions of the impact of immigration on inequality stressed individualistic competition and these conceptions hardly apply to the present American reality. Charles Tilly expresses this discrepancy by mentioning the once popular concept: "the idea of a first-come, first-served sequence of nationalities, queuing for assimilation and opportunity; the notion of wholesale importation of cultural traits whose compatibility with dominant American patterns determined the pace and degree of assimilation; the thought that individual competition in a rapidly expanding labor market was the prime determinant of different immigrant groups' relative success or failure."

Dealing with this discrepancy between ideas and experience, scholars focus on "ways in which common struggle, shared social relations, and group control affected the fates of whole categories of immigrants and their descendants."[62] In short, collectivism in migratory moves is an important subject of research. For this case study in Frisian migration the collective aspects are hard to avoid. Analyzing these aspects gives body to the essence and meaning of the move.

As distinct from earlier historians like Oscar Handlin, who saw individual uprooting (shock), disorganization, and subsequent assimilation as the main characteristics of American immigration, Tilly and others describe continuous processes of collective transformation involving the use of old social *networks* and *categories* to produce new ones. Tilly's main point is that the effective units of migration were neither "individuals, nor households but sets of people linked by acquaintance, kinship, and work experience who somehow incorporated American destinations into the mobility alternatives they considered when they reached critical decision points in their individual or collective lives."[63] Through interpersonal networks the risks were spread and minimized. Network members gave each other information and practical economic aid like tickets for the trip and housing. Networks were a dynamic force; they constantly "moved and changed shape, and sent down new roots without entirely severing the old ones." Tilly makes it clear that in this sense networks migrated. On the other hand, he mentions that immigrants also belonged to categories. They were part of a nationality group, they could be Frisians, Groningers, or Zeelanders. However, not all such categories survived the ocean voyage. According to Tilly the survival of categories depended on "the population mix at the destination and on the previously established categories around which the people already at the destination organized their own lives." Categories stay put and networks create new categories. It may well be that sets of connected immigrants without a common identity at the point of origin identified themselves with new categories. In America, Frisians, Zeelanders and Brabanders tended to become Dutchmen, especially if they shared a common church, but the extent of this transformation depended on their relationship to other groups or on the size of the network.

Tilly distinguishes sending and receiving networks which are linked together. Only rarely did a migrant lose all connection with the sending network. Accepting the network structure implies accepting the involvement in migration of negotiation of new relationships both within and across networks instead of a series of individual transformations in the direction of a dominant American culture. It means the acceptance of collective goals instead of individual status-striving. It also means the selective re-creation of social ties instead of wholesale transplantation.[64] In my opinion, Tilly's concept does not exclude individual characteristics. It more or less is a matter of refusing to reduce the structure of migration to the sum of individualities and recognizing that the decisive, cyclic rules deal with the structure of migration networks themselves.

It is evident that in this perspective the individual and collective factors in northern Frisian migration should be researched. The causes *and* consequences will be an important aspect of this study and the accent will be on the sending communities in the clay area *and* on the receiving communities in the United States. How far do Tilly's use of old social networks and categories produce new ones for the Frisian migrants? Is it possible to find sets of Frisian migrants around the turn of the century linked by acquaintance, kinship and work experience? Tilly's basic assumptions offer a way of departure for further research, especially in the realm of the tradition of migration as described in the first part of this chapter.

### 3.3 Household composition

To find out about the common struggle, the group experience, the shared social relations of the Frisian emigrants, a specification of the heads of household is necessary to analyze the composition of the household and to relate for example the occupational structure to the socio-economic background. As mentioned above, Milton M. Gordon long ago made clear that the study of the social structure of society is synonymous with the study of the nature of its family groups and also its formal and informal organizations. Gordon defines "social structure of a society" as: "the set of crystallized social relationships."[65] Gordon focusses on *crystallized* relationships, that means relationships which are not only occasional but with a repetitious pattern or relationships that can be somehow predicted. What these relationships share, is a kind of common expectation. Or, as John Bodnar notes, families are not only the center of economic production in preindustrial society, they were the focus of life itself.[66] Insight into the social structure of the emigrant group seems fundamental for understanding the migration pattern. Generally, concerning the Frisian emigrants, a clear selection process with regard to sex, civil status and age took place. Focussing on the heads of households, it turns out that in the period 1880-1914, 15.4 percent of the whole group emigrated as husband, 15.2 percent as wife, while the single adult males (or male parent) made up 13.8 percent and adult females (or female parent) 5.5 percent. Together almost 35 percent of the total group of Frisian emigrants was head of household or single individual (male and female parents included).

Most people emigrated as member of the family household. 1,441 couples left Friesland, most (1,249) with children some (192) without, some (40) with servants, most (1,401) without. Only 4 of the couples who brought no children, emigrated with a servant as did 5 of the single parents. Sometimes people did not leave alone, but traveled with a brother, a sister or a friend. 186 of the total of 9,467 emigrants started the journey like that.

Table 3.1  **Composition of heads of household and number of individuals among Frisian clay emigrants 1880-1914:**

| | | |
|---|---|---|
| Singles | 1,643 | 50.1 |
| Couple with children | 1,249 | 38.1 |
| Couple without children | 192 | 5.9 |
| Single parent with children/stepchildren | 196 | 5.9 |

**Source:** J.B.E. Galema, "Frisians to America, 1880-1914. Computer Compilation," (Groningen, 1992)

The exact number of singles who emigrated without any children was 1,643 and this group included three times more males than females. Again it appears that single women did not emigrate as much as single men. Many sources show that the women who did leave by themselves often were part of a network or family. A variety of "love-stories" can be found via oral tradition. For example the following story: in 1911 the Frisian emigrant Sjuk Bergsma from a village twenty kilometers south of Leeuwarden went to America. He left behind his girlfriend Jeltje Scholten, who was only eighteen. After arriving in Washington State Sjuk started to write back home and again and again asked Jeltje to come over. But the girl was not in a hurry and finally Sjuk decided to put an advertisement in *Hepkema's* paper to find a Frisian woman as a life partner in America. It so happened that Jeltje read the advertisement and pretty soon started her way to the United States.[67] This event makes clear that single emigrating women cannot always be characterized as *really* single leaving persons. Very often they were part of social or personal units and very rarely did they simply emigrate to look for a job in America without being certain of the social and familial context. Within the group of single parents who emigrated with children and/or family and/or servants, the sex ratio is completely different: 120 females left as single head of household, while only 76 men did the same. The explanation is clear though. The women more often followed their husbands who had explored the chances and situation in America ahead of them. When a single parent emigrated with the children, he or she most likely was motivated by the opportunities in America for the children or the gathering with family who had already settled overseas. A single parent might have had a more urgent need to find support within the family and when this family for a large part had emigrated, the consequences had to be taken.

Together 4,408 sons and daughters emigrated as children of heads of household to America. Few parents or grandparents of the head of household were recorded as moving as member of the household. Probably some of them later decided to follow their children and therefore were recorded and coded as an individual or independent couple. Some younger family members joined a nuclear family, for example brothers and sisters of the head of household. It is also striking that hardly any servants were present within the emigrating households (only 9 persons).

The average age at which emigration occurred was 40 years for husbands, 38 for wives, while the single male and female or male and female parent was respectively 27 and and 33 years old. A gap of almost a decade existed between the married couples and the single emigrants. It appears that women who emigrated single or without their husband, were on average 6 years older than single men.

There is another striking fact: young single males became an increasingly important element in the emigration from the Frisian clay area as time passed.

Table 3.2 **Emigration rate of singles according to sex and 5-year time periods 1880-1914 (of total number of emigrants):**

|  | single males | single females |
|---|---|---|
| 1880-1884 | 8.9% | 3.5% |
| 1885-1889 | 9.3 | 3.2% |
| 1890-1894 | 13.2% | 6.7% |
| 1895-1899 | 12.7% | 7.6% |
| 1900-1904 | 15.3% | 7..8% |
| 1905-1909 | 20.3% | 6.2% |
| 1910-1914 | 22.9% | 5.6% |

**Source:** Galema, "Frisians to America, 1880-1914. Computer Compilation"

Structurally the share of single male emigrants increased from 9 percent of the number of emigrants between 1880-1884 to 23 percent between 1910-1914,[68] while the share of single females did not i.ncrease at the same rate. On the eve of World War I, single males made up almost one quarter of the whole group of emigrants to the United States, while single females accounted only for a one-twentieth share. The share of heads of household with the status of *husband* decreased between 1880-1914.

Table 3.3 **Percentage of male heads of family (husbands) of total number of emigrants in 5-year periods:**

| 1880-1884 | 17.3% |
|---|---|
| 1885-1889 | 16.0% |
| 1890-1894 | 15.4% |
| 1895-1899 | 15.9% |
| 1900-1904 | 14.1% |
| 1905-1909 | 13.0% |
| 1910-1915 | 14.0% |

**Source:** Galema, "Frisians to America, 1880-1914. Computer Compilation"

Thus we can describe the typical Frisian household that emigrated from the northern clay area to the United States as follows: a couple around 40 years old with three to four children, an already established family. The characterization of the typical single is different: a young (three times more likely to be male than female) person around his or her thirties. As Robert Ostergren discovered for Swedish emigration and Ingrid Semmingsen for Norway, the Frisian emigration also was predominantly a family movement.[69] As time passed, a transition from family to single emigration took place. This happened in other European countries as well, although the transition in this Frisian area was not as distinctive. In the next paragraph some new characteristics concerning the emigrant's socio-economic status will be added to this typology.

### 3.4 Occupation and socio-economic status

Examining the occupational structure of the emigrant group should provide some direct evidence about the motives of these Frisian emigrants. Many scholars have recently used the occupational data of the emigrant population as sources for the complex puzzle of motivation. The Population Registers give the occupation of the individual migrant before departure. The availability of this information makes it possible to compose the socio-economic profile of the Frisian clay emigrant. A division in major economic sectors is made in Figure 3.1.

The proportion of emigrants employed in the primary economic sector of agriculture, fishing and hunting (agricultural laborers included) remained almost the same during the period of research (see also Appendix IV). Between 1885 and 1889 a sharp drop of emigrants from the agricultural

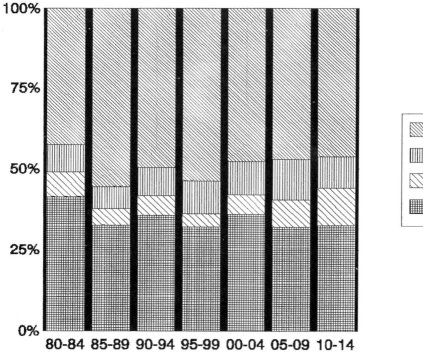

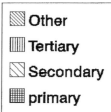

*Figure 3.1*

*Emigrant occupations by major economic sector, 1880-1914.*

**Source:** *Galema, "Frisians to America, 1880-1914. Computer Compilation"*

sector took place, which might have been caused by the increasing unemployment rates due to the agricultural depression. The unemployed emigrants who did not make their specific occupation clear to the governmental officials of the Population Registers, were not categorized as agricultural workers and therefore are included in the major economic sector: Other. We might assume that most of the unemployed emigrants formerly had a job somewhere in the agricultural sector. Generally the share of agriculturally oriented emigrants remained almost the same in the 35 year period. The emigrants of the clay area who worked in agriculture made up 3.7 percent of the total Frisian population working in agriculture in 1909, according to the Occupational Census.[70]

The secondary economic sector showed an increase in the emigrant population, beginning with 7.5 percent between 1880-1884 to 11.8 percent between 1910-1914. This does not reflect the national and provincial pattern of a changing economy after the industrial take-off when the proportion of people employed in the primary and secondary sector gradually decreased and those in the tertiary sector increased.[71] The clay area in Friesland – except for the dairy factories – showed little industrial take-off. Workers in the secondary economic sector of handicraft and food probably were hit later by the agricultural depression than the primary agricultural laborers. And the people in the handicraft sector most likely were more often registered in their own profession than seasonal laborers even when they had no – or hardly any – business in their workshop.[72]

The number of emigrants working in the tertiary economic sector – which includes the professions, service, transport (skippers included), and commerce – slowly increased in synch with the national pattern, and then dropped slightly in the years before World War I.

Almost the entire emigrant labor force in the Frisian clay area was male. It is noticeable that especially in the primary and secondary sectors females were rarely present. This corresponds with the findings of J.L. van Zanden concerning the female share in the agricultural labor force according to the Occupational Census (1889-1909). During the years around 1900, in the province of Friesland only an extremely low percentage of women worked outside the home. However, Van Zanden comments that the Occupational Census of 1889 noted: "The work at home has to be seen as chief ingredient of the activities of the married woman, except when it is perfectly clear that she holds an independent profession or handicraft, distinct from her husband."[73] So the women working in agriculture were not always counted properly and therefore underestimated in the Occupational Census. And because of the general social opinion and *burgerlijke* values many married women probably did not mention their activities outside the home as "real" professions to the Census taker.[74] Anyhow, the female rural proletariat decreased in the last decade of the nineteenth century, also because the real wages for the male laborers became sufficient to support a whole family. The sturdy emigrant Cornelia de Groot who emigrated around 1903 from the village of Deersum in northern Friesland, looked back on her home country in an article in the *San Francisco Chronicle* in 1929 and made the point that "in Holland only a small number of women and girls work outside the home."[75]

The overwhelmingly male emigrant labor force nationally, as reported by Swierenga, is also reflected in the Frisian case. Only 11 percent of the total group of 2,630 female emigrants older than 14 were employed elsewhere. They made up only 4.5 percent of the total emigrant workforce (everybody older than 14). Most of these females were working in the service sector as servants, maids and housekeepers, a few in agriculture as farmer, field laborer or farm girl and some in independent commercial jobs like shopkeepers [winkelierster] and bargewomen [schippersche]. Sewing seemed lucrative because especially young women were seamstress. Only two women worked professionally as teachers.[76] The number of women working as housewives was by far the largest.

Basic information on individual property and wealth is lacking for the mass of Frisian emigrants. Since the Landverhuizerslijsten [Dutch Emigrant Records] are not completely available for the study of Frisian emigration,

Pikking apples in one of the valleys in Washington.

# Noord-Amerikaansche Hypotheekbank.

(NORTH AMERICAN MORTGAGE COMPANY)

## LEEUWARDEN.

TELEFOON INT. 750.

TELEGRAM-ADRES: MORTGAGE.

*Frontpage from brochure of the North American Mortgage Company in Leeuwarden*

hardly any detailed information can be found. But every year the information of the Dutch Emigrant Records was included in the overall account of the provincial reports. This way a survey of the volume of overseas emigration was included. The *Landverhuizerslijsten* contained in the questionnaire an item concerning economic wealth per head of household.[77] Local officials classified emigrants as *welgesteld* [wealthy or well-to-do], *mingegoed* [middling in economic status], or *behoeftig* [impoverished or needy]. This data indicated social class. These lists also contain a remark concerning the migration motivation like: *om zijne positie te verbeteren* [to improve his position], or *om fortuin te maken* [to make a fortune], or *om bij zijne familie te zijn* [to join his family]. Although this basic information for the *individual* Frisian emigrant is lacking because of the loss of the *Landverhuizerslijsten* for Friesland in this time period, some *general* remarks concerning the socio-economic status can be made. The general reports that were conducted from these *Landverhuizerslijsten* were published every year.

Table 3.4  **Socio-economic status of emigrants from Friesland:**

|  | 1880-1894 | | 1901-1920 | |
|---|---|---|---|---|
| Well to do | 220 | 4.3 % | 817 | 5.7 % |
| Middling | 3,449 | 66.9 % | 11,45 | 79.9 % |
| Poor | 1,487 | 28.8 % | 2,073 | 14.4 % |

**Source:** 1880-1894: *Overzicht landverhuizerslijsten*, Rijksarchief Leeuwarden. 1901-1920: R.P. Swierenga, "The Delayed Transition from Folk Migration to Labor Migration; The Netherlands, 1880-1920," *International Migration Review*, 22 (Summer, 1993): 418-19

The Dutch Emigrant Records show the rough social status of the provincial emigrants. For Friesland it appears that between 1880 and 1894 the percentage of emigrants who were well to do was extremely low. The wealthier economic groups were never important in the Frisian emigrant movement around the turn of the century. Most of the emigrants were considered to have a middling status and the percentage of this category increased from 66.9 between 1880-1894 to 79.9 between 1901-1920. The assumption can also be made that in the last two decades of the 19th century more poor people emigrated than in the first two decades of the 20th century. This can be ascribed to the higher unemployment rates during the agrarian depression. However, Y. Schreuder in her research concerning Brabant makes the relevant point that these social status categories are based on subjective judgments made by the government official who was burdened with the compilation of the Emigrant Records.[78]

To avoid this solely subjective judgment, it is worthwhile to obtain a second source of information and make a more balanced judgment concerning the emigrant's social status. The discussion about social class [*klasse* as well as *stand*] has a long history.[79] Usually the sources for constructing a complete social inequality analysis for the total population are not available. And these sources always are related to the specific variables of education, occupation, class and income.[80] Education and class (high-born, low-born etc.) are hard to investigate because of inadequate information. It is possible to relate the municipal Head Tax [*Hoofdelijke Omslag*] to the specific emigrant. But this Head Tax was charged per household and cannot be attributed to many individual emigrants. It is, therefore, logical to rely on the data given in the Population Registers and use the individual occupation as a basis for studying more specific details on social class.

To determine the nature of the occupational hierarchy, one needs a gradation that implies position on the social ladder and the occupational pyramid. And then, as Stephan Thernstrom noted in his study concerning social mobility in a nineteenth century city in New England, it is necessary to justify the use of these methaphors in a specific historical context.[81] I classified the occupations in distinct social categories in order to make possible some immediate generalizations from the data of the Population Registers. An important element in this classification is the fact that we have to deal with a rural area of emigration. It makes sense to consider the differences of rural and urban social structure (table 3.5).

Table 3.5  **Social gradation of occupation clay Frisian emigrants 1880-1914:**

|                               | number | %     |
| ----------------------------- | ------ | ----- |
| Professional, sub-professional | 25     | 0.3   |
| Owner, entrepreneur           | 176    | 1.9   |
| Tenant                        | 108    | 1.1   |
| Skilled                       | 194    | 2.0   |
| Semiskilled                   | 1317   | 13.9  |
| Unskilled                     | 828    | 8.7   |
| No occupation                 | 469    | 5.0   |
| Other                         | 6350   | 67.1  |
| **Total**                     | 9467   | 100.0 |

**Source:** Galema, "Frisians to America, 1880-1914. Computer Compilation"

As noted in table 3.5, the group of professionals includes: doctors, ministers, architects, teachers, nurses, musicians, newspaper editors and submanagerial occupations like police officers, accountants, tax collectors, auctioneers, post office officials. The category of owners and entrepreneurs covers landowners, shipowners, independent farmers, merchants, shopkeepers, brokers and financiers. Tenants include the already mentioned *gardeniers,* small landowners and tenant farmers. The categories of skilled, semiskilled and unskilled are created to indicate the difference in status between for example craftsmen, artisans, sailors, clerks and dressmakers (skilled), craftsmen's apprentices, artisans' apprentices, permanent agricultural laborers and female permanent agricultural and domestic servants (semiskilled), and agricultural day laborers, casual workmen, factory workers, casual servants and hawkers and peddlers (unskilled). The group with no occupation contains people who were unemployed at the moment they left for America. The last category covers the children under fourteen, students, housewives and people whose profession is unknown.

The first conclusion may be that almost all the emigrants were working in manual jobs. The semiskilled category of handicraft apprentices and permanent agricultural and domestic workers is by far the largest. Within the group of "Other," the housewives made up 13.3 percent, the people whose occupation is unknown 21.7 percent, and children 32.2 percent. Emigrants who did not report any occupation may have been unemployed and emigrants reporting a profession may not have had a job at that particular moment. Considering that the data are derived from the Population Registers, it is clear that people who were in the middle and lower ranks of the social ladder left for America. Most of the emigrants came from semiskilled and unskilled ranks of society, while the people without any occupation were also responsible for a large part. In the skilled professions bakers, butchers, carpenters, shoemakers, cheesemakers and cabinet makers left.

Most of the owners, entrepreneurs and those selfemployed as well as most of the tenants who were to emigrate departed in the years 1880-1885; while the period 1890-1914 saw a greater proportion of emigrants who had been agricultural laborers. These peaks correspond with the peaks in emigration. However, the occupational structure changes somewhat over the years, because the percentage of agricultural laborers in the beginning of the eighties is much lower than in the beginning of the second peak of emigration in the nineties (8.4 percent between 1880-1884 and 12.2 percent between 1890-1894). It seems that in the beginning of the period of study more landowners and entrepreneurs with a higher social status left. The people belonging to the skilled professions like butchers, painters and bakers left at the same time.[82] There is no evidence that these professions directly related to agriculture followed those emigrants who had particular agricultural professions. The people with handicrafts who depended upon assignments from the agricultural sector did not show a delayed process of emigration because the agrarian crisis affected the total economic and social order. The people who were recorded as unemployed also did not leave. Between 1880-1884 6.2 percent of the emigrants were unemployed, while between 1890-1894 their share was 5.2 percent. The share of unemployed people was in fact the lowest in the time period 1910-1914 (2.1 percent). But this does not mean that the agrarian crisis was responsible for much higher rates of unemployed emigrants. Between 1885-1889 their share was 5.5 percent, while in the period 1905-1909 the unemployment rate was 4.5 percent of the emigrant population.

It is often said that most of the European emigrants to America did not come from the very lowest ranks of society, because they lacked the means and could not pay for their journey.[83] But this mainly concerns people who left in the first half of the nineteenth century. By the nineties, reduced transportation costs and direct links to America from the port of Rotterdam helped emigrants from the bottom rungs of the social ladder to consider emigration as well. The auction of all the household goods usually left some money for the journey.[84] And those with not even a respectable shirt to wear would be assisted by relatives, neighbors or fellow church members.[85] Martin van der Heide who left the village of Ferwerd in 1914, got enough money for the passage to America because his mother borrowed money for him and his fiancé on the condition that he would pay back soon. In his memoires, Van der Heide writes that he did not feel conscience-stricken about that, because "we were going after all to a land with *a lot of money*."[86] The two brothers Anne and Egbertus Leep from St. Annaparochie in Het Bildt left for Chicago in 1893 with tickets prepaid by two Chicago storeowners who were prompted by earlier emigrants, former neighbors of the Leeps. Anne and Egbertus repaid their tickets after three years of work in Chicago.[87] Generally Frisians who left with prepaid tickets appeared to be the exception which proves the rule. Most of the clay emigrants were able to pay their own fares, because of the relatively cheap prices during the last decades of the nineteenth century.

### 3.5 Motives, pragmatism, and networks

The reflections on the theory of migration in paragraph 3.2 need to be reexamined in the case of the Frisian emigrants. After elaborating the family structure, the composition of the household, and occupational categorization, the patterns of emigration can be profiled more directly. E. Lee's hypotheses seem to be relevant for the Frisians. We may say that the intervening obstacles were enormous in overseas emigration, which is evident from the fact that a lot more people stayed home than emigrated in the clay area. The volume of migration is related to these intervening obstacles. The output [*rendement*] of overseas migration is high because Frisians who crossed the ocean did not return very easily.

The volume of migration also varied with fluctuations in the economy. A potential emigrant judges certain factors differently in economically profitable periods than in more depressed ones. When Pieter Ypes Groustra with his wife Frederica and their two sons Ype and Anton left the village of Ee for America in 1881, he certainly was influenced by the fact that because of the agrarian crisis even an experienced carpenter could not find much work.[88] In the beginning of 1893, when unemployment rates in Friesland were still high, the emigrant Jan W. Bijker wrote from Sioux Center, Iowa:

> What a different world we have, I think many times. In Friesland the laborers get in each other's way and for long periods during the year do not have work and bread, while here where laborers, servants and maids can earn high wages, many of them are necessary.[89]

But depressed economic times were not the only factor in Frisian migration. They could only foster emigration when the land of destination, America, showed some pull effect in economically profitable periods. At the end of the 1870s economic conditions in the United States had improved and the last frontier for farmers had been thrown open by Congress and also by the railroad companies.[90] Frisian emigration especially in the beginning of the

1880s increased rapidly, congruous to the general Dutch emigration situation. When in late 1893 the American economy was hit by an economic depression and bad news was spread concerning swindling practices of emigration agencies with potential emigrants to Colorado, the Frisian emigration dropped in 1894 by 78 percent. In that year Tjerk Zondervan and his wife Maartje Lautenbach wrote from the city of Paterson, New Jersey:

> Labor possibilities are bad here and thousands of people without a job are browsing the streets and this already lasted 10 months...my husband does not have anything to do either...it is a severe winter...and at many homes it's a double winter: within and outside the house. Lots of charitable work is done and if nothing like that was done, thousands would die of hunger and want and those who do have work get low wages and almost every day strikes are present so you can image how times are. We hope that this will change soon because otherwise the situation will be equal to the Netherlands....[91]

At no time before World War I did the overseas migration from the Frisian clay area again reach the high level of the 1880s and the beginning of the 1890s. After the turn of the century Dutch emigration, especially from the *Randstad,* continued to rise, reaching a high point in 1913.[92] But the character of the emigrant stream changed during those years. Twentieth century Dutch emigrants came more from urban areas as the primary emigration field turned from the sea clay areas, to the urban surroundings of Amsterdam and Rotterdam.[93]

Lee's hypothesis that migration tends to take place largely within well defined streams is very true for the northern Frisians. Frisian migration can be characterized as a typical family movement. Many people emigrated as member of a household and most of them had strong family ties in America. Numerous obstacles for potential emigrants disappeared after they got information from family, friends and acquaintances who more or less created cleared paths. It is also easy to confirm Lee's statement that the heightened propensity to migrate is important in the selection of emigrants. The average age of migrating husbands and wives was around 39 years. That means that in the migration process a specific group was selected: people who had been married for some time, who had one or more children, who were part of an established family. D. Thomas' proposition that migrants tend to be young adults holds true for the northern Frisians too. The selection also took place in the group of young single males and females. It occurs that at certain stages of the life-cycle, changes in personal relationships can make people more or less eager to migrate. The younger single adults were more willing to look for fortune in the United States than the younger married couple who had just found a house and had a baby. An established family with no future perspectives for the children made the decision to emigrate often at a point before these children had to enter the labor market. In this respect E.W. Hofstee's remark is important that "migrants" behavior can be understood without positing migratory selection with respect to individual character traits.[94] Personal characteristics surely cannot be denied, but circumstances in which people live determine the migratory move.

In search for historical patterns it seems evident that structural tension within the potential emigrant group also was an important factor in the emigration process. The municipality of Het Bildt had the largest proportion of emigrants from the clay area. In the decades around the turn of the century, Het Bildt also had the highest degree of social tension with bad relations between employers and employees which resulted in many strikes and social upheavals. The process of urbanization also influenced the social relationships in the countryside. Contemporary witnesses like Vitus Bruinsma and K. Reijne did not report in altruistic tones on the depopulation of the countryside. They feared the spector of rural depopulation especially because of the negative social and economic consequences. The sociologist J.E. Ellemers maintains that once a structural process of loosening from the environment already exists, the willingness to migrate is greater. Urbanization and also the tradition of overseas migration already had loosened the psychological ties with the Frisian native soil. Personal characteristics resulting in individual motives for migration can be found in many personal accounts. But I do agree with H.M. in 't Veld-Langeveld that individual causes operate as an answer to expressions of general frustrations or dissatisfaction. When Gerrit Roorda articulated that he had an urge to leave for America to spare his parents because he came home every day very depressed and irritated from a hard day of work and evening lessons at school in Heerenveen, he probably expressed a general feeling of economic dissatisfaction because he wanted to go to America to earn (more) money.[95]

In 1893 the two brothers Anne K. and Egbertus K. Leep, sons of the poor peddler Klaas and his wife Clara Prins, went to America when they were eighteen and sixteen years old. They came from St. Annaparochie in Het Bildt and had heard glowing reports from former neighbors who had gone to the New World earlier. These reports most likely functioned as individual motives to flee a futureless occupational perspective. In three years Anne and Egbertus (in America named Andrew and Edward) saved enough money by doing odd jobs in Chicago and Roseland, to repay their prepaid tickets and to enable the other family members from Friesland to come over. That way father and mother Leep and their five children Doeke, Douwe, Haring, Hendrik and Janke, joined the two oldest boys in Roseland. The individual motive to reunite the family served as encouragement for more general aspirations.[96] These broader ambitions are expressed in the socio-economic profile of the northern Frisian emigrants. In macro-economic terms, the conclusion is that generally the share of agriculturally oriented emigrants – the economic sector with the most emigrants who were part of the work force – remained almost the same between 1880-1914. The secondary economic sector of handicrafts and foods showed an increase in the emigrant population in that period. The number of emigrants working in the tertiary sector slowly increased and only dropped slightly in the years before World War I. These macro-economic developments in overseas migration can be attributed to an almost entirely male emigrant work force. The socio-economic status of the northern Frisian emigrants shows that the percentage of emigrants who were well to do was extremely low. The semi-skilled category of handicraft apprentices and permanent agricultural and domestic workers is by far the largest. It was mainly the people in the middle and lower ranks of the social ladder who left for America, and for their economic and social well-being, they negotiated and were in touch with their fellow countrymen in the United States.

Many potential emigrants relied on personal information of family and acquaintances who already had made the overseas move. The impact of information about America on the motivation of emigrants will be subject of the next chapter.

# *Chapter 4* Fantasy and realism: letters and the image of America

## 4.1 Introduction[1]

A century ago Frederick Jackson Turner tried to explain the character of America and the American people through the frontier experience. In 1893 this young scholar gave a lecture at a meeting of the American Historical Association in Chicago about "The Significance of the Frontier in American History."[2] Turner argued that until 1890 the country had a frontier with uninhabited lands beyond it. Pioneer settlers had moved westward across the American continent, creating all kinds of characteristic institutions. The first settlers symbolized opportunity and opportunism, but also individualism and democracy as well as upward social mobility. Turner's thesis emphasized the fact that the American frontier had constantly expanded westward for four centuries after the discovery of America. After 1890 it was no longer possible to talk about the United States as if there were a frontier line. Turner concluded in his lecture of 1893 that the first period of American history was closed and that the frontier had disappeared.[3]

The distinguishing feature of American history, Turner argued, had been the lure of the open frontier. By giving every person a chance to own property, he stated, and by rewarding democratic virtues of individualism, self-reliance, optimism and resourcefulness, the western frontier had turned Europeans into Americans. This frontier had determined the American character. At this frontier, ordinary people met an extraordinary land. The American institutions were not merely a copy from "The Old World"; no, the years of pioneering had radically changed America into a country with a national character of its own, a country that was different from Europe.[4] According to Turner's thesis, immigrants Americanized and acquired very specific characteristics, recognizable and unique. The frontier was the key to understanding American history and identity, the key to understanding America. The frontier thesis meshed perfectly in 1893 with the confident, nationalistic mood of a young country that was just starting to flex its muscles in the global arena. Turner became a national figure and his theory launched a new academic discipline: the history of the American West. Turner and his supporters were characterized as environmental determinists because they believed that in the struggle of men against nature, the wilderness overwhelmed the pioneer. Frontier settlers abandoned the civilized life and institutions they had known and only later found the chance and ability to build their own society with distinguishable features. In fact, according to Turner and his followers, the frontier settlers went back to the roots of mankind for a while, and afterwards built their own new environment.

In the decades following Turner's seminal essay, there were many critics who were convinced his view was at least half myth. They argued that Turner was ruled by patriotic passions instead of intellectual impulses. In his romantic nationalism, Turner forgot the wild land speculation, the destruction of natural wilderness, the arrogance of American expansionism, and last but not least, the tragedy of the Indians. The frontier thesis though, showed remarkable resilience, and is still being taught at colleges from coast to coast although not without criticism.[5] The prominent Dutch journalist and historian Ben Knapen described the influence of the Turner thesis as follows: in fact, the frontier thesis did not stay alive as a scientific concept, but it did stay alive as a creative metaphor, an American identity, and also as a tribute to American values and uniqueness.[6] The frontier thesis functioned as a specific American introspection, as the image of a nation that was cherished most by the American people. And in a way it still functions like that today. Witness the illegal border crossings. Every year thousands of Mexican immigrants come over to the United States, the land of wealth and freedom of their dreams. This American myth still serves the American people in composing their specific identity.

### 4.2 Observation and analysis

To study the process of image-building between nations is a complex task. The Dutch sociologist A.N.J. den Hollander was convinced that there are various obstacles that hamper a correct perception. He believed that one can only observe another society by breaking through certain barriers, and by realizing that the view is always wrapped in a veil of secrecy.[7] There is always a discrepancy between reality and the muddled perception. Autonomous mental processes are an illusion: these are always influenced by the culture that surrounds it. Den Hollander argued that values, institutions, preoccupations, and taboos of the national culture and subculture always form some kind of screen through which we judge ourselves as well as others. But not only (sub)national values and preferences influence the human mind. There are other important aspects that shape a personal way of thinking, preferences, and presuppositions: the specific personality and characteristics of the observer, his social position and education.[8] The "real" America in fact is obscured by *a prioris* and prejudices.

Den Hollander regarded the veil of secrecy and the screen that surrounds the observer as a mighty obstruction in studying foreign cultures. In fact, Den Hollander created a distorted model in which presuppositions about "the Self" and "the Other" bias true observations. In my opinion, however, we need versions of "Others" to construct an account of ourselves. Of course these versions can be more or less misrecognitions in terms of the version the other produces of itself. But Den Hollander's view suggests a radical subjectivism and individualism that cannot be true in a qualified sense. The *quality* of knowledge of the other will certainly make a difference to subordinated or colonized people. Think about the variations on the topic of American Indians riding around in the wilderness scalping "white men," and capturing their women.

The Dutch historian K. van Berkel argues that the prejudices we have in our observations of foreign cultures should be objects of our studies. Very often the prejudices concerning a foreign nation operate as judgments on one's own country and culture. Whether the images of other nations are right or wrong is more or less irrelevant. The existence of these images is important enough for the historian to pay attention, according to Van Berkel.[9] And anyway, we also want to ask ourselves: in what aspects did the images change in the long run. In this perspective it is not enough to study the changes in American reality. If we follow Van Berkel's point, it is more interesting to study the changes in the imagination of the European observer. It could be the right move to look at the frameworks or structures of feelings themselves as the object of study. But is it really evident that the perception of "right" or "wrong" images of other nations is irrelevant? Isn't "image" (or maybe fantasy) a particular force against other aspects of reality? Speaking of the "image" of America refers, psychologically, to a very complex group of associations, phrases, ideas, fantasies, and attitudes in varying forms and combinations that the name of America evoked in European minds.

Against the background of Turner's romantic nationalism and Den Hollander's and Van Berkel's ideas about observing and interpreting other nations, one might ask how it was possible that in the second half of the nineteenth century so many Netherlanders decided to emigrate to the United States. What was their perception of the New World, and how did the process of image building develop? Why should they abandon the security of their homeland to risk their lives amidst uncertainty and sometimes even violence? After all, they came from a small, relatively well-organized, conveniently arranged country. That thousands upon thousands did migrate is indisputable. Throughout the nineteenth century nearly 20 million immigrants reached the United States, among them 200,000 Dutch.

Until recently, researchers who study migration patterns have not paid much attention to how emigrants imagined their future homeland before they left. And even fewer studies have been made of the immigrants' image of the "old fatherland" after they had settled in the United States. But as soon as the image of other nations became a hot issue in research into nationalism, international scholars started to shed some light on these matters related to the process of migration.[10] In 1990 the historian and migration expert John Bodnar expressed it this way: "The missing dimension of current immigration historiography lies not in the realm of economic detail but in the realm of cultural construction. The predominant scholarly need today is not so much the generation of more social and economic data, although that is needed, but it is the penetration of the structures of meaning or interpretations that immigrants gave to the economic and political systems in which they moved and lived."[11]

In this chapter in the realm of cultural construction, I would like to deal with the image of America that prevailed in the sending communities in the province of Friesland, and how this image was shaped.

### 4.3 Home and future domicile

Almost 10,000 people left the northern Frisian fertile clay area between 1880 and 1914 to settle in the United States.[12] The agricultural depression had deeply affected their area. We might ask ourselves: what made these migrants leave the Netherlands? Did they consider the United States as the land of milk and honey? How did they adopt or embrace certain views and what kind of process created their images?

There are not many sources to investigate the migrants' images of their future country or, as they looked back, of their former homeland. For the group that left the northern Netherlands around the turn of the century, I found that almost all came from the middle and lower classes.[13] They and their families were mostly agricultural laborers. Consequently, the sources are scarce. On the level of private sources, direct personal information about images and image building of the "new" and "old" nations is mainly found in letters, exchanged over the ocean. These letters represent private views or views that circulated within a domestic or personal context and their particular relevance for this study is the glimpse of personal opinions they provide.

On the level of public sources, there was activity of so-called image-makers - travelers[14], promoters, and novelists. The investigation of these image-makers is valuable, because it gives an indication of the huge impact they had on the image-building of America among the emigrants. Private and public sources interacted and they cannot be separated while studying this process of image-building. The Frisian emigrant Martin van der Heide recalls in his autobiographical essay that at the age of ten he became very impressed by a sketch of the American prairies in one of his schoolbooks: "in this sketch we saw a bunch of wild animals running in the long grass; among them: wild horses, buffalos, wolves, swines and other smaller animals. This picture fascinated me enormously and very often I wanted to see it again and again and then I thought: 'Oh would I feel happy if I could be there too and live in such an area where wild animals are around and all that wilderness...'".[15] Fifty years after emigration, Van der Heide still remembers this picture in his schoolbook. This impression was part of the image-making in the Netherlands concerning the United States and also accessible to lower class people in Friesland.

The group of image-makers consisted of agents of steamship and immigration companies, real estate promoters, and employees of immigration agencies. It also included reformers who sought a better future for their fellow country-men, travelers who described their own experiences, and successful immigrants whose letters sometimes glowed with exciting tales of their own prosperity and happiness.

Half a century separated the America described by novelists and travelers in the eighties from that which Tocqueville had surveyed in his famous *De la Démocratie de l'Amerique*. Although general travel accounts and novels enable us to understand more of what the emigrants felt toward the United States around the turn of the century, I will not pay much attention to these travelers' and novelists' views. Rather I wish to emphasize the role of the promoters of emigration in the process of image building. In the next chapter I will also give a glimpse of the specific emigrant travel experiences known through personal accounts of the Frisians who departed from the northern clay area.

### 4.4 Promotors of the "Go!!"

In the city of Harlingen in the 1880s the company Prins & Zwanenburg tried to recruit emigrants for America.[16] They dealt with the Koninklijke Nederlandsche Stoomvaart Maatschappij [Royal Dutch Steamship Company] and from 1883 with the Nederlandsch Amerikaansche Stoomvaart Maatschappij [Netherland American Steamship Company] and also promoted their services as land agents. In glittering brochures and advertisements in local newspapers like *Het Weekblad voor het Kanton Bergum*, Prins & Zwanenburg tried to promote lands that they had bought in different states, because they predestined these areas for Frisian settlement and pointed the emigrants towards the cheap lands, especially of the West.[17]

At the same time the well-known Frisian poet and writer Tjibbe Geerts van der Meulen was an immigration agent. After he had visited his brother Anne in Iowa (who emigrated in 1849), he promoted the New World, but not uncritically.[18] Van der Meulen castigated the land speculators and exposed their nefarious practices. In 1882 he wrote in the *Weekblad voor het Kanton Bergum*:

> America is the land of Cockcaigne, a Wonderland, but before one arrives there, one has to eat one's way through the mountain of pulp and there many perish. Many swindling agents are active; they stir in this pulp and many newcomers have their eyes smeared shut. Many weep when they finally realize where they have actually landed: oh, oh, that pulp mountain.[19]

This article had a very pointed title: "Whoever desires to earn a lot of money should become a recruiter."

The newspapers also published articles in which future emigrants could read about the burdens and hazards of settling in America. In Frisian newspapers like the *Weekblad* and *Het Nieuw Advertentieblad* one could always find an article or letter that emphasized the positive aspects of settlement in the United States. The pros and cons were discussed in almost every newspaper in Friesland in those days. The image of America in newspapers and letters was mainly positive.

Beside the steamship companies and the land agents, other image-makers in the 1880s and 1890s included agents of the Northern Pacific Railroad, carefully selected from the ranks of successful immigrants willing to return to their homelands for a fat fee. Railroad advertising in local newspapers and

*Poster of the* Nederlandsch Amerikaansche Stoomvaart Maatschappij, *around 1885*

*Advertisement in the* Leeuwarder Courant *February 2, 1893*

brochures pictured the northern Great Plains as the Garden of the World, a land with a favorable combination of circumstances unmatched in all the world.[20] Even the smaller railroad lines, unable to afford separate European agencies, sought to grasp their share by linking with immigrant companies. Of course, negative propaganda was spread by people who felt mistreated by the land agents. But generally this negative image did not keep people from emigrating to America. The negative image had less influence and did not appear as frequently as the positive image. According to the Frisian newspapers of the last decades of the nineteenth century, people were well aware of the fact that the goal of these railroad agents was to sell land, and hence their advertisements were suspect. But what happened when an unemployed Frisian laborer fixed his eye upon sentences in the local newspaper proclaiming: "LAND FOR SALE! 60 MILLION BUSHELS GRAIN IN MINNESOTA AND NORTH DAKOTA IN 1882! MONEY TO EARN!."[21] The agents' principal trick was to portray as typical the life stories of the most successful emigrants. This can be illustrated by many published letters, such as one from W. Nauta in Howell County, Missouri. In 1909 he wrote in the newspaper *Het Nieuwsblad van Friesland*:

> After a stay of 28 years in America, I now returned to the fatherland for a while. In early
> next spring, I think I will go back to America. I like to tell you something about the land
> over there, especially concerning Howell-county. The capital city of Howell-county is
> West-Plains with a populations of 4500 souls. One lives right in the middle of the United
> States. Howell-county is crossed from north-west to south-east by the Frisco Railway, which
> makes the transport of fruit, grain, cattle etc. to big cities like St. Louis, Kansas City,
> Memphis, New-York, etc. very easy....
> In the last several years they have planted a lot of peach trees. From this area alone this

*Advertisement of Tjibbe Geerts van der Meulen, agent of the Holland America Line. In:*
Weekblad voor het Kanton Bergum, *March 12, 1881*

year about 800 railway wagons with peaches have been exported as well as 500 wagons with strawberries....

The climate is very healthy. Enough rainfall; the highest temperature is 95 degrees, and the nights are always cool. Winters are short and mild; there is no need to stable the cattle for more than three months. I never heard of foot-and-mouth disease of the cattle, neither of any sheep diseases or swine-plagues. Cattle-breeding and horse-breeding are very profitable. Chicken-farming is also big business. The waters are full of fish, the forests crowded with wild animals, mostly deer, hares, partridges and wild turkeys.

It is possible to buy farms here for the price you pay for rent in Holland, and taxes are very low because the county did not get into debts. We also do have catholic as well as protestant schools here, as well as churches.

Potential emigrants can ask for further information at the American Consulate in Amsterdam.

The undersigned is also very willing to provide information concerning travel, costs of travel, money to bring, settlement, etc....[22]

Nauta came from a small village in the north of Friesland where he had a cattle farm. He and his wife emigrated in 1882. From his letter we may easily draw the conclusion that it was purposely written for a larger public. It was clearly a mixture of private and public sources. Nauta's account was influenced by the fact that he knew it would serve as an information source for an audience larger than his own family. He refers largely to economic perspectives, with hardly any comments concerning social circumstances. What can we say, for example, of the gendered nature of this account? This letter is written by a male person to a male audience. It does not refer to the prospects for women and children in the future country. The economic perspective gets far more attention than social aspects of the immigrant family life. However, the focus on the labor environment may well have to do with the complexity of migration motivation. Economic factors played a great role in encouraging Frisian emigrants to change habitat.

Nauta's letter supports the conclusion that the impact of promotional agents was dwarfed by that of the thousands of "America letters" that spanned the Atlantic. It is not known how many letters arrived in Friesland between 1880 and 1914, but in Denmark in the year 1883 nearly half a million were received. In another study it was calculated that between 1875 and 1914 an average of more than four letters per Dane in the United States were written to the home country.[23]

To Friesland thousands were written, too, based on the many letters published in contemporary newspapers, and those uncovered in a recent national search.[24] The privately written letters are important for several reasons. They give us some insight into personal matters of people from whom there are few extant documents and who did not write public accounts of their daily experiences. America-letters also contain information concerning the multi-ethnic social life and assimilation and acculturation in the New World. We can learn about the immigrants' views and ideas on schools, churches, neighbors, and factories. They also tell us about the discrepancy between norms and values in the "Old" and in the "New" world.

Obviously immigrants made the comparison of both sides of the ocean and in that way they show us the image of a nation. In general we can obtain psychological information concerning the immigrants' experience: their loneliness, hardships, despair, and sometimes tragedies, but also their courage, optimism, sense of adventure, hopes, and hard work.[25]

That letters were written in large numbers is a reflection of the psychological needs of the emigrants. They must have feared exile from the Frisian land. De Vries from San Francisco, for example, wrote a phrase in 1889 that could have been written by many other immigrants:

> Since February this year I received the *Workumer Courant* [The Journal of the city of Workum] and that was it! But I expected you to write something with it, but no letter appeared to be in there.... I think it is stupid that we don't write to each other for such a long time....[26]

Other immigrants felt that they had to justify their move: from many a letter one gets the impression that immigrants experienced a compelling urge to appear better than those left behind, and they were often incapable of admitting error or lack of success. Th. M. Oostenbrug writes in 1882 from the town of Hospers, Iowa:

> I better tell you how things really are in America. The farmers here are all Dutch and Frisian, the same as in your area. Labor is done by horses and machines. So there is no place here for the day laborer. Everyone here is a farmer, or shoemaker.... The soil is in perfect condition, the manure is being burned instead of used. One sees beautiful grain fields... hay can be mowed as much as you want and it's of better quality than ever can be found in Friesland....[27]

These kinds of positive exaggerations might have easily influenced the reality of the immigrants in their new place of settlement. The fact that they were trying to justify their move and their new way of life in America possibly *made* them look back without sorrow or nostalgia. And, of course, in a way a bright and positive outlook on the future was the key to survival.

The arrival of an "America-letter" in a north-Frisian village could be a major event. Many people were readers; the letters circulated among family and friends and sometimes were read in the church. The Dutch historian Bertus Wabeke in his book about Dutch emigration to North America even bore witness that each fresh batch of "America-letters" in a village was responsible for a general exodus.[28] Considering the complexity of the motivation to migrate, Wabeke may have oversimplified. His statement is an exaggeration of one unmistakably important piece of the migration motivation puzzle. But one cannot deny that immigrant letters were a catalyst to emigration.[29] Immigrants wrote to the old country and that was the moment when the image-building started to merge into the efforts of the image-builders. Most immigrant letters provided basic and essential information: cost of land, nature of soils, wages paid, and condition of labor. Most, too, told of the writer's success in simple prose: "I am earning enough money to return to

Holland, if I wanted to. And you cannot imagine what good food I get here,"
Ulbe Eringa wrote in 1892 from Iowa to his sister in Friesland.[30] Or, a few
years later from Runningwater, South Dakota: "Yesterday when I rode to
town with my two horses hitched to our buggy, I was wishing that my wife
and I could ride over to your place that way – that would give you a better
idea of our life here in America". These success stories were mixed with
descriptions of opportunities for those who were thinking of following the
migratory pattern. Eringa writes: "Our brother-in-law, Gerlof, has gotten
work with our neighbor and is earning good money and his board. These
people are very happy to be here. They didn't realize how good it could be –
abundance of work and food so cheap. In comparison the poor day laborer
in Holland has a pitiful, poverty stricken and sorrowful existence."[31]
Finishing his long letter another immigrant from Pensylvania wrote in 1911
in the journal *Nieuwsblad van Friesland*: "In my area, about three hours by
train from New York, more than a hundred farms are for sale. Prices are very
low, about 70 to 80 dollars per acre. In Iowa that kind of land is sold at least
for 150 to 200 dollars per acre. There are good reasons for telling you this,
for I know what I am talking about!"[32]
That the image of America apparently was not always very concrete or that
the image was difficult to express, is shown by the experience of Aukje

Pruiksma from Paterson, New Jersey in 1895. She wrote about her new environment: "the surroundings here are somewhat mountainous and it appears to be a heavy walk upwards."[33] Mrs. Pruiksma had to get used to the hills of New Jersey; Probably she had previously seen nothing but the flat countryside of Friesland. Many, many more of these examples can be mentioned; the new country proved to be a visual collision as well as a culture shock.

Again the gendered nature of the letters can be emphasized. Dictated by their divergent experience of immigrant life, quite often men and women wrote about different subjects. Most Dutch immigrant women, for example, did not have a job outside the home. Some of them never learned to speak English. More than men, immigrant women sometimes felt themselves to be isolated, which is reflected in their written accounts to the old country.[34]

### 4.5 Disappointment overcome by bacon letters

While most of the immigrant letters gave a positive impression of America, more balanced or even negative sentiments are also expressed. Some immigrants were not afraid to tell the people back home that migrating to America was not a blueprint for fortune. Some honestly confessed to being homesick. A lady wrote in 1911 from Iowa City that she had a carefree life but did not enjoy it because she was not able to understand anybody. Although she knew that very many Dutchmen lived in the city, she never met one because the city was so huge and filled with people of many different nationalities![35] J.G Boekhout wrote from Paterson in 1882:

> Now I will write you something about America, because if many people really knew about America, they would decide to stay where they are. Lots of those who live here, want to return because it's a strange world here: Parents cannot boss their own children here, because if the youngsters tell the police that Mum or Dad don't treat them well enough, the parents have to pay 5 dollars. That's how things work here....[36]

According to Boekhout the parental influence in America did not reach far enough and was not independent from authorities as measured by Dutch standards.

Two specific ideas are projected clearly: the social freedom and equality, and the reports of economic success.

During the period, 1880-1914, the Frisian immigrant letters sounded the same refrain: "America is a great country for those who want to work with their hands." In Friesland it was known through immigrant letters that in the silk industry in the city of Paterson one was able to make more money than a land laborer in the old country. In America one could expect immediate rewards and a long term potential for economic and social progress. And it is certainly true that many landless emigrants became farmers and that wages in the United States were higher than in the Netherlands. Therefore the letters exaggerated the fact that there was always plenty to eat, especially meat, butter, and white bread. The so-called *spekbrieven* [bacon-letters] in which the great quantities of inexpensive meat were extolled enticed many future emigrants over the Atlantic.[37]

According to many writers, the supposed scenario for emigrants was as follows: leave your impoverished homeland, modify your culture, work diligently, and the fruits of prosperity will be within easy reach.[38] Social mobility could be achieved by anyone in America. That this did not happen for many ethnic groups in the late nineteenth century is not important because the image of America promised *possible* future social mobility.[39]

If any phrase appeared more often in America letters than "we eat meat three times a day", it was "here we tip our hats to no one!" The immigrant as an image-maker painted America not only as a land of opportunity, but also as the land of equality, where every man saw himself as good as his fellow townsman. An emigrant who settled in South Dakota writes in a Frisian newspaper in 1911 about traveling by train in the United States:

> Our car was full of Dutchmen. You could walk all the cars, because there are no separate classes! It should be like that in the Netherlands. But over there are 'classes' [*standen*]; here we have rich and poor people but 'classes'?. If a rich person passes with his car or buggy he will stop and ask if you want to come along. Here, the millionaire is sitting next to the laborer and very often they look alike.[40]

And W.J. van den Bosch writes in 1893 from Indiana about an American "foreman" in the factory where he works:

> This foreman is the boss of about 50 people. He earns 1100 dollars or 2750 guilders a year. In Holland someone like him would have been properly dressed, with chosen pride constantly commanding his laborers. This person though, walks around in an old shirt and trousers, with a chew of tobacco in his mouth. He helps wherever his help is needed, working side by side with his laborers....[41]

This must have been a startling and appealing prospect to Frisian land laborers. It was the desire to achieve social status, rather than money alone, that was attractive to many potential emigrants and that developed in the European mind an image of America as the land of democracy. One longed for independence from the landlord. In Friesland the emigrants had been accustomed to a life where authority was concentrated in the landed class and where any bridging of the gap between landowners and landless people was almost unthinkable. The status of people was closely connected with the possession of land. American democracy was not lost on the Frisian immigrants. But whether the "egalitarian rhetoric," as the historian Walter Kamphoefner calls it, really was of overriding importance is a question that cannot be answered here.[42]

According to their own correspondence, the emigrants did not decide to move to the United States because their appetite for adventure had been whetted, but because they believed that America offered them a better opportunity for economic and social mobility than their Old Country. As pointed out in the first two chapters, Friesland's people of the northern clay area largely depended on agriculture since little industry had come to this area. During the agricultural crisis many of the land laborers were unemployed or found only seasonal work and they were frustrated because of the absence of social freedom and equality.

Thus, it was not all that surprising that people hoped for a better future for themselves and their children. They had been taught this lesson by image-makers who trumpeted America as the land of promise. The propaganda proved believable and acceptable. The reports from the New World were often difficult to interpret in Friesland and some news was indeed too good to be true. But in general the impact of the America letters was phenomenal. Guidebooks or immigration brochures might stretch the truth now and then, but who could doubt the word of friends and relatives? Until that letter arrived, Iowa and South Dakota had been distant mirages, mere names on a map. But now Ulbe and Maaike were there and the vision cleared to reveal a village, a farm, a family. The people learned about America from those of their own milieu, from the ones they trusted, in their own language, and in their own way of thinking.

### 4.6 Images of the "Old World"

Images of America among Frisian emigrants raise the question of what impressions the immigrants had of the "old fatherland" after they settled in the United States. Letters back to Friesland were part of a two-way communicative process. But the researcher who wants to study Frisian letters to America faces a serious lack of source material. So one has to work with the few sources that are available.[43]

In 1897 members of the Dutch community in Holland, Michigan, concluded concerning their migration history: "A peculiar feature of many of these (Dutch) colonists has been that they preserved their identity, and retained many of their national characteristics without refusing to become fully incorporated with our body politic, preserving their individuality without refusing to be absorbed into the national life."[44]

It is very important to realize that the immigrants' image concerning their home country was not a static view. The longer the immigrant had been settled in the United States, the more his view of the Old Country had been influenced by his impressions of the New World. And of course, the image was also affected by living in a specific Dutch community in the United States or the opposite: by his settlement in a community without other Dutch immigrants or with diverse ethnic groups. The image of the Old Country does not seem to have been a very independent one. In the Netherlands the emigrants had a different view concerning their native country than in the United States. Actually the image of the home country was not very real before they left. This image was clarified after the migrants settled in America.

The American historian Herbert J. Brinks argues that in common American usage, "Old Country" quite often means an immigrant's land of birth or ancestry, but "Old" can also embody a more literal meaning, such as the

*A plea for emigration, 1871*

OPWEKKING

TOT

# LANDVERHUIZING

NAAR DE REPUBLIEK

DER

VEREENIGDE STATEN

VAN

## Noord-Amerika

DOOR

J. A. OBREEN,

EERSTE LUITENANT DER INFANTERIE.

LEIDEN. — A. W. SIJTHOFF. — 1871.

*1415 R*

country of the old folks. I would add to that "Old Country" in the sense of "worn out" or "depreciated." In fact some people believed that Europe had lost its vitality and that progress and future were reserved for the New World, America.

Brinks discovered, as he examined letters to America written from all parts of the Netherlands around the turn of the century, that the second and more literal meaning is often highlighted, "because the Dutch reported more steadily on the vicissitudes of the aged – their ailments, their progressive diminution of powers, and death,– than on the prospects of youthful expectation."[45]

This general characteristic is not very surprising: studying Frisian migration patterns, it appears that the immigrants came largely from the younger ranks of the population. As Brinks points out, the older family members stayed in Holland.

Unquestionably the Frisian correspondents provided the immigrants with a very unpleasant picture of everyday life in Friesland. Although there are not many extant "Friesland letters" to America, much of the news from the area left behind did not paint the Old Country in a very rosy way. This impression corresponds with the findings of Brinks for all of the Netherlands.[46] And in the wake of the agrarian crisis before the turn of the century, the information was dominated with generally unstable or uninviting economic prospects. To cite again: Mr. Algra from Ee in Friesland writes in 1892 to Iowa:

> Because my income is rather slender, I don't have much money to spend. Yes, dear friends, wouldn't it be wonderful if you send me some of your abundance....[47]

Or Mr. Brouwer in 1881 to his family in Iowa:

> The situation is very sorrowful. No one can ever be succesful here. It is real sad and this is not the case in your country, at least that's what they tell around here.[48]

Or the Reverend T. Dalhuijsen in 1899, who worries about the future of his children:

> Our son Hans studies for his teachers' degree, he doesn't like it, is well able, but refuses; he rather wants birds, rabbits, fights etc. What shall I say? Hendrik is 13 years old and wants to become a farmer; as a hobby he learned how to milk cows and earns a quarter a week for that; he would rather be dead than go for an education. So what shall I do with these boys in our poor and miserable and hungry fatherland? To America! There they should go. There they will be able (if they use common sense) to get a farm or so. Here normally nothing else than sand potatoes and grease.[49]

Dutch immigrants' views of the Netherlands must have been influenced by this kind of correspondence from the "Old Country". In contemporary immigrant newspapers in Dutch-American communities, like *De Volksvriend*, letters from the Frisian homeland were often published. Primarily, the letters from home helped the immigrants to stay in touch with a world they knew very well, while the letters from immigrants to Friesland helped to inform Frisians of an unknown world. Or as Oyvind T. Gulliksen writes about Norwegian letters to fellow countrymen in the Midwest: "Letters from home helped to keep alive that private world which had shaped the immigrants before they decided to leave. The letters, for as long as they kept coming, were reminders of a past which the process of assimilation could not eradicate."[50] The immigrants often compared their new environment with the situation they left behind. This comparison functioned in fact as their justification for the move.

This explains part of the criticism immigrants had concerning Friesland. Again the keyword is "equality":

> Isn't it required in Holland for a person A. to have a certain status and income to associate with some person B.? Isn't it true that there is a horrible class distinction? Nobody can deny these distinctions in class! That's why I can take breath in America, thinking how people in Holland have to distinguish themselves from their neighbors' views, with a medal of "class and position!"[51]

Another immigrant, Johannes van Dijk who worked for the first day for a bricklayer's boss in New Groningen, Michigan, recalls that at noon the steam whistle called the workers for "dinner tijm" in the kitchen, "where we had a great dinner together, a manufacturer with his wife, sons and daughter, a bricklayer's apprentice, by which I did understand very well that the division between boss and laborer wasn't the same as in the Netherlands."[52] This perception of Holland is representative. The burdens of class conflicts and class distinction could not be forgotten.

The immigrants had a more positive judgment of Friesland when they wrote about social and religious life. Generally they considered American church life as superficial and they missed the cozy social life of the old village. According to Brinks, the most obvious counter perception to some merciless memories resides in fond romanticization of closely – knit families in the Old-Country – the proximity of grandparents, uncles, aunts, and village companions.[53]

These perceptions of the Netherlands are limited to the province of origin. The immigrants did not consider themselves as Dutchmen in America but more as Groningers, Frisians, and Brabantines. Dutch Americans did not derive their identity from a national horizon, but rather from a subnational, provincial horizon.

### 4.7 Images and migrants reconsidered

At the turn of the century, the exodus of thousands of able-bodied young men and women and their families was a fact. It is very plausible that a connection existed between the better life promised to emigrants, and the rate of flow of the emigrant tide. This, in turn, was linked to conditions in the Netherlands. The more alluring the promises, the less attractive the Frisian homeland appeared during periods of economic stagnation.[54] And the agrarian crisis was a period of stagnation in the province of Friesland. In general there was little opportunity for upward social mobility and daily life was difficult. In the immigrants' accounts the negative voices found their motivation in the difference of culture. The positive sounds, however, mainly originated in a more promising materialistic perspective; once in the new country, the immigrants found it harder to embrace the new cultural values than to adjust to the new working life. We may conclude that the perception of America of the late nineteenth-century emigrants was defined by their socio-economic background.[55]

Against this background, the lure of America is understandable. Turner's thesis that the American frontier was unlimited also became part of the imagination of the Frisian emigrants. The contrast between the old, crumbling Europe and the new, promising America was becoming stronger and stronger.[56] The American example made clear what was needed: a widened franchise, weakened class barriers, proper assurances of respect by the elite, and a certain opportunity for self-improvement and upward social mobility. And if America at a certain time or place did not provide these wants, future emigrants created the America they needed.

To return to the ideas of the sociologist Den Hollander concerning the discrepancy between the real society and the muddled observations: "With some exaggeration one can say: Every human being creates his own outside world." Den Hollander's vision implies that one does not give "the Other world" its own value, but reduces it to a function of one's own world, the "Self"! Images, according to Den Hollander, are clear in the mind: something that once strikes the imagination is not lightly forgotten, even if the image does not agree with reality. Fantasy is often richer, more colorful, and more emotional than reality can ever be. People prefer the satisfying myth rather than the tedious and dreary reality. In his argument Den Hollander makes a clear distinction between fantasy and reality. But what *is* reality, what *is* myth? Is it not true that myth and fantasy often *create* reality and that myth and fantasy are part of reality? This is also the reason why changes in the imagination of the European observer are important. The prejudices in the observations of foreign cultures should be made *object* of study. This assertion also raises the nettlesome issue of the force of "image", or myth or fantasy compared with other aspects of reality. Is it inevitable to accept fantasies as "unreal"? I do not think it is; Den Hollander goes too far in making the distinction between reality and fantasy. Fantasy is as much part of everyday life as, for example, the "fact" of travel abroad. Images and myths have real effects, but only within an already-produced context. Den Hollander considerably exaggerates in saying that every human being creates his own outside world. By accepting this view, one also accepts a radical subjectivism and individualism. This is only true in a very qualified sense. The image of America held by the potential emigrant was not the primary reason for leaving. But without this image most Frisian emigrants would not have left for that faraway land.

# *Chapter 5* Room for maneuvering: geographical and occupational mobility

Frisians on the verge of leaving their native soil sought room for maneuvering. This desire arose from economic, social, or psychological needs and was directed by the experience of crossing the Atlantic, the intended destination, the geographical moves in the United States, the occupational mobility patterns, and the characteristics of family behavior. The ship was ready to maneuver.

## 5.1 Experiences of the Atlantic passage

> *Terpen, marren, bosken, lânnen,*
> *Tûgen fen myn libbenswei!*
> *'k Moat forbrekke sterke bânnen,*
> *'t Skip leit klear, en ik moat mei.*

> *[Terps, lakes, forests, fields,*
> *Witnesses of my path of life!*
> *I have to break off strong bonds,*
> *The ship lies ready, I have to go.]*[1]

Scholars of migration consider the voyage between the continents irrelevant for understanding the general experience and patterns of European migrations to the United States. It was only a short intermezzo in the whole migration process and hardly mentioned. However, the ocean voyage and railroad trip may well have been formative.[2] In Jonathan Raban's remarkable novel of coming to America a memorable sentence can be found: "Before it was anything else, America was the voyage itself".[3] The experience of the transatlantic passage must have been an extraordinarily heartbreaking event. The awful possibility of never experiencing anything of the native country again must have been a cruel reality for many an emigrant.

Dirk Jans Miedema, exponent of the Frisian tradition of overseas migration, put the following notice in the local journal in 1881:

> Dirk Miedema, for 29 years American citizen and now temporarely in Marrum, leaves on April 23, 1881 with the N.A.S.M. [Netherlands American Steamship Company] from Rotterdam to America. Everybody who wants to join this trip can get information and make application at J. Stroosma, innkeeper in Marrum, and J. van der Veen, agent in Dokkum.[4]

Miedema had left for America with his wife and child in April 1852 after suffering a "meager living." He farmed in Holland, Michigan, amid other Dutch immigrants. When he returned to the fatherland he agreed to act as agent for the N.A.S.M. "especially for the less affluent".[5] Johannes K. van Dijk, a young man of 24 working as a contractor, met Miedema in Ferwerd at the home of J.M. Jansma. Van Dijk had not been too successful with putting work out to the lowest bidder in his building business, so he was attracted by Miedema's information about America.[6] After gaining the permission of his parents – he was an only child and this took some gentle insistence – Van Dijk left on May 7, 1881 with the steamship *P. Caland* from Rotterdam.

According to the information in the Population Registers, most of the Frisian emigrants departed in the months of April and May (figure 5.1). This can be easily understood: they waited for better spring weather for the ocean passage, and they also were better off arriving in the United States in early summer because then they still had time to acclimatize and search for jobs before the next severe winter. The monthly pattern did not change much over the decades. The early departure possibly also was related to the fact that the worker's season at the Frisian farms for the steady laborers usually lasted from May 12 to May 12 the next year. The new contract of farm laborers started on that date in spring.[7]

*T.G. van der Meulen's Emigrant-Song in* Ny Frysk Lieteboek, *1886*

This was not important for those without permanent work, but laborers under contract likely wanted to finish their jobs.

Johannes van Dijk's travel account describes the experiences of Frisian emigrants. In the early eighties the journey usually started with horse and buggy to the city of Leeuwarden or Harlingen. From Leeuwarden the train took them to Rotterdam or Amsterdam; from Harlingen people took the boat to these cities. Van Dijk paid 3.01 guilders for his railroad ticket and describes the huge crowd in Leeuwarden. All kinds of people watched the departure of emigrants and discussed the decision while they waved goodbye. It took a whole day before Van Dijk and others reached Rotterdam, where they were given lodging by an agent of the N.A.S.M. The proffered place was very bad, so Van Dijk and friends started to walk the streets of Rotterdam to find decent accommodations. The first four lodgings were too crowded, at the fifth they were lucky and so they slept at the hotel of L. de Valk at the Vlasmarkt for $f$ 2.50 per person for two nights.

For many Frisians the sight of Rotterdam must have been an impressive one. In the years of mass migration, Rotterdam was the temporary residence of thousands of emigrants of all nationalities. In 1880 3,360 Dutch emigrants left via this harbor and they were among a total of 11,549 emigrants. A decade later 2,057 Dutch people left Rotterdam together with 2,640 Germans, 1,589 Austrians, 946 Hungarians, 1,111 Russians and 1,556 others, making a total of 9,899. In 1910 60,897 continental European emigrants steamed from

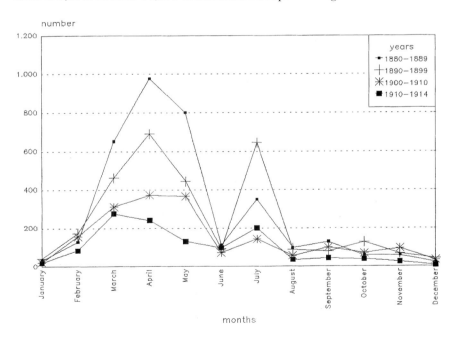

*Figure 5.1*
*Month of departure, Frisian emigrants, 1880-1914:*
**Source:** *Galema, "Frisians to America, 1880-1914. Computer Compilation"*

Rotterdam, among them 2,605 Dutchmen and 35,290 Russians.[8] Generally speaking, Rotterdam was the first internationally-styled city that most Frisian emigrants had ever experienced.

In 1881 Van Dijk paid a total of 96 guilders for his one way trip to the American Midwest. His highest costs were for the transatlantic passage: 42 guilders. Except for an advance for the trip of 10 guilders, the railroad ticket and the transport of luggage (1.65 guilders) to Rotterdam, he paid for food on the ship (1.20 guilders), lodging in New York (3.75 guilders) and for the train ticket New York-Holland, Michigan (32.37 guilders).[9]

Jonathan Raban describes the point of departure strikingly: at that moment "few of the emigrants could think sensibly beyond their coming trial-by-water". At this point the United States was a mere fiction, its unreality supported by the intangible breadth of the ocean.[10] During the ocean voyage many emigrants got seasick. Van Dijk recalls the death of a young German boy and his burial at sea. He also tells about a single German maid who slept with a German man. She was arrested in bed and transported to the upper deck while everyone was shouting "hurray". Van Dijk describes the slaughtering of a cow of 624 pounds on May 14 and also the discovery of four sea "monsters," likely whales. Dirk Jans Miedema traveled in the second class, while Van Dijk used the cheaper third-class or steerage ticket. Van Dijk profited from his acquaintance with Miedema, who showed him all around the ship. Hence, Van Dijk can provide remarkable details of the architecture of the ship in his travel account. The food was adequate, including meat with the warm meal, but this of course is Van Dijk's subjective evaluation. Captain Deddes was assisted by a crew of 31 persons, including a doctor. Most of the 956 passengers traveled in steerage: only 36 were in the first and second class. Van Dijk recalls the bustle on the ship almost as an ethnic adventure. It looked like "a floating small town" where people spoke many different languages and danced, sang, and played cards to while away the time.

After twelve days, on May 19, the *P. Caland* reached New York.[11] Before the passengers disembarked, an American doctor came aboard and together with the captain and the ship's doctor examined with a sharp eye each of the passengers in file. Then the ship was fumigated and the captain got a health certificate. Van Dijk saw the English emigrant steamer *State Nevada* laying in quarantine because there were smallpox patients aboard. This ship had to wait ten days and if the number of sick did not increase during that time, the passengers were allowed to disembark at New York. The *P. Caland* anchored before the N.A.S.M. building in Brooklyn. Van Dijk mentions the wonderful impression of the Brooklyn Bridge, which connected Brooklyn with New York. Then they had to open their luggage and were transported by a steamer to Castle Garden. In this wooden building emigrants could get everything they needed: train tickets, money exchange, information concerning hotels, and work possibilities.

That such services at Castle Garden were not a total luxury for arriving emigrants in the eighties may be clear from the account of Jelle Pelmulder from Bornwerd, who arrived in June 1855:

...And then rapidly a steamer arrived, which dragged us before, or rather into the city, and from that moment the fat was in the fire. Agents of railways, companies, as well as sellers of vegetables and bread, etc. etc., stormed the ship. The one who had money left was able to buy fresh bread, ripe apples and all kind of other things that were for sale. Soon our captain ended this sale by chasing off the ship the uninvited visitors and some of them were not too gently treated by the sailors. The captain did well, because these people only intended to cheat the emigrants by selling their goods far too expensively. A steamer of the railway company came to our ship that day even twice, and all the time the agents tried to approach the ship. Without any consideration our captain refused admittance and this resulted in cursing and swearing, in English, German or Dutch and a bustle that is hard to describe; however, after the moment that one of them had experienced the fists of our first steermen none of them had the guts to come aboard. The poor emigrant is totally at a loss in such a theater. Everybody wants to help and prove to him that there is no safer and better person he can trust, but all those helpers want to profit as much as possible. As far as I can see, that batch of agents of the Erie Railway Company was the scum of all nations....[12]

Castle Garden was erected in the same year that Pelmulder arrived in New York, to regulate and control the immigrant stream and to protect the emigrants from all kinds of swindles during their insecure first visit to the New World.[13]

A quarter of a century later, Miedema and company profited from the *relatively* better organized arrival. In a hotel close to Castle Garden, Miedema contacted an American money changer. For his 105 guilders Johannes van Dijk got 39 dollars and ninety cents. Together with Miedema and his friend the money changer, Van Dijk bought railroad tickets at the Erie ticket office. Van Dijk mentions that Miedema, as a shipping agent, got a free ticket, just as he had earned a second class status on the ocean voyage. One day later, after browsing around in New York – a huge and rich commercial city, according to Van Dijk – they collected their luggage. They showed their "Tjek," a copper tag that identified their luggage, and were transported by steamer from Castle Garden to the Erie Station. It took two more days to reach Holland, Michigan. After a journey of nineteen days, it was a very good experience to sit around the kitchen table with Miedema's family, Van Dijk recalls.

In the next days Miedema showed him around and they met many old acqaintances. Two families that accompanied Miedema's group immediately started working for a brickyard in Zeeland, a village close to Holland. Furthermore, according to Van Dijk, "A. Gelders went for bricklaying to the neigboring village of Overisel. Jan Jansma stayed with Miedema as a farmhand and I was to be called for by Mr. H. Zuidam, a bricklayer's boss in New Groningen, where I was supposed to get work and living."[14] The provisional goal of the journey had been achieved, and there was no doubt that the transatlantic experience would never be forgotten.

Personal experiences of the ocean voyage could differ, depending on circumstances and point of view. Pieter Groustra, who left in 1881, traveled with his wife and two young sons. In a letter Groustra characterized the journey as very tiring and difficult. The family was bothered by bad food, storms, sea sickness, and vermin.[15] A very tragic ocean voyage was made by Rinke van der Wal and his wife in 1882. They lost their two youngest children, one at Castle Garden and the other in New York City.[16] Generally, the ocean experience also depended on the composition of the family: traveling single with no worries concerning young children was clearly easier. However, the agency Prins & Zwanenburg in a brochure of 1882 warned the individual traveler as well:

> Point out to your friends that a voyage to America for husband, wife and children is always a very difficult one and that also those who don't have a family will have to share the discomforts of their fellow travelers; the child of his neighbor can also bother him.[17]

The sturdy Cornelia de Groot from the village of Deersum left around 1902 on the steamer *Vaderland* from Antwerp and "loved the ocean in its every mood."[18] But she traveled most likely as a first class passenger and her knowledge of the English language was more than adequate. Klaas J. Tiemersma from the village of Ee, who left in 1889 on the steamer *P. Caland* with a company of 800 persons, including Germans, Irishmen, Poles, Englismen, Italians, and Dutchmen, found third class accommodations unpleasant.[19]

*Picture of Cornelia de Groot in* When I was a girl in Holland

Jacob Pieters Mellema, who left Sint Annaparochie in the same year, also complained about his trip on the *Leerdam* from Amsterdam. Jacob found that other ships went a lot faster than this steamer and so "the people were released sooner from the misery, as I call it; Misery, nothing else."[20] Hendrik Kroes from Ferwerd two years later had the same opinion: he recalled that the weather actually was quite good but there was hardly any room on the boat to eat and he complained that they never sat at the table. He even saw a passenger take a knife from his pocket and abuse one of the crew members who was carrying a bag with bread. The passenger cut the bag with a fierce stroke and people just grabbed the bread that was spread all over.[21] The conclusion to such a story may be that the people aboard were hungry. However, this is in sharp contrast with the travel account of Anne Bandstra, who left in 1899 on the steamship *Rotterdam* and praised the bountiful meals of soup, potatoes, and meat.[22]

The truth was likely somewhere in the middle. The shipping companies had to provide food and deal with many different ethnic eating habits, which meant that the individual emigrant may not have been satisfied. And the shipping companies had priorities too. A journalist who traveled in 1893 with the *Spaarndam* – an NASM ship –, mentioned that the nationalities were boarded in order: "the Hollanders got the best and airy places, while behind in the dark hold the Arabs and Polish Jews were living." This journalist also described how one of the ship's coal-bunkers was also used to house emigrants: "The Frisians have the best togs, then the Germans follow, the French, the colorful swarthy Italians, the filthy Polish Jews, the Arabs and the Syrians."[23] Ethnic preferences evidently governed.

Food was not always included in the tickets. Hendrik Kroes mentions that he paid 64 dollars for the fare from Leeuwarden to Muskegon, Michigan, for himself and his mother, but this sum was for fare only and did not include the meals. They had to pay extra for the meals and consequently they ate very poorly.[24] During the years after 1880 the eating facilities were improved. Competition between the steamship companies led to better facilities, and this was a challenge in the era of European mass migration. G. Taphorn, agent in northeastern Germany of the Prins & Zwanenburg immigrant agency, reported that in the 1880s the meal menu for third class passengers on NASM vessels was as follows: for breakfast bread, butter, groats with syrup, coffee and tea with milk and sugar; for lunch a two course warm meal with fish or meat that changed every day; for dinner again coffee and tea with milk and sugar as well as bread, butter, herring or cheese. Breakfast and dinner appeared to be the same every day.[25] Martin van der Heide in 1914 admits that he was seasick for many days during his trip with the *Noordam*, but he was very pleased that Jelke Vlietstra from Ferwerd, who wasn't seasick at all, occasionally brought him food from the dining room.[26]

The experience of Ellis Island also differed. In the 1880s the stream of emigrants who entered at New York (76 percent of all emigrants in 1888) overwhelmed Castle Garden, which was not able to guarantee the safety and well-being of all the foreigners. For illness or mental deficiency one could be sent back to the native country. The U.S. government tightened immigration restrictions first with the law of 1882, which excluded diseased and criminals;

later with the law of 1891 which added polygamists because of the Mormons who arrived. In fact the chaos became so great that President Benjamin H. Harrison in 1890 decided to make the reception of immigration a federal task. In 1892 a new "gateway to America" was opened on Ellis Island, a small island off Manhattan.[27]

After the long ocean voyage, Ellis Island meant for emigrants hope, fear, and joy. Martin van der Heide described the procedure in 1914 when he arrived with his fiancé:

> First we had a medical test. We didn't have trouble with that because we were healthy. But after that we went through a moral questioning and there we got stuck, something was wrong, not something awful, only we were not married and therefore we were not allowed to travel on. In the meantime the day was over and the next day we should come for an interrogation. We were not the only ones though, there were quite a bunch. Men and women were separated. We were sent to a hall and a blanket was thrown to each of us and we could go asleep on the marble floor (if something like that was possible). The women were sent to another hall and they had at least beds, and also got a blanket. I did not sleep very much that night, and Anna later on told me she did not either. I think we both were too worried about the future.[28]

The next day Van der Heide and his fiancé had to appear before some kind of immigration court. The officials told them that they were not allowed to enter the United States without being married. The solution was easily found; with their translator – a Dutchman – they went by subway to New York's City Hall and within ten minutes they were spouses. The translator took them to a bar to drink a glass of wine to celebrate the marriage. From there they went to the railway station to continue their voyage.[29]

That unmarried couples could get in trouble was also reported in a letter published in a local Frisian journal in 1911:

> When an engaged couple travels together, the girl should join with another family. If she doesn't, she will get in trouble at the arrival in New York, because then she and her fiancé will be brought to the "gentlemen" who will force them to marry before going further. If they refuse, – and many stick to their guns – they will be asked all kinds of questions that will blush the girls with shame. One would almost think that these "gentlemen" are there for their own amusement because what's the purpose of such questions? If an honorable couple is traveling together and the young man is strong and healthy, what difference does it make for people in New York if they marry there or at their destination a year later?[30]

How many Frisians were sent back by the American authorities is unknown, but the number is certainly small. Sources like emigrant letters and travel accounts never mentioned a forced return. Emigrants were well aware of the regulations, and the first screening took place by the shipping companies, because they had the responsiblity to carry home those rejected free of charge.[31]

Van der Heide had a positive experience, but generally the painful decision of whether to stay or return with a loved one had to be made on the spot.

America letters generally recall that the medical exam at Ellis Island was most to be feared. Medical reasons for refusal of entry were not exceptional. For most emigrants a day spent on Ellis Island seemed like an eternity. It was their first experience in America and left an overwhelming impression. Everybody got poked, palpated, counted, questioned, and weighed before the gate of Eden opened. It certainly was a colorful event; Frisian girls with cap brooch stood in line shoulder to shoulder with sturdy young farmer's sons from Niedersachsen, Groninger land laborers, Russian Jewish families, and Italians on the road to Little Italy. Hope and fear was their common experience. From there they entered the mainstream of America.

The vivid impressions of the voyage to America suggest a generative character in the whole migration process. Rotterdam, Antwerp, and Liverpool indeed were the illustration that everything grew bigger and moved faster. Ellis Island and Miss Liberty were the exponents of big and fast and consequently of better earnings. Debarkation and admission became the most important memory concerning the emigrant's entrance of America. In this sense we may consider the ocean voyage as formative in the migration maneuvering and therefore as part of the geographical and occupational mobility process.[32]

### 5.2 Destination and geographical distribution

Nuclear family ties as well as extended family and neighborhood ties were fundamental in Frisian emigration. These ties also influenced the settlement patterns in the United States. The economic structure of the home communities and the immigrant communities often showed affinity and also directed the process of settlement. Continuity is a very important characteristic of this chain migration. Many studies of ethnic groups confirm the importance of family links.[33] As Dudley Baines points out, the general theme of chain migration is evidently quite simple. Emigration created great insecurity. Everything was new: the transatlantic passage, the new living place, and the prospects of employment. Therefore, "it was usually safer to move from 'the known to the known'."[34] Chains are not static though. Older chains sometimes disappear while new ones are being created. As will be shown below, the spread of Frisian emigration to new regions revealed the beginning of new chains. The emigration of Frisians to Whitinsville, Massachusetts, started in 1886 with two men from Friesland. Using data from 1910 I was able to trace at least 132 immigrants who came directly from the northern Frisian clay area.[35] A study of German emigration demonstrates that it is possible to identify many factors that influenced the location where the emigrants settled. One thing that became clear from this study is that the larger economic forces are inadequate to explain these patterns. This does not mean that economic calculations were not determinants in the decision to emigrate, but the economic information was often transmitted through personal ties.[36]

Where did the Frisians go after they reached the American shore? Did they follow the paths of the Dutch in general or did they create routes directed by their sub-national Frisian compatriots? Or did they follow, in 1882 for example, the Frisian steamship agents A. & H. Kuipers who advertized land for sale in

America: "Thousands of hectares of outstanding Prairie land, very suitable for a **Dutch** colony [*volksplanting*]..."[37]

The database extracted from the Population Register gives some answers to these questions. The potential emigrant was asked for his destination before he left Frisian soil. Many times the governemental clerk wrote down: North-America. But in some cases the particular state or region in the United States was mentioned. Table 5.1 shows the designated destination before departure:

Table 5.1   **Designated destination of Frisian emigrants, 1880-1914:**

| | |
|---|---|
| no specific place | 7886 |
| Michigan | 506 |
| Iowa | 300 |
| Illinois | 239 |
| Wisconsin | 158 |
| New Jersey | 145 |
| Dakotas | 57 |
| Indiana | 52 |
| New York | 36 |
| Minnesota | 35 |
| Montana | 14 |
| Washington State | 9 |
| Nebraska | 7 |
| Oregon | 7 |
| Massachusetts | 3 |
| Maryland | 2 |
| Ohio | 2 |
| Alabama | 2 |
| Wyoming | 2 |
| Pennsylvania | 1 |
| Delaware | 1 |
| Missouri | 1 |
| Colorado | 1 |
| California | 1 |
| **Total** | **9467** |

**Source:** Galema, "Frisians to America, 1880-1914. Computer Compilation.

Although 83 percent of the emigrants did not specify the region of destination, this does not mean that the Frisians did not *know* their goal. The lack of specifity concerning destinations was due to the registration procedure. Government officials simply did not ask for the specific area in the United States. And if they did, they still wrote down: "*Amerika*" or "*Noord-Amerika*". Most of the northern Frisians whose destination was registered left for western Michigan, especially the Dutch settlements at Grand Rapids (212),

Holland (41), Zeeland (17), and Kalamazoo (12). The state of Iowa also attracted many; Pella (41) and Orange City (42) were preferred destinations. In the state of Illinois the Frisians were concentrated in and around the city of Chicago (50), especially in the southern suburbs of Roseland (117) and Kensington (13). In Wisconsin they selected settlements like Sheboygan (52), Prairie du Chien (5), and Waupan (3); and in New Jersey the biggest concentration was in and around the silk city of Paterson (78).

Taking the major states by five-year time periods (see table 5.2), Michigan, Iowa, Illinois, Wisconsin, and New Jersey were the most specified destinations. In the two decades before 1900 all these states had their share of Frisian immigrants, while after the turn of the century especially Michigan and Iowa remained attractive.

Table 5.2   **Major states of destination of Frisians, 5-year periods, 1880-1914:**

| Periods | Michigan | | Iowa | | Illinois | | Wisconsin | | New Jersey | |
|---------|------|------|------|------|------|------|------|------|------|------|
|         | N | % | N | % | N | % | N | % | N | % |
| 1880-84 | 85 | 16.8 | 16 | 5.3 | 15 | 6.3 | 11 | 7.0 | 16 | 11.0 |
| 1885-89 | 125 | 24.8 | 76 | 25.3 | 60 | 25.1 | 17 | 10.8 | 24 | 16.6 |
| 1890-94 | 161 | 31.8 | 46 | 15.3 | 123 | 51.5 | 48 | 30.4 | 57 | 39.3 |
| 1895-99 | 25 | 4.9 | 11 | 3.7 | 14 | 5.9 | 22 | 13.9 | 12 | 8.3 |
| 1900-04 | 27 | 5.3 | 24 | 8.0 | 13 | 5.4 | 2 | 1.3 | 18 | 12.4 |
| 1905-09 | 19 | 3.8 | 62 | 20.7 | 3 | 1.3 | 29 | 18.4 | 2 | 8.3 |
| 1910-14 | 64 | 12.6 | 65 | 21.7 | 11 | 4.6 | 29 | 18.4 | 6 | 4.1 |
| **Total:** | 506 | 0100.0 | 300 | 100.0 | 239 | 100.0 | 158 | 100.0 | 145 | 100.0 |

**Source:** Galema, "Frisians to America, 1880-1914. Computer Compilation"

This configuration is nothing new. It corresponds to that of the Dutch in general, and more importantly, it mirrors the settlement of Frisians in the period 1835-1880.[38]

The geographical distribution of the Frisians within the United States is distorted. Few went to the southern states. Florida, Georgia, Louisiana, Texas, Arizona and New Mexico are absent from the list of destinations in the Dutch Population Registers. This is not exceptional; few Dutch emigrants of the mid-nineteenth century settled in the south.[39] R.P.Swierenga found that in 1870 85 percent of the Dutch immigrants and their families lived in only seven states in the mid-west and in the mid-atlantic regions. Within these seven states the Dutch were even more concentrated: more than 90 percent of the families with a Dutch-born head and the Dutch singles lived in only twenty districts and cities.[40] It is well known that Dutch immigrants and their descendants have made an impact in certain areas in the United States because of their clannish settlement patterns. The confinement of the Dutch to a few states in the United States is also reflected in the fact that in 1930, according to the Census, almost two-thirds of the Dutch immigrants were found in Michigan, New York, Illinois, New Jersey, and Iowa.[41] Nevertheless, although settlement in religiously oriented colonies such as Pella, Orange City, and Holland, explains most of the distinctive features of the distribution, yet perhaps half of the Dutch immigrants between 1835-1880 did not settle in colonies.[42] Recapitulating the above, it seems evident that a good thoroughly research of the areas of settlement of the Frisians within the different states of the United States needs complementary sources.

One research strategy might be to search for all (or a sample) of the Frisian immigrants in the United States censuses, but this task is laborious and forbidding because the censuses are not indexed and they are tabulated by county and not township or precinct. It was not practicable to go through the microfilms of the census of every state of the United States. But to search *only* in the communities that were already known from previous research and literature also was not entirely satisfying. This would result in the same high-density regions being studied. It would also overlook the immigrants who had scattered, and were not connected to a Dutch community.

The search for the Frisian immigrants who scattered over the United States needed another approach. First of all, the sources in archives that specialized on Dutch immigration had to be investigated. Personal documents like death records or autobiograhical writings also provided places of settlement in the United States from which I could then turn to the Census. These sources were very valuable, but again, in order to create a wider geographical sample, these sources also had the disadvantage that they pointed to Pella, Holland, and Grand Rapids.

The solution came from letters written by Frisians to the home country. Writing back was not particularly tied to a person living in a settlement with many people of Dutch origin or to a specific religious or political viewpoint. Therefore, I tried to find immigrant letters in the source areas. In the Frisian clay region many shoeboxes were turned upside down and often I was allowed to make copies of "America letters" written to family in Friesland. Usually these personal writings mentioned the American village, city, or town where these immigrants put pen to paper. With their postmarks on the top of a letter, I turned to the Census again.

To recapitulate, the places of settlement of the Frisian immigrants were derived from the following sources: Dutch Population Registers, Dutch newspapers in the United States, death records, personal writings and genealogies, research and literature concerning Dutch immigration, and the letters written by the Frisian immigrants to their native country, including those published in Frisian newspapers around the turn of the century.[43]

The resulting data file "Frisians in the U.S.A., 1900/1910"[44], shows that most of the northern Frisians after 1880 chose the midwestern states as destination [see Appendix V].[45] They tended to settle in a relatively limited number of locations. Michigan, Illinois, Iowa, New Jersey, and Wisconsin still enjoyed great popularity among the Frisians. But new destinations appeared; the

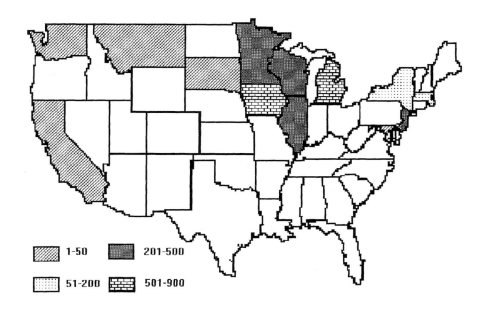

*Map II: Absolute concentration of northern Frisians in the U.S.A., 1900*

midwestern frontier had moved westward in the late 1860s and 1870s and this did not go unnoticed by Frisian immigrants. The states of Minnesota, South Dakota, Montana, Washington, and later California, appeared on the horizon. In the east, Massachusetts also attracted many Frisians in the 1880s and 1890s. They settled in an area without any particular Frisian migration tradition. In the well known surroundings of Paterson, New Jersey, many Frisians started their American life in the 1880s and 1890s, although in the mid-nineteenth century most Dutch immigrants had merely passed through this city and vicinity or only stayed there temporarily. However, in 1880 Paterson had more Dutch-born people than any other American city.[46] In the state of New York Frisians moved to the city of Rochester and surroundings, an area already known to the Dutch for decades.

While many of the Dutch (and among them the Frisian) immigrants of the mid-nineteenth century had settled in rural areas, in the last three decades they increasingly started to discover the growing American cities. They helped supply the labor force in the textile mills and machine shops of Paterson and Passaic, the furniture factories of Grand Rapids, and the Pullman plant of Chicago. On the outskirts of Chicago Dutch settlements evolved from centers of dairying and market gardening into suburban neighborhoods of craftsmen, small business men and, industrial workers.

After browsing through all the different sources, the places of Frisian settlement in the 1900 Census were collected. The names of Frisian emigrants were linked with the names found in the Census. The linkage-variables were: name, sex, year of birth. With the names the Soundex system had to be used because many last and first names became subject to change after settlement in the United States. Table 5.3 shows the result:

Table 5.3  **States of settlement, northern Frisians and descendants, 1900:**

| State | Frisian-born | All stock |
|---|---|---|
| California | 1 | 13 |
| Illinois | 259 | 500 |
| Iowa | 249 | 502 |
| Massachusetts | 57 | 262 |
| Maryland | 1 | 6 |
| Michigan | 483 | 869 |
| Minnesota | 106 | 242 |
| Montana | 9 | 14 |
| New Jersey | 102 | 225 |
| New York | 37 | 76 |
| South Dakota | 25 | 50 |
| Washington | 1 | 10 |
| Wisconsin | 166 | 319 |
| **Total** | 1496 | 3088 |

Note: Only the first generation immigrants are mentioned here: the people who left the northern clay area between 1880-1900.

**Source:** Galema, "Frisians in the U.S.A., 1900/1910. Computer Compilation"

If the counties with more than thirty Frisians and descendants in the 1900 Census are taken, the picture in table 5.4 appears:

Table 5.4  **Counties of settlement, northern Frisians and descendants >30 persons, 1900:**

| State | County | Frisian-born | All stock |
|---|---|---|---|
| Illinois | Cook (Chicago) | 250 | 469 |
| Iowa | Sioux | 200 | 402 |
| | Marion (Pella) | 45 | 85 |
| Massachus. | Worcester (Whitin) | 57 | 262 |
| Michigan | Kent (Grand Rapids) | 202 | 304 |
| | Ottawa (Holland) | 268 | 533 |
| | Missaukee | 12 | 31 |
| Minnesota | Pine | 14 | 36 |
| | Pipestone | 17 | 47 |
| | Chippewa | 23 | 45 |
| | Kandiyohi (Prinsburg) | 36 | 86 |

| State | County | Frisian-born | All stock |
|---|---|---|---|
| New Jersey | Passaic (Paterson) | 102 | 225 |
| New York | Monroe (Rochester) | 32 | 70 |
| South Dakota | Bonhomme | 19 | 36 |
| Wisconsin | Columbia (Friesland) | 77 | 148 |
| | LaCrosse (La Crosse) | 66 | 127 |
| **Total** | | 1420 | 2906 |

**Source:** Galema, "Frisians in the U.S.A., 1900/1910. Computer Compilation"

The next step was to focus more concretely on Frisian clay immigrants who appear in both Frisian and US sources. We find most of these linked individuals in 1900 in and around Chicago; in Sioux Township, Orange City, and Nassau Township in northwestern Iowa; and in Pella; in Whitinsville Village, Massachusetts; in Grand Rapids, Wyoming Township, Zeeland, Holland, Grand Haven, and Blendon Township, Michigan; in Holland Township and Rheiderland, Minnesota; in Paterson, New Jersey; in Rochester and Brighton Township, New York; and in the towns of Holland, Randolph, and Friesland, Wisconsin;

If the results of the linked file are compared with the preferred destination of Frisians according to the Dutch Population Registers (table 5.1 and 5.2), it is evident that most could be found in the five states of their preferred destination: Michigan, Iowa, Illinois, Wisconsin, and New Jersey. Strikingly, the state of Indiana is totally missing in the linked file, although it was cited as a preferred destination in the Dutch Population Registers at least 42 times. This is even more curious because in the mid-nineteenth century immigrants from the provinces of Groningen and Friesland had settled there.[47] The search in the Census of 1900 and 1910 did not provide data on northern Frisian immigrants.[48] Because the reference year is 1900, it does not indicate that northern Frisians did not travel to their intended destination. They may only have stayed there for a while, and then moved on to other places. Martin van der Heide, for example, traveled from Friesland to the small town of Lark in North Dakota where he found the landlord to whom he had arranged to go. For several reasons Van der Heide and his wife were not pleased with the workplace, so they left quickly for another employer. This kind of mobility causes difficulties in tracing the Frisians.

With the example of Frisian Mennonites in Indiana, the problem of definition comes up. Frisians do not appear in the Census as Frisians but as Hollanders. Northern Frisians do not show up with their specified region of origin. But according to the literature, mostly emigrants from southwestern Friesland (Gaasterland) settled near Goshen, Indiana.[49]

Table 5.5    **Foreign-born Dutch immigrants by state by decade, 1850-1920:**

| State | 1850 | 1860 | 1870 | 1880 | 1890 | 1900 | 1910 | 1920 |
|---|---|---|---|---|---|---|---|---|
| California | 63 | 439 | 452 | 694 | 760 | 1,015 | 2,304 | 4,592 |
| Illinois | 220 | 1,416 | 4,180 | 5,012 | 8,762 | 11,916 | 14,402 | 14,344 |
| Iowa | 1,108 | 2,615 | 4,513 | 4,743 | 7,941 | 9,388 | 11,337 | 12,471 |
| Maryland | 106 | 376 | 236 | 362 | 122 | 220 | 203 | 314 |
| Massachus. | 138 | 351 | 480 | 586 | 609 | 993 | 1,597 | 2,071 |
| Michigan | 2,542 | 6,335 | 12,559 | 17,777 | 29,410 | 30,406 | 33,471 | 33,499 |
| Minnesota | | 391 | 1,855 | 1,581 | 1,796 | 2,117 | 3,542 | 5,380 |
| Montana | 103 | 316 | 1,054 | 1,675 | | | | |
| New Jersey | 357 | 1,328 | 2,944 | 4,281 | 7,924 | 10,261 | 12,698 | 12,737 |
| New York | 2,917 | 5,354 | 6,426 | 8,399 | 8,366 | 9,414 | 12,652 | 13,772 |
| S. Dakota | 1,428 | 1,566 | 2,656 | 3,218 | | | | |
| Washington | | | | | | 227 | 632 | 2,157 | 3,097 |
| Wisconsin | 1,157 | 4,906 | 5,990 | 5,698 | 6,252 | 6,496 | 7,379 | 7,473 |
| Western territories | 19 | 79 | 218 | 404 | | | | |

**Source:** *Decennial reports of the Unites States Bureau of the Census*

Comparing the figures of table 5.5 with those of tables 5.3 and 5.4, the conclusion is justified that northern Frisians often moved to settlements in the United States that already had many Dutch settlers. An immigrant in Montana wrote to his native country: "And now we live here as Netherlanders together. We came from almost all the eleven provinces. That is why we gave our settlement the name Holland".[50]

In 1908 a Frisian writer from Preston, Maryland, expressed the general pattern clearly:

> If at one time there is a move to a certain place, if some families already settled there, then it is most obvious (especially if things go fine) that others come to the same settlement. This is the case with every nationality. That way, to mention one example, Grand Rapids became the city where many Hollanders settled. In Grand Rapids, I think one can find 36 Dutch churches. Thus the one person entices the other, although this way there may arrive too many in one place.[51]

It is also clear that Frisians generally moved to settlements that were already primarily Frisian. Referring to the tradition of migration, it is evident that many Frisian immigrants around the turn of the century found their way via the already beaten track of Frisian immigrants in the decades before the 1880s. When the Frisian poet, writer, and orator Tjibbe Geerts van der Meulen visited the United States in 1881, he stopped in many communities with mainly Frisian immigrants. In his letters in the *Weekblad voor het Kanton Bergum*, he mentioned conversations with many compatriots concentrated in specific settlements, such as Pella and vicinity.

Did these various colonizing Frisians hail from the same places of origin?

Was concentration of people from a specific municipality found in a particular settlement in the United States, or were the settlements a mixture of northern Frisians?

According to the 1900 Census, most northern Frisians in Chicago and environs originated from the municipalities of Oostdongeradeel, Ferwerderadeel, and Barradeel. Sioux County, Iowa, migrants came from Barradeel, Het Bildt, and Wonseradeel, while Marion County only had immigrants from Oost- and Westdongeradeel. In Whitinsville, Massachusetts, hardly anyone had origins outside the municipalities of Barradeel and Wonseradeel. In Kent County, Michigan, northern Frisians came from Ferwerderadeel and Wonseradeel, while Ottawa County showed the same lines of origin, including Westdongeradeel. In Renville County, Minnesota, the northern Frisians all came from Het Bildt, in Kandyohi County mainly from Oostdongeradeel. Passaic County, New Jersey, attracted people from Het Bildt and Ferwerderadeel. Monroe County, New York, showed that Frisian immigrants largely came from Het Bildt. Columbia County, Wisconsin, housed people from Oost- and Westdongeradeel, while LaCrosse County appealed to former citizens of Het Bildt. Bonhomme County, South Dakota, was popular among Barradelers. The chain migration from the northern Frisian clay area directed people from single Frisian regions to settle together in single American communities.

An even closer look is possible. Chicago attracted people from all the municipalities in northern Friesland, although the share of Wonseradeel was very low. Northern Frisians in the town of Pella, largely came from Oost- and Westdongeradeel. Grand Rapids housed especially immigrants from Ferwerderadeel and Barradeel. The Wisconsin town of Randolph had most people from Oost- and Westdongeradeel, and not even one from Wonseradeel or Het Bildt. The immigrants in Wisconsin from Het Bildt preferred Holland Town more to the west. In Holland, Michigan, almost all northern Frisians came from Westdongeradeel and Ferwerderadeel, while the nearby town of Zeeland got its inhabitants from Barradeel and Wonseradeel. The industrial city of Paterson grew with inhabitants from Het Bildt and Ferwerderadeel, while Whitinsville attracted immigrants from Barradeel and Wonseradeel.

This further subdivision of northern Frisians into smaller, distinct groups originating in the different municipalities of Friesland can be studied in an even more microscopic perspective [Appendix VI]. People from certain towns in the clay area *en masse* went to certain specified destinations in the United States. From the municipality of Westdongeradeel *only* emigrants from the village of Nes migrated to Pella, and from Oostdongeradeel only those from Lioessens and Ee. From the villages of Blija and Tzummarum emigrants specifically ended up in Grand Rapids.[52] Half of the linked emigrants from Morra and also half of those from Betterwird/Bornwird can be found in 1900 in the town of Randolph, Wisconsin. For those from St. Annaparochie, favored places of settlement were Holland Town, Wisconsin, and Paterson, New Jersey. The villages of Ferwerd, Blija, and Marrum, as well as Betterwird/Bornwird and especially Holwerd sent people to Holland, Michigan. The nearby town of Zeeland, Michigan, housed especially former inhabitants of Almenum, Oosterbierum, Arum, and Piaam.

Many immigrants from Tzummarum, Gaast, and Ferwoude lived in
Whitinsville in 1900. Another striking example of linked villages is Ee. Of
42 linked emigrants of the village of Ee (Oostdongeradeel), 20 were found
in Roseland. From the 85 linked emigrants of the neigboring Hantum,
Hantumhuizen, and Holwerd (Westdongeradeel), 48 went to Ottawa County,
Michigan, 22 of the 40 linked individuals of Ternaard (Westdongeradeel)
went to Marion County, Iowa; Blija sent 90 percent of her linked immigrants
to Michigan, Ferwerd 70 percent. Minnertsga had 37 percent of her linked
emigrants in Sioux County, Iowa, Tzummarum 34 percent.

The pattern of national Dutch settlement before the 1880s described by
Swierenga, and of the province of Noord Brabant described by Schreuder
and Van Stekelenburg, in large measure also holds true for the Frisian
emigrant population around the turn of the century. Frisian emigrants tended
to move to settlements that already had Frisians and Dutchmen. Pieter Ypes
Groustra, who left Ee in 1881, traveled directly to Chicago where he was
given lodging by a former townsman. In one of his first letters Groustra
mentions that he lived among many Frisians and that "everyday we speak as
much Frisian as you do."[53]

The structured character of the Frisian migration, in my opinion, has more
to do with kinship relations than with the individual perception that people
felt they were part of an ethnic group. Frisian settlements in the United
States were often focused on very specific regional ties even within the
province. The clay emigrants largely moved to places where their network
had been established: where former family members and neighbors from
the native village lived. This was the pragmatic outcome of an overseas
migration that in its communication and information relied very much on
personal and community ties.

Comparing data derived from specific areas in the ten year interval between
the 1900 and 1910 censuses, it appears that the Frisian settlements in
Massachusetts and New Jersey remained attractive in the decade after the
turn of the century. In those years the Frisians in Massachusetts almost tripled,
while the northern Frisians in New Jersey multiplied more than five times.
The westward expansion in America can be seen from the Frisian settlement
patterns too. In 1900 hardly any northern Frisians can be found in California
and Washington, while a decade later their presence in these states is much
more evident.

Table 5.6 **States of residence Frisian-born northern Frisians, 1900 and 1910:**

| State | County | 1900 | 1910 |
| --- | --- | --- | --- |
| Washington | Island County | – | 81 |
| | Whatcom County | 2 | 73 |
| | Yakima County | 5 | 42 |
| | Snohomish County | 3 | 12 |

| State | County | 1900 | 1910 |
|-------|--------|------|------|
| California | Humbolt County | 4 | – |
| | San Bernardino County | – | 13 |
| | Los Angelos County | – | 11 |
| New Jersey | Passaic County | 225 | 1111 |
| Massachusetts | Worcester County | 262 | 695 |
| Wisconsin | Columbia County | 148 | 355 |

**Source:** Galema, "Frisians in the U.S.A., 1900/1910. Computer Compilation"

Table 5.6 shows the insignificant share of Dutch settlement in the western states of Washington, Montana, South Dakota, and California before the 1890s.[54] Moving into new land was no simple matter and, although some Dutch settlements go back to the 1870s, the West was really opened for settlement after the construction of the transcontinental railroad lines. After the opening of the Union Pacific Railway in 1869 and the Northern Pacific Railroad in 1883, which linked the eastern and midwestern states with the Far West, Frisians and other Dutchmen also started to move into states like Montana, Washington, and California. This was also due to the availability of homestead land, which was gone by 1890 in the midwestern states. In 1908 a Frisian immigrant wrote to a journal:

> A farmer more or less does not make any difference here. There is space in abundance: 25,000 *pondemaat*. And the land is not as expensive as in the Frisian clay area. We pay 50 dollars per acre, with everlasting water rights. The land that cannot be irrigated only costs 5 dollars per homestead.[55]

Most of these Frisians had emigrated to the United States earlier. In the scenic Gallatin Valley of Montana, Frisians from the settlement areas in Michigan and Iowa established themselves on land of the West Gallatin Irrigation Company.[56] The Weidenaar family from the village of Ee in Oostdongeradeel, after earlier stations of settlement in New Jersey and New Era, Michigan, settled at last in the 1890s in the Gallatin Valley. The brothers Jurjen and Jan Weidenaar emigrated in 1881, while their parents Eelke and Lieuwkje Weidenaar-Bolt arrived the next spring with their married daughter Antje and her husband Johannes Braaksma from the village of Oostrum. Johannes' brother Jacob Braaksma and his family from the region around Betterwird/Bornwird, Westdongeradeel arrived in 1889 in the United States and their intended destination was New Era. Jacob and Ynske Braaksma – Van der Ploeg with their three Dutch – born children, Janke, Klaaske, and Johannes, in 1900 farmed in the Gallatin Valley with three more children, two of them born in Michigan. Close to the farm of Jacob, his brother Johannes with his wife Anna Weidenaar had his own independent farm, where he lived with his daughter Jenny and his parents-in-law Eelke and Lucy Weidenaar.[57]

Thus, the Weidenaars and Braaksmas had a family relationship and most likely relied on each other's knowledge of the New World. Other Dutch migrants like the Groningers Jacob Balda and Willem Broekema also ended up via New Era, Michigan in the Gallatin Valley.[58] All these emigrants to the Gallatin Valley were in fact exponents of a phased migration, a move that was first directed to a certain destination in the United States and later on to a following place of settlement which probably was not decided on beforehand. There are other important areas where the process of settlement and resettlement took place. Pella attracted many Frisian immigrants at the time of its genesis in the 1840s.[59] A few decades later a delegation from the original town went for an excursion to northwest Iowa to investigate the possibilities for a new settlement. Among them was the earlier-mentioned Frisian Jelle Pelmulder, originally from Bornwird. The result was that in the 1870s and 1880s Frisians from Pella went to Sioux County, Iowa, where they were joined by northern Frisians directly from the Netherlands.[60]

Thus, the destination and place of settlement of Frisians was in fact largely based on circumstance. The migrants are traced in *a* certain place at *a* certain time, and it may not be possible to determine their initial destination, which they chose in northern Friesland. Clearly, some immigrants did not end up in their intended destination in the United States. This "secondary settlement" issue is similar to the history of many other European migrants to America. Many first moved in Europe from a rural to an urban environment and then made the big leap over the ocean. In those cases the timing of the decision to emigrate is very hard to determine. This is not the case for the northern Frisians, because they did not move in stages. They tended to emigrate directly overseas. The general conclusion is that the areas of destination of northern Frisian emigrants correspond with those of the Dutch in general, and more importantly, with the areas that Frisians selected in the period 1835-1880. After 1880 they mainly chose the midwestern states as destination, and they generally moved to settlements in the United States that were already primarily Frisian. Concentrations of Frisians from a specific municipality were found in particular settlements in the United States. Chain migration directed people from single Frisian regions to settle together in single American communities. An even more microscopic perspective showed that small distinct groups originated in different villages of Friesland. Emigrants from the towns of Blija and Tzummarum, for example, specifically ended up in Grand Rapids, while almost half of all the emigrants from the village of Ee settled in Roseland, a Chicago suburb. The clay soil emigrants largely moved to places where their network has been established, which was the pragmatic outcome of an overseas migration that in its communication and information relied on personal and community ties, and on the tradition of migration.

As in other ethnic emigrant streams, the westward expansion in America can be seen from the Frisian settlement patterns. Some of these immmigrants were a product of a so-called phased migration, because they first moved to an initial destination in the east or in the Midwest, and only later decided to go on westward. This settlement pattern does not reflect their stable mobility behavior in the premigration period, but more evidently a pragmatic and entrepreneurial bias in a new challenging environment.

## 5.3 Occupational structure and settlement patterns

Upon arrival and entry in the United States, the first object of immigrants was to earn a living. Publicists skillfully created a "cultural mystique of unlimited opportunities and success, freedom and equality, and absence of discrimination."[61] Since by far the largest percentage of the Frisians came from the primary economic sector of agriculture, it is obvious that most sought work in American agriculture or in agriculture-related industries. In the context of the Frisian attachment to the soil as a symbol of social status, this presupposition is even more justifiable.

Research about Dutch emigration before the 1880s provides evidence that the occupation of an immigrant affected his settlement preferences.[62] Other historians of migration have also pointed to this relation – Harald Runblom, Hans Norman, and Robert Ostergren for Sweden, Ingrid Semmingsen and Jon Gjerde for Norway, and Kristian Hvidt for Denmark. It is also known that in the nineteenth century Dutch overseas migration was overwhelmingly a folk or family-oriented migration.[63] The migrants of rural background sought cheap lands that were offered, for example, by the Homestead Act.[64] However, if we think of Frisian migration as an element in the European mass migration of the second half of the nineteenth century, we must place this Frisian migration in the larger context of an Atlantic economy with segmented labor markets. This means that migrating Frisians around the turn of the century were part of a labor market that was internationalized, e.g. a transatlantic occupational labor structure. A recent theory dealing with the world labor market distinguishes two main historical phases: the first contains the emergence and development of the market for labor under colonialism and the second started with industrialization and caused the direct incorporation into the world market of the capitalist metropole.[65] The mass migration from Europe that began in the nineteenth century differs fundamentally from, for example, the transatlantic slave trade, because it was directed by developments within European society and also by the fact that the receiving countries like the United States, Canada, and Australia were "little more than the extension of European societies to other continents."[66] The main point is that European emigrants had a real chance of gaining possession of the means of production in their area of settlement, while for example the African slaves or Asian "coolies" did not have this prospect. The scale and timing of the European emigration was directly related to the capitalization of the agricultural sector and the industrialization within Europe and at the same time to the economic climate and the state of the labor market in the United States and to the prognoses of how such factors might change in the future.

In this context, we might ask whether the Frisian overseas migrants were a product of this international labor market or whether they were more or less responding to their tradition of family- and farm-oriented migration. Or, in other words, in what sense can we think of Frisian migration as part of a single economic phenomenon: the transatlantic labor market, and in what sense was their move defined – consciously or unconsciously – by characteristics of the local areas from which they departed and where they settled?

Figure 5.2 shows the macro occupational structure of the Frisian immigrants and descendants in 1900 after two decades of overseas migratory activity.[67] The Frisians were found 35.4 percent in agriculture, which was only slightly higher than the average of the whole group of northern Frisians between 1880-1914 before they left Friesland [see also Appendix IV]. A real shift took place in the secondary economic sector. An increase of more than 25 percent occurred among those employed in manufacturing and handicrafts. The

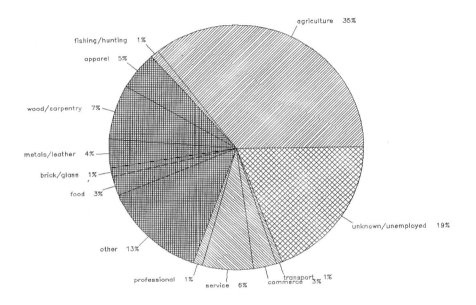

*Figure 5.2*

*Occupations by economic Sector, Frisian immigrants and descendants, 1900, males older than 14.*
***Source:*** *Galema, "Frisians in the USA, 1900/1910. Computer Compilation"*

proportion in the tertiary economic sector remained almost the same. If the occupations are specified in more detail, it is striking to see that especially the major occupational group of farmers and farm managers increased. Before departure this group contained 177 persons or 3.4 percent of the emigrant work force, while in 1900 in the United States Census 280 were farmers and farm managers, or 20.8 percent of the Frisian immigrant work force.[68] The conclusion is that not too many more migrants ended up in the primary sector of agriculture, but that their status changed: already in 1900 many were independent entrepreneurs. Of all the household heads identified in the Census, as many as one third became farmers or farm tenants in the U.S., while the share of farm laborers and farm workers among the heads of households only reached 4.3 percent. I will come back to the aspect of social mobility later.

Another striking result of investigating the general occupational pattern is that hardly any independent single females or wives could be found in the workforce outside the family home. Of the 508 wives of the northern Frisian household heads in the 1900 Census, only three had paid jobs. Of the 11 single female heads of household only 4 were reported in the 1900 Census as farmers, while the other 7 females were listed with the specified occupation of housewife. The 149 immigrant daughters older than 14 showed a totally different pattern. About half held specified jobs. A few worked as spinners and weavers in the silk industry in Paterson, others took jobs as housekeepers, cooks, or servants. Their percentage of the immigrant daughter work force was 52 percent. This is in sharp contrast to the figures for the female heads of household or the female workforce of the Frisian emigrant group before departure.

In the United States Frisians must have revised their ideas about young women working outside the family home. In the perspective of pioneering in the new country, the economic aspect of children bringing home money from paid jobs was an appealing aspect. B.J. Fridsma who emigrated from Friesland as a child of 11 years, recalls in his memoirs that his sisters Jabikje (20) and Jeltsje (19) worked in a yarn factory after arrival in Passaic, while his youngest sister Tryntsje stayed home to help her mother. Fridsma also mentions that his family later on decided to take in a boarder, to "have broader financial means."[69] This clearly shows that the new generation really became part of the new society in which they lived. Among the married females, outside jobs in the United States were not an option.

The occupational stratification can be related to the geographical distribution of Frisians in the United States. In the state of Illinois, especially in and around the city of Chicago, Frisian clay soil immigrants in 1900 can be located in the primary agricultural and in the secondary manufacturing sector. They mainly became farmers, farm managers, and farm laborers, but many of them also worked in the Pullman railway car shops as toolmakers, machinists, and manufacturing laborers, or as salesmen in commerce. In the state of Iowa, most of the Frisians ended up in agriculture and the farmers and farm managers in the workforce outnumbered the farm laborers by 64 against 46 household heads. In Massachusetts, by contrast, hardly any Frisians in 1900 worked in agriculture; almost all worked in the Whitinsville machine shops. In Michigan agriculture absorbed most of the northern Frisians (again farmers outnumbering farm workers) and they also worked in the furniture industry. The western states of Minnesota and Montana mainly offered occupational possibilities in the agricultural sphere, while New Jersey employed most of the Frisians in the silk industry of Paterson. In Wisconsin and South Dakota the Frisians sought farmlands and started their own enterprises.

The general conclusion is that immigrants in the cities tend to have industrial jobs, while those in rural areas were farmers or agricultural laborers. The truth is not always logical: in the urban environment of Chicago, the percentage of Frisians as farm managers and farmers was much higher than the percentage of industrial workers, while in the rural surroundings of Whitinsville, the Frisians in 1900 had industrial jobs rather than agricultural ones. However, this had much to do with the fact that truck gardening around city peripheries was very common. In the next chapter attention will be paid to this phenomenon.

From the occupational data of the 1900 Census it is also possible to determine the social status of Frisian immigrants. The occupational social pyramid is presented in table 5.7.

Table 5.7   **Social gradation of occupation, Frisian immigrants and descendants in the 1900 workforce:**

| Occupational group | Number | % |
|---|---|---|
| Professional, sub-professional | 15 | 1.3 |
| Entrepreneur | 305 | 27.4 |
| Skilled labor | 161 | 14.4 |
| Semiskilled labor | 279 | 25.0 |
| Unskilled labor | 356 | 31.9 |
| **Total** | 1,116 | 100.0 |

**Source:** Galema, "Frisians in the U.S.A., 1900/1910. Computer Compilation"[70]

It is clear that most of the Frisians in the United States in 1900 still worked in manual jobs.[71] The share of professionals (doctors, architects, ministers, and teachers) was not very high. Of course most had only been in the United States for a short time. The biggest change in job status is that many became independent entrepreneurs. Almost 30 percent of the immigrants in the United States are in this group, while this percentage was as low as three percent for the departing emigrant group, evidence of the fabled American upward mobility.

It is surely true that in a relatively short time many of the Frisian immigrants managed to run their own farms. By far the largest part of the category of independent entrepreneurs comprised the self-employed immigrants in agriculture: 90 percent. The conclusion is clear: in the category of entrepreneurs, the Frisian immigrants in the United States sought land and an independent work environment, mainly in agriculture. Their hunger for land showed the affinity with the old country, although only a small group of them had been farmers in Friesland before emigration.

Ulbe Eringa, who was jobless when he left Friesland in 1892, wrote in his very first letter from Hull, Iowa, to his family in Friesland:

> I hired myself out for five months for 25 dollars. For one dollar one gets a Dutch *rijks-daalder*. I could return to Holland in December easily if I wanted, I am earning that much. And you can't image how good the food is here...You surely should not pity me that I am here because it's a beautiful country here and one after another gets ahead. It is just the opposite from Friesland. I really look forward to become a farmer here, then I could lead a lighthearted life.[72]

A year after emigration Ulbe Eringa already had a farm of 240 acres in Runningwater, South Dakota, and in 1894 he and his wife owned 320 acres. Eringa's desire for farmland obviously originated in his native village.[73] The category of unskilled Frisian immigrants shows a larger percentage than before emigration. This may be due to the industrial jobs that were taken in the machine shops, the silk mills and the furniture industry. New immigrants usually had to start in the lowest ranks of the occupational stratum. The percentage of Frisians who were recorded in the 1900 Census as unemployed in fact is quite low. This may be exaggerated because the category "Other" also contains a share (but only 5 percent) of Frisians who were recorded in the Census with their occupation as "unknown" (see also figure 5.2). The conclusion is that not many Frisian immigrants in the workforce were unemployed, and this was also true for the group of departing Frisian emigrants who left for America.

Studying the occupations of the Frisian immigrant group in the United States, it is possible to compare the occupational diversity at the time of emigration (see Appendix IV) and at the moment of tracing in the 1900-Census (see table 5.8). This concerns the linkage group before and after emigration.[74]

Table 5.8   **Ten most frequently listed occupations of the Frisian migrant work force, 15 years and older  1880-1900:**

| Occupation before emigration | | Occupation 1900 Census Frisian born | | Occupation 1900 Census Frisian stock | |
|---|---|---|---|---|---|
| laborer | 267 | farmer | 226 | laborer | 47 |
| farm laborer | 28 | laborer | 127 | farmer | 25 |
| small farmer | 27 | day laborer | 74 | machine maker | 23 |
| farmer | 19 | laborer furniture | 38 | female servant | 15 |
| | | female servant | 38 | | |
| hired hand | 13 | workman | 32 | factory worker | 13 |
| carpenter's | 12 | textile worker | 31 | work man | 11 |
| hand | | carpenter | 31 | | |
| retail man | 8 | farm hand | 9 | | |
| carpenter | 8 | factory worker | 27 | carpenter | 9 |
| workwoman | 7 | peddler | 16 | day laborer | 8 |
| day laborer | 7 | | | | |
| | | | | gardener | 7 |
| **Total:** | 396 | | 640 | | 167 |

**Source:** Galema, "Linked files: Frisians to America and Frisians in the U.S.A. Computer Compilation"

After the northern Frisians emigrated, a remarkable shift in the occupational structure appears. The traditional agrarian-oriented jobs before emigration turned into more industrially oriented occupations in the United States. The newcomers entered different sectors of the economy. Frisians found work especially in the machine shops and furniture industry. Many agricultural laborers managed to start their own farms, either owned or rented, but as independent entrepreneurs. The lure of the land is striking in many ways. The profession of market gardener was a new occupational adventure too, although Frisians had great affinity with this work.[75]

The linked file of the last job before emigration and the first job traced in the United States shows occupational changes very specifically (table 5.9).

Table 5.9   **Pre and post migration jobs, northern Frisians, 1900:**

| Friesland | | United States | |
|---|---|---|---|
| agricultural laborer | 267: | 80 | farmers |
| | | 35 | day laborers |
| | | 37 | laborers, workmen |
| | | 12 | laborer furniture factory |
| | | 8 | machinemakers |
| | | 6 | gardeners |
| | | 5 | storekeepers |
| | | 3 | factory workers |
| | | 3 | fabric dyers |
| | | 78 | other |
| farm laborer | 28: | 7 | workmen |
| | | 6 | farmers |
| | | 3 | day laborers |
| | | 2 | laborers furniture factory |
| | | 10 | other |
| small farmers | 27: | 10 | farmers |
| | | 3 | gardeners |
| | | 3 | day laborers |
| | | 2 | laborers |
| | | 9 | other |
| farmers | 21: | 15 | armers |
| | | 3 | laborers |
| | | 2 | unknown |
| | | 1 | factory worker |

| Friesland | | | United States |
|---|---|---|---|
| day laborer/hired hand | 20: | 8 | farmers |
| | | 2 | laborers furniture factory |
| | | 2 | workmen |
| | | 8 | other |
| carpenters/blacksmiths/ painters/wagonmakers | 15: | 3 | farmers |
| | | 6 c | arpenters |
| | | 2 | painters |
| | | 2 | laborers furniture factory |
| | | 1 | milkbusiness |
| | | 1 | carshop |
| bakers/butchers | 8: | 3 | bakers |
| | | 3 | farmers |
| | | 1 | day laborer |
| | | 1 | fabric dyer |
| none/umemployed | 61: | 11 | laborers, workmen |
| | | 11 | farmers |
| | 8 jobless | | |
| | | 7 | laborers furniture factory |
| | | 6 | unknown |
| | | 2 | bakers |
| | | 2 | day laborers |
| | | 2 | sawyers |
| | | 1 | farmer's hand |
| | | 11 | other |
| housewives | 227: | 207 | housewives |
| | | 14 | unknown 3 farmers |
| | | 1 | housekeeper |
| | | 1 | peddler |
| | | 1 | washwoman |

**Source:** Galema, "Linked files: Frisians to America and Frisians in the U.S.A. Computer Compilation."

Although the occupational progress between the last and first occupation is traced only at one stage in the period 1880-1900, the findings show a remarkable rise in status.[76] The micro occupational data fit in the macro economic and social occupational analysis that is discussed earlier.
In general, northern Frisian overseas migrants reacted to the possibilities of the international labor market. The Atlantic economy provided industrial jobs for part of these Frisians. Hoerder calls this a "quantitatively and

qualitatively new phase in the history of the displacement of labor toward capital."[77] Primarily the Frisian migrants relied on the older traditions of migration. Their decisions directly depended on the economic climate and the state of the labor market in the United States and its future prognosis. But the Frisian migrants for the most part sought agricultural possibilities in the United States, which were compatible with their European occupational backgrounds. In that respect Hoerder's qualification of "a new phase" only partly holds for the Frisians. Around the turn of the century they appear to be an immigrant group in transformation. In one respect they were influenced by the Atlantic economy but in another respect they were a product of their old mobility tradition. The transition from the traditional rural folk migration to a more industrially oriented labor migration was barely evident, and it was in its early stages.[78]

## 5.4 Characteristics of the Frisian-American household

In addition to occupational structure, the data of the American Census of 1900 reveal other biographical information about the Frisian stock. Of the total group, there were 666 two-parent households and only 26 headed by single parents, and only 7 single person households.[79] The composition of the household was typically family oriented. More than in Friesland, the households in the United States also included relatives – grandparents, stepchildren, servants, and boarders.[80] However, the average family included 4.5 members in the United States compared to the premigration average of 5.4 members. The timing of the reference year of 1900 influenced household composition, because many immigrant children had already started their own households. Grandparents sometimes came over later.

The Census data also reveal whether Frisian families owned or rented their homes. Within two decades after emigration 40 percent owned their own home or farm, one fifth were freeholders (see table 5.10), and one fifth held mortgages.

Table 5.10    **Ownership of house or farm, northern Frisian households, 1900 Census:**

| | |
|---|---|
| Owned free | 19 % |
| Owned mortgaged | 21 % |
| Rented | 59 % |
| Unknown | 1 % |
| **Total** | 100 % |

**Source:** Galema, "Frisians in the U.S.A., 1900/1910. Computer Compilation."

These families expressed the migrant's enterprising attitude. In 1909 an immigrant wrote in a Frisian newspaper:

> There are enough farmers here, who started to rent without having any money and who own their farm by now. Among them probably some have their land mortgaged, but

many of them also have their farm 'all paid for' as they say. That is not possible in Friesland, although this is not the fault of the farms, but of course of the high, *too* high rent.[81]

Together with the information concerning the situation of housing, this immigrant's criticism concerning the rent of farms in his old country is undeniable.

In terms of the education of the migratory group, the census taker recorded whether individuals were able to read, write, and speak English (see table 5.11). For the Frisian households these data show clear results.

Table 5.11  **Educational status of northern Frisian immigrants and their descendants, 1900 Census:**

| Education | Linkage group | Non-linkage group* |
|---|---|---|
| Illiterate | 37 | 18 |
| Can read | 21 | 1 |
| Can read and write | 256 | 69 |
| Speaks English | 23 | 12 |
| Reads and speaks English | 3 | 7 |
| Reads, writes and speaks English | 1090 | 820 |
| **Total** | 1430 | 927 |

* Includes northern Frisian immigrants who could not be linked with the departing group, or those who are recorded in the data file "Frisians in the U.S.A., 1900/1910" and who could not be found in the original emigrant file "Frisians to America, 1880-1914," but who were part of the Frisian immigrant household. For example, children born in the United States, boarders, family members who came from other areas in Friesland, and servants belong to this group. The children younger than nine were not included in the table concerning the educational status in 1900, because the Census used nine years as the cut off for the literacy question.

**Source:** Galema, "Frisians in the U.S.A., 1900/1910. Computer Compilation."

The linkage group shows a high level of basic education. In 1900 already 76 percent of the northern Frisians could read, write, and speak English. They also managed to get their children to school. 88 percent of the immigrant descendants and other household members could read, write, and speak English. The immigrant Willem van de Leest wrote in 1883 from Michigan:

Geert [his brother who lived nearby, J.B.E.G.] and his family are quite healthy. Three of his children go to the English school. There are many schools and churches here in America. The children can learn what they want. A poor person has as many rights as the rich.[82]

Although the figures of the Census give a positive idea about the knowledge of English among Frisian immigrants, nevertheless the English language was a problem for most of them. The census taker probably easily wrote down that the specific person was able to speak English after his most elementary questions were answered adequately. But the first sentences that people learn in a foreign country are the ones concerning autobiographical questions: "what's your last name, where are you from, do you have children, what kind of work do you do and who is the person next to you?" Although agents of steamship companies provided potential emigrants with brochures with the most important words and sentences in English, I have the impression from autobigraphical sources that most of the people who left Friesland were not able to speak the English language. Many complain in their letters that they have trouble with understanding non-Dutch people in the work place. Johannes van Dijk several times during his stay in the United States, stated that he did not feel very comfortable when he worked with persons from another ethnic group. An immigrant from Grand Rapids warned the potential emigrants in Friesland via the newspaper:

> Also the english language is a matter that is handled too lightly. The children learn the english language usually very fast, however, for the parents this appears to be a very difficult job, and if they have passed 40 years of age, they never learn the language very well.[83]

Illiteracy was hardly present among Frisian immigrants. The information of the Census, and also the immigrant correspondence shows that the level of illiteracy was low at the moment of departure. The Frisian immigrants really tried to learn the English language. Only a few spoke English who were not also able to read or write it.

The census taker also asked members the place of birth of each person enumerated. If born in the United States, the state or territory was given, if foreign born the country was given. For the linkage group the data are clear: all these immigrants were born in the Netherlands, while *all* their fathers and mothers came from the Netherlands too. Not even one parent from Germany or Belgium was recorded! This again stresses the fact that mobility in the premigration era had not crossed the national border.

Table 5.12 **Citizenship of non-linked household members, Frisian immigrants, 1900:**

| Birthplace self | | Father | Mother |
|---|---|---|---|
| California | 8 | – | – |
| South Dakota | 15 | – | – |
| Illinois | 161 | 2 | 5 |
| Iowa | 215 | | 14 |
| Massachusetts | 57 | – | – |
| Michigan | 317 | – | 15 |
| Minnesota | 68 | – | – |
| Montana | 2 | – | – |
| Nebraska | 1 | – | – |
| New Jersey | 95 | 1 | – |
| New York | 30 | – | 7 |
| Washington | 1 | – | – |
| Wisconsin | 116 | – | 5 |
| The Netherlands | 502 | 1575 | 1533 |
| Germany | 3 | 15 | 12 |
| Belgium | 1 | – | – |
| Switzerland | 1 | 1 | 1 |
| England | 1 | 1 | 2 |
| Norway | – | 1 | 1 |
| Denmark | – | – | 1 |
| **Total** | 1596 | 1596 | 1596 |

**Source:** Galema, "Frisians in the USA, 1900/1910. Computer Compilation."

If the household members other than the linked members are studied, the pattern of citizenship is different. Table 5.12 shows that the Frisian immigrant household contained few members of other ethnic groups. Even the marriages of Frisians or their descendants must have been mostly within their own Dutch circles. Hardly any spouses were of other nationality groups or had parents from another country. The connection of the citizenship with the family status reveals that only one husband was from Germany, two wives were born in Germany and one in England. None of the boarders originated in a European country and only two of the servants were born in Germany. The reference year is again 1900 and this limits the time period studied. Nevertheless, the result is striking. The first years of the Frisian immigrant household in the United States undoubtedly were spent within the ethnic cocoon. In the next chapters I will come back to this aspect of typical Frisian immigrant behavior.

In the Census of 1900 the year of emigration to the United States was recorded as well as the number of years the person lived in the United States. The Census taker also asked adult males whether they were naturalized citizens. From this it appears that in the linked male Frisian immigrant group more

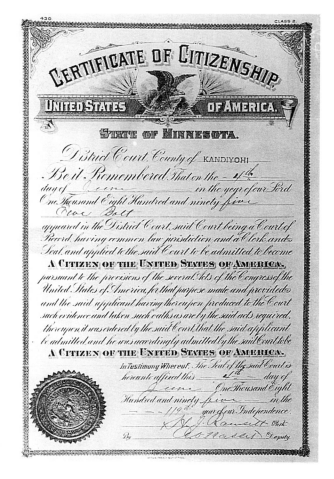

Certificate of Citizenship, State
of Minnesota, 1895.
Calvin College Archives

than one third (37.6 percent) were naturalized. The 1910 Census even shows a higher figure: almost half of the linked males were naturalized (46.3 percent). According to the Second Naturalization Act of January 29, 1795, adult male immigrants could apply for American citizenship after a stay of 5 years. From the naturalized Frisians in 1900, almost 10 percent obtained their Certificate of Citizenship five years after emigration, 20 percent within a decade in the new country, 30 percent within fifteen years, and another 40 percent within 20 years of settlement in the United States In 1900, the relation between the people who were recorded as naturalized and the people who were alien appeared to be respectively 37.6 to 27.1 percent.[84] Naturalized immigrants had advantages. Especially in the typical Dutch immigrant communities, naturalization meant application for political positions within the ethnic group. It also meant the right to vote in local elections in order to control government in the Dutch settlement. Besides the political privilege the Certificate of Citizenship also provided economic privilages. If immigrants wanted to apply for land distributed according to the Homestead Law, they had to be naturalized citizens.[85] The Frisian immigrant Albert Roorda who left around the turn of the century, wrote in a letter of 1903 from Sioux City, Iowa:

This week I have picked up my papers from the court house. When I have been here for five years I have to pick up other forms again and then I will be a real citizen. The first papers only give certain rights. July the 5th to July the 23rd, there will be a lottery for land over here. Land that originally belonged to the Indians, but which is now appropriated by the state. Everyone who has his first papers, has the right to take part in the lottery. There are about 2400 X 160 acres. It will be raffled by 160 acres at a time and it costs 4 dollars per acre. If one manages to get it, one has to pay 1 dollar for every acre immediately, while the rest can come later. Because this land is of very good quality, this is a real cheap deal and I will take my chances. I don't know yet how to get the money, but if I will be that lucky to obtain a piece of land, the money will be all right too. The first thing to do is to possess the land. This land is about 300 miles from here, further west, and nobody ever lived on it, except for the Indians.[86]

Roorda was not lucky in the lottery. He makes clear that some formalities had to be overcome before the newly arrived immigrant could apply for certain privileges. My impression is that even more Frisian immigrants were naturalized after five years than is shown from the Census data, which tended to underreport this information. They needed the Certificate of Citizenship for their economic and political goals, so it is likely that most applied.

### 5.5 Stories of early occupational ventures

Settlement patterns related to occupational mobility of northern Frisian immigrants can be more intensively analyzed through personal stories. The examination of the individual clay-soil emigrant and his quest for occupational success lends insight into typical immigrant behavior. The occupation of an immigrant likely affected his locational preferences. Affinity between the economic structures of sending and receiving areas often influenced where Frisian immigrants settled. This is clear from the fact that the Frisians did not scatter randomly across the United States, but joined others of northern Frisian background.

When Johannes van Dijk arrived in Holland, Michigan, in 1881, he immediately started to work for H. Zuidam, a bricklayer's boss in nearby New Groningen. In an account of his experiences Van Dijk wrote:

New Groningen is a farmer's area, a hamlet as one would say in The Netherlands. There is a school, a small church and a shop where you can buy almost everything. At half an hour distance Zeeland is located, so we live between Holland and Zeeland. The Dutch language is the main language in all these places. The roads are not flat, but run over hills and through valleys, which first did not feel very comfortable to us but later on caused no problem ...My boss brought me to Veneklaasen, the brick factory between us and Zeeland... to do some finishing work on a wagon barn he just had built himself.[87]

For Van Dijk it was easy networking. He immediately met people with whom he could communicate in his own language. In his account he describes the first weeks of work and his earnings: $ 1.50 per day or $ 9 per week. He analyses the situation for immigrants in Michigan:

Still I got the impression that the emigration in the last couple of years went the wrong direction. After all, one arrives here, gets to work, earns good days wages, and therefore has a good living and is satisfied. But more people should go in the forests, to clear land. However, this is hard work, and those who can earn good money in another way, don't have the courage to do this hard work...But it is necessary that it happens, because it provides again work for the factories and all other businesses, while on the other side with the arrival of numerous immigrants work possibilities become fewer and wages become lower, without any land clearings.[88]

Van Dijk's reflection on America as an immigration continent speaks volumes. The wide open country provided occupational possibilities for many, if the right policy was followed according to his diagnosis. While working as a bricklayer in New Groningen, Van Dijk visited acquaintances in the surrounding towns of Holland, Vriesland, Grand Rapids, Zeeland, and Overisel. Through his contacts in the Dutch communities, he and his friend A. Gelders decided to go to Chicago, where they were taken care of by a Mr. De Vries, who emigrated a year before from the village of Hallum, Ferwerderadeel. After some job hunting, Van Dijk again started work as a bricklayer for a foreman of Dutch origin. This did not last long, because his mate Gelders did not like the work and they managed to find a new job in carpentry. They had to buy their own tools with borrowed money from a Dutchman. Van Dijk earned $ 2.50 a day and worked at the same place for a couple of months and learned some English because he had no other Dutchmen at the workplace after Gelders returned to New Groningen for health reasons.

Ulbe Eringa also left as a single young man and was without a job.[89] When he arrived among Dutch friends in Hull, Iowa, in 1892 – 11 years after Van Dijk arrived in Michigan – he immediately got the chance to start at different workplaces. At the home of his friend Murk Abma, a woman who had heard of his arrival drove by and asked him to work for her and her husband at their farm. Eringa started his American work life at the farm of this American family. He wrote positive letters about his boss and about the work, but two years later his letters came from Runningwater, South Dakota, where he owned a big farm together with his new wife Maaike Rijpstra.[90] In 1917 Eringa still lived at his farm in Runningwater. He wrote to Friesland that year:

It's a pity that Frankena is almost poor again too. I am very grateful again that my path of life led to America. Fortunately I still sit here while writing in my own tasteful furnished room with little worries that I will be poor one day.[91]

Eringa did not change places in the United States very often. After he arrived in Hull, Iowa, he went on the way to his own farm without many occupational detours. A Frisian immigrant who also settled in Bonhomme County, South Dakota, wrote in a newspaper in Friesland that there were many Frisian laborers in the surrounding area who worked as farm laborers for the first three or four years after emigration, and then started their own farms. But he also mentioned that the price of land became higher and higher and this was illustrated by the increase in the last five years from 20 to 50 dollars per acre. Laborers seldom remained laborers though, according to this writer. If they were not able to buy the land, they at least started to rent their own farm.[92]

Arjen Hoekstra was another Frisian immigrant who made a shortcut on the way to a farm. He left with his wife and daughter in July, 1896 and settled in LaCrosse County, Wisconsin, where for two years he operated a rented farm. Around 1897 he and his family went to Wood County, Wisconsin, and he bought 40 acres of virgin land in Section 24, Arpin Township. There were no roads to this land and Hoekstra had to follow the old logging trails to reach it. Equipped with only $43 in cash and two oxen, and with the strength and courage that must mark a pioneer, Hoekstra cleared the 40 acres and entered the dairy business, keeping a herd of cattle. After seven years of living here, Hoekstra sold his property and bought 80 acres in Sherry Township. He again cleared 30 acres of land and built a huge barn. After three years he sold his land again and bought a farm, consisting of 120 acres in Section 14 and 15 of Arpin Township. Of this land only 12 acres were already cleared and during Hoekstra's residence on it he completed the clearing of the entire 120 acres and later on another 90 acres in the neighborhood. He carried on general farming and dairying, especially with a herd of Holstein cattle.[93] Hoekstra's clearing practices earned sweat equity, a common American term for work that one invests in one's property. On the frontier, poor squatters and homesteaders developed raw land, built cabins and fences, cut trees, plowed the sod, and then sold their improvements to later comers who had money and wanted to avoid some of the hardship.

Albert Roorda left Friesland around the turn of the century and started a job in Sioux City, Iowa. In one of his first letters he mentioned the land policy in the United States. He recalled the formalities for getting a homestead, and although he was working in a pig slaughterhouse, his thoughts must have often turned to the free land further west. Roorda did not complain about his job as a loader of pork and bacon on wagons, but his remark about the slaughterhouse speaks volumes: "He who works here for a long time, looks like death, so in the long run I will change jobs again".[94] He daydreamed about becoming a photographer in one of the new towns further west, "before another person will practice such a profession." In a letter a couple of months later Roorda compared his American wages with the earnings of a friend in Friesland:

> You are earning 8 guilders per week, I make 8 dollars which is 8 "rijksdaalders" per week but the expenses are correspondingly. This week I made 23 guilders and I worked 54 hours. But 11 guilders are subtracted for boarding and laundry. And then I was one night in the theatre; expenses $f$ 25,– and then a glass of beer 25 cents so after calculation we don't have very much left.[95]

Although wages were higher than in Friesland, Roorda made clear that living and working in a new environment brought other expenses than living in the old country. He was a boarder at different Dutch-American families. In

1904 Roorda was in Chicago where he got board and lodging at another Dutchman's. He worked in the Pullman factories but did not like his job and wages were too low in his opinion. Being a farmer's hand at a huge farm close to Chicago was Roorda's next job: "We were there with three farm laborers and had to milk the cows, plow, harrow and the whole caboodle." He soon had enough of it and returned to Sioux City, Iowa, where he started to work in an egg factory: "we make eggs into powder, so they can last at least 10 years." This job was satisfying and Roorda worked alternately day and night shifts. After his unsuccessfull adventure with the lottery for a homestead further west, he still worked in the egg factory, where he became foreman in 1905, "but I don't think that I will get rich from working like you" he wrote to a friend in Friesland in 1908. In the meantime he had made a journey to San Francisco, where he worked as a waiter in a chic hotel where "almost nobody but millionaires" were guests. However, wages were low, excluding board, and Roorda had to work on Sundays. Besides, "I did not like to pull a sanctimonious face for the rich and to be so darned polite etc." Roorda traveled on to Portland, Oregon, and Vancouver, Canada, and then returned to Sioux City to pick up his job in the egg factory again.[96] Roorda moved over the country like a "rolling stone". Letters after 1908 are not available, but this enterprising story makes one think that many of Roorda's undertakings have been kept secret from us.

Pieter Groustra's occupational career went faster: immediately after arrival

*Pieter and Frederika Groustra-Aukes. ca 1900 (Pieter's second marriage)*

in 1881 in Roseland, he found a job as a carpenter at the Pullman factories. His boss was a Dutch-born foreman and for the next 33 years Pieter stayed at the same job. Later on three of his sons also worked at the Pullman Company.[97]

Van der Heide left the village of Ferwerd in 1914 with his fiancé for America to make money. He had made prior arrangements with a landlord in the small town of Lark, North Dakota. When the couple arrived they were really shocked when they saw the farm. It was all dirt and manure, inside and outside. The cows waded in the dung, even when they were milked. Martin and Anna had to sleep with the sons of the farmer in the garret, with an old rug hung as a curtain. The first weeks the couple helped with all kinds of activities, without being paid. They only got some food. Soon Martin started to accompany the farmer's son to his own farm a few hours from Lark to help him with seeding. Anna found a job at a farm with a widower with children, living in the middle of nowhere. Van der Heide did not see his wife during the week anymore. When he got an offer to work for an American farmer for $ 25 a month, food and board included, he immediately took the job. Like the first farm, this farm also was a sod-house, and still it was far from Anna's workplace. The couple was not very satisfied and Van der Heide wrote in his account:

> Anna had a brother and sister who lived in Edmonton and we often corresponded with them, already when we were in Friesland. It seemed to us that they had a pretty good life there, and we thought it would be a better place than where we were. That's why we thought of going there and we talked about it to the landlord and his wife. Now, they did not agree with us at all, they thought the United States were the best country on earth and we would be stupid to leave it. I think they were right in a certain way, but under this circumstances the U.S. was not very appealing to us. After all we probably had been better off, if we had gone to the manufacturing cities in the east of the United States; there would have been work, we should have done that instead of going to Edmonton... [after arriving in Edmonton, Canada] We experienced pretty soon that Edmonton was not all that rosy either. Anna's sister said when we arrived: 'Och, Och, what are you doing here, Minne [her husband] does not have a job and everybody we know doesn't have one either, and now you are here also'. Oh well, this was the welcome we got. There was no way of return, the money was gone, it was a necessity to stay where we were, at least till we made money again....[98]

When they left the northern Frisian clay area, Van der Heide and his wife intended to go to the United States, but because of occupational difficulties and presuming that their family would give them a hand, they ended up in Canada. For years after the hard times described above, they rushed from job to job in Canada, before settling in British Columbia.

Another Frisian immigrant who appears to be an enthusiastic writer in the *Nieuw Advertentieblad* in 1893, considered himself fortunate because in a relatively short time he managed to find a job in his old profession. In Smith's Grove, Kentucky, he became manager of a dairy factory, "with a salary that even makes many Americans jealous."[99] Jacob Mast wrote in the same paper that he found work for quite some time in Chicago in preparation of the World Exhibition. He wrote that he was among 10,000 colleagues, "a small city in itself". This kind of occasional work absorbed many of the newcomers from Europe and for this Frisian it was a welcome occupational start.[100]

Frederik Dijkstra had a bakery in Hantum, Westdongeradeel and later on in the city of Leeuwarden when he emigrated in 1896 at the age of 44 with his family. He wrote from the village of Bay Shore, New York State, on stationery with his own logo:

> There are hundreds in this town who came here just a little later than I did and they still are as rich or as poor as when they arrived. I have altogether $ 13 to $ 14,000 Dollars, so I am not fearful for the future, financially.[101]

From Dijkstra's letters it is not clear how he made a living, but he enjoyed economic success, according to the sources.[102] Very often immigrants simply accepted jobs that were available after arriving in the United States. This is apparent from the story of Klaas Andeles Hoekema, who left in 1912 for America when he was only sixteen. He "took everything that was available," according to the family's written tradition, and ended up in the farm business in Sunnyside, Washington, in Elmira, Idaho, and later in Spokane, Washington.[103]

Some immigrants tried to stay in their old profession. Albert Vogel, for example, left in 1913 with his parents, brothers and sisters, for Grand Rapids, where he started his career as a house painter, following in his father's footsteps. In 1914 he moved to Orange City, Iowa, and became a successful painter and paperhanger, with some of his younger brothers and his father working for him.[104]

The route to a good and satisfying job in the new country differed greatly for individual immigrants. Unmistakably, their occupational ventures were closely linked to their occupational backgrounds and to their locational preferences, which were determined by their ethnic background.

A real shift in occupational behavior took place in the economic sector of handicrafts and manufacturing. An increase of more than 10 percent occurred after migration among those employed in the secondary economic sector, while within the sector of agriculture the number of farmers and farm managers increased. Hardly any independent females or wives could be found in the workforce outside the family home. However, some younger daughters brought money home from paid jobs in, for example, the silk factories in Paterson, in yarn factories, or as cooks and servants at other families. Generally the women who were farmer's wives cared for the home and children, and the work at the farm was divided according to principles of mutual assistance and Frisian tradition. At their farm in Runningwater, South Dakota, Maaike Eringa-Rijpstra, for example, was successful in raising chickens. Her husband Ulbe wrote about her undertaking in 1903:

> My wife was extremely lucky with chicken farming. She raised about 160 young chicks, half of them cocks and half hens. We partly ate the cocks and partly sold them for a quarter a piece to the hotel. Then the girls brought them and my wife and I plucked them, three in half an hour in the evening at the lamp. We dipped them in boiling water for a moment and then they are clean in an instant.[105]

The occupational social pyramid showed that most Frisians in the United States in 1900 still worked in manual jobs, but compared to premigration many became independent entrepreneurs, especially in agriculture. The occupational diversity showed a remarkable change. The traditional agrarian-oriented jobs of the Frisians before emigration turned into more industrial-oriented occupations in the United States. However, the lure of the land still was striking in many ways, which is expressed, for example, in the fact that Frisians showed great affinity for market gardening.

Although the Frisians experienced much change, the transformation from folk to transatlantic labor migration is only partly evident around the turn of the century. The characteristics of the Frisian American household show a typical family oriented pattern. Most families included two parents, and marriage outside the ethnic group was unthinkable. Grandparents and other relatives more often lived with the nuclear family compared to premigration norms. Within two decades after departure, 40 percent of the households owned their own house and farms.

Illiteracy was rare in the Frisian immigrant group. The English language was a problem for the first generation, and many had to try hard to increase their knowledge in order to operate adequately in occupational or social ventures. But the new country did contain room for maneuvering. Especially in the ethnic enclaves, occupational and geographical mobility was relatively easy and much practised. The migratory moves within the ethnic group also relieved the burdens of unfamiliar language, customs, and homesickness.

In the total experience of the resettlement process of the Frisians, the voyage to America was an integral part and had a formative character. The whole event – from the village of origin through Rotterdam, across the Atlantic Ocean to Ellis Island and a US destination – shaped the immigrant's personality and determined the future experience.

# *Chapter 6* Urban Frisians

### 6.1 The case of settlement

In the process of Frisian migration to the United States, the phenomenon of chain migration deserves further attention. The emigrants from the Frisian clay area entered America through a complex network of kinship, communal associations, and commercial information. In his ambitious book about migrants in urban America, John Bodnar calls such people "transplanted". After settlement in America the old relationships that immigrants brought with them were rejuvenated and once again exploited.[1] Although the term "transplanted" was critized because it does not stress the migrant's *active* participation in the migratory process, I think the paradigm is quite useful in migration research.[2] Especially when the term "transplanted" is combined with the term "networking," the active involvement and the continuous process of transformation are stressed. Charles Tilly's concept of migratory networks as a dynamic force perfectly fits the idea of transplanted communities.[3] Bodnar also wanted to establish links between private lives and large political and economic structures.[4] It is this task of connecting what goes on at the small scale level of the private areas of households and communities with the large scale of economic, political and cultural structures, that inspired me to study particular communities. Rob Kroes's book on Amsterdam, Montana, and Yda Schreuder's book about Dutch Catholics in the Fox River Valley of Wisconsin are exemplary case studies. The following two chapters focus on similar migration communities in which Frisian ties between the old and new world clearly were connected and exploited. Successively, I will concentrate on migration to rural and urban communities in the East and Midwest, then to the upper Midwest, and then to a rural settlement in the Far West.

### 6.2 Fused together: Whitinsville, Massachusetts[5]

In the 1880s Frisians started to settle in Massachusetts, a state that almost equals their home country in size. Worcester, Massachusetts, is a large and productive county with an undulating surface which rises, in general, from two hundred to two thousand feet above sea level. Within its borders, the township of Northbridge incorporates the company village called Whitinsville.[6]

In his personal impression, based on a brief visit in 1921, Jacob van Hinte considered historic Whitinsville to have the same "small town image" as the

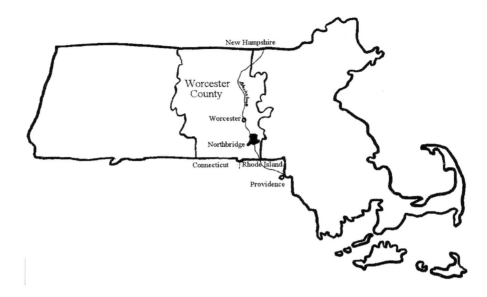

*Map III. The State of Massachusetts with Northbridge on the Blackstone River*

Dutch villages Bussum and Zeist.[7] Since the Revolutionary era, the history of Whitinsville has been chiefly the history of the rise and expansion of various branches of industry. Around 1880, the businessmen of the town belonged to the Whitin family, – hence the village name. In the cotton business and in small manufacturing, the town had a leading position in Worcester County. A National Bank also existed since 1865 in Whitinsville, with one of the members of the Whitin family as president.[8]

Between 1850 and 1875 the population of the region, and especially the village of Whitinsville, increased rapidly and more than doubled between 1875 and 1910.[9] If we follow the description of the contemporary writer Reverend A.P. Marvin in 1879, the marks of thrift were evident on all sides: the buildings were "comparatively new" and kept in "good repair"; the shops and factories were constructed on the basis of improved models and supplied with the best machinery; some of the homes were elegant and splendid, with spacious grounds and colorful gardens. In 1879 Marvin predicted a prosperous future for the town. He wrote:

> It would seem, from an inspection of the town and a survey of its waterpower, that its growth must be mainly in the villages in the river and the railroad.... And as the property in these localities is very much under the control of the members of the family above named [the Whitin family], the gradual development of all the capabilities of the valley of the Blackstone, within the limits of the town, may be expected. As the villages increase, the natural effect will be to raise the value of the land in the Centre, by furnishing a market for all the products of the farms and gardens. The quarries are near for the convenience of builders, and thus many circumstances combine to prophesy a prosperous future to this ancient town.[10]

Why did the northern Frisian emigrants choose the village of Whitinsville for their settlement? The sources reveal that the first Frisians arrived in Whitinsville almost by chance.

According to the recollection of pioneers, the Dutch came as the result of the purchase in 1886 of Holstein-Frisian cattle for John C. Whitin's Castle Hill farm.[11] Whitin was also co-owner of the Whitin Machine Works. After his death in 1882, his widow maintained the farm, but within a few years a scourge of tuberculosis nearly wiped out the herd of registered Jersey cattle. By the early part of 1886 fifteen of the twenty-six registered cows were dead. To restock her herd, Mrs. Whitin, like other American farmers in those days, sent some agents to the province of Friesland and ordered them to find a number of good Holsteins. These Frisian catttle were shipped over in 1886. Two Frisian men accompanied the cows on their ocean voyage: Jan Bosma from the village of Nijland and Hendrik de Boer from Gaastmeer.

According to oral tradition Jan took an immediate liking to the American environment and wanted to stay, but Hendrik got homesick because he had already promised to marry a young lady in the fatherland and therefore he returned to Friesland.[12]

Jan (John) Bosma stayed and worked on the Castle Hill Farm. In May 1887 his sister and her husband Wytse (William) B. Feddema from Tzummarum arrived, followed by Feddema's brother Pieter (Peter) and in September 1888 by Peter's wife Klaske Hoogendijk and five children. All came from Tzummarum.[13] In 1892 Rintje Bosma, Jan's brother, came over with his wife and children. A year after them Albert Rienstra (a brother of Rintje Bosma's wife) with his family settled in Whitinsville, coming from the village of Abbega in southwestern Friesland. Oepke Plantinga with his wife and children had departed a year before from the same place in Friesland. All these names demonstrate that the group of immigrants expanded rapidly, but more importantly, they show connections between the different families or individuals before they crossed the ocean. The ties of kinship, friendship, and regional background are indisputable. Many forces bound the emigrants from Friesland together before they left for Massachusetts. Kith and kin directed the social patterns that were established in Whitinsville after settlement.

The number of Dutch-born in the state of Massachusetts was 993 in 1900 and 1,589 in 1910, according to the U.S. Census. A few of these immigrants were located in the city of Boston; they were largely Jews who were active in diamond-cutting shops and in the cigar-making business.[14] In 1900 Boston had 391 resident Hollanders and 486 in 1910. In other parts of Massachusetts there were only twenty Dutch in 1910 in the industrial towns of Fall River, Lowell, and Worcester, and 18 in the college town of Cambridge.[15]

Hence in 1910 a large part of the Massachusetts Dutch lived in Whitinsville, which accommodated the remarkable number of 987 Dutch immigrants, out of a total population of 8,807, or 11 percent.[16]

J. Jansen, later a minister of the Christian Reformed Church in Whitinsville, mentioned that most of the Dutch immigrants were Frisians who came from the southwestern part of Friesland. This is confirmed by the fact that almost all

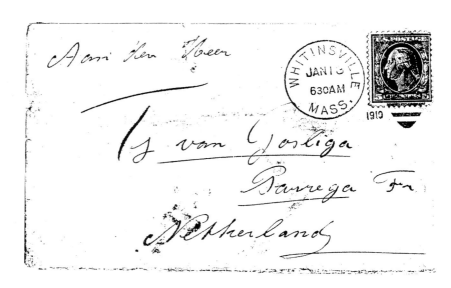

*Letter from R. van Gosliga in Whitinsville, Mass. to Parrega, Wonseradeel, January 13, 1910*

the names of the immigrants are typically Frisian. However, along with migrants from the southwestern corner were some from the northern clay area.[17] From the total group of Dutch migrants in Whitinsville between 1880 and 1910, I was able to link 132 people who came from the six municipalities of Wonseradeel, Barradeel, Ferwerderadeel, Het Bildt, Westdongeradeel, and Oostdongeradeel.[18] Some 83 percent of the linkage group emigrated from only two municipalities in Friesland: Wonseradeel and Barradeel. Even within these two municipalities it is possible to discover some concentration areas. In Barradeel the largest percentage of emigrants to Whitinsville came from the towns of Minnertsga (22 percent) and Tzummarum (39 percent)[19], which towns sent out almost half of the emigrants from the entire municipality (1,777) during the period 1880-1914. In the municipality of Wonseradeel most of the Whitinsville emigrants between 1880 and 1910 departed from the towns of Ferwoude (33 percent) and Gaast (44 percent).[20] They were among 1,401 people who left Wonseradeel in those days for the United States.[21] In Barradeel the population decreased between 1880 and 1914 by nearly 4 percent; that of Wonseradeel increased 1 percent. The province of Friesland increased 11 percent and the Netherlands as a whole showed an increase of 53 percent. As mentioned previously, the contemporary Vitus Bruinsma argued in 1892, as he recalled the population history of Friesland, that the very low population growth in the late eighties and early nineties had nothing to do with birth or death rates. The stagnating Frisian population had everything to do with the emigration rates to the United States.[22]

Emigration was closely tied to the economic structure of the Dutch countryside. Did the emigrants who settled in Whitinsville create a unique work environment? What kinds of jobs did they leave and what kinds did they pick up after arrival?

In 1900 almost half of the labor force in the linkage group worked in industry, mainly in handicrafts. They were factory laborers, machine makers, or foundrymen in the Whitin Machine Shop. Others were employed in the Whitinsville Cotton Mill as weavers, spinners, carpenters, or engineers. What catches the eye is the very small group that worked in agriculture. Only two of the linked Frisian immigrants in 1900 operated as independent farmers, while another two worked as farm hands.[23]

The occupational structure of the 1900 linkage group before they left the province of Friesland is noticeably different from this group in the town of Northbridge. Most were unemployed, due to the agrarian crisis, or they were the elderly or spinsters.[24]

None of the potential emigrants had joined the industrial labor force, which became their future in America. As noted previously, this is not exceptional since northern Friesland was a very rural area where few industrial jobs were available. It also is clear that only the lower social groups emigrated from Friesland to Whitinsville; they were farm workers and day laborers but no independent farmers.

It is interesting to see how the occupational structure of the Whitinsville Dutch remained almost the same over the decade 1900-1910. While the linkage group increased by 23 percent, most of the Frisian immigrants still worked as machinists in the cotton shop or in the Whitin Machine Works. But 14 percent became independent farmers. In 1910 there were nine northern Frisian farmers in the Whitinsville area, five cattlemen (dairy) and four gardeners. Two of the people working in agriculture in 1910 first took jobs in the Whitin Works, to accumulate some financial resources so they could afford to buy or rent a farm. In the valley of the Blackstone River there was a good possibility of finding jobs in gardening. A small part of the work force took advantage of that, although this was not a profession for which they brought extensive experience from their homeland. But neither did the Frisian immigrants who ended up in the industrial sector in Whitinsville. It also seems that nobody had trouble finding work. In the Whitinsville linkage group only a few Frisian males mentioned to the Census marshal in 1910 being unemployed for a couple of months.

Comparing the occupation of Frisians before departure and the job they had in 1910 in Whitinsville, the "factory life" of the Frisians becomes clear:

Table 6.1 **Occupational change of northern Frisians in Whitinsville, Massachusetts before departure and according to the 1910 U.S. Census**

| Premigration Occupation 1880-1910 | | | 1910-Census Occupation | |
|---|---|---|---|---|
| workman, laborer | 14 | >>>>>>>> | farmer | 2 |
| | | >>>>>>>> | machinist | 6 |
| | | >>>>>>>> | machine maker | 6 |
| workwoman, servant girl | 3 | >>>>>>>> | none | 2 |
| | | >>>>>>>> | housewife | 1 |
| day laborer | 2 | >>>>>>>> | machinist | 1 |
| | | >>>>>>>> | milker | 1 |
| baker's apprentice | 1 | >>>>>>>> | farmer | 1 |
| farm hand, hired hand | 2 | >>>>>>>> | machinist | 2 |
| wagonmaker's apprentice | 1 | >>>>>>>> | machine maker | 1 |
| none, unknown | 41 | >>>>>>>> | farmer, gardener | 6 |
| | | >>>>>>>> | farm hand | 1 |
| | | >>>>>>>> | female servant | 3 |
| | | >>>>>>>> | housewife | 1 |
| | | >>>>>>>> | foundry man | 1 |
| | | >>>>>>>> | machine maker | 17 |
| | | >>>>>>>> | machinist | 5 |
| | | >>>>>>>> | painter | 2 |
| | | >>>>>>>> | blacksmith | 1 |
| | | >>>>>>>> | carpenter | 1 |
| | | >>>>>>>> | none | 3 |
| Total | 64 | | | 64 |

**Source:** Galema, "Linked Files: Frisians to America and Frisians in the U.S.A. Computer Compilation"

The occupational pattern of the linkage group in 1900 is representative of all the Frisian immigrants in Northbridge township. Most (43 percent) of the Dutch got jobs in the Whitin Machine Works and the Whitinsville Cotton Mill. Only 5 percent of the Frisian work force in the linkage group became independent farmers, all except one as gardeners. Few were unemployed. Unmarried females mostly stayed at home and worked in the household. However, several single females worked in the cotton mill and as servants in other families. Sometimes people older than 65 did not go out working and women who lost their husbands stayed with their married children or with other families.

In 1910, after the Dutch immigrant group in Whitinsville had almost tripled in number, people laboring in the machine shop and the cotton mill still made up the largest share (43 percent) of the workforce. The change that occurred was that in 1910 more immigrants in the machine factory and the cotton mill worked in jobs with higher socio-economic status than in 1900. In 1900 the Census taker called many of them factory workers, while in 1910 they mostly were described as machinist, engineer, machine operator, or foundry man.[25] It seems that these industrial laborers fared pretty well in their occupational efforts. Only 7 percent were independent farmers and gardeners. Several unmarried women worked as a store clerk, servant, and wash woman. We can conclude that there were few problems in finding nonfarm employment for the Frisian immigrants in Massachusetts around the turn of the century. Their job choices were very pragmatic: they worked in the Whitin Machine Shop or the Whitinsville Cotton Mill, which offered them a relatively stable situation. However, some Dutchmen worked toward the goal of owning a farm. Neglected Yankee farms were bought and restored by Dutch immigrants, according to a Whitinsville resident. This was a phenomenon that happened in other places too. In Fitchburg, Massachusetts, Finnish settlers bought and restored Yankee farms in that area.[26]

The dream of owning their own land was also the reason why some Frisian families from Whitinsville in 1911 filed on homesteads in Edmonton, Canada, where the Christian Reformed Church had a congregation. Among them was Gaele Bakker (later Baker) who had emigrated with his wife and seven children to Whitinsville in 1899. In 1912 Gaele and his son Riemer (Raymond) each filed on land northwest of Edmonton where other Dutch immigrants had taken out homesteads.[27] The conclusion seems to be that although it took some time for realization, the prospect of owning land still was a desirable goal for some of the Frisian immigrants, even years after their ocean crossing. However, in the first decades of Frisian settlement in Whitinsville the occupational patterns were rather stable.

Married women remained in the family home. Even few married immigrant women who for financial necessity worked outside the home in Friesland were housewives in Whitinsville.

Generally there was a marked improvement in the occupational status of the immigrants, who came from the lowest level of the Frisian work force. Some gained the status of independent farmer, and many who had no occupation before departure gained social status by having skilled jobs in carpentry, painting, or factory work.

For the mise-en-scène a closer look at conditions of work, ethnicity, and community life is necessary. The Frisian emigrants landed in a community where the Whitin family was influential; three-quarters of the inhabitants earned their livelihood in their shop. Hence, the terms employee, fellow-citizen, and friend seem to be almost synonymous.

In 1879 a state law established ten hours as a maximum work day. Whitin had been more progressive and had already adopted the ten hour day in 1864. Until 1907, the laborers worked six days a week. Then the shift to a five and a half day week took place. According to the historian T. Navin in his study about the Whitin Machine Works, discipline in the Whitin Shops appears to have been maintained on an easy-going basis and workmen were given considerable freedom on the job. Night work was virtually unknown. The common belief that men worked long and hard in "the old days" does not hold true for Whitinsville, as it had in Friesland. Historian T. van der Wal noted that working conditions for agricultural laborers during the agrarian crisis in Friesland led to social turbulence and that the agrarian crisis caused a general impoverishment. The socio-economic conditions in Friesland during those days became worrisome, especially for those who tilled the land.[28]

The Whitin Company also provided houses for their workers. Navin estimates that two-thirds of the village families were probably company-housed in 1870. In 1900 and 1901 M. Whitin added no less than four hundred dwellings to the three hundred already owned by the Company. Many Frisian immigrants started life in Whitinsville under a Company roof.[29] This is confirmed by the data from the Census concerning home ownership. By far the largest number of all the Frisian immigrants in Whitinsville lived in a rented house in 1900 (81 percent), and this declined only slightly by 1910 (72 percent).[30] Besides housing the Company also had an apprentice training program, which the boys of the village often found more attractive than schooling. Some Frisian sons worked together with their fathers in the machine shop.[31] First generation immigrant Arnold Banning, in an interview, remembered that he came in 1913 at the age of ten, being the oldest son of the family. He went to school in Whitinsville until he was fourteen and then had to make money for the family, especially after his father died of pneumonia when he was sixteen. His younger sister and brother even earned doctoral degrees in sociology and theology. Banning's point was that usually during the first years after migration, the children had to help the family to make a living. Harold Wassenar [changed from Wassenaar] recalls the same point: first-born children were looked upon as additional workers to provide greater security and more "creature" comforts. As the families grew and finances improved, the younger members could go to schools of higher learning. This also happened with Harold's brother and sister, Jacob and Cornelia, who had to work on the recently purchased farm in Whitinsville.[32]

The Whitin Company strategy in the eighties and nineties was to increase its labor force by hiring workers who had only recently come from Europe. This strategy, of course, provided part of the infrastructure for the Dutch and other nationalities in Whitinsville.

Before the 1880s the population of Whitinsville contained mainly descendants of early New England settlers. Those who were not Yankee were either English, Irish, or French Canadian. It is said that the Irish were the first to move into Whitinsville; they came as day laborers in the 1840s and mainly worked in the foundry, a division of the Whitin Machine Works. The second generation Irish refused to endure the hardship of foundry work; thus, in 1886 the foundry was the first to feel the pinch for manpower. One might have expected, therefore, to find many Frisian immigrants in foundry jobs. The census tells us, however, that in 1910 only one Frisian immigrant worked in the foundry; perhaps the jobs in the foundry were not always specified by the census taker because he described them as "laborer machine shop". Most likely the Frisian immigrants deliberately avoided the foundry. T. Navin mentions a large group of French Canadians who started to work in the Whitin Shops after 1886.[33] Two-thirds of them formed a temporary work force, partly in the foundry. A shortage in that department remained until the Whitin family recruited workers from another nationality group, the Armenians. The Armenians arrived in Whitinsville almost the same time as the Frisians. But Arnold Banning recalled that there was not much ethnic tension in the Machine Shop, especially because Whitin had uniform wages for certain work.[34] The heavy influx of foreign nationals, which had begun in the second half of the eighties, had spent its force by 1900, although immigration to Whitinsville did not die out until the beginning of World War I. The immigration stream also caused a movement by a small group of well-educated Yankee reformers to restrict immigration to Massachusetts. They feared being displaced from the centers of power by politicians and industrialists who exploited foreigners' ignorance and poverty.[35]

Knowing that the Dutch in Whitinsville lived among people of Yankee, Irish, French Canadian, and Armenian origin, one would expect a mixture of all these nationalities: Whitinsville as a melting-pot of former European citizens. This was not true. Although the various nationality groups (one writer mentions 14 different ones in 1905![36]) mixed freely in the Machine Shop and the Cotton Mill, they held rather closely to themselves in after-work hours. This was true not only for the French-Canadians and Irish, whose life centered around the Catholic church and numerous affiliated organizations, but also for the Dutch and Armenians. The clannishness of the foreigners caused anxiety among the Yankee restrictionists, because they thought this exacerbated social divisions. The slow pace of assimilation destroyed all hope of restoring the homogeneous, harmonious society that the restrictionists associated with the past, and which they craved.

Proof that the Frisians did not assimilate in the first decade of their settlement in Whitinsville is their marriage-rate with other nationalities. The records of all the Frisians living in the Whitinsville area, according to the U.S. Census of 1910, do not show even one Dutch-born person who married an Armenian, Irish, French-Canadian, or person of a different ethnic group. The Whitinsville Dutch males preferred women from the Netherlands, as is illustrated by a story of Harold Wassenar's grandfather Meindert Krull, who landed in Whitinsville with eight children, five of them females. Dutch women were in scarce supply in the village, according to Wassenar, and the prospect of five ladies coming from Holland was news that spread quickly among the Dutch males. "When they arrived in front of the Whitin Machine Works the Dutch men ran out to greet this wagon full of Dutch females. That would be something to remember. Ha! The first Dutch Beauty Parade and my mother was the "QUEEN."[37] Besides marrying within their own ethnic community, the Dutch families in Whitinsville also did not board persons from other nationalities. They mainly lived in nuclear families as they had before departure.

In Whitinsville, as in so many other villages before the 1880s, the churches served as the principal social centers of the community. Choir rehearsals, church suppers, prayer meetings, and missionary gatherings helped to enliven the workaday drudgery of small-town life. There were several churches: a Methodist, a United Presbyterian, and the two strongest churches: a Congregational and a Roman Catholic.[38] As the population of the town increased and as scepticism reached out to shake religious faith, the churches in Whitinsville began to lose their prominence as the focal points of society. Not so with the church of the Dutch Frisians, who just started to consolidate their church life around the turn of the century.[39] Only a few sources are available to describe the religious life of the Frisian immigrants in Whitinsville. The church records of this community have been preserved by the Christian Reformed Church. There are indications that for most of the Frisians, this church was the nucleus of social existence. The linkage group tells something about the religious conviction of the emigrants before they started their ocean voyage to the new country. Of these Frisians in 1910, 80 percent had belonged to the *Nederlands Hervormde* community, 11 percent had been affiliated with the *Gereformeerde* Church, and 6 percent had been supporters of the *Christelijk Gereformeerde* Church. Thus, only 3 percent had no church affiliation at all. These percentages reflect the general pattern of religious convictions among all the immigrants from the municipalities of Wonseradeel and Barradeel between 1880 and 1914.[40]

In *The Banner*, the organ of the Christian Reformed Church (CRC) edited by Henry Beets in the 1920s, historical reports occasionally appeared concerning individual congregations. There was no Reformed Church of America in Whitinsville. In 1926 Beets reflected on the Frisian church in the village.[41] He reported that a number of Frisian immigrants in the 1880s were not satisfied with Sunday school and preaching services in English. Therefore, they started their own preaching services and used their mother tongue to read sermons and sing psalms. The basement of the United Presbyterian Church and later the townhall were the first meeting-places. In 1895 Reverend F.J. Drost from Wartena in Friesland arrived in Whitinsville, called at a salary of $400 a year, plus housing, to labor among the immigrants.[42] A year later Drost together with Frisian immigrant Mink Beinema sought contact with Classis Hudson (the regional church assembly) of the CRC. Classis Hudson organized a CRC in Whitinsville in October 1896, which comprised thirteen families. In 1897 F.J. Drost became the first minister and a year later a new church building was constructed on Willow Street. So the *nucleus of existence* became real in the village.[43]

After Reverend Drost departed in 1902, a vacancy of two years followed until J. Jansen came from the Netherlands and served the community for almost two years. Jansen is another source who tells something of this settlement. In 1920 he wrote an article in a Dutch journal that dealt with his American experience and mentioned that his parish had about 400 members.[44] Considering that in 1905 a little more than 800 immigrants of Dutch descent lived in Whitinsville, we may conclude that half of them joined the CRC. Jansen describes church life as cheerful [*opgewekt*] and the parish as young, but with a firm base. The services were conducted in the Dutch language and for the immigrant children there was a church-sponsored Dutch language grammar school established to combat the heretical theories of evolution that were being taught in the public schools. The Dutch language was still used by Jansen's successor F. Fortuin who came from Hull, Iowa, in 1906 and served until 1921.[45]

The language problem in the church was, as usual, a prickly one. The first generation did not want to abandon the Frisian language, nor the Dutch. This, however, meant that they spoke only Frisian at home, and in the church Dutch was the language. But soon the children, who had English in school and Frisian at home, did not understand anything of the Dutch sermon.[46] This lead to the often controversial and consequential change in church of Dutch into English, to which I will refer in the last chapter. Although Jansen had an isolated position in Massachusetts, because no other Dutch minister was laboring in that state, he was in touch with the classis of Paterson, New Jersey, which he visited several times a year. Jansen's account has a very contented sound. It almost seems as if Whitinsville was a paradigm of successful settlement and peaceful life. Living conditions for the immigrants were good, Jansen even calls them *ideaal*, in relation to the standard of life in the Frisian source areas in the late nineteenth century. The church had a strong unifying influence in preserving elements of the Dutch culture in the community.

In conclusion, the settling of Whitinsville was a process that involved the use of social networks and categories to produce new social networks and categories.[47] The effective units of migration were neither individuals nor households but sets of people linked by acquaintance, kinship, and work experience. The emigrants commonly drew on information from network members who had already gone to Whitinsville, and often received help as well.[48] The report of people arriving in Whitinsville with tickets prepaid by family members, former neighbors, or friends in the United States, tells us as much. The fact that the Dutch group in Whitinsville was a very homogeneous one, consisting of emigrants from the same Frisian province of origin, shows that this migration was a transplanted network, a knitting together of networks that span place of origin and destination. An immigrant letter to the province of Friesland in the 1950s best captures the community spirit in Whitinsville: "De Friezen binne hjirre hast ien famylje meiinoar en allegearre hast meiinoar forgroeid" [The Frisians here in Whitinsville are one big family closely connected one to another].[49]

## 6.3 Culture island in the city: Paterson, New Jersey

*Alle minsken binn' myn broaren,*
*[All people are my brothers]*
*En de heele wralt myn thus,*
*[And the whole world is my home]*
*Mar 't bloed yn Fryske ieren,*
*[But the blood in Frisian veins]*
*Krupt nei Fries and Fryslan ta.*
*[crawls to Frisian and Friesland].*[50]

The rise in Dutch immigration is reflected in the number of Dutch-born residing in New Jersey, which increased from 357 in 1850 to 12,698 in 1910. In 1910 New Jersey ranked third in the nation in terms of Dutch-born residents, behind Michigan and Illinois. Hollanders in New Jersey ranked behind the English, Irish, Italians, Germans, and Poles.[51] Throughout the nineteenth century Frisians continued to come to New Jersey, despite its urban industrial character.[52]
The city of Paterson had a large Dutch center, numbering more than 10,000 in 1920, including the first American-born generation.[53] A large part of the Dutch ethnic group in Paterson was made up of emigrants from two provinces: Zuid Holland and Friesland. The exact number of Frisians is hard to determine. The general problem is that Frisians are not distinguished from the Dutch in either American or Dutch government records.

In New Jersey the tendency of the Dutch to locate near one another was quite clear; the Dutch presence was more noticeable than if they had scattered throughout the state. The historian G.F. de Jong who studied the Census reports of 1920, found that 60 percent of the Dutch-born in New Jersey in 1920 were living in one county, Passaic. This meant that Passaic County contained the largest community of Dutch immigrants in the East in those days.[54]

Paterson and vicinity are part of Passaic County. Passaic County is the most irregularly shaped of all the counties in New Jersey. J. Whitehead wrote in 1901 about Passaic County that it "has the appearance somewhat of an old fashioned hour-glass, very unsymmetrical, however, and with ill shaped sides."[55] Especially the northern and western part of the county is hilly. Aukjen Pruiksma, who arrived in Paterson in 1895, expressed surprise at the mountainous terrain.[56] Pieter Westerhuis, who migrated in 1881 to Paterson, also expressed his astonishment at the New Jersey landscape:

> You would really be surprised if you came here and if one comes from holland one cannot imagine that it looks like this because one doesn't see canals and ditches like in holland but high mountains from which water runs down and sometimes a river where the water from the mountains runs into...no other waters here while the land that belongs to the owners has fences everywhere...no ditches like yours[57].

Although Westerhuis missed the canals and ditches, Passaic County was certainly well watered. Besides big rivers like the Passaic, Pequannock, and Wanaqua, the county has numerous small streams. Around the turn of the century many railroads also intersected the county in almost every direction, including a good connection to New York City.

Nearly all the people in Passaic in those days were engaged in mechanical and manufacturing pursuits and it was a leading industrial county in the state. In deciding on New Jersey as their new home, some of the Frisian immigrants were attracted by the Dutch (and also Frisian) atmosphere that lingered in parts of the state since the colonial period. The Old-Dutch language was still present, although newly arrived immigrants could hardly understand it. Frisian influence was perceptible too. J. van Hinte recalled the story of an American lady who, wanting to show her devotion to the Dutch language, referred to her grandmother as "een sterke frommes," which means in pure Frisian "a strong woman."[58]

Other evidence of the Frisian spirit in New Jersey is preserved in many letters that were sent over the ocean to the native country. A single letter could swing the opinion of numerous villagers to make the fateful decision.[59] John Faber a Frisian immigrant in Paterson, in 1928 told the Frisian visitor Sjouke de Zee that he had come to America in 1892 for economic reasons and because his sister who already lived in Paterson had "krekt sa lang de angel útsmieten, dat de broer tabiet for emigraesje nei dat nije en greate lân" [thrown the fishing line so well, that her brother bit for emigration to that new and big country].[60]

Although the preservation of Dutch habits, manners, and customs was obvious in New Jersey at the turn of the century, the industrial boom that New Jersey experienced after the Civil War was a greater attraction to Frisian immigrants. Industry was the inducement for many newcomers to settle in ever increasing numbers in cities like Paterson; and also Roseland and Chicago, Illinois; Rochester, New York; and Grand Rapids, Michigan.

Paterson is situated on the "fall line", where the rivers tumble down to the coastal plain, providing water power for industry. In the beginning of the nineteenth century, Paterson was one of the two largest cotton cities in America. The iron industry also settled there, similarly attracted by the water power sites at the Passaic River falls. Silk came later, which was the material that would make this city into the Silk City "par excellence".[61] According to J. van Hinte, there were many Dutch immigrants who arrived in New York and stayed for a while on the other side of the Hudson in the Paterson area, where they usually found work immediately upon arrival. Van Hinte also mentioned the fact that in Paterson the trains to "The West" started.[62] Situated only a dozen miles from Hoboken, which in 1888 became the terminus of the Holland-America Line, Paterson (together with the nearby cities of Lodi and Passaic) was destined to attract Frisian emigrants. In 1890 C.A. Shriner also mentioned that Paterson had steadily increased in her industries. The city's proximity to New York City, which was the trade and commercial center of the country, assured obvious advantages that were virtually bound to give Paterson an unsurpassed industrial position.[63]

Since more than half of the Dutch-born in New Jersey in 1920 lived in one concentration area, Passaic County, one can speak of a culture island of Dutch immigrants. Culture islands are areas in which the population is composed primarily of one ethnic group, surrounded by a less homogeneous native populace. In the nineteenth century in many cities in the United States, Dutch ethnic neighborhoods developed that were even further subdivided according to the province of origin. In Paterson the Dutch settled chiefly in what is now Prospect Park and Peoples Park where an exclusive Frisian neighborhood or culture island existed.[64] By 1853 a Dutch neighborhood had taken shape in that part of Paterson which was known as the town of Wortendyke (later called Midland Park). This settlement pattern does not particularly have to be described as a specific Dutch phenomenon. In 1880 over half of the English-born silk weavers in Paterson were concentrated in a neighborhood that formed the core of the English silk weaving community, known popularly as "Weavertown". According to the historian D.G. Vanderstel, the Dutch residential concentrations were not based upon a common Dutch identity, but reflected the immigrants' diverse provincial origins, denominational affiliations, and time of arrival in the city. In his study of the Dutch in Grand Rapids, Michigan, Vanderstel argues that churches, schools, the press, and other organizations acted to promote Dutch unity. However, they also reflected the differentiation among the Dutch population, based upon ideologies, beliefs, and perceptions of relations with American society.[65]

From the group of Dutch-born in Paterson in 1900 (4,893 persons) and 1910 (4,929), according to the U.S Census Manuscripts[66], I was able to create a linkage group of respectively 102 northern Frisian immigrants in 1900 and 383 in 1910. The total group of Frisians and descendants that was recorded in the Paterson area consisted of 225 people in 1900 and 1168 in 1910. In 1910 the Dutch people in Paterson made up 11 percent of the foreign born and 3.9 of the total population. It can be estimated that the northern Frisians in Paterson made up 0.9 percent of the total population.[67]

Table 6.2   **Northern Frisian immigrants in Paterson, NJ, by Frisian municipality of origin, 1900 and 1910:**

|  | 1900 | | 1910 | |
|---|---|---|---|---|
|  | N | % | N | % |
| Oostdongeradeel | 4 | 3.9 | 18 | 4.7 |
| Westdongeradeel | – | 0.0 | 24 | 6.3 |
| Het Bildt | 46 | 45.1 | 175 | 45.7 |
| Ferwerderadeel | 22 | 21.6 | 68 | 17.8 |
| Barradeel | 13 | 12.7 | 64 | 16.7 |
| Wonseradeel | 17 | 16.7 | 34 | 8.9 |
| **Total** | 102 | 100.0 | 383 | 100.0 |

**Source:** Galema, "Frisians in the U.S.A., 1900/1910. Computer Compilation"

The data of the linkage group show that the largest percentage of northern Frisians came from the municipality of Het Bildt in Friesland (45.7 percent in 1910). The towns of St. Annaparochie and St. Jacobiparochie provided the most important share of these immigrants from Het Bildt. In the municipality of Ferwerderadeel the towns of Ferwerd and Hallum especially contributed people to Passaic County. In Barradeel most of them came from Minnertsga and Tzummarum. Migration from Ferwerderadeel shows a similar pattern for Whitinsville and Paterson.

Comparison of the pre- and post-migration occupational structure of the Paterson linkage group, shows a picture of rural to urban migration. Most of the northern Frisians had worked in agriculture. Of the 1910 linkage group, 38 percent were farming in Friesland, 12 percent were craftsmen, and only 5 percent labored in service and commerce. Almost 46 percent of the workforce was without a job or their profession was recorded in the Dutch Population Registers as unknown.[68] Generally, no professionals were present in the 1900 and 1910 linkage group. A few independent entrepreneurs did change continents; only one farmer was present in the 1910 linkage group, while the 1900 group had no farmer. Three *gardeniers* were in the 1910 linkage group. These small farmers owned or rented a few hectares of land and made a living by growing vegetable crops that were not profitable for larger farmers.[69] Like the Frisian emigrants who left for Whitinsville, those who went to Paterson, also came from the lower ranks of society. There were no white collar workers and no industrial blue collar workers.

After the journey to Passaic County, few northern Frisians could be found in agriculture.

Table 6.3  **Occupations northern Frisians by economic sector in the Paterson area, 1900 and 1910:**

| Economic Sector | 1900 | | 1910 | |
| --- | --- | --- | --- | --- |
| | N | % | N | % |
| Primary (agriculture/fishing) | 5 | 8 | 11 | 4 |
| Secondary (industry/food) | 54 | 82 | 202 | 67 |
| Tertiary (transport/service/commerce) | 6 | 9 | 60 | 20 |
| Other (no job) | 1 | 2 | 27 | 9 |
| **Total** | 66 | 100 | 300 | 100 |

**Source:** Galema, "Frisians in the U.S.A., 1900/1910. Computer Compilation"

The data of the U.S. Census make clear that northern Frisians who settled in the urban surroundings of Paterson found jobs in industry, 82 percent in 1900, and 67 percent in 1910.[70] A classification of the occupations by social categories shows nearly one third in unskilled jobs (32 percent in 1900, and 30 percent in 1910). Most striking is the difference in unemployment rates in Paterson among northern Frisian immigrants: in 1900 only one person in the workforce was unemployed, while a decade later 27 Frisians were recorded without a job (9 percent). The unemployment rate in 1910 was much higher than in 1900. This partly can be ascribed to the fact that the workforce got older; one third of the first generation immigrants who were unemployed in Paterson were older than 65 years of age.

Looking to the specific Frisian occupations, most worked as weavers and fabric dyers in the silk mills. Others found jobs in handicrafts as painters or carpenters or they started their own dairy business or bakery. The progress they made in the decade between 1900 and 1910 is clear: more managed to start an independent farm (64 percent of the farmers in 1910 against 40 percent in 1900) or private business by 1910 and in the silk mills some Frisians became foremen. The occupational progress of the northern Frisians in Paterson can be analysed at the micro level, for example, by comparing the jobs in Friesland to the jobs in Paterson:

Table 6.4  **Occupation in Friesland linked with occupation in Paterson, 1900 and 1910:**

| Occupation in Friesland | Paterson 1900 | N | Paterson 1910 | N |
| --- | --- | --- | --- | --- |
| agricultural worker | farm laborer | 1 | | |
| | day laborer | 2 | day laborer | 2 |
| | milk business | 1 | milk business | 9 |
| | dyer fabrics | 4 | dyer fabrics | 17 |
| | painter | 1 | | – |
| | hotel keeper | 1 | | – |
| | workman | 1 | workman | 1 |

| Occupation in Friesland | Paterson 1900 | N | Paterson 1910 | N |
| --- | --- | --- | --- | --- |
| | store keeper | 2 | storekeeper | 1 |
| | | | businessman | 2 |
| | | | farmer | 3 |
| | | | carpenter | 3 |
| | | | laborer silk | 6 |
| | | | freight driver | 4 |
| | | | unknown | 2 |
| | | | hired hand | 1 |
| | | | fireman | 1 |
| | | | retired | 1 |
| | | | railroad clerk | 1 |
| **Total** | | 13 | | 54 |
| housewife | housewife | 17 | housewife | 52 |
| | | | hired females | 3 |
| | | | unknown/nojob | 12 |
| **Total** | | 17 | | 67 |
| carpenter | milk business | 1 | | |
| carpenter apprentice | carpenter | 3 | carpenter | 2 |
| | farm hand | 1 | | |
| | | | gardener | 1 |
| | | | laborer silk | 1 |
| | | | machine maker | 1 |
| **Total** | | 5 | | 5 |

**Source:** Galema, "Linked Files: Frisians to America and Frisians in the U.S.A. Computer Compilation"

Many Frisian immigrants frequently changed jobs until they found one to their satisfaction. Generally, the wages in Paterson were higher than in Friesland. Durk Willems Zuidema, for example, emigrated with his family from Lichtaard, Ferwerderadeel when he was sixteen. His father died during the ocean passage and was buried at sea. Zuidema had worked fourteen-hour days in Friesland as a carpenter's apprentice. After arrival in Paterson, he took a job driving a team of horses for three dollars a week, and his brother Siemen obtained a job for the same wage. The Zuidemas considered their wages very good compared to those in Friesland. Later Durk had a job in an iron foundry where he made up to eleven dollars during some weeks. After two years he returned to his original profession and became a carpenter's helper, which later led to the beginning of his own successful construction business.[71]

The economic motive was the primary cause for Pieter Westerhuis who emigrated in 1881 from the municipality of Het Bildt in Friesland. He stated in a letter that "work" and "bread" were his reasons for staying in Paterson.[72] F. Ramella found the same motivation for a group of Italian workers that migrated to Paterson and its silk centers in the 1890s. For them America seemed to be synonymous with good wages and a variety of jobs.[73]

In the silk industry, where Frisians worked particularly in dyeing and weaving, before World War I the Netherlanders were outnumbered only by Germans, English, Italians, and Irish.[74] In New Jersey the federal government prepared the figures from information collected in 1907 from 138 of the 218 silk weaving and throwing companies in Paterson. The Dutch made up 8 percent of the employed men of sixteen years and older, while the largest groups in this category were Italians with 24 percent and English with 20 percent. Of the employed women of sixteen years and older, the Dutch at 13 percent ranked behind Irish (20), English (18), Germans (14), and Italians (14). Curious in this respect are the figures for children under sixteen years of age. The number of Dutch children in these factories ranked behind the Italians (30 percent) at the top of this statistic: 21 percent of the children under sixteen in the mills were of Dutch descent.[75]

The Dutch, like the Germans, distinguished themselves as hard workers and therefore were generally considered desirable employees. Frisians particularly worked in the dyeing industry, which only employed men and boys. The dye house was the most dirty and unhealthy part of the silk industry.[76] The jobs of the Frisians in my linkage group sometimes involved precision work, and in some cases they became foremen in the silk industry. The Frisians were sometimes responsible for the finishing touches in the silk mills, where also some women and girls were employed. The very exacting task of "degumming" the silk was assigned to Dutch-Frisians. It involved boiling the raw silk in a soap solution to dissolve the layer of sericin, a process that imparted a beautiful softness and sheen to the silk. This was a very hot job requiring close supervision to prevent part of the sericin from sticking to the silk.

Generally, however, the northern Frisians did the unskilled and semi-skilled tasks in the silk mills. This is in contrast to the Italian and English immigrants who were skilled workers and who stayed in the same professions after migration to Paterson. The Italians and English profited from their old country experience and had a widespread *belief* that opportunities for upward occupational mobility were present in Paterson.[77]

The contemporary belief of better occupational possibilities could also be found among Frisian immigrants.

Around the turn of the century the average pay was $ 12.50 per week. Two decades before, J.G. Boekhout, an immigrant from Het Bildt wrote to Friesland:

> I don't work on the railroad anymore. Nowadays I work in the silk mill and I make seven guilders a week and that doesn't sound too bad to me...[78].

The historian H. Sannes, who wrote a history of Het Bildt, mentions that day laborers with a permanent job earned 5 to 6.5 guilders a week during summer time and 3 to 5 guilders during winter time. These amounts were averages for the Frisian clay areas.[79] A field laborer only made 180 to 290 guilders a year, due to the fact that "rain hours" were subtracted. In the last decades of the nineteenth century, temporary or seasonal laborers were very often unemployed during the winter. We may conclude that the Frisian immigrants considered their wages in the silk industry as good.[80] The same results are found in research concerning the Italian skilled textile workers who migrated to Paterson. F. Ramella states that the local factory workers of Biella in Italy believed that wages in the silk mills of New Jersey were very high.[81] Regarding social status and hierarchy, the labor force in the silk mills was structured along the lines of skill and ethnic origin, with the English and German speaking workers at the top, followed by the skilled Italian weavers and the unskilled Frisians.

As was shown above, many of these Frisian migrants were agricultural laborers primarily from the area of Het Bildt. In the letters of J.G. Boekhout, the emphasis is repeatedly on the fact that he and his fellow immigrants all had jobs. In 1883 he mentions again: "and I still have a job in the factory.... so we do have work close to home and brother Sjoerd again started to dig cellars."[82]

It seems that Pieter Westerhuis in 1882 tried to justify his decision to exchange Friesland for Paterson, because he wrote "home" that he heard that the Frisian field laborers experienced a very bad situation again during that year. So he concluded: "For a man who needs work to make a living, I think there is no better place than Paterson, because those who have children can let them all work in the factory."

More than a decade later Tjerk Zondervan wrote about the work in the silk mills and confirmed that his children Antje and Hiltje also had jobs there.[83] Pieter Westerhuis had other ideas about finding his fortune. The aspiration of buying a farm in the Midwest or in the Far West still seems to have been present in the heart of this Paterson immigrant. In the same letter he wrote:

> but if you have money you can better go West. Iege Mulder bought a farm in the state of Iowa and he got very lucky because in the summer they put a railroad through his land and for that he got so much money that he at once could pay for his whole farm.[84]

When Sjouke de Zee visited the Frisians in the Paterson area, he noticed that some immigrants had worked in the factories to make enough money to start their own farm. Sikke Dijkstra and Rinske Noordbeek from Het Bildt started a chicken and cattle farm in 1918, after Dijkstra had worked in the silk mill for eight years. Dijkstra's Frisian Holstein cattle all were subscribed in the Frisian Holstein Herdbook, the equivalent of the *Fryske Stamboek* and he won an award from the National Dairy Association. Although Dijkstra had some negative experiences with tuberculosis among his cattle he assured Sjouke de Zee in 1928:

I don't have anything to complain though, because when I started to farm 10 years ago, I even was not able to milk cows. The English that I know is not good at all, but I have money in my pocket and then you can manage it here in Amerika. The most stupid farmer very often has the biggest potatoes and my wife and I just stay simple, that's what we like best.[85]

Sjouke de Zee mentions many more immigrants around Paterson from the northern clay area who had started a farm when he visited in 1928. Again it becomes clear that the immigrants from the same region of origin in northern Friesland remained in touch after their move to the United States. It was not very exceptional that Pieter Westerhuis was well informed concerning his fellow Frisian immigrants. It seems they were all eager to know how friends from the old country were doing. And Frisians in Paterson also remained interested in the economic situation in the Netherlands. When W.A. Eisma visited chicken farmer Paulus van Dijk in the surroundings of Paterson in 1936, Van Dijk wanted to know everything about the leading businessmen of Leeuwarden of forty years earlier. This interest is understandable, especially because many emigrants were penniless when they left Friesland. This low socio-economic status made their later desire to compare even more understandable.

The economic situation in Paterson and vicinity could not always bear close scrutiny. There are a few complaints about the hardships of getting a good start in Paterson. In 1895 the Groninger immigrant Klaas Udes wrote from Paterson:

Concerning social matters it is not very good here, everything languishes. Hundreds are without jobs, strikes etc. are the order of the day, sometimes leading to blood and mayhem, the ones who still work make only half of the usual money. However, it is not as bad as last winter. Then they were distributing bread etc to 8,000 persons a day, and then there were probably many more who were ashamed and experienced secret poverty.... Truitje and Hiltje are in the Factory where they make silk worms, and earn 17.50 Dollars in 2 weeks. Jan works in carpentry and earns 4 dollars in 2 weeks. I have not made much money, because we earned half a dollar a day less than usual....[86]

When the Frisians arrived in Paterson, the area was already densely populated with various ethnic groups. The two decades after the Civil War were a period of mill expansion in Passaic County and a great influx of immigrants from Italy, Poland, Russia, and the Austro-Hungarian empire took up the slack in the labor market.[87] Because of the technological changes many older skilled workers were replaced by cheaper unskilled new immigrants. This resulted in animosity which was well established before the turn of the century. As Klaas Udes mentions in his letter, strikes were the order of the day. In 1887, for example, employers fueled group animosity because they used recently arrived southern Italian and Armenian immigrants as strike breakers to frustrate wage increases demanded by older, skilled workers. Living conditions for most of the mill workers usually were overcrowded, unsanitary, and unhealthy. Mill owners had political control and effectively kept the immigrants out of politics during those days.[88] The result was that immigrants stayed among themselves and produced culture islands in the city. In 1900 the total number of foreign born in Paterson was almost 37 percent, and the proportion working in the silk mills was about 50 percent.[89] In a case study of class, status, and community power in Paterson in the nineteenth century Herbert G. Gutman states that in immigrant groups economic power was not easily translated into political power and the changes resulting from rapid industrialization caused opposition to the industrialists.[90] Paterson experienced many strikes; in 1906 the militant Industrial Workers of the World (I.W.W.) staged twenty-four strikes in Paterson alone. In 1913 a gigantic industry wide strike began in the Paterson silk mills. Generally around the turn of the century, the city had a reputation of labor unrest and union activity.[91]

Frisian socialists and prominent leaders in the labor movement, who left for Paterson participated as well. Jan Stap (1859-1908), the field laborer and vice-chairman of the society *Broedertrouw* emigrated in 1896 from St. Jacobi-parochie to Paterson. In the same year Tjeerd Stienstra (1859-1935), radical member of the *Socialistenbond* in Friesland, arrived in the city.[92] After years of radical labor action Jan Stap appeared to be very disappointed concerning the achievements of the social-democratic labor movement in Friesland.

A rift in his labor society *Broedertrouw* in 1891 caused more than 100 people from Het Bildt to emigrate to the United States.[93] Tjeerd Stienstra departed to America for more personal reasons: he had troubles with his wife.[94] Both men had relatives in Paterson when they emigrated.[95]

There is no evidence that these people left for political reasons precisely to Paterson. From a biography of Tjeerd Stienstra it is known that he was involved in a Paterson-branch of the Dutch *Socialistenbond,* where many Frisian immigrants from the area of Harlingen associated for some years. Jan Stap was one of them and their chairman was R. Nakken, former chairman of the Dutch *Sociaal Democratische Bond* in Franeker. Tjeerd was also a member of the Socialist Labor Party for a while, but after 1900 he turned his back on revolutionary socialism.[96] I could not find Stienstra and Stap in the membership list of the Industrial Workers of the World in Paterson.[97]

Tjeerd Stienstra had an older brother Tjibbe, also active in revolutionary Beetgum in the 1890s, who emigrated earlier to the silk city and who made a living in a tailor shop. Tjeerd worked as a tailor too, and first had his shop in Little Falls, and later in Paterson. When in 1900 his younger brother Klaas – with revolutionary spirit too – and his mother came from Friesland to join him, many Stienstra family members were together. Klaas also started in tailoring but later opened a variety store with goods like spices, candy, toys, books, and stationery. Having shops on the opposite side of the street, the brothers Tjibbe and Klaas profited from each others' clientele, according to Sjouke de Zee who visited the Stienstras in 1921 and 1928. De Zee favored Klaas' comedy skills and literary qualities, but he does not mention anything about labor movement participation by these immigrants in their native country or in contemporary Paterson.

In the meantime Tjeerd had returned to his old cause of land nationalization, having founded the Fair Hope Single Tax Colony on Mobile Bay, Alabama. In 1903 he moved there with his two sons.[98] Klaas Stienstra married a Frisian immigrant girl in Paterson and was an intense supporter of the Frisian cultural society *Utspanning troch Ynspanning*. This was not exceptional because Klaas and Tjeerd both were very musical. In Friesland they had been active in the socio-cultural circuit. In 1891 they had their *Socialistische Zang- en Propagandaclub* [Socialist Song and Propaganda Club] together with their cousin, where Tjeerd sang songs written by himself, while Klaas played guitar. In 1895 Klaas appeared to be the first Frisian writer who wrote a play with a revolutionary spirit, called *Dy Godloazen* [The Godless]. After being disappointed by revolutionary socialism in 1896 and 1897, Klaas did not write any play or song with a political theme.[99] He did send all kinds of literary work to the Frisian journal *Sljucht en Rjucht*, but his subjects concerned nature, American seasons, and his youth in the village of Beetgum. In Friesland this literary work has been criticized as parochial and narrow minded. It seems that Klaas Stienstra started a new life in Paterson. Correspondence from Klaas to Friesland and the fact that in the 1970s his son did not know anything about his father's revolutionary background supports this conclusion.[100]

Refraining from politics after immigration seems to have been quite common, although gifts for Jan Stap's *Broedertrouw* came from America.[101] Financial support from socialist sympathizers in America seems to have happened more often. The journal of the Dutch Social Democratic Party (SDP) mentions in 1889 that socialists in America collected money for striking miners in Germany.[102]

There are indications that the denominational preference of the Dutch settlers sometimes determined their chances of getting certain jobs. Van Hinte mentions that, although Hollanders were generally looked upon as desirable employees, employers sometimes preferred members of the Christian Reformed Church, among them many Frisians. Employers liked the idea that these workers considered strikes to be in conflict with their religious beliefs. Van Hinte describes how great this preference of employers could be: it was made evident to him in Paterson that a well-known manufacturer hired only employees who belonged to this denomination.[103]

Sietze J. Boonstra who emigrated in 1910 from St. Annaparochie to Paterson, describes the network that made occupational ventures among Hollanders possible:

> ...at the moment, with the coming winter, I have come into the factory in a surprising way. Willem Rozendal lives here too and he quit working and because his son in law is boss or foreman in the factory, I thought to replace him [Rozendal], but his place was already taken, but he told me he would think of me, and he kept his promise, so I work in a silk factory now and make 9 dollar in 55 hours, so you may think that he who has work here does a lot better than in Holland.[104]

In the last chapter of this study I will come back to aspects of political aspirations among Frisian immigrants in the United States.

To know about other Frisians and to find support was a much easier enterprise once the immigrant belonged to the same religious denomination as other Frisians. The Paterson Frisians showed a more diverse ecclesiastical background. The linkage group contained not only a majority of *Nederlands Hervormde* immigrants, but also 9 percent who had been without any religious affiliation.

Table 6.5 **Netherlands religious affiliation of northern Frisian immigrants, Paterson area, 1910:**

| Denomination | Number | % linkage group |
| --- | --- | --- |
| Nederlands Hervormd | 233 | 61 % |
| Christelijk Gereformeerd | 66 | 17 % |
| Gereformeerd | 37 | 9 % |
| None | 33 | 9 % |
| Unknown | 11 | 3 % |
| Baptist | 3 | 1 % |
| **Total** | 383 | 100 % |

**Source:** Galema, "Linked Files: Frisians to America and Frisians in the U.S.A. Computer Compilations"

Since almost half of the linkage group in Paterson had its origin in the municipality of Het Bildt, the percentage of Frisians without a religious affiliation is understandable. From 1880 until 1910 201 immigrants without any denominational affiliation left Het Bildt for America. But my expectation that Frisian non-believers especially went to the industry of Paterson does not seem to be very realistic. It seems to be true, though, that religious affiliation and emigration in Het Bildt were related. People without religious affinity only started to leave this municipality after the 1890s. It may be possible that a relation between the labor movement and this secular pattern in emigration existed. I will come back to this in the last chapter.

The religious preferences of the Frisian linkage group in Paterson are hard to determine quantitatively. No U.S. Censuses give individual information concerning religion. Other research and sources like ecclesiastical histories or biographical sketches and church membership lists reveal the rapid growth of the Dutch Reformed churches in Passaic County until the close of the nineteenth century. The Sixth Holland Reformed Church of Paterson at that time, for example, had as many as 875 communicant members. Until about the time of World War I, these Dutch churches with many late-nineteenth century Dutch and Frisian immigrants, almost exclusively used the Dutch language in their services.[105]

In an article in the 1980s about his youth in Paterson, an emeritus professor of Calvin College in Grand Rapids, Michigan, stated that "religion did not dominate Paterson as it did Orange City, Iowa, but it dominated the lives of the Christian Reformed churches in Paterson and neighboring areas."[106]

Only some of the Frisian immigrants in Paterson associated with the Reformed and Christian Reformed churches. Some also joined various small house churches which were not covered in any official statistics. Van Hinte remarks that in Pella, Iowa, Sunday worship services were held in seventeen different places for a population of three thousand mostly Dutchmen.[107] Some more independent minded Frisians also may have refused to join any established church. After all, the percentage of non-believers who left Friesland for America has to be considered. It happened that immigrants who were not church members in Friesland did associate with one of the Dutch Reformed churches in America. They needed the ethnic network that Dutch immigrants created for mutual support in all kinds of matters in their new environment. The Frisian writer B.S. Hylkema, who visited the Paterson community pointed out this phenomenon:

> Several of our countrymen, who formerly hardly did not know a reverend, became religious and steady church visiters. Most of them already are swayed on the boat, this is told to me more than once. It is not easy to find a good explanation for that, but it seems to me that the feeling of insecurity and the missing of contacts in a strange environment are the most important causes.[108]

Hylkema also noticed that the *dominies* in America had methods to win support for their churches. He was astonished by shops next to the church building to make money and to encourage churchgoing.[109] That the Dutch language churches in particular, were concerned for newcomers also is clear from a brochure that was published in 1915 in Paterson, with all kinds of information for people who disembarked in Hoboken or Ellis Island. Reverend S. Zandstra from Little Falls, New Jersey, met the newcomers and gave them a "welcome" brochure from the Reformed Church in America that included addresses of preachers in the Dutch language churches all over the country.[110]

A reminder of the old country background was also the Christian schools. Because American public education was deemed too secular, the first Christian School was opened in Paterson in 1892, the second in 1899, and by 1927 four Christian elementary schools and one Christian high school could be found in the Paterson area.[111] All were populated by children of Dutch descent and with faculty members who had graduated from Calvin College, Grand Rapids.
A Dutch-language press also existed in Paterson. The most important newspapers were *De Telegraaf* and *Het Oosten*. The first extensively covered national and international affairs, while the latter concentrated more on local news and religion items relating to the Dutch churches of New Jersey. Cultural pluralism was fostered by the creation of Dutch organizations as well, such as the men's organization *Tot Nut van 't Algemeen* [To Public Welfare], and the ladies society *Harmonie*. These organizations met regularly and planned cultural events such as Dutch songfests and dramas. Secular Frisians in Paterson had their own cultural society *Utspanning troch Ynspanning* [Recreation through Effort]. The organization was founded on June 13,

1893, inspired by a small group of Frisians who had played Sunday handball games [*keatsen*] at the Bunker Hill section of northern Paterson. These Sunday games attracted many spectators and were "looked forward to by many a lonesome toiler somewhat bewildered in a strange country."[112] Dirk (*Richard*) Klazes Hoitsma, who emigrated from the village of Wijnaldum, Barradeel, became the first President.[113] Using his company's stationery ("Richard K. Hoitsma. Real Estate and Mortgage Loans") he wrote to Friesland in 1929 about the first sports events:

> When I came here in 1888, we went to Bunker Hill (a suburb of Paterson) very soon, where all kinds of Frisians gathered and as the *keatse* balls flew over the grass of Bunker Hill, in our minds we were back in the old fatherland.[114]

From 1893 dramatic presentations in the Frisian language were held first in Polak Hall on Fair Street, later on in Highland Hall. The capacity of this hall was soon overtaxed and a larger hall was secured on Lafayette Street and in 1911 a change was made to Schumpf Hall on Cross Street. In the first decade of *Utspanning troch Ynspanning*, about twenty Frisians were members. It was a typical northwestern Frisian society because the first members – like President Richard Hoitsma –, came almost exclusively from the clay area. After 1910 the society grew to 100 members and in 1921 Guild Hall was purchased and restored for its benefit.[115] At first the main entertainment of *Utspanning troch Ynspanning* concerned *keatsen* and picnics in summer, and theater plays and *Onderonsje* [cosy talks] in winter. For example, plays and comedies and other literary works of Klaas Stienstra were performed.[116] Later, they invited entertainers, writers and speakers directly from Friesland. That way, for example, in 1911 the singer Anne Steensma came to sing Frisian songs, the writer Bonne Sjoukes Hylkema visited in 1923, and writer and orator Sjouke de Zee appeared in 1922 and 1928.[117]

Ice skating games were also a favorite, a choir existed for some time, a brass band enlivened the *keats* games for several years, and a steadily increasing library with Dutch and Frisian books served the newcomers and members. Several times a box with silver Frisian spoons was sent over the ocean to honor the winners of the *keats* games. These silver spoons are an old Frisian custom, and also serve as a present for newborns.[118] *Utspanning troch Ynspanning* was in touch with other Frisian cultural *Selskippen* [societies] in Rochester (*Ny Fryslân*), Chicago (*Ut en Thús*), Grand Rapids (*Friso*), and Holland, Michigan (*Jounenocht*). Very often the activities of the society were published in the Dutch newspaper *Het Oosten* in Paterson and results of festivities were also reported to newspapers in Friesland like the *Franeker Courant*, the weeklies *Slucht en Rjucht*, and *It Heitelân.*[119]

It seems clear that the Frisians who founded *Utspanning troch Ynspanning* were not affiliated with the Reformed Church or the CRC in Paterson. Participation in athletics on Sundays was forbidden for members of the both denominations. In Reformed circles only works of necessity or mercy were sanctioned on Sunday. No room existed for organized sports nor for individual or family recreation. This supports the idea that the Frisians who played the *keats* games on Sundays in Paterson in 1893 most likely were not associated with any denomination. Incorporation of recreational sports as a legitimate feature on Sundays was realized much later in the Reformed churches. Only after the 1950s was strict Sunday observance no longer acclaimed without reservation.[120] And of course, individual interpretations always found their way. In 1908 a Frisian woman wrote from Chicago to northern Friesland:

> You probably will think: writing letters on Sunday. I have considered that, but it seems that I can't find a moment's peace to write during week days. After all, it is pure charitable work, this writing.[121]

### 6.4 Frisian immigrants and the American metropole: Chicago

As John Timmerman reminisced about his hometown of Paterson in the 1920s and 1930s, he emphasized living in a homogeneous Dutch community within the circles of the CRC. Timmerman's father was the Reverend John Timmerman, a minister in the Christian Reformed Church. Although his socio-cultural life was largely confined to this homogeneous environment, Timmerman recalls the fascination of his membership in a multicultural baseball team: "it widened my associations with society outside our exclusivistic Dutch community. Without it I would never have been friends of diverse ethnic backgrounds with names like Schillinger, Wentink, Terry, Brewer, Granito, 'Yankee' Renzo, 'Porky' DeLucio, and the like."[122] However, Timmerman's reminisces are not representative for the Frisian community.

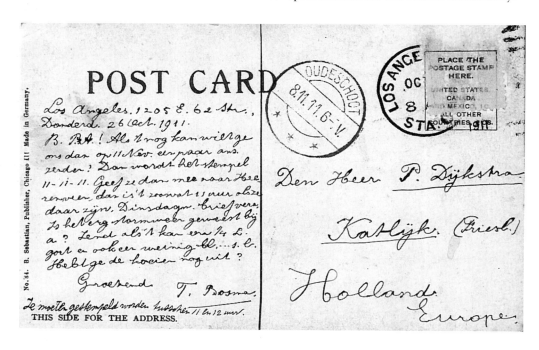

*Postcard written by F. Bosma in Los Angeles to P. Dijkstra in Katlijk, Friesland, October 26, 1911*

It was very common to be a member of a multicultural sporting club, and Timmerman's considerations emphasize a general pattern. The occupational, cultural, and religious life of the Frisian immigrants must have been influenced by their environment. While one might expect that the lives of those who lived in a rural environment in an almost exclusively Dutch community were more dominated by religion than the lives of those who lived in the cities, this was not the case. Although the city provided the multi-cultural perspective, the urban Frisian immigrants drew together more tightly than those in rural environments, because they felt more threatened. It is likely that the city Frisians were stronger ethnics because of the threatening environment.

To obtain ideas about the urban Frisian immigrants in the United States, data on Frisians in other cities than Paterson deserve attention. Timmerman's story of Paterson shows that beliefs and perceptions of relations with American society reflected the differentiations among the Dutch population.
For Frisian immigrants the first impression of American cities usually was an astonishing acquaintance:

> Oh Jantje, what a big city it is here, you can never believe it. They say it almost never ends, and what huge houses. I have seen houses with three hundred windows and if you would be here it would surprise you. One says that about eleven thousand Hollanders live here in Chicago. We live here in a big house. The owner leases seven rooms in this home where we live, she lives here herself too, we live next to her. Its all Hollanders in this house, and what strange faces does one see here, pitch-black men, women and children, and Chinese, they have strange faces too, those men carry long braids in the hair, like women....[123]

The impression of a young lady on the matter of Chicago in the early 1880s shows that becoming acquainted with the big city was an overwhelming experience. At that time Chicago's population had increased to more than 600,000. Two decades later Douwe Dijkstra expresses his admiration for Chicago by writing "it is beautiful again in the city nowadays. At night it looks even greater than it did in the past when we had Prinsesses Birthday on August 31."[124]
In addition to Paterson, Chicago and Grand Rapids were the preferred cities of northern Frisian settlement. In Rochester, New York, I traced only four northern Frisian immigrant households in 1900. Among the Hollanders in Chicago in 1900 I was able to locate 469 Frisian born or of Frisian descent. Most of them lived in the southern suburb of Roseland, which was founded by immigrants from Noord-Holland.[125] The origin of these Frisians was randomly distributed over the clay municipalities, although the share of Wonseradeel was very low. The village of Ee in Oostdongeradeel provided 20 people to Chicago between 1880-1900. Seventy-six northern Frisian households could be linked. The average Frisian family in Chicago was a nuclear family of 5.6 persons. It was a couple with children and usually without any live-in servants or boarders (63 percent). Nearly one quarter (23 percent) of the families had relatives, servants, or other domestics living

*Pieter Groustra with his third wife Jantje de Boer and his son Cornelis and daughter (most likely: Geeske)*

in their home, while 14 percent had no children at the time of the Census report.[126] The Frisian families contained slightly more sons than daughters in 1900 and in the seventy-six linked households only one boarder lived. Of all the household heads only one was a female single parent. This is an amazingly low number, especially after reading so much about immigrant hardships. Immigrants who lost their husband or wife must have remarried after a relatively short time.

Van Hinte speaks highly of the Frisian acumen for business.[127] Occupationally, the northern Frisians in Chicago in 1900 showed a well-known pattern. Menial unskilled and semiskilled jobs prevailed. Some 24 percent were truck farmers. Compared to the figures for the city of Paterson, this percentage is quite high. This was due to the fact that Roseland was an outskirts truck farming village, which was connected to Chicago in the first decade after 1900. Most of the agricultural work of the Frisians was in the vicinity of Chicago, in the southern suburb of Roseland.[128] Around the turn of the century Roseland was the garden center of the city of Chicago, although the huge city was rapidly encroaching. A region with an even bigger concentration of Dutch immigrants in vegetable gardening, the Calumet area a few hours by horseback further south, profited from the transition of Roseland to an urbanized neighborhood of Chicago. Via Chicago and Roseland, the Douma family from Minnertsga, for example, finally settled in the Calumet region where they grew onions, tomatoes, pickles, sugar beets, corn, and wheat.[129] Calumet remains an attractive economic center for Dutch immigrants even to the present. It provided the new settlers with old country values like land ownership and entrepreneurship.[130]

Industrial jobs involved 38 percent of the northern Frisians, while 16 percent worked in services and transport. The remainder (22 percent) can be ascribed to the unemployed (9 percent) and to people whose occupation was unknown or unclear (13 percent). In the linkage group, only three wives of the heads of household had a job outside the home too.[131]

Analyzing the occupational status before and after immigration in Chicago, the northern Frisian linkage group shows the following pattern:

Table 6.6  **Main occupations in Friesland linked with occupations in Chicago and vicinity in 1900:**

| Occupation in Friesland | | Occupation in Chicago | |
|---|---|---|---|
| Workman, laborer | 44 | workman, laborer | 7 |
| | | carshop | 6 |
| | | farmer | 11 |
| | | factory laborer | 5 |
| | | overseer factory | 1 |
| | | carpenter, wagonmaker | 4 |
| | | storekeeper | 3 |
| | | other | 4 |
| | | unknown | 3 |
| | | total | 44 |
| Farm laborer | 3 | workman | 2 |
| | | wagonmaker | 1 |
| | | total | 3 |
| Farmer, small farmer | 3 | carshop | 1 |
| | | workman | 1 |
| | | farmer | 1 |
| | | total | 3 |
| Shipper (peat/coal etc.) | 3 | farmer | 1 |
| | | carshop | 1 |
| | | workman | 1 |
| | | total | 3 |
| Carpenter, wagonmaker | 4 | carpenter | 3 |
| | | carshop | 1 |
| | | total | 4 |
| Store keeper | 1 | carshop | 1 |
| | | total | 1 |
| Buyer, retailer | 3 | farmer | 1 |
| | | peddler | 1 |
| | | bricklayer | 1 |
| | | total | 3 |
| **Total** | **61** | | **61** |

**Source:** Galema, "Linked Files: Frisians to America and Frisians in the U.S.A. Computer Compilation"

The occupational stratification of Chicago (table 6.6) makes clear that in the big city the occupational ventures were more diverse than in a small town like Whitinsville.[132] It is evident though that some concentration of the Frisian workforce took place in the carshop, which means the Pullman factory of railroad cars.

George Pullman had founded his shop in 1880 in Pullman, a few miles east of Roseland. Pullman provided jobs for the Dutch over a long period, among them many northern Frisians. The occupational term "carshop" did not cover the whole category of Frisians working at Pullman. Frisians did all the jobs in building fancy Pullman sleeping coaches with wood-lined interiors. Pieter Groustra and his sons, for example, worked in carpentry at Pullman.[133] Immigrants relied on the factory work of the Pullman shops. In 1881 F.H. Toering wrote about it to his native country with self-confidence:

> I think I will keep my job at *poelman* this coming winter. Anyway, otherwise I will cut reed or in the ice cellar. [on Lake Calumet]. Work enough and the day wages do not become lower....[134]

George Pullman founded an experimental city where his employees could live. This corresponds with company housing at the Whitin Machine Shop in Massachusetts. The offering of houses by employers was an appealing idea for newly arrived Frisian immigrants and evidently attracted many.[135] They felt safer, more comfortable, and healthier. In the linkage group in 1900 only 15 (23 percent) of the 61 households in Chicago owned their home (8 free of mortgage) and 46 rented; one had a farm mortgaged, and thirteen rented. That means that 78 percent of the northern Frisian households in Chicago and vicinity rented in 1900. This percentage was a lot higher than in Grand Rapids, where 61 percent rented in 1900, while

*Board of the Roseland Mutual Aid Society, 1934*

34 percent owned their homes free. It is clear that farms required far more capital, especially around Chicago.

In 1884 Frisians were involved in starting the Roseland Mutual Aid Society [*De Roselandsche Onderlinge Hulpvereeniging bij Overlijden*], which tried to defray the expenses and relieve the material stress connected with the funerals in Dutch families. Some four hundred Dutch members enrolled in the first years, and after twenty-five years there was a total enrollment of more than 4000 members.[136] A Frisian social club was organized much later: in 1925 the society *Ut en Thús* [Away and Home] started activities like *keatsen*, Frisian dancing, and talks on Frisian literature and history. Before this creation of an ethnic social club, Frisians had been members of Dutch clubs like the Sint Nikolaas Society and the Knickerbocker Society. This means that only after Frisians had gained a solid foothold in the urban Chicago environment, their ethnic consciousness was translated into a specific Frisian society.[137]

### 6.5 In the capital city of the Dutch: Grand Rapids

The Dutch settlement patterns in the city of Grand Rapids around 1900 were not based upon a common Dutch identity, but reflected the immigrants' diverse provincial origins, their time of arrival, and their religious affiliation.[138] In Grand Rapids Frisian immigrants similarly congregated in one branch of industry. Of the 52 percent who worked in industry, 32 percent were employed in the furniture business. The number of craftsmen in Grand Rapids was therefore large.[139] There is evidence that not all the immigrants liked factory work. Young people went out of Grand Rapids to do seasonal work on the surrounding farms in lieu of factory jobs. The Lautenbach family reported it to Friesland:

> Steven and Sijts are not at home this summer. They work at a farmer about 3 hours from here. They don't like to work in the factory. Within a few months they most likely will be finished with their work. Then he has to do factory work again. Jan does not go to the factory for 5 years already, because he is ill very often and then they can not handle it very well.[140]

Some immigrants could not find their niche at all. In 1896 a letter of Age Boukes Cnossen to a friend in Paterson reveals the tough situation of mutual help:

> It is probably known that brother Martinus also came over in 1892. Well, he most likely does not belong to the living people anymore. He has had his home at our place, when he was not at a farmer's. But he is not much of an American, and spent most of the winter of 93 to 94 at our home behind the stove. We also had Gerrit, a son of Hotze de Boer, *dito, dito,* he did nothing, so in spring M. was 80 and G. 63 dollars board in debt. Fortunately I had steady income at that time and what happened: on April 17 '94 I came home and my wife said that the boys were in the country for work. I said that was about time, but none of the two came back, neither a dollar. They wrote a post card ten days later from Chicago and wanted to go further....[141]

The story of Martinus Cnossen reveals that he later lived with his cousin and friend Siebren Wybes Cnossen and with their cattle in a hole in the hills (known as a dugout) around Holland, Michigan. When cousin Franke Jelles Cnossen came to visit the two men during winter time when work was slow, he usually found a cosy atmosphere of "eating, smoking, talking and a *slokje* on time" but not a very profitable situation.[142]

Living in the hills was not common among Frisian immigrants. The residential behavior of the Dutch in Grand Rapids showed some extraordinary patterns. In his dissertation David Vanderstel claimed that new immigrants sometimes were hesitant to live in parts of Grand Rapids with older contingents of Dutch settlers, because they perceived a potential threat to their socio-cultural baggage from the already Americanized Hollanders. The locational pattern was also contrary to typical historical premises that immigrants entered the city centers and then later moved to the suburbs, while their homes were occupied by newly arrived immigrants. In Grand Rapids some of the Dutch immigrants at arrival settled in newly developed neighborhoods.[143]

In the last half of the nineteenth century there were twelve distinct clusters of Dutch immigrants in Grand Rapids. Most of the northern Frisians were situated in the West Leonard-Alpine neighborhood. By 1900 more than

A Brook in the Outskirts of Grand Rapids
*Een beekje in de omstreken v. G.R.*

*Postcard of F. Bosma from Webberville, MI, to Langweer in Friesland, January 5, 1906*

1000 Dutch households resided in this northwest sector of the city. The majority of the Frisians originated in the municipalities of Barradeel and Ferwerderadeel. Each Dutch enclave in Grand Rapids had its own uniqueness and showed distinct characteristics compared to other Dutch concentrations, and also to urban enclaves of other nationalities.[144] Frisians in Grand Rapids also settled in the neighborhoods of Canal-North Division in the center of the city close to the Grand River.[145] Vanderstel's detailed description of the Dutch neighborhoods confirms the supposition that Frisian immigrants brought their village identity to urban centers in the new country. This was not typical for Frisian settlers only. Zeelanders, Gelderlanders, and Groningers showed the same residential characteristics. A typical *Groninger Hoek* [Corner] existed in Grand Rapids on Franklin and Madison streets. However, immigrants from other Dutch regions did not establish, like the Frisians, a cultural society based on ethnic background. The *Selskip Friso* promoted the use of the Frisian language, and organized theater plays, parties, and other amusements. It also provided a kind of simple health insurance facility, which took care of sick Frisian members.[146]

In summary, the study of particular Frisian communities in the United States made clear that during the whole period 1880-1914 emigrants from the Frisian clay area entered America through a complex network of kinship, communal associations, and commercial information. After settlement the Frisians tried to rejuvenate and once again exploit old relationships that they brought with them in a continuous process of transformation. In this sense they could be called "transplanted." In Whitinsville, Massachusetts, kith and kin directed the social and economic patterns of the Frisians. These immigrants, coming from two municipalities in Friesland, entered a rapidly growing community where mainly industrial jobs were available. There was no problem in finding jobs, as long as the Frisians were pragmatic in their choice. In the decade 1900-1910 the occupational structure of the Frisians almost remained the same, except for a few who had started as an independent farmer.

Whitinsville, with a population of Yankees, Frisians, Irish, Armenians, and French Canadians, provided the ingredients to test the theory of the American melting pot. The various national-origin groups worked cooperatively in the mill and machine shops, but after hours each group retreated behind familiar social bounderies. The religious and social life of the Frisians was focused on the Christian Reformed Church, the French-Canadians and Irish clustered together around their Catholic church, and the Armenians were similarly clannish. Yankees who expected Europeans to assimilate the social and cultural patterns of traditional New England were disappointed, because the restauration of the homogeneous Yankee past gained little or no support from Whitinsville's newcomers. Like the other groups, Frisians did not abandon their heritage, which is clear from the fact that according to the 1910 Census, none of them married outside the ethnic group.

Frisians who settled in Paterson, New Jersey, entered an urban area which was engaged in mechanical and manufacturing pursuits and which was leading in industry in the state. In Paterson, around the turn of the century in Prospect Park and Peoples Park, exclusive Frisian neighborhoods existed. Most Frisians in the city came from the municipality of Het Bildt. Their pre-migration occupational status was found in agriculture, and in Paterson they mainly had jobs in industry, working in the silk mills, in handicrafts, or as independent painters and bakers. Occupational progress of the Frisians in the decade 1900-1910 was clear from the comparison of jobs before and after emigration.

Frisians faced the social unrest that was present among the Paterson industrial workers around 1900. Some of the Frisian immigrants had been labor activists in the old country. However, there is no evidence that they left for political reasons precisely to Paterson, or, that they took actively part in the American labor organizations like the Industrial Workers of the World. Some of them were active in the Frisian cultural society in Paterson, *Utspanning troch Ynspanning*, but this was not particularly revolutionary minded. Dramatic presentations in the Frisian language were held, summer picnics and the game of *keatsen* was favourite among it's members. Contacts existed between the Frisian societies in different cities, for example *Ny Fryslân* in Rochester, *Ut en Thús* in Chicago, *Friso* in Grand Rapids, and *Jounenocht* in Holland, and the character of the activities showed a secular bias.

Frisians in Chicago concentrated in the southern suburb of Chicago. The origin of these Frisians was randomly distributed over the clay municipalities, and the average family was a nuclear family of 5.6 persons. Many of the Chicago Frisians made a living in truck farming, which provided the settlers with old country values like land ownership and entrepreneurship. The occupational stratification of Chicago made clear that occupational ventures were more diverse than in rural areas in the Midwest, while homeownership was not as common.

In Grand Rapids the majority of the Frisians worked in industry, particularly in the furniture business. Their residential behavior showed some extraordinary patterns. New immigrants sometimes were hesitant to live in parts of Grand Rapids where earlier – already Americanized – Dutch people had settled, because they were experienced as a threat to their socio-cultural baggage. The result was that Frisians as well as other Dutchmen settled in distinct clusters in the city, where they relied on ethnic mutual assitence, although the paths and patterns not always were clearly defined.

It happened that Frisian emigrants left their native country unnoticed. It also happened that an immigrant left America unnoticed to return to the Netherlands according to a letter of Eelkje Dirks Algra:

> Our old landlord disappeared silently to the Netherlands. Oh, he was a bad husband for his household. Also he said nothing to his wife and children. First they thought that he was at our place. And he took a lot of money with him his son told here.[147]

The generalizing aspects of these patterns are important. Frisian communities in the cities also relied on old country networks, influenced by the number of people who arrived in the city and often directed by cultural and religious affiliation. This characterizes the structure of northern Frisian residential behavior in many urban environments.

In the next chapter I will turn to how the West was won. Columbia County, Wisconsin, Amsterdam, Montana, and Lynden, Washington, differed from the urban settlements, but also had some common characteristics.

# *Chapter 7* Rural midwest and frontier Frisians

As many other European immigrants in the United States, Frisians did not
stop their geographical move in the East or in the big cities of the Midwest.
Especially in the 1890s they were part of the immigrant stream that tried to
explore the possibilities further west. Frisians also appeared eager to find
out how the West was won. In this chapter, successively, the settlement
process of Frisians in Wisconsin, Iowa, South Dakota, Minnesota, Montana,
and Washington will be reviewed.

### 7.1 In the wake of T. Tillema: rural Wisconsin

The high rolling prairie of south central Wisconsin shows the Wisconsin
River as the main topographical feature. In this area Columbia county
includes in its northeastern sections the township of Randolph and vicinity,
destination of Frisians in the nineteenth century. The surface area of this
County named after Christopher Columbus is 778 square miles, and the
landscape rises from 200 to 700 feet above Lake Michigan.[1] More than in
Michigan, a continental climate can be found in Wisconsin, because it does
not experience the prevailing southwesterly winds across Lake Michigan.
Severe, long lasting winters and cold nights are the regulators of farming
activities.

The village of Randolph sprang up in 1857, as a station on the Chicago,
Milwaukee & St. Paul Railroad, which opened the area for transportation of
people and goods. The village of Randolph enjoyed a steady growth with the
erection of dwellings and stores and reached a population of about 1200 in
1880.[2] During those years Randolph possessed a post office, three large
elevators, a newspaper, a public school, two hotels, and several churches of
different denominations. In 1872 the manufacture of quality cheese was
started. The milk was bought from the neighboring farmers and this venture
enhanced Wisconsin's enviable reputation as a cheese capital. In 1914
Randolph led the towns of Columbia County as a cheese producer, her brick
cheese being widely famous.[3] Stock raising became quite an industry among
farmers in the 1870s and 1880s.

In the decades before the 1880s, German Lutheran, Scandinavian, Irish and
Welsh people had settled in Columbia County, while the census of 1870
showed a total of 44 Dutch born settlers.[4] That the impact of the Dutch was
not high compared to that of other ethnic groups at that time, is made clear

from a Wisconsin Historical Society study of foreign groups in 1889. The respondent for Columbia County did not even mention the Dutch as a seperate ethnic minority.[5] The U.S. Census reflects the proliferation of the Dutch as the last decade of the century progressed.

The Frisians who came to Columbia County between 1880-1914 were not among the first Dutch settlers in the state of Wisconsin; neither were they the only Frisians who came in these days. The "urban frontier" of Milwaukee and later the Green Bay-Fox River Valley already in the 1840s attracted Dutch immigrants. Especially Gelderlanders and Zeelanders established themselves in Milwaukee, while Dutch Catholics from the province of Noord-Brabant settled in the Fox River Valley. They urged others to come over.[6] Van Hinte complains in his study of the Dutch in America that migration to Wisconsin lacked great leaders and therefore never had the importance of the Van Raalte or Scholte settlements. His judgment of the Wisconsin Dutch is as plain as day: "...little initiative, personality, and originality marked the Wisconsin Dutch settlers, which is more or less the result of their being of average quality among the Dutch immigrants. Another setback in their case was the fact that they had spread out too thinly from the very beginning and lacked great leaders."[7] Recently the studies of migration to Wisconsin by Schreuder and Van Stekelenburg have added nuance to this explanation. Catholic leaders like Father Theodorus J. van den Broek and chaplain Gerardus van den Heuvel appeared to be towers of strength for many an immigrant in the middle of the nineteenth century.[8] Van Stekelenburg states, for example, that one should not compare Father Van den Broek with *koloniestichters* like Van Raalte and Scholte. Van den Broek was more a pioneer for the Roman Catholic Church in the United States, than the advocate of a purely Dutch colony.[9]

Settlement of Netherlanders in Wisconsin was characterized by individual achievement. The majority of the Wisconsin settlers wanted farms. They went to areas with fertile soil and established agricultural and cattle farms. From 1846 on, immigrants from Gelderland in particular, had settled on the slightly rolling farmland near Alto in Fond du Lac County, about seventy miles from Milwaukee. From the beginning an extraordinary amount of grain was produced in the Alto settlement and grasslands provided sustenance for cattle. This success in farming later attracted the Frisians who settled about eighteen miles southwest of Alto in Friesland in Columbia County.[10]

In the more westerly situated county of La Crosse, Frisians followed the tracks of the earlier mentioned Oepke Bonnema, who settled in 1853 close to the Mississippi River in Frysia, later called New Amsterdam, which was part of the town of Holland.[11] In 1880 La Crosse County contained about 17,000 native-born and about 10,000 foreign born, especially Germans and Norwegians. The chief occupations of the people were in agriculture and dairying and the county had a large number of creameries and cheese factories. Jan Siderius, who left his hometown St. Annaparochie with brother Fedde in 1882, reported the next year that they operated a farm in New

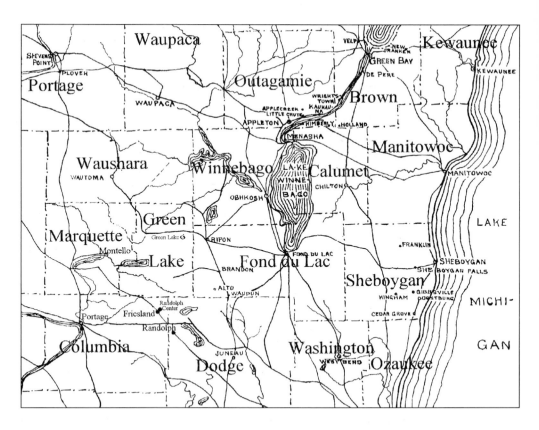

*Map IV. Wisconsin, with the villages of Randolph and Friesland in Columbia county.*
***Source:*** *Van Hinte,* Nederlanders in Amerika, *2: 354*

Amsterdam next to Frisian friends and that they had a good life. Three years
later they were accompanied in La Crosse County by five sisters, two brothers
and their widowed mother.[12] The Frisians especially settled in the towns of
Holland and Onalaska. Excellent farming lands can be found in this area,
and Holland is well-watered because its western and northern boundaries
were the Black and Mississippi rivers. In 1900 the town of Holland had about
1,000 people, most of them of Dutch descent. Onalaska contained about
1,500 inhabitants, with the Dutch as a minority. A woolen mill and a canning
and pickle factory did good business, while the lumber-mills had suffered a
decline around the turn of the century.[13]
In the decades before the 1880s a number of Dutch immigrants also settled
in Sheboygan County, about 45 miles north of Milwaukee including the
villages of Cedar Grove and Oostburg. The Census revealed that in 1900
hardly any Frisians had settled in that area.[14] Racine County in southeastern
Wisconsin did serve as a place of settlement for the Frisians. Some twenty-
five people in 1900 had settled in Mount Pleasant and Dover Townships and
around the village of Union Grove. The streams in this county provided
good natural drainage for the agricultural enterprises.[15]

Columbia County in Wisconsin was the settlement area with the highest concentration of Frisians, according to the U.S. Censuses of 1900 and 1910. In 1854 Tjisse Tillema from Hiaure in Westdongeradeel came with his parents to the United States and settled for one year close to the Van Peymas in Lancaster, New York. In 1855 his family moved westward to Milwaukee, and in 1861 Tillema and his bride Sara van der Velde, originally from Blija in Ferwerderadeel, decided to settle in Columbia County. The Tillemas, with their brother Teunis [George] who came in 1863,[16] and about a dozen other Frisian families founded the village of Friesland and urged other Frisians to come over. Many of the Dongeradelen responded and because of the lack of land in the village of Friesland, they founded with other settlers a new village called Randolph. Until the 1880s Friesland had a steady growth, although the village itself consisted only of a few houses and one large store. Randolph Center nearby, later part of Friesland, also attracted some settlers. Through the Northwestern Railway, the Frisian settlement in the 1880s gained direct contact with markets and prospered. The immigrants in the period 1880 to 1910 arrived in Frisian settlements that already had firm roots in the Wisconsin soil.[17] They were among 6,496 foreign-born Dutchmen in the state in 1900 and among 7,379 in 1910.

The northern Frisians in Columbia County in 1900 outnumbered Frisians in other counties of Wisconsin. In Randolph and vicinity 28 households could be linked, while in La Crosse County 23 Frisian households have been linked in 1900. The total Frisian community in Columbia County included 148 persons, and in La Crosse Frisians and descendants numbered 127 people. In the decade between 1900 and 1910 in Columbia County the Frisian households more than doubled, and increased with 32 linked households to 60 households, or from 148 to 419 persons. Thus, south central Wisconsin was a much desired destination for immigrants from the clay soil in Friesland.

Occupational achievements among the Frisian settlers show a pattern synonymous with the nature of the socio-economic possibilities of central southern Wisconsin. Almost all the members of the workforce around the turn of the century worked in agriculture.[18] More than half of the workforce were farmers or farm managers (55 percent), others worked as laborers in agriculture (22.5 percent), and some were servants or maids (15 percent). The percentage of self-employed people in agriculture catches the eye. It is remarkable to find so many farm managers in 1900, after only two decades of immigration. This does not reflect the socio-economic status of the immigrants before they left Friesland. Of these settlers in Columbia County only one had previously been an independent farmer. Three had been small farmers, the so-called *gardeniers*. In America as many as 22 managed their own farm in 1900. The number of farmers increased over time: in 1910 58 Frisians operated a farm in Columbia County. Only one of them had been a farmer in Friesland, while four were small *gardeniers*. None of the Frisian agricultural laborers in Columbia County had been a farmer in Friesland. In 1900 none of the Frisians possessed a free owned house or farm. But

*Jacob (Jake) van der Meulen and his wife Tietje Gerrits van der Meij from Hantum in Randolph, WI, (circa 1925). Photo dontated by T. Sipma-Dijkstra*

nearly half (11) owned their farm mortgaged, while 12 rented. A decade later three Frisian farmers owned a free farm, and in the meantime the number of mortgaged farms (33) had increased clearly compared to the rented farms (22). S. van den Akker, who lived in southern Wisconsin, told the readers of the *Nieuwsblad van Friesland* in 1909 that many Frisians in the area owned mortgaged farms and some even had their farm all paid for. Van den Akker qualified his positive view by noting that not everyone could become a farmer virtually without money:

> The cattle here are rather expensive, especially the horses...We have four of them, which we bought for 200 dollars per horse average. Good old working horses are about 100 dollars and cows are 40 to 65 dollars. Futhermore, machines are very expensive if one buys new ones, but very often one can buy cheaply at auctions that are organized here even more than in Friesland, because people here always move back and forth. Rents of farms vary from 3 to 5 dollars per acre. Many farm fifty fifty with the landlord, or for one third. We pay 3.50 dollars here per acre, on a farm of 255 acres.[19]

The Frisians improved their occupational status noticeably. But their farm operations were different from those in Friesland. In Wisconsin farmers had more poultry, and while dairying with Holsteins was very common among Wisconsin farmers, Jerseys and Guernseys were also kept for their high butter production. The preserving of hay was very familiar to the Frisians, although in Wisconsin it was stored in silos. Unfamiliar was the fact that during winter the cattle were fed with homegrown corn, because this had a very positive result on the milk production.[20] No evidence was found of Frisians associated with tobacco cultivation, the initial Yankee cash crop that Norwegian immigrants adopted on the land south of Columbia County, in Dane and Jefferson Counties.[21]

It was very normal for a farmer in Friesland to operate his farm with hired hands, "fixed" or steady workers as well as seasonal help. In Wisconsin most of the farm labor came from the nuclear family. Few laborers from outside the family were hired, most likely because hired labor was expensive and especially in the first period of settlement it was too much of a burden on the budget. Recalling the occupational status in the premigration situation, it seems obvious that few of these Frisians came with solid financial means. In the early years of the new start in America the farms were operated by the family members through mutual assistance. Also shared labor by neighborhood exchanges was practised. In Columbia County in 1900 one out of four farmers had a servant in the household. Very interesting is the fact that a decade later in the same expanded group of Frisians, one out of two households had a servant. Most likely the development of settlement was accompanied by more hired labor in the succeeding stages. And industrialization also had its impact, not only in Wisconsin but also in other rural areas. In 1883 Doekele Dijkstra wrote about his farming operations in Iowa:

> ...we are very satisfied. A huge house and 120 acres...Our Simon plows with two horses, sometimes three and it all goes automatically....Really, we do not need a hired hand. Our three boys from now on can take care of everything. At the busiest times we take a hired hand extra. One does not need many people, it all goes as fast as possible. With those machines, you can't imagine. Two boys can labor 100 *pondemaat* in America as well as 10 to 12 persons in Friesland...[22]

The phenomenon of the change in the use of hired labor is also found by Jon Gjerde for Norwegian immigrants who settled earlier in rural Wisconsin south of Columbia County. In fact, Frisians three decades later still had to face the same beginners' difficulties as the Norwegian first settlers. Gjerde notes that it was an additional risk to hire laborers because they were not always reliable. Workers often waited for better future opportunities and the possibility of leaving was the order of the day. This provided uncertainty for the farmer, especially if he intended to increase his acreage on the basis of a workforce outside the family.[23] A curious element in the case of Frisians is that in 1910 half of the hired laborers came from the same northern clay area in Friesland. And since few people from other ethnic groups were members of the Frisian immigrant household, the assumption is correct that farm labor was exchanged through mutual aid within the Frisian community. In contrast to their concentration in such cities as Paterson, Chicago, and Grand Rapids, the Frisians of south central Wisconsin long remained overwhelmingly rural.[24] Their economic situation was quite stable. This had much to do with the fact that most of them used a combination of farming and dairying, which made them less susceptible to economic fluctuations. Dairy prices usually were not as strongly influenced by world trade prices as grain prices. Moreover, the Frisians found seasonal work in the creameries and canning factories in the Randolph area. The cheese factory in Friesland, for example, was built in 1900. Although only few in number, in 1910 Frisian immigrants were found as factory workers in Columbia County (4.2 percent of the workforce). The pattern of Frisian occupations gradually became more complex as Wisconsin's economy developed and the newcomers adjusted.[25]

The social life in Randolph and vicinity centered around the Reformed churches. When Herman Bottema, originally from Gorredijk but a long time resident of Milwaukee, visited the villages of Friesland, Randolph, and East Friesland in 1928, he noticed that many families belonged to the Reformed

*Friesland in America: a garden in Randolph, Wisconsin, 1991*

or Christian Reformed churches. Not one Frisian family in Friesland, he stated, was missed in the church![26]

Bottema's journal of visits at Frisian households in the Randolph neighborhood listed almost all family names originally from the Frisian clay soil area. Among the migrants from that area who had arrived in Columbia County by 1900 were 58 percent *Hervormden*, 26 percent *Gereformeerden*, 13 percent *Christelijk Gereformeerden*, and 3 percent Baptists. In 1910 this picture had slightly changed; the percentage of *Hervormden* was still the same, the share of *Gereformeerden, Christelijk Gereformeerden,* and Baptists was a little lower (24, 10, and 1 percent), but the migrants who were not church-affiliated increased from zero to 6 percent in 1910.[27]

In Randolph and vicinity, especially after the turn of the century, the immigrants had possibilities to join a Dutch oriented church. In 1910 K. Jansma, who had just arrived in Randolph wrote about the religious perspective in his new environment:

> Concerning religion we do not have to complain here. The Gospel truth is brought here clear and bright. Our new Reverend hopes to arrive here this week. This is *Dominee* Homan, someone who was born in *Groningerland,* a man with beautiful gifts and talents....One should not think, though, America is the land that will relieve from all the burdens and pressures. It is true though that the country is big and spacy and there is still a chance here for a lot of people to find their bread. But the voice of God is heard here also, that means that sin and its consequences are not excluded here, and although we have to admire the Lord's Way, we think that we have to admit that it is by his holy advice and wisdom that we were brought and guided here. And we can and may agree every once in a while with the poet: "Who knows the Lord's wise ways?"...Jacob is again organ player in the Dutch Reformed Church in Randolph Center. On Sundays Jacob passes our church here to his own, that is in Center as they call that place. The Reverend over there is pretty good, but the spirit of that church has a lot in common with the *Hervormde* in your area. Our church has a lot in common with your *Afgescheidene* in the past. Therefore much difference will appear in the future. Our church will give a lot more chance for preserving the truth than the one with which Jacob associated.[28]

Jansma emphasized that there were at least two options in church life: the Americanized Reformed Church that had a lot in common with the Dutch *Hervormde* church and the more immigrant-minded Christian Reformed Church that he compared with the *Afgescheiden* church in Friesland. Both churches strongly attracted Dutch immigrants and especially the Christian Reformed Church emphasized worshipping in the Dutch language. From Jansma's information it appears that religious affiliation could split the spirits of the Frisian immigrants. Jansma clearly gave a spiritual superiority to the Christian Reformed Church, which was in his opinion more able to preserve the truth of the Gospel than the Reformed Church. As usual, religiosity and penchant for schism seemed to go hand in hand.

The village of Friesland (then still Randolph Center) had the first officially organized Reformed Church in the area in 1893, and Teunis Tillema had a prominent place in leading the prayers and served as elder until his death in

1910. Teunis also instructed the young people in catechism.[29] A Boy's Society, a summer school for children to keep up with the Dutch language, a Girls' Society, and a Lady's Aid Society were organized within the church in the years between 1900 and 1910. After a number of members from the First Reformed Church of Randolph Center had moved to Randolph and vicinity, they planned to start a Reformed Church in Randolph. In 1908 a committee from the Classis of Wisconsin and the first Consistory were elected. The Randolph Church was known as the Dutch Reformed Church because the Dutch language was used almost exclusively. The congregation continued to grow and in 1928 Bottema writes that in Friesland 93 families were associated with the Reformed Church, while Randolph counted 70 families in that denomination.

The First Christian Reformed Church in Columbia County was organized in 1908 in East Friesland, which is located about six miles northwest of Randolph.[30] Bottema found on his trip that 76 Frisian families were members of this congregation.

To attend worship many had to travel great distances and this was the reason that the Second Reformed Church was built in Randolph. At the time when K. Jansma arrived in Randolph, two new churches in the area had just been organized and he and his fellow immigrants had the choice between association with the Reformed *or* the Christian Reformed Church in Columbia County.

In this perspective it is important to consider that before 1908 the Frisians in Columbia County did not have any religious choice if they wanted to associate with a Dutch oriented denomination, because only the Reformed Church existed in the area. Bottema's conclusion that there was not *any* Frisian family in Friesland who had *not* associated with the Reformed Church in that village proved, according to this Frisian visitor, that the Dutch Reformed Church flourished greatly. Bottema appeared to be surprised by the veneration for the clergy. He compared it with the situation in the Netherlands a century earlier: "The respect for the clergy here is about the same as, for example, in Gorredijk almost a century ago. And in fact this is peculiar, because many changes took place in almost all other fields. In this perspective a total stagnation can be observed."[31] In Randolph another denomination existed, the United Reformed and Lutheran St. Paul's congregation, already organized in 1863. However, it appears that among the mainly German charter members no Frisians names were found. Half a century later the same is true for the Trinity Evangelical Lutheran Congregation that was organized in Friesland in 1917. No Frisians were present among the 13 charter members. This leads to the assumption that the immigrants religiously stayed in their own ethnic group. As was true for other ethnic groups, churches helped to preserve Dutch culture. The impact of religion on immigrant life will be discussed more broadly in the last chapter.

The Dutch language was especially preserved in the church, because no Dutch language schools were present in the Randolph area. The Frisian language was used for verbal communication and in the twentieth century this was still the language used among the immigrants and their children.[32] In fact the Frisian language must have been more widespread than the Dutch, because the Dutch immigrants in Columbia County were almost entirely Frisian. Frisian was spoken in everyday life, so the descendants learned hardly any Dutch. In this respect, immigrant children, when involved in the church, only got education in Sunday School and weekly Bible instruction, which was hardly enough to get them acquainted with the Dutch language.

For first generation immigrants English remained a foreign language. But the Frisian settler soon realized that learning English was the key to survival. It could help to secure employment, and for the rural immigrants it was also essential for such business dealings as the purchase of land and the marketing of crops and dairy products.

That Frisians tried to acclimatize themselves to American society is illustrated by John Siderius' letter, in which he proudly tells that he went to school for a year to learn the English language. At the time of writing he felt strong enough to read the main news in the regional journal.[33] The *Randolph Advance*, a weekly for Randolph and vicinity, did not pay much attention to the Dutch in Columbia County. Investigation of the years 1897 and 1898 did not provide any information or advertizements by or concerning the Frisians.[34] They probably communicated mostly through the ethnic press of the Dutch in America, like *De Volksvriend*.

Another indicator of involvement in American society is that 40 percent of the Frisian males in 1900 were naturalized U.S. citizens.[35] Frisians first maintained a low profile in Randolph politics. The only Frisians who held prominent positions in the town government between 1880 and 1905 were Tjisse and Sam Tillema. Being from the older Frisian stock in the County, they served as chairmen, supervisors, justices of peace, or road commissioner. A few years after the turn of the century, it can be noticed that northern Frisians had their roots more deeply invested in Wisconsin's society. In 1905 Peter Burmania appeared as road commissioner in the town government as did Peter N. Cupery in 1906.[36] In 1910 Watse Haima served as weed commissioner, and Jacob Sterk and Peter D. Westra as road commissioners. In 1912 again new Frisian faces served in the Randolph government: Harke S. Cupery and Henry Streekstra. The Frisian participation remained for years and illustrates the commitment to local governance.[37]

## 7.2 Features of other midwestern settlements

The settlement of Frisians in the rural Midwest was not limited to the Wisconsin borderlands. Other Frisians settled in Iowa, South Dakota, and Minnesota. Data from the 1900 Census do not permit the structural analysis of decadal changes like occupational mobility over time. However, the analysis of the first registration after immigration gives many indicators of the socio-economic status of Frisians in the rural Midwest.

By the turn of the century Frisians had a long migration tradition to the state of Iowa. The midwestern agricultural frontier in the 1840s, 1850s, and

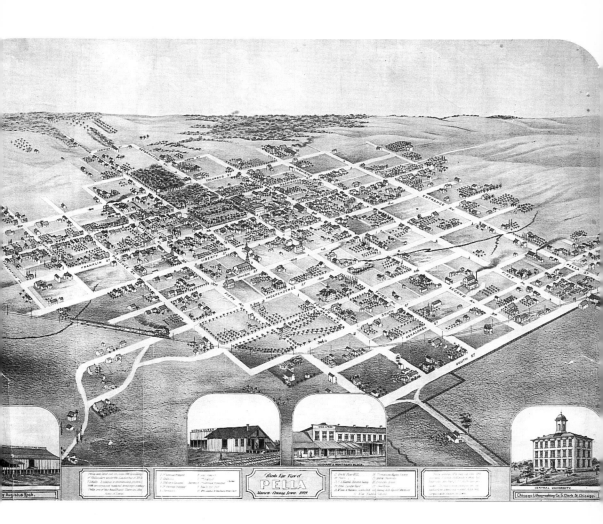

*Birds Eye View of Pella, Iowa, 1869. Drawn by Augustus Koch.*
*Chicago Lithographing Co. S. Clark St., Chicago*

1860s had been a challenge to Frisian settlers like Sjoerd Aukes Sipma, Tjibbe Geerts' brother Anne van der Meulen, and Jelle Pelmulder. Their accounts came from Pella in Marion County's very fertile, sprawling, rolling government lands, and later on from the daughter settlement Orange City in Sioux County's rich, deep prairie soil. In Friesland these experiences aroused much interest, especially since they were published.[38]

In 1870 an 1847 pioneer from Pella came to visit his fellow pioneers in their new environment in Sioux County. He found only a few newcomers who lived in log houses, and a load of planks that expressed future plans. But in the same year Orange City was founded, with a main street called after "William".[39] Several newcomers of Frisian origin played a decisive role in the development of the Sioux County daughter settlement. Tjeerd Heemstra, for example, left with his family of nine children from Michigan, where they had lived in the Van Raalte colony for twenty-three years. He began the first retail business on his farm two miles from Orange City.[40] Henry Hospers, Dutch businessman and former mayor of Pella, started a general store in Orange City and opened the first bank, the Orange City Bank. Hospers also had been asked by the Iowa State Board of Immigration to represent them in the Netherlands in an effort to encourage Dutch immigrants to settle in Iowa. Thus, in 1870 he spent about four months in his native country, holding mass meetings, granting interviews, and answering letters.[41] The new settlement in Sioux County was promoted even before any actual development of the infrastructure had taken place. And news from the settlers' front later on became available. Th.M. Oostenbrug immediately after his journey in 1882 wrote to Friesland that there was no place for laborers in Sioux County because everybody became a farmer or worked as a tradesman. Thus he advised Frisians:

> Sell what you possess, and then make the journey to Iowa and behold the beautiful unin-
> habited creation, such land of milk and honey in abundance and for sale for acceptable
> prices. A tenant farmer in the Netherlands can start his own farm here easily. Clear away
> the yield, clear away the Dutch majesty, because it is poverty and it will remain poverty![42]

In the early seventies travel and transportation was eased by the completion of a section of the St. Paul and Sioux City Railroad. The Dutch in Sioux County got their first railway station at East Orange, four miles east of Orange City. A few years later in 1874, Henry Hospers began publishing *De Volksvriend*, a weekly newspaper in the Dutch language, to help attract and encourage emigrants to come to Sioux County. Frisians like Ebele de Groot from Hallum, Djurre de Boer from Arum, and Jacob Douma from Tzummarum and their families later on got involved.

Without manpower socio-economic improvement was impossible. Migrations from Minnesota, Wisconsin, Illinois, Michigan, and the Netherlands boosted Sioux County's population to 5,426 in 1880 and 24,021 in 1905. In 1875 the Orange City settlement, which also held the county seat, was home to 468 families. 30,000 acres were being tilled, and some 200,000 bushels of wheat were raised that year, according to *De Volksvriend*. Destructive grasshoppers in the seventies visited the area several times, putting many settlers in destitute circumstances. However, pioneer farming in those years put some firm roots in Sioux county's soil.[43]

Investigating the census data for the state of Iowa, it appears that by far the largest number of Frisian immigrants could be found in Sioux County. In 1900 402 people of Frisian origin and their descendants were traced here. Marion County had 85 and Muscatine County 15. The group of linked Frisians in Sioux County included 200 immigrants.[44]

An interesting question is to assess the impact emigration had on the economic prospects of the Frisian immigrants. The occupations of the Sioux County settlers show a remarkably homogeneous pattern. In 1900 58 percent of the workforce (137 in number) labored in the agricultural sector.

A few immigrants worked in handicrafts (including a blacksmith, two carpenters, and an oilseed crusher), and the remainder had jobs in the service sector. Of the farmers five were in vegetable gardening. Compared with the jobs these settlers had in their native country, only one had been a cattle farmer, two had been arable farmers, while five had worked as *gardeniers*. One was a baker. All the others had held no independent positions in Friesland, but had been hired mostly by farmers as laborers or had been unemployed. Generally, three quarters of the workforce entered different occupations from those held in Friesland. This indicates high transoceanic occupational mobility between the Netherlands and the United States. Studies of occupational mobility of the Dutch in Grand Rapids or Holland, Michigan, and also of Pella, Iowa, reveal that in those areas it was lower than for Sioux County. Richard Doyle points out for Pella that only 42 percent of the workforce entered an occupation different from the one in the Netherlands. David Vanderstel concludes that more than 50 percent of the Dutch Grand Rapids settlers experienced transoceanic job mobility, while Gordon Kirk points to almost 60 percent of the Dutch in Holland, Michigan, who entered other professions after migration.[45]

An indicator of improvement of occupational status is also found in data on home ownership. In 1900 only two of the seventy-six Frisian households in Sioux County owned a farm free and eight owned their house free. Seven households possessed a house mortgaged, while sixteen lived on a mortgaged farm. The majority (43) of the households rented their house or farm. These data of the 1900 Census are not available a decade later, and therefore there is no evidence that owning of houses and farms increased syncronically with the years spent in the new country, as was shown for the Frisians in Wisconsin.

Investigating the occupational structure in Sioux County leads to the conclusion that most immigrants sought land. Advertisements for migration to Iowa always emphasized the excellent quality of farmlands.[46] Like other western states, Iowa took a more or less active part in promoting immigration. In the early 1880s it was still possible to obtain a homestead in Sioux County. For the Frisian homeseekers it must have been attractive to invest their lives in vacant lands, especially because they did not bring large amounts of capital. They found that the soil of Iowa lent itself easily to cultivation on account of its looseness and lightness. The farmers could farm on a large scale, although the new immigrants had to get accustomed to this. In 1889 the Frisian immigrant Jurjen Tjerks Dijkstra reported about the threshing machine that he bought on which his sons did custom work for other farmers in the neighborhood. This was an activity that was not practised in Friesland at that time.[47]

Frisian farmers had been used to intensive farming methods in their native country and they first shuddered at the sight of weeds and waste on extensive American farms. However, Dutch immigrant farmers often adopted a middle course and became relatively successful farmers in Sioux County.[48] In 1910 the farmers of Dutch birth or ancestry even formed a majority among the 1,440 foreign-born and 1,275 native-born farmers in

Sioux County. Referring to their conservatism and tendency to work on old-fashioned principles, Jacob van der Zee concludes his reflections on Dutch farming in Iowa in 1912 outspokenly: "they are workers, plodders, savers; and they know how to make farms pay."[49]

Not everyone who operated a farm in Sioux County stayed at the same place for years. Biographical histories reveal that some immigrants operated a variety of farms throughout Sioux County, moving from the vicinity of Orange City to the town of Hull, Sioux Center, Sheldon, Alton (East-Orange earlier), or Maurice, all communities with a large share of Dutch immigrants.[50] Although this mobility seems an adaptation to American conditions and possibilities, it shows that many chose to stay in the environment of their ethnic community. And, as will be discussed later, even movements to places far from the original settlement or ethnic neighborhood should not be perceived as abandonment of ethnic or Old World ties.

Those Frisians who gained a foothold in Sioux County experienced economic improvement. The farmers among them certainly would not have operated a farm independently in their native country and many acquired property to an extent that would not have been possible in Friesland. Sioux County gave opportunities concerning occupational mobility and economic improvement that were hard to gain in Friesland's clay area at the time. However, Frisian immigrants were not the only settlers who exploited these opportunities. A study of the Danish immigrants in Iowa reveals that immigrants managed to achieve a substantial increase in prosperity and many had been able to take a large step upward in the social hierarchy. During the first ten years, the large majority of Danish immigrant farmers in Clay and Sharon Townships worked as farmhands, but by the time they lived in Iowa for thirty years, the great majority owned farms.[51] Doyle's study of the Pella Dutch between 1847 and 1925 makes clear that farmers tended to be more successful in acquiring wealth than were many of their counterparts in the urban segment of the workforce.[52] The Frisians in Sioux County showed similar tendencies.

As settlers continued to flood into Sioux County and into northwestern Iowa, some moved on to more western areas in eastern Dakota.[53] The rapid population increase in Sioux County had boosted land prices and the Homestead and Timber Culture Acts, as well as new lines of the Northern Pacific Railroad forced people to consider Dakota lands. Interest in the Dakotas during the boom period of rapid settlement in the early 1880s was also increased by the favorable climatic condition prevailing in the region at the time. In 1881 in Orange City a meeting was organized to discuss possibilities in southeastern Dakota, in Douglas County. Frisians were involved in these plans and in 1882 these pioneers took claims in Douglas County where government land still could be obtained at a low cost. Dirk van den Bosch and Leendert van der Meer who had participated as leaders in the Sioux County settlement from Pella in the early 1870s, took again leadership.[54] In Douglas County several towns sprang up in a short time:

Harrison, Grand View, New Holland, Joubert, and Armour served the settlers with stores, churches, and handicraft shops in 1885. In that year the total Dutch population in the county had climbed to 3,000.[55]

Northern Frisian immigrants could be found especially in Bon Homme and Charles Mix counties, which neighbored Douglas County on its southwestern border. Already in 1874 the Hornstra family, who left West-Stellingwerf in Friesland in 1872, took claims in Bon Homme County, coming via Sheboygan, Wisconsin, and Sioux County, Iowa, where they had lived for three years. On April 12, when the Hornstras left, ten other families departed for America from the train station in Wolvega. Together they numbered fifty persons, among them Libbe Wybes Dijk and his wife Geeske Theunis Wynia from Wolvega with their ten children. Hendrik D. Dijkstra was a member of this group in South Dakota and more than three decades later he narrated about his first impressions:

> We are here now for 36 years. But what a difference appeared after these years. When we came here in 1874, everything was prairie. And no one lived here in the wide surroundings. It was no wilderness though; the land was covered with plenty of good and nutritious grass. In autumn and winter this was burned, which made the land clean of weeds and bushes. This prairie now is reshaped into fertile agricultural land with big farms and annexes, and beautiful gardens.... The same land that was not very much wanted even as a gift 30 years ago, now is sold for 70 to 80 dollars per acre.[56]

With others Hornstra and Dijkstra settled in Hancock Township about ten miles west of Springfield. Throughout the 1880s the Dutch settlement received additions from Michigan, Sioux County, and directly from the Netherlands. N. Nieuwenhuis mentions that in the course of time Bon Homme County came to consist of 140 Dutch families, of which all but three or four were of Frisian ancestry.[57]

In 1900 the northern Frisian stock in Bon Homme County counted thirty-six people of whom nineteen could be linked directly to the area of research in Friesland.[58] 53 percent of the workforce operated as farmers, 20 percent worked as agricultural laborers, 20 percent were recorded without occupation (unmarried women older than fourteen) and 7 percent was unknown. Thus, the occupational structure in Bon Homme County reflected the pioneer spirit. The land still had to be reclaimed and cultivated for a large part, and Frisians who settled in the area in the 1880s and 1890s only started in agriculture. Of the farmers in Bon Homme two farmed in Friesland, another two were former farm laborers, one was a blacksmith, two had been unemployed, and one had operated a store. Clearly, not much occupational diversity was offered to Frisians who settled in the Dakotas in the two decades before 1900. The challenge was found in starting an independent venture in agriculture or to make money first by working as a farm laborer.[59]

The Frisian households in Bon Homme County were typical nuclear families, some with a (Dutch) boarder. One head of household was a single

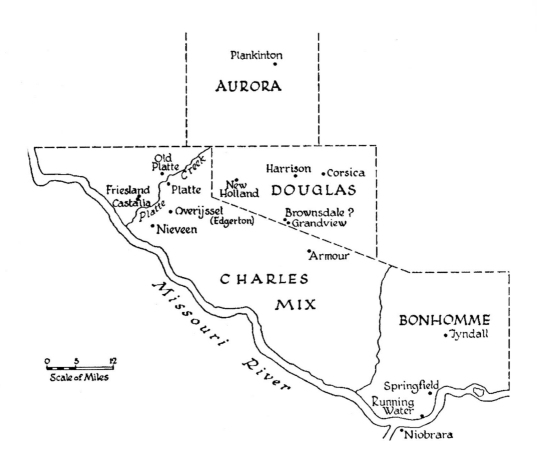

*Map V. Dutch (and Frisian) settlements in South Dakota, about 1900.*
**Source:** *Lucas,* Netherlanders in America, *380*

male who operated his farm with a brother. The households averaged six persons. In 1900 one-third owned their farm free, one-sixth had a mortgaged farm, while another one-sixth rented their farm. One-third of the owner's status was unknown. That it became more difficult to own a farm after the turn of the century because of rising land prizes in Bon Homme County is shown in a letter of T.G. de Vries in 1905:

> As a proof for how much more expensive the land became here, I can report that prices in the last five years increased with 20 to 50 dollars per acre.... The laborers who came here the last three years, almost all had to rent their farms -seldom one remains laborer. To become a renter is rather easy, especially if one enjoys a good reputation.[60]

Northern Frisian settlers also could be found in Charles Mix County, which bordered Bon Homme County on its westside and the banks of the Missouri River on its southside. All of these Frisian households, except one farm laborer, were farmers in 1900. Many of the Frisian settlers in Charles Mix came from southern Friesland. A chief figure in this settlement was Albert Kuipers from Steggerda. Kuipers, born in Workum and brought up in poverty as the son of a poor baker in Drenthe, was an ambitious man. He succeeded in converting a small farm in Steggerda into a profitable business and won 13 medals and more than 500 guilders in prices for his products.[61] Although Kuipers initially was against emigration, he became interested in founding a settlement of Dutch farmers in the Midwest, because opportunities for grain farming seemed greater in America, especially during the first years of the agrarian depression. Kuipers began to act as an agent for Prins & Zwanenburg for the Royal Dutch Steamship Company [*Koninklijke Nederlandsche Stoomvaart Maatschappij*] and sent his son Hendrik in 1881 to investigate the situation in the American Midwest.[62] After his return in October Hendrik did not show much enthusiasm for the Michigan settlement, but preferred the fertile area along the Platte Creek in the Dakotas, especially because homestead land was still available. To promote the uninhabited government land in Dakota, Albert Kuipers started to discuss the idea of emigration at meetings held in the wide surroundings of Steggerda, also in Amsterdam, Groningen, and Zwolle. His farm had been sold by court order to pay off creditors in the summer of 1881, after several very unprofitable years.[63]

There was much negative as well as positive talk about Kuipers' undertaking, according to the many items in the regional newspapers. Even the *Provinciale Groninger Courant* debated with Prins & Zwanenburg and Tjibbe Geerts van der Meulen who at that time was agent for the Red Star Line in Antwerpen.[64] In February 1882 as many as 700 people had shown interest in the operation, but finally 200 subscribed. Due to negative propaganda of, for example, Reverend J.W. Warnshuis who warned against the lonely prairie in the local Frisian press, and extensive writings against the operation of G. Hovens Greve in the *Opregte Steenwijker Courant*, which appeared in Steenwijk but was widely read in West-Stellingwerf, Kuipers' son Hendrik finally left with only 40 families (Lucas mentions 250) on April 8, 1882 for the Dakotas. Albert Kuipers himself had left earlier, "to become President of Kuipers-City", and to welcome the group in Bon Homme County at the Hornstra family house in Dalystown near Springfield.[65] However, in New York the emigrants were assailed by land agents with propaganda against the Dakotas and Kuipers Jr. was not able to calm the roused emotions of insecurity. The group split up and only a few families followed Kuipers to Bon Homme and later Charles Mix County, where they settled around the Platte Creek. Villages like Friesland, Castalia, Platte, Overijssel (later Edgerton), and Nieveen were started and inhabitants came directly from the Netherlands, especially because Kuipers remained an effective publicist who convinced people via Frisian newspapers to come to the Dakotas. In 1897 he even came back to his native country to promote Charles Mix County by giving 151 lectures all over the northern Netherlands with information on settlement in America.[66] An impression of life in Bon Homme County also was easily tossed off by Kuipers in the Frisian *Nieuw Advertentieblad* in 1895:

Per axle from Charles Mix Co. to the most southern part of Bonhomme is a journey of 42 miles east and 42 miles south. This trip I made August 30 accompanied by my sons' wife and youngest daughter. The wife of Cornelis Hornstra and my sons' wife are sisters and they were eager to meet each other. Well, I had time enough to accompany them on this trip and I also was longing to visit the Dutch folks in Bonhomme. The Dutch settlement in Bonhomme County faces a drought this year. The oldest settlers there are the brothers Hornstra, H. Dijkstra, R. Talsma [originally from Oosterlittens, J.B.E.G.], K. Bouma, and H. Wijnie [this is Wynia from Wommels, J.B.E.G.]. They live there already for 20 years and all possess big houses and barns. At Hendrik Dijkstra I saw the best oats; he also had 40 fat pigs. So did Cornelis and Pieter Hornstra. Cornelis Hornstra has 7 children, Fedde Hornstra 9, Rein Talsma 9, Cornelis Bouma 5. The old farmer Jan Hornstra died January 28 this year; his three sons farm in partnership. Hendrik Dijkstra has the highest position in the County administration. He also is a big farmer. The house of Fedde Hornstra looks like a big hotel. The wife of Cornelis Hornstra got a girl of 8 days old as a present from the big city, Sioux City, Iowa. She already had 6 boys, but longed for a girl. Pieter Hornstra is still unmarried; Egbert Hornstra married an American woman.[67]

Douglas, Charles Mix, and Bon Homme Counties marked a new era in Frisian immigration. As other pioneers, the Frisians were touched by the spirit of the westward movement; they were caught by the idea that the West was a place to project wishes and dreams, a symbol for an unknown but promising future. Most of all, for the Frisians this movement was inspired by the compelling urge to search for land. When land was for sale for reasonable prices, the Frisian old country baggage flourished and the immigrant was willing to make his investments. In their opinion land not only was a safe way of gaining property, it also signified social status and economic power.[68] As discussed in the first chapters, the expectation that possession of land would always pay off was a common idea brought from the native country.

Frisian settlers in the Dakotas experienced many hardships. They were severely tried by nature because of storms and drought, aggravated by a seering sun. Winters were severe and often with blinding snowstorms. H.S. Lucas points to some good and some very bad crop years in the 1880s, resulting in disappointment and families leaving the Dutch communities.[69] They faced failed crops in 1894 and the next year experienced a drought. The weather conditions in general may have influenced public opinion because rumor had it that the Dakota settlements faced ruin. Even Kuipers in one of his letters showed doubts concerning the prospects. He mentioned that 400 of the 600 or 700 Dutch families in Douglas and Charles Mix Counties would like to seek their fortune elsewhere.[70] And Kuipers' integrity was questioned. His critics charged that he withheld information about the real circumstances. In 1897 an immigrant in Grand Rapids wrote to Friesland with skepticism:

A while ago I also read an article by that man Kuipers in Hepkema [newspaper, J.B.E.G.], from South Dakota. What does such a man know about it, he is totally isolated from society, he wrote that he sometimes was not provided with mail for a week....[71]

Part of these complaints must have been exaggerated, because people from the afflicted region protested against overstatements in letters that they wrote to newspapers in Friesland and to the Dutch language press in the United States.[72] And not everyone was offended by Kuipers: according to a report in a Frisian newspaper, his seventieth birthday in 1900 was celebrated with great ostentation in the Dutch community of southeastern South Dakota.[73]

Recapitulating all the different stories, it is evident that economic progress in the Dakotas had much to do with climatic conditions. Whenever a favorable summer came and the harvest was plentiful, optimism revived and prognoses for the future were judged positively again. Ulbe Eringa, who farmed in South Dakota for decades, is a clear example of these vicissitudes. He arrived in 1892 and with his wife Maaike Rijpstra went through the whole process of being a farm hand in Iowa, then a tenant farmer in South Dakota, then landowner, then expansion and consolidation even in less fortunate crop years. According to Eringa's writings and reminiscenses, he achieved economic stability in the Dakotas, even when faced with only limited opportunities.[74]

However, the exploitation of these opportunities must have been closely related to the creativity of the individual Frisian immigrant. The widow K. Siderius, who left Het Bildt with her children in 1885 for the Dakotas, after four years of settlement wrote to Friesland and pictured a situation that was representative for many Frisian settlers at that time:

> We now live here at a farm that we rented for three years, and we already spent a year here, but not a good year, we have had three years in a row of bad crops here, that's why I can't speak of advantage here, the farms here are very poor, to say in money. But most of the farmers started very poor too, they almost all are people who came with no financial means, they took land because when this land opened up it cost almost nothing, all the beginnings are difficult: and that is also true for a farmer who starts with nothing. Many then took land, some 160-320, yes some 480 and more acres, this was then all prairie and had to be plowed of course. The first necessity were horses and other agricultural tools, then came the machines; it is true that one is able to achieve a lot here without any money, if you are good, but especially in the first years, when very high interest is being asked for loans. Many are bleeding from that. The first years here were good, and everyone had courage. All the time new machines were invented, new kinds of plows etc., the old one away, newly bought stuff, up to ones ears in debt, now with the bad crops, many can not pay the interest, so the debt is accumulating, and many with some proporty – to say the ones who took land – do have problems right now. That people look forward here to a good crop, is understandable. We rent this farm for 50 percent, but in these bad years we were not able to make a lot of progress, but still we are a lot better off than the workman in your country, food in abundance, and that's the case with everyone here. And also: in fact all the farmers here are former laborers.[75]

The desire for good, cheap land, also inspired Frisians and other Dutchmen to investigate possibilities in the northwestern state of Minnesota. A Minnesota guide in 1901 advertised the state glowingly as follows:

*Advertisement for land in a brochure of the Northern Pacific Railroad, ± 1883*

It is not a prairie state in the sense that there are long stretches of plains such as are found
in some western states. Although three-fourths of the survey is prairie land, it is rolling
prairie, undulating, interspersed with timber, and dotted with innumerable lakes.... This
abundant water surface enriches the land, moderates the extremes of temperature often
found in northern climates.... If you want to be independent, want a home of your
own -Minnesota offers you a chance to help yourself.[76]

As early as 1853 the Frisian Oepke Bonnema bought a farm opposite the
town of New Amsterdam, Wisconsin, on the western side of the Mississippi in
Minnesota. Bonnema never lived on this farm, but rented it to other
settlers.[77]
What catches the eye most in the Minnesota experience of the Dutch is the
fact that a network of promotors and salesmen from the Netherlands was
involved. In 1866 in Amsterdam, the corporation *Maatschappij van Grondbezit
in Minnesota* [Minnesota Real Estate Company] was formed, directed by
N. Kloos and L.A. Bruijn, with J.H. Kloos as the chief representative. Their
aim was to promote land sales alongside the Pacific and St. Paul Railroad,
and to assist in the development of this land. J.H. Kloos published a book in
which he promoted the possibilities of Minnesota. The booklet was also

distributed in Friesland.[78] J.J. Pas, another Netherlander from Hillegom, also published a brochure to promote Minnesota in 1868. Pas and Kloos were successful in attracting Dutch settlers to Minnesota. Before the eighties efforts to establish close-knit Dutch immigrant communities were successful around St. Paul, where Catholics from the province of Limburg settled.[79] The most influential and persistent promotor of Dutch immigration to Minnesota was Theodore F. Koch, who also had much success among Frisians. He finally developed and sold more than one million acres, according to Robert Schoone-Jongen. Koch, who initally was involved in the cattle business, became closely connected with the firm Prins & Zwanenburg and in 1884 he visited the United States with a herd of Frisian-Holstein cattle. He ended up in Minnesota with Martin W. Prins Jr. who was particularly interested in the real-estate possibilities in that area. Together with an experienced land speculator of Danish origin, Nils C. Frederickson, the two men bought 34,000 acres of land in Chippewa, Renville, and Kandiyohi counties for four dollars an acre and opened an office in Chicago, while the immigrant Pieter Haan was stationed as an agent in the heart of the newly bought area.[80]

Frederickson, Prins, and Koch in 1885 began advertising in Dutch language papers in the Midwest and the result was that immigrants originally from Ost-Friesland in Germany and Dutch immigrants who already were in the United States, started buying the land.[81] Ost-Frisian townships like Bunde and Rheiderland (in remembrance of the German homeland) arose as did Clara City (named after Koch's new bride) and Prinsburg (after partner Prins). The company also published a pamphlet in Dutch describing all the blessings of Renville, Chippewa, and Kandiyohi counties, including a list of purchasers of land in 1885. Several Frisian immigrants coming from Michigan, Iowa, Illinois, and Wisconsin, appear on this list of more than 250 buyers.

It must have been the case that after such promotional campaigns, a spirit of enterprise germinated among the Dutch in several communities in the Midwest, with the result that they started to write to each other for detailed information. An informational letter from an immigrant in Minnesota to a fellow countryman in Iowa later was published in a Frisian newspaper.[82] No immigrants who came directly from the Netherlands appeared on the buyer's list of Koch's booklet.[83] Their influx began a few years later, when Koch arranged with a consortium of Dutch farmers and bankers in the province of Groningen, to finance the Prinsburg community. In the beginning Netherlanders and Ost-Frisians settled among each other, but already in 1886 the area of Prinsburg in Kandiyohi County became a Dutch community, whereas Holland in Pipestone County only had a fraction of Netherlanders, and Rheiderland Township in Chippewa County consisted mostly of Germans.

Most of the northern Frisians in 1900 resided in Renville, Chippewa, and Kandiyohi counties. Some others settled in the more northern Pine and Pipestone counties, whereas Kanabec, Mille Lacs, and Rock counties only

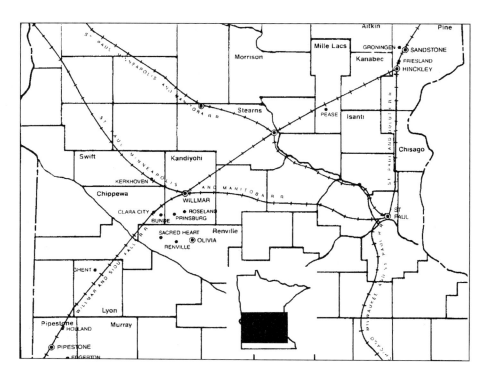

*Map VI. Frisian settlement areas in Minnesota, about 1900.*
**Source:** *Schoone-Jongen, "Cheap land and community,", 217*

housed a handful of Frisians. The northern Frisian stock numbered 242 persons in these counties in 1900, spread over 46 households. Most of them had settled in Holland Township in Kandiyohi County (68); other larger concentrations were found in Fountain Prairie Township in Pipestone County (26), in Dell Grove Township in Pine County, and in Rheiderland in Chippewa County (20). Others were distributed over the counties in smaller numbers. Kandiyohi County had by far the largest number of northern Frisians.[84]

The occupational stratification of other midwestern Frisian rural areas of settlement generally was mirrored among the Minnesota settlers. In 1900 more than 44 percent of the workforce in the linkage group had become independent farmers, whereas 25 percent worked as farm laborers or workmen. Five percent of the workforce had jobs as servant girls and not even 1 percent labored in handicrafts. Only 5 percent of these immigrants had been *gardeniers* or agricultural farmers in Friesland. Occupations had been much more diverse before departure to the United States. Some had been agricultural laborer, baker, servant, innkeeper, carpenter, coach driver, or unemployed. They gained social status by possessing land and being independent. Most of the agricultural laborers in Minnesota had been unemployed in Friesland and without property. In Minnesota in 1900 5 percent owned their farm free, 34 percent had a mortgaged farm, 47 percent rented a farm, and the remainder lived in a (rented) house.

The settlement patterns of the Frisians in Minnesota are characterized by the search for farms and farm lands. All efforts were dedicated to the opening of farms on the frontier. These ventures were risky because most of the immigrants were short of cash and very much dependent on favorable climatic circumstances.[85] As in the Dakotas, in Minnesota good crop years alternated with bad ones. A positive spirit and belief in the future often was crushed by grasshoppers, storms, or droughts, forcing some immigrants to sell everything and leave the community to search for better opportunities. Yet most decided to stay in the hope of a good crop the next year. In 1894, for example, following a disastrous fire in a Dutch community in Hinckly in Pine County, immigrants moved into Pease in Mille Lacs County. Two years later other Dutch immigrants (Frisians among them) fled their scorched fields in Charles Mix County, South Dakota, and also arrived in Pease. After that the area around Pease was promoted among the Dutch in the United States and attracted Dutch settlers from all over, resulting in 110 families living there in 1917.[86]

At the same time, around 1896, Frisians came again to Pine County to settle on the ruined forest lands of the great fire of 1894. Th.F. Koch again was active as intermediary. Many trees had been burned and new settlers tried to start again on the burned off land. They bought the ruined land for 3 to 7 dollars per acre and developed and cultivated the soil. Siebe de Boer, who already lived in Hinckley for 13 years in 1909, stated in a Frisian newspaper that at least a hundred Frisians could be found within 10 miles around. The isolated situation had completely changed compared to a decade earlier. Many farmers had telephones and good roads made communication easier. Hinckley had connections via two railroads to Minneapolis, Duluth, and St.Paul. Four churches, two banks, three hotels, a drugstore, an iron shop, three groceries, a butter factory, and an elementary school served the village in 1909. De Boer described the main source of income too:

> The soil is mostly suitable for dairy farming. Milking cows is therefore the main thing. It is not the milk that is brought to the factory, like in Friesland, but the cream. Every farmer has a hand-separator, to separate the milk from the cream immediately. The skimmed milk is given still warm to the calves and the pigs and the cream is put in a cool place, where it stays three or four days until one has 5 to 10 gallons to deliver. The cream then is judged on its butter percentage and the price is set.[87]

Another immigrant emphasized that a farmer always was able to find a good income, because in summer he could cultivate the fields, while during wintertime he could fell trees, to sell to sawmills in the area.[88]

The main goal in those pioneering years was to create a buffer for sudden economic disappointments. Those without a buffer in unfavorable times had to move from one region to another, along a chain of settlements from Wisconsin westward, from Sioux County to the Dakotas, from there to Minnesota, to Montana, further west, *and* back and forth.

*Advertisement for land and farms in Minnesota,* Leeuwarder Courant, *March 7, 1887*

A buffer was needed not only for economic survival, but even more for social, religious, and psychological well-being. One strategy to reduce risks and uncertainties in frontier settlements was to practise group migration. A businessman like Koch was well aware of the desires and needs of his customers. He named future settlements Friesland and Groningen (in Pine County, Minnesota) even before the first settlers came in.[89] Koch also provided crude dormitories to cover the first period of building homes. In the village of Friesland he helped to build a church and a school, and sometimes he provided settlers with easier credit terms if they were not able to meet the payments. According to Robert Schoone-Jongen, who researched Koch's activities in the upper Midwest, Koch's success lay in the fact that he financed his projects with different sources of capital (like Prins

& Zwanenburg, as well as the Netherlands-American Land Company), he surrounded himself with the best advice money could buy, he invested his own money in the settlements to show his personal commitment and optimism, and he maintained personal and financial control of all his affairs by including his family in his company.[90]

Koch made it perfectly clear: he intended to provide his new settlers with a social and cultural infrastructure that they had known from their native country and he combined this with advantages in the new country. This way language, church, food, and neighbors were combined with fertile, cheap land, independence, and good incomes. An immigrant who moved from Minnesota to South Dakota listed the necessities of the newcomers clearly in his account of the settlement process:

> They started to dig wells and to turn over the promising soil, and now something else had to be done. In order to get more settlers the matter of a school and church must be considered, for if you meet a Hollander from the East and speak about a new colony the first question will be, "Is there a school?" The second, "Is there a church?" These were two necessary matters, but the question was how to get them.[91]

A church usually was organized after a clergyman from another midwestern Dutch settlement had visited the community. After the formal organization of a Reformed or Christian Reformed Church (or both), eastern churches sent money to the pioneers to erect a church building.[92] Already in the early 1880s, Reformed and Christian Reformed congregations were established in many villages and cities in the Dakotas. Lucas mentions that in Harrison, New Holland, Corsica, Old Platte, Overisel, Platte, and Friesland, churches were organized very soon after the first houses in these villages were built.[93] Between 1883 and 1899 the Reformed Church in America (RCA) proceeded with the organization of sixteen congregations in the Dakotas, while the Christian Reformed Church founded four churches.[94] Some founders of new communities like Orange City, Iowa, came from the older settlements like Pella and took with them their familiar ecclesiastical institutions. The Reformed and the Christian Reformed Churches both have a strong Calvinistic heritage and claim the Belgic Confession, the Canons of the Synod of Dordt, and the Heidelberg Catechism as their confessional standards. In the Midwest, both churches stand in the tradition of the nineteenth century movement of the *Afscheiding* [Secessionists], which emphasized Calvinistic orthodoxy and piety and objected to governmental limitations upon their churches and schools.[95]

That Frisian immigrants joined with the established churches of the Dutch in America is not surprising if the religious background of the immigrants in their native country is considered. For the years 1900 and 1910 the U.S. census does not give any specific information concerning the immigrant's religious affiliation, but from the Dutch Population Registers the denomination in Friesland can be determined.

Table 7.1  **Religious background of Frisian immigrants in the (upper) Midwest in 1900 in percentages:**

|  | Nederlands Hervormd | Gereformeerd | Christelijk Gereformeerd | Baptist | None |
|---|---|---|---|---|---|
| Columbia County, WI | 58% | 26 | 13% | 3% | - |
| La Crosse County, WI | 74% | 18% | 5% | – | 3% |
| Sioux County, IA | 64% | 8% | 14% | 1% | 11% |
| Charles Mix County,SD | 71% | – | – | – | 29% |
| Bonhomme County, SD | 63% | 26% | – | 11% | – |

**Source:** Galema, "Linked files: Frisians to America and Frisians in the USA. Computer Compilation"

The majority of the Frisians had been associated with the *Nederlands Hervormde* church in their native villages.[96] Except for a few Baptists and some non-churched, almost all came from Reformed denominations, which comprised the heart of the local Frisian immigrant community in America. Many associated with these churches also because the denominations provided ethnic leaders and social life.

Comparable figures in Friesland in 1899 are shown in table 7.2.

Table 7.2  **Religious affiliation in the province of Friesland, 1899:**

|  | Number | Percentage |
|---|---|---|
| Nederlands Hervormd | 204,902 | 60.2 |
| Gereformeerd | 86,225 | 25.3 |
| Christelijk Gereformeerd | 7,766 | 2.3 |
| Baptist | 13,328 | 3.9 |
| None | 23,356 | 6.9 |
| Other | 4,685 | 1.4 |
| **Total** | 340,262 | 100.0 |

**Source:** *Bijdragen tot de statistiek van Nederland. Uitkomsten der achtste tienjaarlijksche volkstelling (1899)*, vol. 7, province of Friesland ('s-Gravenhage: Belinfante, 1901); H. Knippenberg, *De religieuze kaart van Nederland. Omvang en geografische spreiding van de godsdienstige gezindten vanaf de Reformatie tot heden* (Assen: Van Gorcum, 1992), 80, 97-98, 135, 231, 268.[97]

It is clear that the *Christelijk Gereformeerde* immigrants relatively were more numerous in the Midwest than in Friesland.

Although the primary motive in establishing homes in the upper Midwest was economic, the character of the settlements usually was determined by religion. Across the country the Reformed churches were the binding networks between the Dutch communities. Already in the early days of pioneer settlements in Iowa, South Dakota and Minnesota, churches were organized and built. In the 1880s and 1890s "home missionaries" fanned out to serve the Dutch who lived on the plains and prairies. In South Dakota the Reverend Frederick James Zwemer, the pastor at Platte, worked as missionary to the Frisian farmers in Bon Homme County. When in 1888 a congregation was organized, approved by the Classis of Dakota, eighteen charter members enrolled, of which all but five were Frisians.[98]

In Charles Mix County, Frisians came in 1882 and with other Dutch immigrants first worshipped in homes and in the school. In February 1883 they organized a Christian Reformed congregation under the auspices of the Classis of Iowa. The first elders were Evert Beltman and Jurjen Dijk, the first deacons Jan Wynia and Rein J. Zijlstra, and later Jacob de Lange and Albert Kuipers became elders. Soon these people were split into an east and a west group, because they had to travel long distances. Both groups built their own church, the west group consisting of almost all Frisians, while the east group included many people from the province of Overijsel. The Frisians built their church 5 miles south and 4 miles west of Platte (in the village of Friesland) on 20 acres of land donated by Douwe Zijlstra. Their new elders were Jelle Zijlstra and Wiebe Dijk, their deacons Harm Eerkes and Douwe Zijlstra. Also in the early 1880s the first Reformed Church was organized in Charles Mix County, in the village of Friesland.

In the startup years of struggle, the churches in the East sent boxes and barrels of used clothing to their fellow believers. Settled ministers for the churches were often unavailable, but this problem was solved by visiting pastors and theological seminary students.[99] From the local church histories it generally appears that new congregations relied on older established churches with firm American roots. In the next chapter the impact of religion on migratory matters will be discussed more broadly.

Church life was intermingled with social life. Kerst Huisman's account of the life of Gerrit Roorda, who spent the years 1910-1919 mostly in the American Midwest, shows that the immigrant with little money in his pocket wandered from Dutchman to Dutchman to seek contact with the new country. Roorda got his jobs in carpentry by talking to Frisians who lived in the Orange City area, which resulted in building a barn at one place or replacing a roof at another. Usually Roorda boarded with Frisian families and that way he heard of other jobs in the area. From Sheldon, Iowa, Roorda left to help a Frisian farmer in the Dakotas, came back to Sheldon, then left with another Frisian for Chicago. Next he traveled to Hebron, Illinois, to his friend who worked at a Frisian farmer, went to Lake Will, Illinois, where many of the people from his hometown area lived and did fieldwork, and went back to his Frisian acquaintances in Iowa because of the marriage of one of his friends.[100] Roorda was not a church member, but when visiting in the Frisian families he went to church with them every now and then to meet other Frisian immigrants.

A great driving force behind the many contacts between Frisian immigrants in the Midwest was the circulation of Dutch language newspapers. Henry Hospers in 1874 had launched his newspaper *De Volksvriend* [The People's Friend]. He originally intended to advertise among Netherlanders in the native country or in other areas in America the excellent possibilities of Sioux County and to contradict the negative rumors spread by real estate speculators in other territories.[101] However, *De Volksvriend* soon became the voice for many Dutch immigrants and also the news source for political and governmental matters. *De Volksvriend* gradually developed into one of the most widely read Dutch newspapers in America. It started with only 120 subscribers, but by 1895 it had almost 2,000 and consisted of 8 pages that were read from California to New Jersey, Washington to Michigan, and even in the Netherlands. In that same year the function of *De Volksvriend* as an ethnic associative instrument became clear, when it printed a special red-cover edition on the twenty-fifth anniversary of the Sioux County settlement.[102]

In the settlements public schools were available as soon as enough pupils were in the area. The Dutch (and Frisians among them) also started to organize Christian-oriented schooling themselves. In a letter from Runningwater, South Dakota, Dora Eringa, fourteen year old daughter of Ulbe and Maaike, describes in 1910 the church centered network in which she and her family were involved:

> My brother Pier and sister Jessie go to Catechism together on Saturday morning with horse and buggy, and Jessie does the driving...My sister Jessie is in her last year in the grade school. She will be 13 this winter and then she will go to the Normal School in Springfield. This winter we are getting a new library in the church [the Emmanual Reformed Church of Springfield, established by the Dutch, J.B.E.G.] with English and Dutch books. We have Christmas programs in church and in school. We have 120 students in Sunday School. On sunday evenings we have a young people's meeting. My sister Grace and I and the two hired men go to that. Grace and I also go to the girls' society on Fridays every week. I can read Dutch better than write it, so please excuse the mistakes.[103]

Institutions of higher learning based on Christian principles were created by the Dutch immigrants to preserve a Dutch identity and emphasize their ethno-religious heritage. The year 1882 marked the founding in the Reformed tradition of the Northwestern Classical Academy in Orange City, Iowa, where early courses had a classical emphasis on English, Greek, Latin, and Dutch, as well as rhetoric, elocution, geography, astronomy, and arithmetic. The Academy was a preparatory school for students intending to attend Dutch-oriented colleges and universities. From all over the upper Midwest, immigrant youth attended this school. Three of the Eringa daughters – Jessie, Dora, and Alys – attended the Academy, located 120 miles east of the Eringa farm. Dora later began her college education at Central College in Pella, a Baptist school purchased by the Reformed Church in 1916, and functioning as another educational institute in the Calvinistic ethno-religious tradition.[104]

Frisians in the upper Midwest sought other Frisian (Dutch) immigrants as starting points in every facet of American society. This did not erase the fact that they were living among people of very different ethnic signature. In Minnesota, for example, at the time when the Frisians came in, there was a considerable contingent of foreign-born. In 1880 German-born were the most numerous group, followed by Norwegians, Swedes, Irish, Bohemians, English, Danes, Scots, Swiss, Poles, Russians, and French.[105] The Frisians in Renville and Kandiyohi counties, Minnesota, entered the new settlement area shoulder to shoulder with the German Ost-Frisians. Both groups bought land from Theodore Koch. However, Ost-Frisians as well as Frisians preferred their own settlements, which resulted in Prinsburg made up of Dutch Frisians and Clara City mainly composed of German Frisians. An effort to form a Christian Reformed Church that gathered both nationality groups caused an unresolved conflict between the Dutch and Germans, followed by separation of the churches.[106] Striving against each other instead of cooperating also marked German/Dutch Frisian relationships in settlements in the Dakotas. Generally, this deprived the settlers of unity that would have given them greater capacity to cope with the odds they were already facing without the added religious troubles.[107] Although a large variety of nationalities made up the cultural map of Minnesota and the Dakotas in the 1880s and enlivened its cosmopolitan character, in many cases the preference of seeking and staying in their own ethnic environment appeared to be the highest priority.

### 7.3 Big Sky Country and westward

Jan Willem Schulte Nordholt, historian and poet, described the historical impact of the mythic heliotropic development of civilization, the idea that western culture evolved from east to west synchronous with the movement of the sun. American identity is derived from this historic myth, because it seems that the new nation is the last stage in the heliotropic cycle. History began in the East, moved westward with the sun while civilization increased and resulted, with the discovery of America, in a closed circle, which could mean the end of history or a crisis in western culture. This myth has given western culture its identity and dignity, according to Schulte Nordholt, and justified political and economic expansion.[108]

There is another idea that accompanies this heliotropic myth in the United States. It is the theory of progressive adaptation, the story of successive generations adjusting to new soils and environments with increasing success. Progressive adaptation was an article of faith, a myth of the self-made man, and not always reality. An American historian put it clearly: every force that could make or break the immigrant seemed to turn and dance in his dreams every now and then: faith was attacked by reality.[109] The United States in the nineteenth century became the reservoir where westward dreams gathered and Frisian immigrants participated in this process.

The new settlements in the Dakotas and Minnesota and also older ones in Michigan, Iowa, and Wisconsin, were unable to satisfy the expanding demands of the Frisian immigrants. Crop failures and rising land prices pressed them to alternatives and made them decide to brave the uncertainties of unimproved western lands. Employment in the factories of Grand Rapids, Chicago, or Paterson was no alternative to farm life in the Midwest. Frisians turned their hopes westward to Montana, Washington, and later California, and fresh immigrants from the Netherlands followed in their wake.

In the land of the Crow Indians in Montana, or the Big Sky Country as it is now called, Frisian immigrants in the 1890s and 1900s settled in the villages of Manhattan, Amsterdam, Belgrade, and Church Hill.[110] Rob Kroes analyzed the 19th and 20th century history of these Netherlanders in the Gallatin Valley by entering the community as a stranger, but he became a vicarious insider in the course of investigation.[111] Kroes describes the windmills that now cover Montana as ghostly and spooky skeletons bespeaking misfortune, despair, and failure. But, on the other side, he discovered the friendly replicas on front lawns and in windows, which are reminiscent of successful Dutch settlement.

The Dutch settlement in the western Gallatin Valley emphasizes an unbroken continuity, but also tension and internal strife.[112] Frisians from settlements in Michigan and Iowa were the first Dutch settlers who came around the 1890s. The Weidenaar family, for example, originally from Ee in Oostdongeradeel, came via New Jersey and Michigan to the Gallatin Valley, attracted by the glowing advertisements of Reverend Andreas J. Wormser, who worked for the Board of Domestic Missions of the Presbyterian Church in America, and who was an agent for the West Gallatin Irrigation Company with the task to recruit Dutch farmers from the Netherlands as well as from other parts of America.[113]

Several Frisian immigrants managed to become their own boss or owners of homesteads in the Gallatin Valley. Johannes Koning, who worked briefly for a man named Terpstra, a Frisian farmer in Iowa, investigated possibilities in Montana and wrote in 1905:

> However, I am always glad that I left Iowa, because here – although it does seem a depressive time now – there is a lot more chance to be successful than in the fairly densily populated areas of Iowa, where therefore the top is reached. Had I stayed in Iowa, most likely I still would have been a farm laborer at the Terpstras. Although a farm laborer has a lot of time off here in this country, and although the Terpstras were pleasant people to be with, still I rather am my own boss, that makes me incredibly more free, and although I have more worries, I never will be a farm laborer again.[114]

Willem Koning from Westdongeradeel, Cornelius Lucas from Het Bildt, J. Braaksma from Westdongeradeel, Jacob Veltkamp from Oostdongeradeel, and Hendrik Haga from Ferwerderadeel, among others, operated homesteads. Some of them sold their homestead after the compulsory five years of residence and moved further west or retired like Willem Koning, who considered himself a wealthy man and returned to his native country.[115] Kroes describes the settlement in the Gallatin Valley as a dynamic economic process of buying and selling lands, and not only to those within the ethnic circle.

Consolidation of the Dutch community took place through religion and schooling after the turn of the century, as more Dutch families arrived. A Christian Reformed Church was established on Church Hill in 1903 and

Christian schools were opened next to the system of public schools. Not every Dutch immigrant was involved in the ethnic circle. Some joined the Christian Reformed Church, but did not send their children to the Christian schools or vice versa.

There were Frisians as well as other Dutchmen who moved in the outer boundaries of the Dutch community that were never clear-cut. According to Kroes, communication outside the ethnic group in the Gallatin Valley for socio-economic purposes always was possible. However, it is clear that Dutch farmers often relied on mutual assistance for economic matters, and they often had laborers of Dutch origin. Pieter L. van Dijken (immigrant from the province of Groningen) in 1894, for example, worked in Manhattan in the Gallatin Valley for Jacob Kimm, a farmer originally from Spijk in Groningen. In a letter to the home country he showed in a sketch how the Dutch lived close together in the hills around Manhattan. The same becomes clear in letters from the Frisian immigrants Klaas and Geertje Schuiling-De Jong. This couple in 1905 operated their farm in the Gallatin Valley with the help of Pieter and Lieuwe, laborers originally from Nieuwe Bildtdijk, Friesland.[116]

For the individual immigrant, communication within their own ethnic circles was normal, but it did not prevent the exchange of ideas with the outside world. Consolidation of the ethnic perspective was related to the immigrant group as a whole rather than to each and every individual member.[117]

Besides the Dutch settlement in the Gallatin Valley, several other attempts were made to organize Dutch communities in Montana. However, as in the Dakotas, climatic and soil conditions, the absence of trees, severe droughts and therefore the dependence on irrigation were factors that discouraged immigrants. The urge remained a westward glance. The ever-present desire to secure fertile lands in a region where rainfall, climate, and market conditions were more ideal, directed the Frisian immigrant to the Far West. In 1889 a Frisian woman wrote from the Dakotas that the state of Washington was in the picture:

> There is a lot of land for sale here, and he who is careful can be served quickly for little money of course. If we get more rain here, then there is some future perspective, to make headway. It will hopefully rain some more this summer. Both my sons Dirk and Fedde left for Washington, to see if it is better there.... Fedde wrote that blossoms are on the trees there, and it is beautiful....[118]

The brothers-in-law Hendrik Haga and Jacob Balda, Frisians who came from Michigan to the Gallatin Valley, sold their homesteads and moved with their families to the more rainy Oak Harbor, Washington. In 1895 many Frisians who had experienced weather disasters left Charles Mix and Douglas counties, South Dakota, to find their fortune further west.[119] The real beginnings of Frisian immigration to Washington were the result of the succession of crop failures in the Dakotas and in Montana during the early

1890's. Although a few Netherlanders had settled in Washington during its territorial era, it was around 1894-1895 that Frisians settled in such numbers as to represent a sizeable Dutch immigration. The total number of Dutch-born in the state, according to the census, was 632 in 1900 and 2,157 in 1910.[120]

A catalyst for immigration was the opening of the Northern Pacific and the Great Northern railroads which reached their Seattle terminal in 1883 and 1892, respectively. This drew the attention of Netherlanders in the Dakotas and Montana to the lands of the Puget Sound and Yakima Valley. Another catalyst was enormous lack of mortgage capital (and therefore high interest rates) that limited financial activities of Dutch businessmen in the West. H.A. van Valkenburg, for example, organized in 1886 the Northwestern and Pacific Mortgage Company, which had its main office in Olympia. In 1890 Van Valkenburg created the Northwestern and Pacific Mortgage Bank of Amsterdam, which proved a successful undertaking in investments in real estate in Spokane Falls. In the track of Van Valkenburg's business, other Dutch-American financial institutions became active. In the province of Groningen the *Nederlandsch-Amerikaansche Hypotheek Bank van Uithuizen* was active since 1893, and in Leeuwarden, Friesland the *Noord-Amerikaansche Hypotheek Bank*. This Frisian company operated mainly in Washington and Montana and a brochure shows prominent Frisians on the list of commissioners in Friesland. P.J. Buwalda, who left Witmarsum in Wonseradeel in April 1882, after his move to the Far West in 1896, became agent in North Yakima, Washington. J.P. Fabriek was agent for this company in Bozeman, Montana.[121]

The great difference in interest rates in America compared to the Netherlands, made the mortgage business in the western states very attractive to Dutch investors. H.S. Lucas mentions that the total amount of capital invested by the companies in 1914 was estimated at about $50,000,000.[122] Some of these banks had been forced to change partially into real estate companies, because especially after lean harvest years, banks had to repossess the land. That way mortgage banks like the *Noord-Amerikaansche Hypotheek Bank* in Leeuwarden had an indirect influence on Frisians settling in the Northwest. These banks showed much interest in the increase of land values within decades. In Washington State, for example, the average value per acre between 1900 and 1910 increased by 278 percent and population advanced 120 percent, while Oregon land showed an increase of 214 percent and its population 67 percent.[123]

As mentioned above, the real beginnings of Frisian immigration to Washington were due to crop failures in the early 1890s in the Dakotas and Montana. Yakima County, Oak Harbor on Whidbey Island, and Lynden in Whatcom County, were the chief promotional areas of the Dutch in Washington. The realtors W.E. Werkman and Hein Te Roller, formerly residents of Holland, Michigan, wrote flattering reports of these areas to Dutch newspapers in America, like *De Grondwet* and *De Volksvriend*, and also visited the Dutch settlements in the Midwest and the Dakotas to promote

Whidbey Island. They exhibited some of its produce like large vegetables, sheaves of wheat with kernels as heavy as peas, and excellent grain. Thijs Bakker, for example, left Iowa during the spring in 1895 with twenty-five other Dutchmen to experience the rewards of Whidbey Island.[124] A Frisian immigrant wrote an extensive report about Werkman's visit to Grand Rapids to his family in Friesland:

> At the moment there is a man in this city (a Hollander) – his name is Werkman and earlier he lived in the city of Holland in this state – who comes from the state of Washington, one of the farthest states in the west. He exhibits the products of that state, among them grains, seeds, apples and other fruits, potatoes, different kinds of woods, coal, and other minerals, as well as a big chunk of tree-trunk, cedar wood. I measured it with my own hands and it had a ten foot diameter. The chunk was sawed in the middle. Many America-letters and news are unbelievable for you over there, and if I had never been in this country, for me as well. But what I tell you can be assured. About the other things: everything can be judged positively. Unfortunately I did not meet this man personally yet, I met his servant, because I did not have time during last week and tomorrow I go for work to somebody again. But as soon as possible I will try. That servant said that he came over for a big Land Company, that wants to sell land to Hollanders badly for 10 to 25 dollars per acre, to pay in 8 years, with an interest of 8 percent, and in the first year one can get a house and 10 acres for free to make a living. Mr. Werkman lived on an island, the so-called Whitte Bay, that is 40 miles = 13 hours long and 2-4 hours wide. It is situated on the Pacific Ocean. With not much trouble the land over there is good, transportation by steamship easy, and – the most positive thing about it – the climate with no winter there, at the moment the roses hang in the trees as they do here in summer, and the warmest weather is between 60 and 70 degrees, against 100 here ...It costs 50 dollars for one person from here to go there by train... it costs even more than a trip to the Netherlands.[125]

This letter is clear about the possibilities for newcomers on Whidbey Island; it may be mentioned generally that the promotional material concerning immigration to the state of Washington was abundant and influenced positively decisions to move westward.[126]
Some farmers coming from Iowa, Minnesota, and the Dakotas had lost everything during the drought in Dakota and in the depression of 1893. When they arrived on Whidbey Island they were too poor to buy farms that had already been cleared. They lacked experience with woods. Thus, mostly as ill-prepared frontier immigrants they undertook the formidable task of clearing forest lands and in the first years they were unable to raise large crops.[127] The Frisians experienced many obstacles on Whidbey Island. H.S. Lucas mentions several, like isolation because of an irregular steamboat connection with the mainland, marketing problems, the lack of suitable drinking water, scarcity of money, general poverty, and the lack of knowledge about the art of "squaw farming," that is, raising vegetables and grain among the massive forest stumps, a technique well understood by the frontier woodsman and farmer of western Washington.[128]
Some of the Frisian immigrants did well in 1895 and 1896 on the lush green of Whidbey Island. In 1895 A. Yonker in a letter to *De Volksvriend* compares

the climate of the island with Holland: no burning in summer, no freezing in winter.[129] Coming from Iowa, Levi Sinnema reports to *De Volksvriend* in 1896 that plenty of good farmland was available, while A. Veleke mentions that a Dutch choir was established. The day before Christmas 1896, *De Volksvriend* even published a whole page with promotional letters for Whidbey Island, written by Dutchmen who already lived there. Riekele Zijlstra who came in 1895 from Nieveen, in Charles Mix County, showed optimism concerning the clearing of land:

> ...the best land is most easy clearing, a good feller can cut an acre in four days in rows, in rows is necessary because it burns better. With a stump-puller and a horse a man and boy can clear two acres a week and in some places even three; I have done this work myself, so I can tell you by experience.[130]

H. Hulst makes mention of 37 Dutch families on Whidbey Island in 1897.[131] According to Henry Beets, the pioneer historian of the Christian Reformed Church in America, a Christian Reformed congregation at Oak Harbor on Whidbey Island was organized by the Reverend J.W. Brink in 1897.[132] Although I could not find any northern Frisians on Whidbey Island in the 1900 Census, I was able to trace 14 families in the 1910 Census, consisting of 84 members of northern Frisian stock. All of these families were operating farms. Besides the 14 farm managers, the people in the workforce were recorded as agricultural laborers (10), unmarried females working in the household (11), a teacher and a student. The other family members were housewives and children under fourteen years of age. None of these farmers had operated a farm in Friesland. The conclusion is that northern Frisians came to Whidbey Island after the founding of a firm community of other Frisians (with names such as De Wilde, Piebenga, Pietersma, and Eerkes) and other Dutch immigrants. Most of these northern Frisians did not come directly from the old country, but moved from older settlements in the East, the Midwest, and the upper Midwest.[133] Van Hinte mentions that in 1920 Whidbey Island had more than 800 Dutch inhabitants. Most of them were dairy farmers who later on were engaged in truck gardening and raising poultry.[134]

Frisians also took part in a colonization effort southwest of Spokane in the Yakima Valley of Yakima County, Washington. In 1900 only one family of the Frisian case-study group had found its way to the valley. However, a decade later ten Frisian families were present, together making up a community of forty-five persons. The waste lands of the Yakima Valley were advertised in the Midwest the same way as the areas in Whidbey Island. Dutch agents of land companies or mortgage banks were present in the Yakima Valley and Dutchmen from midwestern settlements were invited at their expense to visit and investigate the region. H. Wayenberg, formerly of Sioux County, Iowa, who had lived in Yakima County since 1886, visited Sioux County in the autumn of 1900 to report that Dutchmen were doing well in Washington State. This visit resulted, according to Lucas, in the arrival of a group of

Gecombineerde Oogst- en Dorschmachine in werking in Eastern Washington.

Vertegenwoordiger in **Washington**:
  P. J. BUWALDA te North-Yakima.
Rechtskundig adviseur: LEE C. DELLE.

Vertegenwoordiger in **Montana**:
  JOHN P. FABRIEK te Bozeman.
Rechtskundig adviseur: GEORG Y. PATTEN.

Bankier in Amerika: FIRST NATIONAL BANK.

N. V. STOOMDR. V/H C. JONGBLOED AZ., LEEUWARDEN.

about seventy Dutch people from Sioux County, Iowa, in December 1900 in the Yakima Valley.[135] Pieter J. Buwalda arrived in North Yakima in 1896 and became agent for the *Noord-Amerikaansche Hypotheekbank*, Leeuwarden. In 1897 his son John wrote to Friesland that they were "delighted with the country" and "the weather is beautiful". Two years later he gave a brief description of the town they lived in:

> We can always see Mt. Rainier and Mt. Tacoma, although they are 60 and 75 miles away. Their snowy sides glisten in the sunshine. The whole mountain seems as though it is one mass of snow. Papa has nearly another artesian well ready. He and another man work at it with a large engine. He drills down about one thousand feet to get water. This town has electric light and water-works. It is a pleasant place and I like to live here.[136]

All but two of the Frisian families in Yakima County operated a farm in 1910. Edgar van Vliet had opened a retail liquor store in North Yakima, while Peter Spoolstra owned a general retail store in Granger City. Of the farmers only John Wijngaarden was involved in fruit farming. A decade later, according to the writings of J. van Hinte, about three hundred Dutchmen mainly active in fruit growing had settled in the Yakima Valley, which had become one of the famous "Apple Valleys" thanks to an effective irrigation system as well as an extensive publicity campaign.[137]

Investigating the place of birth of several immigrant children in Frisian families, it appears that none of the families in Yakima County had come directly from Friesland. Edgar van Vliet moved westward via North Dakota and Kansas, Peter Buwalda via Michigan, the widow Sjoukje Huysman via Iowa, Peter Spoolstra via Illinois, the widow Sophie Sybouts via South Dakota, Hobber De Boer via Massachusetts, and Hyltje Postma with his family first had settled in Iowa before moving to Yakima County.[138]

The most characteristic settlement of Frisians in Washington, however, was at Lynden in Whatcom County, the most northwesterly county in the United States. Lynden became the largest Dutch settlement in the state. This small town in the 1890s mainly found its existence in lumber and was situated in the heart of the fertile Nooksack Valley. The depression of 1893 had forced the shingle mills, upon which Lynden depended, to close down, and many people left, leaving their homes open and empty for newcomers who passed through and inspected the village. From that time the Dutch trek to Lynden began, because three Dutchmen, among them the Frisians Herman Oordt and Douwe J. Zijlstra, from Whidbey Island,[139] visited Lynden in 1896 and found the soil fertile, the climate equable, and the land available for $20 to $25 an acre. Newspaper propaganda on behalf of Lynden in *De Grondwet* and *De Volksvriend* worked to its advantage.[140] The town is situated on the mainland and did not have Whidbey Island's disadvantage of poor access to markets.

After the first Dutchmen came to Lynden, others from Oak Harbor and elsewhere in the Pacific Northwest followed the example of Oordt and Zijlstra. Even fellow countrymen who had experienced many hardships in homestead colonies in Canada crossed the border to join the Dutch settlements in Washington State.[141]

Not many northern Frisians settled in Lynden in the late 1890s. In 1900 only a few members from the Stremler family and the family of Pieter Dijkstra, who originally moved to the United States, respectively, in 1889 and 1883, were living in Lynden. Both families came from Arum in Wonseradeel. The Stremlers were farming on a rented farm, while Pieter Dijkstra made a living as a common laborer and occupied a rented house in Lynden. William Visser, another Frisian, had arrived in 1898 according to the Census, and boarded with the Stremlers, working as a day laborer. He later became a well known farmer and dairyman in Lynden.[142] Pieter Dijkstra first was located in Iowa, and the brothers Fedde and Lieuwe Stremler both had gone other routes too before they arrived in Lynden.

By 1910 the community of northern Frisians in Lynden had grown to 15 families, composed of 79 persons. William Visser owned a mortgaged farm by then and had married a woman of Frisian origin named Grietje Wiersma. Pieter Dijkstra owned a mortgaged dairy farm too with his wife Grietje

*Dairy farm in Washington State in the 1990s*

Wiersma, whom he had married when he returned to Friesland in 1889.
Their six children and Pieter's father Douwe of 85 years old, also lived in.
There were also members of the Stuurmans family, who originally came
from Witmarsum in Wonseradeel. The brothers Sam [Sijbolt] and Albert
[Ale] both had emigrated with their parents and a brother and sister in
1893. On their way via Iowa to Washington Albert met his wife Etta of Frisian
descent but born in Illinois, while Sam ran into Jessie, daughter of Frisian
immigrants in Michigan. Their parents Sasse and Grietje Stuurmans-Visser
also lived in the Lynden area in 1910, while the two other Stuurman
children, Dieuwke and Pieter, lived elsewhere.[143]

The religious life of the Frisians in Lynden was centered around the First
Christian Reformed Church, organized in 1900 especially by Henry Beets,
the later editor of the Dutch weekly, the *Banner*, and in the spirit of Frisian
immigrant D.J. Zijlstra. Thirteen Dutch families and one single man joined
this church, led by Reverend Abel J. Brink who came from Michigan. A
decade later, in 1910, a Christian school was begun by the immigrants with
Dutch as the main language. In her book about the village, Dorothy Koert,
herself a descendant of early settlers in the Lynden area, stresses the
clannishnish of the Dutch immigrants. Although the arrival of people from
England, Sweden, Norway, Switzerland, Germany, France and Belgium was
responsible for a kaleidoscopic range of patterns in family and church life,
the growing Dutch population with their traditions and concepts became
the dominant force in Lynden in the decades after 1900. In many ways,
despite all kinds of internal dissensions, most of the Frisian pioneers in

Washington relied on a way of life supported by religious mores, in which they found security in the fact that they spoke the same Frisian and Dutch languages and defended the same heritage.[144]

This binding spirit also is signaled by B.L. Anderson, who compared the Scandinavian and Dutch rural settlements in the Stillaguamish and Nooksack valleys of Western Washington, where also Frisians had settled. Anderson concludes that the expansion and conservative group spirit of the Dutch settlement was the result of specific agricultural techniques brought from the home country – for example wetland farming – as well as the result of the shared Calvinistic values and faith. The Dutch very much relied on their old country experience, not only in agricultural matters, but also socially and psychologically. Unlike the Dutch, the Scandinavians brought a system of values and agricultural techniques to America that had not proved to be profitable in their home country. As a result, the Scandinavians adapted and in turn discarded many of the agricultural methods of the frontier. By interacting economically and socially with the maturing society in the West, they developed their own composite farming system, and achieved additional income through long hours of labor, a generous use of capital, and an intensive use of the land. In the long run the Scandinavians were not as successful in farming as the Dutch Frisians, although their group spirit remained for decades.[145]

Only a few Frisians of the case-study group went directly to Washington State between 1880-1914. Reflecting on the Dutch in general in 1910, of the western states only California ranked in the ten states with more than 2,200 foreign-born Dutch. Illinois, Iowa, Michigan, New Jersey, New York, and Wisconsin, accounted for a little more than 3 out of 4 Dutchmen in the United States. By contrast, only one out of 55 Dutchmen in the United States in 1910 resided in Washington State.[146]

The same pattern can be found in the case-study group of northern Frisians in 1900. Only one out of these 1,496 Frisian-born had settled as yet in Washington State, while more than two out of three in 1900 had settled in Illinois, Iowa, Michigan, and Wisconsin.[147]

In 1910 there is evidence that more Frisians could be found in Washington State, since they had worked their way west after being in the United States for several years. However, they were still considerably fewer in number than in the eastern or midwestern states. Frisian immigrants in the West had more rural and agricultural options than in the industrially dominated East. They could start jobs that were closely related to those they had in the old country. According to David Nicandri, for example, Italian immigrants faced the same process in the West. Nicandri points out that Italians in the West avoided living in forced close proximity with their own or other ethnic groups as in the eastern cities. The West was different because it was easy going, spacious, yet smaller on the human scale.[148] In a way these western characteristics also worked to the benefit of the Frisian immigrants. The opportunities in an area like Lynden appeared to be favorable and resulted in the following description in a homeseekers' guide to the state of Washington in 1914: The strong colony of Hollanders engaged in dairying near Lynden are of "particular interest" and "the years succeeding the census of 1910 witnessed substantial growth."[149]

In summary, there were clear factors that made the history of the Frisians in the American West different from the eastern and midwestern experience: first, the number of Frisians involved was smaller; secondly Frisian immigrants in the West had been living in the East or Midwest first; and thirdly, as for other immigrants in those years, for Frisians circumstances in the West were dictated by a still evolving society and pioneering spirit. They could not rely upon Frisian roots in western soils. Much more than in the East, Frisians had to pave their own way in social, economic, and religious matters. The West was won differently than the East, and this had consequences for the ethnic identity as well. In the next chapter I will try to construct a framework for understanding Frisian ethnicity, or the interaction between the old country baggage and the new environment.

# *Chapter 8* Ethnic baggage in new suitcases

## 8.1 Introduction

After the poet and writer Sjouke de Zee had visited several Frisian immigrants in the Far West in 1928, he was convinced that they would never be released from their native soil. "Another culture can grow over the deep soul," he proclaimed, "but the inner longing for the old *heitelân* [Frisian homeland] stays alive in their hearts." De Zee was a Frisian himself and his observation in a way was a self-characterization. He wrote the account of his journey to America in the Frisian language and emphasized that this "would strengthen the ties to *Fryslân* over the Ocean."[1]

De Zee's opinion brings up the problem that self-identifications and typifications of strangers are never the same. The discrepancy between the two was also evident in the immigrant letters and the image of America: it was made clear that observation of foreign cultures is a complex issue. Hans Magnus Enzensberger has also referred to this interaction between self-identification and typification of strangers. In his *Van der Leeuw* lecture in Groningen, entitled *Die grosse Wanderung* [the great trek], he attributed to this interaction the role of curiosity and conciliation, defense and offense, resentment and projection, as well as strategies of self-criticism, of irony and disarmament.[2] Enzensberger's characterization suggests that the qualification, "Frisians are stubborn, persistent and stiff," has a totally different meaning depending on whether it is expressed by a Frisian or by a Groninger. Evidence for that can be found in the dissimilar reaction to such a phrase: without producing commotion it can only be articulated by a Frisian among Frisians, not by a Groninger. Ethnicity is a phenomenon that is hard to analyze. Rob Kroes in his study of Dutch immigrants in Amsterdam, Montana, even speaks of "complex processes of cultural struggle." Assimilation and acculturation of this group of Calvinistic pioneers did not appear as a predetermined development but as a continuous process of changing ethnic profiling.[3]

In this chapter attention will be given to aspects of this phenomenon of Frisian ethnic identity. Like other migrants, Frisians were confronted with the daily observation of the "other" and the "self". "Everything is totally different here" is a much voiced comment in nineteenth century immigrant letters. Confrontations with the "other" did raise doubts concerning the obvious "well-known," and influenced the migrant's position in life, while opening new perspectives in thoughts and behavior. However, confrontations with the "other" also produced the fending off of the "other" and, as a result the confirmation of familiar behavior, trustful ideas, and prevailing standards. Interaction with the new society therefore, also brought up the offensive profiling of the "self" as a means to formulate an ethnic identity. And this identity did not appear to be a static state of being; quite the contrary, it was reinvented constantly.[4]

The recent conceptualization of ethnicity formulated by Werner Sollors in his book *The Invention of Ethnicity* runs as follows: "Ethnicity marks an acquired modern sense of belonging that replaces visible, concrete communities whose kinship symbolism may yet mobilize in order to appear more natural." In Sollors' terms ethnicity does not result from any *a priori* cultural difference, but from "the specifity of power relations at a given historical moment and in a particular place." Sollors holds that ethnicity is an invention of collective fiction.[5]

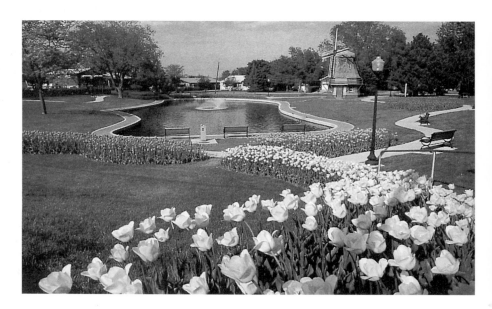

*Dutch windmill and wooden shoe-shaped pond in Pella, Iowa in the 1990s*

Sollors' views concerning ethnicity were discussed recently by a group of leading migration scholars including historians and sociologists. They agreed with Sollors that ethnicity is not primordal "ancient, unchanging, inherent in a group's blood, soul or misty past." But they disputed his idea that ethnicity is a collective fiction by stating that it is rather "a process of construction or invention which incorporates, adapts, and amplifies preexisting communal solidarities, cultural attributes, and historical memories. That is, it is grounded in real life context and social experience."[6] The basic assumption is that ethnicity is constantly reinvented and that contextuality and periodicity affected the process. The authors make plausible that the concept of invention has significant advantages for the study of assimilation and acculturation, because the focus is not so much on individual immigrant behavior in the host society, but more on collective, interactive behavior "in which negotiations between immigrant groups and the dominant ethnoculture are open-ended and ambivalent." This concept brings into question the assumption that the host society is the lone dictator of the process of assimilation and that "change is a linear progression from 'foreignness' to Americanization."[7]

Ethnicity is a flexible idea. Immigrants with the same cultural and racial characteristics may react very differently in various political and economic circumstances. The concept of the invention of ethnicity enables us to profile aspects of Frisian migration to the United States without viewing them as a sterile parochial group that was only cursed with internal vicissitudes.

## 8.2 The role of the family and the immigrant church

The community studies have made clear that the network of kinship and communal associations among the Frisian immigrants was exploited in the new environment to create social and economic networks. The family remained a central component of day to day life. This conclusion moves away from findings of historians of American migration a few decades ago. Scholars like Oscar Handlin argued that immigrants came from a uniformly poor and traditional Europe and that emigration meant a move away from the influence of the family. In Handlin's view emigration symbolized a way in which enterprising individuals could escape the confines of the family and the village community in the old country.

The finding that the family remained the most influential institution in everyday Frisian immigrant life also was accentuated in many recent studies of the experience of immigrants after arrival.[8] S. Sinke's latest study concerning Dutch immigrant women in the United States around the turn of the century, confirms this idea for the Dutch in general. Sinke even considers the family as a distinct economic and emotional base: "It was the bedrock of the realm of social reproduction; it provided the setting and the personnel for a large segment of life as most immigrants knew it...."

The migrants generally tried to preserve rather than restructure the form of the family they knew."[9] Of course, some individual Dutch immigrants fell by the wayside, Sinke argues, but their number must have been small considering the familial nature of Dutch migration in the decades around the turn of the century.[10]

For the Frisian immigrants the nuclear family also was the heart of emotional existence. Bearend J. Fridsma, who came with his parents, two brothers and three sisters, to Passaic in 1911, stresses that all the children contributed their financial share to the family. Two of his sisters worked in the yarn factory immediately after arrival in New Jersey.[11] In the previous chapters it was shown that many sons and daughters worked within the family farm business. Attempts to maximize incomes usually were limited to the nuclear family or extended family first and within the Dutch immigrant community second. Ulbe Eringa with his family ended up in Runningwater,

South Dakota, and first farmed with his brother-in-law. Later on, the two men each went their own way, and Ulbe relied on help from his children.[12] In addition to economic support, the family provided an emotional base that was almost a matter of survival in the new country. For many immigrants, family life was personally meaningful and based on values prior to emigration. Most of the correspondence over the ocean is filled with references to family members and an overwhelming sense of family in general. In Friesland rural life and labor had been organized with the family as a central component, and this arrangement often was brought to the United States and in many cases maintained its strength at least for the first generation.[13] This generalization is convincing even after realizing that opposing arguments concerning the decision to migrate split up families. And the spirit of American family life was not the guarantee of an harmonious home according to immigrant writers:

> Home life is not worth a cent here. When the children reach the age of sixteen, it is an exception if they stay home. They can work out their own salvation and then usually show a clean pair of heels. Also the children of immigrants want to do it that way badly, and turn to morals and habits usually to become American faster.[14]

It also appeared that individual immigrants tried to escape the social control of family ties for a variety of reasons by using the migration process for that purpose. However, this was more the exception than the rule. In many ways the Frisian immigrant remained "traditional" in family relations while at the

*Restaurant in Lynden, WA in the 1990s as a symbol of Dutch heritage*

same time using these family connections for economic purposes and the demands of modern capitalism. Sjouke de Zee not only judged the family life of the Frisians positively in his account of 1928. He was convinced that life for the Frisian Americans was a lot more hurried because of the continued search for economic profit. Therefore, family life was turbulent. Although a lot was accomplished, there was hardly time for "it smûke, it smoute, dat it húslik libben sa ryk meitsje kin" [the cosiness, the homeyness, that can make family life so rich].[15]

The strength of social ties within the families and the nuclear families themselves, influenced immigrant behavior in every aspect of life. What the welfare specialist Charles Murray noted in a late-twentieth century context also fits the Frisians: the nuclear family as the cornerstone of society may well have been a necessity for immigrants in a society with broad, legal freedom, and heavily dependent on non-governmental institutions for the regulation of behavior.[16]

No one who has the impossible desire to penetrate the soul of the United States can neglect American-style religion, A. Lammers wrote a few years ago. And in 1994, J.W. Schulte Nordholt proclaimed that there is hardly a western nation where the people so enthusiastically identify themselves with the kingdom of God on earth as they do in the United States.[17]

The church undoubtedly influenced the New World fundamentally, and often was part of an ethnic identity. Next to the family, the church generally functioned for the Frisian immigrants as a second pillar in American society. When the Reverend Roelof T. Kuiper arrived in Michigan in 1879 he started to write down his impressions of the new land together with hints for prospective immigrants. "In the first place", Kuiper proclaimed, "one should recognize the Lord in all of his ways and in his plans.... Man proposes but God disposes...."[18] This phrase reflects the atmosphere painted in some of the letters of Frisians to the old country. From the different sources it seems that there was an almost unanimous desire among immigrants to assemble in churches. This observation leads to the suggestion that the immigrant church was a harmonious and placid place, where immigrants could interact and worship in an ethnic context that preserved them from the "dangerous outside world." However, that Dutch immigrants found not only solace in their churches, but also competing theories and ideas among themselves and their ecclesiastical leaders, is a notorious fact. In 1888 a Frisian who belonged to the Dutch Reformed Church in America wrote from Grand Rapids, Michigan:

> You write me that you are building a church and I find that a good thing because that's the way it goes here too: every community has to build his own and also has to take care of it. Last year we got a new organ and that cost around 10.000 guilders and here they are almost all laborers who have to make money with their hands, but it comes very slowly. The *Afgescheden* [the 1834 Secessionists] are here in three types *afgescheden* of *afgescheden* and then again *afgescheden*, so three types and everyone builds for himself. Yes, my loving child, a lot is offered to the Religion here and to the schools....[19]

The "feuding over the Faith of the Fathers," as R. Kroes describes it in his book concerning the Dutch in Montana, confirmed their identity and to a certain point kept the community from disintegration and subjection to secular politics. The immigrant churches segregated the Dutch from each other as well as from American society or culture. However, this separatism did not automatically imply disintegration of ethnic identity. Generally, theology seemed to have been a medium for the immigrants to battle out all kind of different conflicts. This tradition was brought from the Netherlands and it was one of the main binding elements of Dutch culture in the United States.[20]

Religious disagreement within the Dutch settlements in 19th century America also led to schisms and turns to different directions. Frisians in this context can be seen as part of the Dutch immigrant communities. I did not find any evidence that they segregated themselves from the religious spirits of the Dutch in general, or that they organized an ethnic church along the lines of their Frisian background. This actually is not very surprising, since in Friesland they had been associated with the Dutch national Protestant churches as well, and the language in church had been Dutch for everyone. The relevant question is, how the Frisian immigrants reacted to religious life in America in general and how their religious commitments affected their ethnic identity.[21]

The Dutch Population Registers only showed one Catholic family in the case-study group of Frisian emigrants, and I did not find any sources that referred to membership of Catholic churches in the United States. Frisian emigrants from the clay area did not associate with the Catholic church. The minority of Catholics in Friesland had no migration tradition. Other major factors play a role in studying the religious behavior of Frisian immigrants. Some did not move into Frisian-American or Dutch-American settlements. Others who did join these communities did not join the Dutch Reformed churches. And, as Sinke indicates appropriately, we should understand that activities of the Dutch American churches aimed at preserving a religious heritage that became a heart of Dutch-American culture.[22] This had consequences for the historical documentation, as is made clear from, for example, the centennial history of the Emmanual Reformed Church of Springfield, South Dakota, a congregation with many Frisian members. In the introduction the author declares:

> There is one intentional omission in this book that perhaps should be mentioned. We have not recorded the unfortunate times when our people did not live up to the standards of Christian love, cooperation, and patience which our Lord Jesus desires of his followers. Whenever a group goes through the process of adjusting from one culture to another, the situation is especially ripe for strained personal relationships. These strains did show themselves from time to time. We confess that such events occurred but we did not record them. Instead, we lift our hearts in thanksgiving to God that He has faithfully carried us forward and continued to love us and in time has healed most of the wounds.[23]

Such lacunae in the historical sources as well as the silence concerning non-church members, have to be considered. All these factors influenced the religious developments within the Frisian-American communities. These had consequences for the individual Frisian immigrant and determined the sources of research.

That religion could be a binding factor and that religious controversies created a completely different atmosphere among Dutch immigrants *within* various communities may be clear from several studies, but it is interesting to see that religion sometimes was a binding or schismatic factor *between* – related – ethnic groups as well. Van Hinte describes the religious life in the Dakotas when Netherlanders settled among Ost-Frisians. From the very beginning first mission stations were established in the settlements and then churches. Reformed preachers made their way to these missions and at the same time Christian Reformed missionaries tried to create churches within the community of Frisians and Ost-Frisians. However, according to Van Hinte, competition and interreligious jealousy became more destructive than constructive among these immigrants, and this resulted in a spirit of divisiveness and weakening of what ethnic solidarity existed between the Ost-Frisians and the Dutch Frisians.[24]

There are other examples of Germans who initially joined with the Dutch in the Reformed churches. H. Brinks recalls the history of the German Bentheimers in Graafschap, Michigan, where they dominated the Christian Reformed Church in the early years. This connection between Dutch and German immigrants not only alters the general perception that the CRC stems exclusively from Dutch immigrants, but it also signifies the influence of old country provincial border relations in new settlements in America. Graafschap Bentheim forms a German border area neighboring the Dutch provinces of Overijssel and Drenthe.[25] Such border relations could be found among Frisian immigrants in Minnesota. Dutch Frisians and Ost-Frisians from the Bunde area in Germany gathered in the Christian Reformed Church of Rheiderland Township in Chippewa County, Minnesota in the late 1880s. A few years later a second Christian Reformed Church called 'Emden' was founded by Dutch and Ost-Frisians together, 7 miles north of Renville in Renville County, Minnesota. After a few years this Church came to the edge of dissolution because the Dutch and Germans were in conflict. Most of the Ost-Frisian families separated themselves and founded a Presbyterian Church, while the Emden CRC became largely Dutch Frisian.[26]

Generally, the church life of the Protestant Frisians moved in their own Dutch (and Frisian) ethnic circles. Like the family, church for them appeared to be part of the linchpin to a Dutch-American identity, and it proved to be a cultural continuum for more than one generation. In a way the church visits provided a platform for intra-ethnic socializing, and at the same time discouraged contacts with non-members or other ethnic groups. That the immigrant church simply was an extension of tradition, a replica from old world culture, has been challenged in migration research for some time now.[27] A traveler from Friesland was astonished at the quite different practices in Dutch American churches to recruit members. In Michigan and

New York he met clerics of Frisian origin and it was made clear to him that a bowling alley in the church basement for leisure use was not an exception. A business-card from a reverend in Rochester appeared to be a tiny little booklet with directions on many aspects of church life. This Frisian traveler also was surprised to see stores around the churches to augment their income.[28]

*Jacob van der Meulen and Tietje Gerrits van der Meij before their home in Randolph, WI. Photograph entitled: "Our car that brings us to church". Donated by T. Sipma-Dijkstra*

Frisians did not participate in Dutch Reformed churches only because they were drawn by their religious background, but also because the church communities provided mutual assistance in a strange land. Hardly any of the Frisian immigrants knew the English language and leaving the homeland with the idea that they would never see their family again could be a lonely venture. Church meetings provided worship services, sharings about the "old"' and "new" countries, and singing psalms in the mother tongue. In many new settlements in the West, in the absence of organized Dutch Reformed churches, these meetings originally started in homes of Frisian immigrants.[29]

The social impact of the church is made clear in a letter of Johannes Koning from Belgrade, Montana, in 1904: "The people (Dutch I mean) are all orthodox here, so I go to church every Sunday too. Also Klaas Rienks, who is here too, has become a steady churchgoer. He works here at a Groninger."[30]

Kl.J. Tiemersma, who spent three years in the United States around 1890, comments on the steady visits to Sunday School by every Dutch member of the immigrant community in Orange City, Iowa, as follows: "no matter if they were churchgoing or not, religious or not....This was just the way it is: an entrenched habit....These Sundays also were my own only days out, except the already mentioned national holiday of the fourth of July."[31] In later decades, with the tiring farm life fairly set, Sunday services were the only respite from the daily routine. These gatherings allowed the farmers to receive religious and theological education. Next to the Bible, other books of a religious and theological nature were found in rural homes and there were unlettered farmers who could discuss ideas of Bavinck, Colijn, Calvin, and Kuyper.[32]

Mutual assistance and socializing could be reasons for Frisians to join the Dutch Protestant churches. Fellow church members could offer help either financially or emotionally during times of unemployment or of death. An immigrant from Orange City, Iowa, wrote to Friesland, for example, that the church members collected money for a group of forty Dutchmen in Colorado to relieve them from their poverty.[33] Reverend Arnold Brink, the son of Home Missionary Abel J. Brink who served in Lynden, Washington, around the turn of the century, recalls mutual assistance in matters of death:

> In the first year that my parents arrived in Lynden as home missionaries, a twelve-year-old girl in the little congregation died. The family had no money. The nearest undertaker was in New Whatcom, nearly twenty miles away, so my father made a casket, my mother lined it with white sheeting. She washed the little girl's body and dressed it for burial. So their first funeral took place. Then and there my father vowed this would not happen again. He persuaded everyone to pledge to contribute a small amount, perhaps no more than ten cents, each time there was a death among them. The money collected was then given to the bereaved family to make possible a suitable funeral. This was the origin of the Monumenta Society, which is still in existence.[34]

As in many other ethnic churches, the Dutch Protestant immigrant churches institutionalized social services by creating homes for the elderly, hospitals, orphanages, women's groups and youth clubs. Many Frisians were anchored to the ethnic enclave through their church membership. The Frisian immigrant community of Whitinsville, Massachusetts, according to the sources, shows a very coherent church life. Only one Dutch Reformed church was created in this settlement. After some heavy discussions, the immigrants in 1896 agreed to join the Christian Reformed Church and sought contacts with the Classis of Hudson. For the following decades the CRC was the ruling immigrant church attended by the Frisians.[35] This coherence of church life probably was influenced by the fact that Whitinsville's immigrant population in the first decades was almost entirely of Frisian origin. It seems that the ethnic background provided an atmosphere of compromise, because everywhere else in Dutch settlements in the United States the different types of Dutch Reformed churches appeared. In Whitinsville as well as in other Dutch immigrant communities, the church was a strong unifying influence in preserving the Dutch culture. This was more so for the general Dutch aspects of Dutch culture than for the specific Frisian aspects.

The language in church always was Dutch. No bible in Frisian was available. Discussions concerning church language in the first decades of the twentieth century were about *Dutch* or English and never about *Frisian* or Dutch or about *Frisian* or English. In fact church life was a key element in language retention among the Dutch in America. In many homes of first generation Frisian immigrants a pluriform situation of three languages existed: English in the outside (often worker's-) world, Dutch in church, and Frisian at home. With regard to church matters this meant that the idea to go over to services in English found response, because the immigrant children who spoke Frisian at home did not appreciate the services in Dutch, since they had trouble understanding it.

Generally, Frisian immigrants preserved the Dutch language longer than immigrants from the Catholic Dutch provinces. Frisians mainly settled in Dutch Protestant communities – corresponding with their religious background – where immigrants often were of homogeneous Dutch origin. Catholic immigrants from, for example, Noord-Brabant ended up in multi-ethnic Catholic communities together with Flemish, Irish, and German immigrants, and therefore were more challenged or provoked to communicate in the shared English language.[36] In this respect Frisian immigrants were clearly part of the Dutch Calvinist immigrant experience in general.

By affiliating with the Dutch-American churches, the Frisian immigrants not only took care of their spiritual well-being in the new environment, but also of the social profiling of their ethnic group in a Dutch national context. That way the Frisians tried to avoid the influences of American society or to assure themselves of personal psychological stability in the economic and social dynamics of a new and strange society. Evidently, the process of acculturation for the Frisians could not be realized without distinction and the ethnic profiling of the self. The ethnic characteristics had to be defined against "the other" in order to create a much needed stabilization of the "self."

### 8.3 Frisian women abroad

When some Frisian women with the traditional silver head cap arrived in Liverpool to take the ocean steamer to America, they were booed by English people who thought that these women were bald. Ethnic differences took a toll soon after leaving the old country.

In this study a lot of attention has been paid to the role of men in the migration process, mainly in economic sense, because they were active in the official labor market. The life of Frisian women who migrated to the United States in the *fin de siècle* period is also characterized by enormous changes, and, therefore, deserves attention. Women did not always come to America for the same reasons men did. As in Friesland, in America immigrant women were occupied with other things than men were. However, the habitual roles of both sexes functioned differently than in Friesland, although immigrants tried to preserve aspects of the Frisian life. Women who migrated left a lot behind and, at the same time, created many opportunities in the New World.

After some years in Roseland, Frederika Groustra-Aukes summarized the emotional reality of leaving people behind:

> I shall put courage into you Brother and Sister; it is a lot better here for a human being to enjoy the necessary needs for physical well-being. One could never picture things so beautiful to me anymore, that it would make me return to the old fatherland; especially since Father and Mother are dead: sisters and Brother who need them so badly in their younger years, it is so disastrous; and what can you do with such a fatherland where you don't have a living even when you are hard working. Well, dear Brother and sister come over to us. Write back soon.[37]

For Frisian immigrant women the firm setting of family relations appeared to be an obstacle in acclimating to the new environment. Family ties always had been a pillar in social life and to leave family members behind was heartbreaking. Especially the care for aging parents was a typical task for daughters. Not to be involved in this duty caused an emotional problem for Frisian immigrant women.

More than 4000 women and girls left the Frisian clay area between 1880 and 1914. Peaks can be found in the years 1881, 1882, 1892, and 1893, when about 250 women a year left for America.

Table 8.1 **Absolute and relative migration of females from the Frisian clay area to the United States, 1880-1914; all ages, married and single:**

|  | Abs. | % |
|---|---|---|
| 1880-1889 | 1531 | 37.2 |
| 1890-1899 | 1312 | 31.9 |
| 1900-1909 | 747 | 18.2 |
| 1910-1914 | 521 | 12.7 |
| **1880-1914** | **4111** | **100.0** |

**Source:** J.B.E. Galema, "Frisians to America, 1880-1914. Computer Compilation," (Groningen, 1992)

Until recently, not much was known about the history of Dutch immigrant women. However, the meaning of gender in the process of migration has been discussed by S. Sinke in her dissertation dealing with Dutch Protestant immigrant women around the turn of the century.[38] Sinke uses the theoretical concept of social reproduction, which emphasizes the idea that there is no production without certain specified conditions like baking bread, cleaning clothes, making contacts with family and friends, and, educating the children. In short, there must be a *home* to take care of body and soul.

It was women who took care of these tasks, and they made little money with it. Nevertheless, these tasks were essential for the production: without these conditions there was no money to earn. Social reproduction contained the part of life beyond the paid job, but at the same time it was needed to do the paid job.

Sinke does not use social reproduction simply as a term to explain reproducing what migrants had known. Reproduction also could mean change. However, this change was created by using old country values, customs and habits. For Frisian immigrant women aspects of social reproduction also could be found in sources like letters, interviews, and biographies.

One of the main characteristics of Frisian migration is the larger number of males who left for the United States. Except for the years 1886, 1894, and 1895, Frisian emigrant women were a minority compared to men. Almost all the women migrated within the family situation. They left together with their husband, fiancé, father, mother, brothers, or sisters. Only a few left all by themselves. This typical Frisian situation differs from migration of females from some other European countries. In Germany, for example, it was quite normal for women and girls to leave as singles and to find servant work in American cities or countryside.[39] That Frisian girls seldom left by themselves most likely was determined by the traditional close family bonds. Also, it was unusual for women in Friesland to work outside the family home, except when economic motives made it absolutely necessary. Women who were active on the official labor market in the native country most likely were more eager to emigrate singly, especially because they felt more self-reliant than their home working counterparts. There were Frisian women or girls who worked as servants for employers. However, when overseas migration was in the picture, they usually quit their jobs and joined their migrating family members. There have been exceptions: the strong and self-confident Cornelia de Groot was one of them, and she deserves attention later, especially because her story makes clear that America for some women served as an escape from existing structures and conditions.

In the clay area during the agrarian crisis, women worked on the land more often than during prosperous times. Economic necessity made whole families active in agricultural labor. A contemporary report about women's and children's labor in Friesland showed discouraging results and concluded that "consequences for the family and for the education of children were disastrous."[40] Considering the fact that most women who emigrated around the turn of the century were from lower economic classes, the bad social situation of women laboring outside the family home also determined the decision to escape life in Friesland.

The decision to emigrate was not only a male matter. Jochum Brouwer in 1881 wrote to his uncle and aunt in Galesburg, Iowa, about the discussions in his family:

> Also from Ee people leave for America.... A whole crowd is thinking about it, but what does it mean, they cannot leave because they don't have any money. I really would like to go, I am thinking of it night and day, almost never my thoughts are without it. My mother

*Minke Jacobs Sikma, after a failed marriage, emigrated around 1885 from Tietjerksteradeel, following 10 of her 12 childeren to Roseland, Chicago. Photo donated by T.G. Hoekstra*

also badly wants to go, she said I should write to you about it.... If my father wanted to go as badly as my mother does, then it was sure that we would come over. But my father does not feel like it yet. Yesterday he said, if Uncle and Aunt write that they like to see us come, than we will leave. My mother and I love to see you writing to father to urge him to leave. We won't have peace before that.[41]

Two months later, after positive migration advice from the family in Iowa, the Brouwers joined them.

Migration motives of Frisian women often were inspired by the idea that a better future for their children was possible in America. Besides, in many immigrant letters the image of America as a so-called "paradise for women" was stressed.[42] In 1893 an immigrant writes about the American women, who were beautifully dressed and "who did the laundry in a dress," without having their hands in the soapy water because "a machine did the work." The same letter recalls that American women sweep their living room with a long broom, "at which they don't have to bend their back at all."[43]

Of course, there were Frisian women who did not think much about emigration to the United States. They just followed their husbands or children and their ideals and in a way felt themselves forced to leave. Sometimes women resisted going because of the care of parents or the long journey. The trip to America often was more troublesome or inconvenient for women than for men. It happened that a child was born on board the ship, or that young children died during the journey, and the food was not all that good. J.W. de Jong writes after his coming to Indiana about his wife Sytske de Bildt: "After arrival in Lafayette...I was depressed about Sytske and the little boy, because they were weak and ailing...but now they bite in the American bacon very well, and they become bloated and get colours like roses."[44]

Frisian immigrant women, who had been used to living in the country side, had to acclimatize in huge American cities like Chicago, Paterson, and Grand Rapids, while others moved to the wide and uninhabited lands of Montana or Washington. Frequently, a positive circumstance in the totally new environment was the fact that others from the old country could be found in the neighborhood. The Old Guard gave support to newcomers. One of the results was that immigrant women spoke the Frisian language sometimes even to the third generation, with positive and negative consequences. Most of the married Frisian women did not work outside the family home and therefore had more difficulties learning English than did men. A decade after immigration, not all of the first generation women could speak English, and some even remained bilingual all their lives.[45]
All in all it seems evident that Frisian women in the New World balanced between the re-creation of practices of their native country and the use of new possibilities, experiences, customs and values in the United States. This balance resulted in new developments in the organization of social life, which can be traced in family circles, women's networks, and in views on the world.
To organize the household, Frisian immigrant women tried to reproduce elements from their daily routines in the homeland. They appreciated thrift and their cooking put potatoes, vegetables, and meat on the table. As in Friesland, household and family ties were considered to be very important. This stressed the role of women as mother and wife, and to get married and to give birth to children was a main goal in life.
Immigrant men often returned to Friesland to search for a mate who ressembled their mother. And Frisian women often knew exactly the unmarried Frisian men they could meet after arrival in the United States. This contradicted the ideas of contemporary scholars, who believed that immigrant single men after settlement would find a wife in the foreign country, which caused an increase in the surplus of women in the homeland.[46] However, Frisian men rarely married outside the ethnic group.

In the United States Frisian women recreated the networks that they had in the old country. Migration caused the networks of traditional informal care to collapse: the woman next door did not automatically give a helping hand when a child was born. The women, therefore, created new networks, which were partly based on elements of the traditional networks. As noted before, parents often followed their children to America. Examples of elderly widows who left are not rare. Froukje Dirks Algra from Minnertsga in 1900 departed at the age of ninety, and Jetske Zwart from Hallum was sixty-three years old when she emigrated.[47] The widow Anna Geertruida Westra from Blija left with three children in 1885 when she was over 50, to follow four of her older children who had already settled in the United States in the early 1880s.[48]

Much energy was used to initiate and preserve ethnic social exchange in the United States. Enormous distances were faced, which was remarkable because before emigration not many immigrants had gone outside the Frisian border. Church and family were significant in this creation of networks in the United States and also determined the world view. Individual experiences of female newcomers differed greatly. The individual woman will be illustrated here by the example of Maaike Rijpstra who was representative for many Frisian immigrant women. Cornelia de Groot, whose migratory experience was totally out of character, will illustrate the atypical case.

In the spring of 1893, at the age of twenty, the maid servant Maaike Rijpstra traveled from the village of Sexbierum, Friesland, to Hull, Iowa, where in the fall she married Ulbe Eringa, age twenty-seven. One of Maaike's first letters came in 1894 from Runningwater, South Dakota, where the couple rented a farm of 320 acres. She acquainted her readers with the new environment and showed some anxiety concerning her new and unknown family-in-law: "Although we don't know each other, and although I don't know if you are interested in an American household, I will tell you something about it."[49] The first impression we get is the idea of a nice, big home surrounded with many fruit trees. Maaike quite often compared her situation with that in the Netherlands and usually her observations could stand the test of comparison: "We have two bedrooms upstairs, where our beds are; we don't have box beds. We also have a cellar, but not as beautiful as the Dutch milk cellar but a good one though and on both sides of the house a *poots* [porch]." Maaike easily explained why she did not have a sewing machine yet, because "a farm at first is very expensive." She showed her joy about the arrival in Runningwater of her sister Teatske with husband Gelf de Roos and three children. Maaike felt at home in America and at the same time realized that for most immigrants it took some time to acclimatize.

In January 1896, when her young daughter Grietje played around in the house, Maaike does not give the impression that she lived a life in the nuclear family only. In her correspondence the contacts with other Frisian immigrants appear frequently: "you both have known Betje from Age Harmes? She was divorced and left for America and married a sturdy American farmer." A few years later a second sister of Maaike came to the Dakotas with a husband and six children. The social life of these families mainly occurred within the Frisian immigrant surroundings. Maaike's children all got Frisian first names, a clear indication of old country attachment.

Not only the Frisian family changed; in her letters Maaike also explained much about material conditions. She reports on a new sewing-machine and 89 guilders received from an inheritance of a childless aunt: "For that money we invited a young hired hand from Sexbierum, who already works at our farm for weeks now."

The division of labor followed Frisian tradition, and Maaike mostly took care of the household. But sometimes we read of exceptional things: in 1903 Ulbe writes about his wife as a succesful chicken farmer.

Often the religious life in the Dutch community in Runningwater is a subject in the letters. Because there was no Christian school in Runningwater at first, Maaike bought a "Kaapsche kinderbijbel" [children's bible] to teach the children the Dutch language, and Ulbe took care of the children's Sunday school, in Dutch. The couple always attended the Emmanuel Dutch Reformed Church in Springfield, more than an hour's walk from Runningwater. Their daughters were members of the church girls' society. American Thanksgiving was also celebrated within the religious community. Two daughters left to go to the Dutch Christian high school in Orange City [now Northwestern College], Iowa, where Maaike came to visit at least once. The oldest daughter Grietje married a Frisian man whose parents still lived in the homeland. In 1926 Maaike left Runningwater with her husband to go to Orange City for retirement.

It is clear that Maaike felt at home in the United States, especially within the framework of the Dutch Reformed Church and the Frisian immigrant community. The new life in America constantly was combined with norms, values, and the intense network of contacts from the fatherland. Maaike is representative for the thousands of Frisian women who left for the American countryside around the turn of the century. She is exceptional, however, in her optimism and overall positive experience. She did not suffer great disappointment concerning her health, and that of her family. And like so many other immigrant women, she never returned to the old fatherland for a visit.

Cornelia de Groot is an exception to the norm. Shortly after 1900 she left for the United States, where she published in 1917 the curious book *When I was a Girl in Holland.*[50] Cornelia was born in the village of Deersum on January 9, 1878, where her father was a cattle farmer. In her book Cornelia described the years of her youth on the farm and focused on the role and position of women in Friesland and on aspects of daily life. As a child she was not satisfied with the future prospect expected for a Frisian farmer's daughter of becoming a local farmer's wife. She was envious of the farmers who did what they wanted during wintertime and who decided themselves if they wanted to spend their time studying, while the women always were working inside the house. The idea that men had far greater challenges and opportunities provoked her. Cornelia succeeded in getting an education and dreamed of travels and jobs in the male world:

> Strange to say, often I did not seem to think of myself as a girl, but as a boy. For instance, I liked variety and a life of sameness seemed to me dreadful, and I wanted to get all out of life there was to be gotten out of it. So at one time I thought, when grown up I should try all the trades, be a carpenter, a blacksmith, a cooper, a sailor, a baker, etc., successively

and each one for a short time only. I read biographies of great men and wanted to
emulate them. My hero and example was always a man, never a woman, and this has been
so with me all through life. Yet I was not a tomboy, due perhaps to my not being very
robust. Neither did I regret my being a girl; on the contrary, I was proud and glad of it,
but I believed myself to be on a perfect equality with boys having the same rights. This
was undoubtedly due to my great love for freedom.[51]

In 1888 Cornelia's brother Lolke had left for California, where he started as
a market gardener. Her sister Antje also crossed the ocean, working as a
stewardess for the Holland America Line and later as a nurse. There is no
doubt that Cornelia was inspired by her family members to move to the
United States.
Cornelia left against her parents' wishes. She took a job in Amsterdam to
save money for the journey, and in 1902 or 1903 she traveled with the
Belgian ocean liner *Vaderland* from Antwerp to New York. She finally ended
up in San Francisco, where her sister Anna lived with her family. Only a few
days later she enrolled in "a prominent business college," and later she
worked for all kind of commercial businesses. But most remarkable is her
writing for the *San Francisco Chronicle*, a prominent newspaper in the city.
Much later, in the thirties and forties, she worked for different Dutch offices

in San Francisco like the Netherlands-American Chamber of Commerce and the Dutch Consulate.

With the book about her youth in the Netherlands, Cornelia de Groot intended to create interest and understanding for the ethnic diversity within and outside of the United States. Her articles in the "World Topic Section" of the *Chronicle* dealt with subjects like the miserable situation of miners and their families, gender differences and the position of women in American society, monuments in the Netherlands like the history of windmills, and alcoholic consumption in the Netherlands compared to American prohibition.

One of these articles, entitled "American and Dutch maids are compared," described the differences of female servants in both countries.[52] Cornelia had recently returned from a visit to Friesland where she found that American women had a bad reputation. The Dutch considered them to be too lazy to care for their children, real spendthrifts, and much too spoiled by American males. Cornelia reported on what she had read in Dutch newspaper articles, especially by expatriated Hollanders:

> One man wrote that American women so dominated their men that when a gathering of men was a spirited, cheerful conversation, and a few women entered their presense, it seemed as if a shadow crept into their midst. Their naturalness and cheerfulness left them and made place for a feeling of uneasiness. The conversation slowed down to perfunctory talk. Another wrote that in choosing a wife the American man preferred the beautiful and dumb. All he cared about was a baby face and a lovely figure so that his friends might admire him for his taste and envy him for his acquisition. He did not concern himself about the intellect or lack of it within the "Queen." It made no difference whether she was educated or not, and whether or not she could carry on an interesting conversation left him cold. What he wanted her for was to "show off."[53]

The earlier mentioned Sjouke de Zee also had outspoken ideas about American women that fit perfectly Cornelia's summary of images in Friesland. He concluded that American females were put on a throne like a queen, which he called idolatry, and warned that laziness and arrogance lead to domineeringness, that will ruin the integrity and the spirit of family life.[54] In her report in the *San Francisco Chronicle*, Cornelia admits that at first she also had not been enthusiastic about American women and their households. Dutch cleaning fits and hominess were hard to find in the United States. However, Cornelia points to the fact that American women usually worked harder, because they had the double job of both wage earner and housekeeper. Laziness is not a characteristic of any one nationality, nor is the spoiling of wives a characteristic of some American husbands only. Cornelia sensibly concluded that human nature does not change much with national bounderies.

Is Cornelia's picture of American women through the eyes of the Dutch realistic? The letters of Frisian immigrant women provide impressions. Most of the newcomers created their social environment through contacts with other Dutch women. It is clear that they adored the ease with which

American women did their household chores, especially because of all the household appliances. Washing machines and new sewing machines were not yet common among Frisian women in America around the turn of the century. Cornelia's stereotypes are also evident. Letters of Frisian immigrants quite often mention laziness and ostentatiousness of American women. One newcomer reported from the Far West that American women looked very slovenly at home, but outside the house they were "rigged out like cockatoos," and they did not have a clue about how to make the home *gezellig* [cozy]. Reverend J. Jansen, who worked in Whitinsville for a few years, after his return to the Netherlands reflected that American women were not as good looking as the Dutch and they did not want to bear "the burdens of motherhood," but in Jansen's opinion Americans were more intelligent than the Dutch.[55]

Most likely, part of the criticism of American women resulted from the fact that first generation Frisian males hardly ever married them. However, according to Cornelia, there was no good reason for Frisian males to be fooled by the negative propaganda concerning American women. Cornelia, nevertheless, was exceptional herself: she never married and her sister Antje married an American. Cornelia de Groot was not representative for all Frisian female newcomers. She emigrated by herself and had many independent jobs outside the home. And more than anyone else, Cornelia was convinced that "no longer can it be said that women are weak! The old favored belief of men is tottering on its foundations."[56]

### 8.4 Education, class, and politics

Before leaving Frisian soil, most emigrants had completed elementary education. Thus, hardly any were illiterate when entering the United States.[57]

In the United States the Dutch also had a reputation of stressing education. This was especially true for the Calvinists because they needed literacy skills to understand the Bible. Therefore, already in the colonial period educational institutes of the Dutch Calvinists often were tied to the immigrant church, which organized tax-supported schools. Catechism instruction in church stressed education informally and the Dutch generally emphasized education formally through public and Christian day schools.[58] Around the turn of the century the Calvinist schools often were viewed as parochial schools. By many Frisian immigrants the *Dutch Christian* character of these schools was more and more critized as sectarian and un-American. This did not concern the Frisians exclusively; the Dutch Protestant immigrants in general in the decades around the turn of the century were influenced by the educational ideas of Abraham Kuyper, who promoted the establishment of independent Christian schools in the Netherlands that were not limited only to a specific Christian church. Kuyper preferred solid, truly American Calvinists rather than sectarian Dutch Calvinists isolated in the United States. A similar opinion could be heard in the *Nieuwsblad van Friesland* by someone in the Frisian homeland:

Elementary school should be a neutral one, also in political matters, it should be accessible for all children. The task of the elementary school can and should be no other than to educate future citizens into thinking adults. And against this, every use of dogmas -whatever kind- is an obstacle....Schools should be there for the children and not to reach grown-up-people's goals through the child.[59]

In contemporary practice the debate concerning education reflected the *schoolstrijd* [school controversy] in the Netherlands, which split the Dutch immigrants into two groups: Christian Reformed folk who established independent schools for their families, and Reformed Church members who considered it their duty to leaven the public schools with a Christian atmosphere. It was also believed that the public schools helped acclimatize and assimilate immigrant children, and transform them into good citizens and hard workers. Native Americans generally viewed the development of all ethnoreligious private schools with mistrust.[60]

Many times the everyday practice of schooling and education was threatened by the immigrant reality. Immigrant letters in contemporary newspapers like the *Nieuwsblad van Friesland,* the *Nieuw Advertentieblad,* and the *Bergumer Courant* did not talk about education or schools. At first the Frisian newcomers did not express any concern about educational matters. More than anything else, immigrants were interested in job possibilities. The demands of the family economy required more than one Frisian immigrant son (and sometimes daughters) to choose a job rather than finish school. Immigrant children generated extra income in the early years of uncertainty. In the *fin de siècle* era the Paterson silk mills and the machine factories in Whitinsville, for example, drew young Frisian workers. Arnold Banning, who emigrated in 1913 at the age of ten, stated in an interview that he did not have the chance to receive a high school education. When his family came to Whitinsville, his father got a job in the Whitin Machine Factory and Arnold went to school until he was fourteen. When his father died of pneumonia, Arnold had to make money in the Whitin factories. However, he "made up his mind that he would not let his brain get dusty;" he became the legendary self-made man.[61]

The problem for most Frisian immigrants was the necessity of learning English. It was quite a transition from the Dutch and Frisian language to English. As pointed out before, hardly anybody learned English before departure. In the United States some of them thought that it was not necessary to learn the language because the settlement would be a Dutch/Frisian community "for ever." Others were convinced that isolation was not the best way to succeed in a foreign country. Most parents were anxious for the socio-economic progress of their children and were well aware of the importance of the English language. Doekele Dijkstra in 1900 invited his young niece Ella to come to Chicago; As a result, he noted, "she profited from the educational system in the Netherlands and now she is in the years – after some schooling – to master the English here, so she will

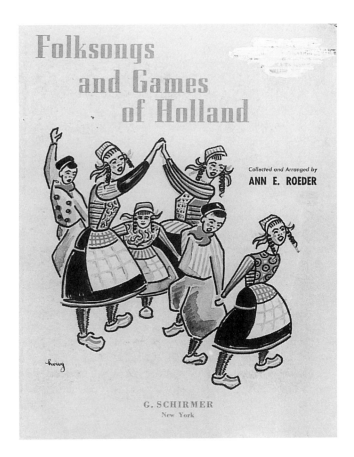

*Cover from:*
*Ann E. Roeder,* Folksongs
and games of Holland
*(New York:*
*G. Schirmer, 1956)*

have the privilege to have a firm grasp of two languages, that will – in the nature of things – make broad-minded views possible."[62]

The link between language and culture is self-evident. The Frisian and Dutch languages represented the homeland culture and brought to life images of the past. The result was that immigrants in the new country faced a language dilemma.

Since the Frisian language was used mostly in conversation only, and the Dutch language for writing and in religious matters, Frisian immigrants faced a complex language retention because of their trilingualism. Where a strong community life existed, the first generation spoke Frisian exclusively in their homes. But in church life, as among the Christian Reformed Frisians in Whitinsville, the Dutch language was used to express religious faith. Nor was Frisian encouraged in the private schools of the Dutch Calvinists. Consequently, the conclusion is justified that worship did not contribute to the formation of a Frisian identity. It contributed to a Dutch national identity.[63] Furthermore, some immigrants went to the English language church in order to learn the language and to worship with others. The widow of K. Siderius wrote after four years in the Dakotas: "...more and more I get used to this country, and learn the language, although the language is very difficult for me, but I start to speak with the people pretty well....Last week we had church every night, so I visited the church six evenings; it is not true that I became so church minded, but the more often I hear [the language], the better I can understand it."[64]

Writing letters was also not a good way of preserving the Frisian language, because it was done in Dutch. This reflected the situation in the old country, where the Frisian language was used nearly exclusively orally. Seldom did first or second generation immigrants write home in English. One of those exceptions was John Peter Buwalda, who arrived as a youngster in 1882, and was schooled in English. He sent his letters in English from North Yakima, Washington, to his cousin in Friesland:

> It grieves me that I am not able to write you in your own language and that I have not mastered several languages, as European students are required to do, but less stress is laid on learning languages in this country; I have spent most of my study-time on the sciences.[65]

The trilingual status made Frisian immigrants distinctive from the Dutch in general. Frisians carried with them a sense of loyalty to their native language that could not be found among *Zeeuwen, Groningers, Brabanders,* or *Drenten.* Generally, the first generation spoke Frisian at home and – like the Dutch – learned rudimentary English for business and political affairs. And sometimes, first generation Frisian immigrant women did not learn English at all, because they mainly spent their lives within the family circle. A woman wrote in 1907:

> You ask if Sjouke works with Frisians, no darling, here are no Frisians in the neighborhood, but at times Hollanders, Groningers or Germans, Englishmen, Swedes, French, Russians, Poles, Irish, Japanese. Black people from all nationalities around us and Chinese. I can hardly understand anybody. Sjouke does understand the people. He speaks English. I am not able to learn it, because that's a bad thing when you get older.[66]

A case study of the linguistic behavior of Frisian immigrants in the United States, with a corpus of data collected in 1966 and based on a linguistic and a socio-demographic component, came to the cautious conclusion that Frisian had been preserved well by the informants.[67] Positive factors in language retention among first and second generation Frisians were the Frisian background of the spouse, the arrival of new Frisian immigrants in the community, and continuing contacts with the homeland.[68] As among the Dutch, second and third generation Frisians replaced conversational Frisian with Yankee Frisian, a mixture of Frisian with English words like postmaster, dollars, mill, company, farm, shop, and all right.[69]

Research concerning the preservation of the Dutch and Frisian languages discerns three major periods: the first was before the turn of the century when immigrants maintained their mother tongue fairly well. This was followed by two decades of language struggles and gradual shift. Finally, after the First World War came the adoption of English.[70] In Frisian

*John Ferwerda, at the age of 90, still wrote from Chicago to Dokkum,*
*Friesland, after 64 years in the USA*

immigrant circles there was not much struggle about language because
Frisian was not used in church and school. But, Frisian remained a language
with a cultural identity. Only later was Frisian cultivated because of its
emotional value for ethnic identity and for cultural education in a broader
sense. In 1928 when Sjouke de Zee visited the Frisian immigrants in the East
and Mid-West, he wondered why he did not find any children's books in
Frisian in the library of Calvin College, the Dutch Calvinist college in Grand
Rapids. He did find a collection of Frisian books, but concluded that the
library was not very well supplied with topical works from fellow countrymen
in Friesland.[71] De Zee's search for Frisian elements in the United States was
wishful thinking in another perspective: he noticed that no clerics of Frisian
descent recognized the great value of preaching in Frisian and subtly De Zee
referred to the "healthy" outcome that such preaching would bring.[72]
Although the Frisian language was not used in church before the 1930s, in
earlier decades there was a lively cultural circuit where the language was
cherished. In cultural societies or *selskippen*, all kinds of activities were
organized to enliven everyday immigrant life. Like so many others, Frisians
experienced the process of creating a culture that was based on past and
present realities. They attempted to give significance to their lives by
manifesting or embracing old and new values and ideas at the same time.[73]
They integrated the *postro* [porridge of buckwheat] with the *turkey* and tried
to make an acceptable immigrant dish that would feed them physically as

well as emotionally. In song, dance, and festivities, Frisian folk life was cherished within the immigrant community, and at the same time it was shown to the outside world and was influenced by the outside world. Around the turn of the century, *selskippen* could be found in many Frisian settlements in the United States. *Utspanning troch Ynspanning* in Paterson was accompanied by *Nij Fryslân* in Rochester, *Ut en Thûs* in Chicago, *Friso* in Grand Rapids, *Helpt elkander* in Indianapolis, and *Jounenocht* in Holland, Michigan.[74] These *selskippen* did not have a political character, neither did they stress the Frisian identity in nationalistic terminology. In the 1920s Bernard Fridsma, an immigrant and advocate of Frisian culture in America, began to criticize Frisians for trivializing the value of the *selskippen*. They only sought for *nocht en wille* [satisfaction and pleasure] instead of promoting the right use of Frisian language and literature.[75] Indeed, sources show that the activities of the *selskippen* mainly included *keatsen,* [the well-known Frisian

*Hessel Brolsma who left Het Bildt in 1892 and who later was secretary in Chicago of* Ut en Thûs

*Sjoerdje Ykema who married Hessel Brolsma in 1902. Photographs donated by J. Brolsma, Leiden*

ballgame], singing, dancing, and acting.[76] Frisians around the turn of the century, supposedly, had no problem with this cultural formula of their societies. Among researchers of the Dutch in America, the idea is widespread that Dutch Americans in the nineteenth century kept a low profile in the political arena.[77] Their relatively small numbers and inclination to religious isolation restricted political activity to the local level. This was not only true for the Dutch immigrants in nineteenth century America. Generally, immigrant politics was ultimately tied to the concerns of family and community, and it is realistic to characterize these politics as an extension of the most immediate concerns, the everyday needs and realities of ordinary people.[78]

Initially, in the 1840s and 1850s urban as well as rural Dutch immigrants in the Midwest favored the Democrats over the Whigs, because they perceived that Democrats stood for the interests of immigrants and the agricultural West. The Dutch rejected Whig nativism and Know-Nothingism. But the increasing dominance during the Civil War era of the southern politicians in the Democratic Party and also the more republican-oriented values of individualism, self-help, free competition and free soil, drove the Protestant Dutch into the Republican camp.[79]

Frisians showed the same pattern. However, it is difficult to imagine that nothing was left over of their political ideals before they left Frisian soil. Especially in the northwest of the province, people had organized socialist societies and anarchism had followers in the area. In the eastern clay area, orthodox Calvinist *kleine luyden* ["little people," plain folk] inspired by the political activism of Abraham Kuyper, gathered in Calvinist labor organizations and had a strong radius of action as well.[80] The roaring final decades of the nineteenth century with their widespread labor unrest suggest some activity of migrants in the American worker's arena. After all, conditions in American industrial centers like Paterson and Chicago were conducive to socialist convictions.

In chapter three it was made clear that most Frisians who left were laborers. Therefore, it is likely that socialist laborers initiated the move to migrate. Van Hinte mentions that two socialist newspaper enjoyed brief success among the Dutch in Michigan, in Grand Rapids in 1908 (the *Volksstem)* and in Holland in 1914 (the *Voorwaarts).*[81] In both places many Frisians had settled. In Grand Rapids in the 1890s the Christian labor organization *Patrimonium* also existed for some years, which published *De Christen Werkman* [The Christian Workman]. This organization was based on the Kuyperian principle of "sphere sovereignty," and the antithetical conceptions like *Christian* and *pagan*.[82] Kuyper was convinced that in a Calvinistic sense family, business, art, science and so forth, were all social spheres, which did not owe their existence to the State, and which did not derive the law of their life from the superiority of the state, but obeyed a higher authority within their own bosom. This authority ruled, by the grace of God, just as sovereignty of the State did.[83] From 1881 on, Abraham Kuyper and other Anti-Revolutionary leaders in the Netherlands had promoted emigration as a solution for over population and social problems. It was reported that a year after the foundation of *Patrimonium* in Grand Rapids, the organization had 40 to 50 members.[84] However, *Patrimonium* had only a short life, as did the two socialist papers.

Frisian laborers in the Paterson area who sympathized with the socialists in Friesland, provided financial support to Frisian organisations. As was true for German immigrants, evidence of mutual socialist understanding was strong when occasion arose to support fellow union members back in Friesland.[85] Gifts for the striking land laborers of Jan Stap's *Broedertrouw* came from immigrant companions in Chicago. A rift in this labor society *Broedertrouw* in 1891 caused more than 100 people from Het Bildt to emigrate to the United States.[86] Frisian labor activists like Tjeerd and Tjibbe Stienstra, R. Nakken, and Jan Stap gathered in Paterson, where more immigrants from north-west Friesland associated in the 1890s.[87]

Refraining from politics after immigration seems to have been quite general. It may be that the image of the United States among Frisian socialists also was constructed by socialist papers like *Recht voor Allen,* that agitated against "Yankee capitalism."[88] These kinds of reports about America may have prevented the move to America. But it is more likely, that official socialist party policy differed from the actual behavior of laborers who found they had no other choice than to emigrate.[89] In some ways America realised the ideas of freedom and equality for Frisian immigrants. As pointed out in chapter four, Frisian immigrants wrote to Friesland that they were asthonished by the fact that they had to "tip their hats to no one." The longing for independence from the landlord is expressed quite often in egalitarian rhetoric from America, and there must have been at least some truth in it. American democracy was not lost on the Frisian immigrants and more than once after migration they ventilated in their letters a negative view of the Frisian "class society."[90]

It appears that only in the individual messages from the new to the old world did Frisian immigrants reveal characteristics of their political ideology. Albert Roorda in 1908 wrote from Sioux City, Iowa, to his friends in the neighborhood of Leeuwarden:

> So, I am glad that you at least get more money now. It's a pity that in such a small village no more unity [*eendracht*] exists. It seems that those people are not aware of the fact that laborers should support each other; that is after all the only thing that counts for a workman. *Eendracht maakt macht* [harmony produces power]. But Hoptille is not the only village where no unity exists. Even here it's almost the same. *De een gunt de ander bijna geen vreeten.* For example, we have a Dutch society here, which could be strong if everyone would enter a membership, because there are at least a hundred [Dutch] males here. At the moment we only have 17 members....[91]

Roorda's sympathy for uniting the laborers shines between the lines. Similar phrases can be found in Gerrit van Dijk's correspondence five years later:

Dad still is pretty healthy and he works in the wagon factory. They work 9 hours a day and get 20 cent per hour, so that is even better than a braker's day rent [in Friesland]. But life here in the last 5 years became much more expensive, the situation is almost comparable with Holland. I bet, only a few years from now and then America is a lot worse than Europe and this is due to the overpowering capitalism and also the ignorance or shiftlessness and the systematic keeping of the masses in ignorance. Oh, how much would I like to attend one of your meetings. I was glad to learn of the fact that there is more activity among the laborers and I hope that your good goals may be fullfilled with success.[92]

Van Dijk noted that he missed the "meetings." It is not clear to which labor society he belonged in Friesland, but the possible interpretation could be that "he was missing" means that he did not join an equivalent labor union in the United States.

Another individual narrative comes from the life of Gerrit Roorda, son of a Frisian teacher and freethinker, born in 1890 in Tijnje, Friesland. When he was sixteen years old, he left with his friend Jeen de Vries for Germany where he worked as a bricklayer. During this time, according to his own opinion, Albert Roorda learned about "the power that you acquire as a laborer, when you are a member of a labor union."[93] After returning to Friesland, he decided to follow his brother Tjerk who had left in 1891 for the United States. In 1910 Roorda (again accompanied by De Vries) took the ocean steamer from Rotterdam to New York, traveled to his brother in Delaware City, and from there to Iowa. He worked for several Frisian immigrants and experienced the conformism of the Frisians in the Dutch communities, especially when dealing with Sabbath observance. His socialist worldview made him oppose U.S. participation in World War I. In 1918 he also became a member of the I.W.W., which made him suspect to the American authorities, not only because of his union sympathies but also because "Dutch" quite often was mistaken for "Deutsch." For a while he was forced to join the American military. Gerrit Roorda returned to Friesland in 1919 and showed himself a faithful follower of the ideas of the Russian Revolution.[94] Frisian socialists or anarchists in America seldom left personal accounts. In the case of Gerrit Roorda, the story was told after he returned to the fatherland. The rediscovery of participation by Frisians in American labor unions or socialist movements remains a tricky problem. Immigration scholars like Rudolph Vecoli sought in vain for a lead for further research, because "in the US, such has been the trauma of the Red Scare and McCarthyism that much of the documentation and even memories of this dimension of immigrant history has been largely destroyed or suppressed."[95]

From the immigrant letters it is also clear that Frisians in the home country often believed that the Democratic Party represented many socialists and socialist ideas. The publicist with the pen name S.A.S., for example, often wrote letters to the editor of *Hepkema's Courant* in which he compared the Democrats with socialists. Age Boukes Cnossen, himself a Democrat, felt the need to refute this in his letters to relatives in Friesland.[96]

In conclusion, it was not only the religious affiliation that served as the central component in day to day immigrant life. In Frisian circles the family was a stable reference point that kept immigrants grounded. Even for obtaining employment it seems that Frisians used family connections in preference to American trade unions or political parties.

Some individual Frisian immigrants were political activists, but not the immigrant group as a whole. Immigrant religious leaders and businessmen often attacked socialism and within their own ethnic group, fragmentation of labor ideas was common. And, of course, the relatively small numbers of Frisian and Dutch immigrants limited their political power in the United States, and limited the continuing vitality of old country working class institutions, as was found for German immigrants.[97] Moreover, the Frisians who remained of a socialist signature were not active within the typical Calvinistic Dutch or Frisian communities. In Paterson, for instance, members of *Utspanning troch Ynspanning* most likely were unchurched, because they gathered for cultural and sporting events on Sundays, which Calvinists would not do.

Generally, economic success brought a loss of interest in socialist ideology. Life also went in other directions: the activist emigrant young men got married and through the years became less revolutionary. It is clear that immigrants left and lived within the structure of the family network. However, no evidence was found that they lived within the political network of the homecountry as well.

# Conclusion

The relationship between migrants and their old homeland often is a complicated one. When Frisians left for the United States, some of their fellow countrymen condemned the move as unpatriotic. Others praised the courage of these emigrants and secretly admired the fact that by leaving they alleviated the unfortunate economic prospects of those left behind. In America during the hard times of acclimatization some Frisians suffered from homesickness; others were sure they never wanted to return to the native soil. This complex connection between Frisian immigrants and Friesland was often reciprocal.

The departure of Frisians to the United States around the turn of the century was a sensational phenomenon and at the same time a saga of people who stayed home. Relatively few families and individuals left Friesland for the United States. By far the biggest part remained in the province and found other ways of dealing with dissatisfaction, dynamism, social unrest, or family obligation. Frisians can not be compared to the Irish, where in some regions one out of two inhabitants left for overseas destinations. At the same time individuals of Frisian birth and ancestry constituted nearly 12 percent of a Massachusetts village's total population in 1910. In Whitinsville Frisians were an immigrant group that was hard to overlook.

This indicates the importance of a regional approach in the study of overseas migration. Around the turn of the century the Netherlands showed an out-migration of 68 emigrants per 100,000 population, but in the Frisian clay area the rate was as high as 498. At that time many voices expressed concern about a depopulating countryside, an "exodus" from Friesland's northern municipalities because of out-migration. It is evident that the clay area in particular lost inhabitants because of emigration and proportionally this high rate of departure for overseas was concentrated in only a few northern Frisian municipalities. Generally, emigration in the Netherlands was particularly important for the agrarian provinces on alluvial soil and at the periphery of the country, where possibilities for expansion of agriculture were minimal and where there was little development of modern industrialization. Therefore, great variation in the rate of emigration from individual regions demands a regional perspective.

For more than a century social scientists have tried to find the causes and effects of migration. Different disciplines have used different approaches. In many of the recently published mobility studies there are complaints about the lack of substantial theoretical generalizations for the phenomenon of migration. As a matter of fact, the generalizing "Laws" of E.G. Ravenstein, formulated in 1885, have stood the test of time and given support to research into migration in many times and places. The theoretical approach has made a shift from monocausal explanations like the religious commitment of the *Afgescheidenen* or Malthus' absolute over-population, to recognition of the complicated and dynamic forces in society that structure the decision to migrate.[1]

As a consequence I chose to consider both individual and collective factors in Frisian migration and also to investigate on both sides of the ocean for the comparative perspective. Ravenstein's Laws and E. Lee's theoretical concept based on those laws guided the approach in this study of the Frisians. I also relied on the concept of social and cultural reality of the sociologist J. Elich and the ideas of C. Tilly concerning migration networks.

A remarkable characteristic of Frisian regional emigration is its continuity. The long term maintainance of ties between native areas and places of destination measured the development of the migration process. The tradition of migration was a determining component, and once the *network* [chain] was established emigration tended to remain. The experiences of people who left the clay area before the 1880s were an indelible ingredient in motivating later ocean crossers.

E.S. Lee's hypothesis that migration tends to take place largely within well-defined streams held true for the northern Frisians. For Frisians patterns of emigration were strongly directed by ties of family and neighborhood. The network was not composed of individual migrants but of nuclear families. As R. Vecoli proclaimed for Italian emigration, it was the nuclear family that made the migration decision and defined what the goals should be.[2] Close interaction with the larger community of townspeople, friends, and relatives provided the broader regional context. Most Frisians emigrated as members of an established family household and the typical household can be profiled as a couple around 40 years old with three to four children, standing on the middle and lower rungs of the rural social ladder. This confirms Lee's statement that the heightened propensity to migrate at certain stages of the life-cycle is important in the selection of emigrants. In general, the share of agriculturally oriented Frisian emigrants remained almost the same in the period 1880-1914.

At no time after 1900 did Frisian overseas migration again reach the high level of the 1880s and 1890s. In this respect Frisian migration differed from the general Dutch pattern. After the turn of the century Dutch emigration continued to rise, reaching a peak in 1913. And, the emigrant stream showed a changed character; most twentieth-century Dutch emigrants did not come from the traditional sea clay areas, but left from urban areas like Amsterdam and Rotterdam.

The volume of Frisian migration is related to the enormous intervening obstacles in overseas migration. This is evident from the fact that many more people stayed home than emigrated. The volume of migration varied with fluctuations in the local economy, and the land of destination also showed some pull effect in economically profitable times. When the United States plunged into an economic depression in 1893, Frisian emigration dropped sharply in 1894. Simultaneously, depressive economic times in Friesland especially in the 1880s and early 1890s caused a real increase in emigration. However, this does not mean that the agrarian crisis was responsible for much higher rates of unemployed emigrants. Between 1885-1889 their share was 5.5 percent, while in the period 1905-1908 the unemployment rate was only slightly lower (4.5 percent of the emigrant population).

Studies of emigration from individual localities have not been able to predict emigration rates simply from the economic and social circumstances.[3] Personal characteristics resulting in individual motives for migration are impossible to overlook. Every Frisian migrant, when interviewed, would have produced individual motives in the context of broader and generalizing motives. A strikingly high percentage of Frisians emigrated from the municipality of their birth, and the percentage of those who left a non-neighboring municipality of their birthplace was extremely low. Frisians did not rush from place to place before taking the decision to go overseas. Many scholars of migration consider the ocean voyage of the emigrants as a short intermezzo in the whole migration process and they hardly mention it. However, in the total experience of the resettlement process, the voyage to America was an integral part and had a formative character. The whole event shaped the emigrant's personality and determined the future experience. Castle Garden and later Ellis Island were the gates of hope, fear, and joy for Frisians before they entered the mainstream of America.
There is not much evidence that many Frisians left with prepaid tickets. Examples of relatives, church members, or wealthy patrons who paid for the tickets are available, but this was far from universal. Maybe the independent Frisian mind prevented relying on others for financial help. In most cases the competitive prices for the ocean voyage seemed to be affordable. Most Frisians departed in the months of April and May in order to lessen the hardships of dangerous storms, winter unemployment, and summer heat. On the steamship the first new contacts with other Frisians and Dutchmen were laid and future plans discussed and sometimes revised. The ship also was the platform where people from different national backgrounds met, and Frisians became acquainted with ethnic diversity for the first time. Some in Friesland specified beforehand to officials where they intended to settle. Most wanted to end up in Michigan, Iowa, Illinois, Wisconsin, and New Jersey, all destinations where the Dutch had settled before. However, in the 1880s and 1890s new destinations appeared, in Massachusetts and as the midwestern frontier moved westward, in Montana, Washington, and later California. The Frisian move westward was largely composed of those who had emigrated to the United States earlier, often first settling in Michigan or other midwestern states before moving to the new frontier.

*Emigrant lodging of the NASM at the Wilhelminakade in Rotterdam around 1900*

At the same time Frisians discovered the growing American cities like Paterson and Passaic, Chicago, and Grand Rapids, where they helped supply the industrial labor force. Working through networks the chain migration from the northern Frisian clay area directed people from single Frisian regions to settle together in single American communities. Grand Rapids, for example, housed Frisians from the municipalities of Ferwerderadeel and Barradeel, while Randolph, Wisconsin became the home of groups of emigrants from Oost- and Westdongeradeel. In an even more microscopic perspective, emigrants moved from a particular village in the Old World to a particular town in the New World. Frisians from the village of Ee settled in Roseland, Illinois; those from Blija chose Holland, Michigan, and those from Minnertsga and Tzummarum selected Whitinsville. The structured character of Frisian migration was the pragmatic outcome of an overseas migration that in its communication and information relied very much on personal and community ties.

To keep the firm relations within the larger overseas migration network, migrants exchanged letters with family in Friesland. In April 1896 Age Boukes Cnossen wrote to his uncle and aunt in Friesland: "Everything is possible here in America; impossible does not exist here."[4] Such statements encapsulated the promise that potential emigrants incorporated in their decision to migrate.

The sociologist A.N.J. den Hollander postulated some theoretical concepts of the process of image-building between nations. Den Hollander believed that one can only observe another society by breaking through certain barriers, and even then the view is always wrapped in a veil of secrecy. He regarded this veil as a mighty obstruction in studying foreign societies. This discrepancy between reality and muddled perceptions can be found among potential Frisian emigrants too. However, in contrast to Den Hollander, it is irrelevant whether the images of America held by Frisian emigrants were true or false. The mere existence of these images is itself an important subject. Therefore, the prejudices and images of Frisian emigrants in their observations of America were made an object of research.

Because of the socio-economic status of the Frisians, public sources about images and image-building are scarce. The group of image-makers consisted of travelers (Sjouke de Zee), novelists (Cornelia de Groot), agents of steamship and immigration companies (Prins & Zwanenburg), real estate promoters (Theodore F. Koch), and employees of immigration agencies (Albert Kuipers). For private sources, direct personal information is mainly found in letters. And even letters were not always clearly a private source. Many were intended for a larger audience, especially those sent to local Frisian newspapers. At that moment public and private sources became a clear mixture. Many published letters came from the most successful Frisian immigrants and contained glowing reports about economic prospects in America. The propaganda of these image-makers who trumpeted America as the land of promise, the guidebooks or immigration brochures of land agents and steamshipcompanies, and the phenomenal impact of America letters, proved believable and acceptable.

Privately written letters reflected the psychological needs of the immigrants. They feared exile from the homeland and by giving information concerning Frisian social life and acculturation in the New World they tried to entice potential emigrants to come. Immigrants compared life on both sides of the ocean and in that way they show us the image of America. The more alluring the promises, the less attractive the Frisian homeland appeared during periods of socio-economic stagnation. The image of America whether true or false, realistic or fantasy, turned out to be the immigrant's promise. With this promise they bought a one-way ticket to America.

Frisian emigrants who in the pre-migration situation had worked in agriculture did not necessarily seek work in this economic sector in the New World. Comparing the data before and after departure showed that only a few more migrants ended up in agriculture. However, a vast difference could be found in their change of status. Of the household heads identified in the 1900 U.S. census, as many as one third became independent farmers or farm tenants. This tendency clearly shows the strong desire for agricultural land. Important in this settlement pattern was the fact that there were still possibilities to find a farm in the western states. Even immigrant sons and daughters were able to become American farmers because there was as yet no shortage of land. If this option had not been available, we may presume that many more immigrants would have joined the industrial labor force in the growing American cities. Or, they would not have left Frisian soil.

One of the hypotheses was that Frisian immigrants in the urban surroundings would show much higher trans-oceanic occupational mobility than Frisians in rural surroundings. Surprisingly enough, in Sioux County, Iowa, in the rural Midwest, three quarters of the first generation Frisian workforce entered different occupations from those held in Friesland. In the urban centers of Grand Rapids, Holland, and Pella, these percentages all were lower than for Sioux County. Part of this difference can be explained by the fact that in the rural Midwest Frisians were successful in becoming independent farmers, which was a transition from their occupational status in Friesland. High trans-oceanic occupational mobility did not necessarily mean that much occupational diversity was available in the Midwest or West. The challenge was found in starting an independent venture, usually in agriculture, or in first making money by working as a farm laborer.

Especially in the Dakotas economic progress had much to do with climatic conditions. The story of Ulbe Eringa and his wife Maaike Rijpstra, is a clear example of the settlers' vicissitudes in the sparsely inhabited midwestern and western lands, and it makes clear that the exploitation of opportunities must have been closely related to the creativity of the individual Frisian immigrant. Often farm operations of Frisian immigrants were different from those in Friesland. In the United States most farm labor came from the nuclear family instead of from steady or seasonal hired hands as was common in Friesland. Another difference was the feeding of cattle during winter with homegrown corn to increase milk production. Dairying with Holsteins was common, but Frisians in America kept Jerseys and Guernseys as well. Frisians also relied on much of their old country experience; in the state of Washington they profited from their specific knowledge of techniques concerning wetland farming and their success can be ascribed to the combination of agricultural background and the shared Calvinistic values and faith that defined the group socially and psychologically.

Immigrants were not undistinguished entities of labor. Like other newcomers Frisians entered the American workforce at the peak of their earning power, carrying with them the costs of their upbringing.[5] To investigate what happened at the small scale level of households and settlements, the study of specific immigrant communities proved useful, especially when connected with the large scale economic, political, and cultural structures. Examination of Frisians in Whitinsville, Massachusetts, for example, reveals that the first emigrants came in 1886, cowboys accompanying Holstein cattle. However, within two decades Frisians constituted more than one-tenth of the Whitinsville inhabitants.

Most Whitinsville Frisians worked as factory laborers, machine makers, or foundrymen in the Whitin Machine Shop, or as weavers, spinners, carpenters, and engineers in the Whitinsville Cotton Mill. By far the largest number of Frisians lived in rented houses in 1900 and some lived in dwellings owned by the Whitin Company. Later on, a few bought rundown

*Business of a Frisian immigrant descendant in Friesland, Wisconsin in hte 1990s*

farms in the area. Whitinsville proved to be an excellent example of Ch. Tilly's theoretical concept of migratory networks and the idea of a transplanted community. The ties of kinship, friendship, and regional background were indisputable. For Whitinsville the effective units of migration were sets of people linked by acquaintance, kinship, and work experience. They somehow incorporated an urban Massachusetts destination into the mobility alternatives they considered when they reached critical decision points in their individual or collective lives.

In urban America, Frisians worked as toolmakers, manufacturing laborers, salesmen in commerce, and as industrial workers. They started in the furniture industry, in the silk mills, in the machine industry, or found jobs in handicrafts as carpenters, bakers, or painters. On Chicago's southside, they combined their Frisian agricultural skills with the urban commercial market by developing truck gardening to supply vegetables to city folk.

In the urban surroundings Frisians worked among people of Yankee, Irish, German, French Canadian, Armenian, Italian, and other national origins. Often they mixed freely with members of different ethnic groups on the work floor. However, in after-work hours they held closely to themselves. Acclimatization in an occupational sense demanded a flexible work attitude, but after work their social life centered around the ethnic organizations often affiliated with the ethnic church. In Whitinsville this pattern was particularly clear. While the Whitin family hired people from many different ethnic groups, this did not lead to ethnic exchange in their social life. The

*Truck-gardening, South Chicago ± 1913. The Groninger Berend Postema bosses immigrant workers.*
*Photo donated by his grandson Jan Postema*

same tendency was found in the cities of Paterson and Chicago, where
Frisians even lived in their own specified neighborhoods.

Between 1880 and 1914 the United States rapidly became urbanized. It has
been estimated that in this time period, a third of the growth of its labor
force was due to immigration.[6] Northern Frisian migrants reacted to the
opportunities offered by this international labor market. Around the turn of
the century the Atlantic economy provided industrial jobs for many of these
Frisians. However, the total transformation from folk to transatlantic labor
migration is only partly evident. Frisians did not show the same pattern as
the Dutch in general or other Western Europeans, whose early twentieth
century emigration differed markedly from previous patterns. A system of
urban labor migration replaced the traditional rural folk movement; instead
of the agricultural regions, the primary emigration fields shifted to the
urban areas, and the families were replaced by single newcomers. At the
same time the primary destination shifted away from the United States.
However, the characteristics of Frisian American households remained
typically family oriented, and Frisian emigration after 1900 still can be
described as a "family affair" with continued settlement in the United States.
In this respect the Frisian experience did not mirror the rural to urban
migration of Dutch Catholics to Wisconsin in the second half of the 19th
century, where no evidence of kinship relationships among emigrant
households was found, and where the migration pattern turned out to be
highly individualistic.[7]

Paterson, Chicago, and Grand Rapids did not evidence the homogeneity that was found in Whitinsville. In the urban neighborhoods Dutch churches, schools, press, and other organizations acted to promote Dutch unity, but they also reflected the differentiation among the Dutch population based upon ideologies, beliefs, geographical background, and differing perceptions of American society. The source areas of Frisians in Chicago were randomly distributed over the clay municipalities and did not show a network as tight as in Whitinsville. Since Chicago had many more Frisians and the city was large, this is to be expected. Menial and semiskilled occupations prevailed among the Frisians in Chicago and there was a lot of diversity in occupational ventures. Industry was the inducement for many Frisian newcomers to settle in ever increasing numbers in American cities where a frequent change of jobs was common, until a satisfying workplace was found.

Compared to Chicago, Paterson showed a different pattern of Frisian source areas, because the immigrants in this New Jersey city mainly came from the municipality of Het Bildt. Even specific Frisian towns like St. Annaparochie and St. Jacobiparochie showed a special link with the city of Paterson. Handships of getting a good start in urban centers in America were numerous. The cities often were densely populated with various ethnic groups that took up the slack in the labor market. Living conditions for most of the industrial workers were overcrowded, unsanitary, and unhealthy. Only around and after the turn of the century was economic power in immigrant groups translated into political power, which caused much labor unrest and strikes. However, there is no evidence that Frisian immigrants took an active part in the American labor movement. Although Frisian labor activists like Jan Stap and Tjeerd and Tjibbe Stienstra, gathered in Paterson, their political activism was limited to the local level. Most political interests were an extension of immediate concerns, the everyday needs and realities of ordinary people. Economic success also contributed to a loss of interest in socialist ideology. Only in individual narratives can we find the old country political ideology expressed.

It seems to have been common to refrain from politics after immigration. In some ways America realized the ideas of freedom and equality because people were convinced that they had to tip their hats to no one. The image of the American Dream, or the belief in achieving economic well-being through individual efforts, directed political behavior. The American Dream led to a low organizational desire among immigrant laborers, and entrepreneurs used ethnic rivalry to keep the masses divided. Furthermore, the relatively small number of Frisians limited their political power in the new arena.

Much of what has been said here about the male migrant's experience applies as well to female Frisians. However, fundamental differences deserve attention. The fact that Frisian women were not part of the workforce determined their specific position in social and cultural life. The Frisian workforce in the United States was totally male-oriented. Few single or married females older than 21 years of age could be found in the workforce

*Mr. and Mrs. Gale Houtman-Houkema.*
*Photograph sent to Ureterp, Friesland*
*from Butte City, California.*
*Donated by J. Feikens*

outside the family home. Immigrant daughters between ages 14 and 21 were the exception; about half held specified jobs, mostly to supplement family income. In this respect Frisians showed revised ideas about young women working outside the family home. Among married Frisian females, outside jobs remained not an option.

Single Frisian women did not chose to emigrate to the United States on their own as was, for example, common for women in Sweden in the same time period.[8] Almost all Frisian women migrated with their families; close family bonds prevented them from going alone or only with other females. This firm setting within the family proved to be an obstacle in acclimating to the new environment. The part of life beyond the paid job kept Frisian women in the United States within the family circle and outside the process of ethnic diversity that men experienced on the job. However, to initiate and preserve ethnic social exchange within Frisian/Dutch circles the women exerted much energy and covered great distances to visit relatives and friends all over the country. Church and family were significant in this creation of networks and were decisive elements in the women's world view. Hardly any of the migrating Frisians were illiterate, but only a few spoke the English language when they arrived. Frisians in the United States faced a trilingual situation: initially they spoke Frisian at home, they worshipped, read the Bible, and wrote letters in Dutch, and they learned rudimentary English for business and political affairs. When the Dutch language in church was abandoned, Frisian remained the family language providing a strong cultural identity.

The Dutch group in Whitinsville was very homogeneous. This community consisted largely of emigrants from the same province of origin, which may have been the reason why the change of language from Dutch to English in the Whitinsville Christian Reformed Church was troublesome, but it was not destructively disruptive to the Frisian subculture. The Frisians likely were not as attached to the Dutch language, because they spoke Frisian at home. When the Whitinsville immigrant children could no longer understand Dutch, the transition to English in church was plausible and not such an intense threat to Frisian identity as it appeared to be to Dutch identity in general. Frisian was spoken at home into the third generation of immigrants. Frisian immigrants also gathered in cultural societies [*selskippen*], where drama, dances, theatre, and literature were enjoyed in the Frisian language, and where the game of *keatsen* found many enthousiastic adherents. These ethnic organizations and the Frisian language itself preeminently served as cultural forces that conserved ethnic consciousness, and that distinguished the Frisian immigrants from the Dutch.

Before leaving the Frisian homeland, the largest part (63 percent) of the emigrants had affiliated with the *Nederlands Hervormde* Church and this group was overrepresented. 27 percent was *Gereformeerd* or *Christelijk Gereformeerd*, while seven percent of the emigrants had no church affiliation. The church undoubtedly influenced Frisian immigrants in the New World

*Seven granddaughters of immigrants Jacob van der Meulen*
*and Tietje van der Meij in Wisconsin (circa 1950)*

and there was almost an unanimous desire to assemble in churches. Most Frisians associated with the Reformed Church in America, or the Christian Reformed Church, both of which were influenced by their counterparts (respectively de *Hervormde* and *[Christelijke] Gereformeerde* churches) in the Netherlands. The existence of these ethnic churches did not lead to harmonious places for worship. Religious disputes and traditions of the homeland were carried to the United States and mixed with everyday immigrant questions such as which language to use in the worship service. This guaranteed a continuous flow of ecclesiastical issues in which ethnicity was part of the discussion. These controversies did not necessarily lead to schisms or disintegration of the ethnic community. In the immigrant community the church often appeared to be the preeminent platform for exchanging ideas and opinions about ethnicity. This finally simplified the adaptation to the new society and kept controversies within their own group. In this respect Frisians took the same routes as the Dutch in general. Generally, the idea that immigrant churches are a threat to the receiving society because of the so-called "natural desire" of newcomers to worship as did their forefathers must be revised. Immigrant churches like the Reformed Dutch churches in the United States served as intense platforms for discussions and not only of religious matters. Economic advancement was part of it as well and, therefore, churches facilitated immigration while preserving an ethnic identity and position in the new society.

In broad perspective the experience of Frisian migration to the United States around the turn of the century indicates that the socio-economic and cultural baggage of the fatherland was fundamental in the process of gaining position in the New World. Frisian Old Country values continuously faced challenges in the United States and this mingling structured the dynamic process of integration. Migration builds bridges between countries. The foundations on both sides determine the nature of the construction.

# Notes

**1** Very recently a program for cooperation in migration research was launched in *Centrum voor de geschiedenis van migranten* (Amsterdam: Het Spinhuis, 1995), 1.

**2** Ibid., 4-5.

**3** R. Vecoli, "New Guidelines and Research Hypotheses for the History of European Emigration" in *Studi sull'emigrazione. Un'analisi comparata*, ed. M.R. Ostuni (Biella, 1989), 47.

**4** For example, in the studies of Y. Schreuder, and H. van Stekelenburg, computer data sets compiled by Swierenga were used for research purposes. See Y. Schreuder, *Dutch Catholic Immigrant Settlement in Wisconsin, 1850-1905* (New York & London: Garland Publishing, 1989); H.A.V.M. van Stekelenburg, *Landverhuizing als regionaal verschijnsel. Van Noord-Brabant naar Noord-Amerika 1820-1880* (Tilburg: Stichting Zuidelijk Historisch Contact, 1991). For the earlier overseas migration from the Netherlands see P.R.D. Stokvis, *De Nederlandse trek naar Amerika 1846-1847* (Leiden: Universitaire Pers, 1977).

**5** J. Lucassen and R. Penninx, *Nieuwkomers. Immigranten en hun nakomelingen in Nederland 1550-1985* (Amsterdam: Meulenhoff Informatief, 1985). A recent historiographical essay concerning the study of migration in the Netherlands can be found in H. Vermeulen and A. Böcker, "De studie van migratie in Nederland. Een bibliografisch overzicht," *Migrantenstudies* 4 (1992): 21-28. A general introduction in the subject is J. Lucassen, *Dutch Long Distance Migration; A Concise History 1600-1900* (Amsterdam: IISG, 1991).

**6** About migration and the transformation of nation states see L. Lucassen, "Het onontkoombare nationaliteitenbeginsel. Enige recente literatuur over (im)migratie en natievorming," *Tijdschrift voor Sociale Geschiedenis* 4 (1993): 489-505.

**7** The need for scholarly attention for the region, or more precisely, the village as the emigration unit recently was stressed by D. Baines, *Emigration from Europe 1815-1930* (London: Macmillan, 1991), 33-34.

**8** R.P. Swierenga, "Dutch International Labor Migration to North America in the Nineteenth Century," in *Dutch Immigration to North America*, eds. H. Ganzevoort and M. Boekelman (Toronto: The Multicultural History Society of Ontario, 1983), 1-34.

**9** R.P. Swierenga, "Dutch Immigration Patterns in the Nineteenth and Twentieth Centuries," in *The Dutch in America; Immigration, Settlement, and Cultural Change*, ed. R.P. Swierenga (New Brunswick: Rutgers University Press, 1985), 15-42.

**10** H. de Vries, *Landbouw en bevolking tijdens de agrarische depressie in Friesland (1878-1895)* (Wageningen: H. Veenman & Zonen, 1971), 13-16.

**11** Swierenga, "Dutch International Labor Migration," 1-34.

**12** T. van der Wal, *Op zoek naar een nieuwe vrijheid. Een kwart eeuw arbeidersbeweging in Friesland 1870-1895* (Leiden: Universitaire Pers, 1972), 369-74.

**13** This statement was made by Hans Magnus Enzensberger in his *Van der Leeuw*-lecture in Groningen entitled "Die grosse Wanderung" [The great Trek]. This lecture was published in H.M. Enzensberger, *De grote trek* (Amsterdam: De Volkskrant, 1992), 16.

**14** International analysis of population data with respect to overseas emigration was pioneered by researchers on Swedish migration to the U.S.A. in The Uppsala Migration Research Project in the 1970s and 1980s. See H. Runblom and H. Norman, eds., *From Sweden to America; A History of Migration* (Minneapolis: University of Minnesota Press, 1976); also R.C. Ostergren, *A Community Transplanted; The Trans-Atlantic Experience of a Swedish Immigrant Settlement in the Upper Middle West, 1835-1915* (Uppsala: Acta Universitatis Uppsaliensis, 1988). Lars-Göran Tedebrand formulated conditions of the quantitative sources in his "Sources for the History of Swedish Emigration," in Runblom and Norman, *From Sweden to America*.

**15** The complicated administrative procedure is described by R.P. Swierenga, "Het bestuderen van de Nederlandse emigratie naar de Verenigde Staten. Nieuwe methoden en begrippen," *Jaarboek Centraal Bureau voor Genealogie* 36 (1982), 252-68; and in Y. Schreuder, *Dutch Catholic Immigrant Settlement in Wisconsin*, 167-74. For specific remarks on sources and methodology of Frisian migration see A. Galema, "'Se binne nei Amearika tein'. Aspekten van Friese landverhuizing naar de Verenigde Staten rond de eeuwwisseling," *It Beaken* 52 (1990) 2: 51-54.

**16** M.L. Samson, *Population Mobility in*

the Netherlands 1880-1910; A Case Study of Wisch in the Achterhoek (Uppsala: Almquist & Wiksell International, 1977), 44-48.

17 For a critique of the U.S. census manuscripts see C. Harzig, "The U.S. Government Census as Source in Immigration Research," in *The Press of Labor Migrants in Europe and North America 1880s to 1930s*, eds. C. Harzig and D. Hoerder (Bremen: Universität Bremen, 1985), 25-37. See also M.J. Anderson, *The American Census; A Social History* (New Haven: Yale University Press, 1988). For an overview about historians and their research based on the Census see R.P. Swierenga, "Historians and the Census; The Historiography of Census Research," *The Annals of Iowa* 50 (1990) 6: 650-73.

18 The linkage program for this research was written by George Welling. References can be found in G.M. Welling, "A strategy for intelligent input programs for structured data," *History and Computing* 5 (1993) 1: 35-46; and G.M. Welling, "Computationele geschiedenis," *Geschiedenis en Bestanden* (Enkhuizen, 1995): 90-99.

A good methodology of record linkage and quantitative approaches in history is E.A. Wrigley, *Identifying People in the Past* (London: Arnold, 1973).

19 The microfilms of the U.S. Passenger lists are available in the National Archives in Washington DC. Copies of these lists are also available in the library of the Carl von Ossietzky University in Oldenburg, Germany. R.P. Swierenga abstracted all arrivals in *Dutch Immigrants in U.S. Ship Passenger Manifests, 1820-1880; An Alphabethical Listing by Household Heads and Single Persons*. 2 Vols. (Wilmington, DE: Scholarly Resources, 1983). I.A. Glazier and P.W. Filby, have worked on a project to transcribe the information in the passenger lists on to computer accessible files which resulted in the publication *Germans to America; Lists of Passengers Arriving at U.S. Ports*, vols. 1-22 (Wilmington DE: Scholarly Resources, 1988-1991 ff). A critique about these volumes as a source can be found in A. Holtmann, "'Wenn man es wagt und seinem Vaterland entsagt'. Auf Seglern und Dampfschiffen zogen sieben

Millionen Deutsche nach Amerika," *Frankfurter Rundschau*, October 10, 1992, 16; also A. Holtmann, "Snares for the Genealogist and the Historian; A Critique," *Society for German-American Studies Newsletter* 14 (September, 1993): 19-24; and A. Holtmann, "New Lures to Entrapment for Genealogists and Historians," *Society for German-American Studies Newsletter* 16 (September, 1995), 1-2. For a reflection on the original passenger lists as a source see R.P. Swierenga, "List Upon List; The Ship Passenger Records and Immigration Research," *Journal of American Ethnic History* 10 (Spring 1991): 42-53.

20 An important point is that prior to 1897 only certain of these variables are reported. This would have been a handicap for the time period studied here.

21 See Gemeentearchief Rotterdam [municipal archives of Rotterdam] where the passenger lists of the Holland America Line of 1900-1962 are preserved.

# Notes – 1

1 Letter of R.J. Algra to J.D. Douma of February 16, 1891. Calvin College Archives, Grand Rapids, MI. In the 1900 U.S. Census I found a Jacob Douma (born May 1858) with his family in Sioux County, IA, in Nassau Township. He lived with his wife Mary (born October 1854) and his children Jacob (born June 1882), Hattie (born January 1890), Susan (July 1894) and Dowe (November 1896). This family emigrated in 1889 and Jacob was a day laborer in 1900, all the children went to school and Jacob and Mary had an owned free house. Their parents Jacob (born September, 1823) and Hattie (born July 1831) Douma lived in the same township with two of their children still at home (Sara, born August 1863 and Oscar, born March 1874). According to the 1900 Census, Jacob still worked as a garden laborer at the age of 78, and he and his family lived in an owned free house.

2 J.H. Veenendaal, *Nederland in 1880* (Tiel: Mijs, 1881), 247.

3 T. van der Wal, *Op zoek naar een nieuwe vrijheid. Een kwart eeuw arbeidersbeweging in Friesland 1870-1895* (Leiden: Universitaire Pers, 1972), 1-49.

4 J.L. van Zanden, *De economische ontwikkeling van de Nederlandse landbouw in de negentiende eeuw 1800-1914* (Utrecht: Hes Uitgevers, 1985), 83-112.

5 Van Zanden, *De economische ontwikkeling van de Nederlandse landbouw*, 85-86.

6 H. Blink, "Friesland als economisch-gewest in den loop der eeuwen en in het bijzonder in den tegenwoordigen tijd," *Tijdschrift voor Economische Geografie* 8 (1917): 337-404.

7 *Uitkomsten der beroepstelling in het Koninkrijk der Nederlanden gehouden op den 31sten December 1899* 12 vols. ('s-Gravenhage: Belinfante, 1902); *Uitkomsten der beroepstelling in het Koninkrijk der Nederlanden gehouden op den 31sten December* 1909 ('s-Gravenhage: Belinfante, 1912-1913).

8 J.J. Spahr van der Hoek, "De weg naar welvaart," in *Geschiedenis van Friesland*, eds. J.J. Kalma, J.J. Spahr van der Hoek, and K. de Vries (Drachten: Laverman, 1968; reprint ed., Leeuwarden: De Tille, 1980), 504.

9 Spahr van der Hoek, "De weg naar welvaart," 499-500.

10 H.E.W. Struve and A.A. Bekaar, "Nijverheidsstatistiek 1888-1890." These statistics had five volumes, one of them dealing with the province of Friesland. Cited in T. van der Wal, *Op zoek naar een nieuwe vrijheid*, 41-42.

11 V. Bruinsma, "De vermindering der bevolking in Friesland," *Vragen des Tijds* 2 (1894): 126.

12 Van der Wal, *Op zoek naar een nieuwe vrijheid*, 41-43.

13 J.J. Spahr van der Hoek, *Geschiedenis van de Friese landbouw*, 2 vols. (Leeuwarden: Friesche Maatschappij van Landbouw, 1952), 1: 555.

14 The historian J.L. van Zanden argues that it is very hard to estimate Dutch dairy production in the nineteenth century. However, from figures of 1910 he concludes that the milk yield in the provinces of Friesland, Utrecht and Holland is the highest in the country. J.L. van Zanden, *De economische ontwikkeling van de Nederlandse landbouw*, 104-08.

15 Blink, "Friesland als economisch gewest," 391-94.

16 Spahr van der Hoek, *Geschiedenis van de Friese landbouw*, 1: 437-80. Also Van Zanden, *De economische ontwikkeling van de Nederlandse landbouw*, 95-100.

17 Letter of Broer J. Soolsma and his wife Taekje A. Lantinga from Franeker, Friesland to G.W. Poelstra in Paterson, NJ, November 7, 1899. Calvin College Archives, Grand Rapids, MI.

18 A steady contract meant that the laborer had a job for a whole year. Every year this contract had to be renewed. Many seasonal contracts only assured the landlaborer a few months' work during the summer.

19 Van der Wal, *Op zoek naar een nieuwe vrijheid*, 51-119.

20 The decline of Friesland's economic and political position is best described in Van Zanden's, *De economische ontwikkeling* and summarized in his article "De Friese economie in de negentiende eeuw," *It Beaken* 1/2 (1992): 7-14.

21 Blink, "Friesland als economisch-gewest," 384.

22 H. de Vries, *Landbouw en bevolking tijdens de agrarische depressie in Friesland (1878-1895)* (Wageningen: H. Veenman & Zonen, 1971), 151.

23 De Vries, *Landbouw en bevolking*, 146. In 1892 A. Rauwerda described the poor conditions in landlaborers' housing facilities. The houses were too small, there was not enough light, and fresh air was hard to find. A. Rauwerda, "Misstanden bij den

veldarbeid in Friesland," *Vragen des Tijds* 2 (1892): 67-96.

**24** *Het Vaandel*, November 2, 1892. Cited in: T. van der Wal, *Op zoek naar een nieuwe vrijheid*, 349-50.

**25** E. van Dijk, "Ontwikkelingen in Oostdongeradeel tijdens de 'Sijtsma-periode,' 1904-1964," *It Beaken* 2 (July 1964): 81-99.

**26** For the socio-economic development of Oostdongeradeel around the turn of the century see S. Zijlstra, *Skiednis fan Eastdongeradiel* (Leeuwarden: Fryske Akademy, 1992), 128-38.

**27** Figure based on data of the Sixth Decennial Census of December 31, 1879. See *Uitkomsten der zesde tienjarige volkstelling in het Koninkrijk der Nederlanden op den 31sten December 1879*, 12 vols. ('s-Gravenhage: Departement van Binnenlandsche Zaken, 1881).

**28** Figures derived from the Census of 1879 and table 1.4. At the end of 1879, for example, 63 percent of the inhabitants of Ferwerderadeel were followers of the Reformed Church, while 34 percent professed ultra Calvinism. Almost 3 percent of the municipal population were Baptists. In 1910 this picture changed to 44 percent *Hervormd* people and 48 percent *Christelijk Gereformeerd*. The influence of other religious groups was insignificant [table 1.3].

**29** The *Afscheiding* of 1834 was a schism in the state Reformed Church. It began with the ministerial labors of Hendrik de Cock in the village of Ulrum in Groningen. De Cock and his followers complained that the *Hervormde Kerk* had departed from its original doctrine. The ministers Henry Pieter Scholte and Albertus van Raalte expressed sympathy with De Cock's faith. In 1834 the Secession (*Afscheiding*) was a fact. In the 1840s Scholte, Van Raalte and Brummelkamp played a decisive role in the emigration of *Afgescheidenen* (Seceders) to the United States.

**30** M. Staverman, *Buitenkerkelijkheid in Friesland* (Assen: Van Gorcum, 1954), 202.

**31** For more detailed information concerning the region see

W.H. Keikes, *Verleden van Frieslands Noordoosten* (Dokkum: n.p., 1968). Also H.M van den Berg, *Noordelijk Oostergo. De Dongeradelen* ('s-Graven-hage: Staatsuitgeverij, 1983).

**32** The village of Peasens was part of the municipality of Oostdongeradeel and Moddergat belonged to the territory of Westdongeradeel. In fact the two villages lay next to each other.

**33** W.P. de Vries, "De visschers van Wierum en Moddergat," *Vragen van den dag* (1894): 180-86.

**34** G.A. Wumkes, *Stads- en dorpskroniek van Friesland* 2 vols. (Leeuwarden: Eisma, 1930-1934), 2: 480.

**35** H. Twerda, *Fan Fryslâns forline* (Bolsward: A.J. Osinga, 1968), 329-**33** Also J.J. Spahr van der Hoek, "Undersyk yn de noardeasthoeke," *It Beaken* 32 (1970): 106.

**36** Data from the report concerning the state of inland and coastal fishing of 1915: "Mededeelingen en verslagen van de visscherijinspectie."

**37** J. Sickenga, *Frieslands gemeentelijke toestanden in woorden en cijfers* (n.p., 1891). T. van der Wal uses Sickenga's figures and he states that the real expenses in fact exceeded the budget. Van der Wal, *Vrijheid*, 113.

**38** A. Rauwerda, *Armenzorg en gemeentegrondbezit* (St. Annaparochie: Kuiken, 1892), 2-4.

**39** J.H. Beucker Andreae, "Rapport ingediend voor het vijfde landhuishoudkundig congres te Leiden, 11, 12 13 Junij 1850, betreffende een onderzoek naar den zedelijken en materiëlen toestand der arbeidende bevolking ten platten lande en van middelen om dien zoveel mogelijk te verbeteren," *Tijdschrift voor Staathuishoudkunde en Statistiek* 6 (1851): 159-61. Together with other reports from 1851, this source has been republished and edited by J.L. van Zanden, *"Den zedelijken en materiëlen toestand der arbeidende bevolking ten platten lande."* *Een reeks rapporten uit 1851* (Groningen: Nederlands Agronomisch-Historisch Instituut, 1991).

**40** Spahr van der Hoek, *Geschiedenis van de Friese landbouw*, 1: 659-63.

**41** *Enkele facetten uit de geschiedenis van de gemeente Westdongeradeel tot de opheffing 1 januari 1984* (Metslawier: Administratief Centrum 'Oostergo', 1984), 34-40.

**42** J.A. de Jonge, *De industrialisatie in Nederland tussen 1850 en 1914* (Amsterdam: Scheltema & Holkema, 1968; reprint ed., Nijmegen: Sun, 1976), 21. For a description of northern Frisian villages around the turn of the century see J. ter Steege, ed., *In vogelvlucht. Geschiedenis van de gemeente Oostdongeradeel* (Aalsum-Wetzens: J. ter Steege, 1971), 1-92.

**43** Van der Wal, *Vrijheid*, 269. Also J. Frieswijk, *Socialisme in Friesland 1880-1900* (Amsterdam: Van Gennep, 1977); T.A. Vonk Noordegraaf, "Oostdongeradeel als 'rechtse' gemeente," *It Beaken. Dongeradeel byda aestersiida der pasen* 26 (1964): 177-94; Spahr van der Hoek, "Undersyk yn de noardeasthoeke," 61-62.

**44** J.J. Bruinsma and J.F. van Hengel, *Bijdragen geneeskundige plaatsbeschrijving van Friesland*, 3 vols. ('s-Gravenhage: Departement van Binnenlandsche Zaken, 1872), 2: 67-68.

**45** H.M. van den Berg, *Noordelijk Oostergo. Ferwerderadeel*, ('s-Gravenhage: Staatsuitgeverij, 1981), 42-45.

**46** *Verslagen en Mededeelingen van de Afdeeling Landbouw van het Departement van Waterstaat, Handel en Nijverheid, 1904*, vol. 1 "Boterproductie en Botercontrole," ('s-Gravenhage, 1904): 26.

**47** D.R. Mansholt, *Mijne zelfverdediging* (St. Annaparochie: Kuiken, 1892), 48.

**48** W.K. van der Veen, *Uit de geschiedenis van de grietenij Ferwerderadeel* (Leeuwarden: n.p., 1958), 35-39.

**49** Public schools existed in the villages of Ferwerd, Hogebeintum, Hallum, Marrum, Wanswerd, Blija, Genum/Jislum, and Lichtaard. Denominational schools could be found in Ferwerd, Hallum, Marrum (2), Wanswerd (2), Blija and Reitsum. A historical comment concerning these schools is given by Van der Veen in his book: *Uit de geschiedenis van de grietenij*

Ferwerderadeel, 113-22. For an overview of the Dutch school system between 1875 and 1895 see J.W.G. Jansing and L. Dasberg, "Onderwijs," *Algemene Geschiedenis der Nederlanden,* vol. 13, (Haarlem, 1978): 129-44. Some notes about education in the village of Ferwerd are in D. Yska, *De geschiedenis van Ferwerd in woord en beeld* (Leeuwarden: Reidsma, 1972), 36-41.

**50** "Immers, de vrouwen- en kinderarbeid op het veld is de hoofdoorzaak van 't ongeregelde schoolgaan ten plattelande". Jan A. Stap, "Het ontstaan en de werking der Vereeniging 'Broedertrouw' te St. Jacobi-Parochie (1891)," *Het Friesch Volksblad*, October 5, 1890 to March 1, 1891.

**51** Rauwerda "Misstanden bij den veldarbeid in Friesland," 72.

**52** *Verslagen betreffende den oeconomischen toestand der landarbeiders in Nederland;* "Friesland" ('s-Gravenhage: J & H van Langenhuysen, 1908), 219.

**53** The region *[gewest]* Holland was the governmental residence of the *Staten Generaal* and the *Raad van State.*

**54** H.S. Buwalda, *Woun op 'e weagen. It Bildt en syn biwenners* (Sneek: Koster, 1946), 7-42.

**55** H. Sannes, *Geschiedenis van Het Bildt,* 3 vols. (Franeker: Wever, 1956), 3B: 469-71. Also H.S. Buwalda, *Woun op 'e weagen,* 47-48.

**56** In 1895, for example, a heavy storm destroyed all the fish traps (about 700) of the fishermen in Barradeel and Het Bildt. Besides the loss of catch and means of subsistence of the season, this caused a loss of F 10,000. Sannes, *Geschiedenis van Het Bildt,* 3A: 278.

**57** Tjepkema had an average annual income of f 272. This was quite high, especially compared to the average yearly income of land laborers which was f 230. See *Enquete Volkspartij,* cited in Van der Wal, *Vrijheid,* 56-57; and S.H. Buwalda, *Geskidenis fan de Bildtse waddenfisserij* (St-Jacobiparochie: Stichting Ons Bildt, 1986), 13. See also two articles in the regional newspaper: "Toen de zalm nog onder de Friese wal kwam," *Leeuwarder*

*Courant,* May 22, 1979 and "'t Brocht gyn bliksum op, maar elk fon 't mooi'," *Leeuwarder Courant,* January 31, 1987. For the regional development of incomes in agriculture in the nineteenth century, see R. Paping, *Voor een handvol stuivers. Werken, verdienen en besteden: de levensstandaard van boeren, arbeiders en middenstanders op de Groninger klei, 1770-1860* (Groningen: Nederlands Agronomisch Historisch Instituut, 1995), 139-224; and P. Priester, *De economische ontwikkeling van de landbouw in Groningen 1800-1910. Een kwalitatieve en kwantitatieve analyse,* A.A.G. Bijdragen 31 (Wageningen: Landbouwuniversiteit, 1991), 186-206.

**58** Buwalda, *Woun op 'e weagen,* 50-51.

**59** Van der Wal, *Vrijheid,* 51-119.

**60** Sannes, *Geschiedenis van Het Bildt,* 3B: 369-403. Speeches were made by Domela Nieuwenhuis, Pieter Jelles Troelstra, B.H. Held from Amsterdam (chairman of the *Algemeen Nederlandsch Werklieden Verbond* [General Dutch Labor Union]), P.J. van der Stad (chairman of the *Nederlandsche Bond voor Algemeen Kies- en Stemrecht* [Dutch Union of Universal Suffrage]), Vitus Bruinsma (chairman of the later *Volkspartij* [People's Party]) and others. Newspapers widely read in Het Bildt were: *De Klok* (since December 1888), *Recht voor Allen* (dayly newspaper from Domela Nieuwenhuis since January 1889) and the *Friesch Volksblad,* paper from the *Volkspartij).*

**61** In his history of Het Bildt, H. Sannes gives even higher numbers for those years. This may be explained by the fact that more people left than those who were actually registered. For a discussion about the data see Chapter 2.4. Also Sannes, *Geschiedenis van Het Bildt,* 3B: 377.

**62** For the origin and rules of *Broedertrouw* see J. Stap, "Het ontstaan en de werking der Vereeniging 'Broedertrouw' te St. Jacobi-Parochie (1891)", *Het Friesch Volksblad,* October 5, 1890 to March 1, 1891.

**63** Sannes, *Geschiedenis van Het Bildt,* 3B: 388.

**64** S.H. Buwalda, *De erbaaiersbeweging*

op 't Bildt in 't leste forndelspart fan 'e negentynde eeuw (St. Annaparochie: Stichting Ons Bildt, 1983), 49.

**65** For more information concerning Broedertrouw and the relationship between employers and employees and the labor movement of Het Bildt in the last two decennia of the nineteenth century, see Sannes, *Geschiedenis van Het Bildt,* 3B: 369-403; Van der Wal, *Vrijheid,* 254-77; Buwalda, *De erbaaierbeweging op 't Bildt,* 1-112; Stap, *Het ontstaan der Vereeniging "Broedertrouw";* Spahr van der Hoek, *Geschiedenis van de Friese landbouw,* 1: 656-66; J. Frieswijk, *Om een beter leven. Land- en veenarbeiders in het noorden van Nederland 1850-1914* (Ljouwert: Fryske Akademy, 1989), 150-61.

**66** The ladies of the House of Orange were: the queen mother Emma and her daughter Wilhelmina. Sannes, *Geschiedenis van Het Bildt,* 3B: 396.

**67** Van der Wal, *Vrijheid,* 270-75.

**68** Wumkes, *Stads- en dorpskroniek van Friesland,* 2: 567.

**69** For statistics concerning irreligiousness in Friesland see M. Staverman, *Buitenkerkelijkheid in Friesland* (Assen: Van Gorcum, 1954), Appendix I; H. Knippenberg, *De religieuze kaart van Nederland. Omvang en geografische spreiding van de godsdienstige gezindten vanaf de Reformatie tot heden* (Assen: Van Gorcum, 1992).

**70** Census 1879.

**71** Census 1909.

**72** In the 1880s in the *Hervormde Kerk,* a movement under the leadership of Abraham Kuyper wanted to focus more upon the confession as it was intented at the confession of the synod of Dordrecht (1618-1619). This led to the education of private ministers and later to the Dutch Nonconformist Church. Some people from the *Christelijk Gereformeerde Kerk* joined this *Doleantie* and the *Gereformeerde Kerken* came into being.

**73** Staverman, *Buitenkerkelijkheid in Friesland,* 165-205. Also H. Knippenberg, "De godsdienstkaart van Friesland in de tweede helft van de negentiende eeuw," *It Beaken* 57 (1995) 2: 100-02.

**74** Staverman, *Buitenkerkelijkheid in Friesland*, 191.

**75** For the information in this paragraph I heavily relied on the book of K. Siderius and J. Siderius, *De geschiedenis van Barradeel* (Franeker: Telenga's Drukkerij, 1950), 5-38.

**76** E. Allershof, *Landhuishoudkundige beschrijving van de kantons Bergum en Beetsterzwaag in de provincie Friesland* (Haarlem: n.p., 1881), 148.

**77** Definitions of the different types of farmers are based on Spahr van der Hoek, *Geschiedenis van de Friese landbouw* 1: 648-84 and Tj.P. Wijngaarden, "Bouwplan en vruchtopvolging op de gardeniersbedrijven in het Noorden van Friesland voor en na het in werking treden van de Wet Bestrijding Aardappelmoeheid van 1949," (Unpublished thesis of the Landbouwhogeschool Wageningen, Oude Bildtzijl, 1955). Wijngaarden specialized in the subject of the *gardenier* and the meaning of his business. (I am indebted to him for his friendly personal information). Wijngaarden mentions that the *gardenier* was also called *kooltjer* or *aardappelaar*. These names suggests that specific crops were more characteristic for the *gardenier* than the size of his business. Wijngaarden also states that the colloquial meaning of *gardenier* among the clay population is totally different from the official terminology. Everywhere in Friesland a *gardenier* means an independent user of land, whether he uses land for mixed agriculture (like in Barradeel or Het Bildt) or only for potatoes and turnips. Even with mixed farming one may speak of a *gardenier* (like in Ferwerderadeel and the Dongeradelen). Besides this geographical description there is a more sociological one. It is also a matter of status when the sharp distinction between a farmer and *gardenier* appears. The latter usually came from the land laboring class, did not own the business buildings, and lacked working capital and machinery. The former got his status

through birth and had his land close to the farm buildings. Wijngaarden finally gives a broad definition of the phenomenon *gardenier*: "a user of land who tries intensively to grow certain crops to create an independent living on a capital extensive farm of about 2 to 10 hectares". The *gardenier* often remained dependent upon the farmer because he had to borrow his buildings and machinery.

**78** Spahr van der Hoek, *Geschiedenis van de Friese landbouw*, 1: 673.

**79** Spahr van der Hoek based his figures on the agricultural reports [*Verslag van den landbouw*] of 1890 and 1891. Spahr van der Hoek, *Geschiedenis van de Friese landbouw*, 1: 684.

**80** Percentages from Spahr van der Hoek, *Geschiedenis van de Friese landbouw*, 1: 683.

**81** This percentage of absenteeism also covers the *gasthuizen* [home for the aged and infirm], *weeshuizen* [orphanages] and *kerkvoogdij* [churchwarden] as landowners. These were institutions within the province. When they are left out of the calculation, the percentage of absentee landlords in the nineties reaches 66 percent. Spahr van der Hoek, *Geschiedenis van de Friese landbouw*, 1: 677; For a discussion concerning absenteeism and possession of land see also M.J.E. Blauw, *Van Friese grond. Agrarische eigendoms- en gebruiksverhoudingen en de ontwikkelingen in de Friese landbouw in de negentiende eeuw* (Ljouwert: Fryske Akademy, 1995), 22-57; and J. Moes, "Absenteïsme van grondbezitters in Friesland en Zeeland 1850-1890," in *Het platteland in een veranderende wereld. Boeren en het proces van modernisering*, eds. H. Diederiks, J.T. Lindblad, and B. de Vries (Hilversum: Verloren, 1994), 255-76.

**82** For the analyses of landprices and rent in the clay area see De Vries, *Landbouw en bevolking*, 65-69. Also A. Venema, "Proeve eener berekening van de koopwaarde der gronden in Nederland bij den landbouw en de veehouderij in gebruik," *De Economist* 2 (1897): 897-908.

**83** Spahr van der Hoek, *Geschiedenis*

van de Friese landbouw, 1: 675-76; also Blauw, *Van Friese grond*, 72-75.

**84** Ibid. 1: 681.

**85** Th. van Welderen Rengers and J.H. Faber, *Friesland en de woningwet 1902-1912* (Leeuwarden: Meijer & Schaafsma, 1913), 22.

**86** For the social position of the farmers, see Spahr van der Hoek, "De weg naar welvaart," 519-22. Also Spahr van der Hoek, *Geschiedenis van de Friese landbouw*, 1: 676-84.

**87** Twerda, *Fan Fryslâns forline*, 319.

**88** Van der Wal, *Vrijheid*, 111.

**89** Spahr van der Hoek, *Geschiedenis van de Friese landbouw*, 1: 662.

**90** Van der Wal, *Vrijheid*, 113-14.

**91** V. Bruinsma, "Hoe is Friesland te helpen?," *Vragen des Tijds* 1 (1894): 343-91. Also quoted in Frieswijk, *Socialisme in Friesland 1880-1900*, 143. Frieswijk describes the miserable situation of the poor in his chapter: '*Honger en werklozenwet*' [Hunger and Unemployment Act].

**92** A. Rauwerda, an agriculture teacher, studied the problem of paupers in Friesland in those years. He tried to figure out how many heads of families were found among the paupers, because he argued this was the only way to find the total percentage of people receiving poor relief in Friesland. However, Rauwerda could not rely on exact information, because the provincial annual reports did not distinguish between heads of families and singles. Rauwerda, *Armenzorg en gemeentegrondbezit*, 2-4.

**93** Siderius, *Barradeel*, 241.

**94** Ibid., 31.

**95** *Verslag van den toestand van handel, nijverheid en fabriekswezen in de gemeenten Franeker, Barradeel en Menaldumadeel* (Franeker: Kamer van Koophandel [Chamber of Commerce], 1880 and 1911).

**96** G.J.A. Bouma, "De lânbou," in *Geakunde Wûnseradiel*, ed. J.J. Spahr van der Hoek (Bolsward: Osinga, 1969), 299.

**97** Blink, "Friesland als economisch gewest", 377.

**98** R. Brougham, *A cruise on Friesland "Broads"* (London: Ward and Downey, 1891), 41-42.

**99** For the discussion about Frisian butter see Spahr van der Hoek,

*Geschiedenis van de Friese landbouw*, 1: 495-565; Twerda, *Fan Fryslâns forline*, 317-20; Bouma, "De lânbou", 304-08; Van Zanden, *De economische ontwikkeling van de Nederlandse landbouw*, 263-73.

**100** Van Zanden, *De economische ontwikkeling van de Nederlandse landbouw*, 266. Blink in his 1917 study, *Friesland als economisch gewest*, 379, mentions the figure of 29 percent for the Frisian share of the total Dutch butter production in 1912.

**101** Van Zanden, *De economische ontwikkeling van de Nederlandse landbouw*, 269. For the development of the first dairy factories see Spahr van der Hoek, *Geschiedenis van de Friese landbouw*, 1: 537.

**102** For the development of the co-operative movement see Van Zanden, *De economische ontwikkeling van de Nederlandse landbouw*, 273-75. Spahr van der Hoek, *Geschiedenis van de Friese landbouw* 1: 555.

**103** Van Zanden, *De economische ontwikkeling van de Nederlandse landbouw*, 271.

**104** Information concerning industry and handicraft see L. Kamminga, "De industrie," in *Geakunde Wûnseradiel*, ed. J.J. Spahr van der Hoek (Bolsward: Osinga, 1969), 332-48.

Van der Wal, *Op zoek naar een nieuwe vrijheid*, 45-46.

**105** Kamminga, "De industrie," 336, 342.

**106** Van der Wal, *Vrijheid*, 56-58.

**107** Census 1879 and 1909. [*Volkstelling 1879 and 1909*].

**108** There was, for example, a vacancy in the village of Lollum between 1886 and 1895, in Wons from 1884 to 1890, and in Gaast and Ferwoude between 1888 and 1895. R. Steensma, "Geastlik libben yn Wûnseradiel," in *Geakunde Wûnseradiel*, 126-225.

# Notes– 2

**1** D. Grigg, *Population Growth and Agrarian Change; A Historical Perspective* (Cambridge: Cambridge University Press, 1980), 59-60, 127-47. Cited in: J.E. Bodnar, *The Transplanted; A History of Immigrants in Urban America* (Bloomington: Indiana University Press, 1985), 34.
**2** J.A. Faber et al., "Population Changes and Economic Development in The Netherlands; A Historical Survey," *A.A.G. Bijdragen* 12 (Wageningen: Landbouwuniversiteit, 1965): 47-113.
**3** See table 1 in E.W. Hofstee, *Korte demografische geschiedenis van Nederland van 1800 tot heden* (Haarlem: Fibula-Van Dishoeck, 1981), 122-23.
**4** Bodnar, *The Transplanted*, 34.
**5** Hofstee, *Korte demografische geschiedenis van Nederland*, 13-17.
**6** H.A. Diederiks et al., *Van agrarische samenleving naar verzorgingsstaat* (Groningen: Wolters-Noordhoff, 1987), 212-13, 218-19. Also Hofstee, *Korte demografische geschiedenis van Nederland*, 49.
**7** Hofstee, *Korte demografische geschiedenis van Nederland*, 21, 27.
**8** J. Kuyper, "Nederlands bevolking," *Tijdschrift van het Nederlandsch Aardrijkskundig Genootschap*, 2 (1885): 240.
**9** K. Reijne, "De uittocht der platte-landsbevolking," *Studies in Volkskracht* 1 (1904): 533-82. Also A. Hallema, "Bloei en verval der Friesche gemeenten in de laatste halve eeuw op grond van haar bevolkingscijfers," *Tijdschrift voor Economische Geographie* 6 (1925): 165-70.
**10** *Uitkomsten der zesde tienjarige Volkstelling in het Koninkrijk der Nederlanden op den 31sten december 1879*, 12 vols. ('s-Gravenhage: Departement van Binnenlandsche Zaken, 1881). Figures per 1000 hectares for all the provinces were: Zuid-Holland 2,659; Noord-Holland 2,456; Utrecht 1,385; Groningen 1,102; Limburg 1,086; Zeeland 1,057; Friesland 993; Gelderland 919; Noord-Brabant 910; Overijssel 817; Drenthe 446.
**11** Taking the absolute population of the census of 1859 and 1879 of Friesland compared to the Netherlands, it appears that Friesland increased with 20 percent and The Netherlands with 21 percent in that time period. Hofstee, *Korte demografische geschiedenis van Nederland*, table 2, 124-25.
**12** Figures based on the census of 1869 and 1879 and quoted in Kuyper, "Nederlands bevolking", 247, 251.
**13** See table 1 of A. Vondeling, *Eat oer it tal biwenners, de migraesje en de bifolkingstichtens yn Fryslân* (Drachten: Fryske Lânboubibleteek, 1943), 8-9. Vondeling gives the population figures of certain years of all the Frisian municipalities between 1714 and 1940. For a comparison of regional figures between 1795 and 1930 see also J.C. Ramaer, *Geschiedkundige atlas van Nederland* ('s-Gravenhage: Martinus Nijhoff, 1931), Appendix 1: 231-72.
**14** Note for figure 2.1: the population figures for 1848 and 1914 are for January 1, while those from 1879 and 1892 are for December 31.
**15** Based on table 2.4, the Netherlands experienced in the period 1881-1900 19.8 deaths per 1000 people per year. In Friesland this figure was 16.7 and this indicated a positive difference for the province of 3.1 persons. In the years after the turn of the century (1901-1915) this number in the Netherlands decreased to 14.4, while Friesland had an average of 13.1. The difference had diminished to 1.3.
**16** These figures come from the *Statistiek van den loop der bevolking in Nederland*. From 1878 on, this source records numbers of birth, death, birth surplus, in- and out-migration and surplus of in- or out-migration, total increase or decrease per year per municipality. The percentages are also given. These figures were collected in Wageningen at the Agricultural University, which generously placed them at my disposal.
**17** Why not compare the clay area to the remainder of Friesland, excluding the clay area? This means that the figures of all the remaining Frisian municipalities have to be analysed. (i.e. 37 municipalities). Only the figures for all of Friesland and for the individual municipalities are available in Wageningen. Analyzing the remainder of Friesland does not give a different perspective concerning my point that death rates and birth rates in the clay area were *not* responsible for the stagnation in the population which took place.

**18** The following numbers were the average in- and out-migration deficit between 1881-1915 (per 1000 per year):

- Friesland -8.4
- Oostdongeradeel -11.2
- Westdongeradeel -12.6
- Het Bildt -12.5
- Ferwerderadeel -10.7
- Barradeeel -13.0
- Wonseradeel -12.3

**19** January 1, 1915 the population of Het Bildt numbered 8548. Source: *Statistiek van den loop der bevolking in Nederland* (Wageningen: Landbouw-universiteit).

**20** The Emigration Records after 1880 from some provinces are kept in the National Archives in The Hague ("Algemeen Rijksarchief"). Swierenga mentions that Groningen records are available until 1901 (with the year 1889 missing), Overijssel until 1918, Utrecht until 1905, Zeeland until 1901 and Zuid-Holland until 1899. For a detailed discussion about migration statistics in the Netherlands see R.P. Swierenga, "Het bestuderen van de Nederlandse emigratie naar de Verenigde Staten. Nieuwe methoden en begrippen", *Jaarboek Centraal Bureau voor Genealogie* 36 (1982), 252-68; and "Dutch International Migration Statistics, 1820-1880; An Analysis of Linked Multinational Nominal Files," *International Migration Review* 15 (Fall 1981): 445-70; Also H.A.V.M. van Stekelenburg, *Landverhuizing als regionaal verschijnsel. Van Noord-Brabant naar Noord-Amerika 1820-1880* (Tilburg: Stichting Zuidelijk Historisch Contact, 1991), 132-36.

**21** Servants and boarders were included in the family recorded in the Population Registers after 1870. Before that year there was a separate register for servants (*Dienstbodenregister*). For the period of research 1880-1914 I found that there was one exception: the municipality of Wonseradeel still had a separate register for servants from 1880 to 1920.

**22** The official decree was dated December 22, 1849, (art. 5), *Staatsblad*, nr. 64.

**23** It is not my intention to pretend that I traced *all* the overseas emigrants from the clay area. This actually is not the important datum. In this study it is more interesting to be sure that the sample has a representative quality. It is also important to know that a crucial measure of reliability of the Population Registers may be assumed. E.W. Hofstee, "De functie van de internationale migratie," *Tijdschrift voor Economische en Sociale Geografie*, 40 (1949): 10-22. The value of the Population Registers is also discussed by M.L. Samson, *Population Mobility in the Netherlands 1880-1910; A Case Study of Wisch in the Achterhoek* (Uppsala: Almquist & Wiksell International, 1977), 44-66 and 115-16 See also H. de Vries, *Landbouw en bevolking tijdens de agrarische depressie in Friesland, 1878-1895* (Wageningen: Veenman & Zonen, 1971), 112-49.

**24** R.P. Swierenga, "Dutch International Migration Statistics," 462-65. The idea that singles could more easily leave unnoticed is shared by Swierenga, Y. Schreuder and H. van Stekelenburg. Schreuder and Van Stekelenburg both studied the emigration from rural Brabant in the nineteenth century. And, of course, the point is that in rural areas social awareness is usually greater than in more densely populated localities like cities. Y. Schreuder, *Dutch Catholic Immigrant Settlement in Wisconsin, 1850-1905* (New York and London: Garland Publishing, 1989); Stekelenburg, *Landverhuizing als regionaal verschijnsel*.

**25** The tradition of the family of Thomas Burmania makes clear that Thomas left Ferwerd to avoid military service, to profess his *Afgescheiden* religion more freely and to improve his economic situation. Thomas had lost his mother when he was 9 years old. His father took him out of school, so he could work for a farmer for meager wages (10 *centen* per day). In 1890 Thomas met Sietske Kuipers (born July 29, 1872) from Blija, one of the two daughters of Jarig Aedes Kuipers and his wife Trijntje Herres Damsma. When Thomas indicated his interest in America to Sietske's father -thinking it would be impossible to leave because he had no possessions-, Jarig Kuipers offered to lend him money for the trip to the United States. Thomas Burmania left in March 1892 and settled in Kalamazoo, Michigan and by working in a factory he earned enough money within a year to pay for his ticket but also to pay for Sietske's ticket to come over. In April 1893 Sietske traveled second class, because Thomas did not want his fiancé to get involved with that *gajes* [scum] of third class passengers. The couple married in Kalamazoo and had five children.

I am indebted to Mrs. K. Feitsema-Boonstra for the information on these emigrants. Sietske Kuipers was her aunt and sister of her mother Ytje. Some letters of Sietske were preserved and generously given to me in 1990. The Population Register gives the date of emigration mentioned above. Mrs. Feitsema recalls that Thomas left in 1890 and Sietske in 1891.

**26** Gerrit's brother Tsjerk had gone to America in 1901 to his uncle Piet, who lived in Orange City, IA. Gerrit Roorda left in May 1910 from Tynje, close to the city of Heerenveen. He returned to Friesland in 1919. His story is told by K. Huisman, *It libben fan Gerrit Roorda/opskrean troch Kerst Huisman* (Bûtenpost: Alternatyf, 1973), 5, 15-16.

**27** J. van Dijk, "Zes maanden in Amerika," 2 vols. (1881) 1: 5-6. A copy of the original hand written text is in Calvin College Archives, Grand Rapids, MI.

**28** R.P. Swierenga, "Dutch Immigration Patterns in the Nineteenth and Twentieth Centuries," in *The Dutch in America; Immigration, Settlement, and Cultural Change*, ed. R.P. Swierenga (New Brunswick, NJ: Rutgers University Press, 1985): 16.

**29** J. Marczewski, "Quantitative History," *Journal of Contemporary History* 3 (April 1968): 190.

**30** I am aware of the disadvantages that accompany the use of specific numerical values for biographical information. But my data files originally were composed to be processed with the SPSS (Statistical Package for the Social Sciences)-program. The numerical values had to be assigned to be capable to use this software.

**31** According to Swierenga's findings, between 1880 and 1914 a total of 117,252 Dutch emigrants went to the USA. See: R.P. Swierenga, "The Delayed Transition from Folk to Labor Migration; The Netherlands, 1880-1920," *International Migration Review* 2 (Summer 1993), table 3 and 5.

**32** Hofstee, "De functie van de internationale migratie," 10-22.

**33** De Vries, *Landbouw en bevolking*, 72. Correlation between the volume of emigration and living costs are demonstrated more often. For example, for Würtemberg, Germany, in W. von Hippel, *Auswanderung aus Südwestdeutschland. Studien zur württembergischen Auswanderung und Auswanderungspolitik im 18./19. Jahrhundert* (Stuttgart: Klett-Cotta, '84), 148-52.

**34** T. van der Wal, *Op zoek naar een nieuwe vrijheid. Een kwart eeuw arbeidersbeweging in Friesland* (Leiden: Universitaire Pers, 1972), 268.

**35** De Vries, *Landbouw en bevolking*, 187.

**36** A "Mr. J." told the story of the swindle in Colorado in the *Denver Republican*, December 18, 1892. It was translated and republished in Friesland in the *Nieuw Advertentieblad*, January 18, 1893.

**37** See below*

**38** W. Kamphoefner states that inheritance systems played a primary role in German emigration history. He concludes that partible inheritance [equal division among heirs] was neither a necessary nor a sufficient condition for heavy emigration. W.D. Kamphoefner, *The*

*Westfalians; From Germany to Missouri* (Princeton NJ: Princeton University Press, 1987), 13. For the Frisian agrarian property ratio see M.J.E. Blauw, *Van Friese grond. Agrarische eigendoms- en gebruiksverhoudingen en de ontwikkelingen in de Friese landbouw in de negentiende eeuw* (Ljouwert: Fryske Akademy, 1995), 167-71.

**39** G. van Roon, "'Long Wave' Economic Trends and Economic Policies in the Netherlands in the 19th and 20th Century," *JEEH* 12 (Fall 1983): 323-37.

**40** Of 160 emigrants the age could not be determined.

**41** For a discussion of the share women's labor outside the home in the late nineteenth and early twentieth century see J.L. van Zanden, *De economische ontwikkeling van de Nederlandse landbouw in de negentiende eeuw 1800-1914* (Utrecht: Hes Uitgevers, 1985), 67-78.

**42** Van Zanden, *De economische ontwikkeling van de Nederlandse landbouw*, 72.

**43** W.P. de Vries, "De visschers van Wierum en Moddergat," *Vragen van den dag* (1894): 180-86; Geertje Posthumus-Zandstra wrote about her mother peddling from door to door. She tells the story about her return migration to Canada in G. Posthumus-Zandstra, *Retour Canada. Een waar verhaal uit het begin van deze eeuw* (Buitenpost: Lykele Jansma, 1978), 28.

**44** The Dutch text was: "Moge er een tijd komen, dat de man voldoende verdient om de vrouw in de huishouding en het kind bij zijne moeder, bij onderwijs en spel te laten". See *De toestand van de arbeiders in Friesland. Uitslag van het onderzoek ingesteld door het Friesch Comité van de*

*Volkspartij,* vol. 1: "Vrouwen en Kinderarbeid," n.p., [1890].

**45** Letter of D. Dijkstra from Chicago to his brother and sister in Friesland in the neighborhood of the city of Dokkum. Thanks to a donation by Mr. de Blécourt a copy of this letter is in my collection of immigrant letters. Douwe Wiegers Dijkstra (born December 21, 1872) emigrated as a single young man in June 1892 from the village of Aalsum in Oostdongeradeel. He was a brush maker and affiliated with the *Christelijk Gereformeerde* Church. Galema, "Frisians to America, 1880-1914. Computer Compilation."

**46** See tables Chapter 1.1.

**47** De Vries, *Landbouw en bevolking*, 104-05.

**48** Schreuder, *Dutch Catholic Immigrant Settlement in Wisconsin*, 51-54.

**49** For the emigration from the municipality of Oostdongeradeel, H. de Vries noticed exactly the same. Looking at the internal migration it appeared that 39 % of the out-migrating heads of household was born in Oostdongeradeel, while the same percentage dealing with overseas emigrants was 71. De Vries, *Landbouw en bevolking*, 186.

**50** Letters from Cathrinus Hoekema from sea and the state of Washington to Wommels 1915-1917. Cathrinus followed his brother Klaas who left in 1912 for America. The letters have been copied in a little booklet, which was generously donated to me by Mr. and Mrs. Slaterus in Leeuwarden. For more details concerning the Hoekema Family see C.P. Hoekema, *Andreas Paulus' Hoekema (1750-1801) en syn neiteam* (Heerenveen: Stifting ffyrug, 1983), 45-47.

**\* 37 Absolute number of emigrants from the clay area, 1880-1914 compared to the population in 1914:**

| Emigrants U.S. | | | Population in 1914 | % |
|---|---|---|---|---|
| Oostdongeradeel: | 1,270 | 8,512 | | 14.9 |
| Westdongeradeel: | 889 | 7,915 | | 11.2 |
| Het Bildt: | 2,341 | 8,451 | | 27.2 |
| Ferwerderadeel: | 1,781 | 8,277 | | 21.5 |
| Barradeel: | 1,777 | 7,658 | | 23.2 |
| Wonseradeel: | 1,401 | 12,999 | | 10.8 |

**Source:** A. Vondeling, "Eat oer it tal biwenners," table 1, 8-9; Galema, "Frisians to America, 1880-1914. Computer Compilation."

**1** This phrase comes from a sonnet called "The New Colossus" written in 1883 by Emma Lazarus, who referred to the Colossus of Rhodes, a statue of the sun god which once stood in the harbor of Rhodes and was known in ancient times as one of the Seven Wonders of the World. Lazarus, from Jewish heritage, is described as the first modern American laureate of Jewish history and culture. Lazarus associated the statue of Liberty with the American promise of new life for the downtrodden of the earth, because at that time after the assassination of Tsar Alexander II a vicious and violent wave of anti-Semitism swept through Russia resulting in hundreds of thousands of refugees streaming toward safety in other countries including the United States. J. Higham, *Send These to Me* (London and Baltimore: John Hopkins University Press, 1984), 72-73.

**2** For a good overview of the Frisians who left for America between 1845 and 1878 see Y.C. Spyksma, *Dutch American Relations; Friesland 1845-1878* (Leeuwarden: Fryske Akademy, 1965); Spyksma compiled his list from the Netherlands Emigration Lists [*De Staat der landverhuizingen naar Noord-Amerika en andere overzeesche gewesten*. Rijksarchief Leeuwarden]. The records contain the following information: *Gemeente* and year of departure, first and last name of head of the family or individual, age, religious affinity, company of wife and number of children, and sometimes the name of the ship is listed. For more complete records of this period see the computer compilation of R.P. Swierenga, *Dutch Emigrants to the United States, South Africa, South America, and Southeast Asia, 1835-1880; An Alphabetical Listing by Households and Independent Persons* (Wilmington, DE: Scholarly Resources, 1983); This list was composed from the Netherlands Emigration Lists, and can be found in the *Rijks-archieven* in The Netherlands.

**3** G.A. Wumkes, *Stads- en dorpskroniek*, 2 vols. (Leeuwarden: Eisma, 1930-1934), 2: 216.

**4** H.S. Lucas, *Netherlanders in America* (Ann Arbor: University of Michigan Press, 1955; reprint ed., Grand Rapids, MI: W.B. Eerdmans, 1989), 165.

**5** S.A. Sipma, *Belangrijke berigten uit Pella, in de Vereenigde Staten van Noord-Amerika*, or *Tweede brief van Sjoerd Aukes Sipma: van daar geschreven aan de ingezetenen van Bornwerd, waarin hij vele bijzonderheden, betreffende de Hollandsche Vereeniging in den staat Iowa, de levenswijze en de gewoonten der Amerikanen, benevens vele nuttige wenken voor hen, die naar de Vereenigde Staten willen verhuizen, voorkomen. Voorzien met eenige aanmerkingen door N.N.* (Dockum: B. Schaafsma, 1849). Swierenga published and edited an English language edition of Sipma's messages as "A Dutch Immigrant's View of Frontier Iowa," *Annals of Iowa* 38 (Fall 1965): 81-120. Also *Brief van Sjoerd Aukes Sipma aan de ingezetenen van Bornwerd in Westdongeradeel, uit wier midden hij in het voorjaar van 1847 als landverhuizer is vertrokken naar Pella, in de Vereenige Staten van Noord-Amerika, voorzien met ophelderende aanmerkingen door N.N.* (Dockum: B. Schaafsma, [1848]). Another report from Pella in the early days is from A.G. van der Meulen, *Eene brief uit Pella van A.G. van der Meulen, uit Bergum naar Noord-Amerika vertrokken den 9 mei 1849* (Bergum: T.G. van der Meulen, 1849).

**6** Lucas, *Netherlanders in America*, 185.

**7** *Brief van Sjoerd Aukes Sipma*, 14-15.

**8** Anne van der Meulen wrote down some of his experiences in a letter: *Eene brief uit Pella van A.G. van der Meulen*.

**9** J.J. Pelmulder, *Eenvoudige maar zeer belangrijke brieven uit Noord-Amerika* (Dockum: A. Schaafsma, 1859).

**10** *Brief van Sjoerd Aukes Sipma*, 16 (note 18).

**11** Pelmulder, *Eenvoudige maar zeer belangrijke brieven*, 2.

**12** *Tiental brieven betrekkelijk de reis, aankomst en vestiging naar en in Noord-Amerika, van eenige landverhuizers vertrokken uit de grietenijen Het Bildt en Barradeel in Vriesland* (Franeker: T. Telenga, 1848), iii. See also for Osinga's travel account: S. Osinga, *Dagboek mijner reize naar Noord-Amerika's Vereenigde Staten in den jare 1847 gedaan* (Franeker: T. Telenga, 1848).

**13** *Tiental brieven*, 15.

**14** B.B. Haagsma, *Lotgevallen van den heer O.H. Bonnema en zijne togtgenooten, op reis uit Friesland naar de Vereenigde Staten van Noord-Amerika* (Harlingen: Houtsma, 1853), 2; also letter of Hendrik Jans Kas of 1853 to his family in Friesland. Kas travelled with Oepke Bonnema and his company. I am indebted to N.J. Jansonius for a copy of the Kas letter.

**15** In Liverpool one family decided to return to Friesland. Bonnema therefore left Liverpool with a Frisian group of 86, about a hundred English and Irish people and 12 Germans. Haagsma, *Lotgevallen van den heer O.H. Bonnema*, 9.

**16** B.B. Haagsma, *Frysia, of schets der Friesche volkplanting in Noord-Amerika, benevens raadgevingen en wenken voor landverhuizers, zijnde een vervolg op het werkje getiteld: O. Bonnema en zijne togtgenooten* (Bolsward: P.M. Feenstra, 1855).

**17** J. van Hinte, *Nederlanders in Amerika. Een studie over landverhuizers en volksplanters in de 19e en 20ste eeuw in de Vereenigde Staten van Amerika*, 2 vols. (Groningen: P. Noordhoff, 1928), 1: 179; J. van Hinte, *Netherlanders in America; a Study of Emigrants and Colonists in the Nineteenth and Twentieth Centuries*, ed. R.P. Swierenga, and trans. A. de Wit (Grand Rapids, MI: Baker Book House, 1985); Lucas, *Netherlanders in America*, 212.

**18** J.H. Karsten, "A Half Century of Dutch Settlement in Wisconsin 1847-1897," in *Dutch Immigrant Memoirs and Related Writings*, ed. H.S. Lucas, 2 vols. (Assen: Van Gorcum, 1955), 2: 139. In 1958 Y. Poortinga wrote about the contradictory opinions concerning Bonnema's settlement in his article "Emigraesje út Westerlauwersk Fryslân nei en festiging yn 'e Foriene Steaten (oant likernôch 1900 ta)," *Frysk Jierboek* (1958), 89-109. See also H.S. Lucas "The Founding of New Amsterdam, La Crosse County," *Wisconsin Magazine of History* 31 (1947-48): 42-60, and A. Brown, "The Life Story of John Tuininga," in *Dutch Immigrant Memoirs*, 2: 188-95.

**19** Almost all the names of the people who left with Ypma are known and mentioned in Lucas, *Netherlanders in America*, 666 (note 102). They were recorded in D. Versteeg, *De pelgrim vaders van het westen. Eene geschiedenis van de worstelingen der Hollandsche nederzettingen in Michigan benevens eene schets van de stichting der kolonie Pella in Iowa* (Grand Rapids, MI: C.M. Loomis, 1886), 46.

**20** A. de Vree, "Ervaringen," *De Grondwet*, February 20, 1912, and T. Ulberg, "Uit de portefeuille van de eerste settlers in de Hollandsche kolonie in Michigan," *Jaarboekje voor de Hollandsche Christelijke Gereformeerde Kerk in Noord-Amerika. Voor het jaar 1883* (Grand Rapids, MI, 1882), 65-79. Both sketches are published in Lucas, *Dutch Immigrant Memoirs*, 1: 272-98. For information about Rev. Ypma and his colony see also Lucas, *Netherlanders in America*, 142-43 and J. Ypma, *Ds Marten Annes Ypma 1810-1863* (Hallum: Fries Dagblad Offset, 1984), 30-31; J.H. Karsten, "Life Sketch of the Rev. Marten Anne Ypma," in *Dutch Immigrant Memoirs*, 2: 384-87; Van Hinte, *Nederlanders in Amerika*, 158-59. Other information about the journey and early northern Frisian settlement in Michigan can be found in *Eene belangrijke brief uit Noord-Amerika, door J.A. van der Meer, voormalig logementhouder op de drie Romers, te Roordahuizum* (Leeuwarden: D. Meindersma, [1848]).

**21** Poortinga, "Westerlauwersk Fryslân," 100.

**22** About Worp van Peyma see J. Swart, "Emigraasje as útwei foar driigjend ûnk," *De Vrije Fries* 64 (1984), 79-93. Also G.A. Wumkes, "Worp van Peyma en zijn vrienden," *De Vrije Fries* 21 (1914), 150-77. Lucas as well as Van Hinte wrote about Van Peyma's migration. See Lucas, *Netherlanders in America*, 246-47, and Van Hinte, *Nederlanders in Amerika*, 1: 172-77. Van Hinte even partly recalled the poem written by Rinse Posthumus, one of Van Peyma's friends and brother in law, a 'Farewell' to accompany the departure of this Frisian farmer to America.

**23** In the Rijksarchief Leeuwarden and in the Provinciale Bibliotheek in Leeuwarden most of Van Peyma's letters from America to Friesland are preserved.

**24** These lines quoted here are not Posthumus' complete poem. Part of the English translation is found in Swierenga's translation of Van Hinte's book *Nederlanders in Amerika*. See Van Hinte, *Netherlanders in America*, 160-61. The original Frisian

text of the poem is as follows and comes from: *Farwol! Taroppen oan myn broer in stalke W. van Peima, bij syn fortjean, mei bern in bernsbern in ore goede kunde, nei Amerika* (Leeuwarden, 1849).

> Ho swier it fâlt, sa fen elkor to skieden,
> It treast, dat jou nei 't lân fen Washington
> En Franklin gonch, ja, troch wans ried en dieden
> De frijheit der de tsjinstberheit oerwon.
> Wij minsken kinne allinne yn frijheit tierje;
> Sa wol it God, hy makket uus sa frij:
> Sa seit Amerika uus yn 't opblierjen
> Fen dy 't der komme yn frijheits skoalle en lij.
> Der is men minske in borger; for de wetten
> Hat nimmen eat foaruut, as troch syn deuchd.
> Nin borgers wurd' troch swiere laest forplette:
> Der groeit in nije wrâd yn bliere jeuchd.
> O Friesen! Nederlân! oer see, yn 't westen,
> Leit 't lân, wer't roemtme for jimme arbeid is.
> Forjitte it lân, wer't men uus widze in fiede
> Mei tate, wer't uus âders stof yn leit,
> Kin nimmen: Nee! it minske-hart mat bliede,
> As it dat lân for 't laeste: farwol! seit.
> Dat de âde en nije wrâd elkoar bystean,
> En dat Amerika uus uut uus slomme
> Opwekket en nij libben oer docht gean
> Yn uus forâde geest.

**25** Van Hinte, *Nederlanders in Amerika*, 2: 95. For more information concerning Tillema and his settlement of Friesland and Randolph, Columbia County, WI, see Lucas, *Netherlanders in America*, 204; Lucas mistakenly calls the first Tillema Teunis. According to reminiscenses of the Tillema family in Randolph, Tjisse was the first who came to the Randolph area, while his brother Teunis arrived in 1863; see *Centennial History of the Town of Randolph, Columbia County, 1849-1950* (n.p., 1950), 21-28. See also H. Bottema, "In America's Friesland," in *Dutch Immigrant Memoirs*, 2: 139-44.

**26** J.H. Karsten, "A Half Century of Dutch settlement in Wisconsin, 1847-1897," in *Dutch Immigrant Memoirs*, 2: 129-39; Bottema, "In America's Friesland," in *Dutch Immigrant Memoirs*, 2: 139-44.

**27** The account of the Yntema's trip on the *Albatross* was kept by Hendrik Dam. The original Dutch text of this account and an English translation can be found in *Dutch Immigrant Memoirs*, 1: 303-10. For more information on the Yntema family see M.E. Yntema, *The Family of Hessel O. Yntema; Frisian Immigrant to Michigan, 1847* (Holland, MI: The Klaasen Printing Company, 1958). Thanks to Mr. J.J. Groeneveld from Eemnes and Mrs. W. Kramer-Yntema from Heerenveen I got a copy of this book.

**28** For more information concerning this departure and settlement of Frisian Mennonites see Van Hinte, *Nederlanders in Amerika*, 1: 180-86; Lucas, *Netherlanders in America*, 247-49; M. Yoder, "Balk Dutch Settlement near Goshen, Indiana, 1853-1889," *Mennonite Quarterly Review* 30 (January 1956): 32-43. For contemporary accounts D.S. Gorter, *De Christelijke lijdzaamheid aangeprezen bij het vertrek der Oud-Doopsgezinden van Balk die om vrijheid van krijgsdienst naar Noord-Amerika verhuisden* (Sneek, 1853); For letters to the Netherlands from Mennonites in America see D.S. Gorter, *Godsdienstige lectuur voor Doopsgezinden* (Sneek, 1854); E.J. Potgieter, "Landverhuizing naar de Vereenigde Staten. Een brief uit Pella, door den Salamagundist," *De Gids* 1 (1855): 528.

**29** For the two percent Baptist emigrants from the northern clay area between 1880-1914 the area in Indiana was not an option. Sjouke de Zee, who visited them in 1928 in New Paris and Goshen concludes that even then many of the immigrants

were Mennonites and most of them came from the region of Gaasterland in Friesland. It seems that this community of Frisians in Indiana was a clear example of chain migration from a specified region in the old country over a timespan of more than half a century.

**30** Jan de Jong wrote with the pen name: John. Around 1888 his travel account was published: John, *Eenige jaren in Amerika. Van Gaasterland naar Indiana en Californië* (Heerenveen, [1888]). About the Frisian Mennonites see also J. van Hinte, "Friesche Mennisten in Indiana," *Neerlandia* 34 (1930): 196-97.

**31** R.P. Swierenga, "Dutch Immigration Patterns in the Nineteenth and Twentieth Centuries," in *The Dutch in America; Immigration, Settlement, and Cultural Change*, ed. R.P. Swierenga (New Brunswick, NJ: Rutgers University Press, 1985), 34-35. Also R.P. Swierenga, "Local Patterns of Dutch Migration to the United States in the Mid-Nineteenth Century," in *A Century of European Migrations, 1830-1930*, eds. R.J. Vecoli and S.M. Sinke (Urbana & Chicago: University of Illinois Press, 1991), 134-57.

**32** For example, M. ten Hoor, "Frisians to the United States," *Michigan Alumnus Quarterly Review* 58 (December 1951): 50-56.

**33** Haagsma, *Lotgevallen van den heer O.H. Bonnema*, 1-3.

**34** *Leeuwarder Courant*, May 11, 1849; *Provinciale Groninger Courant*, March 30, and May 8, 1849; J. Swart, "Emigraasje as útwei foar driigjend ûnk," 79, 93 (note 46).

**35** "Libbensforhael fan in Ferwerter jonge," *Friesch Dagblad*, May 19, 1972. Hendrik Kroes -son of Pope Kroes and Geertje Zuidema- was born on July 16, 1865 and married Aaltje Bouma, also from Ferwerd. Her parents had emigrated in 1888 and two of Aaltje's sisters also had left for America.

**36** For a detailed overview concerning theory on international migration see R. Penninx and F. Selier, "Theorievorming over internationale migratie: een historisch overzicht en een stand van

zaken," *Migratiestudies* 4 (1992): 4-19.

**37** E.G. Ravenstein, "The Laws of Migration," *Journal of the Royal Statistical Society*, 52 (June 1889): 241-301.

**38** In his analysis of mobility in the city of Groningen around the turn of the century, P. Kooij mentions the lack of theoretical approach. Kooij admits that before Ravenstein some studies tried to structure findings by brief statistical investigation, but these statistics were the first unbalanced efforts. P. Kooij, *Groningen 1870-1914. Sociale verandering en economische ontwikkeling in een regionaal centrum* (Ph.D. dissertation, University of Groningen, 1986), 79-80. For a discussion about Ravenstein's laws see also R. Daniels, *Coming to America. A History of Immigration and Ethnicity in American Life* (New York: HarperCollins, 1990), 16-22.

**39** Kooij, *Groningen 1870-1914*, 81-82.

**40** E.S. Lee, "A Theory of Migration," in *Migration*, ed. J.A. Jackson (Cambridge: University Press, 1969), 285.

**41** D.S. Thomas, "Research Memorandum on Migration Differentials," *Social Science Research Council Bulletin* 43 (1938).

**42** S.A. Stouffer, "Intervening Opportunities; A Theory Relating Mobility and Distance," *American Sociological Review* 5 (December 1940): 845-67. This theoretical concept is also used by H. de Vries in his analysis of the migration from the municipality of Oostdongeradeel outside the province. H. de Vries, *Landbouw en bevolking tijdens de agrarische depressie in Friesland, 1878-1895* (Wageningen: H. Veenman & Zonen, 1971), 137-41.

**43** N. Frijda, *Emigranten, niet-emigranten* ('s-Gravenhage: Staatsuitgeverij, 1960); G. Beijer, ed., *Characteristics of Overseas Migrants* ('s-Gravenhage: Staatsuitgeverij, 1961); B.P. Hofstede, *Thwarted Exodus* ('s-Gravenhage: Staatsuitgeverij, 1964); R. Wentholt, *Kenmerken van de Nederlandse emigrant* ('s-Gravenhage: Staatsuitgeverij, 1961).

**44** J.E. Ellemers, "The Determinants of Emigration; An Analysis of Dutch Studies on Migration," *Sociologia*

Neerlandia 2 (1964): 52. This is in agreement with J. Elich's study of Dutch migrants to Australia after World War II. See J.H. Elich, *Aan de ene kant, aan de andere kant. De emigratie van Nederlanders naar Australië 1946-1986* (Ph.D. dissertation, University of Leiden, 1987), 17.

**45** E.W. Hofstee, *Some Remarks on Selective Migration* ('s-Gravenhage: Martinus Nijhoff, 1952).

**46** Ellemers, "Determinants of Emigration," 11.

**47** Kooij, *Groningen 1870-1914*, 82.

**48** H. ter Heide, *Binnenlandse migratie in Nederland* ('s-Gravenhage: Staatsuitgeverij, 1965), 50-53.

**49** H.M. in 't Veld-Langeveld, *Migratiemotieven, migratie-beheersing en hun selektieve betekenis* (Assen: Van Gorcum, 1957), 138-39.

**50** J.J.M. van Amersfoort, *Immigratie en minderheidsvorming. Een analyse van de Nederlandse situatie 1945-1973* (Alphen a/d Rijn: Samson, 1974).

**51** See W.D. Kamphoefner, *The Westfalians; From Germany to Missouri* (Princeton, NJ: Princeton University Press, 1987); J. Gjerde, *From Peasants to Farmers; The Migration from Balestrand, Norway, to the Upper Middle West* (Cambridge: Cambridge University Press, 1985); R.C. Ostergren, *A Community Transplanted; The Trans-Atlantic Experience of a Swedish Immigrant Settlement in the Upper Middle West, 1835-1915* (Uppsala: Acta Universitatis Upsaliensis, 1988; also published by University of Wisconsin Press, 1988).

**52** S. de Schaepdrijver, *Elites for the Capital?* (Amsterdam: Thesis Publishers, 1990), 47.

**53** H.A.V.M. van Stekelenburg, *Landverhuizing als regionaal verschijnsel. Van Noord-Brabant naar Noord-Amerika 1820-1880* (Tilburg: Stichting Zuidelijk Historisch Contact, 1991), 36.

**54** For example the study of P. Kooij about mobility in nineteenth century Groningen and S. de Schaepdrijver's findings concerning foreign migration to mid-nineteenth-century Brussels.

**55** Lee, "A Theory of Migration," 285.

**56** Ibid., 287.

**57** Elich, *Aan de ene kant, aan de andere kant*, 20-21.

**58** Especially in the sociological studies of migration, the concepts of social structure and culture are widely used. See the often cited study of M.M. Gordon, *Assimilation in American Life; The Role of Race, Religion, and National Origins* (New York: Oxford University Press, 1964). Gordon describes social structure as "the set of crystallized social relationships which its members have with each other which places them in groups, large or small, permanent or temporary, formally organized or unorganized, and which relates them to the major institutional activities of the society, such as economic and occupational life, religion, marriage and the family, education, government, and recreation" (30-31). "Culture", Gordon says, "refers to the social heritage of man- the ways of acting and the ways of doing things which are passed down from one generation to the next, not through genetic inheritance but by formal and informal methods of teaching and demonstration" (32).

**59** Gordon, *Assimilation*, 33. Culture, social structure and their dynamic interaction can be analyzed according to a more socio-economic perspective. P. Kooij and associates chose the concept of *integral history* for their in-depth study of the village of Hoogkerk, near Groningen. They limited their analysis to cohort analysis, structural analysis, as well as analyses of municipal accounts and newspapers. They successfully integrated the diverse cohesions between the different social segments, and showed on the local level the "coherence of everything with everything." P. Kooij ed., *Dorp naast een stad. Hoogkerk 1770-1914* (Assen: Van Gorcum, 1993), 1-5, 160-201.

**60** Elich, *Aan de ene kant, aan de andere kant*, 23.

**61** One can think for example of the following questions: what is the hierarchy between different organizations? How much is migration influenced by

bureaucracy? Who determines how many emigrants go where? See Elich, *Aan de ene kant, aan de andere kant*, 27-29.

**62** C. Tilly, "Transplanted Networks," in *Immigration Reconsidered*, ed. V. Yans-McLaughlin (New York: Oxford University, 1990), 81.

**63** Tilly, "Transplanted Networks," 84.

**64** Ibid., 87.

**65** See also paragraph 3.2. and Gordon, *Assimilation*, 30-31.

**66** J.E. Bodnar, *The Transplanted; A History of Immigrants in Urban America* (Bloomington: Indiana University Press, 1985), 38.

**67** I am indebted to Mr. J. van den Bosch from Heerenveen who recalled this story. Van den Bosch even found the advertisement of Sjuk Bergsma in *Hepkema's Courant* of September 17, 1913. Sjuk Bergsma (born in Friens, January 2, 1889) was an uncle of his wife. Bergsma emigrated in 1911 to Renton, Washington. He married Jeltje Scholten (born in Grouw October 4, 1893, daughter of fisherman Pieter Scholten and his wife Margje Berends Stuiver, originally from Nijehaske) in Seattle, Washington June 6, 1914. Sjuk became a dairy farmer and he delivered his bottled milk to private addresses as well as to retailers. Sjuk and Jeltje had seven children. Sjuk died in Renton November 26, 1965 and his wife Jeltje much earlier on December 23, 1949.

**68** This structural increase has also been reported by H. de Vries, but the percentages of single emigrants that he mentions for Oostdongeradeel, are much higher. This originated in the fact that De Vries compared the share of singles to the total number of heads of families, while I related the singles to the total number of emigrants from the northern clay area. See De Vries, *Landbouw en bevolking*, 186.

**69** R.C. Ostergren, *A Community Transplanted*, 122-26. I. Semmingsen concluded that for the early period 1837-1843 four-fifths of the emigration from the Norwegian Tinn in Telemark was family emigration. I. Semmingsen, *Norway to America; A History of the Migration*, trans. E. Haugen

(Minneapolis: University of Minnesota Press, 1978), 37-40; the percentage of Dutch who emigrated as family units also was about 80 percent according to R.P. Swierenga, "Dutch Immigrant Demography, 1820-1880," *Journal of Family History* 5 (1980): 390-405.

**70** The figures of the male occupational population according to the Occupational Census of 1849-1909 can be found in J.L. van Zanden, *De economische ontwikkeling van de Nederlandse landbouw in de negentiende eeuw 1800-1914* (Utrecht: Hes Uitgevers, 1985), 63.

**71** R.P. Swierenga, "The Delayed Transition from Folk to Labor Migration; The Netherlands, 1880-1920," *International Migration Review* 22 (Summer 1993): 406.

**72** It is likely that a farm laborer who had lost his job did not call himself a farm laborer by profession. It may be that before departure to America he registered as 'unemployed'. A carpenter who did not have much work, probably continued to call himself a carpenter by profession.

**73** "De huiselijke bezigheden moeten geacht worden het hoofdbestanddeel uit te maken van de werkzaamheden eener gehuwde vrouw, tenzij duidelijk blijkt, dat zij een zelfstandig beroep of handwerk, afgescheiden van haren man, uitoefent". See citation from *Volkstelling 1889*, Inleiding Deel I [Introduction part I] in Van Zanden, *De economische ontwikkeling van de Nederlandse landbouw*, 67-76.

**74** The nuclear family with the married woman as central person at home was promoted in the *fin de siècle* period by many leading politicians like the well known liberal Ch. Boissevain and others. For an interesting discussion of moral values concerning the role of women in society (personified by the young queen Wilhelmina) see H. te Velde, *Gemeenschapszin en plichtsbesef. Liberalisme en nationalisme in Nederland 1870-1918* ('s-Gravenhage: SDU, 1992), 153-61. The good old fashioned MOTHER was idealized and working outside the home was considered damaging to the education of children. Generally it may be noted that especially in agriculture most of the women worked on the home farm. Butter- and cheese-making was typically their job. Also W.N. Schilstra, *Vrouwenarbeid in landbouw en industrie in Nederland in de tweede helft van de negentiende eeuw* (Amsterdam: Contact, 1940).

**75** C. de Groot, "American and Dutch Maids are Compared," *San Francisco Chronicle*, February 29, 1929. A reprint of this and other articles of C. de Groot can be found in: C. de Groot, *When I was a Girl in Holland* (Boston: Northrop, Lee & Shepard, 1917; reprint ed., Arnhem: Bakker, 1991).

**76** There were 206 *dienstboden*, *dienstmeisjes* and *huishoudsters* counted, 3 farmers, 46 female field laborers or farm girls, 2 barge women, and 14 shopkeepers and buyers.

**77** For sources and methodology see also A. Galema, "'Se binne nei Amerika tein'. Aspekten van Friese landverhuizing naar de Verenigde Staten rond de eeuwwisseling," *It Beaken* 52 (1990) 2: 45-58.

**78** Y. Schreuder, *Dutch Catholic Immigrant Settlement in Wisconsin, 1850-1905* (New York & London: Garland Publishing, 1989), 57.

**79** See especially P. Kooij's analysis of Groningen 1870-1914. Kooij has an exhaustive description of the debate on social inequality in the 19th century and recalls the theoretical discussion of the 1970s in the Netherlands. Kooij, *Groningen 1870-1914*, 28-51.

**80** These criteria are formulated by J. Lucassen and G. Trienekens, "Om de plaats in de kerk. Een onderzoek naar maatschappelijke ongelijkheid voornamelijk in de negentiende eeuw," *Tijdschrift voor Sociale Geschiedenis* 12 (1978): 239-305.

**81** S. Thernstrom, *Poverty and Progress; Social Mobility in a Nineteenth Century City* (Cambridge, MA: Harvard University Press, 1964), 90.

**82** P. Kooij points out that the designation of carpenter or painter in the Population Registers did not always mean that these were independent entrepreneurs. Many times older carpenter's helpers would be registered as carpenter. The same is true for painter's helpers and apprentices. The social categories therefore cannot always be correctly determined. Kooij, *Groningen 1870-1914*, 42.

**83** See, for example, P. Marschalck, *Deutsche Überseewanderung im 19. Jahrhundert. Ein Beitrag zur soziologischen Theorie der Bevölkerung* (Stuttgart: E. Klett, 1973), 52-84; A. Galema and A. Holtmann, "Aus den nördlichen Niederlanden und dem deutschen Nordwesten nach Nordamerika. Motive und Reise-erfahrungen der Auswanderer im 19. Jahrhundert," in *Rondom Eems en Dollard/Rund um Ems und Dollart*, eds. O.S. Knottnerus, et al., (Groningen/Leer: REGIO-PRojekt/ Schuster Verlag, 1992), 447; J.D. Wildeboer concludes that after World War II, about three quarters of the Dutch emigrants from Barradeel and Harlingen emigrated with travel costs subsidized by the government. J.D. Wildeboer, "Friesland verliest zijn kinderen," *It Beaken* 16 (May 1954) 3/4: 100.

**84** See the story of the Hoogstraat family in J. Hoogstraat, *Von Ostfriesland nach Amerika* (Norden: Soltau-Kurier, 1990), 92.

**85** R.P. Swierenga, "The Journey Across; Dutch Transatlantic Emigrant Passage to the United States, 1820-1880," in *Connecting Cultures; The Netherlands in Five Centuries of Transatlantic Exchange*, eds. R. Hoefte and J.C. Kardux (Amsterdam: VU University Press, 1994), 125-26; Galema and Holtmann, "Aus den nördlichen Niederlanden und dem deutschen Nordwesten nach Nordamerika," 437.

**86** M. van der Heide, "Vijftig jaar in Canada en de Ver. Staten," (manuscript by J. Hoekstra, Wester-Nijkerk, 1964), 3. I am indebted to J. Hoekstra in Ferwerd, who provided me with a copy of this manuscript. The original text is: "Ik ben vergeten hoeveel geld de trip zou kosten, maar ik weet nog wel, dat we geen geld genoeg hadden, en moeder was genoodzaakt om geld te lenen, en vanzelf op voorwaarde dat we het zouden terugbetalen. Daar hadden we niets op tegen, we gingen toch naar een land waar **veel geld** was."

**87** For the story of the Leep family who finally went to Montana and Indiana see R. Kroes, *The Persistence of Ethnicity; Dutch Calvinist Pioneers in Amsterdam, Montana* (Urbana and Chicago: University of Illinois Press, 1992), 38-39; also R. Kroes, *Nederlandse pioniers in het Amerikaanse Westen. De geschiedenis van Amsterdam, Montana* (Amsterdam: De Bataafsche Leeuw, 1989), 23-24.

**88** The story of Pieter Groustra based on his letters from America is told in A. Galema, "Over de wereldzee naar de grote stad: Pieter Ypes Groustra met zijn gezin in Chicago rond de eeuwwisseling," *De Nederlandsche Leeuw. Maandblad van het Koninklijk Nederlandsch Genootschap voor Geslacht- en Wapenkunde* 109 (October-November 1992): 450-58.

**89** Letter of Jan W. Bijker, from Sioux Center, Sioux County, IA, of February 2, 1893, *Nieuw Advertentieblad*, February 22, 1893.

**90** R.P. Swierenga, "Exodus Netherlands, Promised Land America; Dutch Immigration and Settlement in the United States" in *A Bilateral Bicentennial; A History of Dutch-American Relations 1782-1982*, eds. J.W. Schulte Nordholt and R.P. Swierenga (Amsterdam: Meulenhoff, 1982), 136.

**91** Letter of Tjerk Zondervan and Maartje Lautenbach from Paterson to Minnertsga, February 25, 1894. This couple left the village of Firdgum (municipality of Barradeel), where Tjerk worked as a landlaborer, with two children (Antje and Jeltje) on April 24, 1889. Part of their correspondence is preserved and became available by kind permission of J. Lautenbach in IJlst.

**92** Swierenga, "Exodus Netherlands," 136.

**93** Swierenga, "The Delayed Transition," 406.

**94** Hofstee, *Some Remarks on Selective Migration*, 23; The importance of personal characteristics and individual decisions in the migration process is also emphasized in

B. Henkes, *Heimat in Holland. Duitse dienstmeisjes 1920-1950* (Amsterdam: Babylon-De Geus, 1995), 29-55.

**95** K. Huisman, *It libben fan Gerrit Roorda/opskrean troch Kerst Huisman* (Bûtenpost: Alternatyf, 1973), 15-16; Loosening from the own environment and becoming alienated as important factors in the migration process are also emphasized in P.H. Pauseback, *Aufbruch in eine Neue Welt. Die Auswanderung aus den schleswig-holsteinischen Kreisen Husum, Eiderstedt und Tondern in die Vereinigten Staaten in königlich-preussischer Zeit 1867-1914* (Bräist/Bredstedt: Nordfriisk Instituut, 1995), 305-06.

**96** E.K. Leep, "The Leep Family in North America; History and Genealogy," (date and place unknown); Calvin College Archives, Grand Rapids, MI. The Leep family can be found in the computerfile Galema, "Frisians to America, 1880-1914." Also Kroes, *The Persistence of Ethnicity*, 38-39.

# Notes – 4

**1** A different version of this chapter has been published in A. Galema, B. Henkes and H. te Velde, eds., *Images of the Nation; Different Meanings of Dutchness 1870-1940* (Amsterdam: Rodopi, 1993): 109-35.

**2** F.J. Turner, *The Frontier in American History* (New York: Henry Holt & Company, 1920).

**3** D.W. Noble, "The American Wests; Refuges from European Power or Frontiers of European Expansions?," in *The American West as Seen by Europeans and Americans*, ed. R. Kroes (Amsterdam: VU University Press, 1989), 20.

**4** M.P. Malone, "The West in American Historiography," in *The American West as Seen by Europeans and Americans*, 1-19.

**5** *The Washington Post*, October 10, 1989, A3.

**6** B. Knapen, "De veroveringsdrang van het goede Amerika," *NRC Handelsblad*, December 23, 1989. Knapen also describes Turner's thesis in his book *De grenzen van Amerika* (Amsterdam: Prometheus, 1990), which includes essays based on newspaper articles he wrote earlier.

**7** A.N.J. den Hollander, *Americana. Studies over mensen, dieren en een kaktus tussen Rio Grande en Potomac* (Meppel: Boom, 1970), 7.

**8** M. Mooijweer, "Waarnemen vanuit de verte," *Intermediair*, June 20, 1986, 11. Also A. Lammers, "Amerikanist van het eerste uur: A.N.J. den Hollander," in *Amerika in Europese ogen*, ed. K. van Berkel ('s-Gravenhage: SDU Uitgeverij, 1990), 181-93.

**9** K. van Berkel, *Denken over cultuur*

(Groningen: Historische Uitgeverij Groningen, 1990), 29-30.

**10** The tenth International Economic History Congress in Leuven, Belgium (August, 1990) had a specific session on "Emigration from Northern, Central and Southern Europe, 1880-1939". Quite a few papers dealt with illusions and reality in the expectations of migrants.

**11** J. Bodnar, "Reworking Reality; Polish Immigrants and the Meaning of the Immigrant Experience." Paper presented at the Tenth Economic History Congress, Leuven, August 20-24, 1990.

**12** J.B.E. Galema, "Frisians to America, 1880-1914. Computer Compilation," (Groningen, 1992).

**13** A. Galema, "'Se binne nei Amearika tein'. Aspekten van Friese landverhuizing naar de Verenigde Staten rond de eeuwwisseling," *It Beaken*, 52 (1990) 2: 45-58. Also ibid., "Transplanted Network; A Case Study of Frisian Migration to Whitinsville, Mass., 1880-1914," in *The Dutch in North-America; Their Immigration and Cultural Continuity*, eds. R. Kroes and H-O. Neuschäfer (Amsterdam: VU University Press, 1991), 174-88.

**14** There are many travel accounts of people who made a trip to the United States in the late nineteenth and early twentieth century. Among them C.J. Wijnaendts Francken, *Door Amerika. Reisschetsen, indrukken en studiën* (Haarlem: H.D. Tjeenk Willink, 1892). For an overview of Dutch America-travelers see J.W. Schulte Nordholt, "Dutch Travelers in the United States; A Tale of

Energy and Ambivilance," in *A Bilateral Bicentennial; A History of Dutch-American Relations 1792-1982*, eds. J.W. Schulte Nordholt and R.P. Swierenga (Amsterdam: Meulenhoff, 1982), 251-65. A. Lammers, *Uncle Sam and Jan Salie* (Amsterdam: Balans, 1989). Very interesting essays and novels are C.V. Gerritsen and A.H. Jacobs, *Brieven uit en over Amerika* (Amsterdam: F. van Rossen, 1906); N.A. de Vries, *De Nieuwe Wereld. Amerika 1923* (Groningen: J.B. Wolters, 1924); L.R. Scholte, *Een vreemdelinge in een vreemd land* (Goes: Oosterbaan & Le Cointre, 1960).

**15** M. van der Heide, "Vijftig jaar in Canada en de Ver. Staten," (manuscript, trans. by J. Hoekstra, Wester-Nijkerk, 1964), 1. Personal Collection Author.

**16** In the *Provinciale Groninger Courant* of May 8, 1867, an advertisement can be found about the partnership founded by Arend Martens Prins in Groningen and Anne Zwanenburg in Harlingen. On March 1, 1867 the partnership was started and the firm planned to "het ondernemen van een algemeen expeditie-kantoor ter bevordering van landverhuizers en goederen, en voorts daaraan te verbinden zoodanige transactiën als bij nadere overeenkomst zal worden goedgevonden". Prins & Zwanenburg functioned as a shipping office for emigrants and goods to America, but later on also operated as a land company. In 1883 an agreement was reached by the Royal Dutch Steamship Company -the KNSM,

mainly operating from Amsterdam-
and the Netherland American
Steamship Company -the NASM,
which had Rotterdam as homebase-
that finally ended in the
incorporation of the KNSM by the
NASM. The NASM also took over a
number of KNSM commitments,
including those with the Harlingen
firm Prins & Zwanenburg. See
C. Zevenbergen, *Toen zij uit Rotterdam
vertrokken. Emigratie via Rotterdam door
de eeuwen heen* (Zwolle: Waanders,
1990), 40.
**17** There was a lot of competition
among the steamship companies,
especially in the early 1880s. A
brochure from the firm of Prins &
Zwanenburg makes this competitive
business clear; in a comment for
emigrants Prins & Zwanenburg
wrote: "...many efforts were made to
make the Amsterdam-line [KNSM]
suspicious by seditious pamphlets.
Some newspapers even did not
hesitate to copy articles from an
American journal with accusations
concerning fake situations, things
that even were not possible to
happen; dirty articles are published,
'signed' with fictitious names, and
also with names of persons who wrote
the opposite to their inlaws". See
*Naar Amerika. Inlichtingen over de
expeditie Prins & Zwanenburg, per
Koninklijke Nederlandsche Stoomboot-
Maatschappij, directe lijn Amsterdam-
New York* (Groningen: B. Jacobs,
1882), 1. Prins & Zwanenburg also
had stiff competition from the
Norddeutsche Lloyd Company who
operated in Bremen and in earlier
days from the firm of Wambersie and
Crooswijk. See A. Galema, W. Grams,
and A. Holtmann, eds., *Van de ene en
de andere kant. Noordnederlandse en
Noordwestduitse migratie naar de
Verenigde Staten in de negentiende
eeuw/Nordniederländische und
Nordwestdeutsche Auswanderung nach
Amerika im 19. Jahrhundert*
(Groningen: Universiteitsbiblio-
theek/Oldenburg: Stadtmuseum,
1993), 19-20; R.P. Swierenga, "The
Journey Across; Dutch Transatlantic
Emigrant Passage to the United
States, 1820-1880," in *Connecting
Cultures; The Netherlands in Five*

*Centuries of Transatlantic Exchange,*
eds. R. Hoefte and J.C. Kardux
(Amsterdam: VU University Press,
1994), 101-33. A detailed discussion
of the agency system or recruiting
and selling passage in Germany can
be found in A. Bretting and H.
Bickelmann, *Auswanderungsagenturen
und Auswanderungsvereine im 19. und
20. Jahrhundert*, vol. 4: *Von
Deutschland nach Amerika: Zur
Sozialgeschichte der Auswanderung im
19. und 20. Jahrhundert* (Stuttgart:
Franz Steiner Verlag, 1991).
**18** Van der Meulen visited his
brother in 1881. At the same time he
became an agent for the *Red Star Line*
in Antwerp, so he boarded a ship of
this company -the *Belgenland*- to the
United States. In the years after his
brother's emigration, Tjibbe Geerts
had been an agent for the shipowners Van Es & Co. in Rotterdam.
Later on it appears that he also
worked for the firm of Prins &
Zwanenburg (see advertisement of
Prins & Zwanenburg with the title
'Naar Amerika' in *Weekblad voor het
Kanton Bergum*, 19 February, 1881).
Reading Van der Meulen's travel
account in the journal *Weekblad voor
het Kanton Bergum* (about 70 letters
from 1881-1883), it can be discovered
that he became so indignant about
the 'scandalous' manner in which
Prins & Zwanenburg in the end
housed and generally treated the
emigrants that he no longer wanted
to have anything to do with the
company, in particular since it was
becoming involved in American land
sales. In this *Weekblad* (see March 20,
1882), Van der Meulen also sneered
at A.H. Kuipers from Steggerda who
was involved in the transatlantic
passage business as well. For a
detailed account on Tjibbe Geerts'
concern with emigration and
America see G.N. Visser, "Tsjibbe
Gearts en it lân fan dream en
winsken," in *Tsjibbe Gearts van der
Meulen. Wâldman en wrâldboarger*
(Leeuwarden: Fryske Akademy nr.
466, 1974), 182-208. The information
from Visser does not correspond with
what Van Hinte tells about Tjibbe
Geerts. Van Hinte, for example,
mentions that Tjibbe Geerts' brother

-with the name Bastiaan- left with a
group of people from the vicinity of
Bergum in 1853. His sources were
two letters (in 1922 and 1926) from
W.A. van der Meulen, the son of
Tjibbe Geerts. See J. van Hinte,
*Nederlanders in Amerika. Een studie over
landverhuizers en volksplanters in de 19e
en 20e eeuw in de Vereenigde Staten van
Amerika*, 2 vols. (Groningen: P.
Noordhoff, 1928), 2: 156-58. This
study is republished in English
translation in one volume as
*Netherlanders in America; a Study of
Emigrants and Colonists in the Nineteenth and Twentieth Centuries*, ed. R.P.
Swierenga, trans. A. de Wit (Grand
Rapids: Baker Book House, 1985).
**19** T.G. van der Meulen, "Wie veel
geld wil verdienen worde werver,"
*Weekblad voor het Kanton Bergum*,
February 25, 1882.
**20** For example: the agent J. Wijkstra
in the village of Ee in Friesland,
operated for the agency of Prins &
Zwanenburg with a glittering
brochure in which he showed the
advantages of the railway land.
Wijkstra told his readers something
about the climate, about tourism and
about the cities and villages alongside
the Northern Pacific Railway. A huge
map of the Northern Pacific Railway
completed the brochure. See
"Informatie voor ontginners van de
landerijen langs den Noordelijken
Pacific Spoorweg," collection
immigrant letters P.Y. Groustra 1881-
1941, Rijksarchief Leeuwarden. How
many agents were active in the
northern clay area can be seen from
an advertisement of Prins &
Zwanenburg in the *Franeker Courant*,
March 3, 1882. Agents were located
in the villages of Ee, Waaxens,
Steggerda, Marrum, Oude Bildtzijl,
Oldekerk, Oenkerk, St.
Jacobiparochie, Tzum, Blija, Kollum,
Drogeham, Holwerd, Appelscha,
Hallum, Hantum, St. Annaparochie,
Ferwerd, Hogebeintum, Dokkum,
Stiens, Gorredijk, Koudum, Berlicum
and Hardegarijp.
**21** "Informatie voor ontginners...". A
very curious example of the shocking
experience of immigrants who were
fleeced by unscrupulous promotors
can be found in H. Ganzevoort,

"Sharks in Wooden Shoes," in *Dutch Immigration to North America* eds. H. Ganzevoort and M. Boekelman (Toronto: The Multicultural History Society of Ontario, 1983), 147-68. The wide range of possible views to which the potential emigrant was exposed can be found in a publication of a German bibliography and essay on this subject: S.W. Görisch, *Quellen und Forschungen zur Hessischen Geschichte*, Vol. 84 (Darmstadt: Hessischen Historischen Kommission, 1991).

**22** Letter of W. Nauta in *Nieuwsblad van Friesland*, September 15, 1909.

**23** K. Hvidt, *Flight to America; The Social Background of 300,000 Danish Emigrants* (New York: Academic Press, 1975), 186; N.P. Stilling and A.L. Olsen, *A New Life; Danish Emigration to North America as Described by the Emigrants Themselves in Letters 1842-1946* (Aalborg: Danes Worldwide Archives, 1994), 17.

**24** In the fall of 1990, in cooperation with professor H.J. Brinks, Calvin College, Grand Rapids, I coordinated a national campaign in the Netherlands to find letters of Dutch immigrants to America in the nineteenth and twentieth century. In a time period of three months a few thousand letters were collected, mostly donated by private persons who had family overseas. A great many of these letters were written in the nineteenth century and many times we were able to obtain series of letters written by one and the same person or family. Part of these letters are published in H.J. Brinks, ed., *Dutch American Voices; Letters from the United States* (Ithaca and London: Cornell University Press, 1995).

**25** For a discussion about immigrant letters as sources for migration research see Brinks, *Dutch American Voices;* W. Helbich and U. Sommer, "Immigrant Letters as Sources," in *The Press of Labor Migrants in Europe and North America 1880s to 1930s*, eds. C. Harzig and D. Hoerder (Bremen: Universität Bremen, 1985), 39-58. Several impressive immigrant letter editions have been published in the last two decades: H.A. Barton, *Letters from the Promised Land; Swedes in America, 1840-1914* (Minneapolis: University of Minnesota Press, 1975; H.J. Brinks, *Schrijf spoedig terug. Brieven van immigranten in Amerika, 1847-1920* ('s-Gravenhage: Boekencentrum, 1978); C. Erickson, *Invisible Immigrants; The Adaptation of English and Scottish Immigrants in 19th-Century America* (Coral Gables, FL: University of Miami Press, 1972; reprint ed., Ithaca and London: Cornell University Press, 1990); W. Helbich, W. Kamphoefner and U. Sommer, eds. *Briefe aus Amerika. Deutsche Auswanderer schreiben aus der Neuen Welt, 1830-1930* (München: Beck, 1988); L. Schelbert and H. Rappolt, *Alles ist ganz anders hier. Auswandererschicksale in Briefen aus zwei Jahrhunderten* (Olten and Freiburg: Walter, 1977). A study in depth of letters of an individual immigrant is A. Holtmann, ed., *"Ferner thue ich euch zu wissen..." Briefe des Johann Heinrich zur Oeveste aus Amerika (1834-1876)* (Bremen: Edition Temmen, 1995).

**26** Letter from O.H. de Vries from San Francisco, November 17, 1889 to Friesland.

**27** Letter from Th.M. Oostenbrug from Hospers, IA, June 11, 1882 to the town of Roodkerk near Leeuwarden.

**28** B. Wabeke, *Dutch Emigration to North America 1624-1860* (New York: Netherlands Information Bureau, 1944), 98.

**29** This point is also made by Niels Peter Stilling concerning Danish emigration to the United States in his article "Letter from America: The Emigrant Letter as Stimulus to Emigration," in *Danish Emigration to the U.S.A.*, eds. B. Flemming Larsen and H. Bender (Aalborg: Danes Worldwide Archives, 1992), 363-65.

**30** Letter of Ulbe Eringa from Hull, IA, to Friesland, July 4, 1892. Calvin College Archives, Grand Rapids, MI. Part of the letters of Ulbe Eringa are published in *100 Years of God With Us; Emmanuel Reformed Church, Springfield South Dakota 1888-1988* (Freeman, SD: Pine Hill Press, 1988). Also in *Ons Friese Platteland*, July 4, 1981.

**31** Letter of Ulbe Eringa from Runningwater, SD, to Sneek in Friesland, April 8, 1894.

**32** Letter from an immigrant in Pennsylvania to *Nieuwsblad van Friesland*, August 5, 1911.

**33** Letter of Aukjen Pruiksma from Paterson, NJ, to Friesland, May 16, 1895. Calvin College Archives, Grand Rapids, MI.

**34** For specific information on Dutch immigrant women see S. Sinke, "Home is Where You Build It; Dutch Immigrant Women and Social Reproduction," in *The Dutch in North-America; Their Immigration and Cultural Continuity*, 410-21; also Sinke's "Dutch Immigrant Women in the Late Nineteenth Century," (M.A. thesis, Kent State University, 1983); and *Home is Where You Build it; Dutch Immigrant Women in the United States, 1880-1920* (Ph. D. dissertation, University of Minnesota, 1993; Ann Arbor: UMI, 1993). A recent study about gender and America-letters is H. Krogh, "'We Meet Only to Part'; Norwegian Immigrants in Transition," (Ph.D. dissertation, University of Colorado, 1990).

**35** Letter of Mrs. Duba from Iowa City in 1911 to the Netherlands, published in Brinks, *Schrijf spoedig terug*, 139.

**36** Letter of J. Boekhout from Paterson, NJ, August 22, 1882, to J.J. Hoogland in St. Annaparochie. "Collectie Hoogland," Rijksarchief Leeuwarden.

**37** Van Hinte, *Nederlanders in Amerika*, 1:166.

**38** J. Bodnar, *The Transplanted; A History of Immigrants in Urban America* (Bloomington: Indiana University Press, 1985), 169.

**39** Examples of important mobility studies are S. Thernstrom, *The Other Bostonians; Poverty and Progress in the American Metropolis, 1880-1970* (Cambridge, MA: Harvard University Press, 1973), and his *Poverty and Progress; Social Mobility in a Nineteenth Century City* (Cambridge, MA: Harvard University Press, 1964). Also R.L. Doyle, "Wealth Mobility in Pella, Iowa 1847-1925," in *The Dutch in America; Immigration, Settlement and Cultural Change*, ed. R.P. Swierenga (New Brunswick: Rutgers University Press, 1985), 156-71; Also G.W. Kirk

Jr., *The Promise of American Life; Social Mobility in a Nineteenth-Century Immigrant Community, Holland, Michigan, 1847-1894* (Philadelphia: The American Philosophical Society, 1978).

**40** *Nieuwsblad van Friesland,* August 27, 1911, 77.

**41** *Nieuw Advertentieblad,* July 8, 1893.

**42** W.D. Kamphoefner, *The Westfalians; From Germany to Missouri* (Princeton, NJ: Princeton University Press, 1987), 135; M. Curti and K. Birr, "The Immigrant and the American Image in Europe, 1860-1914," *The Mississippi Valley Historical Review* 37 (September 1950): 220.

**43** At Calvin College, Grand Rapids, MI, serious efforts have been made to preserve as many letters as possible from "The Old Country" to Dutch immigrants in the United States and Canada. But the source material concerning immigrant letters to the old fatherland is much more extensive.

**44** H.S. Lucas, ed., *Dutch Immigrant Memoirs and Related Writings,* 2 vols. (Assen: Van Gorcum, 1955), 2: 5.

**45** H.J. Brinks, "Impressions of the 'Old' World 1848-1940," in *The Dutch in North-America; Their Immigration and Cultural Continuity,* 34-47.

**46** Brinks, "Impressions," 35.

**47** Letter of R.J. Algra from Ee to J.D. Douma in Pella, IA, January 3, 1892; Calvin College Archives, Grand Rapids, MI.

**48** Letter of E.J. Brouwer from Ee to D.J. Douma in Pella, IA, April 8, 1881; Calvin College Archives, Grand Rapids, MI.

**49** Letter of T. Dalhuijsen from Wanswerd to America, April 5, 1899; Calvin College Archives, Grand Rapids, MI.

**50** O.T. Gulliksen, "Letters to Immigrants in the Midwest from the Telemark Region of Norway," *Norwegian-American Studies,* 32 (1989): 157-75.

**51** *Nieuw Advertentieblad,* July 8, 1893.

**52** J. van Dijk, "Zes maanden in Amerika," 2 vols. (Manuscript, 1881); Calvin College Archives, Grand Rapids, MI.

**53** Brinks, "Impressions," 2.

**54**. Franco Ramella found the same for Italian workers who went to New Jersey at the turn of the century. America seemed to offer what potential emigrants were looking for: "jobs in abundance, good pay and freedom to express themselves politically." See F. Ramella, "Across the Ocean or over the Border; Expectations and Experiences of Italians from Piedmont in New Jersey and Southern France," in *Distant Magnets; Expectations and Realities in the Immigrant Experience, 1840-1930,* eds. D. Hoerder and H. Rössler (New York: Holmes & Meier, 1993), 121-22.

**55** This is in contradiction to the group of emigrants who left for America with their leader Rev. H.P. Scholte in the middle of the nineteenth century. Their nation image of America was defined by their religious concept. See R. Kuiper, *Zelfbeeld en wereldbeeld. Antirevolutionairen en het buitenland* (Kampen: Kok, 1992).

**56** For a beautifully written reflection on images of America of Dutch Calvinist immigrants in the middle of the nineteenth century see J.W. Schulte Nordholt, "Perceived in Poetry; Poetical Images of America for Dutch Immigrants," in *The Dutch in North-America; Their Immigration and Cultural Continuity,* 3-15.

# Notes – 5

**1** This poem, "Ofskie fen in lânforhûzer" [goodbye to an emigrant], by an author named "Y", was published in the *Weekblad voor het Kanton Bergum*, March 9, 1889. There are more well-known lyrics of contemporaries who wanted to give attention to the phenomenon of emigration. Harmen S. Sytstra, teacher and co-founder of the society for language and culture *Frysk Selskip*, wrote "Ofskied fen frjeonen, dy nei de foriene Steaten fen Noard-Amerika teagen" [Goodbye to friends, who emigrated to the United States of America]. See O.H. Sytstra, *Blom-lêzing ût 'e gedichten fen H.S. Sytstra* (Ljouwert: R. van der Velde, 1894), 75-78. The renowned poet, writer and agent of a steamship company, Tjibbe Geerts van der Meulen, paid a tribute to the emigrants that is still noted. He concluded with: America, you have given me bread and wealth, but I still pray heaven: give me a grave in Friesland's soil. See T.G. van der Meulen, "Lânforhuzerssang," *Ny Frysk lieteboek* (Heerenveen: A.L. Land, 1886), 54-56. Van der Meulen also wrote farces, e.g. *Nei Roaselân* (Heerenveen: J. Hepkema, 1888), about Frisian emigrants who left for Roseland, a southern suburb of Chicago. Even the socialist leader Pieter Jelles Troelstra wrote about emigrants. The theme of his poem mainly focused on the economic circumstances that forced especially poorer people to leave Friesland. See P.J. Troelstra, "De lânforhûzer," *Rispinge. Alde en nije fersen fen Pieter Jelles* (Den Haag: De Atlas, 1909),

248-49. I also found a lyrical expression from the other side of the ocean. An immigrant in Grand Rapids, Michigan in 1889 from the area around Dokkum wrote a poem about overseas migration and sent it to a Frisian newspaper. He emphasized the poor situation in Friesland as the motivation for leaving. See C. Helmus, "De lânforhûzers ût de Dokkumer-Wâlden," *Friesch Nieuws en Advertentieblad*, June 5, 1889.
**2** D. Hoerder makes this point in his review of J. Bodnar, *The Transplanted,* in "The Transplanted; International Dimensions," *Social Science History* 12 (Fall 1988): 261-62.
**3** J. Raban, *Hunting Mr. Heartbreak* (London: Pan Books, 1991), 9.
**4** *Het Noorden*, March 15, 1881. Reference to Miedema can also be found in A. Galema, "'Se binne nei Amearika tein'. Aspekten van Friese landverhuizing naar de Verenigde Staten rond de eeuwwisseling," *It Beaken* 52 (1990), 2: 45-58. In the 1900 U.S. Census Miedema was in Holland, MI, where he lived as a widower, aged 76, with a servant of Dutch descent (Miss Jenie DeVries, 26 years old, born in Michigan and parents from Holland). In 1900 Miedema was a naturalized U.S. citizen and lived in his own home free of mortgage. Miedema was not exceptional in giving lectures about America for future emigrants. Advertisements show that in numerous Frisian villages people came to tell about their American experiences. See f.e. "Lezing over Amerika en de Nieuwe Hollandsche

Kolonie 'Nederland' in Zuid-Oost Texas...," *Franeker Courant*, January 9, 1898. I am indebted to Jacob Lautenbach for information concerning advertizing in the *Franeker Courant.*
**5** Handwritten account of J. van Dijk, "Zes maanden in Amerika," 2 vols. (1881), 1: 1. Manuscript, Calvin College Archives, Grand Rapids, MI.
**6** At the time of the decision to leave for America, Van Dijk had applied with specifications and drawings for a parsonage in the village of Midlum. His parents gave him permission to leave for America at the moment when it turned out that he was not the lowest bidder for the project. The same day Van Dijk heard about his failed attempt, he went to Miedema to subscribe for a ticket to America.
**7** H. Goren and H. Heger, *Per mud of bij de week gewonnen. De ontwikkeling van beloningssystemen in de Groningse landbouw, 1800-1914* (Groningen: Nederlands Agronomisch Historisch Instituut, 1993), 28-32. R.P. Swierenga found in the U.S. ship passenger manifests, 1820-1880, that in the early decades the Dutch emigrated even in winter. To lessen the hardships of dangerous storms, winter unemployment and summer heat, the planning started to be more careful after the Secessionists Van Raalte and Scholte left with their groups in 1846 and 1847. Around the middle of the 19th century 40 percent or more of the Dutch emigrants arrived in May or June. See R.P. Swierenga, "The Journey Across; Dutch Transatlantic Emigrant Passage to the United States, 1820-

1880," in *Connecting Cultures; The Netherlands in Five Centuries of Transatlantic Exchange,* eds. R. Hoefte and J.C. Kardux (Amsterdam: VU University Press, 1994), 130; J.B.E. Galema, "Frisians to America, 1880-1914. Computer Compilation," (Groningen, 1992), shows the following figures: month of departure: January 119; February 544; March 1689; April 2281; May 1724; June 373; July 289; August 278; September 350; October 301; November 247; December 105; Unknown 1193.

**8** These figures can be found in C. Zevenbergen, *Toen zij uit Rotterdam vertrokken. Emigratie via Rotterdam door de eeuwen heen* (Zwolle: Waanders, 1990), 45. That most of the Dutch emigrants after 1860 left via Rotterdam is also reported in Swierenga, "The Journey Across," 106-07.

**9** Van Dijk, "Zes maanden in Amerika," 2: 84. The exchange rate for Van Dijk was f2.50 for $ 1. As noted many times before, the voyage was prepaid by family members or friends who already had emigrated to the United States. Hendrik Kroes from Ferwerd who left in 1891 with his wife Aaltje Zuidema, recalls in his life story that the voyage was paid by his wife's family: 64 dollars for the two of them was sent over from Muskegon, MI. See "Libbensforhael fan in Ferwerter jonge," *Friesch Dagblad,* May 25, 1972.

**10** Raban, *Mr Heartbreak,* 9. Besides Rotterdam, Amsterdam also was used as harbor of departure. Even in the last decades of the nineteenth century, some emigrants from Friesland steamed to Hull in England and then went to Liverpool to board an ocean steamer to the United States. Liverpool competed with the continental European steamship companies. Some accounts that describe the journey via Liverpool may be mentioned: for the story of Dirk Pieter van den Bergh who came from Bussum and traveled with his family in March 1906, having Frisian fellow travelers, see G. Read, "Liverpool. The Flood-Gate of the Old World; A Study in Ethnic

Attitudes," *Journal of American Ethnic History* 13 (Fall 1993): 44; also H.T. Kamp, "Account of the Trip of the Kamp Family, Emigrating from Almelo, Province of Overijsel, Netherlands, June 18 to July 5, 1904." Translated by his son, G. Kamp. Manuscript, Calvin College Archives, Grand Rapids, MI; also D. de Vries, "Naar Canada," *Franeker Courant,* June 30, 1893 (in a letter from Yorkton, June 4, 1893).

**11** A little more than a decade later it was possible to reach New York in about 6 days. This was quite fast, especially compared to the sailing emigrant trade of the mid-nineteenth century, when the passage took 40 to 50 days. See B. Greenhill, *The Great Migration; Crossing the Atlantic under Sail* (London: National Maritime Museum, 1968). In advertizments in the newspapers, the shipping companies emphasized the faster voyage. See an advertisement of the White Star Line, "Geregelde wekelijksche dienst naar Amerika...," *Leeuwarder Courant,* February 2, 1893. It was also common for the companies to advertise names of new agents in the local papers. This can be concluded from advertisements like one from the White Star Line in the *Franeker Courant,* December 2, 1894 in which the general agent T.G. van Slooten in Harlingen introduces the new agents Jacob Hiemstra in the village of Tzummarum and IJpe Bonnema in Witmarsum.

**12** Letter of J.J. Pelmulder of June 1855 to his friend Swarte van Loon in Westdongeradeel. See J.J. Pelmulder, *Eenvoudige maar zeer belangrijke brieven uit Noord-Amerika* (Dockum: A. Schaafsma, 1859), 58. About the swindles and fraud that could be experienced by newcomers in the U.S., especially if they were not acquainted with the language, see J.C.C. Sandberg, "De uitbuiting van den immigrant in de Vereenigde Staten van Noord-Amerika," *Tijdschrift van den Nederl. Werkloosheidsraad* 73 (1918): 611-23.

**13** Another experience of Castle Garden can be found in a letter of Sietze Haveman and Arjen Meierhof, originally from the Frisian village of

Beets, *Nieuw Advertentieblad,* February 7, 1894. Also H.J. Brinks, "Castle Garden," *Origins* 2 (1984) 1: 6-8. For a good overview concerning the travel experiences of European emigrants in general, see D. Hoerder and D. Knauf, eds., *Aufbruch in die Fremde/Fame, Fortune and Sweet Liberty* (Bremen: Edition Temmen, 1992), 75-116. For the departure from Bremerhaven see D. Hoerder, "The Traffic of Emigration via Bremen/Bremerhaven; Merchants' Interests, Protective Legislation, and Migrants' Experiences," *Journal of American Ethnic History* 13 (Fall 1993): 68-101. For the travel experiences of the Dutch emigrants in the period 1820-1880 see H.J. Brinks, "Crossing the Atlantic," *Origins* 2 (1984) 1: 2-5; Swierenga, "The Journey Across," 101-33. About the ocean passage of northern Dutch and northern Germans, see A. Galema and A. Holtmann, "Aus den nördlichen Niederlanden und dem deutschen Nordwesten nach Nordamerika. Motive und Reiseerfahrungen der Auswanderer im 19. Jahrhundert," in *Rondom Eems en Dollard/Rund um Ems und Dollart,* eds. O.S. Knottnerus et al., (Groningen/Leer: REGIO-PRojekt/Schuster Verlag, 1992), 433-49; For the official regulations and restrictions in The Netherlands concerning the transportation of emigrants see *Staatsblad van Het Koninkrijk der Nederlanden,* (No. 81) "Besluit van den 28. December 1837, houdende nadere bepalingen omtrent den doortogt van landverhuizende personen" and (No. 53) "Wet van den 1sten Junij 1861, houdende bepalingen omtrent den doortogt en het vervoer van landverhuizers."

**14** Van Dijk, "Zes maanden in Amerika," 1: 26. For travel experiences see also L.A. van der Valk, "Landverhuizersvervoer via Rotterdam in de negentiende eeuw," *Economisch- en Sociaal-Historisch Jaarboek* 39 (1976): 148-71; for the history of the Holland America Line see A.D. Wentholt, *Brug over den oceaan. Een eeuw geschiedenis van de Holland Amerika Lijn* (Rotterdam: Nijgh & Van Ditmar, 1973); and D.

Schaap, *Brug naar de zeven zeeën. Holland Amerika Lijn honderd jaar* (Rotterdam: Holland Amerika Lijn, 1973). A shrewd and sympathetic observer of emigrant travel is also the writer Robert Louis Stevenson, who sailed from Scotland and left for America in 1879 with a passenger ship full of immigrants. His account is contemporary and very informative about the travel circumstances for steerage passengers. See R.L. Stevenson, *The Amateur Emigrant* (1892; reprint ed., London: The Hogarth Press, 1984).

**15** For the story of Pieter Ypes Groustra and Frederica Aukes see: A. Galema, "Over de wereldzee naar de grote stad: Pieter Ypes Groustra met zijn gezin in Chicago rond de eeuwwisseling," *De Nederlandsche Leeuw. Maandblad van het Koninklijk Nederlandsch genootschap voor geslacht- en wapenkunde* 109 (October-November 1992): 450-58.

**16** Letter of Rinke van der Wal from Spring Lake, MI, to a friend. *Franeker Courant*, 23 April 1882. I am indebted to Otto de Vent for this information.

**17** *Naar Amerika. Inlichtingen over de expeditie Prins & Zwanenburg, per Koninklijke Nederlandsche Stoomboot-Maatschappij, directe lijn Amsterdam-New York* (Groningen: B. Jacobs, 1882), 49-50.

**18** C. de Groot, *When I was a Girl in Holland* (Boston: Northrop, Lee & Shepard, 1917; reprint ed., Arnhem: Bakker, 1991), 205.

**19** Kl.J. Tiemersma, *Drie jaren in Amerika* (Leeuwarden: Eisma, 1894), 5.

**20** "Mellema Papers." Diary of J.P. Mellema in Calvin College Archives, Grand Rapids, MI. Jacob Pieters Mellema was born August 10, 1835 and left for America with his wife Elizabeth Pieters Koning, born November 14, 1833. Two daughters, Maartje and Froukje were with them. Sierts van der Wal traveled on the same boat and Mellema recalls that this man lost a child during the trip.

**21** "Libbensforhael fan in Ferwerter jonge," *Friesch Dagblad*, May 25, 1972. See also the translation of Hendrik Kroes' account by his son Herman, "Autobiography of Henry P. Kroes,"

Manuscript, Calvin College Archives, Grand Rapids, MI.

**22** "The Anne Bandstra Story." Travel account of Anne Bandstra, who left May 24, 1899. Translated by Mrs. H. DeVries. Manuscript, Calvin College Archives, Grand Rapids, MI.

**23** This journalist is cited in Zevenbergen, *Toen zij uit Rotterdam vertrokken*, 58-67.

**24** "Autobiography of Henry P. Kroes." Kroes left in 1891. In those years food mostly was included in the ticket price. Kroes's ticket without meals was exceptional.

**25** The archive of G. Taphorn who worked for Prins & Zwanenburg in Essen, Germany is preserved at the research institute Niedersächsische Auswanderer in den USA (NAUSA) at the Carl von Ossietzky University of Oldenburg, Germany. That Prins & Zwanenburg got many passengers from the East-Frisian border region in Germany is indisputably clear from their information brochure, *Naar Amerika. Inlichtingen over de expeditie Prins & Zwanenburg*, 50-75. They mention passengers on their ships by name in the brochure.

**26** M. van der Heide, "Vijftig jaar in Canada en de Ver. Staten," trans. by J. Hoekstra (Wester-Nijkerk, 1964), 4-5. Personal Collection Author.

**27** In 1990 there was a great deal of publicity about the history of Ellis Island, because it was reopened for the general public as the Ellis Island Immigration Museum. The press was unanimously positive about the new museum. See M. Delaere, "De gouden toegangspoort tot Amerika als museum heropend," *Haagsche Courant*, September 20, 1990; J. Groen, "De mythe van de Nieuwe Wereld," *De Volkskrant*, September 15, 1990, 9; R. Hollander, "De gouden deur naar Amerika als museum heropend," *NRC Handelsblad*, September 15, 1990, 6; K.M. Eggers, "Nadelöhr zur Freiheit," *Zeit/Magazin* (September, 1990), 22-28; "Museen," *Der Spiegel* (1990/37), 244-45; A.J. Hall, "New Life for Ellis Island," *National Geographic* 178 (1990): 88-101. The history of Ellis Island is told in L.D. Scucs, *Ellis Island; Gateway to America* (Salt Lake City: Ancestry,

1986); P. Reeves, *Ellis Island; Gateway to the American Dream* (New York: Dorset Press, 1991).

**28** Van der Heide, "Vijftig jaar", 5-6.

**29** Ibid., 6.

**30** Letter from Springfield, SD, September 1911, in *Nieuwsblad van Friesland*, September 27, 1911.

**31** I found more evidence of the fact that the Dutch emigrants in general were well aware of the American immigration regulations. In research concerning dossiers of mentally ill persons of psychiatrical clinics at Medemblik and Grave between 1870 and 1930, it is mentioned that Netherlanders who became insane in foreign countries were transferred to Medemblik and Grave. But also many foreigners who got insane in the Netherlands were placed in these clinics. A group of emigrants who were not allowed to enter the U.S.A. because of alleged insanity is mentioned: they were returned with the Holland America Line to Rotterdam and transferred to Medemblik or Grave. These people mainly consisted of emigrants from the Eastern European countries. Hardly any Dutch people were among these returnees. See *Notitie betreffende een reglement voor behoud van historische patiëntendossiers* (Utrecht: Nederlands centrum Geestelijke volksgezondheid, 1989), 19-20. I am indebted to Geertje Dimmendaal for this information.

**32** Hoerder, "The Transplanted; International Dimensions," 261. The *Journal of American Ethnic History* had a special issue dealing with European ports of emigration in the fall of 1993. This publication demonstrates the acceptance of the voyage as formative in the migration process. See especially D. Hoerder, "Introduction," *Journal of American Ethnic History* 13 (Fall 1993): 3-5.

**33** J. Gjerde, *From Peasants to Farmers; The Migration from Balestrand, Norway, to the Upper Middle West* (Cambridge: Cambridge University Press, 1985); W.D. Kamphoefner, *The Westfalians; From Germany to Missouri* (Princeton, NJ: Princeton University Press, 1987); R.C. Ostergren, *A Community Transplanted; The Trans-Atlantic*

*Experience of a Swedish Immigrant Settlement in the Upper Middle West, 1835-1915* (Uppsala: Acta Universitatis Upsaliensis, 1988); Y. Schreuder, *Dutch Catholic Immigrant Settlement in Wisconsin, 1850-1905* (New York & London: Garland Publishing, 1989); H. Runblom and H. Norman, eds., *From Sweden to America; A History of the Migration* (Minneapolis: University of Minnesota Press, 1976); K. Hvidt, *Flight to America; The Social Background of 300,000 Danish Emigrants* (New York: Academic Press, 1975).

**34** D. Baines, *Emigration from Europe, 1815-1930* (London: Macmillan, 1991), 33.

**35** A. Galema, "Transplanted Network: A Case Study of Frisian Migration to Whitinsville, Mass., 1880-1914," in *The Dutch in North-America; Their Immigration and Cultural Continuity*, eds. R. Kroes and H-O. Neuschäfer (Amsterdam: VU University Press, 1991), 174-94.

**36** Kamphoefner, *Westfalians*, 71.

**37** *Nieuw Advertentieblad*, January 21, 1882.

**38** R.P. Swierenga, "Local Patterns of Dutch Migration to the United States in the Mid-Nineteenth Century," in *A Century of European Migrations, 1830-1930*, eds. R.J. Vecoli and S.M. Sinke (Urbana & Chicago: University of Illinois Press, 1991), 151-52.

**39** Ibid., 144-55.

**40** R.P. Swierenga, "Het bestuderen van de Nederlandse emigratie naar de Verenigde Staten. Nieuwe methoden en begrippen," *Jaarboek Centraal Bureau voor Genealogie* 36 (1982): 258, 267-68.

**41** In 1930 the Dutch-born population in the United States was at its peak for any decennial census year. See G.F. DeJong, "Four Generations of a Dutch American Community," in *Dutch Immigration to North America*, eds. H. Ganzevoort and M. Boekelman (Toronto: The Multicultural History Society of Ontario, 1983), 221. This clannish settlement pattern can also be found in other nationality groups. At the turn of the century, f.e., 80 percent of the Norwegians in America were concentrated in the six midwest states of Illinois, Iowa, Wisconsin, Minnesota, and the Dakotas according to I. Semmingsen, *Norway to America; A History of the Migration*, trans. E. Haugen (Minneapolis: University of Minnesota Press, 1978), 122.

**42** R.P. Swierenga, "Dutch Immigration Patterns in the Nineteenth and Twentieth Centuries," in *The Dutch in America; Immigration, Settlement, and Cultural Change* (New Brunswick, NJ: Rutgers University Press, 1985), 39.

**43** This research strategy has a minor impact on the sample population. There is a bias toward the cities where Frisians entered the industrial work force (Rochester, Whitinsville, Paterson, Grand Rapids and Roseland). If the sample of northern Frisians in the U.S.A. was truly random, the rural proportion would be 63.7 percent.

**44** See J.B.E. Galema, "Frisians in the USA, 1900/1910. Computer Compilation" (Groningen, 1993). Because of restricted research time in the USA, I chose 1900 as the reference year for the places of settlement of the northern Frisians. The Census Schedules of 1890 were lost by fire. As far as possible, I supplemented the 1900 Census with the one of 1910, also to make it possible to analyze a decade of immigration in personal and general characteristics. Some of the emigrants were found in the 1900 and in the 1910 Censuses. It would have been a possibility to use the 1920 Census, instead of the 1900 Census, but the risk of not finding immigrants who had died seemed too obvious. The time span 1880-1920 is enough to lose many first generation Frisians in the 1920 Census.

**45** After the collection of *possible* settlements of Frisian immigrants, the counties below (or part of them) were researched through microfilms of the United States Census. Although I principally searched for Frisians from the northern clay area, my sources did not specify these clay Frisians from the Frisians in general. That explains why, in spite of the specifity of some sources, the search in the microfilms occasionally was in vain. The Census was screened for the following counties: Arkansas: White County; California: Santa Clara, San Joaquin, Sacramento, San Bernardino, Riverside, San Benito, Merced, Sonoma, Stanislous, Los Angeles, Kings, Humbolt, and Fresno counties; Colorado: Boulder, Conejos, and Costilla counties; Illinois: Cook, McHenry, Whiteside, and Dupage counties; Indiana: St.Joseph, Fayette, Fountain, Elkhart, and Floyd counties; Iowa: Shelby, Sioux, Muscatine, Franklin, Hardin, Wayne, O'Brien and Marion counties; Kansas: Ottawa county; Kentucky: Warren county; Maryland: Caroline county; Massachusetts: Worcester county; Michigan: Clinton, Ottawa, Oakland, Midland, Missaukee and Kent counties; New Jersey: Passaic county; Minnesota: Ottertail, Pipestone, Pine, Hubbart, Isanti, Itasca, Jackson, Kanabec, Rock, Marshall, Martin, Meeker, Millelacs, Chippewa, Kandiyohi, Cottonwood, and Renville counties; Missouri: Howell county; Montana: Madison, Ravalli, Fergus, Gallatin and Yellowstone counties; New York: Monroe, Suffolk, Erie, Oswego, and Cayuga counties; North Dakota: Wells county; Ohio: Cuyahoga county; Pennsylvania: Bucks county; South Dakota: Bonhomme, Walworth, Turner, Campbell, Charles Mix, Brookings, Brown, Brule, Buffalo, and Butte counties; Vermont: Windsor county; Virginia: Amelia county; Washington: Yakima, San Juan, Snohomish, Chehalis, Whatcum, and Island counties; Wisconsin: Clark, Manitowoc, Washington, Dane, Dodge, Ozaukee, Outagamie, Columbia, La Crosse, Racine and Sheboygan counties. Most of these counties were screened for the 12th Census (1900) and some were also screened for the 13th Census (1910).

**46** J.P. Allen, *We the People; An Atlas of America's Ethnic Diversity* (New York: Macmillan, 1988), 60.

**47** The pioneer from Groningen, Klaas Jans Beukma, settled close to

Lafayette, Indiana in 1835. See J. van Hinte, *Nederlanders in Amerika. Een studie over landverhuizers en volksplanters in de 19e en 20ste eeuw in de Vereenigde Staten van Amerika*, 2 vols. (Groningen: Noordhoff, 1928), 1: 124-28; H. Bras, "Tussen twee werelden. De migratiemotieven van Klaas Jans Beukma (1789-1860), een Groninger pionier in Amerika" (M.A. thesis, University of Groningen, 1993). Immigrants from the Frisian municipalities -then called *grietenijen*- of Het Bildt and Barradeel joined Beukma in 1847, according to the letters of these pioneers in *Tiental brieven betrekkelijk de reis, aankomst en vestiging naar en in Noord-Amerika, van eenige landverhuizers vertrokken uit de grietenijen Het Bildt en Barradeel in Vriesland* (Franeker: T. Telenga, 1848).

48 The following counties were screened in the 1900 Census: Elkhart, Fayette, Floyd, St. Joseph, and Fountain County. St. Joseph County, for example, was on my list of microfilms because I found a letter of a Frisian immigrant who wrote from South Bend, Indiana to the *Nieuw Advertentieblad* to report about his experiences in the United States. This Frisian, W.J. van den Bosch, does not express any connection with the nearby Frisian Mennonite settlement in Goshen and New Paris. See *Nieuw Advertentieblad*, July 8, 1893.

49 References to the Mennonite settlement of the Frisians in Indiana can be found in Chapter 3, when the tradition of migration is discussed. See also Sj. de Zee, *Myn twadde Amerika-reis* (Heerenveen: Handelsdrukkerij Hepkema, 1929), 150-68; and R.P. Swierenga, "The Low Countries," *Encyclopedia of Indiana Ethnic Groups* (1996, forthcoming). According to my database, "Frisians to America," the share of Baptists (*Doopsgezinden*) in the total northern Frisian emigrant group was only 2 percent. They did not go to the area where the Mennonites of Balk settled originally, neither to Lafayette, where the Groninger farmer Klaas Jans Beukma had started a

settlement in 1835. Beukma even was in touch with immigrants from the northern Frisian clay area and also with the group of Frisian immigrants around Worp van Peyma in Lancaster, NY. H.S. Lucas mentions possible other places in Indiana where Netherlanders have settled in the decades after 1850: the offshoot of the Lafayette settlement at Fowler, in Benton County and along the Indiana-Illinois line at Hammond. See H.S. Lucas, *Netherlanders in America* (Ann Arbor: University of Michigan Press, 1955; reprint ed., Grand Rapids, MI: W.B. Eerdmans, 1989), 245.

50 Letter from P.R. Zwolle from Holland, Yellowstone County, MT to the *Nieuwsblad van Friesland*, January 9, 1909.

51 Letter of S.A.S. from Preston, Maryland to the *Nieuwsblad van Friesland*, December 16, 1908.

52 The pattern of migration from a certain Frisian village to a specified American or Dutch-American community can also be analyzed from the emigrating church members of the *Gereformeerde Kerk* in Tzummarum, Barradeel. From this list it is apparent that in the decades around the turn of the century almost all typical Dutch immigrant communities in the U.S.A. were chosen as destination. See J. Lautenbach, *Zij durfden het aan. Gereformeerden in Tzummarum* (Tzummarum: Gereformeerde Kerk, 1990), 115-20.

53 Letter of Pieter Groustra from Chicago to Ee, August 15, 1881. Rijksarchief Leeuwarden.

54 In the 1900 Census, some counties like Island County, WA did not show any northern Frisian settlement, which led me to search in the 1910 Census. The choice of other areas like Worcester, MA and Passaic County, NJ was directed by an opposite motivation: in 1900 I found so many northern Frisians in these counties, that it became important to see whether they had settled permanently.

55 Letter from P.R. Zwolle December 21, 1908 from Holland, MT to the *Nieuwsblad van Friesland*, January 9, 1909.

56 R. Kroes, *The Persistence of Ethnicity. Dutch Calvinist Pioneers in Amsterdam, Montana* (Urbana and Chicago: University of Illinois Press, 1992). This study first was published in Dutch with the title *Nederlandse pioniers in het Amerikaanse Westen. De geschiedenis van Amsterdam, Montana* (Amsterdam: De Bataafsche Leeuw, 1989).

57 These data are derived from the two combined computer files of this research J.B.E. Galema, "Linked files: Frisians to America and Frisians in the USA. Computer Compilation." The linkage program is composed by George Welling and reference can be found in G.M. Welling, "A Strategy for Intelligent Input Programs for Structured Data," *History and Computing* 5 (1993): 35-46; and G.M. Welling, "Computationele geschiedenis," in *Geschiedenis en Bestanden* (Enkhuizen 1995): 90-99. The difficulties in tracing the Frisians in the U.S. Census is clearly shown from the data on Eelke and Lieuwkje Weidenaar; they were found in John [Johannes] Braaksma's home and the Census taker wrote down their names as Eelke and Lucy Widner.

58 Kroes, *Nederlandse pioniers*, 29.

59 The primary works for the history of the Dutch in Iowa are J. van der Zee, *The Hollanders of Iowa* (Iowa City: The State Historical Society, 1912); K. van Stigt, *Geschiedenis van Pella, Iowa en omgeving* (Pella: Weekblad Print Shop, 1897); C.L. Dyke, *The Story of Sioux County* (Dixon, IL: Print Shop, 1983); Van Hinte, *Nederlanders in Amerika*; Lucas, *Netherlanders in America*; *The Centennial Book Orange City, Iowa 1870-1970* (Orange City, IA: The Ad-Visor, 1970).

60 A. Galema, "'Forjit my net'. Friese emigratie naar de Verenigde Staten aan het eind van de negentiende eeuw," *Groniek* 96, (1986): 89-101.

61 D. Hoerder, "An Introduction to Labor Migration in the Atlantic Economies, 1815-1914," in *Labor Migration in the Atlantic Economies; The European and North American Working Classes During the Period of Industrialization*, ed. D. Hoerder (Westport, CT: Greenwood Press, 1985), 3.

62 R.P. Swierenga and H.S. Stout, "Socio-Economic Patterns of Migration from The Netherlands in the Nineteenth Century," in *Research in Economic History*, ed. P. Uselding (Greenwich, CT: JAI Press, 1976), 1: 310-12.

63 R.P. Swierenga, "Dutch International Labour Migration to North America in the Nineteenth Century," in Ganzevoort and Boekelman, eds., *Dutch Immigration to North America*, 1-34.

64 The Homestead Act of 1862 granted 160 acres to any citizen who promised to cultivate the land for a period of five years. The only charge was a modest sum to pay for the cost of surveying.

65 L. Potts, *The World Labour Market; A History of Migration* (London and Atlantic Highlands, NJ: Zed Books, 1990), 200-03. trans. *Weltmacht für Arbeitskraft: Von der Kolonisation Amerikas bis zu den Migrationen der Gegenwart*, (Hamburg: Junius, 1988).

66 Potts, *The World Labour Market*, 200.

67 Of the total of 3,089 persons in 1900, the group of housewives and children younger than or 14 years old (1,750 individuals) are excluded, because they were not active in paid jobs *outside* the family home.

68 For the farm laborers or farm workers a different pattern can be found. According to Galema, "Frisians to America, 1880-1914. Computer Compilation," 20.8 percent of the emigrant work force were land laborer or farm worker in agriculture. The file "Frisians in the USA, 1900/1910. Computer Compilation," shows that only 14.6 percent of the northern Frisian immigrant and descendant work force were reported as farm laborers or farm hands.

69 B.J. Fridsma, *Nea ferbrutsen bân. 60 jier Fryske aksje yn Amearika* (Leeuwarden: De Tille, 1991), 22-24.

70 From 230 immigrants the social gradation was unknown. They are excluded in the table.

71 In the comparable table of the social status before departure, the category of tenants -mostly tenant farmers or *gardeniers*- was separated from the group of farm owners and land owners. In this table for 1900 they are included in the category of entrepreneurs. There is a variable in the Census included through which information can be obtained of the living place. The census taker asked the inhabitants if they rented or owned the house they lived in, and if it was mortgaged or not. I will come back to this information later. One must also note about the *gardeniers*, that during the agricultural crisis in Friesland some of these small farmers had fallen back to the level of farm laborer. And then emigration to the United States followed. But these ex-*gardeniers* or farmers most often had the knowledge that a farmer needed, and with that baggage they were able to take advantage of the American agricultural possibilities.

72 Letter of Ulbe Eringa from Hull, IA, July 4, 1892 to Sneek, Friesland, Calvin College Archives, Grand Rapids, MI. Part of the letters of Ulbe Eringa and Maaike Rijpstra were also published in *Ons Friese Platteland*, May-August 1981.

73 According to the Dutch Population Registers, Ulbe Eringa was born April 21, 1866 in the village of Hidaard on the edge of the municipality of Wonseradeel. He left May 16, 1892 from the village of Oostrum in Oostdongeradeel. According to the Population Registers he was *Nederlands Hervormd*, unemployed and single, destination Iowa. See Galema, "Frisians to America, 1880-1914. Computer Compilation." Eringa's great grandson Brian W. Beltman, wrote a history of this remarkable Frisian immigrant and prepared the letters of Ulbe and Maaike Eringa for publication. B.W. Beltman, *A Dutch-American Immigrant in the Rural Midwest; The Life and Letters of Ulbe Eringa, 1866-1950* (Urbana & Chicago: University of Illinois Press, 1996). Coming from a farmer's family in Friesland Ulbe Eringa, according to Beltman's findings, worked as an agricultural laborer for ten years before he came to the United States.

74 For a very clear and complete overview of the occupational change among Dutch immigrants in the time period 1820-1880 see R.P. Swierenga, "Dutch International Migration and Occupational Change; A Structural Analysis of Multinational Linked Files," in *Migration Across Time and Nations* eds. I. Glazier and L. De Rosa (New York/London: Holmes & Meier, 1986), 95-124.

75 Many of the occupations of Frisians in America are identical with the ones that were promoted or discussed in articles and brochures concerning immigrant letters in the local newspapers. The article originating from the *Vereeniging "Landverhuizing"* with information concerning the United States is interesting in that aspect: see F.E.H. Groenman, "Iets over landverhuizing naar de Vereenigde Staten van Amerika," *Economische Verslagen* (Bijlage van *Handels-berichten*), 5 (1915): 1-16.

76 Emigrants who did not have a job in Friesland, or who were recorded without a profession in the United States, might have been special cases. It is, for example, unknown whether these people were disabled, or for one or another reason not capable of joining the work force.

77 Hoerder, "Labor Migration in the Atlantic Economies," 3.

78 For an analyses of the general Dutch patterns see R.P. Swierenga, "The Delayed Transition from Folk to Labor Migration; The Netherlands, 1880-1920," *International Migration Review* 22 (Summer 1993): 406-24.

79 The total group was mainly biased, which resulted in the fact that relatively few singles were in the linkage group.

80 Composition of Frisian-American linked households in 1900:

692 heads m/f
815 sons
762 daughters
69 boarders
63 servants
24 step-sons
23 step-daughters
16 brothers of head
15 mothers in law
15 fathers in law
10 fathers

| | |
|---|---|
| 10 | brothers in law |
| 9 | mothers |
| 7 | granddaughters |
| 7 | nephews |
| 7 | nieces |
| 7 | sisters in law |
| 6 | grandsons |
| 6 | sons in law |
| 3 | sisters |
| 2 | adopted sons |
| 2 | housekeepers |
| 2 | partners |
| 1 | uncle |
| 1 | cousin |
| 1 | adopted daughter |
| 1 | step-mother |
| 1 | kinship tie unknown |

To compare the households before and after migration (see also table 3.10), in fact, is a comparison between apples and oranges. The factor *time* is the determinator of the composition of the household. They were traced in the U.S. in 1900 and this could be a minimum of one year after emigration and a maximum of 20 years.

**81** Letter of S. van de Akker of August 14, 1909 from Franksville, WI to the *Nieuwsblad van Friesland,* September 11, 1909.

**82** Letter of Willem van der Leest from Muskegon, MI, to the province of Groningen, December 25, 1883.

**83** Letter of Leendert Visser March 1912, from Grand Rapids, MI, to the *Nieuwsblad van Friesland*, April 6, 1912.

**84** Only males could be naturalized before women suffrage in 1919. An original Certificate of Citizenship can be found in Calvin College Archives, Grand Rapids, MI. An illustration of this document concerning the Groninger immigrant Ewe Bolt in Minnesota in 1895 is included in A. Galema, A. Holtmann, and W. Grams eds., *Van de ene en de andere kant. Noordnederlandse en Noordwestduitse migratie naar de Verenigde Staten in de negentiende eeuw/Nordniederländische und Nordwestdeutsche Auswanderung nach Amerika im 19. Jahrhundert* (Groningen: Universiteitsbibliotheek/Oldenburg: Stadtmuseum, 1993), 104.

**85** The Homestead Law of May 20, 1862, stated that any American citizen or alien who had filed his or her intention papers, if 21 years of age or over, or if he was the head of the family, or if he had served at least 14 days in the army or navy of the USA, was permitted for a fee of $10 to file a claim to as many as 160 acres of unappropriated public land. After residing on and cultivating the land for five years, he could obtain a patent if he was then a citizen of the US. See *US Statutes at Large,* vol. 12, 392-93.

**86** Letter of Albert Roorda from Sioux City, IA, to Friesland (probably Wartena) June 13, 1904. I am indebted to Mr. and Mrs. F. Roorda-Dongstra for copies of this letters.

**87** Van Dijk, "Zes maanden in Amerika," 1: 29-30. Jan Hendrik Veneklaassen came to Groningen, MI, in 1851 with his wife and eight children. Veneklaassen started a brick factory where he produced bricks by hand from a mixture of sand and clay. These bricks were dried in the sun and baked in the ovens in his yard. In southwestern Michigan about 120 'Veneklaassen-houses' can be found with characteristic façades with contrasting red and white brick colors. Supposedly many of these houses are built by Groninger bricklayers, because these kind of architecture can also be found in the Dutch province of Groningen. See Galema ed., *Van de ene en de andere kant,* 108.

**88** Van Dijk, "Zes maanden in Amerika," 1: 40; 2: 41-42.

**89** Eringa left without a job according to the Dutch Population Registers. The truth is though that before departure he worked in various agricultural jobs in Friesland. Eringa's life and reminiscenses are described in Beltman, *A Dutch-American Immigrant in the Rural Midwest* (University of Illinois Press, 1996).

**90** According to my file "Frisians to America, 1880-1914," Maaike Rijpstra left from the village of Sexbierum, Barradeel for the United States, May 1, 1893. She was twenty years old (born December 15, 1872) and traveled by herself. Her destination was unknown: 'Amerika'. She was recorded as a servant when she left. From the letter collection of the Eringas it is known that Maaike had a brother, Hedser, who already emigrated earlier and who worked with Ulbe Eringa.

**91** Letter of Ulbe Eringa from Runningwater, SD, to Friesland July 29, 1917, Calvin College Archives, Grand Rapids, MI.

**92** Letter of T.G. de Vries from Runningwater, SD, in the *Bergumer Courant,* July 7, 1906.

**93** According to the data of the Dutch Population Register, Arjen Hoekstra was born November 2, 1865. He left in 1896 with his wife Hinke Meinderts Dijkstra, born September 28, 1865, and his daughter Klaasje, who was born August 9, 1893. The family left the village of Minnertsga, where they had a store according to the records. See Galema, "Frisians to America 1880-1914. Computer Compilation." Information in the occupational career of Arjen Hoekstra is found in G.O. Jones, *History of Wood County, Wisconsin* (Wood County, WI: H.C. Cooper, Jr. & Co., 1923), 700. The year 1895 is mentioned as his year of emigration to America. There is a note on the marriage date of Arjen Hoekstra: May 12, 1888. The couple had three children according to this source, namely Clara, born August 10, 1895, Minard, born January 19, 1899 and Theodore, born October 23, 1902. The data of Clara is either wrong or she must have been the second daughter with the name Klaasje (Clara), while the first had possibly died. Hoekstra is not recorded in my file of "Frisians in the USA, 1900/1910," because in 1900 he already had left LaCrosse County for Wood County, the Census enumeration of which was not screened.

**94** Letter of A. Roorda from Sioux City, IA, to Friesland October 17, 1902. Personal Collection Author.

**95** Letter of Albert Roorda from Sioux City, IA, to Friesland January 25, 1903. Personal Collection Author.

**96** Letters of Albert Roorda 1904/1906/1908 to Friesland. Personal Collection Author. It may very well be that this Albert Roorda was a member of the Roorda family described in the book *Roorda Family History* (Des Moines, IA, n.d.). In this book the Roorda family appears to be an early emigrated Frisian family who already came in the 1850s to Iowa. One of the Roorda's, Izaak E. Roorda, even made the trip across the Atlantic in the year 1853 with the shipwrecked *William and Mary*. His account can be found in the book mentioned above.

**97** See A. Galema, "Over de wereldzee naar de grote stad," 450-58. This article is based on the letter collection of Pieter Groustra in the Rijksarchief Leeuwarden. Many Dutch immigrants started to work in the Pullman factories, although the employment possibilities changed over the years. The immigrant Andries van Ek wrote in 1888 from Sioux County, IA, that the notion was not correct that all the newcomers immediately could get work at Pullman. See letter of Andries van Ek from Sioux County, IA, to the *Nieuwsblad van Friesland*, March 28, 1888.

**98** M. van der Heide, "Vijftig jaar in Canada en de Ver. Staten," 10-12.

**99** Letter of W.I. van den Bosch from Smith's Grove, KY, in the *Nieuw Advertentieblad*, August 9, 1893.

**100** Letter of Jacob Mast from Chicago in the *Nieuw Advertentieblad*, May 10, 1893.

**101** Letter of Frederick Dykstra from Bay Shore, NY, June 19, 1922 to his family in northern Friesland. I am indebted to F. Boersma in Oranjewoud for copies of some of Dijkstra's letters. Frederik Dijkstra was born in Wierum, April 15, 1852. He married Hiltje Douma in Westdongeradeel on September 4, 1873. He left for America in 1896. His brother Fedde, born in Wierum, January 15, 1862, also had a bakery in Lioessens and emigrated in May 1905 and settled in Kalamazoo, MI. He had married twice, first with Maria Bienses Vogel and later on April 4, 1895 with Teatske de Vries, who was born in Ee, April 23, 1877. Fedde Dijkstra died in Kalamazoo in 1938, and his wife on December 21, 1961. Galema, "Frisians in the USA, 1900/1910. Computer Compilation."

**102** The same can be said for Jan Jans de Vries, who left the village of Dantumawoude in northern Friesland in 1894 with his wife and five of their six children. De Vries was a carpenter in Friesland. His profession in Lowell, Ada, and Grand Rapids, MI, is unknown, but his oldest son Jan, who left about two decades later was an agricultural

laborer in Friesland and became a farmer in Lowell, MI, after emigrating with his wife Saakje Boonstra and their five children. Jan and Jan must have been reunited in Michigan. For the information concerning this family I am indebted to Mr. B.D. van der Meulen from Drachten. See B.D. van der Meulen et al., *Van der Zwaag, Wouterswoude, Friesland* (Wouterswoude: compilers, 1991), 48-67.

**103** C.P. Hoekema, *Andreas Paulus' Hoekema (1750-1801) en syn neiteam* (Heerenveen: Stifting Ffyrug, 1983), 66-67. I am indebted to T. Hoekema in Zuidhorn for this source.

**104** For the Vogel family history see the unpublished manuscript "Vogel," written by members of the Vogel family, Harlingen, n.d.

**105** Letter of Ulbe Eringa from Runningwater, SD, December 20, 1903 to Friesland, Calvin College Archives, Grand Rapids, MI. Also A. Galema and S. Sinke, "Paradijs der vrouwen? Overzeese migratie naar de Verenigde Staten van Friese vrouwen rond de eeuwwisseling," in *Vrouwen in den vreemde. Lotgevallen van emigrantes en immigrantes*, eds. A. Dassen, C. van Eerd, and K. Oppelland (Zutphen: Walburg Pers, 1993), 44.

# Notes – 6

**1** J.E. Bodnar, *The Transplanted; A History of Immigrants in Urban America* (Bloomington: Indiana University Press, 1985), 57-84.
**2** D. Hoerder, "The Transplanted; International Dimensions," *Social Science History* 12 (Fall 1988): 257-58.
**3** C. Tilly, "Transplanted Networks," in *Immigration Reconsidered*, ed. V. Yans-McLaughlin (New York: Oxford University Press, 1990), 84.
**4** J.E. Bodnar, "Response," *Social Science History* 12 (Fall 1988): 266.
**5** Earlier versions of the history of the Whitinsville Frisians appeared as A. Galema, "Transplanted Network; A Case Study of Frisian Migration to Whitinsville, Mass., 1880-1914," in *The Dutch in North-America; Their Immigration and Cultural Continuity*, eds. R. Kroes and H-O. Neuschäfer (Amsterdam: VU University Press, 1991), 174-88; and A. Galema, "Whitinsville, Massachusetts," *Origins*, 12 (1994) 2: 2-7. For further information concerning Whitinsville I am greatly indebted to Whitinsville resident Theodore E. Haringa, who organized an informational and historical tour during my research visit in spring 1991.
**6** E.B. Crane, *History of Worcester County, Massachusetts* (New York & Chicago: Lewis Historical Publishing Company, 1924), 1-2; *History of Worcester County, Massachusetts; Embracing a Comprehensive History of the County from its First Settlement to the Present Time, with a History and Description of its Cities and Towns*, 2 vols. (Boston: C.F. Jewett and Company, 1879), 2: 140.

**7** J. van Hinte, *Nederlanders in Amerika. Een studie over landverhuizers en volksplanters in de 19e en 20ste eeuw in de Vereenigde Staten van Amerika*, 2 vols. (Groningen: P.Noordhoff, 1928), 2: 305.
**8** An informative and pictorial idea about the Whitin factory, its offices and leading persons can be found in *A Trip through the Whitin Machine Works; Manufacturers of Textile Machinery* (Whitinsville: Whitin Machine Works, 1925).
**9** T.W. Baldwin, *Vital Records of Northbridge Massachusetts to the Year 1850* (Boston: [S.N.], 1916).
**10** *History of Worcester County, Massachusetts* (1879), 149. An interesting study about industrialization in rural Massachusetts and the rapid rise of unprecedented water-powered factories, can be found in J. Prude, *The Coming of Industrial Order; Town and Factory Life in Rural Massachusetts 1810-1860* (New York: Cambridge University Press, 1983).
**11** J. Jansen, "Een verblijf in Amerika," *Vragen van den Dag* 35 (August 1920): 624-35. T.R. Navin, the chronicler of the Whitin family, published *The Whitin Machine Works Since 1831* (Cambridge: Harvard University Press, 1950), 162. The story of the first Dutch settlers was also recalled by Arnold Banning, who came from Makkum, Friesland in 1913 with his parents when he was ten years old. I interviewed A. and M. Banning in their home in Whitinsville, March 11, 1991. See also P. Hacket, "The Stone Walls of Castle Hill," *Tribune*, May 15, 1974.

**12** J. Kooistra, "Brief út Whitinsville fan in âld-Grouster," *Frysk en Frij*, March 24, 1950, and April 7, 1950.
**13** This opposes Y. Poortinga in his article "Emigraesje út Westerlauwersk Fryslân nei en festiging yn è Foriene Steaten (oant likernôch 1900 ta)," *Frysk Jierboek* (1958): 107. Poortinga marked Wytse Feddema from Feinsum in the province of Friesland as the number one Frisian in Whitinsville.
**14** R.P. Swierenga, *The Forerunners; Dutch Jewry in the North American Diaspora* (Detroit: Wayne State University Press, 1994), 164-87; J. van Hinte, *Nederlanders in Amerika*, 2: 307.
**15** The Census records of the township of Northbridge in 1900 and 1910, linked with the data from the Dutch Population Registers of the northern Frisian clay area between 1880 and 1910, reveal some clear migratory patterns. Unfortunately, no accurate information concerning the population of the village of Whitinsville has ever existed. Never having had a separate legal status, the community has always been considered for census purposes as a part of the town of Northbridge. For that reason, it was necessary to search for the Frisian immigrants in the U.S. Census of 1900 and 1910 throughout the entire town of Northbridge. For data see J.B.E. Galema, "Whitinsville, all Frisians, 1880-1910. Computer Compilation," (Groningen, 1989).
**16** For the purpose of having complete source materials, I extracted *all* the Dutch-born people in the town of Northbridge from the U.S. Census of 1900 *and* the Census

of 1910. Almost all of the Dutch inhabitants of Whitinsville were Frisians. See J.B.E. Galema, "Frisians in the U.S.A., 1900/ 1910. Computer Compilation," (Groningen, 1993).

**17** Galema, "Frisians in the USA, 1900/1910. Computer Compilation." Jansen, "Een verblijf in Amerika," 624-35.

**18** J.B.E. Galema, "Linked Files: Frisians to America and Frisians in the USA. Computer Compilation," (Groningen, 1995).

**19** Percentages derived from total emigration from Barradeel to Northbridge township, 1880-1910.

**20** Percentages derived from total emigration from Wonseradeel to Northbridge township, 1880-1910.

**21** For the figures of emigration from the northern clay area see earlier chapters and also J.B.E. Galema, "Frisians to America, 1880-1914. Computer Compilation," (Groningen, 1992).

**22** V. Bruinsma, "Hoe is Friesland te helpen?," *Vragen des Tijds* 1 (1894): 343-91.

**23** This settles the common idea that the Dutch immigrants in Whitinsville almost all became farmers or farmworkers. G.F. DeJong, *The Dutch in America, 1609-1974* (Boston: Twayne Publishers, 1975), 169.

**24** We may assume that when the Dutch Population Register reports 'unknown' for the occupation of a male adult, the specific job of that person was not a very steady one or he had no job at all.

**25** This could be the result of the census taker in 1910 being more precise and careful in specifying occupations.

**26** Interview with Harold Wassenar, Whitinsville, March 11, 1991.

**27** Gaele Bakker was born July 31, 1858 in Koudum, Friesland. His parents owned a bakery, which Gaele later took over. He married Catharina Visser (born March 9, 1864) on May 17, 1884 in Witmarsum, Wonseradeel. The couple migrated in 1899 to Whitinsville with their seven children: Jan (John) of 14, Jouke (Joseph) 12, Jacobje (Jenny) 11, Riemer (Raymond) 8, Magdalena 6, Dirk (Dick) 4, and Grietje (Katie) 2.

Catharina Visser's parents had immigrated to Whitinsville years earlier and her brother Dirk Visser had returned to Friesland with reports of the good conditions there. Gaele found work immediately in the Whitin Machine Works. See E. Navis and J. Siebring-Wieringa eds., *A Furrow Laid Bare* (Edmonton, Alberta: Friesen Printers, 1985), 41-49, 144-52. I am indebted to Gilbert Baker, a descendant of Gaele Bakker in Whitinsville. Gilbert Baker worked for many years in the Whitin Machine Works with other Frisians. Interview with Gilbert and Catharine Baker, Whitinsville, March 13, 1991.

**28** T. van der Wal, *Op zoek naar een nieuwe vrijheid. Een kwart eeuw arbeidersbeweging in Friesland 1870-1895* (Leiden: Universitaire Pers, 1972), 369-74.

**29** The U.S. Census records show the specific street where inhabitants lived. The Company housing used by Frisian immigrants was also described in interviews with Whitinsville residents. Arnold Banning's father, who came in 1913, started a job at the Whitin Machine Works and lived in a Company house. See interview Banning and interview Baker, Whitinsville, March 11, 1991.

**30** Of all the Frisian households in Whitinsville in 1900, 6 percent had a free owned house, 6 percent had a free owned farm, another 6 percent operated rented farms, 81 percent had a rented house, and for 1 percent ownership was unknown. In 1910 6 percent owned a house free, 3 percent owned a house mortgaged, 2 percent had an owned free farm, while 9 percent had a farm mortgaged, 72 percent lived in a rented house, and the remaining 8 percent was unknown. It is important to consider that in the decade 1900-1910 new Frisian immigrants came to Whitinsville, which explains the low increase in free owned houses in this time period.

**31** R.H. Bloem, "Dutch Immigration to Whitinsville," Thesis, May 1981; Calvin College Archives, Grand Rapids, MI.

**32** Interview Banning, Whitinsville, March 11, 1991. Half a year later

Arnold Banning died in Whitinsville at the age of 88 (October 5, 1991). His father Hermanus Banning (born July 8, 1879) and his wife Sijtske van der Sluis (born October 5, 1885) came to America with their four children: Arnoldus 10, Oene 8, Alle Dirk 4 and Frederika Wilhelmina 2 years old. They traveled in March, 1913 directly to Whitinsville. See Galema, "Frisians to America, 1880-1914. Computer Compilation." The interview with Harold Wassenar occurred the same day in 1991. Afterwards Wassenar wrote down his ideas about Dutch immigration in Whitinsville in a paper: "Some Notes on the Meeting with Annemieke Galema of Holland," (April 1, 1991).

**33** Navin, *Whitin Machine Works*, 161.

**34** Interview Banning.

**35** R.D. Brown, *Massachusetts; A Bicentennial History* (New York: W.W. Norton & Company, 1978), 185-239.

**36** J. Jansen, "Verblijf," 633.

**37** Wassenar, "Some Notes on the Meeting with Annemieke Galema," 3-4. The Krul family also can be found in my database Galema, "Frisians in the U.S.A., 1900-1910. Computer Compilation." Harold Wassenar's sister Ethel Baker also wrote down some impressions concerning her family in "The Maynard J. Krulls Immigrated to America in 1896." Manuscript, Personal Collection Author. Ethel Baker's father, Beert Wassenaar, emigrated in 1895 and came from Minnertsga. The Wassenaars can be found in the database Galema, "Frisians to America, 1880-1914. Computer Compilation."

**38** E.B. Crane, *History of Worcester County*, 703.

**39** The first period of nineteenth century Dutch migration to the U.S. really started with the settlement of two groups of Separatist people, who went with their reverends H.P. Scholte and A.C. van Raalte to Iowa and Michigan, respectively. Initally these Separatists joined the existing Reformed Church of America (a creation of earlier Dutch settlers), but many devout persons had begun to wonder whether or not Van Raalte and his closest friends had "sold the churches to an impure denomination". The result was that in 1857 a permanent separation occurred and a denomination of secessionists was formed. The new church was named The Christian Reformed Church. See H. Beets, *The Christian Reformed Church in North America* (Grand Rapids, MI: Grand Rapids Printing Company, 1923); D.H. Kromminga, *The Christian Reformed Tradition from the Reformation till the Present Time* (Grand Rapids, MI: W.B. Eerdmans, 1943); A. Hyma, *Albertus C. van Raalte and his Dutch Settlements in the United States* (Grand Rapids, MI: W.B. Eerdmans, 1947), 193-239.

**40** Galema, "Frisians to America, 1880-1914. Computer Compilation."

**41** H. Beets, "Our Frisian Settlement in Whitinsville, Mass.," *The Banner*, October 1, 1926.

**42** Rev. Drost wanted a higher salary a year later, which can be read in his letter of October 26, 1896 to the CRC church council in Whitinsville. Calvin College Archives, Grand Rapids, MI.

**43** R.H. Bloem, "Whitinsville", 4. See also W. Van Gorp-Vander Baan, "The History of the Dutch people in Whitinsville," article at the request of the Northbridge Bicentennial Celebration Committee in 1972. Personal Collection Author; also a poem "Een terugblik" written by P. Glashouwer (translation Steve De Haan) about the creation of the CRC in Whitinsville; Calvin College Archives, Grand Rapids, MI. Also "The Pleasant Street Christian Reformed Church of Whitinsville, Massachusetts; 75th Anniversary 1896-1971," Manuscript, Calvin College Archives, Grand Rapids, MI; and "Fiftieth Anniversary, October 20, 1946, Christian Reformed Church, Whitinsville, Mass. 1896-1946," Manuscript, Calvin College Archives, Grand Rapids, MI. A picture of the first church building as well as a short history can be found in *Souvenir for the Dedication of the New Church Building of the Christian Reformed Church Whitinsville, Massachusetts June 25, 26, 1930* (Whitinsville: Eagle Press, 1930).

**44** Jansen, "Verblijf," 624-36.

**45** Van Gorp-Vander Baan, "Dutch people in Whitinsville," 4. For more information on the Whitinsville CRC see "Historical Sketch Fairlawn Christian Reformed Church Whitinsville, MA.," (written for 25th anniversary 1958-1983). Manuscript, Calvin College Archives, Grand Rapids, MI.

**46** J. Daan, "Trouw aan het Fries in de U.S.A.," in *Flecht op 'e koai. Stúdzjes oanbean oan Prof.Dr. W.J. Buma ta syn sechstichste jierdei*, ed. by T. Hoekema et al., (Groningen: Wolters-Noordhoff, 1970), 178.

**47** Tilly, "Transplanted Networks," 81-84. In his theoretical essay on migration to the U.S.A. Tilly distinguishes *networks* from *categories*, stating that networks migrate and categories stay put.

**48** The fact that people drew on information of earlier settlers is also known from letters in the Frisian newspapers. H. Bakker, for example, wrote from Whitinsville, February 10, 1901 about his journey of August 1900 on the *Rotterdam* of the Holland America Line. The last sentence of his letter in the *Nieuw Advertentieblad* was: "For he who wants more information concerning this environment, I will provide this". I also found an envelope of a letter of January 1910 from P. van Gosliga from Whitinsville to the village of Parrega. According to my data this must have been Pier van Gosliga (born June 4, 1889) who left Parrega in 1909 by himself. Most likely Pier came back to The Netherlands and returned with his younger brother Jan (born November 3, 1887) in 1913.

**49** Kooistra, "Brief út Whitinsfield," April 7, 1950. Personal Collection Author.

**50** Verse of J.H. Halbertsma. These lines (with spelling errors) were written in a letter from Paterson of Richard K. Hoitsma to Y. Rypma in Leeuwarden, September 9, 1929; *KNKB-Archief*, De Trije, Franeker.

**51** H.S. Lucas, *Netherlanders in America* (Ann Arbor: University of Michigan Press, 1955; reprint ed., Grand Rapids, MI: W.B. Eerdmans, 1989), 642-43. Information

concerning population derived from H. Bischoff, *Data on New Jersey Urban Immigration and Migration; Maps, Statistics and Charts* (n.p., 1985), 5-9; and J.E. Brush, *The Population of New Jersey* (New Brunswick: Rutgers University Press, 1956), 2-17.

**52** S. Thernstrom, ed., *Harvard Encyclopedia of American Ethnic Groups* (Cambridge, MA: Harvard University Press, 1980), 401-03.

**53** Van Hinte, *Nederlanders in Amerika*, 2: 376.

**54** G.F. DeJong, "Dutch Immigrants in New Jersey before World War I," *New Jersey History* 94 (1976) 2: 69-88.

**55** J.L.D. Whitehead, *The Passaic Valley New Jersey* (New York: The New Jersey Genealogical Company, 1901), 229. For the history of Passaic County see also W. Nelson and C.A. Shriner, *History of Paterson and its Environs*, 2 vols. (New York and Chicago: Lewis Historical Publishing Company, 1920), 1: 185-196.

**56** Letter of Aukjen Pruiksma, May 16, 1895, from Paterson, NJ, to the province of Friesland; Rijksarchief Leeuwarden.

**57** "Gij zout verwonderlijk op zien zoo als gij hier ook eens kwam men kan het zen zoo niet voor stellen die en holland woont dat het hier er zoo uit ziet want varten en slotten ziet men hier niet zoo als in holland maar hoge bergen daar het water uit loopt en dan zoms een riever daar het water en langs loopt dat uit de bergen komt maar ander ziet men hier geen waters want het land dat aan eigenaaren behoort daar zijn allemaal stekken om maar geen slotten zoals bij u...". Letter of Pieter Westerhuis, June 6, 1881, from Paterson, NJ, to J.J. Hoogland, St. Annaparochie; Collectie Hoogland, Rijksarchief Leeuwarden.

**58** Van Hinte, *Nederlanders in Amerika*, 1: 65. For the Dutch colonial spirit in New Jersey see also: A.C. Leiby, *The Early Dutch and Swedish Settlers of New Jersey* (Princeton, NJ: D. Van Nostrand, 1964), 109-21.

**59** G. Schnücker, *Die Ostfriesen in Amerika. Eine illustrierte Geschichte ihrer Kolonien bis zur Gegenwart* (Cleveland, OH: Central Publishing House, 1917), 5-10.

60 S. de Zee, *Myn twadde Amerika-reis* (Heerenveen: Handelsdrukkerij Hepkema, 1929), 61.

61 C.A. Shriner, *Four Chapters of Paterson History* (Paterson, NJ: Lont & Overkamp, 1919), 53-101.

62 Van Hinte, *Nederlanders in Amerika*, 1: 374. Also H.J. Brinks, "The Beginnings of the CRC in New Jersey 1855-1866," *Origins* 2 (1984) 1: 17-21.

63 C.A. Shriner, *Paterson, New Jersey* (Paterson: The Press Printing and Publishing Company, 1890), 28.

64 The term 'culture island' is used mainly in geographical research. B.L. Anderson in his study *The Scandinavian and Dutch Rural Settlements in the Stillaguamish and Nooksack Valleys of Western Washington* (Ann Arbor: University Microfilms International, 1957), used the term to describe two different ethnic communities. See also *A History of Paterson and Its Relations with the World* (Union City, NJ: Hudson Dispatch Printer, 1932), 108-15.

65 D.G. Vanderstel, *The Dutch of Grand Rapids, Michigan, 1848-1900; Immigrant Neighborhood and Community Development in a Nineteenth Century City* (Ann Arbor: University Microfilms International, 1986), 539.

66 *United States Population Census Manuscripts, Bureau of the Census. 13th Census (1910)*, vol. 1, Population, General Report and Analysis (Washington: Bureau of the Census, 1910), 856-57; Microfilm reels National Archives for 1900: T623-990, T623-991, T623-992; for 1910: T624-904, 905, 906, 907.

67 The total population in Paterson in 1910 was 125,600. Bischoff, *Data on New Jersey*, 8.

68 Housewives and children younger than 14 years of age are not included in the workforce.

69 J.J. Spahr van der Hoek, *Geschiedenis van de Friese landbouw*, 2 vols. (Leeuwarden: Friesche Maatschappij van Landbouw, 1952), 648-51. For the definition of *gardenier* see chapter 1.6 of this book.

70 Housewives and children younger than 14 years of age are not included in the workforce.

71 In 1974 the American historian Gerald F. DeJong interviewed Durk

(*Richard*) Zuidema in Paterson. See DeJong, "Dutch Immigrants in New Jersey," 77-78. According to the data file Galema, "Frisians to America, 1880-1914" Zuidema left in 1892 with his parents Willem Jans Zuidema and Ytje Durks Offringa and his brother Siemen Willems. DeJong recalls that there was a sister too. This sister was not recorded with the other members of the family, but in the data I found a Dieuwke Zuidema from Lichtaard who was married to Sijbren Jans Teitsma and left with a daughter named Ytje in 1894 to Paterson.

72 Letter of Pieter Westerhuis, January 3, 1882 from Paterson to J.J. Hoogland, St. Annaparochie. "Collectie Hoogland," Rijksarchief Leeuwarden.

73 F. Ramella, "Across the Ocean or over the Border; Expectations and Experiences of Italians from Piedmont in New Jersey and Southern France" in *Distant Magnets; Expectations and Realities in the Immigrant Experience, 1840-1930*, eds. D. Hoerder and H. Rössler (New York: Holmes & Meier, 1993), 109.

74 J.W. Jenks and W.J. Lauck, *The Immigration Problem* (New York and London: Funk & Wagnals Co., 1917, first publ. in 1912), 516-17; for the experience of the Frisians Tjerk Zondervan and Maartje Lautenbach in Paterson see H.J. Brinks, "Silk City; News from Paterson's Mill Workers," *Origins* 11 (1993) 2: 2-11; for the working conditions in the silk mills see P.B. Scranton ed., *Silk City; Studies on the Paterson Silk Industry, 1860-1940* (Newark: New Jersey Historical Society, 1985), 35-72.

75 *Report on Condition of Woman and Child Wage-Earners in the United States*, vol. 4, "The Silk Industry," (Washington DC, 1911), 66.

76 *Report on Condition of Woman and Child Wage-Earners*, "The Silk Industry," 1911, 189. An article about work in the Dye House is S. Bell, "A Paterson Dyer's Story," *Solidarity* (May 3, 1913): 2; also D.W. Dodyk and S. Golin, *The Paterson Silk Strike of 1913* (Paterson, 1987), 59-60. The hard and unhealthy work in the dye house is also recalled by the Woudenberg

family in H. Westra, "Fear and Hope Jostled; Dutch Immigrant Life and Death in Paterson, New Jersey," *Origins* 8 (1990) 2: 1-15.

77 Ramella, "Across" in *Distant Magnets*, 113; R.D. Margrave, "Technology Diffusion and the Transfer of Skills; Nineteenth-Century English Silk Migration to Paterson," in *Silk City; Studies on the Paterson Silk Industry, 1860-1940*, ed. P.B. Scranton (Newark: New Jersey Historical Society, 1985), 12-13. Margrave's study on the English silk workers makes clear that the contemporary view of rapid and easy upward mobility in the Paterson silk industry was a distortion of reality. Margrave states that opportunities were present, but contemporary accounts considerably overstated the case.

78 "Ik werk nu niet meer aan het spoor ik werk nu in een siede molen en verdien daar 7 gulden de week en dat komt mij niet zo slim aan...". Letter of J.G. Boekhout, December 1, 1881, from Paterson to J.J. Hoogland St. Annaparochie, "Collectie Hoogland," Rijksarchief Leeuwarden.

79 Amounts based on research of the "Friesch Comité van de Volkspartij" [Frisian committee of the People's Party] of 1891 and described by H. Sannes, *Geschiedenis van Het Bildt*, 3 vols. (Franeker: Wever, 1956), 3B: 371-72.

80 Netherlanders already started to come to New Jersey beginning in the 1850s because they were attracted by good wages in the factories of Lodi, Paterson, Passaic, and other New Jersey cities. See Lucas, *Netherlanders in America*, table 2, 642-43; Also R.J. Vecoli, *The People of New Jersey* (Princeton, NJ: D. Van Nostrand Company, 1965), 99.

81 Ramella, "Across," 107.

82 Letter of J.G. Boekhout, March 19, 1883, from Paterson to J.J. Hoogland St. Annaparochie, "Collectie Hoogland," Rijksarchief Leeuwarden.

83 Letter of Tjerk Zondervan from Paterson to his brother Sijds in Friesland, November 13, 1893. Thanks to Jacob Lautenbach in IJlst.

84.- Yge Mulder (born August 19,

1827) was an immigrant who also came from Het Bildt. He emigrated in April 1881 from St. Annaparochie as a widower with his five sons Jouke, Gerrit, Gerke, Wiltje, and Abe, and his daughter Dirkje; Letter of Pieter Westerhuis November 21, 1882, "Collectie Hoogland," Rijksarchief Leeuwarden. Letters from the Hoogland Collection are also described in "In de winter hoeft men in Amerika niet te vlasbraken," *Leeuwarder Courant*, April 26, 1986; and in "Brieven uit het beloofde land," in *Friesland vroeger. Uit de archiefkast van het Rijksarchief in Friesland*, eds. S. de Haan and J. Hoving, (Drachten/Leeuwarden: Friese Pers Boekerij, 1987), 93-97. Pieter Doekes Westerhuis was the son of Doeke Westerhuis (who was born in Hyum, February 2, 1824, and died in St. Annaparochie, June 5, 1869) and Adriaantje Wiebes Nieuwsma and born January 14, 1860. He left from St. Annaparochie to America on April 4, 1881, with his step father Klaas Dirks de Jong (*gardenier*, second husband of his mother), his sister Froukje Klazes de Jong (born July 26, 1866), and his mother (born December 30, 1823). I am indebted to Mr. W.G. Westerhuis in The Hague, who provided me with documents from the Dutch Population Register and birth certificate of Pieter Doekes Westerhuis.

**85** De Zee, *Myn twadde Amerika-reis*, 60-61. See also Galema, "Frisians to America, 1880-1914. Computer Compilation." Some Dutch immigrants stayed in New Jersey only long enough to earn sufficient money to go to the Dutch communities in the MidWest, or to buy a farm and start as an independent entrepreneur. See Vecoli, *The People of New Jersey*, 99; Also DeJong, "Dutch Immigrants in New Jersey," 76.

**86** Letter of Klaas Udes from Paterson, NJ, January 1895 to Bedum. Also letter from H. Husselman from Paterson, December 29, 1908 to Grand Rapids, MI; Calvin College Archives, Grand Rapids, MI.

**87** Factors which drew various immigrant workers to the Paterson silk mills are described in United States Immigration Commission, *Immigrants in Industries; Silk Goods Manufacturing and Dyeing*, part 5 (Washington DC, 1907-1910), 18-19.

**88** M.C. Mooney, "The Industrial Workers of the World and the Immigrants of Paterson and Passaic, NJ, 1907-1913," (M.A. thesis, Seaton Hall University, 1969), 28-44; Living conditions for immigrants in urban areas conspicuously; evaluation can be found in D. Ward, *Cities and Immigrants; A Geography of Change in Nineteenth-Century America* (New York: Oxford University Press, 1971), 105-23.

**89** J.E. Wood, "History of Labor in the Broad-Silk Industry of Paterson, NJ." (Dissertation, University of California, 1941), 135.

**90** H.G. Gutman, "Class, Status, and Community Power in Nineteenth-Century American Industrial Cities - Paterson, New Jersey; A Case Study," in *The Age of Industrialism in America; Essays in Social Structure and Cultural Values*, ed. F.C. Jaher (New York: Free Press, 1968), 281-83.

**91** For the labor movement generally, and especially about Paterson, see P.S. Foner, *History of the Labor Movement in the United States*, vol. 4: The Industrial Workers of the World; 1905-1917 (New York: International Publishers, 1965), 351-72; also P.S. Foner, *Women and the American Labor Movement* (New York: Free Press, 1979), 440-57.

**92** Galema, "Frisians to America, 1880-1914. Computer Compilation." Also Van der Wal, *Op zoek naar een nieuwe vrijheid*, 255-57, 301-02.

**93** Van der Wal, *Op zoek naar een nieuwe vrijheid*, 272.

**94** Johan Frieswijk wrote a biography of Tjeerd Stienstra and focused mainly on his active period in the Frisian labor movement. J. Frieswijk, "Een socialisties propagandist in revolutionaire jaren. Biografie van Tjeerd Stienstra (1859-1935)," *Tijdschrift voor Sociale Geschiedenis* 6 (October, 1976): 221-56. Tjeerd Stienstra's wife was Grietje Kijlstra. See also P.R.D. Stokvis, "Socialistische immigranten in de Verenigde Staten. Vrijheid versus gelijkheid," *Groniek* 96 (1986): 103-16; G. Jelsma, "Twa revolúsjonaire toanielskriuwers út de

ein fan de foarige ieu," *It Beaken* 5/6 (1979): 295.

**95** For the Stienstras who left from the village of Beetgum see also T. Kingma, *Bitgum. De skiednis fan Bitgum en Bitgummole* (Leeuwarden: Fryske Akademy, 1988), 128-35, 275-77.

**96** J. Frieswijk, "Een socialisties propagandist," 219-56. The Socialist Labor Party was in contact with European revolutionary groups. Especially immigrants from Germany and the Netherlands were members of the SLP, that focused on Marxism with a revolutionary perspective.

**97** In the Paterson city directories [to be found in the Public Library, Paterson, NJ], John Stap is listed in 1901 in the milk business, and he lived at 132 East 7th Avenue, on the northeastern side of Paterson. In the 1904 directory Stap was listed as a filecutter at the same address. The 1906 and 1907 directories did not list Stap. Maybe this was because he was out of the labor market due to a serious illness. Stap died in Paterson on December 15, 1908. See H. Sannes, *Geschiedenis van Het Bildt*, 3B: 369-403, particularly 394 note 18.

**98** Later Tjeerd Stienstra remarried and moved to St. Louis and vicinity, MO, where he worked as a tailor again. Frieswijk, "Een socialisties propagandist," 249-51.

**99** De Zee, *Myn twadde Amerika-reis*, 56-57. Also Stokvis, "Socialistische immigranten," 109-10, and P.R.D. Stokvis, "Dutch-Speaking Peoples," in *The Immigrant Labor Press in North America, 1840s-1970s*, ed. D. Hoerder (New York: Greenwood Press, 1987), 263-78. Klaas and Tjeerd Stienstra both got involved in the controversial *Hogerhuis Zaak*, in which innocent people were imprisoned. In 1899 Tjeerd made an official statement concerning this case after he had emigrated to Paterson. See G. Jelsma, "Twa revolusjonaire toanielskriuwers út de ein fan de foarige ieu," 291-310; G.A. Wumkes, *Stads- en dorpskroniek van Friesland*, 2 vols. (Leeuwarden: Eisma, 1930-1934), 2: 603. All the details of the participation of Klaas and Tjeerd in the *Hogerhuis* conflict before and after emigration can be found in H. Sleurink and J. Frieswijk,

*De zaak Hogerhuis. Eene gerechtelijke misdaad* (Leeuwarden: Friese Pers Boekerij, 1984).

**100** G. Jelsma, "Twa revolútionaire toanielskriuwers," 296, 300-01. Klaas Stienstra died in 1929 in Paterson, according to Jelsma.

**101** Sannes, *Geschiedenis van Het Bildt*, 3B: 388.

**102** "Brieven uit Amerika," *Recht voor Allen*, June 14, 1889. Special thanks to Homme Wedman for this information.

**103** Van Hinte, *Nederlanders in Amerika*, 2: 378. That Dutch church-affiliated immigrants in Paterson refused to strike is also clear from the letters of the Woudenberg family from Amersfoort. See H. Westra, "Fear and Hope Jostled," 6.

**104** Letter of Sietze J.Boonstra from Paterson to his sister-in-law Antje Dijkstra in St. Annaparochie, December, 1910. Sietse Boonstra (born August 19, 1849) emigrated with his wife Hinke P. Koning (born May 24, 1852) to Paterson on April 25, 1910 with their son Pieter (born November 18, 1892). Their son Jacob and daughter Sytske with their families already had gone to Paterson on October 26, 1907. I am indebted to D. Boonstra from Gasselte for this information.

**105** For the information on the religious life of Dutch immigrants in Paterson I heavily relied on DeJong's "The Dutch in New Jersey." Also Brinks, "The beginnings of the CRC in New Jersey 1855-1866," 17-21.

**106** J.J. Timmerman, "Growing up in New Jersey," *Origins* 3 (1985) 2: 25.

**107** Van Hinte, *Nederlanders in Amerika*, 1: 412.

**108** B.S. Hylkema, "Op reis nei Amerika," *Sljucht en Rjucht*, 25 (1923): 301.

**109** Hylkema, "Nei Amerika," 301-02.

**110** *Beknopte inlichtingen voor Hollandsche emigranten* (Paterson: De Telegraaf, 1915); Calvin College Archives, Grand Rapids, MI.

**111** DeJong, "Dutch Immigrants in New Jersey," 83. Also *A History of Paterson and Its Relations with the World*, 128-29.

**112** *Golden Jubilee of Utspanning troch Ynspanning Paterson, New Jersey* (June

13, 1943), *KNKB-Archief*, De Trije, Franeker. Very informative about *keatsen* and its language is P. Breuker, *Keatserstaal* (Groningen: Frysk Ynstitut University of Groningen, 1983).

**113** Galema, "Frisians to America, 1880-1914. Computer Compilation." Hoitsma was born October 26, 1866. When he left Friesland he was unmarried with profession unknown in the Dutch Population Registers. For Hoitsma's career see also De Zee, *Myn twadde Amerika-reis*, 64.

**114** Letter of Richard K. Hoitsma to U. Rypma in Leeuwarden, September 9, 1929; *KNKB-Archief*, De Trije, Franeker.

**115** *Golden Jubilee of Utspanning troch Ynspanning*. Guild Hall was also rented to other societies or for private weddings and banquets. After the Frisians had made alterations and additions to Guild Hall, it had a capacity of 400 persons. The twenty members in 1895 were Y. Stienstra, J. de Roo, R. Zondervan, J. Tjepkema, J. Wiersma, H. Stienstra, H. Poelstra, D. Hoitsma, S. Reijenga, Tj. Zondervan, L. Zwerver, G. Elgersma, Sj. Sinnema, R. Nakken, J. Schurenga, W. Bakker, J. Schuurmans, P. Stienstra, J. Koster, A. Dykstra, G. Visser, F. v.d. Valk, J. Pape, and P. Sinnema. Most of these people's family names are in the datafile Galema, "Frisians to America, 1880-1914. Computer Compilation."

**116** G. Jelsma, "Twa revolúsjonaire toanielskriuwers," 297.

**117** In 1924 Dirk Driebergen, in 1925 Yme Schuitmaker, and in 1929 Dora Terpstra were other performing Frisians who visited and entertained in Paterson.

**118** The boy or girl who is named after a certain family member gets a decorated silver spoon at birth from this particular person.

**119** See, for example, the *Franeker Courant* June 28, 1900; July 29, 1900; October 5, 1926; October 10, 1926; *Het Oosten*, February 1, 1923; July 18, 1929; *Sljucht en Rjucht* April 23, 1921; August 11, 1934; *It Heitelân*, 31 (1924); 32( 1924); 26 (1925); 41 (1925);

**120** J. Byl, "Sports and Sabbath

Desecration," *Origins* 8 (1990) 2: 25-29.

**121** "Een Calvinist onder stoom," *Nieuwsblad van Noord-Oost Friesland*, May 11, 1990.

**122** John J. Timmerman's family came from Ost-Friesland to America. Timmerman, "Growing up in New Jersey," 26.

**123** Letter of Geeske Bandringa from Chicago, Il, October 3, 1884 to Pieterburen, Groningen. Calvin College Archives, Grand Rapids, MI.

**124** Letter of Douwe Dijkstra from Chicago, December 18, 1900 to Friesland. August 31 was the birthday of Princess Wilhelmina, who was born in 1880 as the only child of King Willem III and his second wife Emma van Waldeck-Pyrmont. After the death of her half-brother Alexander in 1884, Wilhelmina became the heiress to the throne and was inaugurated September 6, 1898.

**125** A *Groninger Hoek* existed on the west side of Chicago. See H. Krabbendam, "The West Side Dutch in Chicago," *Origins* 9 (1991) 2: 4-8; H. Stob, "Henry Stob," *Origins* 9 (1991) 2: 9-17; H. Stob, "Church and School on Chicago's West Side 1913-1921," *Origins* 10 (1992) 2: 14-19 and *Origins* 11 (1993) 1: 24-29; R.P. Swierenga, "Chicago's Groninger Hoek; The Origins and Development of the Dutch Colony on the 'Old West Side' in the Nineteenth Century," (paper delivered at the University of Groningen, 1988).

**126** For all the data concerning Frisians in Chicago see Galema, "Frisians in the USA, 1900/1910. Computer Compilation." The couples without children were mainly in their twenties.

**127** Van Hinte, *Nederlanders in Amerika*, 2: 389-90.

**128** See Galema, "Frisians in the USA, 1900/1910. Computer Compilation." Roseland became the largest homogeneous Dutch urban city in the U.S. in 1900-1920, with 10,000-20,000 Dutch and they numbered about 80 percent of the total population. For a description of life among the Dutch in Roseland and the many Frisians in that community see S. Dekker, "History of Roseland and Vicinity," (Calumet,

1938; Typescript, Calvin College Archives, Grand Rapids, MI); also R.R. Tiemersma, "Growing Up in Roseland in the 20's & 30's," *Origins* 5 (1987) 1: 2-19; and Van Hinte, *Nederlanders in Amerika*, 2: 388-89; and R.A. Cook, *South Holland Illinois; A History* (South Holland: South Holland Trust and Savings Bank, 1966), 58-85; and "Dutch Immigration to Laage Prairie." Manuscript, Herrick Publick Library, Holland, MI; and R. Ettema, *The Dutch Connection in South Cook County* (South Holland, IL: Park Press, 1984); and "South Holland, Illinois; 75th Anniversary, 1894-1969." Manuscript, Herrick Publick Library, Holland, MI.

**129** D. Zandstra, "The Calumet Region; A Land Flowing with Milk and Honey," *Origins* 4 (1986) 1: 16-21. Also H. Eenigenburg, *The Calumet Region and it's Early Settlers* (Chicago: Arrow Printers, 1935), 26-27. Hein Ruurd Douma and his wife Lijsbert Dirks Vis left the village of Minnertsga on June 5, 1903. They took their children Dirk, Fokje, Marten, and Ruurd with them. Hein Douma was registered as a field hand before he left. Shortly after arrival in Chicago, Lijsbert died of anemia. See also Galema, "Frisians to America, 1880-1914. Computer Compilation."

**130** D. Zandstra, "The Calumet Region; Toward Success," *Origins* 4 (1986) 2: 48-54; also A. Vandenbosch, *The Dutch Communities of Chicago* (Chicago: the Knickerbocker Society of Chicago, 1927), 75-77.

**131** Galema, "Frisians in the USA, 1900/1910. Computer Compilation." Housewives and children younger than 15 are excluded from the workforce.

**132** This pattern was also shown for German laborers in Chicago around the turn of the century. See H. Keil and J.B. Jentz, ed., *German Workers in Industrial Chicago, 1850-1910; A Comparative Perspective* (Dekalb, IL: Northern Illinois University Press, 1983), 134-38.

**133** A. Galema, "Over de wereldzee naar de grote stad. Pieter Ypes Groustra met zijn gezin in Chicago rond de eeuwwisseling," *De Nederlandsche Leeuw. Maandblad van het Koninklijk Nederlandsch Genootschap voor Geslacht- en Wapenkunde* 109 (October-November, 1992): 450-58.

**134** Letter of F.H. Toering from Roseland, IL, December 11, 1881, to Friesland. I am indebted to Luky van der Wal in Hindeloopen, who provided me with some of the correspondence of the Toering family.

**135** For a report about Pullman from a contemporary Dutch visitor see R.D. Nauta, "Een bezoek bij Pullman," *Vragen van den dag* 9 (1894): 550-57. R.P. Swierenga's great grandfather Anne Lolle Hoekstra and Lolle's brothers and their sons worked for Pullman and lived in company housing in the 1890s.

**136** "Fiftieth Anniversary Roseland Mutual Aid Society, 1884-1934." Brochure of the fiftieth anniversary by the board of directors. Calvin College Archives, Grand Rapids, MI.

**137** R.P. Swierenga, "Dutch Social Clubs in Chicago." Paper presented to the Association for the Advancement of Dutch-American Studies Conference, Orange City, IO, October 26-28, 1995.

**138** Vanderstel, *Dutch of Grand Rapids*, 539.

**139** That many people in Grand Rapids worked in the furniture industry and lived with other relatives in the same neighborhood is clear from the letter collection of the Renzema family. Durk Harmens Renzema (1823-1911) and his wife Klaaske Jacobs Wiersma (1829-1899) left the village of Sexbierum in 1876 with six children and a mother. Three more children came later. All the letters are addressed to their son Simon Durks Renzema and his wife Jacoba Dirks Lautenbach in Berlikum, Friesland. The collection runs from 1884-1911 and Durk Renzema of Dokkum graciously provided copies.

**140** Letter of Antje Lautenbach-Herrema from Grand Rapids to Tzummarum, Friesland, October 1, 1901. Antje was married with Jan Lautenbach and emigrated to Grand Rapids on April 27, 1881. Jan's sister Maartje also left April 24, 1889 with her husband Tjerk Zondervan and settled in Paterson. I am indebted to Jacob Lautenbach from IJlst who provided me with this correspondence.

**141** Letter of Age Boukes Cnossen from Grand Rapids to Paterson, September 28, 1896. Age Cnossen was born in Hommerts May 3, 1859 and married in 1884 Grietje Herres Andringa. Age Cnossen was a buyer and also had a café in Hommerts before he left for America. See archive *Familievereniging "C(K)NOSSEN."*

**142** *Cnossen-Knossen, geschiedenis van een Friese familie.* See archive *Familievereniging "C(K)NOSSEN."*

**143** Vanderstel, *Dutch of Grand Rapids*, 247-306.

**144** D.G. Vanderstel, "Dutch Immigrant Neighborhoods in the City of Grand Rapids 1848-1900," *Origins* 2 (1984) 1: 22-27.

**145** Ibid., 24.

**146** Letter of Jan Scheffer, Grand Rapids, to the *Nieuwsblad van Friesland*, April 1, 1914.

**147** Letter of Eelkje Dirks Algra from Grand Rapids to her family in Suawoude, Friesland (around 1910). Eelkje Algra (born May 19, 1854 in Rinsumageest) married Sijmen Fokkes Fokkema in 1893 and left with twelve children and a son in law to Grand Rapids in 1893. Some of her correspondence has been preserved and given to me thanks to Bouwe D. van der Meulen in Drachten.

# Notes – 7

**1** J.N. Kane, *The American Counties; Origins of County Names, Dates of Creation and Organization, Area, Population Including 1980 Census Figures, Historical Data, and Published Sources* (Metuchen, NJ and London: The Scarecrow Press, 1983).
**2** *History of Columbia County, Wisconsin,* 2 vols. (Chicago: Western Historical Co., 1880), 2: 723. For population statistics of Wisconsin see *History of La Crosse County, Wisconsin* (Chicago: Western Historical Co., 1881), 250.
**3** J.E. Jones, *A History of Columbia County, Wisconsin* (Chicago & New York: The Lewis Publishing Company, 1914), 127.
**4** *History of La Crosse County,* 259.
**5** "John R. Roesler's Correspondence on Nationality Groups, 1885-1890;" Wisconsin Manuscript Collection, State Historical Society of Wisconsin, Madison, WI.
**6** Y. Schreuder, *Dutch Catholic Immigrant Settlement in Wisconsin, 1850-1905* (New York & London: Garland Publishing, 1989), 65-69; H.A.V.M. van Stekelenburg, *Landverhuizing als regionaal verschijnsel. Van Noord-Brabant naar Noord-Amerika 1820̃1880* (Tilburg: Stichting Zuidelijk Historisch Contact, 1991), 82-110; H.S. Lucas, *Netherlanders in America* (Ann Arbor: University of Michigan Press, 1955; reprint ed., Grand Rapids, MI: W.B. Eerdmans, 1989), 196-201. About the Dutch in Milwaukee see also G. van Steenwijk, "Milwaukee," *De Recensent, algemeen letterkundig maandschrift* (1851): 1-16; H.S. Lucas, "Reminiscenses of Arend Jan Brusse on Early Dutch Settlement in Milwaukee," *Wisconsin Magazine of*

*History* 30 (September 1946): 85-90.
**7** J. van Hinte, *Nederlanders in Amerika. Een studie over landverhuizers en volksplanters in de 19e en 20ste eeuw in de Vereenigde Staten van Amerika,* 2 vols. (Groningen: P. Noordhoff, 1928), 2: 92-93.
**8** *The Story of Father Van den Broek, O.P.; A Study of Holland and the Story of the Early Settlement of Wisconsin* (Chicago: Ainsworth & Company, 1907).
**9** Van Stekelenburg, *Landverhuizing,* 110.
**10** Lucas and Van Hinte both refer in detail to the Alto settlement in Fond du Lac County. Also E.J. Bruins, "The Dutch-Immigrant Congregations of Alto, Wisconsin 1845-1900," *Origins* 7 (1989) 1: 23-33.
**11** For Oepke Bonnema see chapter 3.1.
**12** Letter of John Siderius from New Amsterdam, Wisconsin to J.J. Hoogland in St. Annaparochie, Friesland, March 22, 1883. "Collectie Hoogland," Rijksarchief Leeuwarden.
**13** B.F. Bryant, *Memoirs of La Crosse County* (Madison: Western Historical Association, 1907), 181-85, 227-31.
**14** For the Dutch in Sheboygan County see besides Van Hinte and Lucas, S.F. Rederus, "The Dutch Settlements of Sheboygan County," *Wisconsin Magazine of History* 1 (March 1918): 256-65; R.J. De Smith, "Jacobus DeRooy; Rural Wisconsin Diarist and Preacher," *Origins* 2 (1984) 2: 27-36; H. Harmeling, "History of Amsterdam and Cedar Grove," and P. Daane "Sketch of Cedar Grove and Oostburg," in *Dutch Immigrant Memoirs and Related Writings,* ed. H.S. Lucas, 2 vols.

(Assen: Van Gorcum, 1955), 2 :110-28; W. Wilterdink, *Winterswijkse pioniers in Amerika* (Winterswijk: 'Het Museum', 1990); G.H. Ligterink, *De Landverhuizers. Emigratie naar Noord-Amerika uit het Gelders-Westfaalse grensgebied tussen de jaren 1830-1850* (Zutphen: De Walburg Pers, 1981).
**15** F.S. Stone, *History of Racine County Wisconsin,* vol. 1 (Chicago: S.J. Clark Publishing Co., 1916), 17-18, 499-501; also letter of G. van Dijke from Racine, WI, to St. Jacobiparochie, Friesland, January 16, 1913. I am indebted to J.J. Buikstra for a copy of this letter.
**16** Teunis Tillema married Marie Jozina Kettelle who was born August 17, 1850, in Milwaukee. Teunis and his brother Meindert left in 1853, a year before his brother Tjisse and sister Tjitske left with their parents. Meindert started a farm in Iowa. See P.J. Schreiber, ed., *Centennial History of the Town of Randolph, Columbia County, 1849-1950* (n.p., 1950), 26-27; The family of Saape and Wopkje van der Velde-Dijkstra left at the same time from Blija and finally settled in Town Eight, Milwaukee. See C. Van der Velde, "Saape van der Velde-Wopkje Dijkstra Descendants," (n.p.), 1979. Manuscript, Herrick Public Library, Holland, MI). For more information on the VanderVelde family from Ee and Engwierum in La Crosse and Friesland, WI, see the genealogical record of Reinder, Pope, Jogchum, Geert, and Martinus Vandervelde [van der Velde]. I am indebted to R.H. Postma for copies of this record.
**17** For the history of the Dutch in

Wisconsin see also "J.H. Karsten "A Half Century of Dutch Settlement in Wisconsin 1847-1897," in *Dutch Immigrant Memoirs*, Lucas ed., 2 :129-39. Lucas makes the appropriate remark that Karsten fails to mention the Dutch Catholic settlements in the Fox River Valley, which were numerically larger than all other Dutch settlements in Wisconsin combined. See also H.J. Brinks, *Schrijf spoedig terug. Brieven van immigranten in Amerika 1847-1920* ('s-Gravenhage: Boekencentrum, 1978), 66-75.

**18** The total linked number of persons in the workforce was 40 in 1900 in Columbia County. Housewives and children younger than 15 are excluded from the workforce.

**19** Letter of S. van den Akker from Franksville, WI, to the *Nieuwsblad van Friesland*, September 11, 1909.

**20** Letters of S. van den Akker and J. Kooistra from Franksville, WI, to the *Nieuwsblad van Friesland*, September 11, 1909; also letter of Hendrik van der Wal from Onalaska, La Crosse County, WI, to Beetgumer-molen, Friesland, March 23, 1909. I am indebted to Andries Elsma in Beetgum for a copy of this letter.

**21** R.J. Fapso, *Norwegians in Wisconsin* (Madison: The State Historical Society, 1982), 29-30.

**22** A *pondemaat* is an old Frisian surface measurement and equals 36.75 *are* or 3,675 m2 [an acre equals 4,046 m2]. Letter from Doekele Dijkstra from Sioux Center, IA, to his cousins in Friesland, September 18, 1883. I am indebted to Klaas Oosterbaan and his sister Sjoukje de Jong-Oosterbaan for this information.

**23** J. Gjerde, *From Peasants to Farmers; The Migration from Balestrand, Norway, to the Upper Middle West* (Cambridge: Cambridge University Press, 1985), 171-75.

**24** This was similar to the Swiss. See F. Hale, *The Swiss of Wisconsin* (Madison: The State Historical Society of Wisconsin, 1984), 7-8.

**25** That this also was true for the Danish immigrants in Wisconsin is described in F. Hale, *Danes in Wisconsin* (Madison: The State

Historical Society of Wisconsin, 1981), 28.

**26** H. Bottema, "In het Amerikaansche Friesland," *Leeuwarder Courant*, August 8,9, 1928. Bottema's article is also published in Lucas, *Dutch Immigrant Memoirs*, 2: 139-44.

**27** J.B.E. Galema, "Linked files: Frisians to America and Frisians in the U.S.A., 1880-1914. Computer Compilation," (Groningen, 1995); In 1892 the *Dolerenden* (the Reformed people around Abraham Kuyper) merged with a part of the *Afgescheidenen* (Seperatists of 1834) and called themselves *Gereformeerde Kerken in Nederland* (Reformed Church in the Netherlands). Another part of the *Afgescheidenen* remained auto-nomous as *Christelijk Gereformeerden* (Christian Reformed).

**28** Letter of K. Jansma from Randolph, WI, to Hantumhuizen, Westdongeradeel, October 31, 1910. The person named Jacob probably is the brother in law of the addressee, Jan Sipma. I am indebted to Mrs. T. Sipma-Dijkstra for this information. The name of Randolph Center around 1910 was changed to Friesland because authorities demanded a different name for this place if the village wanted to apply for a post office. In 1915 the First Reformed Church of Randolph Center then changed its name to the First Reformed Church of Friesland, WI. Schreiber, *Centennial History of the Town of Randolph*, 36.

**29** The foundation of the First Reformed Church was laid in 1861 and 1863 when Tjisse and Teunis Tillema came to the Randolph area. The members met in the homes of these immigrants. Later on at stated times the Pastor of the Alto congregation, the Reverend J.H. Karsten, would come to serve them. See "75th Anniversary First Reformed Church, Friesland, Wisconsin 1893-1968," (Manuscript, Herrick Public Library, Holland, MI), 5-10.

**30** N. Schreiber, ed., *Randolph Centennial 1870-1970* (n.p.: Hutchinson, 1980), 42-47. This Church started out with approximately 15 Frisian families.

**31** Bottema, "In America's Friesland," in *Dutch Immigrant Memoirs*, 2: 142-43.

**32** Ibid., 140.

**33** Letter of John Siderius, 1883.

**34** *The Randolph Advance*, 1897 and 1898. The State Historical Society of Wisconsin, Madison.

**35** That newcomers from Friesland did not always bring blessings to the community is shown in a horrible event in the year 1900. In the early spring the Gerrit van der Hoek family had arrived from Jislum, Ferwerderadeel in Randolph, with their ill infant Aukje. They first stayed at the Peter D. Westra home, where the child soon died. Mary Tillema, Teunis' wife, went there to help. Soon thereafter the children of Peter Westra became ill and doctors were not able to diagnose the malady. Dannie Westra died in March, Hubert Tillema (son of Teunis and Mary) in April and his sisters Nina and Josie followed in May. Other children of the Westra family also died, making a total of eight victims. It was a real tragedy in the immigrant community. Later on it was believed that the disease was a very violent form of scarlet fever combined with diphteria. No one knows if this epidemic originated during the ocean voyage of the Van der Hoek family. But the tragedy caused despondent feelings for a long time. See Schreiber, *Centennial History of the Town of Randolph*, 29-30. Also J.B.E. Galema, "Frisians to America, 1880-1914. Computer Compilation," (Groningen, 1992).

**36** Pieter Tjeerds Burmania came from the village of Ternaard in Westdongeradeel in 1892 directly to Randolph with his wife Jitske Gerrits Kok and their son Tjeerd. The Cuperij family already had come to Wisconsin in 1881. Pieter emigrated from Westdongeradeel with his parents Klaas Harkes Cuperij and Martha Pieters Westra, his two sisters and one brother. See Galema, "Frisians to America, 1880-1914. Computer Compilation."

**37** Schreiber, *Centennial History of the Town of Randolph*, 64-79.

**38** For references concerning correspondence of the first Frisian

Pella settlers see Chapter 3.1. For a Frisian look on the Iowa frontier see the letter of 1848 of Sjoerd Aukes Sipma translated and edited by R.P. Swierenga, "A Dutch Immigrant's View of Frontier Iowa," *Annals of Iowa* 38 (Fall 1965): 81-120; For the history of Pella see besides H.S. Lucas and J. van Hinte: J. van der Zee, *The Hollanders of Iowa* (Iowa City: The State Historical Society, 1912); *Souvenir History of Pella, Iowa* (Pella: The Booster Press, 1922); *History of Pella, Iowa, 1847-1987*, 2 vols. (Dallas: Pella Historical Society, 1988-1989).

**39** The city was named after the royal house of the Netherlands, while the main street honored to King *Willem van Oranje*. Van Hinte, *Nederlanders in Amerika*, 1: 21.

**40** Tjeerd Heemstra was born November 8, 1824 at Marrum, Ferwerderadeel in Friesland. He married Sijke Hoekstra on March 19, 1846. The couple emigrated to Michigan in 1847. Heemstra died at Orange City, IA, April 13, 1901. See *The Centennial Book Orange City, Iowa, 1870-1970* (Orange City, IA: The Ad-Visor, 1970), 51.

**41** N.G. Nieuwenhuis, *Siouxland; A History of Sioux County, Iowa* (Orange City, IA: The Sioux County State Historical Society, 1983), 110; Van Hinte, *Nederlanders in Amerika*, 2: 35.

**42** Letters of Th.M. Oostenbrug from Hospers, IA, to Roodkerk near Leeuwarden, June 11 and December 18, 1882. Oostenbrug left in 1882 and from his first letter it appears that he had a farm in Friesland, which he sold before departure. I am indebted to F.J. Koning for this information.

**43** *The Centennial Book Orange City, Iowa*, 12-13; C.B. Kennedy, "The Sioux County Dutch," in *The Dutch in America*, ed. E.J. Bruins (Holland, MI: Hope College, 1984), 29-40; J.W. Warnshuis, "The History of Sioux County," (n.p., 1879, trans. by P. Vander Kooi. Manuscript, Calvin College Archives, Grand Rapids, MI). For figures see W.H. Bender, *Iowa* (New York, 1908), 44-51.

**44** J.B.E. Galema, "Frisians in the USA, 1900/1910. Computer Compilation," (Groningen, 1993).

**45** R.L. Doyle, *The Socio-Economic Mobility of the Dutch Immigrants to Pella, Iowa 1847-1925* (Ph.D. dissertation, Kent State University, 1982), 369-70; D.G. Vanderstel, *The Dutch of Grand Rapids, Michigan, 1848-1900; Immigrant Neighborhood and Community Development in a Nineteenth Century City* (Ann Arbor: University Microfilms International, 1986), 440-44; G.W. Kirk, Jr., *The Promise of American Life; Social Mobility in a Nineteenth-Century Immigrant Community, Holland, Michigan, 1847-1894* (Philadelphia: The American Philosophical Society, 1978), 89. A general article on occupational mobility of the Dutch which covers the period 1835-1880 is R.P. Swierenga, "Dutch International Migration and Occupational Change; A Structural Analysis of Multinational Linked Files," in I. Glazier and L. De Rosa, *Migration Across Time and Nations* (New York/London: Holmes & Meier, 1986), 95-124.

**46** For a contemporary immigrant information guide to Sioux County and vicinity see *Iowa. Het land voor emigranten* (Pella: Iowa commissie van emigratie, 1873).

**47** Letter of Jurjen Tjerks Dijkstra from Orange City, IA, to Arum, Wonseradeel November 1, 1889.

**48** Jacob van de Zee describes in 1912 that the Dutch farmers in Iowa, for example, destroyed weeds especially if they could exploit the labor of their large families. Van der Zee, *The Hollanders of Iowa*, 329-36. Also B.W. Beltman, "Ethnic Persistence and Change; The Experience of a Dutch-American Family in Rural Iowa," *The Annals of Iowa* 52 (Winter 1993): 1-49.

**49** Van der Zee, *Hollanders of Iowa*, 336.

**50** Klaas and Aaltje Pietens-Huisman with their son left Oudega in 1883 and traveled directly to Sioux County where they were met by Fokeltje (Aaltje's step-sister) and Berend de Jong who had come there the previous year. Both couples operated different farms in Sioux County. See "A Pietens Family Chronicle," (n.p., 1979; manuscript, Herrick Public Library, Holland, MI); *The Centennial*

*Book Orange City, Iowa*, 34-61; That many Frisians settled in the Sioux County area and that they were acquainted with each other is also clear from the letter collection of Jurjen Tjerks Dijkstra who's letters from Orange City and Middleburgh, Iowa to Arum in Wonseradeel from 1884 to 1905 have been preserved and offered thanks to R.J. Miedema.

**51** J. Mackintosh, "The Lure of Prosperity; Economic Development among Danish Immigrants to Iowa," in *On Distant Shores*, eds. B. Flemming Larsen, H. Bender, and K. Veien (Aalborg: Danes Worldwide Archives, 1993), 177-90. Frisian immigrants also worked as farm laborers for a few years, before investing in a farm. See letter of J.W. Bijker in *Nieuw Advertentieblad*, February 22, 1893.

**52** Doyle, *The Socio-Economic Mobility of the Dutch Immigrants to Pella*, 391.

**53** In 1889 the territory was divided into the states of North and South Dakota.

**54** Nieuwenhuis, *History of Sioux County*, 114; Van Hinte, *Nederlanders in Amerika*, 2: 17.

**55** Van der Zee, *Hollanders of Sioux County*, 379; N.G. Nieuwenhuis, "A History of Dutch Settlements in South Dakota to 1900," (Masters thesis, University of South Dakota, Vermillian, 1948), 20-23; E. Van der Laan, "South Dakota," *Origins* 5 (1987) 1: 32-37; H. Vander Pol, *On the Reservation Border; Hollanders in Douglas and Charles Mix Counties* (Stickney, SD: Argus Printers, 1969), 90-132.

**56** Letter of Hendrik D. Dijkstra from Springfield, SD, to the *Nieuwsblad van Friesland*, February 5, 1910.

**57** Nieuwenhuis, "A History of Dutch Settlements in South Dakota," 18. Nieuwenhuis does not mention his source for the amount of Frisians in Bon Homme County. In a letter in the *Nieuw Advertentieblad* of August 31, 1898, Albert Kuipers writes that 'many Frisians' live in Bon Homme County and he mentions the farmers Folkert van Gespen, Harmen Visser [from Langweer] and Jan Woudsma [from Weststellingwerf].

**58** Data derived from Galema, "Linked Files: Frisians to America and Frisians in the USA. Computer Compilation."

**59** G.J. de Jong wrote about his experience as a farm laborer in Bon Homme County to Friesland after he had been gone for 2.5 years. See letter of G.J. de Jong from Springfield, SD to the *Nieuwsblad van Friesland*, August 5, 1911.

**60** Letter of T.G. de Vries from Runnningwater, SD, to the *Bergumer Courant*, July 7, 1906.

**61** For the details on A. Kuipers' medals and other prizes I am indebted to Otto de Vent, who informed me orally and by written communication. De Vent is working on a publication focusing on Albert Kuipers and his impact for migratory patterns in the *Stellingwerven*. Lucas' opinion that Kuipers' son Hendrik investigated areas in the USA in 1880, appears to be wrong, according to De Vent. This must be 1881, which I found confirmed in Vander Pol's, *On the Reservation Border*, 295.

**62** The first advertisement showing A. Kuipers' connection as an agent for the Prins & Zwanenburg firm appeared in the *Steenwijker Courant*, December 27, 1880.

**63** See letter of A. Kuipers to the *Nieuw Advertentieblad*, July 19, 1899. An advertisement of the auction can be found in the *Nieuw Advertentieblad*, July 6, 1881. Albert Kuipers initially was against emigration because he thought it was possible to make economic progress in Friesland as well. He thought of *landverhuizers* as mainly people "who refused to work and who were good for nothing." (See account of his lecture in *Bolswardsche Courant*, March 25, 1897). Kuipers became interested when the agrarian crisis hit (he himself mentions 1878), and he also once pronounced the idea that emigration was not necessary if "the capitalists wanted to invest their money in the development of wastelands, that are still in huge quantities available in our country." (see "De landverhuizing naar Noord-Amerika," *Handelsblad*, February 18, 1882). See also Vander Pol, *On the Reservation Border*, 293-96; G.F. DeJong, *The Dutch in America,*

*1609-1974* (Boston: Twayne Publishers, 1975), 155-59.

**64** An article with encouraging words in favor of settlement in the Dakotas can be found in the *Franeker Courant*, February 16, 1882. Arguments against the Dakotas as destination are ventilated by Reverend J.W. Warnshuis who served in Sioux County at that time. His writings were published in the *Franeker Courant*, February 26, 1882 and in the *Nieuw Advertentieblad*, May 13, 1882. He warned against settlement in uninhabited lands, without other countrymen in the surroundings and with no provision and facilities. In the *Provinciale Groninger Courant* the Dakotas and Kuipers were discussed September 8 and 11, 1882 and March 6, 16, 22, 23, 28, and 30, 1883. See also *Nieuw Advertentieblad*, January 7, 11, 18, March 15, 18, April 5, 1882, February 21, 1894.

**65** This was Kuipers' personal story. The truth was that he left Friesland secretly to avoid committal to prison because of his debts. A wanted notice had even appeared in the newspaper. Information on Kuipers, the number of emigrants, and the Hornstra family is from Otto de Vent. The Hornstras originally came from West-Stellingwerf. Kuipers Sr. corresponded with this family in the 1870s to gather information concerning the Dakotas. A son of Hornstra later became the brother in law of Kuipers Jr. For the number of people who left with Kuipers Jr. see also one of Kuipers' lectures of 1897 in the *Enkhuizer Courant*, August 10, 1897.

**66** Letter of A. Kuipers of January 13, 1897 in the *Nieuw Advertentieblad*, January 15, 1897. For an overview of Kuipers' lectures see his letter in the *Nieuw Advertentieblad*, July 24, 1897, entitled "My Lectures." Kuipers was able to return to Friesland only after he had paid a debt in the old country of 7000 guilders. For Kuipers' promotional letters see also the *Nieuw Advertentieblad*, April 4, 11, 18, 1888, March 3, May 10, 1893, April 25, 1894, June 25, 1898; *Nieuwsblad van Friesland*, April 18, 1888; an example of Kuipers' promotional letters in the Dutch language press in

America is found in *De Volksvriend*, March 18, 1884. Information concerning the number of lectures Kuipers gave in 1897 I obtained from Otto de Vent, who also published an example of Kuipers' practices in "Johannes Nieuwenhuis, laandverhuzer van Steggerde," *De Ovend* (May 1994): 15-17; also K. Berkenbosch, "Laandverhuzen is drama," *De Ovend* (May 1994): 12-14.

**67** Letter of A. Kuipers to the *Nieuw Advertentieblad*, October 5, 1895.

**68** The emphasis on land opportunities in the Dakotas can be found in a letter of Petrus van der Wal from Castalia, Charles Mix County, who left Friesland in October 1892. See *Nieuw Advertentieblad*, March 1, 1893.

**69** Lucas, *Netherlanders in America*, 383; also H.J. Brinks, "The Vanden Hoeks in Harrison 1884-1895," *Origins* 5 (1987) 1: 38-41.

**70** Letter of Albert Kuipers to the *Nieuw Advertentieblad*, June 12, 1895.

**71** Letter from Age Boukes Cnossen from Grand Rapids to Petrus Harings Nauta and Pietje Ages Cnossen in Friesland, January 6, 1897, *Archief Familievereniging "C(K)NOSSEN."* Jan Woudsma, in a letter from Wanari, SD, in the *Nieuw Advertentieblad*, June 21, 1893, warned against Kuipers' optimism. He concluded that many farmers had trouble surviving.

**72** Letter of W.F. Meerwalt from Harrison, SD, to *De Volksvriend*, March 18, 1884. H.S. Lucas mentions that the editor of *De Grondwet* reported that in 1890 he received letters from readers who wanted to make a statement against the negative reports concerning the Dakotas. See Lucas, *Netherlanders in America*, 384.

**73** Letter from R.J. Feenstra from Hurley, SD, to the *Nieuw Advertentieblad*, March 24, 1900.

**74** B.W. Beltman, *A Dutch-American Immigrant in the Rural Midwest; The Life and Letters of Ulbe Eringa, 1866-1950* (Urbana & Chicago: University of Illinois Press, forthcoming).

**75** Letter from the widow K. Siderius from Ashton, SD, to the widow J.J. Hoogland in Het Bildt, March 27,

1889. "Collectie Hoogland," Rijks-archief Leeuwarden.

**76** *Minnesota, "The Bread and Butter State" of the Union, to the Pan-American Exposition Visitors* (n.p., July 1901), 8-12.

**77** Van Hinte, *Nederlanders in Amerika,* 1: 177-80; Lucas, *Netherlanders in America,* 362.

**78** J.H. Kloos, *Minnesota, (Vereenigde Staten van Noord-Amerika) in zijn hulp-bronnen, vruchtbaarheid en ontwikkeling geschetst voor landverhuizers en kapitalisten* (Amsterdam: H. de Hoogh, 1867).

**79** Lucas, *Netherlanders in America,* 364; For the Catholic immigrants from Limburg see A.F.M. Koeweiden-Wijdeven, "Vergeten emigranten. Landverhuizing van noord- en midden-Limburg naar Noord-Amerika in de jaren 1847-1877," (M.A., Venlo, May 1982); and A.F.M. Koeweiden-Wijdeven, "Vergeten emigranten," *Spiegel Historiael* 3 (March 1984): 120-24, 154.

**80** R. Schoone-Jongen, "Cheap Land and Community; Theodore F. Koch, Dutch Colonizer," *Minnesota History* 53 (Summer 1993): 214-24; Lucas, *Netherlanders in America,* 366-67.

**81** N.G. Nieuwenhuis, "Orange City and the Western Movement," in *Proceedings of The Association for the Advancement of Dutch American Studies Conference,* " (Orange City, September 1985), 26; G. Schnücker, *Die Ostfriesen in Amerika. Eine illustrierte Geschichte ihrer Kolonien bis zur Gegenwart* (Cleveland, OH: Central Publishing House, 1917), 260-66; Trans. K. De Wall, *The East Friesens in America; An Illustrated History of their Colonies to the Present Time,* (Topeka, KS: Jostens Printing and Publishing, 1986).

**82** Letter of E. Veenhoven, Pine City, MN, to J. Gosliga in Iowa of January 26, 1894, published in the *Nieuw Advertentieblad,* March 17, 1894.

**83** *Beschrijving en inlichtingen over de nieuwe Hollandsche kolonie Prinsburg in Renville, Kandiyohi, en Chippewa counties, Minnesota* (Chicago: Fergus Printing Co., n.d.), 18-24; also F. Curtiss-Wedge, *The History of Renville County, Minnesota,* 2 vols. (Chicago: H.C. Cooper, 1916), 2: 761-836.

**84** Galema, "Frisians in the USA, 1900/1910. Computer Compilation."

**85** This shortness of cash was not typical for the Frisian immigrants, but was for most of the new Dutch settlers who came in the last quarter of the 19th century. See R. Schoone-Jongen, "Cheap Land and Community," 214; R. Morgan ed., *Progress and Pride go Hand in Hand; Platte's 75th Anniversary 1900-1975* (n.p., 1975), 10.

**86** Lucas, *Netherlanders in America,* 373-74.

**87** Letter of Siebe de Boer, Hinckley, Pine County, MN, to the *Nieuwsblad van Friesland,* March 17, 1909.

**88** Letter of E. Veenhoven, Pine City, MN, to J. Gosliga in IL, published in the *Nieuw Advertentieblad,* March 17, 1894.

**89** Schoone-Jongen, "Cheap Land and Community," 221.

**90** Ibid., 222-23.

**91** "G.W. Rensker's History of Settlement in Campbell County." Netherlands Museum, Special Files, Holland, MI.

**92** Ibid., 3.

**93** Lucas, *Netherlanders in America,* 382-83.

**94** Brinks, "The Vanden Hoeks in Harrison," 38.

**95** J.D. Bratt, *Dutch Calvinism in Modern America; A History of a Conservative Subculture* (Grand Rapids, MI: W.B. Eerdmands, 1984), 3-13.

**96** In the counties researched in Minnesota a similar pattern appeared: 69 percent were *Nederlands Hervormd,* 3 percent *Gereformeerd,* 14 percent *Christelijk Gereformeerd,* 10 percent was not associated with any denomination and 4 percent had joined with the *Vrijzinnige Gemeente* in the old country.

**97** The comparable figures for the Netherlands in 1899 were: *Nederlands Hervormd:* 48.6 percent; *Gereformeerd:* 7.1 percent; *Christelijk Gereformeerd:* 1.1 percent; *Baptist:* 1.1 percent; *None:* 2.3 percent. H. Knippenberg, *De religieuze kaart van Nederland. Omvang en geografische spreiding van de godsdienstige gezindten vanaf de Reformatie tot heden* (Assen: Van Gorcum, 1992), 97, 231.

**98** Beltman, *A Dutch-American Immigrant,* chapter 3, 17.

**99** Morgan, *Progress and Pride go Hand in Hand,* 13-16; *100 Years of God with us; Emmanuel Reformed Church, Springfield, South Dakota, 1888-1988* (Freeman, SD: Pine Hill Press, 1988), 10-11.

**100** K. Huisman, *It libben fan Gerrit Roorda/opskrean troch Kerst Huisman* (Bûtenpost: Alternatyf, 1973), 28-40.

**101** For a discussion concerning northwest Iowa in the Dutch language newspapers *De Hollander, De Grondwet, Pella's Weekblad, De Hope, and De Wachter* (these last two religious oriented) see Lucas, *Netherlanders in America,* 346-51.

**102** Nieuwenhuis, *Sioux Land,* 114; A. Galema, "'Forjit my net'. Friese emigratie naar de Verenigde Staten aan het eind van de negentiende eeuw," *Groniek* 96 (1986): 96.

**103** Letter of Dora Eringa from Runningwater, SD, November 15, 1910 to Friesland, published in Beltman, *Dutch-American Immigrant,* (forthcoming), chapter 5, 13.

**104** Ibid., chapter 5, 12.

**105** T.C. Blegen, *Minnesota; A History of the State* (St.Paul: University of Minnesota, 1975), 307-13.

**106** Schnücker, *Die Ostfriesen in Amerika,* 267-69; Van Hinte, *Nederlanders in Amerika,* 2: 117-23.

**107** Van Hinte, *Nederlanders,* 2: 114-15.

**108** J.W. Schulte Nordholt, *De mythe van het Westen. Amerika als het laatste wereldrijk* (Amsterdam: Meulenhoff, 1992).

**109** M.B. LaDow, "Chinook, Montana, and the Myth of Progressive Adaptation," *Montana* 39 (Autumn 1989): 10.

**110** For reflections on Montana's history and attractiveness see R.W. Rydell, "Montana; Big Sky Country," *Amerika,* Winter 1993, 6-13; E.J. Bell, *Homesteading in Montana; Life in the Blue Mountain Country* (Bozeman: Big Sky Books, 1975).

**111** R. Kroes, *Nederlandse pioniers in het Amerikaanse Westen. De geschiedenis van Amsterdam* (Amsterdam: De Bataafsche Leeuw, 1989); A revised edition in English was published as R. Kroes, *The Persistence of Ethnicity; Dutch Calvinist Pioneers in Amsterdam, Montana* (Urbana and Chicago: University of Illinois Press, 1992), i.

112 Kroes, *The Persistence of Ethnicity*, 42; R. Kroes, "Amsterdam, Montana; In America, Not Of It? A Fractured History of Ethnic Continuity," in *The Dutch in North-America; Their Immigration and Cultural Continuity*, ed. R. Kroes and H-O. Neuschäfer, (Amsterdam: VU University Press, 1991), 219-39.

113 R. Kroes, "Windmills in Montana; Dutch Settlement in the Gallatin Valley," *Montana* 39 (1989): 42; R. Kroes, "There're Dutch in them thar Hills! Ethnicity in the Mountain West," in *The American West as Seen by Europeans and Americans*, ed. R. Kroes (Amsterdam: VU University Press, 1989), 166-82; *Manhattan, Montana; From its Beginning in the 1860's, through the Present 1986* (Dallas, TX: Taylor Publishing Company, 1986), 4; M. Schuurmans, "The Church and Assimilation in an Isolated Nationality Group" (M.A. thesis, Michigan State College of Agriculture, 1941), 7; *A Goodly Heritage; A History of the Churchill and Amsterdam Area of Montana* (Bozeman: Churchill-Amsterdam Historical Society, 1989), 69-86.

114 Letter of Johannes Koning, Belgrade, MT, to Stiens in Friesland, October 23, 1905. Johannes Koning left Friesland in 1894. I am indebted to Tine van Eck-Brolsma for donation of some of Koning's letters.

115 These economic practices are also confirmed by accounts of the lectures of Albert Kuipers in 1897, for example, in the *Bolswardsche Courant*, March 25, 1897, and in the *Telegraaf*, March 31, 1897.

116 Letter of P.L. van Dijken, Manhattan, MT, to the Netherlands, April 21, 1894. Letter of Klaas Schuiling, Manhattan, MT, n.d., "Collectie Hoogland," Rijksarchief Leeuwarden.

117 Kroes, *The Persistence of Ethnicity*, 51-61. On the mid-nineteenth century schism among Dutch Protestant immigrants in the Mid-West see R.P. Swierenga, "Local-Cosmopolitan Theory and Immigrant Religion; the Social Basis of the Antebellum Dutch Reformed Schism," *Journal of Social History* 14 (Fall 1980): 113-36.

118 Letter of Mrs. K. Siderius from Ashton, Spink County, Dakotas to Mrs. J.J. Hoogland in St. Anna-parochie March 27, 1889. "Collectie Hoogland," Rijksarchief Leeuwarden.

119 Letters of Albert Kuipers from South Dakota to the *Nieuw Advertentieblad*, November 27, 1895, and February 5, 1896.

120 Data derived from the *Decennial Reports of the United States Bureau of the Census*.

121 Commisionners for the *Noord-Amerikaansche Hypotheekbank* were Jhr. Mr. J.M. van Beyma, major of Engwirden, B. van Haersma Buma, director of the *Dordtsche Bank* in The Hague, Cor. Visser, First Class Member of the National Organisation of Accountants in Leeuwarden, Mr. E.H.Ph. Boschloo, member of the firm *Boschloo & Pothaar* in Heerenveen, Jhr. O.B. van Vierssen Trip, Member of the firm *Mrs. Van Vierssen Trip & Feith* in Groningen, K.J. Rienks, landlord in Tzummarum and J.H. Heep, insurer in Leeuwarden. See brochure *Noord-Amerikaansche Hypotheekbank* (n.p., n.d.), Personal Archive Author, thanks to a donation of J. Meinema, Groningen.

122 Lucas, *Netherlanders in America*, 415; also J.C.J. Kempees, "De Nederlandsche hypotheekbanken in de Vereenigde Staten van Noord-Amerika en in Canada," *De Economist* (October-December 1919): 655-695.

123 Kempees, "Nederlandsche hypotheekbanken," *De Economist* (October-December, 1919): 760-62.

124 Letter of Thijs Bakker from Oak Harbor, WA to the *Franeker Courant*, February 2, 1897. I am indebted to Mr. Veltman for this information. Bakker originally came from Sexbierum and left Friesland in 1892.

125 Letter from Age Boukes Cnossen, Grand Rapids, MI, April 12, 1896, to Petrus Harings Nauta and Pietje Ages Cnossen, Jutrijp, Friesland; *Archief Familievereniging "C(K)NOSSEN"*.

126 In 1889 the Union Pacific Railroad Company, for example, published *The Resources and Attractions of Washington for the Home Seeker, Capitalist, and Tourist* (Chicago: Rand McNally & Co, 1889). This guide gives information on climate, soil,

farming, stock raising, dairying, fruit growing, lumbering, mining, scenery, game, and fish. The Bureau of Statistics and Immigration of the State of Washington published *A Review of the Resources and Industries of Washington* (Olympia, WA: E.L. Boardman, 1909), and the *Homeseekers' Guide to the State of Washington* (Olympia, WA: F.M. Lamborn, 1914). Both brochures give descriptions and statistics on natural sources, industries and agriculture in the different counties of Washington.

127 Some Dutchmen had daily experience in digging up tree stumps. Onno Heller who arrived in 1890 in Holland, MI, with his wife Klaaske Noorda, practised stump digging in Michigan for a couple of years, before moving to Oak Harbor in the mid- nineties. See letters of Onno Heller and Klaaske Noorda from Holland, MI, and Oak Harbor, WA, 1890-1900; Calvin College Archives, Grand Rapids, MI.

128 Lucas, *Netherlanders in America*, 420.

129 *De Volksvriend*, June 6, 1895.

130 Letter of Riekele Zijlstra, July 20, 1895, from Oak Harbor, WA, *De Volksvriend*, December 24, 1896.

131 Letter of H. Hulst from Whidbey Island, August 2, 1897, *De Volksvriend*, August 19, 1897

132 *De Volksvriend*, May 14, 1896; H. Beets, *De Christelijk Gereformeerd Kerk in Noord-Amerika* (Grand Rapids, 1918), cited in Van Hinte, *Nederlanders in Amerika*, 2: 247-48.

133 For data on northern Frisians see Galema "Frisians in the U.S.A. 1900/1910. Computer Compilation." For data of other Frisians on Whidbey Island see United States Bureau of the Census, 13th Census (1910), Roll T624-1656, Vol. VIII-Island County, WA; National Archives Washington DC; the idea that the West was mostly settled by people who had been longer in America is also revealed by J.C.J. Kempees, "De Nederlandsche hypotheekbanken," 765.

134 Van Hinte, *Nederlanders in Amerika*, 2: 249-50.

135 Lucas, *Netherlanders in America*, 421.

136 Letters of John Buwalda from North Yakima, WA to Jochum B. Kingma in Schettens, Friesland,

March 13, 1897 and February 11, 1899. I am indebted to J. Meinema for this information.

**137** Van Hinte, *Nederlanders in Amerika*, 2: 245-50.

**138** Information derived from Galema, "Frisians in the USA, 1900/1910. Computer Compilation." The names of these Frisians are written the way they are included in the 1910-Census.

**139** D.J. Zijlstra, born in Drachten, Friesland in 1859 emigrated to Friesland, SD, around 1880. In 1889 he was elected County Commissioner of Charles Mix County, SD. In 1895 after a severe drought, he moved to Whidbey Island, WA, and from there to Lynden, WA, because his wife Dieuwerke Dijksterhuis objected to living on an island. D. Koert, *Portrait of Lynden* (Lynden: Lynden Tribune, 1976), 61-64.

**140** A. Brink, "Lynden-A Home Far Away From Home", in *Proceedings of the Association of Dutch American Study Conference* (Orange City, IA, 1985), 89-90; L.R. Roth, *History of Whatcom County*, 2 vols. (Chicago: Pioneer Historical Publishing Company, 1926), 1: 838-53; Lucas, *Netherlanders in America*, 423-24.

**141** It also happened that there was recruitment for new settlers to Dutch settlements in Canada. In Yorkton, MB, efforts were made to attract Dutch settlers from communities in the United States. See J.Th.J. Krijff, *"100 Years Ago"; Dutch Immigration to Manitoba in 1893* (Windsor, ON: Electa Press, 1993), 92-93.

**142** Galema, "Frisians in the USA, 1900/1910. Computer Compilation;" L.R. Roth, *History of Whatcom County*, 2: 331.

**143** Galema, "Frisians in the USA 1900/1910. Computer Compilation."

**144**. Koert, *Portrait of Lynden*, 61; Brink, "Lynden," 91-95.

**145** B.L. Anderson, *The Scandinavian and Dutch Rural Settlements in the Stillaguamish and Nooksack Valleys of Western Washington* (Ann Arbor: University Microfilms International, 1957), 169-73.

**146** Data from the decennial reports of the United States Bureau of the Census.

**147** Galema, "Frisians in the USA, 1900/1910. Computer Compilation."

**148** D.L. Nicandri, *Italians in Washington State; Emigration 1853-1924* (n.p.: The Washington State American Revolution Bicentennial Commission, 1978), 25-28.

**149** *Homeseekers' Guide to the State of Washington*, 18.

# Notes – 8

**1** Sj. de Zee, *Myn twadde Amerika-reis* (Heerenveen: Handelsdrukkerij Hepkema, 1929), 7.
**2** H.M. Enzensberger, *De grote trek* (Amsterdam: De Volkskrant, 1992), 14.
**3** R. Kroes, *The Persistence of Ethnicity; Dutch Calvinist Pioneers in Amsterdam, Montana* (Urbana and Chicago: University of Illinois Press, 1992), 122-34, 153.
**4** Ideas about the "other" and the "self" were earlier formulated in an essay in: A. Galema, ed., W. Grams, and A. Holtmann, *Van de ene en de andere kant. Noordnederlandse en Noord-westduitse migratie naar de Verenigde Staten in de negentiende eeuw/ Nordniederländische und Nordwest-deutsche Auswanderung nach Amerika im 19. Jahrhundert* (Groningen: Universiteitsmuseum/Oldenburg: Stadtmuseum, 1993), 98-107.
**5** W. Sollors, ed., *The Invention of Ethnicity* (New York and Oxford: Oxford University Press, 1989), xiv, xvi.
**6** K. Neils Conzen et al., "The Invention of Ethnicity; A Perspective from the U.S.A.," *Journal of American Ethnic History* 12 (Fall 1992) 1: 4-5.
**7** Neils Conzen et al, "The Invention of Ethnicity," 31-32.
**8** V. Yans-McLaughlin, *Family and Community; Italian Immigrants in Buffalo, 1880-1930* (Ithaca: Cornell University Press, 1977), 260; J.E. Bodnar, *The Transplanted; A History of Immigrants in Urban America* (Bloomington: Indiana University Press, 1985), 57-84; G.E. Pozzetta ed., *Immigrant Family Patterns; Demography, Fertility, Housing, Kinship, and Urban Life* (New York: Garland Publishing,

1991); R.J. Vecoli, "The Formation of Chicago's 'Little Italies'" in *Migrations Across Time and Nations*, eds. I. Glazier and L. De Rosa (New York: Holmes & Meier, 1986), 287-301.
**9** S.M. Sinke, *Home is Where You Build it; Dutch Immigrant Women in the United States, 1880-1920* (Ph. D. dissertation University of Minnesota, 1993, Ann Arbor: University Micro-films International, 1993), 78-79.
**10** Sinke, *Home is Where You Build it*, 128.
**11** B.J. Fridsma, *Nea ferbrutsen bân. 60 jier Fryske aksje yn Amearika* (Ljouwert: De Tille, 1991), 20-24.
**12** B.W. Beltman, *A Dutch-American Immigrant in the Rural Midwest; The Life and Letters of Ulbe Eringa, 1866-1950* (Urbana & Chicago: University of Illinois Press, forthcoming), 1-28.
**13** For example the letter collections of the P. Groustra-Aukes family, Rijksarchief Leeuwarden; the Ulbe Eringa-Rijpstra collection, Calvin College Archives, Grand Rapids, MI; and the Klaas Schuiling-De Jong family, "Collectie Hoogland," Rijksarchief Leeuwarden, show this commitment to family bonds clearly.
**14** Letter of Leendert Visser from Grand Rapids, MI, March 1912, to the *Nieuwsblad van Friesland*, April 6, 1912.
**15** De Zee, *Myn twadde Amerika-reis*, 211-12.
**16** M. Huygen, "Amerika zoekt weer naar het gezinsverband," *NRC-Handels-blad*, January 17, 1994.
**17** A. Lammers, *Helden van het geloof. Amerika in de greep van de dominees* (Amsterdam: Balans, 1988), 7; J.W. Schulte Nordholt, "Geloven in Amerika," *Amerika*, Spring 1994, 79.

**18** R.T. Kuiper, *A Voice from America about America*, trans. E.R. Post (Grand Rapids, MI: W.B. Eerdmans, 1970), 92; On R.T. Kuiper see also H. Krabbendam, "R.T. Kuiper; Developer of Churches," *Origins* 12 (1994) 1: 9-16.
**19** Letter of Durk Harmens Renzema and his wife Klaaske Jacobs Wiersma from Grand Rapids, MI, to Berlikum, Friesland November 9, 1888. The spelling was used by Renzema. I am indebted to
D. Renzema for copies.
**20** Kroes, *The Persistence of Ethnicity*, 99-121; F. Stoffels, "'s Heren wegen in de USA," *VU Magazine*, September 8, 1985, 301-06; As early as 1929 A. Eekhof concluded that the internal struggle of the Calvinist emigrants finally lead to group cohesiveness. See A. Eekhof, "De Nederlandsche kolonisatie in Noord-Amerika," *Haagsch Maandblad* 3 (March 1929): 230. A similar argument is made for the Germans in D. Peterson, "'From Bone Depth'; German-American Communities in Rural Minnesota Before the Great War," *Journal of American Ethnic History* 11 (Winter 1992): 27-55.
**21** An important study of the Dutch immigrant church with detailed descriptions of theological issues is J.D. Bratt, *Dutch Calvinism in Modern America; A History of a Conservative Subculture* (Grand Rapids, MI: W.B. Eerdmans, 1984); R.P. Swierenga attempts to explain the mid-nine-teenth century religious conflict among Dutch Protestant immigrants in the Midwest by using comparative statistical analysis of Old and New

World religious behavior in "Local-Cosmopolitan Theory and Immigrant Religion; the Social Bases of the Antebellum Dutch Reformed Schism," *Journal of Social History* 14 (Fall 1980): 113-36.

**22** Sinke, *Home is Where You Build it*, 256.

**23** *100 Years of God With Us; Emmanuel Reformed Church, Springfield, South Dakota 1888-1988* (Freeman, SD: Pine Hill Press, 1988), vii-viii.

**24** J. van Hinte, *Nederlanders in Amerika. Een studie over landverhuizers en volksplanters in de 19e en 20ste eeuw in de Vereenigde Staten van Amerika*, 2 vols. (Groningen: P. Noordhoff, 1928), 2: 112-15.

**25** H.J. Brinks, "Germans in the Christian Reformed Church, 1857-1872," *Origins* 9 (1991) 2: 36-43.

**26** "Remarks on Christian Reformed, East Frisian Rheiderland Township, Minnesota," *Frisian News Items* (June 1981): 26; G. Schnücker, *Die Ostfriesen in Amerika. Eine illustrierte Geschichte ihrer Kolonien bis zur Gegenwart* (Cleveland, OH: Central Publishing House, 1917), 260-69; J. Hoogstraat, *Von Ostfriesland nach Amerika* (Norden: Soltau-Kurier, 1990), 123-38.

**27** An important chapter about the role of the immigrant church is to be found in Bodnar, *The Transplanted*, 144-68. On religion of the Dutch see R.P. Swierenga, "Religion and Immigration Behavior; The Dutch Experience," in *Belief and Behavior*, eds. Ph.R. Vandermeer and R.P. Swierenga (New Brunswick: Rutgers University Press, 1991), 166 ff.

**28** B.S. Hylkema, "Op reis nei Amerika," *Sljucht en Rjucht* 25 (1923): 302.

**29** *Emmanuel Reformed Church, Springfield, South Dakota*, 7.

**30** Letter of Johannes Koning, born at Stiens in 1878 and emigrated to America in 1894, of July 1904 to the city of Groningen. I am indebted for copies to T. van Eck-Brolsma in Ede.

**31** Kl.J. Tiemersma, *Drie jaren in Amerika* (Leeuwarden: Eisma, 1894), 17-18. The point that non-religious Frisians did associate with the church after migration is also emphasized by B.S. Hylkema who made a trip to

America and wrote about it in *Sljucht and Rjucht*, 25 (1923): 301-03.

**32** David Zandstra makes this point for the vegetable farmers in the Calumet Region close to Chicago, where numerous Frisians had settled in the first two decades of the twentieth century. D. Zandstra, "The Calumet Region; A Land Flowing with Milk and Honey," *Origins* 4 (1986) 1: 16-21.

**33** Letter of P. van Steinvoorn and E.R. Leegsma from Orange City, IA, to Friesland, December 16, 1893. I am indebted to J.A. Postema for copies.

**34** A. Brink, "Lynden," *Origins*, 4 (1986) 2: 33; the same article can be found in *Proceedings of the Association for the Advancement of Dutch American Studies Conference* (Orange City, IA, 1985), 89-98.

**35** H. Beets, "Our Friesian Settlement in Whitinsville, Mass.," *The Banner* (October 1, 1926); J. Jansen, "Een verblijf in Amerika," *Vragen van den Dag* 35 (August 1920): 629-31; W. Van Gorp-Vander Baan, "The History of the Dutch People in Whitinsville," (Whitinsville, manuscript written at the request of the Northbridge Bicentennial Celebration Committee, 1972): manuscript donated by the author. Personal Collection Author.

**36** For southern Dutch Catholic immigrants and their ethnicity see Y. Schreuder, *Dutch Catholic Immigrant Settlement in Wisconsin, 1850-1905* (New York & London: Garland Publishing, 1989), 132-35; H.A.V.M. van Stekelenburg, *Landverhuizing als regionaal verschijnsel. Van Noord-Brabant naar Noord-Amerika 1820-1880* (Tilburg: Stichting Zuidelijk Historisch Contact, 1991), 220-25.

**37** Letter of Frederica Groustra-Aukes from Roseland to Ee, October 22, 1888. Rijksarchief Leeuwarden.

**38** Sinke, "Home is Where You Build it."

**39** M. Blaschke and C. Harzig, eds., *Frauen wandern aus. Deutsche Migrantinnen im 19. und 20. Jahrhundert* (Bremen: Universität Bremen, 1990).

**40** *De toestand van de arbeiders in Friesland. Uitslag van het onderzoek ingesteld door het Friesch Comité van de*

*Volkspartij*, [1890], vol. 1: Vrouwen en kinderarbeid.

**41** Letter from Jochum Brouwer from Ee, to Douwe Jans Douma in Galesburg, IA, February 15, 1881. Calvin College Archives, Grand Rapids, MI.

**42** Van Hinte, *Nederlanders in Amerika*, 1: 113.

**43** Letter of Minne Zonneveld of June 10, 1893, from Hull, IA, to Friesland in *Nieuw Advertieblad*, June 21, 1893.

**44** Y. Poortinga, "Bildtske emigranten yn 'e foarige ieu," *Estrikken* 30 (1960), 67-70.

**45** Studies have shown similar conditions for women from other nationalities. Norwegian immigrant women in the rural Upper Middle West in 1900 appeared to be monolingual twice as often than Norwegian men. J. Gjerde, *From Peasants to Farmers; The Migration from Balestrand, Norway, to the Upper Middle West* (Cambridge: Cambridge University Press, 1985), 227.

**46** For example, A. Sevenster, *Het bevolkings- en emigratievraagstuk in Nederland en in den Nederlandschen landbouw* (Ph.D. dissertation, Wageningen, 1930), 112.

**47** Galema, "Frisians to America, 1880-1914. Computer Compilation."

**48** K. Huisman, "De dramatyske libbensein fan emigrante Anna," *Leeuwarder Courant*, February 26, 1994. Also Galema, "Frisians to America, 1880-1914. Computer Compilation."

**49** Letter of Maaike Rijpstra and Ulbe Eringa from Runningwater, SD, to Friesland, April 11, 1894. Calvin College Archives, Grand Rapids, MI.

**50** C. de Groot, *When I was a Girl in Holland* (Boston: Northrop, Lee & Sheppard, 1917; reprint ed., Arnhem: Bakker, 1991). Cornelia de Groot's story is also told in A. Galema, "Um eines bequemeren Lebens willen in die Neue Welt? Auswanderung friesischer Frauen in die Vereinigten Staaten um 1900," in *Hoffnung Amerika. Europäische Auswanderung in die Neue Welt*, ed. K. Schulz (Bremerhaven: NWD-Verlag, 1994), 137-150.

**51** De Groot, *When I was a Girl in*

Holland, 179-80. Two other autobiographies of Frisian immigrant writers are David Cornel De Jong, *With a Dutch Accent. How a Hollander Became an American* (New York and London, 1944); and Henry Kay Pasma, *Close-Hauled* (New York, 1930). De Jong was born in Blija in 1901 and Pasma in 1881 in Oosterbierum. A comparison of their experiences can be found in P. Stokvis, "Drie emigranten over het leven in Friesland rond 1900," *It Beaken* 3 (1984): 153-63.

**52** *San Francisco Chronicle*, February 10, 1929.

**53** Ibid.

**54** De Zee, *Myn twadde Amerika-reis*, 214.

**55** J. Jansen, "Een verblijf in Amerika," 626.

**56** C. de Groot, "Nine Farmerettes. They Prove Woman is not Weak," [1906? Magazine unknown]. Published in *When I was a Girl in Holland*, reprint ed., Supplement, 11.

**57** The American Census reported whether persons were able to read and write in any language and to speak English. No illiteracy was found among the Frisian immigrants. See J.B.E. Galema, "Frisians in the USA, 1900/1910. Computer Compilation," (Groningen, 1993).

**58** R.P. Swierenga, "The Dutch," in *Harvard Encyclopedia of American Ethnic Groups*, ed. S. Thernstrom (Cambridge, MA, and London: Harvard University Press, 1980), 293.

**59** *Nieuwsblad van Friesland*, January 5, 1910.

**60.** Bodnar, *The Transplanted*, 189-91.

**61** Interview with Arnold Banning, Whitinsville, March 11, 1991. Arnold Banning's brother got a Ph.D. in theology, and his sister one in sociology.

**62** Letter of Doekele Dijkstra from Chicago, June 1900, to Kimswerd in Friesland. One curious detail in this letter is that the writer is talking about *two* languages, which means the English and the Dutch. The Frisian language was not considered a language for official use.

**63** John E. Zucchi in his study about Italians in Toronto convincingly makes clear that worship was one of the contributing factors in preserving a national identity. By joining an ethnic parish, immigrants became more aware of their Italian national background. See J.E. Zucchi, *Italians in Toronto; Development of a National Identity, 1875-1935* (Kingston & Montreal: McGill-Queen's University Press, 1988), 118-40.

**64** Letter of Mrs. K. Siderius from Ashton, Spink County, Dakotas, March 27, 1889 to Mrs. J.J. Hoogland in St. Annaparochie. "Hoogland Collectie," Rijksarchief Leeuwarden.

**65** Letter of John Peter Buwalda from North Yakima, WA, to Friesland, January 20, 1909.

**66** Letter of A. Brouwer from Harvey, IL, to her brother in Haskerdijken in Friesland, March 25, 1907. I am indebted to W. Veenbaas in Dedemsvaart for this letter.

**67** This corpus comprised a considerable number of tapes, recorded in a number of Dutch immigrant communities, among them Whitinsville, which were originally meant to document the history of the Dutch language, its dialects, and the Frisian language. Tapes were created by Jo Daan and Henk Heikens and are archived at the P.J. Meertens Instituut in Amsterdam. See "Dutch Immigrant Language Collection," composed by Jo Daan and Henk Heikens. Also T. Anema, T. de Graaf, and H.F. Schatz, "The Frisian Language in America," *Nowele* 12 (May 1988): 91-108.

**68** In this sense there is much similarity among the *Friezen om utens* [Frisians abroad] in the Netherlands. A study concerning the use of the Frisian language in provinces outside of Friesland concludes that Frisians abroad even with a good motivation for retaining the language, in the long run (in the second and third generation) had to give up speaking Frisian. See L.G. Jansma and G.H. Jelsma, "Friezen om utens. Migraasje en taalbehâld by de Fryske Kriten en studinteferienings," *It Beaken* 3 (1993): 116.

**69** J. Daan, "Trouw aan het Fries in de U.S.A.," in *Flecht op 'e koai: Stúdzjes oanbean oan Prof.Dr.W.J. Buma ta syn sechstichste jierdei*, ed. by T. Hoekema

et al., (Groningen: Wolters-Noordhoff, 1970), 177-181. Also "Dutch Immigrant Language Collection," P.J. Meertensinstituut," tape 1107.

**70** J. Daan, *Ik was te bissie. Nederlanders en hun taal in de Verenigde Staten* (Zutphen: De Walburg Pers, 1987), 82-83. For the use of the Dutch language in Iowa see P.E. Webber, *Pella Dutch; The Portrait of a Language and Its Use in One of Iowa's Ethnic Communities* (Ames, IA: Iowa State University Press, 1988). For the immigrant's literary expressions see W. Lagerwey, *Neen Nederland, 'k vergeet u niet. Een beeld van het immigranten-leven in Amerika tussen 1846 en 1945 in verhalen, schetsen en gedichten* (Baarn: Bosch & Keuning, 1982).

**71** De Zee, *Myn twadde Amerika-reis*, 94.

**72** Ibid., 123-24. Preaching in Frisian took place for the first time in 1935, and between 1957 and 1981 there were 25 years of continuity of Frisian sermons in the Christian Reformed Church of Grand Rapids. See B.J. Fridsma, *Nea ferbrutsen bân. 60 jier Fryske aksje yn Amearika*, 102-03, 351-52.

**73** Bodnar, *The Transplanted*, 184.

**74** I found reports of Frisian ballgames (*keatsen*) in Indianapolis in the *Franeker Courant*, August 9, 1897; August 26 1899.

**75** Fridsma, *Nea ferbrutsen bân*, 37-38. In his autobiography Fridsma characterizes his criticism as "under the influence of *Jongfrysk* thought." This was a nationalist movement promoting the use of the oral and written Frisian language. See, for example, G.R. Zondergeld, *De Friese beweging in het tijdvak der beide wereldoorlogen* (Leeuwarden: De Tille, 1978), 31-37; 51-94.

**76** Information about the game of *keatsen*, and especially the language of *keatsen*, is to be found in P. Breuker, *Keatserstaal* (Groningen: Frysk Ynstitut, University of Groningen, 1983). Sources concerning the *keats* society in Paterson are in the *KNKB-Archief* in Franeker. For the Frisian societies see also the account of De Zee, *Myn twadde Amerika-reis*.

**77** See the research on voting among the Pella Dutch in the 1840s and 1850s in R.P. Swierenga, "The Ethnic

Voter and the First Lincoln Election," *Civil War History* 11 (1965): 27-43.
**78** Bodnar, *The Transplanted*, 108-09, 197; D. Baines, *Emigration from Europe 1815-1930* (London: Macmillan, 1991), 67.
**79** R.P. Swierenga, "The Dutch," in *Harvard*, 293-94; P.R.D. Stokvis, "Dutch-Speaking Peoples," in *The Immigrant Labor Press in North America, 1840s-1970s*, ed. D. Hoerder (New York, Westport, London: Greenwood Press, 1987), 268-69.
**80** J. Frieswijk, "The Labour Movement in Friesland, 1880-1918," *Tijdschrift voor sociale geschiedenis* 18 (1992): 376-77.
**81** Van Hinte, *Nederlanders in Amerika*, 2: 467.
**82** Stokvis, "Dutch-Speaking Peoples," 269; R. Kuiper, *Zelfbeeld en wereldbeeld. Antirevolutionairen en het buitenland, 1848-1905* (Kampen: Kok, 1992), 156. For a song of the Christian labor unions see Lagerwey, *Neen Nederland, 'k vergeet u niet*, 87-88.
**83** A. Kuyper, *Calvinism; Six Stone-Lectures* (Amsterdam and Pretoria: Höveker & Wormser, 1898), 116.
**84** *Patrimonium*, March 18, 1893, quoted in T. van der Wal, *Op zoek naar een nieuwe vrijheid. Een kwart eeuw arbeidersbeweging in Friesland 1870-1895* (Leiden: Universitaire Pers, 1972), 359.
**85** H. Keil, "Socialist Immigrants from Germany and the Transfer of Socialist Ideology and Workers' Culture," in *A Century of European Migrations, 1830-1930*, eds. R.J. Vecoli and S.M. Sinke (Urbana & Chicago: University of Illinois Press, 1991), 322.

**86** Van der Wal, *Op zoek naar een nieuwe vrijheid*, 272; J. Frieswijk, "De beweging Broedertrouw op Het Bildt (1889-1892)," in *Jaarboek voor de geschiedenis van socialisme en arbeidersbeweging in Nederland* (Nijmegen: Socialistische Uitgeverij, 1978), 120; H. Sannes, *Geschiedenis van Het Bildt* 3 vols. (Franeker: Wever, 1956), 3B: 388.
**87** J. Frieswijk, "Een socialisties propagandist in revolutionaire jaren. Biografie van Tjeerd Stienstra (1859-1935)," *Tijdschrift voor Sociale Geschiedenis* 6 (October 1976): 248-51. I was not able to find one of these activists listed on the I.W.W. [International Workers of the World] membership lists of those days.
**88** *Recht voor Allen*, March 21-22, 1891.
89. Keil, "Socialist Immigrants from Germany," 323.
**90** *Nieuw Advertentieblad*, July 8, 1893; *Nieuwsblad van Friesland*, August 27, 1911; K.J. Tiemersma, *Drie jaren in Amerika*, 74, 111-12.
**91** Letter of Albert Roorda from Sioux City, IA, to a village near Leeuwarden, March 11, 1908. I am indebted to F. Roorda in Oosterwolde for copies of this letter.
**92** Letter of Gerrit van Dijk from Racine, WI, to A. Buikstra in St. Jacobiparochie in Het Bildt in Friesland, January 16, 1913. I am indebted to J.J. Buikstra in Roden for a copy of this letter.
**93** K. Huisman, *It libben fan Gerrit Roorda/opskrean troch Kerst Huisman* (Bûtenpost: Alternatyf, 1973), 13.
**94** Roorda's story by K. Huisman was also summarized by P.R.D. Stokvis,

"Socialistische immigranten in de Verenigde Staten. Vrijheid versus gelijkheid," *Groniek* 96 (1986): 113. See Huisman, *It libben fan Gerrit Roorda*, 1-123.
**95** R. Vecoli, "New Guidelines and Research Hypotheses for the History of European Emigration," in *Studi sull'emigrazione. Un'analisi comparata*, ed. M.R. Ostuni (Biella, 1989), 53.
**96** The pen name S.A.S. must have been the pseudonym of S.A. Schilstra. For Schilstra's writings to inform potential Frisian emigrants see, for instance, *Nieuwsblad van Friesland*, December 16, 1908; January 13, 1909; April 10, 1909; May 5, 1909; November 11, 1909; January 5, 1910; November 5, 1910; December 21, 1910; December 25, 1910; January 1, 1911; January 28, 1911; March 3, 1911; March 15, 1911; May 13, 1911; August 5, 1911; October 28, 1911; November 4, 1911; March 30, 1912; April 6, 1912; June 14, 1913; April 1, 1914; Schilstra, mostly writing from Preston, Maryland and Perkasie, Bucks County, Pensylvania, debated the pros and cons of the USA with Cornelis Beeling and J.P. Leffertstra. Also letter of Age Boukes Cnossen from Grand Rapids to his aunt and uncle Petrus Harings Nauta and Pietje Ages Cnossen in Jutrijp, Friesland, March 15, 1894; March 11, 1900; Cnossen tells that he voted for the Democrats and refuted the idea that Democrats were socialists. *Archief Familievereniging "C(K)NOSSEN."*
**97** Keil, "Socialist Immigrants from Germany," 331.

# Bibliography

## I. Archival Sources

For the period 1880-1914 the following newspapers and periodicals have been used:
*De Hollander* (Allegan and Holland, MI)
*De Grondwet* (Holland, MI)
*Pella's Weekblad* (Pella, IA)
*De Hope* (Holland, MI)
*De Wachter* (Grand Rapids, MI)
*De Volksvriend* (Orange City, IA)
*San Francisco Chronicle* (San Francisco, CA)
*Provinciale Groninger Courant* (Groningen)
*Nieuw Advertentieblad* (Heerenveen)
*Nieuwsblad van Friesland* (Heerenveen and Leeuwarden)
*Bergumer Courant* (Bergum)
*Weekblad voor het Kanton Bergum* (Bergum)
*Franeker Courant* (Franeker)

– Allershof, E. *Landhuishoudkundige beschrijving van de kantons Bergum en Beetsterzwaag in de provincie Friesland.* Haarlem: n.p., 1881.
– "The Anne Bandstra Story, 1899." Translated by Mrs. Henry DeVries. Manuscript, Calvin College Archives, Grand Rapids, MI.
– "75th Anniversary First Reformed Church, Friesland, Wisconsin 1893-1968." Manuscript, Herrick Public Library, Holland, MI.
– *Archief Familievereniging "C(K)NOSSEN.* "Sneek, private collection.
– "Archives of G. Taphorn." Niedersächsische Auswanderer in den USA, Carl von Ossietzky University of Oldenburg, Germany.
– "Autobiography of Henry P. Kroes." Translated by H. Kroes. Calvin College Archives, Grand Rapids, MI.
– Baker, C., and Baker, G. Whitinsville, MA. Interview, March 13, 1991.
– Baker, E.; Baker, J.; and Wassenar, H. Whitinsville, MA. Interview, March 11, 1991.
– Baker, E. "The Maynard J. Krulls Immigrated to America in 1896." Manuscript, Personal Collection Author.
– Banning, A, and Banning, M. Whitinsville, MA. Interview, March 11, 1991.

– *Beknopte Inlichtingen voor Hollandsche emigranten.* Paterson: De Telegraaf, 1915. Calvin College Archives, Grand Rapids, MI.
– Bell, S. "A Paterson Dyer's Story." *Solidarity*, May 3, 1913.
– Bender, W.H. *Iowa.* New York, 1908.
– *Beschrijving en inlichtingen over de nieuwe Hollandsche kolonie Prinsburg in Renville, Kandiyohi, en Chippewa counties, Minnesota.* Chicago: Fergus Printing Co., n.d.
– Beucker Andreae, J.H. "Rapport ingediend voor het vijfde landhuishoudkundig congres te Leiden, 11, 12, 13 Junij 1850, betreffende een onderzoek naar den zedelijken en materiëlen toestand der arbeidende bevolking ten platten lande en van middelen om dien zoveel mogelijk te verbeteren." *Tijdschrift voor Staathuishoudkunde en Statistiek* 6 (1851): 159-61.
– *Bijdragen tot de statistiek van Nederland. Uitkomsten der achtste tienjaarlijksche volkstelling (1899).* Vol. 7, province of Friesland. 's-Gravenhage: Belinfante, 1901.
– *Bolswardsche Courant*, Lecture Albert Kuipers, March 25, 1897.
– *Brief van Sjoerd Aukes Sipma aan de ingezetenen van Bornwerd in Westdongeradeel, uit wier midden hij in het voorjaar van 1847 als landverhuizer is vertrokken naar Pella, in de Vereenigde Staten van Noord-Amerika, voorzien met ophelderende aanmerkingen door N.N.* Dockum: B. Schaafsma, [1848].
– Brougham, R. *A Cruise on Friesland "Broads".* London: Ward and Downey, 1891.
– Bruinsma, J.J., and Hengel, J.F. van. *Bijdragen geneeskundige plaatsbeschrijving van Friesland.* 3 vols. 's-Gravenhage: Departement van Binnenlandsche Zaken. (1870-1875): 7-172.
– Bruinsma, V. "Hoe is Friesland te helpen?." *Vragen des Tijds* 1 (1894): 343-91.
– Bruinsma, V. "De vermindering der bevolking in Friesland." *Vragen des Tijds* 2 (1894): 117-44.
– Bruinsma, V. "De Friesche gemeenten en het wetsontwerp betreffende gemeentefinanciën." *Vragen des Tijds* 2 (1897):
– Bryant, B.F. *Memoirs of La Crosse County.* Madison: Western Historical Association, 1907.
– Bureau of Statistics and Immigration of the State of Washington. *A Review of the Resources and Industries of*

*Washington.* Olympia, WA: E.L. Boardman, 1909.

– Bureau of Statistics and Immigration of the State of Washington. *Homeseekers' Guide to the State of Washington.* Olympia, WA: F.M. Lamborn, 1914.

– "Collectie Holland Amerika Lijn." Gemeente Archief Rotterdam. -"Collectie Hoogland." Rijksarchief Leeuwarden.

– *Decennial Reports of the United States Bureau of the Census.* 1900 and 1910.

– *Denver Republican,* December 18, 1892.

– *Derde deel van de uitkomsten der negende tienjaarlijkse Volkstelling.* 's-Gravenhage: 1911.

– Dijk, J. van. "Zes maanden in Amerika." 2 vols. (1881). Manuscript, Calvin College Archives, Grand Rapids, MI.

– *Dienstbodenregister.* Separate population register for servants. Municipality of Wonseradeel, 1880-1914.

– "Dutch Immigrant Language Collection." Composed by J. Daan, and H. Heikens. Amsterdam: P.J. Meertensinstituut, 1966.

– "Dutch Immigration to Laage Prairie." Manuscript, Herrick Publick Library, Holland, MI.

– *Dutch Population Registers.* Municipalities of Wonseradeel, Barradeel, Het Bildt, Ferwerderadeel, Oost- and Westdongeradeel, 1880-1914.

– *Eene belangrijke brief uit Noord-Amerika, door J.A. van der Meer, voormalig logementhouder op de drie Romers, te Roordahuizum.* Leeuwarden: D. Meindersma, [1848].

– *Enkhuizer Courant,* August 10, 1897.

– "Fiftieth Anniversary, October 20, 1946, Christian Reformed Church, Whitinsville, Mass. 1896-1946." Manuscript, Calvin College Archives, Grand Rapids, MI.

– "Fiftieth Anniversary Roseland Mutual Aid Society, 1884-1934." Brochure of the fiftieth anniversary by the board of directors. Calvin College Archives, Grand Rapids, MI.

– *Franeker Courant,* June 28 and July 29, 1900.

– *Het Friesch Volksblad,* October 5, 1890.

– Gerritsen, C.V., and Jacobs, A.H. *Brieven uit en over Amerika.* Amsterdam: F. van Rossen, 1906.

– Glashouwer, P. "Een terugblik." Translated by S. de Haan. Calvin College Archives, Grand Rapids, MI.

– *Golden Jubilee of Utspanning troch Ynspanning Paterson, New Jersey.* June 13, 1943. *KNKB-Archief,* De Trije, Franeker.

– Gorter, D.S. *De Christelijke lijdzaamheid aangeprezen bij het vertrek der Oud-Doopsgezinden van Balk die om vrijheid van krijgsdienst naar Noord-Amerika verhuisden.* Sneek, 1853.

– Gorter, D.S. *Godsdienstige lectuur voor Doopsgezinden.* Sneek, 1854.

– "G.W. Renker's History of Settlement in Campbell County." Special Files. Netherlands Museum, Holland, MI.

– Haagsma, B.B. *Frysia, of schets der Friesche volkplanting in Noord-Amerika, benevens raadgevingen en wenken voor landverhuizers, zijnde een vervolg op het werkje getiteld: O.*

*Bonnema en zijne togtgenooten.* Bolsward: P.M. Feenstra, 1855.

– Haagsma, B.B. *Lotgevallen van den heer O.H. Bonnema en zijne togtgenooten, op reis uit Friesland naar de Vereenigde Staten van Noord-Amerika.* Harlingen: Houtsma, 1853.

– Heide, M. van der. "Vijftig jaar in Canada en de Ver. Staten." Manuscript, translated by J. Hoekstra. Wester-Nijkerk, 1964. Personal Collection Author.

– Helmus, C. "De lânforhûzers ût de Dokkumer-Wâlden." *Friesch Nieuws en Advertentieblad,* June 5, 1889.

– "Historical Sketch Fairlawn Christian Reformed Church Whitinsville, Mass." Manuscript, Calvin College Archives, Grand Rapids, MI.

– *History of Columbia County, Wisconsin.* 2 vols. Chicago: Western Historical Co., 1880.

– *History of La Crosse County, Wisconsin.* Chicago: Western Historical Co., 1881.

– *History of Worcester County, Massachusetts; Embracing a Comprehensive History of the County from its First Settlement to the Present Time, with a History and Description of its Cities and Towns.* 2 vols. Boston: Jewett and Company, 1879.

– *Immigrant Letter Collection.* Calvin College Archives, Grand Rapids, MI.

– *Immigrant Letter Collection.* Personal Collection Author.

– "Informatie voor ontginners van de landerijen langs den Noordelijken Pacific Spoorweg." Collection immigrant letters P.Y. Groustra 1881-1941. Rijksarchief Leeuwarden.

– *Iowa. Het land voor emigranten.* Pella: Iowa commissie van emigratie, 1873.

– Jenks, J.W., and Lauck, W.J. *The Immigration Problem.* New York and London: Funk & Wagnals Co., 1917. First published in 1912.

– John, [Jan de Jong]. *Eenige jaren in Amerika. Van Gaasterland naar Indiana en Californië.* Heerenveen, [1888].

– "John R. Roesler's Correspondence on Nationality Groups, 1885-1890." Wisconsin Manuscript Collection, State Historical Society of Wisconsin, Madison, WI.

– Jones, J.E. *A History of Columbia County, Wisconsin.* Chicago & New York: The Lewis Publishing Company, 1914.

– Kamp, H.T. "Account of the Trip of the Kamp Family, Emigrating from Almelo, Province of Overijsel, Netherlands, June 18 to July 5, 1904." Translated by G. Kamp. Manuscript, Calvin College Archives, Grand Rapids, MI.

– Kloos, J.H. *Minnesota, (Vereenigde Staten van Noord-Amerika) in zijn hulpbronnen, vruchtbaarheid en ontwikkeling geschetst voor landhuizers en kapitalisten.* Amsterdam: H. de Hoogh, 1867.

– *KNKB-Archief.* De Trije, Franeker.

– Kuyper, A. *Calvinism; Six Stone-Lectures.* Amsterdam and Pretoria: Höveker & Wormser, 1898.

– Kuyper, J. "Nederlands bevolking." *Tijdschrift van het Nederl. Aardrijkskundig Genootschap* 2 (1885): 240-54.

– "De landverhuizing naar Noord-Amerika." *Handelsblad*, February 18, 1882.

– Leep, E.K. "The Leep Family in North America; History and Genealogy." N.d., n.p. Manuscript, Calvin College Archives, Grand Rapids, MI.

– "Letter Collection Tjerk Zondervan and Maartje Lautenbach." Private collection of J. Lautenbach, IJlst, Friesland.

– "Letter Collection P.Y. Groustra, 1881-1941." Rijksarchief Leeuwarden.

– Mansholt, D.R. *Mijne zelfverdediging*. St. Annaparochie: Kuiken, 1892.

– "Mededeelingen en verslagen van de visscherijinspectie, 1915."

– "Mellema Papers." Calvin College Archives, Grand Rapids, MI.

– Meulen, A.G. van der. *Eene brief uit Pella van A.G. van der Meulen, uit Bergum naar Noord-Amerika vertrokken den 9 mei 1849*. Bergum: T.G. van der Meulen, 1849.

– Meulen, T.G. van der. *Ny Frysk lieteboek*. Heerenveen: A.L. Land, 1886.

– Meulen, T.G. van der. *Nei Roaselân*. Heerenveen: J. Hepkema, 1888.

– Meulen, T.G. van der. "Wie veel geld wil verdienen worde werver." *Weekblad voor het Kanton Bergum*, February 25, 1882.

– *Minnesota, "The Bread and Butter State" of the Union, to the Pan-American Exposition Visitors*. N.p., July 1901.

– *Naar Amerika. Inlichtingen over de expeditie Prins & Zwanenburg, per Koninklijke Nederlandsche Stoomboot-Maatschappij, directe lijn Amsterdam-New York*. Groningen: B. Jacobs, 1882.

– Nauta, R.D. "Een bezoek bij Pullman." *Vragen van den dag* 9 (1894): 550-57.

– *Noord-Amerikaansche Hypotheekbank*. N.p, n.d. Brochure, Personal Collection Author.

– *Het Noorden*, March 15, 1881.

– *Het Oosten*, February 1, 1923; July 18, 1929.

– Obreen, J.A. *Opwekking tot landverhuizing naar de republiek der Vereenigde Staten van Noord-Amerika*. Leiden: A.W. Sijthoff, 1871.

– Osinga, S. *Dagboek mijner reize naar Noord-Amerika's Vereenigde Staten in den jare 1847 gedaan*. Franeker: T. Telenga, 1848.

– *Paterson City Directories*. 1900-1908. Public Library, Paterson, NJ.

– *Patrimonium*, March 18, 1893.

– Pelmulder, J.J. *Eenvoudige maar zeer belangrijke brieven uit Noord-Amerika*. Dockum: A. Schaafsma, 1859.

– "A Pietens Family Chronicle." N.p., 1979. Manuscript, Herrick Public Library, Holland, MI.

– "The Pleasant Street Christian Reformed Church of Whitinsville, Massachusetts; 75th Anniversary 1896-1971." Manuscript, Calvin College Archives, Grand Rapids, MI.

– Posthumus, R. *Farwol! Taroppen oon myn broer in stalke W. van Peima, bij syn fortjean, mei bern in bernsbern in ore goede kunde, nei Amerika*. Leeuwarden: 1849.

– Potgieter, E.J. "Landverhuizing naar de Vereenigde Staten. Een brief uit Pella, door den Salamagundist." *De Gids* 19 (1855) 1: 465-530.

– *The Randolph Advance*, 1897 and 1898. Wisconsin State Historical Society, Madison.

– Rauwerda, A. *Armenzorg en gemeentegrondbezit*. St. Annaparochie: Kuiken, 1892.

– Rauwerda, A. "Misstanden bij den veldarbeid in Friesland." *Vragen des Tijds* 2 (1892): 67-96.

– Ravenstein, E.G. "The Laws of Migration." *Journal of the Royal Statistical Society* 52 (June 1889): 241-301.

– *Recht voor Allen*, "Brieven uit Amerika." June 14, 1889. March 21-22, 1891.

– Reijne, K. "Ontvolking van het platteland." *Vragen des Tijds* 2 (1902): 205-18.

– Reijne, K. "De uittocht der plattelandsbevolking." *Studies in Volkskracht* 1 (1904): 533-82.

– "Renzema family. Letter collection, 1884-1911." Personal Collection Author.

– *Report on Condition of Women and Child Wage-Earners in the United States*. Vol. 4, "The Silk Industry." Washington, DC, 1911.

– *Roorda Family History*. Des Moines, IA, n.d.

– Shriner, C.A. *Paterson, New Jersey*. Paterson: The Press Printing and Publishing Company, 1890.

– Sickenga, J. *Frieslands gemeentelijke toestanden in woorden en cijfers*. N.p., 1891.

– Sipma, S.A. *Belangrijke berigten uit Pella, in de Vereenigde Staten van Noord-Amerika of Tweede brief van Sjoerd Aukes Sipma: van daar geschreven aan de ingezetenen van Bornwerd, waarin hij vele bijzonderheden, betreffende de Hollandsche Vereeniging in den staat Iowa, de levenswijze en de gewoonten der Amerikanen, benevens vele nuttige wenken voor hen, die naar de Vereenigde Staten willen verhuizen, voorkomen. Voorzien met eenige aanmerkingen door N.N*. Dockum: B. Schaafsma, 1849.

– "South Holland, Illinois; 75th Anniversary, 1894-1969." Manuscript, Herrick Publick Library, Holland, MI.

– *Staat der landverhuizingen naar Noord-Amerika en andere overzeesche gewesten*. Rijksarchief Leeuwarden.

– *Staatsblad van het Koninkrijk der Nederlanden*. (No. 81) "Besluit van den 28. December 1837, houdende nadere bepalingen omtrent den doortogt van landverhuizende personen." (No. 53) "Wet van den 1sten Junij 1861, houdende bepalingen omtrent den doortogt en het vervoer van landverhuizers."

– Stap, J. A. "Het ontstaan en de werking der vereeniging 'Broedertrouw' te St. Jacobi-Parochie." *Het Friesch Volksblad*, October 5, 1890 to March 1, 1891.

– *Statistiek van den loop der bevolking in Nederland, 1881-1915*. Wageningen: Landbouwuniversiteit.

– Steenwijk, G. van. "Milwaukee." *De recensent, algemeen letterkundig maandschrift* (1851): 1-16.

– *De Steenwijker Courant*, December 27, 1880.

– Stigt, K. van. *Geschiedenis van Pella, Iowa en omgeving*. Pella: Weekblad Print Shop, 1897.

– *The Story of Father Van den Broek, O.P.; A Study of Holland and the Story of the Early Settlement of Wisconsin*. Chicago:

Ainsworth & Company, 1907.

– Sytstra, O.H. *Blom-lêzing út 'e gedichten fen H.S. Sytstra.* Ljouwert: R. van der Velde, 1894.

– Tiemersma, Kl.J. *Drie jaren in Amerika.* Leeuwarden: Eisma, 1894.

– *Tiental brieven betrekkelijk de reis, aankomst en vestiging naar en in Noord-Amerika, van eenige landverhuizers vertrokken uit de grietenijen Het Bildt en Barradeel in Vriesland.* Franeker: T. Telenga, 1848.

– *De toestand van de arbeiders in Friesland. Uitslag van het onderzoek ingesteld door het Friesch Comité van de Volkspartij.* Vol. 1: "Vrouwen en kinderarbeid." N.p., [1890].

– Troelstra, P.J. *Rispinge. Alde en nije fersen fen Pieter Jelles.* Den Haag: De Atlas, 1909.

– *Uitkomsten der beroepstelling in het Koninkrijk der Nederlanden gehouden op den 31sten december 1899* 12 vols. 's-Gravenhage: Belinfante, 1902.

– *Uitkomsten der beroepstelling in het Koninkrijk der Nederlanden gehouden op den 31sten december 1909.* 's-Gravenhage: Belinfante, 1912-1913.

– *Uitkomsten der zesde tienjarige volkstelling in het Koninkrijk der Nederlanden op den 31sten december 1879.* 12 vols. 's-Gravenhage: Departement van Binnenlandsche Zaken, 1881.

– Union Pacific Railroad Company. *The Resources and Attractions of Washington for the Home Seeker, Capitalist, and Tourist.* Chicago: Rand McNally & Co, 1889.

– *United States Population Census Manuscripts, Bureau of the Census. 12th Census (1900).* Washington: Bureau of the Census, 1900.

– *United States Population Census Manuscripts, Bureau of the Census. 13th Census (1910).* Washington: Bureau of the Census, 1910.

– United States Immigration Commission. *Immigrants in Industries; Silk Goods Manufacturing and Dyeing,* part 5. Washington DC, 1907-1910.

– *United States Statutes at Large.* Vol. 12. 1862. *Het Vaandel,* November 2, 1892.

– "Vandervelde [van der Velde]." Record of Reinder, Pope, Jogchum, Geert, and Martinus Vandervelde. Personal Collection Author.

– Vandervelde, C. "Saape van der Velde-Wopkje Dijkstra Descendants." N.p., 1979. Manuscript, Herrick Public Library, Holland, MI.

– Veenendaal, J.H. *Nederland in 1880.* Tiel: Mijs, 1881.

– Venema, A. "Proeve eener berekening van de koopwaarde der gronden in Nederland bij den landbouw en de veehouderij in gebruik." *De Economist* 2 (1897): 897-908.

– *Verslag van den toestand van handel, nijverheid en fabriekswezen in de gemeenten Franeker, Barradeel en Menaldumadeel.* Franeker: Kamer van Koophandel, 1880.

– *Verslag van den toestand van handel, nijverheid en fabriekswezen in de gemeenten Franeker, Barradeeel en Menaldumadeel.* Franeker: Kamer van Koophandel, 1911.

– *Verslagen betreffende den oeconomischen toestand der landarbeiders in Nederland.* "Friesland." 's-Gravenhage: J&H van Langenhuysen, 1908.

– *Verslagen en mededeelingen van de afdeeling landbouw van het Departement van Waterstaat, Handel en Nijverheid, 1904.* 's-Gravenhage: 1904. Vol. 1: Boterproductie en botercontrole.

– Versteeg, D. *De pelgrim vaders van het westen. Eene geschiedenis van de worstelingen der Hollandsche nederzettingen in Michigan benevens eene schets van de stichting der kolonie Pella in Iowa.* Grand Rapids, MI: C.M. Loomis, 1886.

– Vries, W.P. de. "De visschers van Wierum en Moddergat." *Vragen van den dag* (1894): 180-86.

– Warnshuis, J.W. "The History of Sioux County." N.p., 1879. Translated by P. Vander Kooi. Manuscript, Calvin College Archives, Grand Rapids, MI.

– Wassenar, H. Whitinsville, MA. Interview, March 11, 1991.

– Wassenar, H. "Some Notes on the Meeting with Annemieke Galema of Holland." Whitinsville, MA: April 1, 1991. Manuscript, Personal Collection Author.

– Welderen Rengers, Th. van., and Faber, J.H. *Friesland en de woningwet 1902-1912.* Leeuwarden: Meijer & Schaafsma, 1913.

– Whitehead, J.L.D. *The Passaic Valley New Jersey.* New York: The New Jersey Genealogical Company, 1901.

– Wijnaendts Francken, C.J. *Door Amerika. Reisschetsen, indrukken en studiën.* Haarlem: H.D. Tjeenk Willink, 1892.

– Y. "Ofskie fen in lânforhûzer." *Weekblad voor het Kanton Bergum,* March 9, 1889.

– Zee, J. van der. *The Hollanders of Iowa.* Iowa City: The State Historical Society, 1912.

## II. Books and Articles

– Allen, J.P. *We the People; An Atlas of America's Ethnic Diversity.* New York: Macmillan, 1988.

– Amersfoort, J.J.M. van. *Immigratie en minderheidsvorming. Een analyse van de Nederlandse situatie 1945-1973.* Alphen a/d Rijn: Samson, 1974.

– Anderson, B.L. *The Scandinavian and Dutch Rural Settlements in the Stillaguamish and Nooksack Valleys of Western Washington.* Ann Arbor: University Microfilms International, 1957.

– Anderson, M.J. *The American Census; A Social History.* New Haven: Yale University Press, 1988.

– Baines, D. *Emigration from Europe, 1815-1930.* London: Macmillan, 1991.

– Baldwin, T.W. *Vital Records of Northbridge Massachusetts to the Year 1850.* Boston: [S.N.], 1916.

– Barton, H.A. *Letters from the Promised Land; Swedes in America, 1840-1914.* Minneapolis: University of Minnesota Press, 1975.

– Beets, H. *The Christian Reformed Church in North America.* Grand Rapids: Grand Rapids Printing Company, 1923.

– Beets, H. *De Christelijk Gereformeerde Kerk in Noord-Amerika.* Grand Rapids, 1918.
– Beijer, G., ed. *Characteristics of Overseas Migrants.* 's-Gravenhage: Staatsuitgeverij, 1961.
– Bell, E.J. *Homesteading in Montana; Life in the Blue Mountain Country.* Bozeman: Big Sky Books, 1975.
– Beltman, B.W. "Ethnic Persistence and Change; The Experience of a Dutch-American Family in Rural Iowa." *The Annals of Iowa* 52 (Winter 1993): 1-49.
– Beltman, B.W. *A Dutch-American Immigrant in the Rural Midwest; The Life and Letters of Ulbe Eringa, 1866-1950.* Urbana & Chicago: University of Illinois Press, 1996.
– Berg, H.M. van den. *Noordelijk Oostergo. Ferwerderadeel.* 's-Gravenhage: Staatsuitgeverij, 1981.
– Berg, H.M. van den. *Noordelijk Oostergo. De Dongeradelen.* 's-Gravenhage: Staatsuitgeverij, 1983.
– Berkel, K. van., ed. *Amerika in Europese ogen.* 's-Gravenhage: SDU Uitgeverij, 1990.
– Berkel, K. van. *Denken over cultuur.* Groningen: Historische Uitgeverij Groningen, 1990.
– Bischoff, H. *Data on New Jersey Urban Immigration and Migration; Maps, Statistics and Charts.* N.p., 1985.
– Blaschke, M., and Harzig, C., eds. *Frauen wandern aus. Deutsche Migrantinnen im 19. und 20. Jahrhundert.* Bremen: Universität Bremen, 1990.
– Blauw, M.J.E. *Van Friese grond. Agrarische eigendoms- en gebruiksverhoudingen en de ontwikkelingen in de Friese landbouw in de negentiende eeuw.* Ljouwert: Fryske Akademy, 1995.
– Blegen, T.C. *Minnesota; A History of the State.* St. Paul: University of Minnesota, 1975.
– Blink, H. "Friesland als economisch-gewest in den loop der eeuwen en in het bijzonder in den tegenwoordigen tijd." *Tijdschrift voor Economische Geografie* 8 (1917): 337-404.
– Bodnar, J.E. *The Transplanted; A History of Immigrants in Urban America.* Bloomington: Indiana University Press, 1985.
– Bodnar, J.E. "Response." *Social Science History* 12 (Fall 1988): 265-68.
– Bottema, H. "In America's Friesland." In *Dutch Immigrant Memoirs and Related Writings*, 2: 139-44. Edited by H.S. Lucas. Assen: Van Gorcum, 1955.
– Bouma, G.J.A. "De lânbou." In *Geakunde Wûnseradiel*, 293-312. Edited by J.J. Spahr van der Hoek. Bolsward: Osinga, 1969.
– Bratt, J.D. *Dutch Calvinism in Modern America; A History of a Conservative Subculture.* Grand Rapids, MI: W.B. Eerdmans, 1984.
– Bretting, A., and Bickelmann, H. *Auswanderungsagenturen und Auswanderungsvereine im 19. und 20. Jahrhundert.* Vol. 4: *Von Deutschland nach Amerika: Zur Socialgeschichte der Auswanderung im 19. und 20. Jahrhundert.* Stuttgart: Franz Steiner Verlag, 1991.
– Breuker, P. *Keatserstaal.* Groningen: Frysk Ynstitut, University of Groningen, 1983.
– "Brieven uit het beloofde land." In *Friesland vroeger. Uit de archiefkast van Rijksarchief in Friesland*, 93-97. Edited by S. de Haan, and J. Hoving. Drachten/Leeuwarden: Friese Pers Boekerij, 1987.
– Brink, A. "Lynden-A Home Far Away From Home." In *Proceedings of the Association of Dutch American Study Conference.* Orange City, IA, 1985.
– Brinks, H.J. *Schrijf spoedig terug. Brieven van immigranten in Amerika 1847-1920.* 's-Gravenhage: Boekencentrum, 1978.
– Brinks, H.J. "Impressions of the 'Old' World 1848-1940." In *The Dutch in North-America; Their Immigration and Cultural Continuity*, 34-47. Edited by R. Kroes, and H-O. Neuschäfer. Amsterdam: VU University Press, 1991.
– Brinks, H.J., ed. *Dutch American Voices; Letters from the United States.* Ithaca and London: Cornell University Press, 1995.
– Brown, A. "The Life Story of John Tuininga." In *Dutch Immigrant Memoirs and Related Writings*, 2: 188-95. Edited by H.S. Lucas. Assen: Van Gorcum, 1955.
– Brown, R.D. *Massachusetts; A Bicentennial History.* New York: W.W. Norton & Company, 1978.
– Bruins, E.J., ed. *The Dutch in America.* Holland, MI: Hope College, 1984.
– Brush, J.E. *The Population of New Jersey.* New Brunswick: Rutgers University Press, 1956.
– Buwalda, H.S. *Woun op 'e weagen. It Bildt en syn biwenners.* Sneek: Koster, 1946.
– Buwalda, S.H. *De erbaaiersbeweging op 't Bildt in 't leste fordelspart fan 'e negentynde eeuw.* St. Annaparochie: Stichting Ons Bildt, 1983.
– Buwalda, S.H. *Geskidenis fan de Bildtse waddenfisserij.* St. Jacobiparochie: Stichting Ons Bildt, 1986.
– *Centennial History of the Town of Randolph, Columbia County, 1849-1950.* N.p., 1950.
– *The Centennial Book Orange City, Iowa, 1870-1970.* Orange City, IA: The Ad-Visor, 1970.
– Conk, M. "Occupational Classification in the United States Census: 1870-1940." *Journal of Interdisciplinary History* 9 (1978) 1: 111-30.
– Conzen, K. Neils; Gerber, D.A.; Morawska, E.; Pozzetta, G.E.; and Vecoli, R.J. "The Invention of Ethnicity; A Perspective from the U.S.A." *Journal of American Ethnic History* 12 (Fall 1992) 1: 3-41.
– Cook, R.A. *South Holland Illinois; A History.* South Holland: South Holland Trust and Savings Bank, 1966.
– Crane, E.B. *History of Worcester County, Massachusetts.* New York & Chicago: Lewis Historical Publishing Company, 1924.
– Curti, M., and Birr, K. "The Immigrant and the American Image in Europe, 1860-1914." *The Mississippi Valley Historical Review* 37 (September 1950): 203-30.
– Curtiss-Wedge, F. *The History of Renville County, Minnesota.* 2 vols. Chicago: H.C. Cooper, 1916.
– Daan, J. "Trouw aan het Fries in de U.S.A." In *Flecht op 'e koai. Stúdzjes oanbean oan Prof.Dr. W.J. Buma ta syn*

*sechstichste jierdei*, 177-81. Edited by T. Hoekema.
Groningen: Wolters-Noordhoff, 1970.

– Daan, J. *Ik was te bissie. Nederlanders en hun taal in de Verenigde Staten*. Zutphen: De Walburg Pers, 1987.

– Daane, P. "Sketch of Cedar Grove and Oostburg." In *Dutch Immigrant Memoirs and Related Writings*, 2: 117-28. Edited by H.S. Lucas. Assen: Van Gorcum, 1955.

– Dam, H. "Description of my Journey." In *Dutch Immigrant Memoirs and Related Writings*, 1: 303-10. Edited by H.S. Lucas. Assen: Van Gorcum, 1955.

– Daniels, R. *Coming to America. A History of Immigration and Ethnicity in American Life*. New York: HarperCollins, 1990.

– Dassen, A.; Eerd, C. van.; and Oppelland, K., eds. *Vrouwen in den Vreemde. Lotgevallen van emigrantes en immigrantes*. Zutphen: Walburg Pers, 1993.

– De Jong, D.C. *With a Dutch Accent. How a Hollander Became an American*. New York and London: Harper and Brothers, 1944.

– De Jong, G.F. *The Dutch in America, 1609-1974*. Boston: Twayne Publishers, 1975.

— De Jong, G.F. "Dutch Immigrants in New Jersey before World War I." *New Jersey History* 94 (1976) 2: 69-88.

– De Jong, G.F. "Four Generations of a Dutch American Community." In *Dutch Immigration to North America*, 221-37. Edited by H. Ganzevoort, and M. Boekelman. Toronto: The Multi Cultural History Society of Ontario, 1983.

– Diederiks, H.A.; Noordam, D.J.; Quispel, G.C.; and Vries, P.H.H. *Van agrarische samenleving naar verzorgingsstaat*. Groningen: Wolters-Noordhoff, 1987.

– Dijk, E. van. "Ontwikkelingen in Oostdongeradeel tijdens de 'Sijtsma-periode', 1904-1964." *It Beaken* 2 (July 1964): 81-99.

– Dodyk, D.W., and Golin, S. *The Paterson Silk Strike of 1913*. Paterson, 1987.

– Doyle, R.L. *The Socio-Economic Mobility of the Dutch Immigrants to Pella, Iowa 1847-1925*. Ph.D. dissertation, Kent State University, 1982.

– Doyle, R.L. "Wealth Mobility in Pella, Iowa 1847-1925." In *The Dutch in America; Immigration, Settlement and Cultural Change*, 156-71. Edited by R.P. Swierenga. New Brunswick: Rutgers University Press, 1985.

– Dyke, C.L. *The Story of Sioux County*. Dixon, IL: Print Shop, 1983.

– Eekhof, A. "De Nederlandsche kolonisatie in Noord-Amerika." *Haagsch Maandblad* 3 (March 1929): 219-30.

– Eenigenburg, H. *The Calumet Region and it's Early Settlers*. Chicago: Arrow Printers, 1935.

– Elich, J.H. *Aan de ene kant, aan de andere kant. De emigratie van Nederlanders naar Australië 1946-1986*. Ph.D. dissertation, University of Leiden, 1987.

– Ellemers, J.E. "The Determinants of Emigration; An Analysis of Dutch Studies on Emigration." *Sociologia Neerlandia* 2 (1964) 1: 41-52.

– *Enkele facetten uit de geschiedenis van de gemeente Westdongeradeel tot de opheffing 1 januari 1984*. Metslawier: Administratief Centrum 'Oostergo', 1984.

– Enzensberger, H.M. *De grote trek*. Amsterdam: De Volkskrant, 1992.

– Erickson, C. *Invisible Immigrants; The Adaptation of English and Scottish Immigrants in 19th-Century America*. Coral Gables, Fla: University of Miami Press, 1972; reprint ed., Ithaca and London: Cornell University Press, 1990.

– Ettema, R. *The Dutch Connection in South Cook County*. South Holland, IL: Park Press, 1984.

– Faber, J.A.; Roessingh, H.K.; Slicher van Bath, B.H.; Woude, A.M. van der.; and Zanten, H.J. van. "Population Changes and Economic Development in The Netherlands; A Historical Survey." *A.A.G. Bijdragen* 12: 47-113. Wageningen: Landbouwuniversiteit, 1965.

– Fapso, R.J. *Norwegians in Wisconsin*. Madison: The State Historical Society, 1982.

– Flemming Larsen, B., and Bender, H., eds. *Danish Emigration to the U.S.A.* Aalborg: Danes Worldwide Archives, 1992.

– Foner, P.S. *History of the Labor Movement in the United States*. Vol. 4: The Industrial Workers of the World; 1905-1917. New York: International Publishers, 1965.

– Foner, P.S. *Women and the American Labor Movement*. New York: Free Press, 1979.

– Fridsma, B.J. *Nea ferbrutsen bân. 60 jier Fryske aksje yn Amearika*. Leeuwarden: De Tille, 1991.

– Frieswijk, J. "Een socialisties propagandist in revolutionaire jaren. Biografie van Tjeerd Stienstra (1859-1935)." *Tijdschrift voor Sociale Geschiedenis* 6 (October 1976): 221-56.

– Frieswijk, J. *Socialisme in Friesland 1880-1900*. Amsterdam: Van Gennep, 1977.

– Frieswijk, J. "De beweging Broedertrouw op het Bildt 1889-1892." In *Jaarboek voor de geschiedenis van socialisme en arbeidersbeweging in Nederland*, 83-139. Nijmegen: Socialistische Uitgeverij, 1978.

– Frieswijk, J. *Om een beter leven. Land- en veenarbeiders in het noorden van Nederland 1850-1914*. Ljouwert: Fryske Akademy, 1989.

– Frieswijk, J. "The Labour Movement in Friesland, 1880-1918." *Tijdschrift voor sociale geschiedenis* 18 (1992): 370-88.

– Frijda, N. *Emigranten, niet-emigranten*. 's-Gravenhage: Staatsuitgeverij, 1960.

– Galema, A. "'Forjit my net'. Friese emigratie naar de Verenigde Staten aan het eind van de negentiende eeuw." *Groniek* 96 (1986): 89-101.

– Galema, A. "'se binne nei Amearika tein.' Aspekten van Friese landverhuizing naar de Verenigde Staten rond de eeuwwisseling." *It Beaken* 52 (1990) 2: 45-58.

– Galema, A. "Transplanted Network; A Case Study of Frisian Migration to Whitinsville, Mass., 1880-1914." In *The Dutch in North-America; Their Immigration and Cultural Continuity*, 174-94. Edited by R. Kroes, and H-O. Neuschäfer. Amsterdam: VU University Press, 1991.

– Galema, A. "Over de wereldzee naar de grote stad: Pieter Ypes Groustra met zijn gezin in Chicago rond de eeuwwisseling." *De Nederlandsche Leeuw. Maandblad van het Koninklijk Nederlandsch Genootschap voor Geslacht- en Wapenkunde* 109 (October-November 1992): 450-58.

– Galema, A., and Holtmann, A. "Aus den nördlichen Niederlanden und dem deutschen Nordwesten nach Nordamerika. Motive und Reiseerfahrungen der Auswanderer im 19. Jahrhundert." In *Rondom Eems en Dollard/Rund um Ems und Dollart*, 433-49. Edited by O.S. Knottnerus; P. Brood; W. Deeters; and H. van Lengen. Groningen/Leer: REGIO-PRoject/Schuster Verlag, 1992.

– Galema, A.; Grams, W.; and Holtmann, A., eds. *Van de ene en de andere kant. Noordnederlandse en Noordwestduitse migratie naar de Verenigde Staten in de negentiende eeuw/Nordniederländische und Nordwestdeutsche Auswanderung nach Amerika im 19. Jahrhundert.* Groningen: Universiteitsbibliotheek/Oldenburg: Stadtmuseum, 1993.

– Galema, A., and Sinke, S. "Paradijs der vrouwen? Overzeese migratie naar de Verenigde Staten van Friese vrouwen rond de eeuwwisseling." In *Vrouwen in den vreemde. Lotgevallen van emigrantes en immigrantes*, 30-46. Edited by A. Dassen; C. van Eerd; and K. Oppelland. Zutphen: Walburg Pers, 1993.

– Galema, A.; Henkes, B.; and Velde, H. te., eds. *Images of the Nation; Different Meanings of Dutchness 1870-1940.* Amsterdam: Rodopi, 1993.

– Galema, A. "'Now I will write you something about America...'; Dutch Migrant's Views of the United States around the Turn of the Century." In *Images of the Nation; Different Meanings of Dutchness 1870-1940*, 106-31. Edited by A. Galema; B. Henkes; and H. te Velde. Amsterdam: Rodopi, 1993.

– Galema, A. "Um eines bequemeren Lebens willen in die Neue Welt? Auswanderung friesischer Frauen in die Vereinigten Staaten um 1900." In *Hoffnung Amerika. Europäische Auswanderung in die Neue Welt*, 137-50. Edited by K. Schulz. Bremerhaven: NWD-Verlag, 1994.

– Galema, A. "Culture Island in the City: A Case Study of Frisian Migration to the USA (1880-1914)." In *Emigration and Settlement Patterns of German Communities in North America*, 223-36. Edited by E. Reichmann. Indianapolis: Max Kade German-American Center, 1995.

– Galema, A. "Views of the United States, 1880-1914; The Case of Dutch Migrant's Transatlantic Correspondence." In *Images of America.* Edited by W.L. Chew. Brussels: forthcoming, 1996.

– Ganzevoort, H. "Sharks in Wooden Shoes." In *Dutch Immigration to North America*, 147-68. Edited by H. Ganzevoort, and M. Boekelman. Toronto: The Multicultural History Society of Ontario, 1983.

– Ganzevoort, H., and Boekelman, M., eds. *Dutch Immigration to North America.* Toronto: The Multicultural History Society of Ontario, 1983.

– Gjerde, J. *From Peasants to Farmers; The Migration from Balestrand, Norway, to the Upper Middle West.* Cambridge: Cambridge University Press, 1985.

– Glazier, I., and De Rosa, L., eds. *Migration Across Time and Nations.* New York/London: Holmes & Meier, 1986.

– Glazier, I.A., and Filby, P.W. *Germans to America; Lists of Passengers Arriving at U.S. Ports.* Vols. 1-22, Wilmington, DE: Scholarly Resources, 1988-1991 ff.

– *A Goodly Heritage; A History of the Churchill and Amsterdam Area of Montana.* Bozeman: Churchill-Amsterdam Historical Society, 1989.

– Gordon, M.M. *Assimilation in American Life; The Role of Race, Religion, and National Origins.* New York: Oxford University Press, 1964.

– Goren, H., and Heger, H. *Per mud of bij de week gewonnen. De ontwikkeling van beloningssystemen in de Groningse landbouw, 1800-1914.* Groningen: Nederlands Agronomisch Historisch Instituut, 1993.

– Görisch, S.W. *Quellen und Forschungen zur Hessischen Geschichte.* Vol. 84. Darmstadt: Hessischen Historischen Kommission, 1991.

– Greenhill, B. *The Great Migration; Crossing the Atlantic under Sail.* London: National Maritime Museum, 1968.

– Grigg, D. *Population Growth and Agrarian Change; A Historical Perspective.* Cambridge: Cambridge University Press, 1980.

– Groenman, F.E.H. "Iets over landverhuizing naar de Vereenigde Staten van Amerika." *Economische Verslagen* (Bijlage van *Handelsberichten*) 5 (1915): 1-16.

– Groot, C. de. *When I was a Girl in Holland.* Boston: Northrop, Lee & Shepard, 1917; reprint ed., Arnhem: Bakker, 1991.

– Groot, C. de. "Nine Farmerettes. They Prove Woman is not Weak." Published in *When I was a Girl in Holland*; reprint ed., Supplement, Arnhem: Bakker, 1991.

– Gulliksen, O.T. "Letters to Immigrants in the Midwest from the Telemark Region of Norway." *Norwegian-American Studies* 32 (1989): 157-75.

– Gutman, H.G. "Class, Status, and Community Power in Nineteenth-Century American Industrial Cities - Paterson, New Jersey; A Case Study." In *The Age of Industrialism in America; Essays in Social Structure and Cultural Values*, 263-87. Edited by F.C. Jaher. New York: Free Press, 1968.

– Hale, F. *Danes in Wisconsin.* Madison: The State Historical Society of Wisconsin, 1981.

– Hale, F. *The Swiss of Wisconsin.* Madison: The State Historical Society of Wisconsin, 1984.

– Hallema, A. "Bloei en verval der Friesche gemeenten in de laatste halve eeuw op grond van haar bevolkingscijfers." *Tijdschrift voor Economische Geographie* 6 (1925): 165-70.

– Harmeling, H. "History of Amsterdam and Cedar Grove." In *Dutch Immigrant Memoirs and Related Writings*, 2: 110-17. Edited by H.S. Lucas. Assen: Van Gorcum, 1955.

– Harzig, C., and Hoerder, D., eds. *The Press of Labor*

Migrants in Europe and North America 1880s to 193 0s. Bremen: Universität Bremen, 1985.

– Harzig, C. "The U.S. Government Census as Source in Immigration Research." In *The Press of Labor Migrants in Europe and North America 1880s to 1930s*, 25-37. Edited by C. Harzig, and D. Hoerder. Bremen: Universität Bremen, 1985.

– Heide, H. ter. *Binnenlandse migratie in Nederland*. 's-Gravenhage: Staatsuitgeverij, 1965.

– Helbich, W., and Sommer, U. "Immigrant Letters as Sources." In *The Press of Labor Migrants in Europe and North America 1880s to 1930s*, 39-58. Edited by C. Harzig, and D. Hoerder. Bremen: Universität Bremen, 1985.

– Helbich, W.; Kamphoefner, W.; and Sommer, U., eds. *Briefe aus Amerika. Deutsche Auswanderer schreiben aus der Neuen Welt, 1830-1930*. München: Beck, 1988.

– Henkes, B. *Heimat in Holland. Duitse dienstmeisjes 1920-1950*. Amsterdam: Babylon-De Geus, 1995.

– Higham, J. *Send These to Me*. London and Baltimore: John Hopkins University Press, 1984.

– Hinte, J. van. *Nederlanders in Amerika. Een studie over landverhuizers en volksplanters in de 19e en 20ste eeuw in de Vereenigde Staten van Amerika*. 2 vols. Groningen: P. Noordhoff, 1928.

– Hinte, J. van. *Netherlanders in America; a Study of Emigrants and Colonists in the Nineteenth and Twentieth Centuries*. Edited by R.P. Swierenga, and translated by A. de Wit. Grand Rapids, MI: Baker Book House, 1985.

– Hippel, W. von. *Auswanderung aus Südwestdeutschland. Studien zur württembergischen Auswanderung und Auswanderungspolitik im 18. und 19. Jahrhundert*. Stuttgart: Klett-Cotta, 1984.

– *A History of Paterson and Its Relations with the World*. Union City, NJ: Hudson Dispatch Printer, 1932.

– *History of Pella, Iowa 1847-1987*. 2 vols. Dallas: Pella Historical Sòciety, 1988-1989.

– Hoefte, R., and Kardux, J.C. *Connecting Cultures; The Netherlands in Five Centuries of Transatlantic Exchange*. Amsterdam: VU University Press, 1994.

– Hoekema, C.P. *Andreas Paulus' Hoekema (1750-1801) en syn neiteam*. Heerenveen: Stifting Ffyrug, 1983.

– Hoerder, D., ed. *Labor Migration in the Atlantic Economies; The European and North American Working Classes During the Period of Industrialization*. Westport, CT: Greenwood Press, 1985.

– Hoerder, D., ed. *The Immigrant Labor Press in North America, 1840s-1970s*. New York: Greenwood Press, 1987.

– Hoerder, D. "The Transplanted; International Dimensions." *Social Science History* 12 (Fall 1988): 255-63.

– Hoerder, D., and Knauf, D., eds. *Aufbruch in die Fremde/ Fame, Fortune and Sweet Liberty*. Bremen: Edition Temmen, 1992.

– Hoerder, D. "The Traffic of Emigration via Bremen/Bremerhaven; Merchants' Interests, Protective Legislation, and Migrants' Experiences."

*Journal of American Ethnic History* 13 (Fall 1993): 68-101.

– Hoerder, D. "Introduction." *Journal of American Ethnic History* 13 (Fall 1993): 3-5.

– Hofstede, B.P. *Thwarted Exodus*. 's-Gravenhage: Staatsuitgeverij, 1964.

– Hofstee, E.W. *Korte demografische geschiedenis van Nederland van 1800 tot heden*. Haarlem: Fibula-Van Dishoeck, 1981.

– Hofstee, E.W. *Some Remarks on Selective Migration*. 's-Gravenhage: Martinus Nijhoff, 1952.

– Hofstee, E.W. "De functie van de internationale migratie." *Tijdschrift voor Economische en Sociale Geografie* 40 (1949): 10-22.

– Hollander, A.N.J. den. *Americana. Studies over mensen, dieren en een kaktus tussen Rio Grande en Potomac*. Meppel: Boom, 1970.

– Holtmann, A., ed. *"Ferner thue ich euch zu wissen..." Briefe des Johann Heinrich zur Oeveste aus Amerika (1834-1876)*. Bremen: Edition Temmen, 1995.

– Holtmann, A. "Snares for the Genealogist and the Historian; A Critique." *Society for German-American Studies Newsletter* 14 (September 1993): 19-24.

– Holtmann, A. "New Lures to Entrapment for Genealogists and Historians." *Society for German-American Studies Newsletter* 16 (September 1995): 1-2.

– *Homeseekers' Guide to the State of Washington*. Olympia, WA: F.M. Lamborn, 1914. Hoogstraat, J. *Von Ostfriesland nach Amerika*. Norden: Soltau-Kurier, 1990.

– Hoor, M. ten. "Frisians to the United States." *Michigan Alumnus Quarterly Review* 58 (December 1951): 50-56.

– Huisman, K. *It libben fan Gerrit Roorda/opskrean troch Kerst Huisman*. Bûtenpost: Alternatyf, 1973.

– Hvidt, K. *Flight to America; The Social Background of 300,000 Danish Emigrants*. New York: Academic Press, 1975.

– Hyma, A. *Albertus C. van Raalte and his Dutch Settlements in the United States*. Grand Rapids, MI: W.B. Eerdmans, 1947.

– Jackson, J.A., ed. *Migration*. Cambridge: University Press, 1969.

– Jansing, J.W.G., and Dasberg, L. "Onderwijs." *Algemene Geschiedenis der Nederlanden*. Vol. 13: 129-44. Haarlem: 1978.

– Jansma, L.G., and Jelsma, G.H. "Friezen om utens. Migraasje en taalbehâld by de Fryske Kriten en studinteferienings." *It Beaken* 3 (1993): 107-23.

– Jelsma, G. "Twa revolúsjonaire toanielskriuwers út de ein fan de foarige ieu." *It Beaken* 5/6 (1979): 291-310

– Jones, G.O. *History of Wood County, Wisconsin*. Wood County, WI: H.C. Cooper, Jr.& Co., 1923.

– Jonge, J.A. de. *De industrialisatie in Nederland tussen 1850 en 1914*. Amsterdam: Scheltema & Holkema, 1968; reprint ed., Nijmegen: Sun, 1976.

– Kamminga, L. "De industrie." In *Geakunde Wûnseradiel*, 332-48. Edited by J.J. Spahr van der Hoek. Bolsward: Osinga, 1969.

– Kamphoefner, W.D. *The Westfalians; From Germany to*

*Missouri.* Princeton, NJ: Princeton University Press, 1987.

– Kane, J.N. *The American Counties; Origins of County Names, Dates of Creation and Organization, Area, Population Including 1980 Census Figures, Historical Data, and Published Sources.* Metuchen, NJ and London: The Scarecrow Press, 1983.

– Karsten, J.H. "Life Sketch of the Rev. Marten Anne Ypma." In *Dutch Immigrant Memoirs and Related Writings*, 2: 384-87. Edited by H.S. Lucas. Assen: Van Gorcum, 1955.

– Karsten, J.H. "A Half Century of Dutch Settlement in Wisconsin 1847-1897." In *Dutch Immigrant Memoirs and Related Writings*, 2: 129-39. Edited by H.S. Lucas. Assen: Van Gorcum, 1955.

– Keikes, W.H. *Verleden van Frieslands Noordoosten.* Dokkum: n.p., 1968.

– Keil, H., and Jentz, J.B. ed. *German Workers in Industrial Chicago, 1850-1910; A Comparative Perspective.* Dekalb, IL: Northern Illinois University Press, 1983.

– Keil, H. "Socialist Immigrants from Germany and the Transfer of Socialist Ideology and Workers' Culture." In *A Century of European Migrations, 1830-1930*, 315-38. Edited by R.J. Vecoli, and S.M. Sinke. Urbana & Chicago: University of Illinois Press, 1991.

– Kempees, J.C.J. "De Nederlandsche hypotheekbanken in de Vereenigde Staten van Noord-Amerika en in Canada." *De Economist* (October-December 1919): 655-95, 759-93, 866-909.

– Kennedy, C.B. "The Sioux County Dutch." In *The Dutch in America*, 29-40. Edited by E.J. Bruins. Holland, MI: Hope College, 1984.

– Kepley-Mahmood, C. *Frisian and Free; Study of an Ethnic Minority of The Netherlands.* Prospect Heights, IL: Waveland, 1989. -Kero, R. *Migrations from Finland to North America in the Years between the United States Civil War and the First World War.* Turku: Turun Yliopisto, 1974.

– Kingma, T. *Bitgum. De skiednis fan Bitgum en Bitgummole.* Leeuwarden: Fryske Akademy, 1988.

– Kirk, G.W., Jr. *The Promise of American Life; Social Mobility in a Nineteenth-Century Immigrant Community, Holland, Michigan, 1847-1894.* Philadelphia: The American Philosophical Society, 1978.

– Knapen, B. *De grenzen van Amerika.* Amsterdam: Prometheus, 1990.

– Knippenberg, H. *De religieuze kaart van Nederland. Omvang en geografische spreiding van de godsdienstige gezindten vanaf de Reformatie tot heden.* Assen: Van Gorcum, 1992.

– Knippenberg, H. "De godsdienstkaart van Friesland in de tweede helft van de negentiende eeuw." *It Beaken* 57 (1995) 2: 80-105.

– Koert, D. *Portrait of Lynden.* Lynden: Lynden Tribune, 1976.

– Koeweiden-Wijdeven, A.F.M. "Vergeten emigranten." *Spiegel Historiael* 3 (March 1984): 120-24, 154.

– Kooij, P. *Groningen 1870-1914. Sociale verandering en economische ontwikkeling in een regionaal centrum.* Ph.D. dissertation, University of Groningen, 1986.

– Kooij, P., ed. *Dorp naast een stad. Hoogkerk 1770-1914.* Assen: Van Gorcum, 1993.

– Krijff, J.Th.J. *"100 Years Ago"; Dutch Immigration to Manitoba in 1893.* Windsor, ON: Electa Press, 1993.

– Kroes, R., ed. *The American West as Seen by Europeans and Americans.* Amsterdam: VU University Press, 1989.

– Kroes, R. "Windmills in Montana; Dutch Settlement in the Gallatin Valley." *Montana* 39 (1989): 40-52.

– Kroes, R. "There're Dutch in them thar Hills! Ethnicity in the Mountain West." In *The American West as Seen by Europeans and Americans*, 166-82. Edited by R. Kroes. Amsterdam: VU University Press, 1989.

– Kroes, R. *Nederlandse pioniers in het Amerikaanse Westen. De geschiedenis van Amsterdam, Montana.* Amsterdam: De Bataafsche Leeuw, 1989.

– Kroes, R. *The Persistence of Ethnicity; Dutch Calvinist Pioneers in Amsterdam, Montana.* Urbana and Chicago: University of Illinois Press, 1992.

– Kroes, R. "Amsterdam, Montana; In America, Not Of It? A Fractured History of Ethnic Continuity." In *The Dutch in North-America; Their Immigration and Cultural Continuity*, 219-39. Edited by R. Kroes, and H-O. Neuschäfer. Amsterdam: VU University Press, 1991.

– Kromminga, D.H. *The Christian Reformed Tradition from the Reformation till the Present Time.* Grand Rapids, MI: W.B. Eerdmans, 1943.

– Kuiper, R. *Zelfbeeld en wereldbeeld. Antirevolutionairen en het buitenland, 1848-1905.* Kampen: Kok, 1992.

– Kuiper, R.T. *A Voice from America about America.* Translated by E.R. Post. Grand Rapids, MI: W.B. Eerdmans, 1970.

– LaDow, M.B. "Chinook, Montana, and the Myth of Progressive Adaptation." *Montana* 39 (Autumn 1989): 10-23.

– Lagerwey, W. *Neen Nederland, 'k vergeet u niet. Een beeld van het immigrantenleven in Amerika tussen 1846 en 1945 in verhalen, schetsen en gedichten.* Baarn: Bosch & Keuning, 1982.

– Lammers, A. *Uncle Sam and Jan Salie.* Amsterdam: Balans, 1989.

– Lammers, A. *Helden van het geloof. Amerika in de greep van de dominees.* Amsterdam: Balans, 1988.

– Lammers, A. "Amerikanist van het eerste uur: A.N.J. den Hollander." In *Amerika in Europese ogen*, 181-93. Edited by K. van Berkel. 's-Gravenhage: SDU Uitgeverij, 1990.

– Lautenbach, J. *Zij durfden het aan. Gereformeerden in Tzummarum.* Tzummarum: Gereformeerde Kerk, 1990.

– Lee, E.S. "A Theory of Migration." In *Migration*, 282-97. Edited by J.A. Jackson. Cambridge: University Press, 1969.

– Leiby, A.C. *The Early Dutch and Swedish Settlers of New Jersey.* Princeton, NJ: D. Van Nostrand, 1964.

– Ligterink, G.H. *De landverhuizers. Emigratie naar Noord-Amerika uit het Gelders-Westfaalse grensgebied tussen de jaren 1830-1850.* Zutphen: De Walburg Pers, 1981.

– Lintelman, J.K. "'On My Own': Single, Swedish, and

Female in Turn-of-the-Century Chicago." In *Swedish-American Life in Chicago; Cultural and Urban Aspects of an Immigrant People 1850-1930*, 89-99. Edited by Ph.J. Anderson, and D. Blanck. Uppsala: Acta Universitatis Upsaliensis, 1991.

– Lucas, H.S. "Reminiscenses of Arend Jan Brusse on Early Dutch Settlement in Milwaukee." *Wisconsin Magazine of History* 30 (September 1946): 85-90.

– Lucas, H.S. "The Founding of New Amsterdam, La Crosse County." *Wisconsin Magazine of History* 31 (1947-1948): 42-60.

– Lucas, H.S. *Netherlanders in America*. Ann Arbor: University of Michigan Press, 1955; reprint ed., Grand Rapids, MI: W.B. Eerdmans, 1989.

– Lucas, H.S., ed. *Dutch Immigrant Memoirs and Related Writings*. 2 vols. Assen: Van Gorcum, 1955.

– Lucassen, J. *Migrant Labour in Europe 1600-1900*. London: Croom Helm, 1987.

– Lucassen, J. *Dutch Long Distance Migration; A Concise History 1600-1900*. Amsterdam: Internationaal Instituut voor Sociale Geschiedenis, 1991.

– Lucassen, J. "Het onontkoombare nationaliteitenbeginsel. Enige recente literatuur over (im)migratie en natievorming." *Tijdschrift voor Sociale Geschiedenis* 4 (1993): 489-505.

– Lucassen, J., and Penninx, R. *Nieuwkomers. Immigranten en hun nakomelingen in Nederland 1550-1985*. Amsterdam: Meulenhoff Informatief, 1985.

– Lucassen, J., and Trienekens, G. "Om de plaats in de kerk. Een onderzoek naar maatschappelijke ongelijkheid voornamelijk in de negentiende eeuw." *Tijdschrift voor Sociale Geschiedenis* 12 (1978): 239-305.

– Mackintosh, J. "The Lure of Prosperity; Economic Development among Danish Immigrants to Iowa." In *On Distant Shores*, 177-90. Edited by B. Flemming Larsen; H. Bender; and K. Veien. Aalborg: Danes Worldwide Archives, 1993.

– Malone, M.P. "The West in American Historiography." In *The American West as Seen By Europeans and Americans*, 1-19. Edited by R. Kroes. Amsterdam: VU University Press, 1989.

– *Manhattan, Montana; From its Beginning in the 1860's, through the Present 1986*. Dallas, TX: Taylor Publishing Company, 1986.

– Marczewski, J. "Quantitative History." *Journal of Contemporary History* 3 (April 1968): 179-91.

– Margrave, R.D. "Technology Diffusion and the Transfer of Skills; Nineteenth-Century English Silk Migration to Paterson." In *Silk City; Studies on the Paterson Silk Industry, 1860-1940*, 9-34. Edited by P.B. Scranton. Newark: New Jersey Historical Society, 1985.

– Marschalck, P. *Deutsche Überseewanderung im 19. Jahrhundert. Ein Beitrag zur soziologischen Theorie der Bevölkerung*. Stuttgart: E. Klett, 1973.

– Meulen, B.D. van der.; Schoppink, M.; Zwaag, B. van der.; and Zwaag, H. van der. *Van der Zwaag, Wouterswoude, Friesland*. Wouterswoude, compilers, 1991.

– Moes, J. "Absenteïsme van grondbezitters in Friesland en Zeeland 1850-1890." In *Het platteland in een veranderende wereld. Boeren en het proces van modernisering*, 255-76. Edited by H. Diederiks; J.T. Lindblad; and B. de Vries. Hilversum: Verloren, 1995.

– Morgan, R., ed. *Progress and Pride go Hand in Hand; Platte's 75th Anniversary 1900-1975*. N.p., 1975.

– Navin, T.R. *The Whitin Machine Works Since 1831*. Cambridge: Harvard University Press, 1950.

– Navis, E., and Siebring-Wieringa, J. eds. *A Furrow Laid Bare*. Edmonton, AB: Friesen Printer, 1985.

– Nelson, W., and Shriner, C.A. *History of Paterson and its Environs*. 2 vols. New York and Chicago: Lewis Historical Publishing Company, 1920.

– Nieuwenhuis, N.G. *Siouxland; A History of Sioux County, Iowa*. Orange City, IA: The Sioux County State Historical Society, 1983.

– Nieuwenhuis, N.G. "Orange City and the Western Movement." In *Proceedings of The Association for the Advancement of Dutch American Studies Conference*. Orange City, September 1985.

– Nicandri, D.L. *Italians in Washington State; Emigration 1853-1924*. N.p.: The Washington State American Revolution Bicentennial Commission, 1978.

– Noble, D.W. "The American Wests; Refuges from European Power or Frontiers of European Expansions?" In *The American West as Seen by Europeans and Americans*, 19-36. Edited by R. Kroes. Amsterdam: VU University Press, 1989.

– *Notitie betreffende een reglement voor behoud van historische patiëntendossiers*. Utrecht: Nederlands Centrum Geestelijke Volksgezondheid, 1989.

– Ostergren, R.C. *A Community Transplanted; The Trans-Atlantic Experience of a Swedish Immigrant Settlement in the Upper Middle West, 1835-1915*. Uppsala: Acta Universitatis Upsaliensis, 1988.

– Paping, R. *Voor een handvol stuivers. Werken, verdienen en besteden: de levensstandaard van boeren, arbeiders en middenstanders op de Groninger klei, 1770-1860*. Groningen: Nederlands Agronomisch-Historisch Instituut, 1995.

– Pauseback, P.H. *Aufbruch in eine Neue Welt. Die Auswanderung aus den schleswig-holsteinischen Kreisen Husum, Eiderstedt und Tondern in die Vereinigten Staaten in königlich-preussischer Zeit 1867-1914*. Bräist/Bredstedt: Nordfriisk Institut, 1995.

– Penninx, R., and Selier, F. "Theorievorming over internationale migratie: een historisch overzicht en een stand van zaken." *Migrantenstudies* 4 (1992): 4-19.

– Peterson, D. "'From Bone Depth'; German-American Communities in Rural Minnesota Before the Great War." *Journal of American Ethnic History* 11 (Winter 1992): 27-55.

– Poortinga, Y. "Emigraesje út Westerlauwersk Fryslân nei en festiging yn 'e Foriene Steaten (oant likernôch 1900 ta)." *Frysk Jierboek* (1958): 89-109.

– Posthumus-Zandstra, G. *Retour Canada. Een waar verhaal uit het begin van deze eeuw*. Buitenpost: Lykele Jansma, '78.

– Potts, L. *The World Labour Market; A History of Migration.* London and Atlantic Highlands, NJ: Zed Books, 1990. Translated from German: *Weltmarkt für Arbeitskraft. Von der Kolonisation Amerikas bis zu den Migrationen der Gegenwart.* Hamburg: Junius, 1988.

– Pozzetta, G.E., ed. *Immigrant Family Patterns; Demography, Fertility, Housing, Kinship, and Urban Life.* New York: Garland Publishing, 1991.

– Priester, P. *De economische ontwikkeling van de landbouw in Groningen 1800-1910. Een kwalitatieve en kwantitatieve analyse.* A.A.G. Bijdragen, 31. Wageningen: Landbouwuniversiteit, 1991.

– Prude, J. *The Coming of Industrial Order; Town and Factory Life in Rural Massachusetts 1810-1860.* New York: Cambridge University Press, 1983.

– Raban, J. *Hunting Mr. Heartbreak.* London: Pan Books, 1991.

– Ramaer, J.C. *Geschiedkundige atlas van Nederland.* 's-Gravenhage : Martinus Nijhoff, 1931.

– Ramella, F. "Across the Ocean or over the Border; Expectations and Experiences of Italians from Piedmont in New Jersey and Southern France." In *Distant Magnets; Expectations and Realities in the Immigrant Experience, 1840-1930,* 105-25. Edited by D. Hoerder, and H. Rössler. New York: Holmes & Meier, 1993.

– Read, G. "Liverpool. The Flood-Gate of the Old World; A Study in Ethnic Attitudes." *Journal of American Ethnic History* 13 (Fall 1993): 31-47.

– Rederus, S.F. "The Dutch Settlements of Sheboygan County." *Wisconsin Magazine of History* 1 (March 1918): 256-65.

– Reeves, P. *Ellis Island; Gateway to the American Dream.* New York: Dorset Press, 1991.

– Roeder, A.E. *Folksongs and Games of Holland.* New York: G. Schirmer, 1956.

– Roon, G. van. "'Long Wave' Economic Trends and Economic Policies in the Netherlands in the 19th and 20th Century." *JEEH* 12 (Fall 1983): 323-37.

– Roth, L.R. *History of Whatcom County.* 2 vols. Chicago: Pioneer Historical Publishing Company, 1926.

– Runblom, H., and Norman, H., eds. *From Sweden to America; A History of the Migration.* Minneapolis: University of Minnesota Press, 1976.

– Samson, M.L. *Population Mobility in the Netherlands 1880-1910; A Case Study of Wisch in the Achterhoek.* Uppsala: Almquist & Wiksell International, 1977.

– Sandberg, J.C.C. "De uitbuiting van den immigrant in de Vereenigde Staten van Noord-Amerika." *Tijdschrift van den Nederl. Werkloosheidsraad* 73 (1918): 611-23.

– Sannes, H. *Geschiedenis van Het Bildt.* 3 vols. Franeker: Wever, 1956.

– Schaap, D. *Brug naar de zeven zeeën. Holland Amerika Lijn honderd jaar.* Rotterdam: Holland Amerika Lijn, 1973.

– Schaepdrijver, S. de. *Elites for the Capital?* Amsterdam: Thesis Publishers, 1990.

– Schelbert, L., and Rappolt, H. *Alles ist ganz anders hier. Auswandererschicksale in Briefen aus zwei Jahrhunderten.* Olten and Freiburg: Walter, 1977.

– Schilstra, W.N. *Vrouwenarbeid in landbouw en industrie in Nederland in de tweede helft van de negentiende eeuw.* Amsterdam: Contact, 1940.

– Schnücker, G. *Die Ostfriesen in Amerika. Eine illustrierte Geschichte ihrer Kolonien bis zur Gegenwart.* Cleveland, OH: Central Publishing House, 1917.

– Schnücker, G. *The East Friesens in America; An Illustrated History of their Colonies to the Present Time.* Translated by K. De Wall. Topeka, KS: Jostens Printing and Publishing, 1986.

– Scholte, L.R. *Een vreemdelinge in een vreemd land.* Goes: Oosterbaan & Le Cointre, 1960.

– Schoone-Jongen, R. "Cheap Land and Community; Theodore F. Koch, Dutch Colonizer." *Minnesota History* 53 (Summer 1993): 212-24.

– Schreiber, N., ed. *Randolph Centennial 1870-1970.* N.p.: Hutchinson, 1980.

– Schreiber, P.J., ed. *Centennial History of the Town of Randolph, Columbia County, 1849-1950.* N.p., 1950.

– Schreuder, Y. *Dutch Catholic Immigrant Settlement in Wisconsin, 1850-1905.* New York & London: Garland Publishing, 1989.

– Schulte Nordholt, J.W. "Dutch Travelers in the United States; A Tale of Energy and Ambivilance." In *A Bilateral Bicentennial; A History of Dutch-American Relations 1792-1982,* 251-65. Edited by J.W. Schulte Nordholt, and R.P. Swierenga. Amsterdam: Meulenhoff, 1982.

– Schulte Nordholt, J.W. "Perceived in Poetry; Poetical Images of America for Dutch Immigrants." In *The Dutch in North-America; Their Immigration and Cultural Continuity,* 3-15. Edited by R. Kroes, and H-O. Neuschäfer. Amsterdam: VU University Press, 1991.

– Schulte Nordholt, J.W. *De mythe van het Westen. Amerika als laatste wereldrijk.* Amsterdam: Meulenhoff, 1992.

– Schulte Nordholt, J.W., and Swierenga, R.P., eds. *A Bilateral Bicentennial; A History of Dutch-American Relations 1782-1982.* Amsterdam: Meulenhoff, 1982.

– Scranton, P.B., ed. *Silk City; Studies on the Paterson Silk Industry, 1860-1940.* Newark: New Jersey Historical Society, 1985.

– Scucs, L.D. *Ellis Island; Gateway to America.* Salt Lake City: Ancestry, 1986.

– Semmingsen, I. *Norway to America; A History of the Migration.* Translated by E. Haugen. Minneapolis: University of Minnesota Press, 1978.

– Sevenster, A. *Het bevolkings- en emigratievraagstuk in Nederland en in den Nederlandschen landbouw.* Ph.D. dissertation, Wageningen, 1930.

– Shriner, C.A. *Four Chapters of Paterson History.* Paterson, NJ: Lont & Overkamp, 1919.

– Siderius, K., and Siderius, J. *De geschiedenis van Barradeel.* Franeker: Telenga's Drukkerij, 1950.

– Sinke, S. "Home is Where you Build It; Dutch Immigrant Women and Social Reproduction." In *The Dutch in North-America; Their Immigration and Cultural Continuity,* 410-21. Edited by R. Kroes, and H-O.

Neuschäfer. Amsterdam: VU University Press, 1991.

– Sinke, S.M. *Home is Where You Build it; Dutch Immigrant Women in the United States, 1880-1920*. Ph.D. dissertation, University of Minnesota, 1993. Ann Arbor: University Microfilms International, 1993.

– Sleurink, H., and Frieswijk, J. *De zaak Hogerhuis. Eene gerechtelijke misdaad*. Leeuwarden: Friese Pers Boekerij, 1984.

– Sollors, W., ed. *The Invention of Ethnicity*. New York and Oxford: Oxford University Press, 1989.

– *Souvenir for the Dedication of the New Church Building of the Christian Reformed Church Whitinsville, Massachusetts June 25, 26, 1930*. Whitinsville: Eagle Press, 1930.

– *Souvenir History of Pella, Iowa*. Pella: The Booster Press, 1922.

– Spahr van der Hoek, J.J. "De weg naar welvaart." In *Geschiedenis van Friesland*, 493-514. Edited by J.J. Kalma; J.J. Spahr van der Hoek; and K. de Vries. Drachten: Laverman, 1968; reprint ed., Leeuwarden: De Tille, 1980.

– Spahr van der Hoek, J.J. "Undersyk yn de noardeasthoeke." *It Beaken* 32 (1970): 61-118.

– Spahr van der Hoek, J.J. *Geschiedenis van de Friese landbouw*. 2 vols. Leeuwarden: Friesche Maatschappij van Landbouw, 1952.

– Spyksma, Y.C. *Dutch American Relations; Friesland 1845-1878*. Leeuwarden: Fryske Akademy, 1965.

– Staverman, M. *Buitenkerkelijkheid in Friesland*. Assen: Van Gorcum, 1954.

– Steege, J. ter., ed. *In vogelvlucht. Geschiedenis van de gemeente Oostdongeradeel*. Aalsum-Wetzens: J. ter Steege, 1971.

– Steensma, R. "Geastlik libben yn Wûnseradiel." In *Geakunde Wûnseradiel*, 126-225. Edited by J.J. Spahr van der Hoek. Bolsward: Osinga, 1969.

– Stekelenburg, H.A.V.M. van. *Landverhuizing als regionaal verschijnsel. Van Noord-Brabant naar Noord-Amerika 1820-1880*. Tilburg: Stichting Zuidelijk Historisch Contact, 1991.

– Stekelenburg, H.A.V.M. van. *'Hier is alles vooruitgang...'Landverhuizing van Noord Brabant naar Noord-Amerika, 1880-1940*. Tilburg: Stichting Zuidelijk Historisch Contact, 1996.

– Stevenson, R.L. *The Amateur Emigrant*. 1892; reprint ed., London: The Hogarth Press, 1984.

– Stilling, N.P. "Letter from America: The Emigrant Letter as Stimulus to Emigration." In *Danish Emigration to the U.S.A.*, 363-65. Edited by B. Flemming Larsen, and H. Bender. Aalborg: Danes Worldwide Archives, 1992.

– Stilling, N.P., and Olsen, A.L. *A New Life; Danish Emigration to North America as Described by the Emigrants Themselves in Letters 1842-1946*. Aalborg: Danes Worldwide Archives, 1994.

– Stokvis, P.R.D. *De Nederlandse trek naar Amerika 1846-1847*. Leiden: Universitaire Pers, 1977.

– Stokvis, P.R.D. "Socialistische immigranten in de Verenigde Staten. Vrijheid versus gelijkheid." *Groniek* 96 (1986): 103-16.

– Stokvis, P.R.D. "Dutch-Speaking Peoples." In *The Immigrant Labor Press in North America, 1840s-1970s*, 263-78. Edited by D. Hoerder. New York: Greenwood Press, 1987.

– Stone. F.S. *History of Racine County Wisconsin*. 2 vols. Chicago: S.J. Clark Publishing Co., 1916.

– Stouffer, S.A. "Intervening Opportunities; A Theory Relating Mobility and Distance." *American Sociological Review* 5 (December 1940): 845-67.

– Struve, H.E.W., and Bekaar, A.A. "Nijverheidsstatistiek 1888-1890." 5 vols. Cited in T. van der Wal *Op zoek naar een nieuwe vrijheid. Een kwart eeuw arbeidersbeweging in Friesland 1870-1895*. Leiden: Universitaire Pers, 1972.

– Swierenga, R.P. "The Ethnic Voter and the First Lincoln Election." *Civil War History* 11 (1965): 27-43.

– Swierenga, R.P. "A Dutch Immigrant's View of Frontier Iowa." *Annals of Iowa* 38 (Fall 1965): 81-120.

– Swierenga, R.P., and Stout, H.S. "Socio-Economic Patterns of Migration from The Netherlands in the Nineteenth Century." In *Research in Economic History*. Vol. 1, 298-333. Edited by P. Uselding. Greenwich, CT: JAI Press, 1976.

– Swierenga, R.P. "Dutch Immigrant Demography, 1820-1880." *Journal of Family History* 5 (1980): 390-405.

– Swierenga, R.P. "The Dutch." In *Harvard Encyclopedia of American Ethnic Groups*, 284-95. Edited by S. Thernstrom. Cambridge, MA, and London, England: Harvard University Press, 1980.

– Swierenga, R.P. "Local-Cosmopolitan Theory and Immigrant Religion; the Social Bases of the Antebellum Dutch Reformed Schism." *Journal of Social History* 14 (Fall 1980): 113-36.

– Swierenga, R.P. "Dutch International Migration Statistics, 1820-1880; An Analysis of Linked Multinational Nominal Files." *International Migration Review* 15 (Fall 1981): 445-70.

– Swierenga, R.P. "Exodus Netherlands, Promised Land America; Dutch Immigration and Settlement in the United States." In *A Bilateral Bicentennial; A History of Dutch-American Relations 1782-1982*, 127-47. Edited by J.W. Schulte Nordholt, and R.P. Swierenga. Amsterdam: Meulenhoff, 1982.

– Swierenga, R.P. "Het bestuderen van de Nederlandse emigratie naar de Verenigde Staten. Nieuwe methoden en begrippen." *Jaarboek Centraal Bureau voor Genealogie* 36 (1982), 252-68.

– Swierenga, R.P. "Dutch International Labor Migration to North America in the Nineteenth Century." In *Dutch Immigration to North America*, 1-34. Edited by H. Ganzevoort, and M. Boekelman. Toronto: Multicultural History Society of Ontario, 1983.

– Swierenga, R.P. *Dutch Emigrants to the United States, South Africa, South America and, Southeast Asia, 1835-1880; An Alphabetical Listing by Households and Independent Persons*. Wilmington, DE: Scholarly Resources, 1983.

– Swierenga, R.P. *Dutch Immigrants in U.S. Passenger Manifests, 1820-1880; An Alphabethical Listing by*

*Household Heads and Single Persons*, 2 vols. Wilmington, DE: Scholarly Resources, 1983.

– Swierenga, R.P. "Dutch Immigration Patterns in the Nineteenth and Twentieth Centuries." In *The Dutch in America; Immigration, Settlement, and Cultural Change*, 15-42. Edited by R.P. Swierenga. New Brunswick, NJ: Rutgers University Press, 1985.

– Swierenga, R.P. "Dutch International Migration and Occupational Change; A Structural Analysis of Multinational Linked Files." In *Migration Across Time and Nations*, 95-124. Edited by I. Glazier, and L. De Rosa. New York/London: Holmes & Meier, 1986.

– Swierenga, R.P. "Historians and the Census; The Historiography of Census Research." *The Annals of Iowa* 50 (1990): 650-73.

– Swierenga, R.P. "Local Patterns of Dutch Migration to the United States in the Mid-Nineteenth Century." In *A Century of European Migrations, 1830-1930*, 134-57. Edited by R.J. Vecoli, and S.M. Sinke. Urbana & Chicago: University of Illinois Press, 1991.

– Swierenga, R.P. "List Upon List; The Ship Passenger Records and Immigration Research." *Journal of American Ethnic History* 10 (Spring 1991): 42-53.

– Swierenga, R.P. "Religion and Immigration Behavior; The Dutch Experience." In *Belief and Behavior*. Edited by Ph.R. Vandermeer, and R.P. Swierenga. New Brunswick: Rutgers University Press, 1991.

– Swierenga, R.P. "The Delayed Transition from Folk to Labor Migration; The Netherlands, 1880-1920." *International Migration Review* 22 (Summer 1993): 406-24.

– Swierenga, R.P. "The Journey Across; Dutch Transatlantic Emigrant Passage to the United States, 1820-1880." In *Connecting Cultures; The Netherlands in Five Centuries of Transatlantic Exchange*, 101-33. Edited by R. Hoefte, and J.C. Kardux. Amsterdam: VU University Press, 1994.

– Swierenga, R.P. *The Forerunners; Dutch Jewry in the North American Diaspora*. Detroit: Wayne State University Press, 1994.

– Swierenga, R.P. "The Low Countries." *Encyclopedia of Indiana Ethnic Groups*. Forthcoming.

– Tedebrand, L-G. "Sources for the History of Swedish Emigration." In *From Sweden to America; A History of Migration*, 76-93. Edited by H. Runblom, and H. Norman. Minneapolis: University of Minnesota Press, 1976.

– Thernstrom, S. *Poverty and Progress; Social Mobility in a Nineteenth Century City*. Cambridge, MA: Harvard University Press, 1964.

– Thernstrom, S. *The Other Bostonians; Poverty and Progress in the American Metropolis, 1880-1970*. Cambridge, MA: Harvard University Press, 1973.

– Thernstrom, S., ed. *Harvard Encyclopedia of American Ethnic Groups*. Cambridge, MA: Harvard University Press, 1980.

– Thomas, D.S. "Research Memorandum on Migration Differentials." *Social Science Research Council Bulletin* 43 (1938).

– Tilly, C. "Transplanted Networks." In *Immigration Reconsidered*, 79-95. Edited by V. Yans-McLaughlin. New York: Oxford University Press, 1990.

– *A Trip through the Whitin Machine Works; Manufacturers of Textile Machinery*. Whitinsville: Whitin Machine Works, 1925.

– Turner, F.J. *The Frontier in American History*. New York: Henry Holt & Company, 1920.

– Twerda, H. *Fan Fryslâns forline*. Bolsward: A.J. Osinga, 1968.

– Ulberg, T. "Uit de portefeuille van de eerste settlers in de Hollandsche kolonie in Michigan." *Jaarboekje voor de Hollandsche Christelijke Gereformeerde Kerk in Noord-Amerika. Voor het jaar 1883*, Grand Rapids, MI: 1882. Reprinted in *Dutch Immigrant Memoirs and Related Writings*, 1: 272-89. Edited by H.S. Lucas. Assen: Van Gorcum, 1955.

– Valk, L.A. van der. "Landverhuizersvervoer via Rotterdam in de negentiende eeuw." *Economisch- en Sociaal-Historisch Jaarboek* 39 (1976): 148-71.

– Vandenbosch, A. *The Dutch Communities of Chicago*. Chicago: the Knickerbocker Society of Chicago, 1927.

– Vanderstel, D.G. *The Dutch of Grand Rapids, Michigan, 1848-1900; Immigrant Neighborhood and Community Development in a Nineteenth Century City*. Ann Arbor: University Microfilms International, 1986.

– Vander Pol, H. *On the Reservation Border; Hollanders in Douglas and Charles Mix Counties*. Stickney, SD: Argus Printers, 1969.

– Vecoli, R.J. *The People of New Jersey*. Princeton, NJ: D. Van Nostrand Company, 1965.

– Vecoli, R.J. "The Formation of Chicago's 'Little Italies'." In *Migrations Across Time and Nations*, 287-301. Edited by I. Glazier, and L. De Rosa. New York: Holmes & Meier, 1986.

– Vecoli, R. "New Guidelines and Research Hypotheses for the History of European Emigration." In *Studi sull'emigrazione. Un'analisi comparata*, 45-58. Edited by M.R. Ostuni. Biella, 1989.

– Vecoli, R., and Sinke, S.M., eds. *A Century of European Migrations, 1830-1930*. Urbana & Chicago: University of Illinois Press, 1991.

– Veen, W.K. van der. *Uit de geschiedenis van de grietenij Ferwerderadeel*. Leeuwarden, n.p., 1958.

– Veld-Langeveld, H.M. in 't. *Migratiemotieven, migratiebeheersing en hun selektieve betekenis*. Assen: Van Gorcum, 1957.

– Velde, H. te. *Gemeenschapszin en plichtsbesef. Liberalisme en nationalisme in Nederland 1870-1918*. Den Haag: SDU, 1992.

– Vermeulen, H., and Böcker, A. "De studie van migratie in Nederland. Een bibliografisch overzicht." *Migrantenstudies* 4 (1992): 21-28.

– Vermooten, W.H. "Oorzaken van de toenemende urbaniseering in Nederland." *Mens en Maatschappij* 8 (1932): 161-82.

– Visser, G.N. "Tsjibbe Gearts en it lân fan dream en winsken." In *Tsjibbe Gearts van der Meulen. Wâldman en wrâldboarger*, 182- 208. Leeuwarden: Fryske Akademy nr. 466, 1974.

– Vondeling, A. *Eat oer it tal biwenners, de migraesje en de bifolkingstichtens yn Fryslân.* Drachten: Fryske Lânboubibleteek, 1943.

– Vonk Noordegraaf, T.A. "Oostdongeradeel als 'rechtse' gemeente." *It Beaken. Dongeradeel byda aestersiida der pasen* 26 (1964): 177-94.

– Vree, A. de. "Ervaringen." *De Grondwet*, February 20, 1912. Reprinted in *Dutch Immigrant Memoirs and Related Writings*, 1: 292-99. Edited by H.S. Lucas. Assen: Van Gorcum, 1955.

– Vries, H. de. *Landbouw en bevolking tijdens de agrarische depressie in Friesland (1878-1895).* Wageningen: H. Veenman & Zonen, 1971.

– Vries, H. de. "The Labor Market in Dutch Agriculture and Emigration to the United States." In *The Dutch in America; Immigration, Settlement, and Cultural Change*, 78-101. Edited by R.P. Swierenga. New Brunswick NJ: Rutgers University Press, 1985.

– Vries, N.A. de. *De Nieuwe Wereld. Amerika 1923.* Groningen: J.B. Wolters, 1924.

– Wabeke, B. *Dutch Emigration to North America 1624-1860.* New York: Netherlands Information Bureau, 1944.

– Wal, T. van der. *Op zoek naar een nieuwe vrijheid. Een kwart eeuw arbeidersbeweging in Friesland 1870-1895.* Leiden: Universitaire Pers, 1972.

– Ward, D. *Cities and Immigrants; A Geography of Change in Nineteenth-Century America.* New York: Oxford University Press, 1971.

– Webber, P.E. *Pella Dutch; The Portrait of a Language and Its Use in One of Iowa's Ethnic Communities.* Ames, IA: Iowa State University Press, 1988.

– Welling, G.M. "A strategy for intelligent input programs for structured data." *History and Computing* 5 (1993): 1: 35-46.

– Welling, G.M. "Computationele geschiedenis." *Geschiedenis en Bestanden* (Enkhuizen 1995): 90-99.

– Wentholt, R. *Kenmerken van de Nederlandse emigrant.* 's-Gravenhage: Staatsuitgeverij, 1961.

– Wentholt, A.D. *Brug over den oceaan. Een eeuw geschiedenis van de Holland Amerika Lijn.* Rotterdam: Nijgh & Van Ditmar, 1973.

– Wildeboer, J.D. "Friesland verliest zijn kinderen." *It Beaken* 16 (May 1954) 3/4: 65-120.

– Williamson, J.C. "American Prices and Urban Inequality since 1820." *Explorations in Economic History* 2 (1974).

– Wilterdink, W. *Winterswijkse pioniers in Amerika.* Winterswijk: 'Het Museum', 1990.

– Wrigley, E.A. *Identifying People in the Past.* London: Arnold, 1973.

– Wumkes, G.A. *Stads- en dorpskroniek van Friesland.* 2 vols. Leeuwarden: Eisma, 1930-1934.

– Yans-McLaughlin, V. *Family and Community; Italian Immigrants in Buffalo, 1880-1930.* Ithaca: Cornell University Press, 1977.

– Yans-McLaughlin, V., ed. *Immigration Reconsidered.* New York: Oxford University, 1990.

– *100 Years of God With Us; Emmanuel Reformed Church, Springfield, South Dakota 1888-1988.* Freeman, SD: Pine Hill Press, 1988.

– Yntema, M.E. *The Family of Hessel O. Yntema; Frisian Immigrant to Michigan, 1847.* Holland, MI: The Klaasen Printing Company, 1958.

– Yoder, M. "Balk Dutch Settlement near Goshen, Indiana, 1853-1889." *Mennonite Quarterly Review* 30 (January 1956): 32-43.

– Ypma, J. *Ds Marten Annes Ypma 1810-1863.* Hallum: Fries Dagblad Offset, 1984.

– Yska, D. *De geschiedenis van Ferwerd in woord en beeld.* Leeuwarden: Reidsma, 1972.

– Zanden, J.L. van. *"Den zedelijken en materiëlen toestand der arbeidende bevolking ten platten lande." Een reeks rapporten uit 1851.* Groningen: Nederlands Agronomisch-Historisch Instituut, 1991.

– Zanden, J.L. van. *De economische ontwikkeling van de Nederlandse landbouw in de negentiende eeuw 1800-1914.* Utrecht: Hes Uitgevers, 1985.

– Zanden, J.L. van. "De Friese economie in de negentiende eeuw." *It Beaken* 1/2 (1992): 7-14.

– Zee, Sj. de. *Myn twadde Amerika-reis.* Heerenveen: Handelsdrukkerij Hepkema, 1929.

– Zevenbergen, C. *Toen zij uit Rotterdam vertrokken. Emigratie via Rotterdam door de eeuwen heen.* Zwolle: Waanders, 1990.

– Zijlstra, S. *Skiednis fan Eastdongeradiel.* Leeuwarden: Fryske Akademy, 1992.

– Zondergeld, G.R. *De Friese beweging in het tijdvak der beide wereldoorlogen.* Leeuwarden: De Tille, 1978.

– Zucchi, J.E. *Italians in Toronto; Development of a National Identity, 1875-1935.* Kingston & Montreal: McGill-Queen's University Press, 1988.

## III. Periodicals and Newspapers

– Anema, T.; Graaf, T. de.; and Schatz, H.F. "The Frisian Language in America." *Nowele* 12 (May 1988): 91-108.

– Beets, H. "Our Frisian Settlement in Whitinsville, Mass." *The Banner*, October 1, 1926.

– Berkenbosch, K. "Laandverhuzen is drama." *De Ovend* (May 1994): 12-14.

– Bottema, H. "In het Amerikaansche Friesland." *Leeuwarder Courant*, August 8,9, 1928.

– Brink, A. "Lynden." *Origins* 4 (1986) 2: 28-39.

– Brinks, H.J. "The Beginnings of the CRC in New Jersey 1855-1866." *Origins* 2 (1984) 1: 17-21.

– Brinks, H.J. "Castle Garden." *Origins* 2 (1984) 1: 6-8.

– Brinks, H.J. "Crossing the Atlantic." *Origins* 2 (1984) 1: 2-5.

– Brinks, H.J. "The Vanden Hoeks in Harrison 1884-1895." *Origins* 5 (1987) 1: 38-41.

– Brinks, H.J. "Germans in the Christian Reformed Church, 1857-1872." *Origins* 9 (1991) 2: 36-43.

– Brinks, H.J. "Silk City; News from Paterson's Mill Workers." *Origins* 11 (1993) 2: 2-11.

– "'t Brocht gyn bliksum op, maar elk fon 't mooi'."

*Leeuwarder Courant*, January 31, 1987.

– Bruins, E.J. "The Dutch-Immigrant Congregations of Alto, Wisconsin 1845-1900." *Origins* 7 (1989) 1: 23-33.

– Byl, J. "Sports and Sabbath Desecration." *Origins* 8 (1990) 2: 25-29.

– "Een Calvinist onder stoom." *Nieuwsblad van Noord-Oost Friesland*, May 11, 1990.

– Delaere, M. "De gouden toegangspoort tot Amerika als museum heropend." *Haagsche Courant*, September 20, 1990.

– De Smith, R.J. "Jacobus DeRooy; Rural Wisconsin Diarist and Preacher." *Origins* 2 (1984) 2: 27-36.

– Eggers, K.M. "Nadelöhr zur Freizeit." *Zeit/Magazin*, September 1990, 22-28.

– Galema, A. "Whitinsville, Massachusetts." *Origins* 12 (1994) 2: 2-7.

– Groen, J. "De mythe van de Nieuwe Wereld." *De Volkskrant*, September 15, 1990.

– Groot, C. de. "American and Dutch Maids are Compared." *San Francisco Chronicle*, February 29, 1929.

– Hacket, P. "The Stone Walls of Castle Hill." *Tribune*, May 15, 1974.

– Hall, A.J. "New Life for Ellis Island." *National Geographic* 178 (1990): 88-101.

– Hinte, J. van. "Friesche Mennisten in Indiana." *Neerlandia* 34 (1930): 196-97.

– Hollander, R. "De gouden deur naar Amerika als museum heropend." *NRC Handelsblad*, September 15, 1990.

– Holtmann, A. "'Wenn man es wagt und seinem Vaterland entsagt'. Auf Seglern und Dampfschiffen zogen sieben Millionen Deutsche nach America." *Frankfurter Rundschau*, October 10, 1992, 16.

– Huisman, K. "De dramatyske libbensein fan emigrante Anna." *Leeuwarder Courant*, February 26, 1994.

– Huygen, M. "Amerika zoekt weer naar het gezinsverband." *NRC-Handelsblad*, January 17, 1994.

– Hylkema, B.S. "Op reis nei Amerika." *Sljucht en Rjucht* 25 (1923): 301-03.

– "In de winter hoeft men in Amerika niet te vlasbraken." *Leeuwarder Courant*, April 26, 1986.

– *It Heitelân* 31 (1924); 32 (1924); 26 (1925) 41 (1925).

– Jansen, J. "Een verblijf in Amerika." *Vragen van den Dag* 35 (August 1920): 624-35.

– Knapen, B. "De veroveringsdrang van het goede Amerika." *NRC Handelsblad*, December 23, 1989.

– Kooistra, J. "Brief út Whitinsville fan in âld-Grouster." *Frysk en Frij*, March 24, 1950, and April 7, 1950.

– Krabbendam , H. "The West Side Dutch in Chicago." *Origins* 9 (1991) 2: 4-8.

– Krabbendam, H. "R.T. Kuiper; Developer of Churches." *Origins* 12 (1994) 1: 9-16.

– "Libbensforhael fan in Ferwerter jonge." *Friesch Dagblad*, May 25, 1972.

– Mooijweer, M. "Waarnemen vanuit de verte." *Intermediair*, June 20, 1986.

– "Museen." *Der Spiegel*, 1990/37, 244-45.

– *Ons Friese Platteland*, May-August, 1981.

– Poortinga, Y. "Bildtske emigranten yn 'e foarige ieu." *Estrikken* 30 (1960): 67-70.

– "Remarks on Christian Reformed, East Frisian Rheiderland Township, Minnesota." *Frisian News Items* (June 1981): 26.

– Rydell, R.W. "Montana; Big Sky Country." *Amerika*, Winter 1993-1994, 6-13.

– Schulte Nordholt, J.W. "Geloven in Amerika." *Amerika*, Spring 1994, 79-83.

– *Sljucht en Rjucht*, April 23, 1921. August 11, 1934.

– Stob, H. "Henry Stob." *Origins* 9 (1991) 2: 9-17.

– Stob, H. "Church and School on Chicago's West Side 1913-1921." *Origins* 10 (1992) 2: 14-19, and *Origins* 11 (1993) 1: 24-29.

– Stoffels, F. "'s Heren wegen in de USA." *VU Magazine*, September 8, 1985, 301-06.

– Swart, J. "Emigraasje as útwei foar driigjend ûnk." *De Vrije Fries* 64 (1984): 79-93.

– Tiemersma, R.R. "Growing Up in Roseland in the 20's & 30's." *Origins* 5 (1987) 1: 2-19.

– Timmerman, J.J. "Growing up in New Jersey." *Origins* 3 (1985) 2: 18-26.

-"Toen de zalm nog onder de Friese wal kwam." *Leeuwarder Courant*, May 22, 1979.

– Vanderstel, D.G. "Dutch Immigrant Neighborhoods in the City of Grand Rapids 1848-1900." *Origins* 2 (1984) 1: 22-27.

– Vander Laan, E. "South Dakota." *Origins* 5 (1987) 1: 32-37.

– Vent, O. de. "Johannes Nieuwenhuis, laandverhuzer van Steggerde." *De Ovend* (May 1994): 15-17.

– Westra, H. "Fear and Hope Jostled; Dutch Immigrant Life and Death in Paterson, New Jersey." *Origins* 8 (1990) 2: 1-15.

– Wumkes, G.A. "Worp van Peyma en zijn vrienden." *De Vrije Fries* 21 (1914): 150-77.

– Zandstra, D. "The Calumet Region; A Land Flowing with Milk and Honey." *Origins* 4 (1986) 1: 16-21.

– Zandstra, D. "The Calumet Region; Toward Success." *Origins* 4 (1986) 2: 48-54.

## IV. Unpublished Works

– Bloem, R.H. "Dutch Immigration to Whitinsville." Thesis, May 1981. Calvin College Archives, Grand Rapids, MI.

– Bodnar, J.E. "Reworking Reality; Polish Immigrants and the Meaning of the Immigrant Experience." Paper presented at The Tenth Economic History Congress, Leuven, Belgium; August 20-24, 1990.

– Bras, H. "Tussen twee werelden. De migratiemotieven van Klaas Jans Beukma (1789-1860), een Groningse pionier in Amerika." M.A. thesis, University of Groningen, 1993.

– Dekker, S. "History of Roseland and Vicinity." Calumet, 1938; Typescript, Calvin College Archives, Grand Rapids, MI.

– Galema, J.B.E. "Whitinsville, all Frisians, 1880-1910."

Computer Compilation." Groningen, 1989.

– Galema, J.B.E. "Frisians to America, 1880-1914. Computer Compilation." Groningen, 1992.

– Galema, J.B.E. "Frisians in the U.S.A., 1900/1910. Computer Compilation." Groningen, 1993.

– Galema, J.B.E. "Linked Files: Frisians to America and Frisians in the U.S.A. Computer Compilation." Groningen, 1995.

– Koeweiden-Wijdeven, A.F.M. "Vergeten emigranten. Landverhuizing van noord- en midden-Limburg naar Noord-Amerika in de jaren 1847-1877." M.A. thesis, Venlo, May 1982.

– Krogh, H. "'We Meet Only to Part'; Norwegian Immigrants in Transition." Ph.D. dissertation, University of Colorado, 1990.

– Mooney, M.C. "The Industrial Workers of the World and the Immigrants of Paterson and Passaic, NJ, 1907-1913." M.A. thesis, Seaton Hall University, 1969.

– Nieuwenhuis, N.G. "A History of Dutch Settlements in South Dakota to 1900." M.A. thesis, University of South Dakota, Vermillian, 1948.

– Peters, J.P.M. "Landbouwcrisis en emigratie. Een onderzoek naar het verband tussen de landbouwcrisis en het verschijnsel emigratie in drie landbouwgebieden (1875-1900)." Thesis, University of Nijmegen, 1978.

– Schuurmans, M. "The Church and Assimilation in an Isolated Nationality Group." M.A. thesis, Michigan State College of Agriculture, 1941.

– Sinke, S.M. "Dutch Immigrant Women in the Late Nineteenth Century." M.A. thesis, Kent State University, 1983.

– Swierenga, R.P. "Chicago's Groninger Hoek; The Origins and Development of the Dutch Colony on the 'Old West Side' in the Nineteenth Century." Paper delivered at the University of Groningen, 1988.

– Swierenga, R.P. "Dutch Social Clubs in Chicago." Paper presented to the Association for the Advancement of Dutch-American Studies Conference. Orange City, IA, October 26-28, 1995.

– Van Gorp-Vander Baan, W. "The History of the Dutch People in Whitinsville." Manuscript written at the request of the Northbridge Bicentennial Celebration Committee, 1972. Personal Collection Author.

– "Vogel." Unpublished manuscript written by the Vogel-family. Harlingen, n.d.

– Wijngaarden, Tj. P. "Bouwplan en vruchtopvolging op de gardeniersbedrijven in het Noorden van Friesland voor en na het in werking treden van de Wet Bestrijding Aardappelmoeheid van 1949." Thesis, Landbouwhogeschool Wageningen, Oude Bildtzijl, 1955.

– Wood, J.E. "History of Labor in the Broad-Silk Industry of Paterson, NJ." Dissertation, University of California, 1941.

# Appendix I: Codebook of datafile: J.B.E. Galema, "Frisians to America, 1880-1914. Computer Compilation." Groningen, 1992

-Name of emigrant
-First name
-Sex
1 Male
2 Female

-Family status
01 husband
02 wife
03 single individual or single parent
04 single male individual or single male parent
05 single female individual or single female parent
10 son
11 step-son
12 adopted son
20 daughter
21 step-daughter
22 adopted daughter
30 child
31 infant
40 son-in-law
41 daughter in law
42 grandson
43 granddaughter
44 grandchild
50 mother of householdhead
51 mother in law
52 step-mother
53 father of householdhead
54 father in law
55 step-father
56 grandfather
60 brother
61 brother-in-law
62 sister
63 sister-in-law
64 niece
65 nephew
66 uncle
67 aunt
68 cousin

69 grandmother
70 servant
71 servant's daughter
72 servant's son
73 boarder
74 spinster
75 widow
76 widower
77 housekeeper
78 domestic
79 matron
80 kinship tie unknown
81 step-grandchild
82 orphan
83 partner

-Date of birth
-Emigration geographic
1 place of birth
2 neighbourhood of place of birth
3 neighbouring municipality of place of birth
4 non-neighbouring municipality of place of birth
5 same municipality as place of birth
9 unknown

-Frisian born
1 frisian born
2 non frisian born
9 unknown

-Civil status
1 married
2 unmarried/singl
3 widow(er)
4 divorced
9 unknown
5 married twice
6 married thrice

-Number of women in family
-Number of children in family
-Number of servants in family
-Number in family
-Family type
1 single
2 couple with children
3 couple with children + servants + relatives + dome
4 couple without children + servant/stepchildren
5 single parent + children + servant
6 single parent + servant/domestic
7 single parent + children
8 couple without children or servants
9 other (2 brothers + 1 sister etc.)

-Religion
1 nederlands-hervormd
2 gereformeerd
3 christelijk gereformeerd
4 doopsgezind
5 katholiek
6 other
7 none
8 missing
9 vrijzinnige gemeente

-Occupation
Major occupation
99 architects, engineers and surveyors
01 chemists, physicists, geologists and physical scientists
02 biologists, veterinarians and related scientists
03 physicians, surgeons and dentists
04 nurses and midwifes
05 other professional medical workers
06 teachers
07 clergy and related members of religious orders

08 other professional, technical and related workers, contractors (aannemers)

09 artists, writers, and related workers

10 administrators and executives, government

11 directors, managers, and working proprietors

12 wholesale and retail trade (koopman)

13 insurance and real estate salesman

14 manufacturer's agents

15 salesmen, shop assistants and related workers (winkelier)

20 bookkeepers and cashiers

21 stenographers and typists

22 clerks-governments

23 clerk retail

24 clerk manufacturing

29 other clerical workers

30 new workers seeking employment

32 workers reporting occupations unidentifiable or inadequately described

33 workers not reporting any occupation (vrouw/geen)

40 farmers and farmmanagers

41 farm workers not elsewhere classified (arbeider, boerenknecht, stalknecht, tuinknecht.

42 hunters and related workers

43 fishermen and related workers

44 loggers and other forestry workers (tuinman)

50 miners and quarrymen

51 well-drillers and related workers

52 mineral treaters

59 miners, quarrymen and related workers not elsewhere classified

60 desk officers, enigeer officers and pilots,ship

61 deck and egine-room ratings (ship), barge crews and boatmen

63 drivers and firemen, railway engine

64 drivers, road transport

65 conductors, and brakemen railway

66 inspectors, supervisors, traffic controllers and dispatchers, transport

67 telephone, telegraph, and related telecommunication operators

68 postmen and messengers

69 workers transport and communication occupation not elsewhere classified,teamster

70 spinners, weavers, knitters, dyers, and related workers

71 tailors, cutters, furriers, and related workers.

72 leather cutters, lasters and sewers (except gloves and garments) and related wor

73 some furnacemen, rollers, drawers, moulders and related metal making workers

74 precision-instrument makers, watch-makers, jewellers and related workers

75 toolmakers, machinists, plumbers, welders, platers and related workers

76 electricians and related elictrical and elictronics workers

77 carpenters, joiners, cabinetmakers, coopers and related workers

78 painters and paperhangers

79 bricklayers, plasterers and construction workers not elsewhere classified

80 compositors, pressmen, engravers, bookbinders and related workers

81 potters, kilnmen, glass and clay formers and related workers

82 millers, bakers, butchers, brewmasters and related food and beverage workers

83 chemical and related process workers

84 tobacco preparers and tobacco-product makers

85 craftsmen and production process workers not elsewhere classified (speederfender

86 packers, labellers and related workers

87 stationary-engine and excavating and lifting equipment operators and rel.workers

88 longshoremen and related freight handlers

89 labourers not elsewhere classified (dienstbode)

90 fire-fighters, policemen, guards and related workers

91 housekeepers, cooks, maids and related workers (host, dienstmeid)

92 waiters, bartenders and related workers (cafe-houders)

93 military officers and enlisted men (soldaat)

94 barbers, hairdressers,beauticians and related workers

95 launderers, dry cleaners and pressers

96 athletes, sportsmen and related workers

97 photographers and related camera operators

98 embalmers and undertakers.

Social occupational group

01 professional (onderwijzer)

02 sub-professional

03 owner, entrepreneur (schipper)

04 sub-managerial

05 employee-clerk

06 agriculture, self-employed

07 agriculture, tenant

08 agriculture, laborer (arbeider)

09 high commercant, salesman

10 shopkeeper, petty entrepreneur (winkelier,kruidenier)

11 hawker pedler (marskramer)

12 skilled labor (verwer, timmerman, electricien)

13 semiskilled labor (verwersknecht, visser)

14 unskilled labor (dienstbode, dienstmeid, stalknecht, werkman, fabriek)

15 jobless

16 rentier, independant means, gentleman

19 student

21 child under 14 years

22 retired

23 no occupation (geen beroep)

24 housewife

25 unknown (geen opgave)

20 code 20 (fout)

Specific/real occupation

001 aannemer-building contractor

002 agent-agent

003 advocaat-atterney,lawyer

004 akkerbouwman-farmer

005 ambtenaar-government official, civil servant

006 ambtenaar hoofd-head government official

007 apotheker-druggist, pharmaceutical chemist

008 ambachtsman-artisan

009 apotheker's bediende- druggist clerk (apprentice)

010 aardwerker-earthware or pottery worker

011 arbeider-workman

012 arts-doctor

013 arbeidster-workwoman

014 architect

015 aschkooper-ash buyer
016 azijnmaker-vinegar maker
017 bakker (brood,koek,banket)-
    baker
018 bakkers' knecht-baker's helper
019 bakkersleerling-baker's
    apprentice
020 barbiersleerling-barber's
    apprentice
021 barbier-barber
022 meid-maid
023 beddenschoonmaakster-
    chambermaid
024 bediende-servant
025 beeldhouwer-sculptor
026 begrafenis baas-
    undertaker,mortician
027 behanger-wall paper hanger
028 besteller-postman
029 besteller van boodschappen-
    messenger boy,delivery man
030 behangersknecht-wallpaper
    hanger's hired hand
031 bierbrouwer-beer brewer-
    bottelaar mineraalwater
032 balansmaker-scale(balance)-
    maker
033 bijzonder hoofdonderwijzer-
    teacher
034 bijker- bee keeper
035 binnenvaarder-canal boatman
036 bierbrouwersknecht-beer
    brewer's hired hand
037 blauwverver-dyer (blue dyer)
038 blauwverversknecht-dyer's hired
    hand
039 bleeker-bleacher
040 bleekersknecht-bleacher's hired
    hand
041 blikslager-tinsmith
042 biljardmaker-billiard table maker
043 bloemist,bloemwerker-florist
044 automobielshop-carshop
045 blokkenmaker-pulley maker, clog
    or woodenshoemaker
046 blokmastknecht-pulley man's
    hired hand
047 boekbinder-bookbinder
048 boekdrukkersknecht-publisher's
    hired hand
049 boeketmaker-bouquet maker
050 boekhanderlaarsbediende-
    bookstore clerk
051 boekdrukker-printer
052 boekhandelaar,boekverkoper-
    bookstore owner
053 boekhouder-
    bookkeeper,stenograaf

054 boer,boerenbedrijf-farmer
055 boerenknecht,
    boerenarbeider,boerenwerker-
    farmer's hand
056 boerenmeid,boerwerkster-
    farmer's hand (female)
057 borstelmaker-brush maker
058 boomkweker-tree planter/
059 boschbaas-forest administrator,
    ranger
060 boterkoper-butter merchant
061 boerwerkster-farmer's hand
    (female)
062 boomkweker-tree husbandry
063 bouwkundige-architect
064 brandweerman-fireman
065 bouwman-farmer
066 bouwmansknecht-farmer's hand
067 brandersknecht-distiller's hand
068 buitenberoep-job outdoors
069 buitenvaarder-coastal boatman
070 chemist
071 candidaat notaris-notary
072 chirurgijnmajoor-major surgeon
073 cigarenmaker-cigar maker
074 candidaat jurist-law student
075 cigarenmakersknecht-cigar
    maker's hired hand
076 cichoreidroger-chicory dryer
077 civiel ingenieur-civil engineer
078 conducteur op stoomboot-
    steamboat conductor
079 commisionair-commision
    agent,stock broker
080 controleur-inspector
081 dagloner-day laborer (male)
082 commies-government official
083 dagloonster-daylaborer(female)
084 draaijer-turner
085 drooger in een meestof-dryer
086 dekker,uitdekker-roofer
087 deurwaarder-usher,process
    server
088 decatiseur van laken-cotton
    decorator
089 diamantslijper-diamond cutter
090 docent-teacher
091 dienstbode-hired girl, female
    servant
092 dijkwerker-dyke worker
093 dienstknecht-hired hand (male)
094 draaijer-turner
095 dienstmeid-(farm)servant girl
096 essayeur-essayer
097 fabrikant-manufacturer

098 fabrikant directeur-factory
    manager

099 fabrieksarbeider/bediende-
    factory worker
100 gareelmaker-harness maker
101 gardenier-small farmer,gardner
102 evangelist
103 geen-none/without any job
104 geestelijke-clergy man
105 gemeente ontvanger-municipal
    official
106 gastheer-hostler/housekeeper
107 geneesheer/physician
108 gepensioneerd officier(militair)-
    pensionated millitary officer
109 geweermaker-gunsmith
110 electricien-
111 gistkooper-yeast buyer
112 brandweerman-fireman
113 glasblazer-glass blower
114 glaszetter-glass
115 goud en zilversmid-gold-and
    silver smith
116 eierkoopman-eggbuyer
117 gouvernante-governess
118 grafdelger-grave digger/laborer
    cemetary
119 graanhandelaar-graindealer
120 graveur-engraver
121 grofsmid-blacksmith(crude iron)
122 groente/fruithandelaar-
    vegetables/fruit merchant
123 grofsmidsknecht-blacksmith's
    hand
124 huizenverkoper-buyer and seller
    of houses
125 grutter-grocer, corn handler
126 gruttersknecht-grocer's hand
127 haam of gareelmaker-horse
    collar maker
128 handelsman, handelaar-buyer
129 heelmeester-doctor
130 huizenbouwer-builder of houses
131 hulponderwijzer-assistant teacher
132 hofmeester-purser
133 herbergier-hotel keeper
134 huishoudster-
    housekeeper(female)
135 hoedenmaakster-hat
    maker,milliner
136 huurman-hired man
137 hoefsmid-blacksmith,horse shoer
138 instrumentmaker
139 houtzaagmolenaar-sawmill
    operator
140 houtzaagmolenaarsknecht-
    sawmill operator's hand
141 holdraaijer-ditch digger
142 hovenier-gardener
143 horlogemaker-watchmaker

144 houthakker-woodman, timber farmer
145 houtdrager,houtzager-wood carrier, sawyer
146 huisknecht-domestic hired hand
147 huisschilder-house painter
148 industrieel-industrialist
149 huisvrouw-housewife
150 ijzergieter-foundry man
151 ijzersmidsknecht-blacksmith's hand
152 ingenieur-engineer
153 inlandse kramer-peddler
154 jager-hunter
155 krantenjongen-newsboy
156 juwelier-jewler
157 kabinet en schrijfwerker,kastenmaker-cabinet maker
158 kaarsenmakersknecht-candle maker's helper
159 kantoorbediende-office clerk
160 kapelaan-chaplain, assistant priest
161 kapper-barber,hairdresser
162 kassier-cashier
163 kastelein-innkeeper
164 kaasman-cheese man
165 katoenspinner-cotton spinner/dyer/worker
166 keukenmeid-kitchen maid, maid
167 kleermaker-clothes maker,tailor,cloth inspector
168 kleermakersknecht-tailor's helper
169 klerk-clerk
170 kolenbrander-charcoal burner, maker
171 klompenmaker-wooden shoemaker
172 klooster zuster-nun
173 kleimaker-clay maker
174 kok-cook
175 kooiman-wild duck trapper
176 kooiboer,kooiker-wild duck trapper, chickenfarmer
177 koehouder,koemelker-milker,cattleman
178 koetsier-driver,coach man
179 koopman-buyer,retailer, merchant, middleman
180 koopman bediende-buyer's helper
181 koopvrouw-buyer (woman)
182 koffiehuishouder-cafe proprieter
183 koperslager,kopergieter-coppersmith
184 koperslagersknecht-

coppersmith's hand
185 korenschippersknecht-grain ship hand
186 kapelaan-r.C. Curate, assistant priest,chaplain
187 kostganger-boarder
188 kelner-waiter
189 koster-church custodian
190 kooltjer-charcoal dealer,laborer coal
191 kramer-pedler
192 koopvaardij kapitein,stuurman-merchant mariner
193 kraamster-pedler(female)
194 kribbaat-
195 kroeghouder-cafe owner
196 karreman-carter,cartman
197 kroeghoudster-bar owner(female)
198 ketelmaker-boilermaker
199 kuiper-cooper
200 kanaalwerker-canal worker
201 kuipersknecht-cooper's hand
202 kweeling-pupil
203 kunat kolenbrander-charcoal maker
204 kurkenmaker-cork maker
205 kunstschilder-artist,painter
206 kunstrijder-circus performer or figure skater
207 labelmaker
208 laarsenmaker-bootmaker
209 landbouwer-farmer
210 landbouwster-farmer(female)
211 landbouwersleerling-farmer's apprentice
212 kleinlandbouwer-small farmer
213 landgebruiker-landdeveloper,landlord(realtor)
214 leemvormer-clay molder,potter
215 leraar-teacher,minister
216 kaasmaker-cheesmaker
217 leerlooijer-leather preparer,tanner
218 linnenwever-linenweaver
219 leerlooijersknecht-leather tanner's hand
220 lettergieter-type fouder
221 linnen fabrikant-linnen manufacturer
222 lintwerker-draper
223 landmeter-land assessor, surveyor
224 letter zetter-type setter
225 leemvormer-clay molder,potter
226 lettergieter-type founder
227 leurder-peddler
228 liefdezuster-nun, sister of charity
229 likeurstoker-distiller

230 lichtwachter-lantern watcher(lichter)
231 ligmatroos-sailor
232 kasteleinsknecht-bar owner's hand
233 lithograaf-lithographer
234 logementhouder-hotelkeeper
235 portier-doorman
236 loodgietersleerling-plumber's hand
237 loodgieter en leydekker-plumber and roofer
238 machinist katoenfabriek-machinist cotton shop
239 loodsschipper-ship pilot
240 machinemaker machinefabriek-machinemaker machine shop
241 machinist-engineer,steam-engine operator machine shop
242 magnetiseur-mesmerizer
243 makelaar-broker
244 machinebediener,timmerman machinefabriek-speeder fender
245 mandenmaker-basket maker
246 manufacturier-manufacturer
247 marsdrager-peddler
248 landheer-landlord
249 matroos sailor
250 medische dokter-doctor
251 arbeider meubelfabriek-laborer furniture shop
252 meid-maid
253 melkboer-dairy farmer
254 melktapper-milkbusiness
255 messelaar-knif3e grindler
256 metselaarsknecht-bricklayer's helper
257 metselaar-bricklayer,mason
258 meubelmaker-furniture maker
259 militair-military
260 mineur-miner
261 modemaakster-milliner(female)
262 melkrijder,melkfabrieksarbeider-milk driver,laborer dairyfac
263 modiste-milliner
264 melker-milker
265 molenaar-miller
266 pelmolenaar-seashell grinder
267 molenaarsknecht-miller's hand
268 opzichter zijde fabriek-foreman silk mill
269 molenmaker-windmillmaker
270 mouter-maltster in malt house
271 muziek direkteur-music director
272 natuurkundige-physicist
273 naaister-seamstress
274 nachtwacht-night watchman
275 officier-officer

276 olieslager-oilseed crusher (cooking oil business man)

277 olieslagersknecht-oil seed cruscher's hand, seller oil

278 officier van gezondheid-health officer

279 onderwijzer-teacher

280 opzigter-overseer

281 onderwijzeres-teacher(female)

282 oppasser-caretaker

283 orgelmaker-organ maker

284 paarddriller-horse trainer

285 pakkendrager-delivery man

286 pakhuisknecht-warehouse man

287 papier fabriekant-paper manufacturer

288 paraplumaker-umbrella maker

289 particulier-independent man

290 pastoor-pastor

291 pelmolenaarsknecht-seashell grinder's hand

292 pachter-tenant farmer

293 pettenmaker-cap makerf

294 ploeger-plow man

295 fotograaf-photographer

296 planter

297 poelier-poulterer,chicken raiser

298 politieagent-policeman

299 pompenmaker-pump maker

300 polderwerker-excavator, dirthauler, polderworker.

301 Postbode-mailman

302 plankhouwer-plank hewer (sawmill worker)

303 pottenmaker-pot maker

304 pottenbakker-potter,ceramist

305 predikant-preacher

306 priester-r.C.Priest

307 proponent-ministerial candidate (protestant)

308 professor-doctor of letters, university professor

309 pred.Chr.Afg-christian reformed minister

310 religieus-r.C. Nun

311 radmaker-maker of wheels

312 reizigende handelaar-traveling salesman

313 resident-resident(district governor in east indies)

314 rentenier-retired business man

315 rijksschatter-governmental financial worker

316 reitdekker-thatcher

317 rijkswegarbeider-federal highway worker

318 rijtwig-harness maker

319 renteniersche-lady of

independent means(retired woman)

320 schafthuishouder-restaurant owner

321 schaapherder-shepherd

322 scheepsgezagvoerder-ship captain

323 scheepstimmerman-ship carpenter

324 scheepstimmermansknecht-ship carpenter's helper

325 schaarslijper-scissors sharpener

326 scheepsmaat-shipmate

327 schilder-painter,artist

328 schildersknecht-painter's helper

329 schipper-sailor

330 scheepsmaker-ship builder

331 schippersknecht-sailor's hand

332 stenograaf-stenographer

333 schoenmaker-shoemaker

334 scheepsbevrachter-ship chartering,broker

335 schoenmakersknecht-shoe maker's hand

336 schoolhoudster-school keeper(female)

337 schoorsteenveger-chimney sweper

338 schoolmeester-school teacher

339 schrijnwerker-joiner, cabinet maker, furniture maker

340 schrijnwerkersknecht-joiner's hand

341 schrijver-writer,author

342 schuitenvoerder-bargeman

343 schuurster-buffer(female)

344 scheepsjager-barge towman(by horse)

345 sleutelmaker-keymaker

346 secretaris-secretary general (government official)

347 smid-blacksmith

348 schippersche-sailor(female)

349 smidsknecht-blacksmith's hand

350 sjouwerman-porter, dock hand

351 slagter,slachter-butcher

352 slagersknecht-butcher's hired hand

353 spekslagter-butcher pigs

354 spoorwegbeambte-railroad official, worker

355 stalknecht-stableman, groom

356 steenbakker-brick maker

357 steenbakkersknecht-brickmaker's hand

358 stoffenverversleerling-apprentice fabric dyer

359 steenhouwer-mason

360 spinster,spinner-spinning mill worker

361 stoelenmaker-chair (stool)maker

362 stamper-masher,oil mill worker

363 stoffenverver-specialist fabric dyer,dry cleaner

364 sleper-carter,tug-boat

365 stroodekker-roofer straw

366 student-

367 student in de theologie-theology student

368 stuurman ter zee-ship helmsman

369 stukadoor-plasterer

370 tapper-tavern owner(male)

371 tabaksplanter-tobacco planter

372 tapster-tavern owner(female)

373 tegelbakkersknecht-tile baker's helper

374 tapijtwerker-carpetmaker

375 tekenaar-house designer

376 takelaar-rigger,tackler

377 telegrafist-telegrapher

378 taakwaarnemer-employment agent

379 theewerker-teamaker

380 strijker van kleding-ironer

381 timmerlieden-carpenter

382 stationchef-railway station worker

383 timmerman-carpenter

384 terpbaas-

385 timmermansknecht-carpenter's hand

386 telefoonkantoorhoudster-telefooncompany owner

387 tolgaarder-toll collector

388 textielwerker(ster)-textile worker

389 tolpachter-toll collector (road or canal)

390 transportarbeider-laborer transport

391 touwslager-rope maker

392 truck groenteboer-truck gardener

393 tuinder,tuinier,tuinbouwboer-gardener

394 veenwerker,veenman,turfmaker, turfdrager-peat worker

395 turfschipper-peat-coal dealer (shipper)

396 tuinknecht-gardener's helper

397 twijnder-twister silkmill

398 verlakker-pottery painter

399 veearts-vetinarian

400 uitgever-publisher

401 veehouder,veehandelaar-cattleman

402 veehoudersknecht-cattleman's hand

403 veerman-ferry operator
404 uitdekker-roofer
405 uitdrager-second hand dealer
406 uurwerkmaker-watchmaker,clockmaker
407 veldarbeider-field hand
408 vergulder-gilder
409 veldwachter-village policeman, county constable
410 venter-peddler
411 verhuizer-mover
412 vlasbaas-flax foreman
413 verkoper-salesman
414 vletter-flatboatman
415 verloskundige-midwife (or veterinarian)
416 voermansknecht-coach driver's hand
417 verfmaker-paintmaker
418 verpleegster-nurse
419 verversknecht-painter's hand
420 vervener,verlakker-painter,varnisher
421 vleeshouwer-butcher,meat cutter
422 verver-house painter
423 voerman-coach driver
424 verbouwer-agricultural farmer
425 vrachtrijder-freigt driver
426 visser-fisherman
427 visserwerk repareerder-fish net repair
428 voddenkoopman-rag dealer
429 wagenmaker-wagon maker,car builder
430 warmoezier-market gardener
431 wasvrouw-wash woman, laundry woman
432 wagenmakersknecht-wagon maker's hand
433 weefster-weaver(female)
434 wagenaar-freigt driver
435 werkbode-work servant
436 wegarbeider-road worker
437 werktuigkundige-mechanic (small appliances)
438 volontair-volontary worker
439 werkman-workman
440 veldarbeidster-field laborer(female)
441 werkvrouw, werkster-work lady
442 arbeider vloerbedekkingfabriek-laborer carpet mill
443 wever-weaver silk and cotton
444 wijnkopersknecht-wine merchant's helper
445 wielendraaijer-wheel turner
446 wielster-wheel turner(female)
447 winkelbediende-store clerk(male)
448 winkelbediende-store clerk(female)
449 winkelier-store keeper, grocery owner
450 wolkammer-wook comber
451 winkelierster-store keeper(female)
452 verzekeringsagent-insurance agent
453 wollenaaister-woolen seamstress
454 zaakwaarnemer-soliciter
455 zadelmaker-saddle maker
456 zadelmakersknecht-saddle maker's helper
457 zakkendrager-bag carrier
458 zandman-sandhauler
459 zeelieden-sailor
460 zeilmaker-sail maker(manufacturer)
461 zeeman-sea sailor
462 zeepzieder-soapmaker
463 zendeling-missionary
464 zeevarende-seafarer
465 zonder-without occupation
466 zijde-industrie arbeider-silk industry worker
467 zonder beroep-without occupation
468 zijde afmaker-silk finisher
469 zoutzieder-saltmaker
470 wolkammer-woolcomber
471 drukker-printer
472 wasserijbeheerder-laundry owner
473 drukkersknecht-printer's hand
474 zijdewinder-silk winder
475 kurkenmaker-cork maker
476 zager-sawyer

-Date of emigration
-Destination
  1 usa-unidentified region
1000 Maine
1100 Vermont
1300 Massachusetts
1301 Boston,mass.
1302 Worcester,mass
1400 Rhode island
1401 Woonsocket,providence co.
1500 Connecticut
1501 Willimantic,windham co.
1700 New Jersey
1701 Clinton
1702 Hackensack
1703 Lodi
1704 Newark
1705 Paterson
1800 Pennsylvania
1801 Erie, pa
1802 Hanover,pa
1803 Philadelphia
1804 Pittsburgh
1900 Washington State
2000 Delaware
2100 Maryland
2101 Baltimore
2102 Frederick
1600 New York
1601 Albany
1602 Brooklyn
1603 Buffalo
1604 Lancaster,erie co.
1605 Long Island
1606 Pultneyville, wayne co.
1607 Punteville
1608 Rochester
1609 Staten Island
1610 Utica
1611 West Canal
1612 Yonkers
1613 Hampton
3200 Illinois
3201 Calumet
3202 Chicago
3203 Danforth
3204 Fulton
3205 Roseland
3206 Kensington
3300 Michigan
3301 Allegan
3302 Bay City
3303 Detroit
3304 Drenthe
3305 Filmore
3306 Friesland
3307 Fulton City
3308 Graafschap
3309 Grand haven
3310 Grand Rapids
3311 Grandville
3312 Groningen
3313 Holland
2200 District of Columbia
2300 Virginia
2301 Williamsburg
2400 North Carolina
2500 South Carolina
2600 Georgia
2700 Florida
3000 Ohio
3001 Cincinnati
3002 Cleveland
3004 Toledo
3305 Troy
3100 Indiana
3101 Elkhart

3102 Evansville
3103 Fort Wayne
3104 Goshen
3105 Goshen
3106 Indianapolis
3106 Lafayette
3107 Munster
3108 Terre Haute
3109 Brownstown
3413 Prairie du Chien
3414 Sheboygan
3415 Waupan
3500 Minnesota
3501 Benton Carver
3502 Kanton Carga
3503 Minneapolis
3504 Silver Creek
3505 St.Paul
3506 Clara City
3600 Iowa
3601 Appleton
3602 Cedar Rapids
3603 Chariton
3604 Davenport
3605 Dubuque
3606 Grundy Center
3607 Keokuk
3608 Muscatine
3609 Orange City
3610 Pella
3611 Sioux City
3612 Waterloo
3613 Ackley
3614 Otley
3615 Hull co.sion
3314 Kalamazoo
3315 Lowell
3316 Muskegon
3317 Ottawa
3318 Overijsel
3319 Plainfield
3320 Saugatuck
3321 Zeeland
3322 Colmerson
3323 Vieuw New Era
3400 Wisconsin
3401 Alto
3402 Cumberland
3403 Dupere
3404 Gibbsville
3405 Green bay
3406 Lacross
3407 Little chute
3408 Madison
3409 Manitowoc
3410 Milwaukee
3411 New Amsterdam
3412 Oostburg

3413 Midway
3414 Randolf Center Columbia co.
3415 Racine
4200 Alabama
4201 Mobile
4300 Mississippi
4400 Louisiana
4401 New orleans
4500 Texas
4501 Rio grande
4600 Arkansas
5000 Montana and Wyoming
5100 Colorado
5200 New Mexico and Arizona
5300 Utah and Nevada
5400 Idaho
5500 Oregon
5501 Portland, Oregan
5600 California
5601 Auckland
3700 Missouri
3701 Jefferson City
3702 Kansas City
3703 St.Louis
3704 Atchison
3705 Laflin
3800 Dakotas
3801 New Holland s.D.
3802 Charle Alise Platte,s.D.
3803 Springfield s.D.
3900 Nebraska
3901 Omaha Nebraska
3902 Grand Island Nebraska
4000 Kentucky
4001 Louisville
4100 Tennessee
4101 Memphis
3324 Ferrysburg

**-Last residence**

<u>Municipality</u>
1 Oostdongeradeel
2 Westdongeradeel
3 Het bildt
4 Ferwerderadeel
5 Barradeel
6 Wonseradeel

<u>Village/dorp</u>
101 Aalsum
102 Anjum
103 Ee
104 Engwierum
105 Jouswier
106 Lioessens
107 Metslawier
108 Morra

109 Niawier
110 Nijkerk
111 Oostrum
112 Paesens
113 "Schippers"/boatmen
114 Wetzens
201 Betterwird,bornwird etc
202 Hantum,hantumhuizen etc
203 Holwerd
204 Nes
205 Ternaard
206 Wierum
301 St.Anna Parochie 1880-99
302 St.Jacobi Par. 1880-1899
303 Vrouwenparochie 1880-1914
312 Het bildt 1900-1914
401 Blija
402 Ferwerd
403 Genum
404 Hallum
405 Hogebeintum
406 Jislum
407 Lichtaard
408 Marrum
409 Nijkerk
410 Reitsum
411 Wanswerd
501 Almenum
502 Firdgum
503 Kloosterlidlum
504 Minnertsga
505 Oosterbierum
506 Pietersbierum
507 Sexbierum
508 Tzummarum
509 Wijnaldum
601 Allingawier
602 Arum
603 Burgwerd
604 Cornwerd
605 Dedgum
606 Engwier
607 Exmorra
608 Ferwoude
609 Gaast
610 Greonterp
611 Hartwerd
612 Hichtum
613 Hieslum
614 Idsegahuizen
615 Kimswerd
616 Lollum
617 Longerhouw
618 Makkum
619 Oldeklooster
620 Parrega
621 Piaam
622 Pingjum

623 Schettens
624 Schraard
625 Tjerkwerd
626 Ugoklooster
627 Witmarsum
628 Wons
629 Zurich


**-Householdnumber related to
number of original copies**

# *Appendix II:* Absolute number of emigrants per year from six Frisian clay municipalities 1880-1914

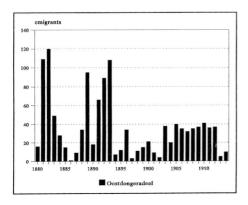

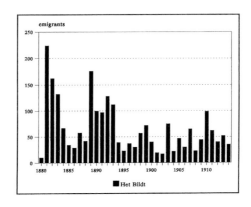

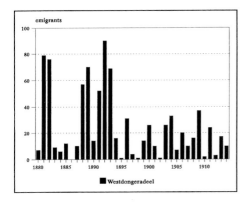

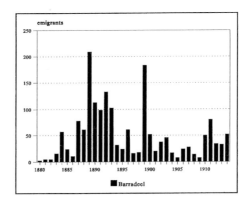

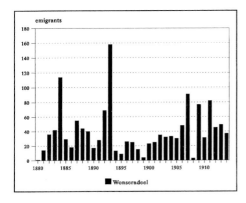

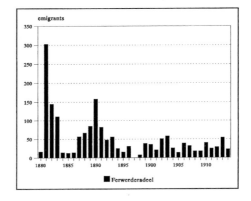

**Source:** Dutch Population 1880-1914

# Appendix III: Absolute emigration 1880-1914 in proportion to absolute population in different villages according to the Volkstelling of 1909:

|  |  | Number of emigrants 1880-1914 | 1909 census |
|---|---|---|---|
| Ferwerderadeel: | Blija | 240 | 977 |
|  | Ferwerd | 508 | 1690 |
|  | Genum | 14 | 214 |
|  | Hallum | 477 | 2247 |
|  | Hogebeintum | 70 | 249 |
|  | Jislum | 61 | 120 |
|  | Lichtaard | 30 | 162 |
|  | Marrum | 165 | 1125 |
|  | Nijkerk | 33 | 314 |
|  | Reitsum | 38 | 129 |
|  | Wanswerd | 145 | 622 |
|  |  |  |  |
| Het Bildt | St.Anna 1880-1899 | 671 | 3042 |
|  | St.Jacob 1880-1899 | 703 | 2809 |
|  | Vrouwenp 1880-1899 | 2792 | 419 |
|  | Het Bildt 1900-1914 | 688 | 8416 |
|  |  |  |  |
| Westdongeradeel: | Betterwird etc | 152 |  |
|  | Hantum etc | 102 |  |
|  | Holwerd | 306 | 1942 |
|  | Nes | 89 | 1351 |
|  | Ternaard | 167 | 1231 |
|  | Wierum | 73 | 838 |
|  |  |  |  |
| Oostdongeradeel: | Aalzum | 43 | 755 |
|  | Anjum | 326 | 1503 |
|  | Ee | 284 | 1127 |
|  | Engwierum | 85 | 920 |
|  | Jouswier | 8 | 71 |
|  | Lioessens | 102 | 542 |
|  | Metslawier | 50 | 496 |
|  |  |  |  |
|  | Morra | 99 | 402 |

|  |  |  |  |
|---|---|---|---|
|  | Niawier | 66 | 400 |
|  | Nijkerk | 73 | 794 |
|  | Oostrum | 55 | 442 |
|  | Paesens | 52 | 537 |
|  | Schippers | 12 |  |
|  | Wetzens | 15 | 137 |
|  |  |  |  |
| Barradeel: | Almenum | 66 | 756 |
|  | Firdgum | 70 | 213 |
|  | Kloosterlidlum | 21 | 83 |
|  | Minnertsga | 302 | 1411 |
|  | Pietersbierum | 55 | 435 |
|  | Sexbierum | 378 | 1504 |
|  | Tzummarum | 530 | 1511 |
|  | Wijnaldum | 64 | 627 |
|  |  |  |  |
| Wonseradeel: | Allingawier | 16 | 173 |
|  | Arum | 353 | 1513 |
|  | Burgwerd | 34 | 466 |
|  | Cornwerd | 21 | 168 |
|  | Dedgum | 15 | 180 |
|  | Engwier | 2 | 21 |
|  | Exmorra | 14 | 316 |
|  | Ferwoude | 40 | 348 |
|  | Gaast | 45 | 354 |
|  | Greonterp | 1 | 161 |
|  | Hartwerd | 7 | 148 |
|  | Hichtum | 32 | 157 |
|  | Hieslum | 6 | 158 |
|  | Idsegahuizen | 15 | 161 |
|  | Kimswerd | 45 | 745 |
|  | Lollum | 8 | 409 |
|  | Longerhouw | 3 | 91 |
|  | Makkum | 154 | 2044 |
|  | Oldeklooster | 1 | 51 |
|  | Parrega | 56 | 519 |
|  | Piaam | 21 | 135 |
|  | Pingjum | 93 | 969 |
|  | Schettens | 37 | 287 |
|  | Schraard | 16 | 292 |
|  | Tjerkwerd | 24 | 608 |
|  | Ugoklooster | 3 | 23 |
|  | Witmarsum | 297 | 1434 |
|  | Wons | 26 | 375 |
|  | Zürich | 16 | 260 |

**Source:** Galema, "Frisians to America, 1880-1914. Computer Compilation,"; *Volkstelling*, 1879 and 1909

# Appendix IV: Emigrant occupations by economic sector per period 1880-1914:

| Major Occupation — Economic sector | 80-84 N | 80-84 % | 85-89 N | 85-89 % | 90-94 N | 90-94 % | 95-99 N | 95-99 % | 00-04 N | 00-04 % | 05-09 N | 05-09 % | 10-14 N | 10-14 % | PERIOD N | PERIOD % |
|---|---|---|---|---|---|---|---|---|---|---|---|---|---|---|---|---|
| **Primary** | | | | | | | | | | | | | | | | |
| 1. agriculture | 405 | 41.1 | 232 | 32.5 | 438 | 35.5 | 154 | 31.8 | 192 | 35.7 | 178 | 31.7 | 223 | 32.1 | 1822 | 35.0 |
| 2. fishing/hunting | 2 | 0.2 | 1 | 0.1 | 1 | 0.1 | 1 | 0.2 | 2 | 0.4 | 2 | 0.4 | 3 | 0.4 | 12 | 0.2 |
| Totals 1 and 2 | 407 | 41.3 | 233 | 32.6 | 439 | 35.6 | 155 | 32.0 | 194 | 36.1 | 180 | 32.1 | 226 | 32.5 | 1834 | 35.2 |
| **Secondary** | | | | | | | | | | | | | | | | |
| 3. apparel | 7 | 0.7 | 4 | 0.5 | 9 | 0.7 | 2 | 0.4 | 5 | 0.9 | 2 | 0.4 | 2 | 0.3 | 31 | 0.6 |
| 4. wood | 31 | 3.2 | 17 | 2.4 | 34 | 2.8 | 10 | 2.1 | 14 | 2.6 | 8 | 1.4 | 34 | 4.9 | 148 | 2.8 |
| 5. metals/leather | 8 | 0.8 | 2 | 0.3 | 5 | 0.4 | 1 | 0.2 | 1 | 0.2 | 2 | 0.4 | 4 | 0.6 | 23 | 0.4 |
| 6. brick/glass | 1 | 0.1 | 0 | 0.0 | 0 | 0.0 | 0 | 0.0 | 1 | 0.2 | 1 | 0.2 | 2 | 0.3 | 5 | 0.1 |
| 7. food | 19 | 1.9 | 12 | 1.7 | 22 | 1.8 | 4 | 0.8 | 6 | 1.1 | 30 | 5.3 | 31 | 4.5 | 124 | 2.4 |
| 8. other | 8 | 0.8 | 2 | 0.3 | 5 | 0.4 | 3 | 0.6 | 5 | 0. | 5 | 0.9 | 8 | 1.2 | 36 | 0.7 |
| Totals 3-8 | 74 | 7.5 | 37 | 5.2 | 75 | 6.1 | 20 | 4.1 | 32 | 5.9 | 48 | 8.6 | 81 | 11.8 | 367 | 7.0 |
| **Tertiary** | | | | | | | | | | | | | | | | |
| 9. professional | 7 | 0. | 2 | 0.3 | 7 | 0.6 | 1 | 0.2 | 2 | 0.4 | 1 | 0.2 | 4 | 0.6 | 24 | 0.5 |
| 10. service | 30 | 3.0 | 17 | 2.4 | 48 | 3.9 | 28 | 5.8 | 32 | 5.9 | 38 | 6.8 | 27 | 3.9 | 220 | 4.2 |
| 11. commerce | 23 | 2.3 | 22 | 3.1 | 30 | 2.4 | 12 | 2.5 | 14 | 2.6 | 14 | 2.5 | 16 | 2.3 | 131 | 2.5 |
| 12. transport | 24 | 2.4 | 7 | 1.0 | 21 | 1.7 | 8 | 1.6 | 7 | 1.3 | 16 | 2.8 | 20 | 2.9 | 103 | 2.0 |
| Totals 9-12 | 84 | 8.4 | 48 | 6.8 | 106 | 8.6 | 49 | 10.1 | 55 | 10.2 | 69 | 12.3 | 67 | 9.7 | 478 | 9.2 |
| **Other** | | | | | | | | | | | | | | | | |
| 13. none/unknown/unemployed | 419 | 42.6 | 397 | 55.5 | 613 | 49.7 | 261 | 54.0 | 257 | 47.8 | 265 | 47.2 | 321 | 46.2 | 2533 | 48.6 |
| **Grand TOTAL** | 984 | 100.0 | 715 | 100.0 | 1233 | 100.0 | 485 | 100.0 | 538 | 100.0 | 562 | 100.0 | 695 | 100.0 | 5212 | 100.0 |

# Appendix V: Codebook of datafile:
# J.B.E. Galema, "Frisians in the USA, 1900/1910.
# Computer Compilation." Groningen: database, 1993.

**Source:** Galema, "Frisians to America, 1880-1914. Computer Compilation"

**-Name of immigrant**
**-First name**
**-Last recidence household number/linkage number**
**-State county township householdnumber**

State
91 Alabama
92 Alaska
93 Arizona
94 Arkansas
95 California
96 Colorado
97 Connecticut
98 South Dakota
99 North Dakota
10 Delaware
11 Florida
12 Georgia
13 Groenland
14 Idaho
15 Illinois
16 Indiana
17 Iowa
18 Kansas
19 Kentucky
20 Louisiana
21 Maine
22 Massachusetts
23 Maryland
24 Michigan
25 Minnesota
26 Mississippi
27 Missouri
28 Montana
29 Nebraska
30 Nevada
31 New Hampshire
32 New Jersey
33 New Mexico

34 New York
35 North Carolina
36 Ohio
37 Oklahoma
38 Oregon
39 Pensylvania
40 Rhode Island
41 South Carolina
42 Tennessee
43 Texas
44 Utah
45 Vermont
46 Virginia
47 Washington
48 West Virginia
49 Wisconsin
50 Wyoming
51 The Netherlands
52 Friesland
53 Germany
54 Ireland
55 Belgium
56 Norway
57 Switserland
58 England
59 Denmark
60 Australia

County
2201 Boston
2202 Worcester
3201 Passaic
1701 Sioux
1702 Marion
1703 Muscatine
4901 Columbia
4902 LaCrosse
4903 Dodge
4904 Racine
4905 Sheboygan
1501 Cook
1502 Whiteside
1503 DuPage

2401 Kent
2402 Ottawa
2403 Missaukee
2404 Oakland
9801 Charles Mix
9802 Bonhomme
2301 Caroline
4701 Snohomish
4702 Yakima
4703 Island
4704 Whatcom
9501 Humbolt
9502 Los Angeles
9503 San Bernardino
9504 Riverside
3401 Monroe
3402 Erie
2801 Gallatin
2501 Pine
2502 Pipestone
2503 Kanabec
2504 Mille Lacs
2505 Rock
2506 Renville
2507 Chippewa
2508 Kandiyohi

**-Census**
1 Census 1900
2 Census 1910

**-Family status**
see codebook appendix i
**-Sex**
see codebook appendix i
**-Date of birth**
**-Age of last birthday**
**-Civil status**
see codebook appendix i
**-Number of years married**
**-Mother of how many children**
**-Number of living children**
**-Nativity**

a place of birth of this person
b place of birth of father
c place of birth of mother
see codebook appendix i (state)
**-Family type**
see codebook appendix i
**-Citizenship**
year of emigration
number of years in usa
naturalization
1 naturalised
2 alien
9 unknown

**-Occupation**
major occupation

see codebook appendix i
social occuapation
see codebook appendix i
specific occuapation
see codebook appendix i
months not employed

**-Education**
0 illiterate
1 read
2 write
3 read and write
4 speaks english
5 reads and speaks english
6 writes and speaks english
7 reads, writes and speaks english

9 blank

**-Ownership house**
1 owned house free
2 owned house mortgaged
3 owned farm free
4 owned farm mortgaged
5 rented farm
6 rented house
9 unknown
0 blank, not applied to

# *Appendix VI:*
# Examples of Northern Frisian-Linked migrants, 1880-1900

| | | | |
|---|---|---|---|
| Ee, | Roseland, Illinois | 20 | |
| Oostdongeradeel | Welcome Tp, Iowa | 1 | |
| | Pella, Iowa | 6 | |
| | Summit Tp, Iowa | 1 | |
| | Grand Rapids, Michigan | 4 | |
| | Blendon Tp, Michigan | 1 | |
| | Richland Tp, Michigan | 2 | |
| | West Gallatin, Montana | 2 | |
| | Paterson, New Jersey | 4 | |
| | Onalaska, Wisconsin | 1 | **Total: 42** |
| | | | |
| Holwerd, | Chicago, Illinoi | 8 | |
| Westdongeradeel | Fulton, Illinois | 1 | |
| | Wyoming Tp, Michigan | 2 | |
| | Grand Rapids, Michigan | 8 | |
| | Holland, Michigan | 28 | |
| | Blendon Tp, Michigan | 5 | |
| | Randolph, Wisconsin | 4 | **Total: 56** |
| | | | |
| Vrouwenparochie, | Chicago, Illinois | 12 | |
| Het Bildt | Orange City, Iowa | 2 | |
| | Wyoming Tp, Michigan | 2 | |
| | Grand Rapids, Michigan | 1 | |
| | Blendon Tp, Michigan | 3 | |
| | Sandstone Tp, Minnesota | 1 | |
| | Woods Tp, Minnesota | 2 | |
| | Rheiderland Tp, Minn. | 4 | |
| | Paterson, New Jersey | 6 | |
| | Onalaska, Wisconsin | 9 | |
| | Holland, Wisconsin | 5 | |
| | Barretown, Wisconsin | 8 | **Total: 55** |

| | | | |
|---|---|---|---|
| Blija, | Chicago, Illinois | 2 | |
| Ferwerderadeel | Grand Rapids, Michigan | 11 | |
| | Zeeland, Michigan | 2 | |
| | Olive Tp, Michigan | 4 | |
| | Holland, Michigan | 31 | |
| | Blendon Tp, Michigan | 9 | |
| | Paterson, New Jersey | 4 | **Total: 63** |
| | | | |
| Sexbierum, | Chicago, Illinois | 8 | |
| Barradeel | Center Tp, Iowa | 1 | |
| | Holland, Iowa | 15 | |
| | Nassau Tp, Iowa | | |
| | Sherman Tp, Iowa | 4 | |
| | Wyoming Tp, Michigan | 10 | |
| | Grand Rapids, Michigan | 7 | |
| | Zeeland, Michigan | 1 | |
| | Holland, Michigan | 5 | |
| | Clam Union Tp, Michigan | 2 | |
| | Dell Grove Tp, Minnesota | 1 | |
| | Sandstone Tp, Minnesota | 1 | |
| | Fountain Prairie, Minn. | 2 | |
| | Burke Tp, Minnesota | 3 | |
| | Holland, Minnesota | 3 | |
| | Tyndall, South Dakota | 6 | **Total: 72** |
| | | | |
| Piaam, | Orange City, Iowa | 2 | |
| Wonseradeel | Zeeland, Michigan | 13 | |
| | Blendon Tp, Michigan | 1 | **Total: 16** |

**Source:** Galema, "Linked files: Frisians to America and Frisians in the USA. Computer Compilation"

# Appendix VII:
## Occupations by Economic Sector Northern Frisian Immigrants and Descendants, 1900

| Economic Sector | M | F | Total | Percentage |
|---|---|---|---|---|
| Primary | | | | |
| Agriculture | 466 | 11 | 477 | 35.4 |
| Fishing/Hunting | 14 | - | 14 | 1.0 |
| **Sector Totals** | 480 | 11 | 491 | 36.4 |
| Secondary | | | | |
| Apparel | 43 | 25 | 68 | 5.1 |
| Wood/Carpentry | 96 | – | 96 | 7.1 |
| Metals/Leather | 48 | 2 | 50 | 3.7 |
| Brick/Glass | 16 | - | 16 | 1.2 |
| Food | 31 | 3 | 34 | 2.5 |
| Othe | 162 | 16 | 178 | 13.2 |
| **Sector Totals** | 396 | 46 | 442 | 32.8 |
| Tertiary | | | | |
| Professional | 15 | 1 | 16 | 1.2 |
| Service | 31 | 57 | 87 | 6.5 |
| Commerce | 38 | 2 | 40 | 3.0 |
| Transport | 10 | - | 10 | 0.7 |
| **Sector Totals** | 94 | 60 | 153 | 11.4 |
| Other | | | | |
| None/Unknown/Unemployed | 123 | 137 | 260 | 19.3 |
| **Grand Totals** | 1092 | 254 | 1346 | 100.0 |

**Note:** Housewives and children younger than 15 are not included in the workforce. The secondary economic sector includes day laborers, because they often were not part of the agricultural field. This differs from the Dutch Population Registers, where the same designation *dagloner* can be classified within the Primary Agricultural Sector. See M. Conk, "Occupational Classification in the United States Census: 1870-1940," *Journal of Interdisciplinary History* 9 (1978) 1: 111-30.

**Source:** Galema, "Frisians in the USA, 1900/1910. Computer Compilation."

# Samenvatting

Zoals in vele landen staat ook in Nederland het verschijnsel van internationale migratie de afgelopen decennia veelvuldig in de belangstelling. Steeds weer blijkt een aanzienlijk gedeelte van de mensheid, om de meest uiteenlopende redenen, in beweging. De transformatie van Europa van een emigratie- in een immigratiecontinent heeft de aandacht voor migratievraagstukken doen toenemen. Op nationaal niveau leeft het bewustzijn dat nieuwkomers die na de Tweede Wereldoorlog naar Nederland kwamen, permanent zullen blijven. In deze eigentijdse context past de bestudering van Nederlanders als landverhuizers in historisch perspectief. De studie *With the Baggage of the Fatherland; Frisians to America 1880-1914*, sluit aan bij de interesse voor het vraagstuk van migratie en wil een bijdrage leveren aan de geschiedenis van de Nederlandse landverhuizing naar de Verenigde Staten. Daarbij staat het begrip van de sociaal-economische en culturele werkelijkheid van de migrant centraal. Friezen hebben een lange migratietraditie naar de Verenigde Staten. Reeds in het midden van de 19e eeuw waagden zij de overtocht om in soms onherbergzame Amerikaanse streken een nieuw leven te beginnen. Met name in de tweede helft van de negentiende eeuw drukte de Friese emigratie een onmiskenbaar stempel op de regio. Tussen 1880-1914 vertrok in sommige streken een op de vier inwoners naar Amerika. In 1881 kozen uit de dunbevolkte kleigemeentes Oost- en Westdongeradeel, Het Bildt, Ferwerderadeel, Barradeel en Wonseradeel, maar liefst meer dan 700 emigranten voor een overzeese bestemming, in 1893 ongeveer 600, terwijl in 1913 nog steeds meer dan 200 Friezen uit deze regio de oversteek maakten. In *With the Baggage of the Fatherland* staat een groep van bijna 10.000 landverhuizers centraal, die in de periode 1880-1914 uit de noordelijke kleistreek van Friesland vertrok. Deze emigranten worden belicht vanuit een trans-Atlantisch gezichtspunt, waardoor een vergelijking tussen vertrek- en vestigingsgebied mogelijk is. Gezien de diversiteit in de migratiefrequentie op provinciaal niveau, is de nadruk gelegd op een regionale benadering van het migratieproces. De migranten zijn gelokaliseerd in hun oorspronkelijke woonplaats, tijdens de tocht naar de nieuwe wereld, en in hun vestigingsplaatsen overzee. Daarbij zijn onder meer de aantallen landverhuizers in kaart gebracht, wie zij waren, of zij individueel of in groepsverband vertrokken, wanneer zij Friesland verlieten en met welke motivatie, hoe zij reisden, waar zij zich vestigden in de Verenigde Staten, in welke beroepen zij terechtkwamen, hoe zij positie toegewezen kregen en hoe zij positie verwierven in de Amerikaanse samenleving. Bij de analyse van deze vragen is met name gebruik gemaakt van overheidsstatistieken en ego-documenten.

Om de comparatieve benadering van het migratieproces vorm te geven, is gekozen voor een kwantitatief prosopografische opzet van het onderzoek. Dit betekent dat zoveel mogelijke biografische gegevens van de Friese landverhuizers zijn verzameld, zodat de sociaal-economische en culturele achtergrond van de migranten gekarakteriseerd kon worden door de bestudering van de individuele kenmerken. In het algemene beeld komt daarbij ook de persoonlijke context van de individuele landverhuizer aan de orde.

Het boek kent zowel een chronologische als thematische invalshoek. In hoofdstuk I wordt door middel van een thematische benadering van de verschillende gemeenten uit het onderzoeksgebied, een beeld geschetst van de regio van vertrek. Bestudering van facetten als boeren en hun grond, arbeiders en verzet, visserij, onderwijs en religie, leveren een totaalbeeld van de noordelijke kleistreek in Friesland rond de eeuwwisseling. Het gebied was voornamelijk afhankelijk van de landbouw en visserij. Mogelijkheden voor het vinden van een bestaan in handel en industrie waren zeer beperkt. In de laatste twee decennia van de negentiende eeuw drukte de agrarische depressie zwaar op deze regio, waardoor wijdverbreide sociale onrust ontstond. De meerderheid van de bevolking van het kleigebied was gelieerd aan de Hervormde Kerk. Onderwijs en educatie hadden een lange traditie van publieke dorpsscholen, die in de jaren zeventig van de vorige eeuw concurrentie kregen van het bijzonder onderwijs. In dit klimaat ontstonden de push- en pull-factoren die -in de periode 1880-1914- leidden tot het vertrek van bijna 10.000 landverhuizers naar de Verenigde Staten.

In het tweede hoofdstuk ligt de nadruk op de demografische factoren die ten grondslag lagen aan het migratieproces. Samen met Gelderland, Noord-Brabant, Overijssel en Drenthe, behoorde Friesland tot de minst dicht bevolkte provincies van Nederland. Friesland werd daarbij gekenmerkt door een relatief lage huwelijksleeftijd, een relatief hoge huwelijksfrequentie, en een relatief lage vruchtbaarheid. De provinciale bevolking groeide met name in de laatste decennia van de 19e eeuw veel minder snel dan de nationale. Uit analyse van de geboorte- en sterftecijfers, alsmede de vestigings- en vertrekoverschotten, blijkt dat Friesland vooral haar bewoners kwijtraakte door migratie naar andere delen van Nederland en door emigratie naar overzee.

De landverhuizing uit het kleigebied kende met name pieken in de jaren 1881, 1882, 1889, 1892, en 1893. In de periode 1880-1893 vertrok bijna 60 procent van het totale aantal emigranten tussen 1880-1914. Nederland vertoonde toentertijd een aantal van 68 landverhuizers per 100.000 inwoners, terwijl het kleigebied 498 telde. Een opvallende conclusie is gelegen in het feit dat slechts een zeer klein percentage van de emigranten vertrok uit een woonplaats welke niet direct in de buurt van hun geboortegrond lag. Voordat zij zich opmaakten voor de langste reis van hun leven, betoonden de Friezen zich zeer honkvast.

Hoofdstuk III handelt over de factoren die de motivatie in zowel de collectieve als individuele landverhuizing hebben vormgegeven. Naast beweegredenen van sociaal-economische aard, wordt aandacht besteed aan de migratietraditie, waarin duidelijke samenhang met de motivatie is te constateren. Daarin past de benadering van het migratieproces door middel van recente en minder recente theorievorming. Onder meer de netwerk-theorie van Charles Tilly bleek behulpzaam. In de praktijk betonen de Friese landverhuizers zich een geselecteerd gezelschap, in doorsnee bestaande uit een gezin met drie tot vier kinderen, waarbij de ouders een leeftijd hadden van rond de veertig, en een niet al te hoge sociaal-economische status. In hoofdstuk IV komt het Amerikabeeld Van de landverhuizers aan de orde name bronnen als brieven geven daarover informatie. Brieven over de oceaan blijken echter niet altijd alleen bestemd te zijn geweest voor de particuliere lezer in de eigen familie- of kennissenkring. Menige brief werd geschreven vanuit de gedachte dat een groot lezerspubliek de aantrekkingskracht van de Nieuwe Wereld kon vergroten en dus meer landverhuizers zou bewegen naar Amerikaanse oorden te trekken. De zogenoemde "spekbrieven", die de kwantiteit van het Amerikaanse vlees op de immigrantendis roemden, werden gepubliceerd in plaatselijke kranten in Friesland en gebruikt als promotiemateriaal door de scheepvaart-maatschappijen en reisagentschappen. Particuliere brieven functioneerden als publieke bronnen die het Amerikabeeld bepaalden. Zodoende wisten nieuwkomers zich te vergewissen van het gezelschap van streekgenoten uit het Friese kleigebied. Of de denkbeelden van de landverhuizers over Amerika de werkelijkheid benaderden valt te bezien. De realiteit van deze beeldvorming gaf echter genoeg aanleiding tot bestudering. Zonder een door de potentiële landverhuizer gecomponeerd Amerikabeeld was migratie naar overzee geen werkelijkheid geworden. De ervaringe van de trans-atlantische reis, het aankomen in de plaatsen van vestiging, nieuwe beroeps-structuren en de karakteristieken van het Friese immigrantengezin, staan centraal in hoofdstuk V. In reisbeschrijvingen is de overtocht in alle toon-aarden bezongen. Immense indrukken, prijzen, voedsel en accomodatie gaven de Friezen aanleiding de pen ter hand te nemen. De meeste landverhuizers streken neer in de staten Michigan, Illinois, Iowa, Massachusetts, Wisconsin en New Jersey, en later Minnesota, Montana, Washington en California. Op basis van de Amerikaanse Census konden zij getraceerd worden in gemeenschappen waar veelal reeds eerder landgenoten zich hadden gevestigd. In de Verenigde Staten vond tevens een gefaseerde migratie plaats. Friezen die zich eerst in het oosten of in het midden-westen hadden gevestigd, besloten later hun heil in het verre westen te zoeken. Zij vervulden een voortrekkersrol voor landverhuizers die direct uit Friesland voor het Amerikaanse westen kozen.

Vergelijking tussen de beroepsstructuur voor en na de landverhuizing leverde een beeld van een duidelijk agrarisch georiënteerde groep.

Verhoudingsgewijs kwamen ongeveer net zoveel immigranten in de agrarische sector terecht als er in Friesland in dezelfde sector werkzaam waren geweest. Wat echter in het oog sprong was de verandering van status. Van de gezinshoofden die in de Census van 1900 werden geïdentificeerd, bleek maar liefst een derde deel onafhankelijk een boerenbedrijf te bestieren. Deze tendens duidt op een sterke begeerte naar land. Om deze wens te realiseren werden aanvankelijk allerlei beroepsmatige omwegen bewandeld, zolang deze maar leidden naar startkapitaal. Het agrarische bedrijf in de Verenigde Staten werd door de Friezen met name door de eigen familieleden bewerkt, wat in tegenstelling was met de bedrijfsvoering in Friesland.

In hoofdstuk 6 en hoofdstuk 7 wordt aan de hand van studie van specifieke stedelijke en plattelandsgemeenschappen duidelijk gemaakt dat het fenomeen van migratienetwerken voor Friese immigranten bij uitstek gold. Hier werd het private leven verbonden met overkoepelende economische en politieke structuren. Contacten tussen Friese nieuwkomers in de Verenigde Staten, en tevens tussen geëmigreerde en niet-geëmigreerde Friezen, werden intensief geëxploiteerd en leverden concreet positieverwerving op in de Amerikaanse maatschappij. Friezen in steden als Chicago, Paterson en Grand Rapids, vonden werk in de zijde- en meubelindustrie, meestal als fabrieksarbeiders. Zij waren min of meer exponent van een internationale arbeidsmarkt, die zich in de tweede helft van de negentiende eeuw manifesteerde en mede bewerkstelligde dat de massale migratie van het Europese continent naar de Verenigde Staten op gang kwam.

In het laatste hoofdstuk wordt aandacht besteed aan de Friezen als etnische groep en hun integratie in de Amerikaanse samenleving. Aan de hand van thema's als de rol van het gezin, de immigrantenkerk, sexeverschillen, onderwijs en taal, wordt duidelijk gemaakt dat ook de Friezen in het alledaagse leven werden geconfronteerd met "het andere" en "het eigene". Door hun drietaligheid en associatie met de eigen immigrantenkerk, manifesteerden zij zich als etnische groep in de Amerikaanse maatschappij. Daarbij springen de sterke familiebanden in het oog, welke met overgave werden bewaakt. De familie toonde zich een stabiel referentiepunt, waardoor Friese immigranten vaste grond onder de voet kregen. Mede gesteund door de piëteit die hun gemeenschappen domineerde, zochten zij als etnische groep naar een situatie die van het "andere" het "eigene" maakte.

Hopelijk draagt deze studie bij tot meer inzicht in dit proces en tevens tot meer begrip van de economische en culturele werkelijkheid van mensen die grenzen overschrijden.

# Curriculum vitae

Annemieke Galema was born March 1, 1956 in Burgwerd, in the province of Friesland, the Netherlands. After finishing highschool in Bolsward, she started the study of history at the University of Groningen and got her degree in 1981. She worked at the history department of the University of Groningen and in 1985 received a research grant to study the history of migration at Kent State University, Ohio, for a year.

Galema wrote several articles on Frisian and Dutch migration to the United States and is co-author of the volumes *Images of the Nation; Different Meanings of Dutchness* (1993), and *Van de ene en de andere kant. Noordnederlandse en Noordwestduitse migratie naar de Verenigde Staten in de negentiende eeuw/Nordniederländische und Nordwestdeutsche Auswanderung nach Amerika im 19. Jahrhundert* (1993). In 1996 she received her PhD. from the University of Leiden.

Since 1988 Galema works at the Faculty of Arts of the University of Groningen.

# Index